D1616428

Digital Empires

Digital Empires

The Global Battle to Regulate Technology

ANU BRADFORD

OXFORD
UNIVERSITY PRESS

OXFORD
UNIVERSITY PRESS

Oxford University Press is a department of the University of Oxford. It furthers
the University's objective of excellence in research, scholarship, and education
by publishing worldwide. Oxford is a registered trade mark of Oxford University
Press in the UK and certain other countries.

Published in the United States of America by Oxford University Press
198 Madison Avenue, New York, NY 10016, United States of America.

© Oxford University Press 2023

CIP data is on file at the Library of Congress

ISBN 978–0–19–764926–8

DOI: 10.1093/oso/9780197649268.001.0001

Printed by Sheridan Books, Inc., United States of America

For Oliver, Sylvia, and Vivian

Contents

Contents

Introduction

WHEN THE INTERNET became widely commercialized in the 1990s, it arrived with the promise of freedom: freedom for individuals to access information, exercise their voices, engage in debates, and shape societies. Early internet pioneers saw online platforms as the guardians and amplifiers of those freedoms, enhancing democracy by providing an inclusive platform for promoting diverse voices around the world. Today, this techno-optimist promise of an enhanced human experience has, at least in part, been realized: the internet has indeed democratized access to content and vastly expanded individuals' ability to receive, create, and disseminate all kinds of data, fundamentally transforming human beings' relationship with both information and with each other. This enhanced access to information and conversations has redefined the very fabric of human experience and undoubtedly generated immeasurable benefits for individuals and societies. And as the internet evolves in the years ahead, it will almost certainly continue to deliver significant new benefits in ways individuals and societies cannot yet even imagine.

Alongside these many benefits, however, the internet has also altered societies and individual lives to their detriment. While the internet has cultivated human connections and civic engagement, it has also been a channel for exposing vast segments of society to different forms of harmful content. Internet sites often serve as platforms for disinformation, bullying, hatred, and repulsive content, undermining the safety and dignity of individuals while dividing societies and destabilizing democracies. Algorithms designed to tailor online content to each user's preferences have fueled polarization and fragmentation, cultivating more extremist ideas and further eroding societal cohesion.[1] Instead of only increasing freedom, enhancing democracy, and nurturing an egalitarian and inclusive communitarian culture, the internet has also been used repeatedly to diminish these values, creating an ecosystem in which surveillance capitalism can thrive and societal divides deepen.[2]

Mitigating the individual and societal harms that arise from the internet is just one piece of the broader governance challenge facing regulators of today's digital economy. Digital transformation has ushered in an exceedingly concentrated economy where a few powerful companies control vast economic wealth and political power, restricting competition and widening the gap between winners and losers in the digital economy. The five largest tech companies—Amazon, Apple, Google, Meta, and Microsoft—collectively recorded over $1 trillion in revenue in 2020, while earning an income of $197 billion and having a market capitalization of $7.5 trillion by the end of 2020.[3] In 2021, the combined market capitalization of Apple, Alphabet, Meta, and Amazon exceeded the value of the over 2,000 companies listed on the Tokyo Stock Exchange; Apple and Meta together were worth more than the one hundred companies with the highest market cap listed on the London Stock Exchange; and Amazon alone eclipsed the entire German DAX Index, which represents around 80 percent of the market cap of companies publicly listed in Germany.[4] No doubt these tech companies would not have grown this big without developing products and services that consumers around the world value. But the law has also been on their side. For example, weak antitrust enforcement has amplified these companies' growth, allowing them to amass even more power through a staggering number of acquisitions. Over the past three decades, Amazon, Apple, Google, Meta, and Microsoft combined have acquired 770 startups.[5] According to Apple's CEO Tim Cook, Apple alone has acquired approximately one company every three to four weeks for the past six years.[6] Looking at this recent history, the power of these companies seems to only be growing stronger and more concentrated as the industry matures, with few obvious limits to how that power is deployed.

There are several reasons to be concerned about this concentration of economic, political, and cultural power in a few large tech companies.[7] First, this handful of companies controls a large proportion of the sector's wealth, allowing them to buy any competitor that threatens their market power. Second, their economic power buys them political influence that can be deployed to lobby for favorable regulation to further entrench that power. Third, these same companies increasingly control public discourse by moderating content on platforms where societal conversations, including political speech, take place. This allows them to exercise power over online infrastructures for democracy and public discourse. Fourth, these companies control much of the personal data that every user generates on a daily basis, which they have every incentive to extract for economic gain. These stores of data vest them with power over individual users. The cumulative effect of these different dimensions of power is to make these companies central to modern economic, political, and social life. The power vested in these companies is so vast that it increasingly competes with the power exercised by nation states, a phenomenon that has raised significant concerns among governments around the world.

Because of this accumulation of power, decisions by tech companies on how to wield their influence are becoming more consequential and controversial, opening up important questions about how societies and individual lives are being shaped by this multifaceted power. For example, when tech companies moderate content on their platforms, they face significant challenges in seeking to curtail harmful speech without suppressing free speech. To be sure, these companies err constantly in their efforts to achieve this balance—both in failing to restrict harmful speech in some cases and in censoring speech that has public value in others. Despite their efforts to take down detrimental content, major platforms such as Facebook, YouTube, and Twitter overflow with content that is hateful, dangerous, and often illegal. Perhaps most disturbingly, the platforms still host terrorist propaganda and abhorrent violence all too frequently. For example, in 2019, a perpetrator who carried out a hate-motivated massacre of fifty people in a mosque in Christchurch, New Zealand, livestreamed his killings on Facebook.[8] This tragedy received a large number of views on Facebook and various other online platforms, where the footage was replayed while the companies struggled to take down the various copies of the video appearing online. On the other hand, there are numerous examples where platforms' content removal efforts have been overzealous. In 2011, YouTube removed a video of a thirteen-year-old boy killed in the war in Syria in accordance with its policy prohibiting display of "dead bodies."[9] The image of the boy's dead body was shocking. But the image was meant to shock. The video was posted to awaken the international community to the horrors of the unfolding war, with the hope of galvanizing a global condemnation of the repressive Syrian regime. But as these examples reveal, drawing lines between permissible and impermissible speech in ways that are socially acceptable is exceedingly difficult. Yet, despite the delicate nature of content moderation, many government regulators have largely abdicated these types of decisions to the platforms themselves.

In addition to the flawed outcomes from content moderation, the methods used in content moderation can be disconcerting as well. For example, alongside their reliance on algorithms, all platforms use human moderators that deploy so-called community guidelines to decide what content stays up and what is removed. But as revealed by the German newspaper *Sueddeutsche Zeitung* in a 2018 story,[10] there is a massive human toll borne by these moderators who work on the frontlines "cleaning" the internet. In return for meager pay and few employment protections, content moderators are exposed to a constant stream of graphic violence and cruelty. The story reported that a single Facebook moderator in Germany, for instance, was expected to handle 1,300 reports a day.[11] A 2014 article published in *Wired* documented the work of Facebook's content moderators in the Philippines, who clean the platform of illegal content while being paid $1–4 per hour for their work. These moderators are exposed hour after hour to the worst possible content posted to these internet platforms. One Google moderator estimated having to filter through 15,000 images a day, including images of child pornography, beheadings, and animal abuse.[12] In 2020, Meta settled a lawsuit brought by over 10,000 of its content moderators, agreeing to pay $52 million in mental health compensation.[13] Content moderators pay an enormous psychological price in helping to keep the platforms safer and more civil for users around the world, but their plight also lays bare the distance between the highly compensated and powerful tech executives in Silicon Valley and the behind-the-scenes labor employed to scour the internet for harmful content. This human toll further calls into question the early, techno-optimist vision of the internet as an emancipatory force that would inevitably dismantle existing institutions of power and lead to a "more humane and fair" world.[14]

Another reason to be concerned about the concentration of power among a few tech companies relates to their collection of user data as part of their business model and the impact of that data collection on user privacy. This "surveillance capitalism" describes how tech companies extract vast data on their users' private lives and commercialize that information through targeted advertising, which threatens those people's rights to privacy and individual self-determination.[15] At worst, users' personal data can be harnessed to serve not only commercial, but also political goals. The Cambridge Analytica scandal—where a British political consulting firm acquired Facebook users' private data and used it in political campaigns—illustrates this problem in no uncertain terms.[16] In this case, internet users' private data was deployed with the goal of influencing the election in favor of President Trump. This or any similar attempt to manipulate voters compromises individuals' decisional privacy and undermines their trust in democracy.[17]

Internet users are not only vulnerable to surveillance by private tech companies, but also to digital surveillance by governments who rely on tech companies and their digital tools to further their national security or law enforcement objectives. The Chinese government's surveillance of its citizens, including its deployment of facial recognition technology, is particularly far-reaching. Hundreds of millions of surveillance cameras are already installed across China where the government can now match the video footage to personal data collected elsewhere, identifying individuals in real time and potentially predicting or even preventing political resistance before it even happens.[18] The government has rolled out AI-driven surveillance programs such as Sharp Eyes,[19] the goal of which is to create an "omnipresent, fully integrated, always working and fully controllable" nationwide surveillance system, built and supported by Chinese tech companies.[20] Yet it is not only authoritarian governments that deploy the internet as a tool for surveillance. Democratic governments, including the United States, also conduct extensive surveillance operations, as former US National Security Agency (NSA) contractor Edward Snowden revealed as part of the unprecedented leak of sensitive US intelligence data in 2013. Those Snowden revelations exposed how the NSA had engaged in a mass surveillance of individuals by harvesting data available through Facebook.[21] Without proper oversight, it is both tempting and feasible for any government to utilize the surveillance capabilities of tech companies to advance their political goals or national security objectives, even when that surveillance undermines individuals' civil liberties.

Many of these concerns are now amplified with the rapid advances in artificial intelligence (AI). The innovations in so-called generative AI technologies, in particular, have the potential to revolutionize the way we work and interact with information and each other. At best, generative AI will allow humans to reach new frontiers of knowledge and productivity, leading to unprecedented levels of economic growth and societal progress. At the same time, the pace of AI development is unsettling technologists, citizens, and regulators alike. AI is already used to power both private and government surveillance and to manipulate human behavior, but those activities can now reach new heights with larger training datasets and more sophisticated AI tools. A growing fear is that these technologies will give powerful tools for bad actors to exploit and defraud people or commit other illegal acts. They might also soon be used by anyone to unleash waves of disinformation. Even ardent techno-enthusiasts are now issuing dire warnings on how unregulated AI can lead to these and many other uncontrollable harms, posing severe threats to individuals and societies. The direst predictions presage the AI's ability to obliterate labor markets and make humans obsolete or—under the most hyperbolic scenario—even destroy humanity.

As people have become increasingly aware of the risks and potentially harmful effects associated with the use of these digital tools and with tech companies' vast economic power and social impact, it is not surprising that calls for greater regulation of these companies are growing. Recently, several governments have begun to respond to these popular demands by asserting their regulatory powers, leading prominent news outlets to proclaim how "A Global Tipping Point for Reining In Tech Has Arrived,"[22] and to describe how "Big Tech Braces for a Wave of Regulation."[23] For the past decade, the European Union has been leading this fight, frequently leveraging its antitrust laws, data protection laws, and other regulatory instruments to reclaim control over the industry.[24] But the EU is no longer the lone crusader in taking on the leading tech giants. The Chinese government has initiated an unprecedented crackdown on its tech sector in the name of advancing "common prosperity" and in order to ensure that tech giants do not overpower the Chinese state.[25] The tide may finally be turning even in the US, where Congress is reassessing the need to rewrite US antitrust laws, enact a federal privacy law, or revisit the Communications Decency Act of 1996, which shields internet platforms from liability for the content they host.[26] However, even if the problems associated with the tech industry have led to a broadening consensus that the digital economy needs to be regulated, there is no consensus among governments on what that regulation should look like.

Digital Empires: Three Competing Regulatory Models

Today, there are three dominant digital powers—the US, China, and the EU—who can metaphorically be thought of as "digital empires." These modern empires of the internet era are the leading technology, economic, and regulatory powers, each with the ambition and capability to shape the global digital order toward their interests and values. They have each developed a distinct governance model for their domestic digital economies, consistent with their different ideological commitments. Not unlike the empires of the past, they have further exported their domestic models in an effort to expand their respective spheres of influence, thus pulling other countries into the orbits of the American, Chinese, or European digital empires. The digital empires find their closest analogue, not in the former territorial empires, but in various informal empires of the twentieth century that projected economic, military, and cultural power across their borders, creating power asymmetries that vested them with influence over foreign societies. Today's digital empires are primarily exporting their tech companies, technologies, and rules governing those technologies, thus shaping countries and individuals that fall under their influence toward the norms and values they espouse.

Each digital empire holds a different vision for the digital economy, which is reflected in the regulatory models they have adopted at home and promoted abroad. These three leading regulatory models could be thought of as representing three "varieties of digital capitalism"—drawing on different theories about the relationship between markets, the state, and individual and collective rights.[27] As described throughout this book, the US has pioneered a largely *market-driven* model, China a *state-driven* model, and the EU a *rights-driven* model. Each of these regulatory models involves societal choices that rest on diverging economic theories, political ideologies, and cultural identities. In deciding how to regulate the digital economy, governments in the three jurisdictions have all had to balance their support of technological innovation with the implications those technologies have for civil liberties, the distribution of wealth, international trade, social stability, and national security, among other key policy concerns. This balancing effort has led to some similarities but also notable differences across the leading regulatory models. As each model is associated with contested policy choices that subject them to criticism—each for different reasons—there is no global consensus on which of the three dominant regulatory models best serves the goal of building a vibrant and resilient digital economy and society.

The US has traditionally followed a *market-driven* regulatory model, which has provided the foundation for the global digital economy as it exists today.[28] The American regulatory approach centers on protecting free speech, the free internet, and incentives to innovate.[29] It is characterized by its discernible techno-optimism and relentless pursuit of innovation. The US government has historically viewed the internet as a source of economic prosperity and political freedom and, consequently, as a tool for societal transformation and progress. The American market-driven model exhibits uncompromising faith in markets and embraces a limited role for the government. According to this techno-libertarian view, government intervention not only compromises the efficient operation of markets; it also undermines individual liberty. Thus, while the US's commitment to innovation and growth provides the economic rationale against government intervention, its commitment to individual liberty and freedom is often invoked as a political reason to limit the government's role. Minimizing government interference is seen as essential to producing a vibrant democratic society characterized by free speech and the engagement of diverse voices in civic life. From this perspective, the government is only expected to step in to protect national security—on cybersecurity issues, for example, the US government has a role to play alongside tech companies.

Few would dispute that many of the prized innovations that shape our everyday lives today can be traced to Silicon Valley—innovations that the American market-driven model has directly facilitated. At the same time, privacy advocates and other critics argue that this zealous pursuit of innovation has come at the expense of protecting individual internet users' rights. The EU has joined these advocates in arguing that, absent regulatory safeguards, public and private surveillance thrive under the US model and severely compromise individuals' rights to privacy and political autonomy. Seen from this vantage point, a world governed by tech companies' business models subjects internet users to behavioral advertising and manipulation that subvert individual choice, liberty, and self-governance.[30] By allowing for this, the US model thus compromises individuals' abilities to exercise their agency and participate in democracy. Several recent high-profile scandals illustrate the problem, including the Snowden revelations and the Cambridge Analytica scandal mentioned above. The EU and other critics of the market-driven regulatory model can also point out how Facebook, Twitter, YouTube, and other platforms have repeatedly failed to remove dangerous disinformation on topics ranging from the COVID-19 pandemic to democratic elections. And they can replay the images of the January 6, 2021, insurrection at the US Capitol, which originated in a rampant social media–fueled disinformation campaign about a stolen election.[31] Consequently, when looking strictly at innovation and economic growth, the American market-driven model can be praised for its ability to nurture tech companies, but that economic benefit comes at the expense of risking fundamental rights, human dignity, political autonomy, and democracy.

In contrast to the American market-driven regulatory model, the Chinese regulatory model rests on a *state-driven* vision for the digital economy.[32] The Chinese government seeks to maximize the country's technological dominance while maintaining social harmony and control over its citizens' communications.[33] China is determined to leverage technology to fuel its economic growth and development. It is currently engaged in an unprecedented state-led effort geared toward becoming the world's leading technology superpower. In addition to pursuing this economic goal, the government is focused on tightening the political grip of the Chinese Communist Party (CCP) by deploying the internet as a tool for control, surveillance, and propaganda. To achieve these goals, the CCP has harnessed the power of its private tech companies: in return for the initially lax regulatory approach that helped them grow and flourish, Chinese tech companies have acted as the CCP's surrogates, performing the surveillance and control functions of the state over their users. However, the Chinese government is increasingly adopting the view that the largest tech companies have grown too powerful. It has recently leveraged its antitrust laws to rein in domestic giants such as Alibaba and Tencent—the opening salvo of an unprecedented assault on its domestic tech industry. Yet even this newest turn in digital regulation serves the fundamental goal of the

Chinese government: cementing the state's control of the digital economy as a defining feature of China's regulatory model.

Like the US, China has been tremendously successful in fostering technological innovations, allowing leading tech companies such as Alibaba, Tencent, and Huawei to emerge. At the same time, the Chinese state-driven regulatory model has also come under increasing criticism in democratic countries, as the Chinese government systematically harnesses the internet as a tool for censorship and political control. Many foreign governments, including the US and the EU, condemn the Chinese government's policy of banning and filtering online content on a large scale—a policy colloquially known as the Great Firewall. Many foreign companies have become a direct casualty of this policy, including Google, Meta, and Twitter, which have largely abandoned the Chinese market due to the government's extensive censorship policies.[34] China's large-scale deployment of facial recognition techniques for law enforcement purposes is also widely condemned abroad.[35] Its social credit scheme, which rates citizens for their trustworthiness based on issues such as paying taxes or committing a crime, is similarly met with deep suspicion.[36] These examples illustrate how the Chinese government has converted the internet from a tool for advancing democracy to an instrument in service of autocracy. Thus, China's practice of deploying data as a tool for social control represents a stark departure from the shared European and American view where the internet is seen as key to promoting individual liberty and advancing freedom in society. Through its model, China has shown the world how freedom is not inherent in the character of the internet, but rather vulnerable to political choices by those with the power to limit that freedom.

The European regulatory model differs from both the American and Chinese models in being distinctly *rights-driven*.[37] The EU embraces a human-centric approach to regulating the digital economy where fundamental rights and the notion of a fair marketplace form the foundation for regulation.[38] According to this view, regulatory intervention is needed to uphold the fundamental rights of individuals, preserve the democratic structures of society, and ensure a fair distribution of the benefits from the digital economy. Technology must be harnessed toward human empowerment and with the aim of safeguarding the political autonomy of digital citizens. In contrast to the US model, which focuses on protecting free speech as *the* fundamental right, the EU model seeks to balance the right to free speech with a host of other fundamental rights, including human dignity and the right to privacy. In contrast to the Chinese model—which also reserves a strong role for the state in steering the digital economy—the EU model is geared at enhancing, not curtailing, the rights of citizens vis-à-vis both tech companies and the state.

The EU's regulatory model also emphasizes that digital transformation needs to be firmly anchored in the rule of law and democratic governance. Whereas the American market-driven model often emphasizes how governments do not understand technology and should hence refrain from regulating it, the European rights-driven model is more concerned that tech companies do not understand the pillars of constitutional democracy or the fundamental rights of internet users.[39] As a result, under the European regulatory model, the government must steer the digital economy with the goal of protecting those rights they view as foundations of a liberal democratic society.

Civil rights advocates often praise the EU for its commitment to fundamental rights, dignity, and democracy, including its efforts to steer the digital economy toward those values through regulation. At the same time, many industry advocates and companies in both the EU and foreign markets— particularly the US—view the European rights-driven regulatory model in a less positive light. They describe it as overly protective, compromising tech companies' incentives to innovate, and thereby curtailing the technological and economic progress that societies depend on. Few successful tech giants are emerging from Europe, which is often attributed to the EU's protective regulations that interfere with tech companies' innovative zeal.[40] Many US politicians, tech companies and other proponents of the free speech ideals underlying the American regulatory model also allege that the European rights-driven model risks undermining free speech and stifling public debate. In particular, US tech companies like Google have argued that the EU's approach toward content moderation—including its online hate speech rules and the "right to be forgotten" provision in the EU's General Data Protection Regulation (GDPR)—could to lead to harmful censorship.[41] In other words, these critics argue that the EU overdoes its rights-driven regulation, damaging economic progress and political freedom in the process.

Even this cursory overview of the three leading regulatory models reveals significant distinctions among them. However, the models also have elements in common. Despite prioritizing the market, the state, or individual and collective rights differently, each model ultimately maintains aspects of each. Markets do not always win in the US; the state does not control everything in China; and the rights of internet users do not always prevail over other policy imperatives in the EU. Nevertheless, when faced with critical policy trade-offs and the balancing of various interests in regulating the digital economy, each jurisdiction often falls back on those foundational principles that are intrinsic to their distinctive regulatory models: the US tends to draw on its pro-market instincts to limit government intervention, China responds in ways that ensure the government's interests are protected, and the EU acts in a manner that elevates the rights of digital citizens to the heart of its policymaking. It is these persistent differences across the three models that fuel tension and conflict, paving the way for the contested battles that have become a defining feature of today's digital economy.

Imperial Rivalries: A Battle Fought on Two Levels

Due to the global nature of the digital economy, these leading regulatory models extend across jurisdictions, impacting foreign societies and shaping lives of foreign individuals. As a result, these models frequently collide in the international domain, leading to fierce battles both within and across the digital empires. These imperial rivalries are thus central to the evolution of the global digital order, revealing how that order is shaped not only by the empires themselves but by their mutual contest for influence. These rivalries take place at two levels. First, there is a *horizontal battle among different governments*, as illustrated by the conflicts among the US, China, and the EU over the norms and values that govern the digital economy. However, this horizontal battle among the governments is shaped by—and often fought through—*vertical battles between governments and the tech companies* that these governments are seeking to regulate. These vertical battles have evolved differently in each jurisdiction, consistent with the differences in the three regulatory models. Various horizontal and vertical battles are further deeply intertwined, constraining the strategies that any government can deploy in each battle. For example, the US government is reluctant to regulate its tech companies too aggressively for fear of stifling these companies' ability to innovate as such a strategy could, in turn, weaken the US in its horizontal rivalry over technological supremacy against China. Such interconnections across the various horizontal and vertical battles often lead to a strategy of restraint, bringing about periods of de-escalation alternated with periods of escalation. This dynamic sustains a persistent, yet ultimately manageable, conflict that prevents a full-blown tech war from emerging but also keeps a lasting truce at bay.

A Contest Among Governments: The Horizontal Battles Between the US, China, and the EU

Most of the public commentary on the great power contest in the digital sphere focuses on technological rivalry between the US and China as the leading technology powers.[42] This narrative often dismisses the EU as a bystander, caught between the two powers battling for technological supremacy while struggling to create a vibrant tech industry of its own.[43] However, the EU has asserted itself in this contest as the most powerful regulator of the digital economy, giving it unique leverage to shift the digital economy toward its values. This often elicits strong criticism, especially from US tech companies and the US government, and leads to heated regulatory battles between the US and the EU.[44] As a result, this book frames the horizontal battle for the digital economy as one taking place between the US, China, and the EU.

In their contest for influence over the digital economy the US, China, and the EU each approach their horizontal battles with their distinct policy goals in mind. For the US, the primary objective has been to advance open markets and internet freedoms, at home and abroad.[45] This policy agenda blends the economic interests of US tech companies seeking to expand internationally with the foreign policy interests of the US government promoting democracy and freedom abroad. In pursuit of this agenda, the US has challenged foreign regulations that compromise the economic interests of its tech companies and condemned various attempts at online censorship that undermine free speech and political freedoms around the world. More recently, the US has turned its focus to technological competition with a determination to ensure its leadership over China. For China, this horizontal battle has initially been a defensive one. The Chinese government has focused on regime survival, political control, and its right to make its own rules for the "sovereign internet." A key concern has been to protect the Chinese market and citizens from harmful foreign influences.[46] But the Chinese government is also increasingly fighting an offensive battle for technological supremacy, both to become more self-reliant in a volatile world but also to prevail over the US in the two superpowers' contest for greater relative economic, geopolitical, and even military power.[47] For Europe, the battle has primarily focused on safeguarding the fundamental rights of European citizens in a globalized world.[48] The EU is seeking to rein in surveillance capitalism and protect European citizens from being exploited by US tech giants. But the EU is also seeking to protect Europeans from American and Chinese government surveillance, which has become easier to conduct in the digitalized world. In addition to this defensive agenda, the EU is now increasingly seeking to bolster its "digital sovereignty" in an effort to shed its dependencies on American and Chinese technologies by building its own technological capabilities.[49]

This horizontal conflict has morphed into several battles, the most prominent one being the unfolding US–China tech war.[50] This battle has reinvigorated the US export control regime, as the US government is restricting outflows of critical technologies from the US to China.[51] It has also galvanized a vigorous investment screening process in the US, limiting

Chinese investors' ability to acquire control of US technologies.[52] China has responded in kind, further constraining US tech companies' access to its domestic market while placing additional limits preventing its own critical technology assets, including sensitive data, from leaving China.[53] Even the stock market is now the target of mutual decoupling, with both China and the US tightening their rules that apply to foreign listings.[54] Both powers have also engaged in a relentless capacity-building effort to gain new technological capabilities while reducing their dependencies on each other. This battle has fueled a subsidy race in semiconductors, batteries, and artificial intelligence, setting off techno-nationalist impulses in other governments as well.

In addition to battling China for the mastery of new technologies, the US is battling Europe over the regulations that govern those technologies.[55] This transatlantic regulatory battle has focused on data flows, with the US and the EU asserting different views on the way individuals' right to privacy can, or cannot, be reconciled with the needs for government surveillance for law enforcement or national security purposes.[56] Another key tension relates to the taxation of the digital giants, with the Europeans insisting on their right to tax some of the revenue that large American tech companies generate in Europe.[57] Europeans have also forcefully leveraged their antitrust laws to constrain the business practices of US companies.[58] In these battles, Europeans are concerned about US tech firms' alleged overreach, while Americans are concerned about European regulators' alleged overreach. The US views the EU's regulatory efforts as both excessive and protectionist, unfairly targeting European companies' more successful American rivals. The EU has responded by insisting on its sovereign right to preserve a competitive and fair marketplace while ensuring that the fundamental rights of Europeans are protected. Thus, at the heart of the US–EU regulatory battle are the questions of who gets to set the rules for the digital economy and what kind of digital society emerges from those rules.

Vertical Battles Between Governments and Tech Companies

The US, China, and the EU are not only engaged in horizontal battles with each other. They are simultaneously fighting vertical battles vis-à-vis the tech companies operating in their markets—tech companies who wield private power so vast and so global that they have been compared to emerging empires themselves.[59] Two features render these vertical battles particularly complex today. First, tech companies are both targets as well as tools for governments. Governments seek to restrain these companies while simultaneously deploying them in fighting horizontal battles, turning the vertical relationship into a delicate balancing act. For example, China relies on its tech companies to conduct surveillance and enforce censorship, the US harnesses its tech sector to pursue its national security goals, and the EU delegates to these companies the task of enforcing many of its data privacy and content moderation norms. The US, China, and the EU further need these companies to promote economic growth and technological progress in order to enhance their relative economic and geopolitical standing in their horizontal battles. This suggests that tech companies should be seen as both allies and enemies to the governments, helping them to achieve some policy goals while undermining others. The challenge for the governments therefore is to inflict some regulatory constraints on these companies without undermining their roles as forceful instruments in other battles where governments rely on their powerful capabilities.

Second, these vertical battles are complicated by the nature of the global marketplace, where tech companies have multiple masters.[60] These companies often face conflicting demands from different governments, making it impossible for them to comply with all of those demands at the same time. In a nearly decade-long battle that began in 2013, Microsoft was asked by US law enforcement officials to hand over personal data stored on its servers in Europe while simultaneously facing demands by European regulators not to hand over such data under the EU's data protection rules.[61] In 2021, Apple and Google bowed to the demands of the Russian government and removed an app designed by allies of opposition leader Aleksei Navalny to coordinate protest voting in Russian elections, their commitment to freedom and democracy at home notwithstanding.[62] Now, leading tech companies are navigating the Russian invasion of Ukraine, facing conflicting demands from Ukraine, Russia, the EU, and the US on how to handle the disinformation and propaganda on their platforms that are shaping the narrative about the war.[63]

US tech companies operating in China face a particularly difficult balancing act.[64] For example, Apple has been a vocal advocate of data privacy and civil liberties in the US and EU. However, the company has made several concessions in return for being able to operate in China. It has agreed to store the data of its Chinese users locally in a datacenter in Guiyang, where Chinese state employees manage the stored data. Apple also proactively censors its Chinese App Store with the help of algorithms and employees who flag and block apps that do not meet the approval of the Chinese leadership. In another example, in 2017, Google took steps to build a censored search engine for China in an effort to retain its right to operate in the country, only to back down the following year in response to growing criticism in the US that the company was capitulating to China's censorship demands.[65] More recently, Chinese tech companies abroad have also had to navigate the difficult terrain of regulators' conflicting demands. In 2020, TikTok, a social media company owned by the Chinese company ByteDance, was attempting to comply with the US government's requirement that the company must find a US buyer—under the threat of being banned from the US market—only to learn that the Chinese government responded by prohibiting all artificial intelligence exports, thereby threatening the very sale that the US government required.[66] Similarly, the Chinese ride-hailing company DiDi Chuxing found itself caught between the conflicting demands of the Chinese and US governments regarding the disclosure requirements associated with Chinese companies' initial public offerings (IPOs) in the US. The US Securities and Exchange Commission asked DiDi to hand over data, which the Chinese government maintained could not leave China. This led the company to ultimately delist its shares from the New York Stock Exchange.[67] These examples illustrate how distinct vertical battles often collide, leaving companies with the difficult—and at times impossible—task of choosing which government's demands to comply with.

How the Horizontal and Vertical Battles Intersect and Encourage Restraint

The horizontal and vertical battles intersect in important ways, forcing governments to simultaneously reconcile various, and at times conflicting, imperatives. This interplay across the battles—both horizontal and vertical—leaves governments more constrained in terms of the regulatory policies they can pursue and often forces them toward a strategy of restraint. In the horizontal battles, governments are locked in conflict, yet the countries also need each other. For example, the US government wants to restrict China's technological ambitions, but it needs to preserve US companies' access to the large and lucrative market that China offers. The US export control regime illustrates this tension well. The US requires an export license for many sensitive technologies that US companies want to export to China; in practice, the government often grants those licenses to mitigate the costs imposed on US companies exporting those technologies to China.[68] The US also opposes many EU regulations targeting US tech companies but has an incentive to de-escalate any transatlantic tensions as it needs the EU to join forces with the US government in its battle against China.[69]

Governments are similarly constrained in their vertical battles against tech companies, which are necessary instruments for the governments to win their horizontal battles. For example, the US government needs strong tech companies to stay ahead of China in the AI race and preserve its overall technological dominance. When the US Congress recently debated more assertive antitrust action, leading US tech companies warned that their ability to compete with the Chinese tech giants would be compromised should their business practices be curtailed by overzealous regulatory action.[70] European regulators also face a delicate balancing act. The EU's ability to set the rules for the global digital economy depends on multinational tech giants concluding that the costs of complying with European rules remain lower than the costs of pulling out of the European market—and that the benefits associated with globalizing EU rules outweigh the benefits of offering customized products in different markets. Should the EU overshoot its mark, these companies might conclude that they will abandon the European market, seeking profits elsewhere.[71] Such a move would fundamentally dissolve the EU's power to shape the digital economy, also undermining the EU's standing in its horizontal battles. Thus, we observe more moderation and de-escalation than we would if vertical and horizontal battles proceeded in isolation from one another.

This interplay across the various battles forces all players toward a strategy of restraint, keeping the battles alive yet de-escalating conflicts and making them more manageable. These interdependencies also explain why we are less likely to see outcomes as stark or extreme as those often predicted in the public conversation about the future of the digital economy.[72] This public commentary often envisions binary outcomes—arguing that the world is forced to choose between the US and China;[73] that the future will feature a global internet or a fragmented "splinternet";[74] or that either governments or tech companies will set the rules.[75] However, this binary way of framing the questions often blinds us to the more complex dynamics that shape the global digital economy. A closer examination of the interdependencies across the key battles suggests that the internet will not be global, nor will we witness full decoupling; China will not triumph over the US, nor will the US triumph over China; governments will not declare a complete victory over tech companies, but neither will tech companies detach themselves from government regulation. Instead, the digital world will likely be characterized by what Mark Leonard, the Director of the European Council of Foreign Relations, calls "the age of unpeace": a geopolitical order where states are too interconnected to fight an all-out war but too discordant to live in genuine peace.[76] In this highly connected and conflict-ridden world, battles will be costly and differences lasting, yet ultimately manageable—producing victories that will be relative as opposed to absolute.

Imperial Expansion: Global Consequences of the Regulatory Models

In addition to engaging in rivalries with each other, the three digital empires are also competing for global influence by exporting their regulatory models to other countries. This way, the US, China, and the EU are each seeking to shift the rest of the world closer to the norms and values inherent in their market-driven, state-driven, and rights-driven models. As a result, the question is not only whether the US or China prevails in their tech war against each other but, even more fundamentally, whether the global digital economy ultimately evolves toward the norms underlying the American market-driven or the Chinese state-driven model. Similarly, the success of the EU model will be judged not only by its ability to curtail US tech companies' market power in the US–EU regulatory battles, but also by its ability to shape the global digital order toward the values that are fundamental to the European rights-driven regulatory model.

When these regulatory models are exported to foreign jurisdictions, they generate both "positive externalities" and "negative externalities" in those jurisdictions. Those externalities are positive, for example, when foreign citizens use US companies' digital technologies to enhance their productivity or to access conversations they find valuable; when foreign governments improve public safety with the help of Chinese surveillance technologies to the benefit of their citizens; or when foreign privacy advocates witness data protection standards elevated around the world thanks to the global effect of the EU's regulation. However, those externalities can also be negative, affecting foreign societies in harmful ways, and evoking of negative connotations associated with expansionist digital empires.[77] Although these three digital empires may not be self-consciously imperial in search for domination over unwilling populations and governments, critics may accuse, for example, the US of "free-trade imperialism," China of "surveillance imperialism," or the EU of "regulatory imperialism." These allegations reflect a perception that the digital empires' global expansion often leads to power asymmetries between the center and the periphery of those empires.

The American market-driven regulatory model is increasingly becoming a source of global concern. Because of the global nature of the digital economy, the effects of the US model are felt everywhere, every day. Limited privacy protections, lenient antitrust laws, and the generally hands-off approach to internet platforms in the US have enabled and nourished a world dominated by large American tech giants. These tech giants are now shaping the lives of digital citizens across all continents. WhatsApp allows its two billion users across 180 countries to send 100 billion messages a day.[78] Google operates in over 200 countries, where internet users make over five billion Google searches a day.[79] Nobody can deny that these tech giants are fostering global connections among individuals and providing valuable services to internet users around the world.

But these companies are also often shaping foreign societies in deeply disturbing ways. For example, the growing criticism that US companies have pursued technological innovation and commercial rewards at the expense of individual and collective rights of citizens is a global one. To illuminate how the failings of the American regulatory model are felt around the world, consider the role that Meta played in the Brexit campaign that led the United Kingdom to leave the EU in 2020. Its Facebook algorithms amplified the more emotional and controversial messages that were associated with the pro-Brexit campaign, overshadowing the less inflammatory social media messaging of the Remain campaign.[80] During the lead-up to the Brexit vote, Twitter also enabled Russian meddling in the referendum. More than 150,000 Russian Twitter accounts posted about Brexit in the days leading up to the referendum, mostly encouraging people to vote to leave the EU.[81] In another disturbing episode involving Myanmar, Meta admitted in 2018 that it failed to intervene and remove content posted by military and radical Buddhist groups. These groups utilized the Facebook platform to spread hate and racially motivated discrimination against the Rohingya minority, including messages using dehumanizing language and calling for the destruction of Rohingya as a people.[82] Instead of removing posts that were fueling hatred toward the country's Muslim minority, Meta provided a platform for advocating racist attacks and ethnic cleansing.[83] These disturbing developments around the world can be traced to the business models of US tech companies—but also to the US regulatory model that enables those business models to emerge and continue to thrive.

The Chinese state-driven regulatory model is also increasingly having global implications, elevating foreign governments and citizens' concerns about the influence that Chinese tech companies—and the CCP that is widely believed to exert control over those tech companies—have over foreign societies. It is common knowledge that the Chinese government is deploying the internet as a tool for control and surveillance.[84] Much of this surveillance is domestic, geared at controlling political dissent and maintaining social stability within China. However, there is a growing concern among democratic governments and civil rights advocates that Chinese digital authoritarianism is also entrenching around the world as Chinese companies build digital infrastructures in many jurisdictions as part of the country's expansive "Digital Silk Road" project.[85]

One example of such concerns materializing involves the headquarters of the African Union (AU) located in Addis Ababa, Ethiopia.[86] The Chinese government built and financed the building complex hosting the AU, and the Chinese information and communications technology giant Huawei was contracted to provide most of the IT solutions for the building. But in January 2018, the leading French newspaper *Le Monde* reported that it had uncovered a multiyear hacking operation of the headquarters.[87] The report disclosed that, between January 2012 and January 2017, servers inside the AU building transferred data every night between 12:00 a.m. and 2:00 a.m. to unknown servers hosted in Shanghai. After this data theft was discovered, a further investigation revealed microphones hidden in the desks and walls of the building.[88] While it is often difficult to prove that Chinese companies transfer data gained through their overseas operations to the Chinese government, the suspicion of this potential for espionage is already shaping business opportunities for companies such as Huawei.[89] The US is now leading the quest to rein in Huawei's—and, according to the US, the Chinese government's—global influence by banning Huawei from US networks and urging other nations to do the same.[90] This battle involving the US government and China's Huawei illustrates how the reach of one digital empire into the territory of another can morph into a conflict with global implications.

If the US and Chinese models reach across the global marketplace, so does the European rights-driven model. The externalities associated with the EU model relate to the global reach of European regulations. The most interventionist laws constraining the power of today's tech companies can often be traced to European civil servants writing them in Brussels and European judges interpreting them in Luxembourg. These laws call for more data privacy, greater competition, and less harmful content, often shaping tech companies' global business practices and thus affecting digital citizens around the world.[91] As a result, foreign internet users today have more privacy and are exposed to less hate speech online because of the EU. While many of them welcome the global reach of the European laws, others criticize the EU for engaging in digital protectionism and regulatory imperialism while tampering with innovation and free speech—not just in Europe, but around the world.[92]

Whatever one's normative views on the merits of the EU regulations, few can dispute that its impact is felt far outside of the EU. Consider the highly consequential decision in June 2020 in which the European Court of Justice invalidated the US–EU Privacy Shield agreement that had previously provided a legal basis for transatlantic data transfers, citing inadequate data privacy protections in the US.[93] That decision threw much transatlantic commerce into disarray, as unhindered data flows are critical in sustaining the $7 trillion transatlantic economic relationship. In its 2022 annual report to the US Securities and Exchange Commission, Meta even warned that, absent a government-negotiated solution to the transatlantic data transfers, the company may need to pull out its key services—such as Facebook and Instagram—from the EU.[94] Should this happen, internet users across Africa, Asia, Australia, and North and South America would be disconnected from their friends and family in Europe. This is but one example of what the critics describe as "regulatory imperialism," accusing the EU of externalizing its data privacy norms around the world without seeking the consent of foreign regulators, companies, or internet users.[95]

These examples illustrate how the US, China, and the EU each export their models abroad, expanding their respective spheres of influence as expansionist empires, each with their own global ambitions and distinct methods of influence. The US's global influence today manifests through the dominance of its tech companies that exercise *private power* across the global digital sphere.[96] China's global influence can be traced to its *infrastructure power*, where Chinese firms—all with close ties to the Chinese state—are building critical digital network infrastructures in countries near and far.[97] The EU exercises global influence primarily through *regulatory power* that entrenches European digital norms across the global marketplace.[98] Like traditional empires, these digital empires' growth and expansion is constrained by the efforts of the other digital empires to extend their own influence using their preferred mechanisms. As a result, unaligned foreign markets often turn into critical battlefields, with local governments navigating the effects of American companies, Chinese infrastructure, and European law on their markets. These governments need to decide issues such as whether to allow China's Huawei to build their digital infrastructure, generously financed by the Chinese government while actively opposed by the US government. They must also decide whether to allow the outsized presence of US companies in their markets to shape their economies and societies or to instead join the EU's efforts to restrain them.

This imperial projection has ingrained American private power, Chinese infrastructure power, and European regulatory power deep into the economic, physical, and legal foundations of foreign societies. While there is legitimate criticism of these digital empires' efforts to extend their influence abroad, foreign stakeholders often view the US, China, and the EU operating as "empires by invitation."[99] For example, many foreign consumers welcome the presence of American tech companies in their markets, embracing their products and services increasingly depending upon them. Many foreign citizens also relish the global reach of EU digital regulations that protect their privacy or help ensure a safer online environment, the same way several foreign governments often willingly emulate EU regulations which they believe benefit their societies. The Chinese Digital Silk Road is also not merely a manifestation of Chinese government's deliberate expansionist strategy; instead, many foreign governments—in particular those across the developing world—welcome Chinese infrastructure (and capital) as a pathway for digital development. Thus, today's digital empires can be both admired and reviled across the territories that fall under their influence.

What Is at Stake: The Battle for the Soul of the Digital Economy

A key question for the coming years is how these battles will evolve and which regulatory model—if any—will dominate in the future. In the public conversation and news commentary, there is a commonly repeated narrative that suggests that the main contest over the future of the digital economy takes place between the US and China. These two powerful digital regimes not only compete for technological supremacy but also engage in a fundamental battle of values as they advance two competing visions for the global digital order: the American vision of economic and political freedom and the Chinese vision of technological progress fused with state control. But this narrative, which leaves the EU and other countries to choose between these two variants of digital worlds, is flawed in drawing the main battleline between the American and Chinese models. Instead, as this book explains, the American market-driven regulatory model is fading as countries around the world are rejecting the free market and free speech as cornerstones of their digital economies.[100] Even the US itself is now questioning the virtues of an unregulated digital marketplace, with the American public supporting stronger tech regulations and Congress debating the need for legislative reform. In deserting the US's regulatory approach, countries around the world are left with choices that lead them to either coalesce behind a version of the Chinese state-driven model or adopt the core tenets of the European rights-driven regulatory models; in that scenario, it is likely that the US will be forced to choose between joining forces with the EU and the rest of the democratic world, or acceding to China's growing influence over the global digital economy.

The prospect of the Chinese state-driven regulatory model prevailing is as real as it is disconcerting for the US and its allies. A growing number of countries in Africa, Asia, and South America in particular are now embracing

Chinese technology for both financial and geopolitical reasons, importing China's state-driven regulatory norms in the process. The US and other democratic countries remain concerned about the way the Chinese government engages in censorship, suppresses individual rights, and deploys the internet as a tool for surveillance. But these very features of the Chinese model are welcomed by many authoritarian leaders seeking to maintain their own political control, suppress dissent, and hold onto power. The number of such authoritarian leaders is also rising in today's world where democracy is on the decline in a growing number of countries.[101]

In contrast, in the democratic world, the European rights-driven regulatory model is emerging as the most desirable alternative to the waning American market-driven regulatory model.[102] The European model is associated with a set of values—fundamental rights, fairness, and democracy—that are often undermined by today's tech giants. The EU's regulatory approach has also been validated by numerous high-profile data privacy and disinformation scandals that have further eroded citizens' trust in tech companies, elevating the EU's standing in the debate and facilitating the global emulation of its regulatory model. Increasingly disillusioned with free markets, toxic online speech, repeated privacy violations, and other harms associated with unregulated tech companies, many American citizens would also welcome the US shifting toward the European rights-driven regulatory model.

At the same time, others remain cautious about emulating the EU model, fearing a loss of technological and economic progress if the government steps in and replaces companies' freedom to innovate with the state's authority to regulate. However, as this book will argue, more digital regulation does not necessarily mean less innovation. Instead, the EU's inability to produce its own tech giants to date can be attributed not to digital regulation, but to various other policies that have thwarted European technological progress. This observation should alleviate the concerns of American policymakers and other stakeholders about the consequences of endorsing EU-style digital regulations, paving the way for their adoption in the US. An additional reason for the US to more closely align itself with the EU arises from the perceived urgency to consolidate a democratic front to restrain China's growing influence. The US is already calling for closer cooperation of the world's "techno-democracies" to counter the growing influence of China and other "techno-autocracies,"[103] suggesting that this contest—where battlelines are drawn according to fundamental political and ideological convictions—is now increasingly central in defining the evolution of the digital economy.

The stakes in the unfolding horizontal and vertical battles cannot be overstated. These regulatory conflicts are taking place in an era of mounting geopolitical tensions, entangling questions of technology, trade, and innovation with questions of national security and global power politics. The resolution of these battles has a direct bearing on economic prosperity, political stability, and the individual freedom of every person that uses the internet. But the most consequential battle is the one being fought over the very future of liberal democracy itself. As this book shows, there are two likely pathways for liberal democracy to potentially deteriorate through these battles. First, democratic institutions in any jurisdiction will be undermined if the US, the EU, and their democratic allies lose their horizontal battle to China, and governments around the world shift toward a state-driven model. China's victory in this battle would usher in a world where technology is harnessed to empower the state, not its people, subjugating individual rights and freedoms to state control. However, democratic institutions can also be weakened if the US and the EU are to ultimately lose their vertical battle to tech companies—a realistic possibility given the power of these companies and the many challenges the EU has faced to date in implementing its ambitious digital regulations in practice. Victory for the tech giants would leave internet users and societies at the mercy of these companies' business models, even when those business models compromise individual rights or undermine democratic elections. In the end, it is this existential battle over the fate of liberal democracy as a form of government that will provide the US and the EU with the greatest impetus to join forces in both their horizontal and vertical battles—knowing that, if that fight is lost, the battle for the soul of the digital economy is also lost.

The Structure of the Book

Understanding how the global digital economy has evolved to date, and how it is likely to evolve going forward, requires integrating numerous scholarly and policy conversations that span across different jurisdictions and policy domains. This book is an effort to provide such an integrated approach, identifying and analyzing the key forces that determine the legal and political foundations of today's and tomorrow's digital societies. It is divided into three parts, with each part contributing key elements toward the book's larger argument regarding the present and future state of the global digital economy. The chapters in the first part introduce the three *digital empires*—the US, China, and the EU—and describe their regulatory models that provide competing visions for the digital economy; the chapters in the second part focus on *imperial rivalries*, outlining the key battle lines being contested as the regulatory models collide in the global marketplace; and the chapters in the third part address the strategies employed by each for the *expansion of their empires*, explaining how the US, China, and the EU are battling for global influence, exporting their regulatory models and shaping the digital destinies of the societies and individuals around the world.

Part I (Chapters 1–3) discusses the three digital empires' competing visions of how the digital economy ought to be regulated. In governing the tech industry, the US draws on its market-driven instincts whereas China elevates the role of the state to the heart of its regulatory model. The EU differs from both the American market-driven model and the Chinese state-driven model in its focus on the individual and collective rights of its citizens in the digital economy. Despite many differences across the three jurisdictions' regulatory philosophies, the book shows how all three models also have some overlapping commitments that coexist alongside those differences. All models also evolve over time, which both amplifies their similarities and makes starker some of their differences.

Chapter 1 discusses the American market-driven regulatory model, which centers on protecting free speech, the free internet, and incentives to innovate. This regulatory approach rests on a policy view that places notable faith in markets and embraces a limited role for the government. According to this view, the government needs to step aside to maximize the private sector's unfettered innovative zeal—except when it comes to protecting national security, including cybersecurity, where the government can and must work alongside private companies. The chapter traces the ideological origins of the US model and shows how the values and principles underlying that model have been deeply engrained in existing legal frameworks and actual government policy. However, the political winds are turning in the US as well. The public and political leaders are starting to question the virtues of the free internet and the growing role of the largest tech companies in ordering our societies. At the same time, many voices remain skeptical of change and maintain that market-driven values are deeply entrenched in Americans' institutions and mindsets, making it difficult to reverse the regulatory model that, despite all its limitations and false promises, continues to be associated with tremendous wealth and technological progress.

Chapter 2 examines the Chinese state-driven regulatory model. It shows how the Chinese government leverages technology to fuel the country's economic growth and development. In the name of social stability, the government also uses technology as a tool for political control, surveillance, and propaganda, entrenching digital authoritarianism deeply into the Chinese society. These two factors—economic development and social stability—are central to the survival of the Chinese Communist Party (CCP). The chapter engages with criticism of the Chinese regulatory approach, detailing how the state-driven model infringes individual rights and deprives Chinese citizens of key civil liberties. At the same time, it acknowledges that technological breakthroughs can also emerge under a state-driven regulatory model, suggesting that freedom may not be necessary for a dynamic culture of innovation. However, the future of the Chinese tech industry is uncertain. As with the US, the Chinese regulatory model is undergoing a drastic shift as the Chinese government is abandoning its traditionally lax approach toward tech regulation, and forcefully leveraging its powers to crack down on the tech industry in the name of "common prosperity" while facing little resistance from the industry. This unfolding change further reinforces the core tenet of the state-driven regulatory model by ensuring that the Chinese government, not tech companies, reigns supreme over the digital economy in China.

Chapter 3 brings into view the third major model of digital regulation—the European rights-driven model. The chapter illustrates how the EU asserts its regulatory power in the name of upholding individual and collective rights, protecting democratic values, and ushering in a fair and human-centric digital society. To further these goals, the EU model distributes power away from large tech companies to smaller firms, internet users, and platform workers. The EU often refers to the "digital society of rights and values," which, it claims, cannot be realized under the market-based model that permits the exploitation of personal data by tech companies, nor under the state-centric model that permits censorship and surveillance by governments. The EU further engrains those rights and values in binding regulatory instruments, reflecting its belief that digital transformation needs to be firmly anchored in the rule of law and democratic institutions. Despite the many benefits associated with the EU's regulatory model, the chapter also addresses its shortcomings, including the common criticism that extensive regulation impedes innovation, thereby explaining the EU's inability to date to produce tech companies akin to those that have emerged and thrived under American and Chinese regulatory models.

Part II (Chapters 4–6) turns to analyze conflicts that ensue when the three regulatory models collide in the international domain. Those conflicts manifest both as vertical battles, involving governments and tech companies, and as horizontal battles, involving the governments themselves. It starts by examining the difficult choices faced by tech companies caught between conflicting demands of different regulatory models, before moving to examine the US–China tech war and the evolving regulatory conflicts between the US and the EU.

Chapter 4 specifically examines how American and Chinese tech companies straddle between the market-driven and state-driven regulatory models as they fight vertical battles against the US and Chinese governments, facing increasingly irresolvable regulatory dilemmas. At worst, tech companies are forced to choose which of the models they comply with—while knowing that their compliance with one regulatory model is deemed to violate another. For example, a Chinese tech company listed in the US stock exchange cannot at the same time obey the US government's request to disclose certain data and the Chinese government's request not to disclose that same data. Similarly, US tech companies operating in China must acquiesce to the Chinese government's demands to censor online content, which puts them directly at odds with the American regulatory model emphasizing free speech, and exposes them to criticism among US lawmakers, their US-based customers, and their own employees. These conflicts have grave implications for the companies involved but also for the broader digital economy, as they risk partially decoupling the leading tech ecosystems.

Chapter 5 shows how the individual vertical battles discussed in Chapter 4 are now evolving into a broader horizontal conflict between the US and China as the two digital powers are fighting for technological supremacy. Over the past few years, the US has taken a number of measures to restrict China's access to strategic technologies, citing national security concerns. China is responding in kind, imposing extensive export and investment restrictions on US companies. This ongoing rivalry has also fueled a subsidy race as the US and China both seek to shore up their capabilities in critical technologies such as semiconductors. Other countries, including those in the EU, are also turning to industrial policy in the midst of the growing US–China tensions and unraveling global supply chains. As a result, the tech war risks entrenching techno-nationalism as a global norm. This can be seen as a victory for the Chinese state-driven model as governments are abandoning the US's vision of an open, free, and global digital economy. The chapter predicts that the US–China conflict is likely to continue, even intensify. But it also shows how deeply intertwined supply chains and commercial pressures in both the US and China are likely to prevent a full decoupling of US and Chinese technological assets. As a result, the horizontal conflict will remain costly, yet will also feature elements of restraint, ultimately denying both satisfactory resolution and averting a complete balkanization of the digital economy.

Chapter 6 closes out Part II by discussing transatlantic regulatory battles, revealing how the US tech companies and the US government are in a much more tenuous position than widely understood. They have over the past years been fighting a two-front battle, not just with China, but also with Europe. One of the most notable areas of transatlantic disagreement relates to data protection, where the EU's focus on fundamental rights clashes with the US's focus on national security. This disagreement has become a major obstacle for data flows between the EU and the US. Other dominant conflicts revolve around antitrust policy and digital taxation, both realms where the US government has perceived the EU's attempts to impose obligations on American tech giants as acts of digital protectionism. However, on many of these issues, the transatlantic gap seems to be gradually closing. The US is conceding that more regulation of the tech industry is needed and thus moving toward the European regulatory approach, paving the way for transatlantic rapprochement and cooperation. What gives an even greater impetus for bridging the remaining transatlantic differences is the EU and US's shared concern about China's rise and the impact of that rise on the future of liberal democracy. Both parties acknowledge that their policy differences seem manageable compared to China's AI-powered mass surveillance, internet censorship, and government propaganda, all of which are antithetical to the values of democracy and freedom that the EU and the US have long embraced at home and championed abroad.

Part III (Chapters 7–9) extends the discussion from various bilateral battles between digital empires to a global battle that reaches across all continents. In addition to engaging in mutual rivalries, the US, China, and the EU each seek to expand their respective spheres of influence, looking to gain relative influence by shifting the global digital marketplace toward their competing norms and values. In reaching across jurisdictions, each is relying on different forms of influence, with the US leveraging its private power, China its infrastructure power, and the EU its regulatory power.

Chapter 7 examines how the US has exported its market-driven ideals primarily through the penetrating influence of its leading tech companies, which have shaped digital economies around the world through their business practices. Private tech companies have thus been key in not just defending the American market-driven ideals at home, but also in universalizing them through the often-unmitigated influence they exercise over the digital lives of internet users abroad. The US government has further paved the way for its companies' global influence by actively promoting its "internet freedom agenda" as a key element of its foreign policy, urging governments around the world to commit to the economic and political freedoms that underlie the US regulatory model. However, the US model is now becoming a victim of its early success. The outsized influence of the US tech companies and their harmful practices are creating a backlash across jurisdictions. This growing resentment is further contributing to the decline of the US regulatory model and, with that, the dwindling of the influence of the values associated with the most powerful digital empire.

Chapter 8 turns to examine how China is gaining global influence by building digital infrastructures around the world. Country by country, Chinese tech companies—all with varying ties to the CCP—have built the physical components of digital infrastructures, provided critical telecommunications and electronic commerce (e-commerce) services, and supplied surveillance technologies along the Digital Silk Road. This chapter shows how Chinese tech companies have made inroads into numerous markets across Asia, Africa, and Latin America and even parts of Europe. China has also gradually assumed control of key positions in relevant international organizations involved in standard setting across technologies, further allowing the Chinese government to entrench its regulatory standards and surveillance practices—and, with that, its values—around the world. Many receiving countries have welcomed Chinese technologies and accompanying regulatory standards as a path toward digital sovereignty and development. For authoritarian governments, an additional motivation has been to gain access to surveillance technologies that they eagerly use toward illiberal ends. The chapter discusses the unease the US and its allies have regarding the growing sphere of China's influence yet also acknowledges the difficulties they face in countering that influence.

Chapter 9 moves to examine how the EU has also wielded significant international influence through its digital regulations that have spread around the world. By adopting laws such as the GDPR, the EU often shapes the global business practices of leading tech companies, which often extend these EU regulations across their global business operations in an effort to standardize their products and services worldwide—a phenomenon known as the "Brussels Effect." While the GDPR may be the posterchild of the EU's global regulatory influence, this chapter shows how antitrust law, regulation of online content, and rules for emerging technologies such as artificial intelligence can be similarly exported through the Brussels Effect. European digital regulations have not only been incorporated into tech companies' global business practices, but often ingrained in legislation by foreign governments. As democratic governments are turning away from the American market-driven model, they are increasingly embracing the European rights-driven model as an alternative way to govern their digital economies. At the same time, while many foreign stakeholders welcome the EU's global regulatory power, others criticize the EU for engaging in regulatory imperialism and thus undermining the authority of governments to regulate their digital economies in accordance with their national interests and democratic preferences.

The conclusion asks whether the American, the Chinese, or the European regulatory model will prevail in their horizontal battles and quest for global influence, while simultaneously examining whether the tech companies or governments will ultimately triumph in their various vertical battles. It predicts that the European rights-driven regulatory model is likely to prevail over the American market-driven model within the democratic world. At the same time, the continuing appeal of the Chinese regulatory model limits the EU's ability to entrench its norms and values outside of the democratic world. In addition, the EU model is haunted by the difficulties of enforcing its regulations against powerful tech companies, threatening to render its victory in the battle of values a hollow one. In this state of the world, the US needs to decide whether to align itself more closely with the European regulatory model—in part in response to a shift in domestic policy preferences and in part to contain China's growing influence over the digital economy. If the US can be convinced that embracing the European rights-driven model will not impede innovation and compromise its technological progress, this choice to emulate the EU model will be easier to embrace. Ultimately, the most compelling argument for closer transatlantic alignment comes from a shared perception that the US and the EU both need to focus on the battle that matters the most: the battle that will be fought over the fate of liberal democracy. That battle will ultimately determine the soul of the digital economy, defining what kind of society we will live in for years and decades to come—a battle that neither the US nor the EU can afford to lose.

PART I

Digital Empires

I

The American Market-Driven Regulatory Model

THE AMERICAN MARKET-DRIVEN regulatory model and the US tech giants that grew under its influence have provided the foundation for much of the global digital economy as it exists today. The US model, in particular, centers on protecting free speech, a free internet, and incentives to innovate. It is shaped by discernible techno-optimism, relentless pursuit of innovation, and uncompromised faith in markets as opposed to government regulation. Under this worldview, the internet is viewed as a source of economic prosperity and political freedom and as a tool for societal transformation and progress. The market-driven regulatory model places trust in tech companies' ability to self-regulate and embraces a limited role for government. Proponents of this model argue that the government needs to step aside to maximize the private sector's unfettered innovative zeal—except when it comes to protecting national security, including cybersecurity, where both the government and private sector play a role. This pro-market ethos is deeply embedded in the existing US regulatory framework, which consists of weakly enforced antitrust laws, an absence of a federal data privacy law, and permissive content moderation rules that shield tech companies from liability, leaving them free to decide whether or not to remove certain harmful content from their platforms.

The origins of the American market-driven regulatory model can be traced to California: not only the home of pathbreaking technological innovations, but also certain countercultural ideals that shaped the internet revolution and championed internet freedom.[1] Most of today's leading tech giants, including Apple, Google, and Meta, hail from California. A thriving venture capital (VC) industry, characterized by risk-seeking investors pursuing rare but, when successful, astronomical awards, have fueled these companies' innovations.[2] These VC investors, enthralled by audacious innovations and "lust for riches," have channeled both capital and talented employees into countless tech startups, incubating a fertile tech industry and establishing California's—and in particular Silicon Valley's—preeminence in the global digital economy.[3] Silicon Valley's tech companies have benefited from unparalleled access to engineering talent, in no small part thanks to their proximity to the thriving research cluster built around Stanford University.[4] Stanford has invested heavily in science and engineering research, and cultivated close contacts with the technology industry, including by building a large research park around its campus. Stanford itself has benefited from extensive federal research grants and military contracts, further amplifying its scale advantages.

However, the techno-libertarian thinking that has emanated from California has not been shaped by the Silicon Valley engineers, the startup founders, the venture capitalists, or Stanford University alone. Instead, it stems from diverse communities knit together by their shared optimism about technology. Richard Barbrook and Andy Cameron have described the ethos behind the rise of the American internet economy as a reflection of a distinct "Californian ideology," in that it combines the "freewheeling spirit of the hippies" and the "entrepreneurial zeal of the yuppies."[5] These different West Coast communities—writers, artists, hackers, community media activists, and capitalists—shared a profound faith in the "emancipatory potential" embedded in information technologies.[6] Given its diverse foundation, the American market-driven model thus extends beyond traditional neoliberal thinking. It blends the cultural bohemianism of San Francisco with the high-tech industries invented in Silicon Valley, bringing together these seemingly different worldviews under a shared rubric of profound techno-optimism.

These early techno-libertarians found common purpose reaching across the political spectrum. These varied groups were united in their goals by their distrust of authorities, hierarchies, and government, and coalesced around the idea that technology allows them to transcend the existing dominant institutions.[7] For the left-leaning techno-libertarians, technology offered a way to empower individuals and community activists at the expense of corporate and bureaucratic elites.[8] Several prominent scholars, including Yochai Benkler, and influential NGOs, such the Electronic Frontier Foundation, advanced their techno-optimist argument from the political left, emphasizing the internet's potential to enhance individual freedom and civil liberties.[9] For the right-leaning proponents of the market-driven model, technology presented the opportunity to weaken big government and entrench their laissez faire ideology by reducing the power of the nation state, fueling competition, and empowering technology entrepreneurs.[10] Even though the early days of the internet combined left and right ideologies under a shared Californian ideology, the free-market ideology has subsequently come to transcend the original countercultural roots of the market-driven model as the internet has further commercialized.[11]

Even with its faith in markets and reliance on venture capital, there is more to the American techno-libertarian spirit than sheer profit-making. Scholars studying Silicon Valley's culture emphasize its meritocratic mindset and the ability to reward creativity, individualism, and risk-taking.[12] But what makes Silicon Valley truly special, they argue, is its tech entrepreneurs' innovative zeal that often goes beyond the desire to make money. Many West Coast insiders of the tech community emphasize American tech entrepreneurs' aspiration to "change the world" through revolutionary technologies. Often, these entrepreneurs consider themselves as "revolutionaries" and "visionaries" engaged in remaking the world through technology.[13] This distinct Silicon Valley mentality can be contrasted with that of Chinese tech entrepreneurs in Shenzhen, which is China's hub for technology innovations and manufacturing. In Shenzhen, the Silicon Valley's dual motivation—making money while changing the world—is reduced to the first motivation—making money. Kai-Fu Lee, a prominent Chinese technology investor and the former president of Google China, describes Chinese tech entrepreneurs as market-driven individuals whose goal is to get rich. Unlike many of Silicon Valley's leaders, the Chinese tech entrepreneurs did not have the luxury of growing up having their parents encourage them to think how they might change the world. These individuals are often a mere generation away from severe poverty and were raised with a single-minded focus on survival.[14] Silicon Valley's dual motivational structure and certain idealism are therefore seen as a quintessential product of its distinct mindset and hence part of the American techno-libertarian ethos.[15]

This chapter outlines the main tenets of the American market-driven regulatory model, a model that emerged out of these techno-libertarian origins. It explains how this model developed around a skepticism of government regulation and a fear that such regulation hinders innovation and reduces economic growth. Next, the chapter turns from this economic rationale for limited government intervention to the political rationale for keeping the government at bay. According to this view, the internet must be the bastion of free speech. Only by defending free speech and condemning censorship can the internet advance individual freedom and democracy. Both these freedoms— economic and political—have also been deeply engrained in law, enjoying the full backing of every branch of the US government, and further entrenching self-regulation as the norm in the US. However, despite its faith in markets, the market-driven regulatory model has accommodated a prominent role for the government in funding several key innovations. Since the onset of the US–China tech war, the US government has also assumed greater control over the tech industry as the country's national security and technological self-sufficiency have gained new salience in policymaking. These examples reveal how the US model is hardly absolutist in its market-driven commitments but also accommodates state intervention when viewed as necessary to ensure technological progress or fulfill other policy goals. As this chapter shows, there has also been a notable recent turn in the public conversation about the digital economy in the US. The general public and political leaders alike are starting to question the virtues of the free internet and the outsized role of the largest tech companies in ordering the American economy and society. This chapter delves into this criticism of the market-driven regulatory model, revealing how it is pushing the US toward a potentially larger rethink of the techno-libertarian foundations of its regulatory model, and its suitability to address the challenges of today's digital economy.

Markets Outperform Government Regulation

The early internet pioneers in California took an extreme view against regulation, arguing that regulation was both undesirable and unfeasible. According to this view, the internet should be a self-ordering space that writes its own rules without government interference. Only when left alone can the internet deliver its full potential. At the 1996 World Economic Forum meeting in Davos, John Perry Barlow, the founder of the Electronic Frontier Foundation, published "A Declaration of the Independence of the Cyberspace," which captured the core tenet of the internet freedom agenda.[16] In the Declaration, Barlow declares the cyberspace to be its own "global social space" that is independent from government "tyranny." National governments have no moral right or legal authority to impose their laws on this space that is detached from state sovereignty, Barlow proclaims. The internet is a self-ordering place that forms its own social contract and sets its own rules. Barlow also advances a view that is optimistic and empowering. Capturing the emancipatory spirit of the Californian ideology, he describes the cyberspace as "a world that all may enter without privilege or prejudice" and as a place that is "more humane and fair than the world your governments have made before."

The Declaration advances a vision that the internet cannot, and should not, be regulated. Numerous scholars, commentators, and political leaders have since endorsed this view, and it is a perspective that has played an important role in shaping the American regulatory model.[17] There are several strands to these anti-regulation arguments. The first argument is that cyberspace is different from the real world and hence by its very nature eludes government control. In the early years of the internet, the Clinton administration largely subscribed to this view that controlling the internet is "impossible,"[18] or, as President Clinton famously put it in 2000, any attempt to regulate it was "like trying to nail Jell-O to the wall."[19] Second, even if the internet in theory could be regulated, an attempt to do so would be ill-advised, even illegitimate. Some commentators argue that the government is too slow to regulate fast-developing technologies, making such regulation ineffective to address any problems that may emerge in cyberspace.[20] Private parties are better positioned to develop responsive, adaptive, and flexible norms that govern the online world.[21] Critics also argue against regulation on the grounds that territoriality-based government regulation is ill-suited for the borderless internet.[22] Any nation's attempt to exercise jurisdiction over cyberspace would inevitably have undesirable spillover effects in other jurisdictions, resulting in jurisdictional conflicts and excessive regulation, in addition to being by its nature anti-democratic.[23]

Others have refuted the argument that the internet cannot be regulated. Lawrence Lessig has written against the idea that cyberspace is immune from control. Instead, he argues that cyberspace is governed and controlled by *code*—the internet's underlying architecture—written by programmers coding websites and other software. This code instructs the technology to perform a certain way. According to Lessig, how this code is written determines whether cyberspace is a space for freedom or oppressive control. This view maintains that "code is law," which makes it crucial that policymakers and citizens influence the values that the code embodies.[24] Jack Goldsmith has offered another early critique of the view that the internet by its very nature does not lend itself to regulation.[25] He refutes the argument that cyberspace activity is fundamentally different from the activity taking place in the real world.[26] Even in the offline world, people from one territorial jurisdiction frequently transact with people from another territorial jurisdiction, and existing laws are capable of handling such multijurisdictional regulatory problems. Also, while spillover effects of cyberspace regulation are common, so are the spillover effects of the cyberspace activity itself.[27] This adds legitimacy to government efforts to regulate any online activity that produces effects in their respective jurisdictions.[28]

Even if one accepts that regulation of cyberspace is feasible, an ideological disagreement remains over the optimal amount of regulation. The market-driven regulatory model rests on an idea that even if governments had the ability and the legal authority to regulate, they should take a backseat and make space for self-regulation. According to this view, cyberspace lends itself particularly well for self-governance.[29] First, the digital economy is characterized by easy access to information, which promotes fair bargaining between all parties. Digital communication lowers transaction costs, further facilitating private contracting across all online transactions. Second, entry and exit are near costless, making it easy for parties to switch across internet service providers and hence opt in and out of rules that correspond to their preferences. This view assumes an online space where different internet service providers tailor their products and services to differing consumer preferences. For example, some online platforms may permit offensive language while others may ban it. The internet user can then choose the service that corresponds to that user's preferences on the optimal boundaries of free speech.[30] This characterization of the online marketplace rests on an idea of almost limitless consumer choice as well as efficient and highly competitive markets that call for little government involvement—an assumption that recently has come under increasing criticism, as discussed further below.[31]

A key argument for relying on free markets and limiting regulatory intervention has been the belief that this policy approach best supports innovation and economic growth.[32] From this perspective, when the government stays out of the way, it will not dampen the innovative zeal of the entrepreneurs. Venture capital will identify winners better than governments, allowing for the most innovative companies to thrive. Regulation is viewed as an impediment to innovation as excessive regulation increases costs and further constrains the behavior of innovators. Of course, even the proponents of free markets concede that markets are not perfect and private companies do not always get it right. For example, many Americans acknowledge the problems associated with the massive extraction of personal data by large tech companies, such as Google and Meta. However, their conclusion has often been that, in choosing between the two evils, the government should be feared more than the corporations.[33] Violation of privacy is seen as an inevitable side effect of doing business. Or, as Scott McNealy, the CEO and cofounder of Sun Microsystems, stated back in 1999: "You have zero privacy anyway. Get over it."[34] Even while boundaries of data privacy may be transgressed by the tech companies and their data-driven business practices, many retort that the "bigger concern is the government" and that markets are likely to eventually solve the problem anyway.[35] A more interventionist regulatory approach, this argument suggests, would not only risk curtailing these key freedoms but also constrain the entrepreneurial zeal and innovative drive of platform companies that have generated tremendous wealth and driven new innovations.[36]

Among those who advocate for the market-driven model, many espouse a view that regulation should be strictly confined to addressing market failures.

Yet the most ardent techno-libertarians do not see the need for regulation even where markets fail. Instead, they present technology as the solution wherever technology is a problem.[37] If harmful speech appears online, tech companies will develop technologies to filter such speech. If internet users worry about privacy, tech companies will develop technologies that preserve user privacy. Government regulation is rarely the solution—technology is. According to this view, when technology is harnessed to address any regulatory challenges, several benefits will ensue.[38] For one, while law often offers a singular solution, technological remedies can better respond to the different perceptions of the problem and the plurality of the views held by internet users. Second, they can be deployed more nimbly, making these market-based remedies more responsive to evolving technologies as well as changing business and social practices. Technological remedies can also deploy the vast resources of the private sector, harnessing the expertise of tech companies with deep knowledge of the technologies they have generated in the first place. In contrast, government regulation would often consist of a single solution, deployed with a delay, and implemented with limited knowledge and resources.

This faith in self-regulation as a core tenet of the American regulatory model sets it apart from the European rights-driven regulatory model, where the government, not the tech companies, is in charge of solving regulatory problems. Apple's development of a technological solution to eradicate child sexual abuse from its phones illustrates this contrast between the two models well. In 2021, Apple announced that it had developed a new technology called neuralMatch that is designed to scan child sexual abuse imagery in iPhones.[39] The technology would alert a team of human reviewers if illegal images are detected, and the reviewers would then pass the information to law enforcement after verification. This feature is part of Apple's new child protection systems, which the company had planned to introduce first in the US alongside the release of its iOS 15 phone. While some privacy advocates have expressed concern that this technology paves the way for broader surveillance practices—which is why Apple has, for now, postponed the introduction of the technology—others hailed the company's commitment to deploying technology to solve online harms that governments have tried to regulate with only moderate success.[40] Apple's efforts to find a way to ensure that its products are not being used for illegal activity—even in the absence of a legal requirement to do so—is an example of self-regulation that the US model encourages. In comparison, in 2022, the European Commission proposed new legislation that, if adopted, will oblige tech companies to detect, report, and delete any child sexual abuse material from their platforms.[41] These two examples involving self-regulation by Apple on the one hand, and government regulation by the Commission on the other, reveal in a concrete way the distinctiveness of the American regulatory model, which believes that tech companies—not governments—should lead the way in regulating the digital economy.

A Free Internet Advances Freedom and Democracy

Inherent in the American market-driven regulatory model is also the idea that government intervention not only compromises the efficient operation of markets, but also undermines individual liberty. Thus, while the US's commitment to innovation and growth provides an economic rationale to argue against government intervention, its commitment to individual liberty and freedom is often invoked as a political reason to limit government interference. This is seen as central to vibrant democratic society characterized by free speech and the engagement of diverse voices in public conversation and civic life. One of the core beliefs underlying the market-driven model is its faith in technology as an instrument to advance democracy. Among the internet pioneers in California, technology was viewed as offering a path toward individual freedom and an elevated state of participatory democracy. In the early days of the internet economy, the techno-optimists believed that these technologies would create an "electronic agora," a virtual place for everyone to express their opinions free of censorship or the mediating influence of the government and corporations.[42] What fueled their optimism was the idea that a direct democracy within all institutions was within reach.

The internet's potential to advance democracy also informed US government policy across different administrations. Ira Magaziner, Chief Policy Advisor to President Clinton, delivered a speech at The Progress & Freedom Foundation's annual summit on Cyberspace and the American Dream in 1998, in which he described the internet as "a force for the promotion of democracy," explaining how "dictatorship depends upon the control of the flow of information." Magaziner suggested that, with access to the internet, people around the world can gain access to information, which allows them to "participate fully in the democratic process." This led him to conclude that the internet has "tremendous potential for promoting individual freedom and individual empowerment."[43] Over the subsequent decades, this idea of democracy-enhancing properties of technology has persisted. In her famous 2010 speech on internet freedom, then-Secretary of State Hillary Clinton emphasized how technologies can transform societies. In her words,

"online organizing has been a critical tool for advancing democracy and enabling citizens to protest suspicious election results. And even in established
democracies like the United States, we've seen the power of these tools to
change history."[44] This belief in the internet's potential to advance democracy
and freedoms abroad has also been central to the US's foreign policy agenda,
as discussed in Chapter 7.

Few would dispute that the wide dissemination of digital technologies has
empowered individuals, giving them new economic, political, and cultural
opportunities. As billions of people around the world have gained access to the
internet, their ability to access information, transact professionally, and connect personally has expanded. In a best-case scenario, this more democratized
access to conversations and opportunities should also usher in a more inclusive democracy that empowers the voiceless and diminishes the importance
of elite referees—whether established media or political parties—that have
traditionally controlled access to public space and political conversations.[45]
The internet's ability to enable community organizing and to change history,
as Secretary Clinton suggested, has also been vividly illustrated in some recent social movements that have gained visibility online and shifted national,
even international, conversation about the need for social justice and change.
For example, it took less than a year for the hashtag #MeToo to be shared over
19 million times globally, contributing to the social movement against sexual
harassment.[46] The hashtag #BlackLivesMatter was being shared on average
3.8 million times a day in the period following the brutal killing of an un-
armed black man, George Floyd, at the hands of a white police officer in May
2020.[47] These examples reveal how social media campaigns can be effective
in elevating the political salience of issues and paving the way for social and
political reforms.

The US regulatory model rests on a belief that the internet contributes to
vibrant democracy by fostering public debate and elevating diverse voices. The
internet can amplify freedom of speech, which again can amplify democratic
discourse, the techno-libertarian argument goes. The US's commitment to
free speech is one the country's defining values. The First Amendment of the
US Constitution codifies this freedom, and the courts have defended it vigorously ever since. It is this unyielding commitment to free speech—together
with a firm belief that the internet ought to be a bastion of such speech—
that most sets the American market-driven regulatory model apart from the
Chinese state-driven regulatory model, which views online censorship as necessary to maintain an orderly society. But the US model also departs from that
of the EU in its approach toward online speech even while both Europeans
and Americans consider free speech to be a fundamental right. The protection

of free speech in the US rests on a notion of a "marketplace of ideas," which emphasizes the societal benefit of preserving an uninhibited environment where all ideas can be voiced without government censorship or control.[48] As a result, the US is prepared to defend free speech even in instances where the EU is prepared to restrict it, protecting even hateful speech or repulsive ideas that, under the European regulatory model, are seen as compromising individual dignity and leading to societal harm that the government needs to address. In contrast, under the American regulatory model, there is a guiding belief that as long as this marketplace of ideas remains free, truth will ultimately emerge and prevail. This freedom of speech also serves democratic culture through deliberation and participation. These opportunities for participation can be magnified through digital technologies, providing a strong political argument for a free internet leading the way toward a more robust and inclusive democracy. This understanding of technology's relationship to democracy has remained a lodestar for the American market-driven regulatory model.

Codifying the Free-Market Ethos in Law

This market-driven ethos underlying the American regulatory model is codified in statutes and court judgments, thus illustrating that the ideas around economic and political freedom have enjoyed the full backing of the US government. This way, the roots of the market-driven model can be traced not only to Silicon Valley but also to Washington, DC. Since the 1990s, all branches of the US government—Congress, the Executive branch, and the courts—have been reinforcing the market-driven regulatory model by enacting and interpreting the US Constitution and various statutes in ways that have enhanced the private power of the tech companies at the expense of the government.[49] This reflects a widely held view that the government ought to set the tech companies free to innovate in order to maximize the country's economic growth. Thus, since the early years of the digital revolution, the tech companies and the US government have largely acted in unison toward upholding the same vision of an unregulated, innovative, market-driven digital economy.

How Congress Liberated Tech Companies with Section 230 of the Communications Decency Act

Congress deserves much of the credit—or, as some would argue, much of the blame—for setting the tone that underpins the deregulatory architecture of today's digital economy. No other law better captures the spirit of the American market-driven regulatory model than Section 230 of the Communications Decency Act (CDA) of 1996.[50] This law provides immunity for online intermediaries, precluding these companies from being held legally liable for any third-party content that they host on their platforms. For example, YouTube cannot be held responsible when a user uploads a video that promotes violence, and Meta cannot be accused of defamation when a Facebook user posts a libelous comment about someone on that platform. At the same time, if YouTube chose to take the illegal video down or Meta chose to remove the defamatory post, these companies would be free to do so without a fear that they are violating the user's free speech rights. The assumption underlying this liability shield is that these platforms are not considered publishers of the content, which relieves them of certain legal obligations. This immunity that runs both ways—protecting platforms' action and inaction alike—has been viewed as essential for online services to grow and flourish. It has even led some commentators to describe Section 230 as "the law that matters most for speech on the Web."[51]

Congress enacted Section 230 in response to a concern that arose in 1995 when the New York Supreme Court ruled in the case of *Stratton Oakmont v. Prodigy* that Prodigy, an internet service provider that hosted online bulletin boards, was held liable for defamatory postings on those bulletin boards.[52] At the time, Prodigy had two million subscribers and it received 60,000 postings a day, which was far too many for the company to review systematically. However, by engaging in content moderation and deleting many offensive messages, the court found that Prodigy had assumed the role of a "publisher," which made the company responsible for defamatory postings published on its site. Thus, an attempt to moderate *some* posts led the company to be held liable for *all* posts. To avoid liability, Prodigy would have had to give up moderating altogether and simply act as a blind host of third-party posts. Several members of Congress reacted to the court decision with alarm. To preserve tech companies' incentives to develop new, innovative, and beneficial services—including moderator tools, as Prodigy had done—Congress moved to shield these companies from liability, claiming this was necessary to ensure the internet could serve its users and continue to flourish.[53]

The contested *Stratton Oakmont* decision thus provided the impetus for Congress to enact the CDA in 1995, which became the first piece of legislation to regulate online speech in the US.[54] This law regulated obscenity and indecency and made it illegal to knowingly expose minors to such content online.[55] It was introduced alongside a sweeping bill to update the Telecommunications Act of 1934.[56] During the passage of the bill,

Representatives Chris Cox and Ron Wyden introduced an amendment to the CDA that would end up becoming Section 230.[57] The bipartisan Cox-Wyden Amendment was specifically designed to overrule *Stratton-Oakmont v. Prodigy* and ensure that internet service providers would not be treated as publishers of third-party content, thus distinguishing online services from publications such as newspapers that are held accountable for the content they print. According to Representative Cox, the amendment was designed to serve two purposes. First, it would protect online service providers from liability in instances where they decide to remove indecent and offensive material for their customers. Second, "it will establish as the policy of the United States that we do not wish to have content regulation by the Federal Government of what is on the Internet."[58]

A key goal of Section 230 was to vest private parties, such as parents or internet service providers, with the authority to regulate offensive content, rather than have the Federal Communications Commission regulate such content.[59] According to Representatives Cox and Wyden, parents and families were better suited than "government bureaucrats" to protect children online, which is why it was important that internet service providers such as Prodigy remained free to develop tools to help these customers determine the content they see.[60] The fear was that too much government regulation would prevent the market from coming up with innovative solutions or undermine the internet as "a forum for a true diversity of political discourse" that flourishes with a minimum of government regulation.[61] Representatives Cox and Wyden stated this unambiguously when clarifying that "our intent in writing this law was to keep the [Federal Communications Commission] out of the business of regulating websites, content moderation policies, and the content of speech on the internet."[62] This vision was firmly enshrined in Section 230, which states that "it is the policy of the United States . . . to preserve the vibrant and competitive free market that presently exists for the Internet and other interactive computer services, unfettered by Federal or State regulation."[63]

In shielding online platforms from legal liability and by encouraging self-regulation, Section 230 captures the core philosophy of the American market-driven regulatory model. While it is the hallmark of Congress's attempts to codify the free market and free speech ideas into the US's digital legislation, this same philosophy has also guided many other legislative acts and proposals in Congress. The 1998 Digital Millennium Copyright Act, for example, shields internet service providers from liability with respect to copyright-infringing material posted on their platforms as long as these companies follow certain policies, including taking down illegal content once requested to do so by the copyright owner.[64] Other laws introduced in Congress largely embody this same spirit of minimalist regulation in the name of innovation and technological progress. When Representative William Tauzin introduced the Internet Protection Act of 1997, he emphasized the need to support efficient technological innovation and deployment of information technology services. This, according to Tauzin, required the US to "rely on private initiative and to avoid, to the maximum extent possible, government restriction or supervision of such services."[65] Two years later, Senator John McCain struck a similar tone in introducing the Internet Regulatory Freedom Act, designed to "prohibit the FCC and state commissions from regulating . . . Internet access or online services."[66] The Children's Online Privacy Protection Act (COPPA) of 1998,[67] which has been described as the "first US privacy law written for the Internet," enhances data protections for children under the age of thirteen, including calling for website operators to publish a privacy policy and seek parental consent in some instances. Yet even COPPA allows for companies to request the FTC's approval of self-regulatory guidelines to govern their compliance, showing how Congress's legislative activity has been guided by its pro-market instincts.[68]

What Congress has *not* done in terms of legislation is perhaps even more telling than what it has done to regulate the digital economy. Even as most countries in the world have adopted laws to regulate data privacy, no comprehensive federal privacy law has emerged from Congress. Congress has also not updated its age-old antitrust statutes that, according to many, are ill-suited to address the problems of today's digital economy. Nor has Congress acted to regulate artificial intelligence, protect the rights of gig workers, or imposed obligations on platforms to share revenue with creators of copyright-protected content. This bare-bones US legislative framework stands in stark contrast to the EU institutions, which have legislated extensively across these and many other domains of the digital economy, as discussed in Chapter 3. Over the past few years, several members of Congress have started to question the idea that free markets and self-regulation best serve today's digital economy. Several bills calling for more governmental oversight are pending in both the House of Representatives and the Senate, as will be discussed below. However, the partisan gridlock has ensured that Congress has failed to harness the needed political consensus to pass any such proposed legislation to date. Thus, Congress—through its inaction—continues to sustain the market-driven regulatory model as the foundation of the digital economy even today.

Tech Companies Protected by the Courts: Judicial Interpretation of Section 230

While Congress played a key role in setting tech companies free by legislating Section 230, the US judiciary has been crucial in protecting, and even expanding, the freedoms embedded in that legislation. US courts have upheld both the content and rationale behind Section 230's two-way liability shield, including in a famous case *Zeran v. America Online, Inc.*, which was decided by a US federal court in 1997.[69] The *Zeran* case concerned AOL's liability over defamatory statements a third party had posted on AOL's message board. The court upheld AOL's Section 230 immunity, highlighting the need to protect "freedom of speech in the new and burgeoning internet medium" and noting how imposing liability on AOL would constitute "intrusive government regulation of speech."[70] In interpreting Section 230 immunity and the congressional intent behind it, the court emphasized two key objectives: first, Section 230 incentivizes the platforms to filter obscenity and other offensive material without the fear of liability. Second, it encourages "unfettered and unregulated development of free speech on the Internet," which allows the internet economy and e-commerce to develop.[71]

The US Supreme Court has also endorsed strong free speech norms in its jurisprudence. Shortly after the CDA was adopted, advocates of internet freedom as well as representatives of the tech industry challenged certain provisions of the CDA on the grounds that it violated free speech rights guaranteed by the First Amendment of the US Constitution.[72] The contested provisions were intended to protect minors from unsuitable internet material and criminalized the intentional transmission of "obscene or indecent" or offensive sexual messages. In 1997, the case reached the US Supreme Court, which struck down the CDA's anti-decency provisions in *Reno v. American Civil Liberties Union*.[73] In invalidating the law, the Court held that the CDA placed an "unacceptably heavy burden on protected speech" that "threaten[ed] to torch a large segment of the Internet community."[74] The Court also wrote that "the interest in encouraging freedom of expression in a democratic society outweighs any theoretical but unproven benefit of censorship."[75] The Court left Section 230's liability shield untouched and used the ruling as the opportunity to portray the internet as a virtual town square where speech of any kind contributes to democratic discourse.

The Supreme Court has maintained a similar tone even in its recent rulings, extending its defense of the internet as a bastion of free speech to the modern era of the digital economy where the value of free speech online has become more contested. For example, in *Packingham v. North Carolina*,[76] decided in 2017, the Supreme Court struck down a statute that permitted a state to prohibit a person convicted of a sex crime from accessing social media. In invalidating the contested statute, the Supreme Court issued a sweeping ruling where it compared online platforms to a modern public park or town square, thus portraying platforms as quasi-state actors that should be limited by the First Amendment from using their power to silence citizens. According to the Court, "a fundamental principle of the First Amendment is that all persons have access to places where they can speak and listen."[77] The Court then went on to rule that the most important place for the exchange of views today is "cyberspace—the 'vast democratic forums of the Internet' in general, and social media in particular."[78] By prohibiting sex offenders from using social media, these individuals were prevented from "speaking and listening in the modern public square," and were thus stripped of the "most powerful mechanisms available to a private citizen to make his or her voice heard."[79] In writing for the majority, Justice Kennedy acknowledged that the impact of the internet on speech was not fully understood and that it might someday even be used for "anti-social ends."[80] However, according to Justice Kennedy, "until then, extreme caution was in order so the Internet's democratic potential could be realized."[81] This suggests that even today—with ample evidence of the internet being deployed for "anti-social ends"—for the US Supreme Court, the internet remains a stronghold of free speech that amplifies, not undermines, democracy. The US courts' steadfast defense of internet freedoms in this and earlier cases reveals how the judiciary has repeatedly lent its legitimacy to the free-market ethos that underlies the US regulatory model, thus contributing to the model's influence and endurance.

The Executive's Commitment to Internet Freedoms

Like the legislative and judicial branches of the US government, the Executive branch has embraced the market-driven regulatory model, advocating very similar policies as Congress in shielding the tech industry from extensive regulation. The Clinton administration, which oversaw the critical period of commercializing the internet, promoted nonregulation as the governing principle for the internet.[82] However, the early years of the Clinton presidency might be characterized as reflecting a more ambivalent stand as the administration was straddling its commitment to nonregulation with the need to ensure law enforcement's access to electronic devices. In 1994, the White House announced its endorsement of a "clipper chip," which was an encryption device developed by the US National Security Agency that contained a back door for law enforcement officials to break encryption and thus access voice and data transmissions in electronic devices. However, extensive criticism of the clipper chip led the Clinton administration to back down and more unequivocally embrace self-regulation as the heart of the American regulatory model.[83]

A 1997 policy document released by the Clinton administration—*A Framework for Global Electronic Commerce*—reflects this commitment to self-regulation.[84] This strategy document outlined the US policy orientation toward e-commerce, emphasizing the benefits of a market-oriented approach over government regulation. In describing the framework, Ira Magaziner, Chief Policy Advisor to President Clinton at the time, stressed how "competition and individual choice should be the watchwords of the new digital economy." Rules for the digital economy should therefore be set by private parties and multistakeholder groups, not the government.[85] President Clinton himself endorsed this market-oriented approach to e-commerce in a memorandum sent to the heads of executive departments and agencies in 1997. He emphasized the "unique nature" of the internet and how, "for electronic commerce to flourish, the private sector must lead. Therefore, the Federal Government should encourage industry self-regulation wherever appropriate and support private-sector efforts to develop technology and practices that facilitate the growth and success of the Internet."[86] He further stressed that the government should exercise restraint and avoid imposing unnecessary regulations, taxes, or tariffs on internet-based commercial activities.

This techno-optimist view reflects the prevailing political climate in the 1990s—a key decade when the internet was commercialized. That decade was also a heyday of globalization and deregulation. This era informed the views of the policymakers and the public alike, further institutionalizing the market-driven regulatory model as the norm in the US. Regulation skeptics pointed to the recently deregulated telecommunications industry, which showed that deregulated companies performed better than government-owned firms.[87] This lent additional support to the view that the private sector outperforms the government. The main concern was to avoid any harm that government might cause at a time when the world was on the brink of a new technological revolution.

This free-market dogma has continued from the 1990s into subsequent decades, characterizing the Bush and Obama administrations alike. The Bush administration's 2003 "National Strategy to Secure Cyberspace" advocated for the market-driven regulatory approach, stating how "our traditions of federalism and limited government require that organizations outside the federal government take the lead in many of these efforts."[88] This market-driven policy orientation necessitated that action by the federal government in this area was "only justified when the benefits of intervention outweigh the associated costs. This standard is especially important in cases where there are viable private sector solutions."[89] The Obama administration continued to emphasize the benefits of free markets, free speech, and the important role of the private sector in internet governance. The administration's 2011 International Strategy for Cyberspace identified the promotion of open markets as a policy priority, explaining that "Competition in these markets drives innovation, while a free-trade environment enables manufacturers to keep prices competitive and standards high . . . The United States will work to sustain that free-trade environment, particularly in support of the high-tech sector, to ensure future innovation."[90] His administration also remained skeptical of regulating the internet on grounds that any such effort could lead to harmful censorship. For example, it opposed the 2011 Stop Online Piracy Act (SOPA)—a proposed piece of legislation intended to combat online piracy— citing fears that an attempt to fight online piracy risked censoring lawful activity online.[91] The Obama administration further highlighted the important contribution of the private sector in governing the digital economy. The 2011 strategy included an ongoing commitment to its partnerships with the tech industry in internet governance, which it viewed as "essential to upholding its multi-stakeholder character."[92]

In a stark policy reversal, however, the interests of the US government and the US tech companies began to diverge during the Trump administration. President Trump, who was often seen as governing via social media platforms like Twitter, turned against the tech companies after he felt that these companies had turned against him. For example, after Twitter added fact check warnings to his tweets,[93] President Trump threatened to institute policies comparable to those deployed by authoritarian regimes, suggesting that he had the power to shut down social media or the internet to protect US national security.[94] In the name of protecting free speech and preventing online censorship, President Trump sought to root out the conservative bias that social media companies were allegedly harboring by issuing a 2020 executive order.[95] The executive order referred to US tech companies engaging in "selective censorship that is harming our national discourse" and sought to mandate them to carry certain political speech, thus interfering in these platforms' right to decide on what kind of content they host—something traditionally seen as an important part of their freedom.[96] Thus, what President Trump labelled as a defense of free speech, his critics viewed as an attack on the free press and media. President Trump's efforts to discipline social media companies may have driven a wedge between the US government and its leading tech companies, but those efforts fell short of overhauling the market-driven regulatory model as a hallmark for governing the digital economy in the US.

The Stickiness of the Free-Market Ethos in American Law

The free-market, anti-statist policy has been the cornerstone of the US regulatory approach toward the digital economy until recently, enjoying support at the highest levels of the US government. This philosophy has been deeply entrenched in existing legal frameworks and actual government policy, most notoriously in defending the liability shield under Section 230. Courts have repeatedly struck down legal challenges that would erode the core protections that tech companies enjoy under the CDA, and Congress has refused to adopt legislation that would dilute those protections. Thus, Section 230 remains the crown jewel of the US's market-driven regulatory model to this day. Congress's and the courts' tendency to default to free speech and refrain from regulating online content likely reflects their habit of seeing digital regulation primarily through the lens of First Amendment law and ideology that is pervasive in American legal culture. Any attempt to regulate online speech remains vulnerable to a legal challenge under the First Amendment, reinforcing Congress's deregulatory instinct over content moderation. First Amendment principles are also guiding the US Supreme Court's approach toward regulating the digital economy. If anything, the Supreme Court has recently taken an even more libertarian turn in interpreting the First Amendment, delivering a set of rulings that weaponize the First Amendment to keep economic and social regulation at bay.[97] Given the government's hesitancy to depart from this free speech orthodoxy, online platforms are largely left in charge, free to develop their own content moderation policies. However, even these companies' policies tend to be written in the shadow of the First Amendment thinking that permeates their corporate policies.[98] This entrenches free speech doctrine as the foundation of the American market-driven regulatory model.

These pro-market ideas have also penetrated US antitrust law, resulting in a light regulatory touch and contributing to highly concentrated technology markets. The leading technology companies—Amazon, Apple, Google, Meta, and Microsoft—have grown to dominate large swaths of the digital economy, controlling the market for e-commerce, smartphones, internet search, social media, online advertising, cloud services, and operating systems. These companies have also engaged in relentless merger activity, acquiring at least five hundred companies over the last decade and facing few regulatory constraints along the way.[99] As a manifestation of its commitment to the market-driven regulatory model, the US government has let all these mergers proceed unchallenged. The US antitrust agencies have also chosen not to deploy their powers to challenge the monopolistic behavior of these companies, bringing no cases since the US Department of Justice (DOJ) sued Microsoft in 1998.[100] Not until late 2020—over two decades since the antitrust challenge against Microsoft—did the DOJ and the Federal Trade Commission (FTC) bring antitrust suits against Google and Meta, respectively.[101] However, as explained below, it is not clear if the US judiciary is prepared to abandon its long-held commitment to market-driven principles that have defined US antitrust regulation for the past fifty years.

Another area that is highly illustrative of the market-driven regulatory model relates to the US government's approach to data privacy. The US is a global outlier in not having a federal privacy law, even as regulating data privacy has become a standard feature of legal regimes around the world.[102] President Obama sought to regulate privacy but was ultimately unsuccessful in persuading Congress to act. In 2012, the Obama administration unveiled a Consumer Privacy Bill of Rights as part of a comprehensive blueprint to protect individual privacy rights and give users more control over how their information is handled.[103] This initiative, by giving users new legal and technical tools to safeguard their privacy, sought to protect all Americans from having their information misused. In defending the bill, President Obama emphasized its consistency with key values underlying the American market-driven regulatory model, noting how "as the Internet evolves, consumer trust is essential for the continued growth of the digital economy . . . By following this blueprint, companies, consumer advocates and policymakers can help protect consumers and ensure the Internet remains a platform for innovation and economic growth."[104] He also emphasized that consumer privacy is a basic American right, noting that privacy has been "at the heart of our democracy from its inception, and we need it now more than ever."[105] However, the Privacy Bill of Rights was attacked from all sides, and eventually failed to spur legislative action in Congress.[106] Tech companies decried the bill, lamenting that it would lead to burdensome regulations, stifle innovation, and prevent their ability to develop new online services that could benefit consumers. At the same time, privacy advocates attacked the bill as weak, filled with loopholes that tech companies could exploit. Ultimately, Congress decided not to pursue this legislation, leaving US digital regulation firmly anchored in companies' self-regulation and thus preserving the market-driven foundations of its regulatory model.[107]

Efforts to overturn the American free-market consensus in digital regulation have rarely been successful. One of the few legislative victories that ended up qualifying the Section 230 immunity was legislation designed to fight on-line sex trafficking known as the Allow States and Victims to Fight Online Sex Trafficking Act of 2017 or "FOSTA." FOSTA was a response to Congress's concern that Section 230 improperly shields certain online service providers, which are actively promoting criminal sex trafficking on their platforms. It was adopted in the aftermath of the 2016 decision in *Doe v. Backpage.com*, discussed further below, in which a US federal court ruled that a website called Backpage could not be held liable even though it knowingly facilitated criminal sex trafficking through its online service.[108] FOSTA amends Section 230 by excluding from its liability shield internet service providers' conduct that violates federal sex trafficking or criminal prostitution laws.[109] FOSTA's preamble clarifies Section 230 by noting that it "was never intended to provide legal protection to websites that unlawfully promote and facilitate prostitu-tion and websites that facilitate traffickers in advertising the sale of unlawful sex acts with sex-trafficking victims."[110] However, FOSTA has been criticized for its lack of effectiveness and unintended adverse consequences. For ex-ample, a 2020 survey measuring the impact of FOSTA found that the law caused platforms to preemptively crack down on consensual sex workers as well, making their jobs more dangerous and difficult.[111] By being able to ad-vertise on websites such as Backpage.com, voluntary sex workers were able to develop their own customer base instead of relying on pimps to facilitate their encounters with customers. Thus, FOSTA was accused of pushing sex workers back to the streets, which made their work even more dangerous.[112] Thus, even this modest curtailment of Section 230 liberties has had a mixed effect on its intended regulatory goals, at best, illustrating the difficulties asso-ciated with any attempt to readjust the market-driven foundations of the US digital economy.

How the US Has Begun to Rethink the Market-Driven Regulatory Model

The free-market ethos underlying the American regulatory model has shown its resilience over the years, guiding the policy-making across all branches of the US government. However, in recent years, an ever broader segment of American society has started to question the techno-libertarian foundations of the digital economy, and criticism of the market-driven regulatory model is growing. This emerging ideological shift acknowledges that the downsides of the US model have become too obvious to ignore in public discourse. Diverse voices—consisting of scholars, public intellectuals, journalists, civil society activists, small businesses, and, increasingly, political leaders—are raising concerns about the unmitigated power of the leading tech giants and the harmful impact these companies have on society. They point out how these companies have grown simply too big, possessing the kind of economic power and political influence that was unimaginable at the time the internet pioneers in California were dreaming of a new era of democracy, freedom, and societal progress enabled by technology. With dominant companies exploiting the marketplace, pressures to revive antitrust laws are growing. With every data privacy scandal that unfolds, critics are starting to wonder how these companies handle the users' personal data that they control and monetize as their core business model. With rampant hate speech and other detrimental content online, calls are mounting to hold large platforms accountable for the speech they host on their platforms. In this economic and political climate, few today are prepared to defend the argument that the internet can be a self-ordering place where, left to their own devices, large technology companies will deliver economic progress and enhance freedom and democracy.

Platform immunity and unregulated cyberspace are concepts that are no longer endorsed unequivocally by scholars, politicians, citizens—or even the by platforms themselves. Jack Balkin, who emphasized the internet's democratizing potential in its early days,[113] has tempered his optimism and acknowledged the dangers of private companies controlling online speech norms.[114] Danielle Citron, who has been more critical throughout the years, is advocating greater "cyber civil rights" and calling for the Section 230 liability shield to be conditional on platforms having reasonable content moderation practices in place.[115] Politics may also be gradually changing, potentially paving the way for tighter regulation of online speech. With its passing of the FOSTA legislation in 2018, the US Congress for the first time curtailed the Section 230 liability shield by lifting the immunity in instances where platforms and website operators knowingly hosted sex trafficking ads.[116] Several critics in the US have begun to urge regulators to go further and rethink the Section 230 safe harbor,[117] and many expect the Biden administration to take on this task.[118] In 2019, Nancy Pelosi, Speaker of the US House of Representatives at the time, called for the tech industry to assume greater responsibility for online content, alluding to the idea that "it is not out of the question" that Section 230 immunity would be removed.[119] This shift in political rhetoric reflects public opinion, which is turning against online platforms, including their toleration of hateful content.[120]

Congress is also holding hearings and deliberating bills that would revive antitrust laws, reflecting a realization that the market-driven regulatory model has delivered an economy of excessive concentration, where a few tech companies can abuse monopoly power that the lax regulatory framework has allowed them to accumulate. A 2020 House Antitrust Report contains a condemning assessment after a sixteen-month investigation into the sector, declaring that Amazon, Apple, Google, and Meta all engaged in forms of monopolistic behavior.[121] In introducing their report, leading lawmakers described in their joint statement: "Our investigation leaves no doubt that there is a clear and compelling need for Congress and the antitrust enforcement agencies to take action that restores competition, improves innovation, and safeguards our democracy."[122] At the time of writing in 2022, there are several bills advancing in Congress seeking to impose tighter antitrust constraints on the larger tech companies, including the 2021 American Innovation and Choice Online Act.[123] This bill would impose several constraints on large tech companies, including preventing them from misusing data to gain an unfair advantage over their rivals or manipulating search results to favor a search engine's own products. The Executive branch is also finally deploying its existing powers to enforce existing antitrust laws, with the DOJ and the FTC challenging Google's and Meta's business practices via lawsuits brought in 2020.[124] These lawsuits have been described as "the greatest threat yet to big tech."[125] A more robust approach toward antitrust enforcement against the tech companies has the full backing of President Biden. He appointed prominent tech critics Tim Wu, Lina Khan, and Jonathan Kanter to key antitrust positions in the White House, the FTC, and the DOJ, respectively. This suggests that the pressure is growing to rewrite the permissive antitrust doctrine either through legislative reform or through more robust enforcement of existing antitrust laws.

Lawmakers are also turning their sights on data privacy. Sensing the urgency to act, some individual states have gone ahead and enacted a GDPR-type state privacy law, not waiting for the federal government to act. Most prominently, California adopted the California Consumer Privacy Act in 2018, amending it with an even more rights-protecting California Privacy Rights Act in 2020.[126] At the federal level, while President Obama's proposed Privacy Bill of Rights went nowhere, it seems to have spurred other congressional proposals, including the Internet Bill of Rights and the CONSENT Act. The Internet Bill of Rights—proposed in 2018 by Representative Ro Khanna, whose California district is home to Apple, Intel, and Yahoo—builds on the Obama administration's Internet Bill of Rights proposed in 2015.[127] The CONSENT Act would enhance data privacy by, for example, requiring internet service providers to obtain opt-in consent from users to use, share, or sell users' personal information.[128] In introducing the bill, Senator Edward Markey emphasized that "the avalanche of privacy violations by Facebook and other online companies has reached a critical threshold, and we need legislation that makes consent the law of the land. Voluntary standards are not enough; we need rules on the books that all online companies abide by that protect Americans and ensure accountability."[129] President Biden also elevated privacy in his 2022 State of the Union address, calling for Congress to protect the privacy of American children. According to Biden, tech companies are conducting "a national experiment" on our children for profit, and set forth that "it's time to strengthen privacy protections, ban targeted advertising to children, demand tech companies stop collecting personal data on our children."[130]

It is possible that this backlash against tech companies—unfolding in the US but also around the world—will pose the biggest threat yet to the American market-driven regulatory model. The coming years will reveal whether the ongoing debate about the downsides of techno-libertarian ideals, and the proposed legislation that harnesses that sentiment, will usher in a new era of regulation in the US, radically shifting the ideological foundations of the digital economy. While others are optimistic, more skeptical voices maintain that the market-driven values are deeply entrenched in American institutions and in the American mindset, making it difficult to reverse the behavior of the largest tech companies that are the product of this unconstrained techno-optimism. Deeply entrenched pro-market views may still be shaping, for example, the views of the US judiciary, which might not yet be prepared for an "antitrust revolution."[131] It is also not certain that Congress will fundamentally overhaul Section 230, the law that sustains the current norms of free speech online. Reforming content moderation is genuinely difficult, and the threat of government censorship remains a danger that Americans are hard-wired to avoid. Thus far, any legislative reform has been limited to a few issues such as protecting children or limiting illegal sex trafficking where political compromise is relatively easy to reach—but even those laws have turned out to be weak or counterproductive, as the criticism over FOSTA illustrates.

Tech companies' outsized influence over the political process in the US is also hindering attempts to reform digital regulation. The techno-libertarian distaste for regulation has been sustained over the years through the tech industry's persistent lobbying efforts. In 2018, a former congressional aide explained that a privacy reform was hindered by the leverage tech companies wield in Washington, DC, commenting how "lobbyists outnumber consumer privacy advocates in Washington 20 to 1 or 30 to 1."[132] These tech companies' significance to the US economic growth and innovation base is undeniable, making the political leaders more susceptible to their views. For example, Apple, Amazon, Google, and Meta combined spent more than $55 million on lobbying the federal government in 2021, up from $34 million in 2020.[133] In 2021, Amazon alone spent a record-high $19 million,[134] and Meta over

$20 million.[135] These companies were not only seeking to fend off antitrust regulation, but also to defend their other policies in the aftermath of high-profile public complaints or scandals. Amazon faced labor complaints after suppressing its workers' unionization efforts,[136] whereas Meta was left to defend its content moderation practices following the incident where Frances Haugen, a former Facebook product manager, leaked documents to Congress that raised questions about the company's handling of hate speech and disinformation.[137] These tech companies have advanced in their defense various narratives when lobbying Congress. For example, in 2022, they argued that more robust antitrust legislation would "give a free pass" to foreign companies, hurting US competitiveness.[138]

But the biggest impediment to legislative reform is the political dysfunction that has to date paralyzed any meaningful legislation in Congress. Even when the Democrats and Republicans agree that regulation is needed, they cannot agree on the content of that regulation. While Republicans are concerned that platforms are censoring conservative speech, Democrats worry about rampant hate speech and other harmful content that is littering the internet as platforms take advantage of their Section 230 liability shield. If Congress will not act, one question is whether the courts will cause the US to retreat from its market-driven regulatory model. The Supreme Court will soon have the opportunity to rule on the boundaries of Section 230 in a number of cases, including in one where litigants are challenging a Texas law known as HB20.[139] This particular law prohibits online platforms from moderating content based on "the viewpoint represented in the user's expression," which reflects the perception among conservatives that tech companies hold a liberal ideological bias and that their content moderation practices ascribe to that bias. The courts will also rule in the near future on the anticompetitive practices of Google and Meta in two separate lawsuits bought by the DOJ and the FTC that are currently pending. These cases will test how entrenched the market-driven model is within the US judiciary.

Absent Congress or the courts rewriting the key principles underlying the market-driven regulatory model, there may be a way to reform the digital economy in a manner that constrains the power of the large tech companies yet does so while respecting some fundamental tenets of techno-libertarian thinking. Jack Balkin has argued that large online platforms should be conceived as "information fiduciaries," which vests them with special responsibilities toward their customers.[140] These fiduciary duties dictate that these companies owe a special duty of care toward the people whose data they collect and distribute, conditioning the Section 230 immunity to their acceptance of these duties. Danielle Citron and Benjamin Wittes have similarly argued for making the Section 230 liability shield conditional, available only for platforms that commit to restricting unlawful use of their service in situations that create serious harm to others.[141] These compromise proposals would preserve the Section 230 immunity to some degree, thus extending a lifeline to the American market-driven model in today's more critical political environment. Arguably, such modest reforms would inch the US model closer—even if only timidly so—to the European rights-driven regulatory model while avoiding the kind of radical reform that, some would argue, is destined to fail.

Regardless of the outcome of the emerging regulatory push, there is a fundamental tenet of the market-driven regulatory model that is not fading in the US political discourse. The US's commitment to political freedom and individual liberty remains a guidepost that continues to define the US's approach toward regulation of the digital economy—even as there is less certainty that the market-driven model has been enhancing democracy and freedom in the US. The criticism of authoritarian states' efforts, including those by China, to deploy the internet as a tool for control and surveillance remains a shared concern among different factions that shape the US's digital policy. Both Democrats and Republicans agree on the need to rein in the Chinese surveillance state and its exportation of digital authoritarian values across the world. China's rising dominance has also become a battle cry in the US's efforts to convince its allies, including European governments, that techno-democracies must unite to defeat the use of the internet as the tool for oppression, as opposed to freedom. Freedom therefore remains the defining value in the American regulatory model today even if its pursuit now takes place in a very different digital, economic, geopolitical, and cultural reality than the freedom agenda advocated by the internet pioneers of 1990s California.

How the American Regulatory Model Overlaps with the Chinese and European Models

Although the US regulatory approach is steeped in its historical commitment to the free market and free speech as key organizing principles of the digital economy, there are areas where the American regulatory model bears similarities to the European rights-driven model—or even the Chinese state-driven model. Despite its general aversion to regulation, several examples reveal that the US's commitment to a market-driven model has never been absolute. A preference for markets among the US policymakers does not entail that markets always prevail. Embedded within the US regulatory framework is a significant concern about individual rights, a concern that incorporates elements of the European rights-driven model. Similarly, the US government has often played a prominent role as a facilitator of the digital economy, resembling at times the role that the Chinese government has assumed in funding big technology innovations. The US government's national security objectives also dictate that the government and private tech companies collaborate closely on some domains of the digital economy, including cybersecurity and digital surveillance, qualifying any claim that marginalizes the role of the state in the digital economy.

The US and EU regulatory models share a commitment to free speech as a fundamental right that shapes their respective regulatory approaches toward the digital economy. Given the prominent role of Section 230 in shaping the US digital economy, the US model could also be described as rights-driven— even with its narrower focus on free speech as the principal fundamental right worth protecting. However, while the US approach can be viewed as more absolutist in its defense of free speech, the EU approach often balances free speech with other fundamental rights such as the right to privacy or human dignity, which leads the EU to at times ban harmful speech, such as hate speech. Also, while Europeans believe that defending free speech sometimes requires the government to step in and mandate platforms to moderate content in the name of civility, dignity, decency, or public safety, the American view tends to defer more to markets and self-regulation in finding the right balance in the marketplace of ideas. Thus, the US model implements its vision of individual rights more commonly by leaving it to the markets to realize those rights. In addition, while free speech is the most visible fundamental right embedded in the American regulatory model, it would be mistaken to assume that the US does not care about other rights, such as the right to privacy, even if there is no federal data privacy law akin to the GDPR. James Whitman has persuasively referred to "two western cultures of privacy," a European variant focusing on dignity and an American variant focusing on liberty.[142] Also, while there is no federal privacy law in the US, California and some other states have legislated on data privacy,[143] illustrating that the American regulatory model embeds elements of the European rights-driven model, even if primarily at the state level.

The American market-driven regulatory model also typically downplays the role of the state in generating technological progress. However, even in the US, the government has still played a pivotal role in fostering many of the central innovations that underpin today's digital economy, suggesting that it also incorporates elements of a state-driven regulatory model.[144] The political motivation behind state involvement can be traced back to the Cold War, when, for decades, the US government invested heavily in its arms race and the space race against the Soviets. It also has roots in the US's efforts to prevail in the economic competition against Japan in the 1980s. These geopolitical battles called for massive state investments in technology, leading the US to disburse large research grants to universities and offer lucrative military contracts to private tech companies. However, instead of picking winners or investing in a few state-owned companies, the US government implemented its state-driven investment model in a way that was more true to its market-driven instincts, channeling its public funding in a more decentralized fashion that encouraged private entrepreneurship as opposed to large monopolies.[145]

These state investments have been important in the broader development of the US digital economy, thus qualifying the market-driven regulatory model. Several path-breaking technologies have their origins in a US government agency called the Defense Advanced Research Project Agency (DARPA), which operates under the US Department of Defense. DARPA can be credited for funding many US innovations in their early development. For example, DARPA financed the ARPANET, which was the predecessor of the internet. Email was similarly developed as a result of DARPA-funded research projects at the Massachusetts Institute of Technology and Stanford University.[146] Even the Apple iPhone is not a posterchild of private entrepreneurship but a beneficiary of DARPA funding.[147] The iPhone's touch-screen technology was developed by a company called FingerWorks, which was founded by researchers at the publicly funded University of Delaware, which benefitted from US government research grants.[148] The iPhone's personal assistant "Siri" that relies on voice-recognition technology was developed as a spinoff from a DARPA-backed artificial intelligence project.[149] Further, Apple's iMac benefited from the startup capital provided by the US government's Small Business Administration.[150] The US National Science Foundation further supported research that led to the development of Google's search algorithm.[151]

More recently, the US government has again turned to industrial policy to boost the country's technological development as it is facing technological and geopolitical rivalry from China. As will be discussed in Chapter 5, the US and China are now vying for leadership and self-sufficiency in key technologies, such as semiconductors. This rivalry has fueled a subsidy race, which in the US culminated in Congress passing the CHIPS and Science Act in 2022, which allocates over $50 billion for American semiconductor research and development.[152] In addition to granting subsidies to shore up domestic manufacturing of key technologies, the US government is imposing extensive restrictions on technology exports and investments in an effort to limit China's access to strategically important technologies. These measures, adopted as part of the US's escalating technological rivalry with China, are quickly becoming the most visible aspect of US tech policy, moving the US further away from its traditional focus on promoting an open and global digital economy. These recent developments reveal how even in the US—which has been the most vocal champion of the private sector–led, free-market orthodoxy—the market-driven regulatory model has never existed in a pure form but has at different times incorporated elements of other leading regulatory models as well.

Government also plays an important role in shaping the US digital economy given the ways that digital economy intersects with national security, law enforcement, and other traditional public functions of the state. National security ranks high among the US government's policy priorities, affecting the government's regulatory approach in several other policy domains, including the digital economy. Cybersecurity and government surveillance are hence domains where the American market-driven model yields to a public-private partnership model, featuring a collaborative, even if uneven and sometimes contested, relationship between state and market actors. In a speech delivered in 2015, President Barack Obama remarked how "neither government, nor the private sector can defend the nation alone. It's going to have to be a shared mission—government and industry working hand in hand, as partners."[153]

Private companies and governments are both vulnerable to cyberattacks, making collaboration in preventing and responding to such attacks a joint endeavor. Kristen Eichensehr has argued that the US's approach toward cybersecurity reflects a distinct public-private partnership model, where the private sector assumes a quasi-governmental role on key cybersecurity issues, while the federal government acts less like a traditional public regulator and more like a market participant.[154] Cybercrime is growing both in frequency and sophistication, and there are several examples showing how vulnerable the US digital infrastructure, whether public or private, is to intrusion by hackers. For example, in 2020, thousands of US targets became victims in what became known as the "SolarWinds hack," which was one of the largest cyberbreaches of the century.[155] The incident was later attributed to Russian state-sponsored actors, who had deployed a malicious code through software company SolarWinds' IT performance monitoring system called Orion. Among the US government departments affected were the Department of Commerce and Homeland Security as well as the US Treasury. Private companies that suffered from the attack included large and sophisticated players such as Microsoft, Deloitte, and Cisco. This incident illustrates how the interests of the government and private sector often align, both benefiting from more robust cybersecurity governance.

Surveillance operations provide another example of public-private collaboration in the domain of the digital economy. The US government conducts extensive digital surveillance, both domestically and internationally, as was infamously revealed by a former National Security Agency (NSA) contractor, Edward Snowden, who exposed the US government's mass surveillance program to the world in 2013.[156] These practices have become a major source of controversy between the US and the EU, as will be discussed in Chapter 6. The Snowden revelations also show that the NSA relies on partnerships with major US telecom and internet companies in conducting its surveillance operations, leveraging these private actors to gain access to high-capacity international fiber-optic cables and other key infrastructures. The NSA also ran a program called "Prism," which relied on data collection from Google, Meta, Apple, Yahoo, and other US tech companies. This has led to criticism of the role of tech companies in sustaining the US government's surveillance apparatus.[157]

However, tech companies have also restrained the US government's surveillance operations, highlighting a difference in how the surveillance state operates in the US and China. Alan Rozenshtein—a law professor who formerly served in the US Department of Justice National Security Division—has argued that tech companies have both financial and ideological incentives to resist government surveillance.[158] They often choose minimal compliance and aggressive litigation to resist government requests for user data. These companies also use product design such as end-to-end encryption or offshore data storage as a way to make surveillance harder, in addition to rallying public opinion against surveillance. In its 2022 Comprehensive Cyber Review, the US Department of Justice affirmed the claim that powerful tech companies have on several occasions resisted government requests for assistance.[159] When the Obama administration sought US tech companies' collaboration on cyber defense, the Chamber of Commerce and other business associations blocked the proposed cybersecurity bill, criticizing it for being too interventionist and hence "un-American" in that it would have mandated information sharing about cyber hacks or even joint defense strategies that are "antithetical to free-market capitalist ideals."[160] In another example, Apple engaged in a high-profile court fight with the FBI in 2016 when the company challenged a court order compelling it to help unlock the iPhone of one of the perpetrators involved in the 2015 terrorist attack in San Bernardino, California, that left fourteen people dead and twenty-two seriously injured.[161] While condemning the terrorist attacks, Apple CEO Tim Cook published an open letter on the company's website defending Apple's decision not to unlock the phone and "hack our own users," describing the FBI's request as "undermin[ing] the very freedoms and liberty our government is meant to protect."[162] These are examples of tech companies' practices that constrain, as opposed to simply enable, government's surveillance programs.

Nevertheless, numerous other examples reveal how tech companies have occasionally been willing partners of the government's national security and law enforcement efforts, further underscoring the inevitable place of the government in a market-driven regulatory model. In the post-9/11, national security–driven political climate, major telecommunications operators helped the government fight the war on terror by assisting in information collection.[163] For example, they granted warrantless access to the NSA to monitor international telephone calls and correspondences. These companies also agreed to transfer vast amounts of telephone and other digital records, including purely domestic telephone calls and emails, to the NSA. More recently, as cybersecurity threats have become increasingly salient, tech companies are again collaborating more closely with the US government. In the wake of the Russian invasion of Ukraine in March 2022, the White House issued an executive order that requires US companies running critical infrastructure to report cyber hacks within seventy-two hours.[164] The war in Ukraine has also thrown tech companies into the middle of the conflict, given that it is often the tech companies, not governments, that first observe various cybersecurity threats. For example, shortly before the Russian invasion began, Microsoft's Threat Intelligence Center detected "wiper" malware that seemed to have been aimed at erasing data on Ukrainian government computers. Microsoft notified Ukraine's cyber defense units and alerted the White House, which then asked the company to share the details of the code with European nations, which were potential targets of the cyberattack as well.[165] In describing the company's role in the conflict, Microsoft's president Brad Smith noted that "we are a company and not a government or a country" yet acknowledged that the company's role was "not a neutral one." Instead, Microsoft was collaborating closely on cybersecurity with the Ukrainian, American, EU, and NATO governments.[166] In the wake of the war, the US's private-public collaboration on cybersecurity is reported to be intensifying. Tech company executives, armed with security clearances, are receiving NSA and US Cyber Command briefings, while the US government is relying on tech companies' capabilities to help detect and deter those cyberattacks.[167]

These above examples qualify the American market-driven regulatory model by illustrating how even the US model incorporates elements of the rights-driven and state-driven regulatory approaches in its governance of the digital economy. The US model does include a strong focus on fundamental rights in its digital regulation—indeed, Section 230 is as much a story about free speech as a fundamental right as it is a story about the faith in markets to uphold that right. But the market-driven model also features a strong role for the government, whether underwriting risky early investments in technology or by joining forces with tech companies in advancing its cybersecurity or broader national security goals. Yet even when the government does play a role, the American regulatory model tends to remain true to some of its market-driven qualities, whether by allocating government funding in more market-driven ways or by vesting tech companies with a role not just to facilitate government surveillance but also to check and to limit that surveillance.

Criticism of the Market-Driven Model in the US and Abroad

The virtues of the American market-driven regulatory model are undeniable. The US government's staunch support of free enterprise has contributed to a thriving, innovative tech industry that has generated tremendous wealth by producing products and services that are valued by consumers, many of whom are entranced with—or, some would argue, addicted to—the convenience they bring. Whether measured by their user numbers or stock price, the US tech companies are an unprecedented economic success story. At the same time, that success has come with a price. The American regulatory model has been blind to many market failures, which have been left to fester, unacknowledged or unaddressed. It is these failures that are now driving the recent and ongoing conversation about the future of the market-driven regulatory model.

Several academics and other political commentators have pointed out both fallacies and unrecognized downsides of the market-driven regulatory model. For example, lax antitrust laws have created a highly concentrated marketplace with a small number of firms exercising an unprecedented amount of economic, political, and cultural power. There is little competition left to keep the biggest tech behemoths in check, stripping consumers of choice and leaving them at the mercy of the business models of the leading platforms. Tim Wu is among those who have warned about the "curse of bigness," arguing that excessive corporate power feeds inequality and weakens the democratic structures of society.[168] While a free market and free internet were supposed to empower the individual, the critics of the American regulatory model argue that this market-driven ideology has instead empowered a few big technology companies while leaving large swaths of the society without the benefits of the internet revolution. This suggests that the emancipatory promise behind the Californian ideology has failed to materialize, raising a question whether

a self-governing cyberspace can ultimately deliver individual freedom and societal progress, as the proponents of the market-driven model have argued.

Societal harms associated with unconstrained free speech, encouraged by
Section 230, also illustrate the fallacies of unmitigated speech online. Section
230 shields platforms from liability even when those platforms enable and
amplify truly outrageous content, calling into question the wisdom behind
the law's unyielding commitment to free speech and platform immunity.
There are countless examples to illustrate how far reaching the courts have
interpreted the Section 230 immunity to be. For example, in 2016 and 2017,
a man with the name Oscar Juan Carlos Gutierrez deployed a gay dating platform called Grindr to send countless men to his ex-boyfriend Herrick, leading
these men to expect sex and drugs as part of those encounters. Gutierrez accomplished this by creating fake profiles on Grindr, pretending to be Herrick.
Over the course of ten months, more than 1,400 men—as many as twenty-
three in a single day—arrived in person at Herrick's home and workplace to
demand sex.[169] Despite fifty pleas to remove the posts and block Gutierrez
from the platform, Grindr refused to help, which led Herrick to bring a lawsuit against Grindr. However, the complaint was dismissed and the Supreme
Court refused to hear the case, given that Grindr had no obligation to remove
the posts under Section 230.[170] Another case, Doe v Backpage.com, reveals
a similar hyperextension of Section 230.[171] Backpage was a website hosting
online advertising for illegal commercial sex in the United States—referred
to as "world's largest online brothel"—until California's attorney general ordered the site to be shut down in 2018.[172] In a lawsuit challenging Backpage's
practices, the United States Court of Appeals for the First Circuit ruled that
Backpage is immune from liability connected to sex trafficking under Section
230 even though the site proactively helped sex traffickers to avoid getting
caught. As the content was generated by users and only hosted by Backpage,
Section 230 protected the company even though Backpage was aware of the
illegal activity and had even consciously designed the site to evade detection
by law enforcement.[173] These examples reveal how Section 230 can enable
and protect bad behavior, including egregious sexual harassment and sex
trafficking, in the name of free speech and the benefits of an unregulated
marketplace.

It is also increasingly doubtful whether the market-driven model is
delivering on its promise to enhance democracy as hatred and disinformation are often replacing the civic debates that were supposed to thrive online. Instead of nurturing inclusive democracy, online engagement has often
increased societal polarization. Cass Sunstein has warned about the perils of
polarization resulting from online platforms delivering a highly "personalized

experience" for each user.[174] Social media has become a venue characterized by filter bubbles and "information cocoons" where citizens are no longer exposed to alternative viewpoints.[175] This feeds social divisions and nurtures more extremist ideas. Deprived of shared conversations and experiences, a society cannot address social problems collectively. This undermines the potential for the internet to be a genuine public sphere where a conversation enhances understanding and paves the way for compromises.[176]

Social media not only feeds polarization, but also risks simply lowering the quality of information that citizens consume. Algorithms empowering social media are designed to reward virality over veracity, which inevitably deteriorates the quality of information and crowds out verified, factual information.[177] Online content that is controversial or sensationalist elicits the most user engagement.[178] This serves the internet platforms' business interests as more user engagement means more advertising revenue, giving the platforms the incentive to amplify it. The digital public space is also increasingly compromised by rampant disinformation, in particular as disinformation gets disseminated more than truth online. A 2018 study examining news stories that were shared in Twitter from 2006 to 2017 reveals how false information spreads "farther, faster, and deeper" than truth, and how this effect is particularly pertinent in the case of political news.[179] Finally, the traditional press is also today less capable of checking and balancing the divisive content that gets elevated in social media. It has lost its place to shape public discourse, further contributing to the decline of the quality of news that users are exposed to. These news outlets face a growing strain on their business model as advertising has increasingly moved online, reducing revenue streams that are needed to pay for investigative reporting, local news, and other high-quality journalism.[180]

Additional concerns relate to the role that the leading online platforms play in elections through moderating—or failing to moderate—the conversations that take place online and thus influence public opinion and voter behavior. Online platforms' content-moderation decisions influence what kind of messaging voters are exposed to. This could manipulate the electorate if these platforms harbored a political bias, determining through their algorithms what kind of messages reach, or fail to reach, voters. Twitter and Facebook have both been accused of demoting speech that reflects conservative views while elevating liberal messages,[181] even though recent research finds no evidence of such a liberal bias.[182] But given their access to users' personal data, these internet platforms could—at least in theory—deploy their power to "engineer elections."[183] They could selectively display information to influence voting behavior, drawing on their vast knowledge of the internet users' political beliefs or affiliations. While this has not been shown to happen in practice, even the prospect that platforms *could* manipulate an election outcome this way is unsettling.

What online platforms have actually been shown to do, however, is further contribute to the polarization of the electorate through the algorithms behind political advertising. A recent study reveals that online platforms' algorithms make it harder for political advertisers to reach voters who do not agree with them, thus contributing to the polarization discussed earlier.[184] For example, Facebook delivers political advertisements disproportionately to the internet users that share the political leaning with the organization behind the ad while charging extra for having the ad reach someone across the political divide. Polarization, the researchers conclude, is hence part of Facebook's business model. Perhaps the most potent charge today is that even if these platforms were not advancing an explicit political agenda, manipulating citizens, or tilting voter turnout toward their desired outcome, they are enabling election interference by failing to filter content that spreads disinformation or calls into question the integrity of elections, both before and after voting takes place. As long as these platforms tolerate disinformation, voters can be misled, causing them either to vote based on false information or refrain from voting if such disinformation undermines their faith in the integrity of the electoral process. There is no more vivid illustration of this than the January 6 insurrection at the US Capitol following a rampant social media–fueled disinformation campaign about a stolen election.

The unregulated digital economy is also rife with privacy scandals. This is exactly what happened in the infamous Cambridge Analytica scandal that involved the harvesting of Facebook data to build psychological profiles that were then used in political campaigns—without obtaining consent of those individuals whose data had been used.[185] While the Cambridge Analytica scandal was rather extreme in its scope and impact, large online platforms have tremendous leeway to infringe user privacy and individual autonomy on a daily basis. These platforms engage in what Shoshana Zuboff has termed "surveillance capitalism," extracting users' data for commercial gain and compromising their "decisional privacy" in the process.[186] This surveillance capitalism enables behavioral advertising and other forms of manipulation, which then subvert individual choice, liberty, and self-governance.[187] This way, technology suppresses human autonomy and individual freedom and, with that, deprives individuals of the ability to exercise their agency and to participate in democracy.

A different example of the American market-driven digital model becoming the victim of its own success arises in the national security sphere.

Jack Goldsmith and Stuart Russel have argued that many virtues of the US model—including its commitment to free speech, rule of law, and limited government regulation—have become vulnerabilities that malicious actors, in particular authoritarian foreign adversaries, can exploit.[188] This, in part, explains why the US has been a frequent victim of cyber operations such as cyberespionage, cybertheft, information operations, ransomware attacks, and other so-called soft cyber operations. For example, the success of US tech companies also entails that the US is the most attractive target for cyber operations. There are simply more valuable trade secrets and intellectual property to steal, creating an asymmetric vulnerability for the US. Former NSA Director Keith Alexander has acknowledged this, describing how hundreds of billions of dollars of US business secrets have been stolen in the last decade as a result of various cyberespionage operations. Alexander refers to it as the "greatest transfers of wealth in history."[189] Thus, the US's economic strength in technology has at times become a liability compared to other countries that have much less to lose from such espionage operations.

Several features of the US's digital governance model also contribute to this asymmetric vulnerability compared to the US's rivals, in particular authoritarian countries such as China.[190] The US is a deeply digitally connected society, which exposes it to offensive cyber operations. The free and open nature of US society further adds to its relative weakness compared to closed and authoritarian societies that can better shield themselves from adverse cyber operations. For example, the US government does not control social media and news outlets, making it easier for adversaries to infiltrate those outlets with disinformation operations. Such operations can be deployed to manipulate elections or otherwise undermine democratic institutions—as happened, for example, in 2016 when Russian hackers stole emails from the Democratic National Committee in connection to Hillary Clinton's presidential campaign and subsequently released those emails to the public in a major doxing operation. The US is also more constrained in responding to cyberattacks due to its commitment to the rule of law—both domestic and international—in ways that its authoritarian counterparts are not. Unlike China, the US government has limited access to private networks and communications in the US, which makes it harder to detect attacks and respond to them. Yet the US is also more vulnerable than the European governments and societies because of its stand against regulation. The US government's hands-off approach toward regulation also means that the state imposes weak cybersecurity requirements on private actors. These companies do not face significant mandated security measures or information-sharing requirements, nor do they face liability for cybersecurity harms they generate or contribute to.

These various examples show that the US's digital economy often falls short on its techno-libertarian promise to be the amplifier of liberal democracy and individual freedoms, questioning the long-held assumption that democracy and freedom will inevitably ensue as long as we leave technology companies alone. It also suggests that the US has for too long been focusing on the benefits of the market-driven regulatory model, unwilling to revisit it for fear of losing the benefits of the free market and a free society, while refusing to admit its drawbacks that are now cascading and fueling resentment against tech companies. The discontent with abuses of market power, repeated privacy violations, and repugnant speech online are shaking the US's own faith in the regulatory model that it created and has championed for the past twenty-five years. Consequently, US regulators must now rethink their own commitment to the market-driven regulatory model. Its deficiencies are weakening the US's position in its horizontal battle against the EU and China and explain why the market-driven model is quickly losing its domestic and global appeal, while also undermining the US government's efforts to counter the growing attractiveness of the Chinese state-driven regulatory model.

2

The Chinese State-Driven Regulatory Model

IN STARK CONTRAST to the American market-driven regulatory model, the Chinese state-driven regulatory model seeks to harness technology in strengthening government control as opposed to protecting individual freedom. Although the American model helped generate world-changing technological innovations, China's equal success in building tech companies has demonstrated that significant technological breakthroughs can also emerge under a state-driven regulatory model; its command-and-control system propelled the country's tech industry into the leading global force it is today. As they have grown and matured into powerful national champions, these Chinese tech companies have contributed to China's economic growth and geopolitical prominence in recent decades. This perceived success of the Chinese regulatory model has enhanced the model's legitimacy in the eyes of Chinese citizens while also contributed to its growing appeal internationally. Foreign governments seeking a viable alternative regulatory path to the American market-driven approach are now increasingly turning to the Chinese state-driven approach for guidance on how to effectively manage their digital economies and control their digital societies.

While there are important similarities between the Chinese state-driven model and the American and the European regulatory models, the Chinese model departs from those other models in fundamental ways. Principally, the Chinese government seeks to leverage technology to fuel the country's economic growth and development while maintaining social harmony and control over its citizens' communications. In addition to its efforts to turn China into the world's leading technological superpower, the government is focused on tightening the grip of the Chinese Communist Party (CCP) over the domestic digital economy by deploying technology as a tool for control, surveillance, and propaganda, entrenching digital authoritarianism deeply into Chinese society. These two factors—economic development and social stability—are central to the survival of the Chinese leadership.[1] Economic development allows the CCP to maintain popular support and legitimacy by serving the material interests of the people. Social stability allows the CCP to preempt criticism and resistance to Party rule, which further protects its ability to hold onto power.[2] Acutely aware of these policy imperatives, China's government has geared its state-driven regulatory model toward attaining these broader political goals.

Chinese political leadership has articulated the country's state-driven vision for the digital economy in several high-profile statements. In a prominent speech delivered at the 2015 World Internet Conference in Wuzhen, China, President Xi Jinping—the General Secretary of the CCP—underscored how digital governance in China is rooted in state sovereignty. In a clear rebuke of the US's cyber hegemony and global influence over internet governance, President Xi called for each country to be able to independently choose its own "path of cyber development,"[3] stressing countries' sovereign right to set their internet policies and other digital regulations. In a 2018 speech, President Xi emphasized that "accelerating the development of a new generation of AI is an important strategic handhold for China to gain the initiative in global science and technology competition, and it is an important strategic resource driving our country's leapfrog development in science and technology, its industrial optimization and upgrading, and a comprehensive leap ahead in productivity."[4] At the same time, President Xi has made it clear that this goal of reaching a cyber-superpower status cannot undermine political discipline.[5] For instance, in 2010, China's top information bureau—the State Council Information Office—published a white paper titled "The Internet in China," which highlighted how the internet is "an issue that concerns national economic prosperity and development, state security and social harmony, state sovereignty and dignity, and the basic interests of the people."[6] It must be free of "information that contains content subverting state power, undermining national unity, infringing upon national honor and interests."[7] These statements reveal how China harnesses digital technologies to reinforce three key sources of Chinese leadership's legitimacy: economic growth, social stability, and nationalism.[8]

The Chinese state-driven regulatory model has fostered a powerful tech industry. Despite the state-led economic policy—which is often viewed as antithetical to a dynamic and innovative marketplace—China is today rivaling the US in technological dominance, as shown in Chapter 5. Different metrics can be used to capture China's technological prowess. Measured by market capitalization, China has eight of the twenty largest public internet companies—Tencent, Alibaba, Meituan, and JD among the top ten as of August 2022.[9] When private internet companies are included, ByteDance also joins the top ten based on June 2022 data.[10] In some domains of technology, including electronic payments, China has leapfrogged the US, leading the way with the development and market uptake of such technologies.[11] Chinese cellphone maker Xiaomi briefly surpassed Apple and became the second largest smartphone maker globally in 2021.[12] China also leads as a producer of telecom network equipment and commercial drones.[13] TikTok's popularity—as demonstrated by the company surpassing Facebook as the most visited social media website in 2021[14]—has further shown that Chinese tech companies' innovations extend into social media, a space traditionally dominated by US companies.

These companies did not emerge in a vacuum. The Chinese government has directly facilitated the growth of China's tech sector, nurturing the industry with generous subsidies while also shielding it from foreign competition. Until recently, the industry also benefited from relatively more lax regulation as the government was adamant to let the industry flourish and innovate. Overall, the Chinese regulatory model rests on particularly close ties between the government and private tech companies, each helping the other reach their goals. In return for permissive regulation, these tech companies have often acted as the CCP's surrogates in performing surveillance and control functions vis-à-vis their users. However, this symbiotic relationship between government and tech companies has recently morphed into a more confrontational phase. The government policy toward its tech industry shifted—suddenly and dramatically—in 2021, when the Chinese leadership began to emphasize the importance of economic fairness and redistribution alongside the pursuit of aggregate economic growth. Like the US, the Chinese government is increasingly assuming a view that the largest tech companies and their high-profile leaders have grown too powerful to be left unchecked. It has recently leveraged its antitrust laws to rein in companies such as Ant Group, Alibaba, and Tencent as part of an unprecedented regulatory assault on its domestic tech industry. This newest uptick in regulation may transform the existing bargain between the Chinese government and its tech companies, yet it leaves the core tenet of the Chinese regulatory model intact: the model serves the goals of the Chinese state by preserving the survival and legitimacy of the CCP.

This chapter looks closely at how China's state-centric vision of the digital economy is focused on the dual goals of technological dominance and economic development on the one hand, and the maintenance of social stability through political control on the other. It shows how, in pursuit of these goals, the government has made concerted efforts to enhance China's technological leadership and digital sovereignty, while also leveraging the internet as a tool for control, propaganda, and state surveillance. The chapter also examines the role of Chinese tech companies in the state's censorship and surveillance operations and describes the experiences and responses of Chinese internet users whose digital lives are shaped by these operations. Although China's state-driven regulatory model is designed to amplify the government's autocratic goals, no regulatory model—including the Chinese one—is absolutist in its policy commitments. Instead, this chapter reveals how the Chinese model also incorporates elements of the European rights-driven and the American market-driven regulatory models. This chapter further highlights how the Chinese model has evolved in recent years, exploring the recent government crackdown on the tech industry in the name of "common prosperity"[15] and analyzing the drivers and implications of this policy shift for digital governance in China. Finally, it brings into view some of the common criticisms levied at the state-driven regulatory model, both from inside China and from abroad.

China's Push for Technological Supremacy and Reliance on Digital Protectionism

The Chinese state-driven regulatory model seeks to leverage digital technologies toward enhancing China's economic growth and geopolitical prominence. To grow the country's tech industry, the government initially opted for more permissive regulation at home, while imposing tight restrictions on foreign companies. The goal was to isolate domestic tech companies from foreign competition so that they could achieve sufficient scale in their home market, and at the same time exert political control over foreign firms. Today's tense geopolitical environment, including the ongoing US–China tech war, has given the Chinese government an additional impetus to invest in the domestic tech industry and thereby enhance the country's technological capabilities. The government is conscious that it cannot rely on international technology supply chains in accessing products such as semiconductors in an era where the US and several of its allies actively seek to decouple their domestic markets and technologies from those of China. Today's geopolitical reality thus further pushes China toward greater technological self-sufficiency and digital protectionism.

The Pursuit of Technological Self-Sufficiency

The Chinese regulatory model has sought to facilitate the growth of China's tech industry by enhancing the country's technological capabilities while reducing its dependencies on foreign technologies. On many metrics, China has already succeeded in becoming a technological superpower. Chinese tech companies are market leaders in many domains of the digital economy: Alibaba, Baidu, Tencent, and JD.com lead as software developers while Huawei and Xiaomi are some of the world's leading hardware companies. These and several other Chinese companies' tremendous success is a tribute to both the companies' innovation and to an enabling regulatory environment that has nurtured growth of these companies.

The government's hands-off approach to the tech industry throughout the 2010s laid the groundwork for Chinese tech companies' eventual success. Angela Zhang attributes this initial policy orientation to three factors.[16] First, the Chinese government was adamant in supporting the growth of the country's tech industry, in particular in the aftermath of the 2008 financial recession when the growth of the Chinese economy slowed down.[17] The CCP staked its economic development strategy and, consequently, its legitimacy, on the adoption and promotion of new technologies as a way to revitalize the Chinese economy.[18] But Chinese tech firms' lobbying also contributed to this lax regulation.[19] Unlike their US tech counterparts, Chinese tech companies do not lobby through contributing to election campaigns. Instead, they play an active role in politics. For example, Alibaba and Ant Group founder Jack Ma is a member of the CCP.[20] Chinese tech entrepreneurs, including Tencent's founder Pony Ma, also submit proposals to key government bodies such as the National People's Congress or the Political Consultative Conference, even if those proposals may be viewed as political gestures rather than serious policy initiatives.[21] The tech companies rely on their connections to the political elites, former government officials, or academics, who act as their intermediaries in lobbying for favorable regulatory policies.[22] Finally, Zhang shows how bureaucratic inertia contributed to lax regulation. Chinese regulators are not as independent as their counterparts in the US and the EU. Instead, all government agencies and local governments depend on the support of the top leadership in Beijing.[23] Conscious of the national policy agenda focused on fostering innovation, various lower-level regulatory authorities opted to follow the top leadership and tread cautiously, thus adopting a lax enforcement approach toward the country's tech companies.[24] Of course, even under this permissive approach, Chinese tech companies likely still engaged in some degree of preemptive self-regulation or self-censorship of behavior, always keenly aware of the government's policy objectives and mindful not to contradict them. But overall, this accommodating approach toward China's native tech companies in the early years of China's digital development was notable and consequential. It became an integral part of the Chinese regulatory model and helped the country's tech industry become a dominant player in the global digital economy.

In addition to passively refraining from regulating the tech industry with burdensome measures, the Chinese regulatory model has also evolved around a proactive industrial policy. The Chinese government has extended generous state subsidies and adopted other industrial policy measures to further accelerate the country's technological development and to ensure China will become self-sufficient in all key technologies. The government's goal with these policies is to make China a technological superpower that dominates all technologies that are key to the country's economic, geopolitical, and military power, including artificial intelligence, quantum computing, and robotics. As part of this ambitious strategy, in 2015, the Chinese government launched a ten-year plan known as the "Made in China 2025" program, a state-led industrial policy effort aimed at ensuring that China becomes a globally dominant player in high-tech manufacturing.[25] The program leverages China's state-owned enterprises to invest in strategically important technologies, while also extending generous government subsidies—estimated to be in the range of hundreds of billions of dollars—to domestic firms developing these technologies. The program also encourages investments in foreign technologies through the acquisition of foreign companies and the negotiation of technology transfer agreements with companies that do business in China.[26]

The broader policy objectives of the Made in China 2025 program reflect the Chinese government's efforts to diminish its dependency on foreign technologies and thus enhance the country's "technological sovereignty." This policy goal is reflected in the precise targets the program sets out.[27] For example, China's tech industry is currently dependent on foreign companies for most of its semiconductor needs, which presents a significant vulnerability given that semiconductors are critical components for almost all electronic products. In 2019, China accounted for 60 percent of the global demand for semiconductors but was responsible only for 13 percent of the global supply.[28] Determined to address this vulnerability, the program sets a 70 percent self-sufficiency target in high-tech industries by 2025.[29] This paves the way for an even more ambitious goal by 2049, which marks the 100th anniversary of the People's Republic of China. By then, the Chinese government's goal is to achieve a status of a "manufacturing powerhouse" featuring a "world-leading technology system and industrial system."[30] The deteriorating US–China political relationship and the accelerating tech war is further incentivizing China to pursue technological dominance and self-sufficiency, including to subsidize its strategic industries, as discussed in Chapter 5.

The Made in China 2025 program has been heavily criticized abroad for its protectionist goals and effects. The US government has accused China of stealing intellectual property and engaging in cyberespionage operations, in addition to discriminating against foreign investors and mandating technology transfers that force foreign companies to share their technologies with Chinese firms and other local entities.[31] This foreign criticism has led the Chinese government to forgo references to the Made in China 2025 program in public while continuing to pursue its goals in practice.[32] The Chinese leadership has also continued to set ambitious goals that reaffirm technological dominance as the central tenet of the country's digital policy. In the government's 2017 Next Generation of Artificial Intelligence Development Plan, China pronounced several goals, including its intention to become the world's premier AI innovation center by 2030.[33] For its part, the US has acknowledged the significant strides that China is making in its race against the US for technological supremacy. For example, a 2021 report by the US National Security Commission on AI warns that China will soon replace the US as the "AI superpower."[34] This warning echoes earlier comments by the Commission's chair, former CEO and Executive Chairman of Google, Eric Schmidt, who warned back in 2017 that China was going to overtake the US in AI development if the US government did not act soon.[35] The Chinese leadership also envisions China surpassing the US as the world's largest economy by 2035, largely thanks to a massive investment in China's technological leadership.[36] These developments suggest that the Chinese state-driven regulatory model possesses the ambition and the strategy—and increasingly the capabilities—to meet its goals to reach technological superpower status.

The Pursuit of Digital Protectionism

Protectionism has been pervasive in China's efforts to grow its tech sector, making digital protectionism or "techno-nationalism" a fundamental element of the Chinese state-driven regulatory model. The government has cultivated a large and protected home market where Chinese companies can develop and test their technologies, build scale, and benefit from extensive state subsidies—all while shielded from foreign competition.[37] Although China has opened some sectors to foreign competition, foreign companies' entry is difficult in the strategic industries that are of the greatest significance to

China's high tech–driven growth and development model. This type of restric-tive industrial policy can be self-defeating elsewhere in that it often stifles the benefits of competition that sustain companies' innovative zeal and produc-tivity. However, Chinese companies may at least in the short run avoid such pitfalls as they operate in a sizable domestic market featuring more internet users than the US and EU markets combined. In this large and dynamic do-mestic market, protectionist policies often prevent foreign companies from challenging Chinese players' market share. However, the protected Chinese companies still retain the incentive to innovate as they continue to face competition—from other Chinese players.

China has used various forms of market restrictions on foreign companies to boost its domestic tech industry. At times, these market restrictions con-sist of requiring foreign companies who wish to invest in China to form a joint venture with a local partner. These joint ventures often help Chinese companies secure valuable technology transfer agreements from foreign tech companies.[38] Many innovative foreign tech companies consider these joint venture requirements with local companies costly, forcing them to give away their most important technological assets. Other types of restrictions consist of discriminatory procurement practices or burdensome domestic standards that can be hard for foreign companies to meet.[39] For example, the US-based multinational tech company IBM was expected to buy supplies from Chinese vendors in the IT market.[40] To retain its ability to operate in China, IBM was forced to trade technology for market access. The company ended up supplying software and hardware blueprints to local vendors, which allowed them to produce a version of the leading IBM Power8 processor and manufac-ture servers that compete with similar IBM products. IBM acknowledged that this "will create a new and vibrant ecosystem of Chinese companies producing homegrown computer systems for the local and international markets."[41] In addition to such technology transfer requirements, the Chinese government's strict censorship rules and requirement to share user data with the Chinese government pose further market barriers.[42] These restrictions contribute to the techno-nationalist foundations of the Chinese model and reveal a stark contrast with the American regulatory model, which has traditionally been as-sociated with economic openness and a frictionless investment environment.

The Chinese government has blocked websites or apps that fail to abide by these government regulations, affecting also numerous US tech companies, as discussed in more detail in Chapter 4. For instance, Facebook was blocked in 2009, following riots in western China where the protesters had used Facebook for their communications. Instagram was blocked in 2014 in connection with pro-democracy protests in Hong Kong. Twitter was first blocked in June 2009 in the lead-up to the twentieth anniversary of the 1989 Tiananmen Square protests. YouTube was blocked multiple times before being permanently banned in 2009.[43] And the list goes on: companies or websites such as Snap Inc., Google, Reddit, Tumblr, Pinterest, Slack, Twitch, Discord, Dropbox, Quora, A Medium Corporation, Wikipedia, Vimeo, Flickr, SoundCloud, DuckDuckGo, and Dailymotion have all been blocked since the late 2000s.[44] Google shut down its China-specific search engine in 2010 following a censorship and hacking dispute between the company and the government.[45] Facebook has explored ways to comply with Chinese censorship demands in order to reenter the Chinese market, which, in Facebook's absence, is dominated by Weibo and WeChat. To date, these efforts have been unsuccessful.[46] While these restrictions are mainly motivated by political control and censorship, as discussed below, they have also helped the Chinese government shield local tech companies from foreign competition. This has directly facilitated these companies' efforts to grow and reach their current scale, unencumbered by foreign tech giants that dominate the industry elsewhere.

These various market restrictions imposed by the Chinese government—coupled with the government's proactive industrial policy measures—have hindered foreign tech companies' efforts to pursue growth opportunities in China and contributed to China becoming an increasingly prominent technological superpower. China's success has accelerated the country's technological, economic, and political rivalry with the US, while also challenging the American market-driven model as the most conducive model for fostering technological innovation and contributing to economic progress.

How China Harnesses Technology for Censorship and Surveillance

Political control lies at the heart of China's state-driven regulatory model. In the name of social stability, the Chinese government deploys technology to engage in extensive surveillance of its citizens while also censoring the information that those citizens can access online. Under President Xi, China has assumed even tighter government control over online communications. The Chinese president has warned that the internet may foster "hidden negative energy" that can be detrimental to social stability,[47] and decisively moved to purify the internet of such energy. The government's fear is that its citizens are deploying various online platforms to question the political ideology underlying the communist system and to undermine the public order. As a result, the government has adopted a host of measures—both technological and legal—designed to censor the internet and thereby ensure the CCP's control of the Chinese cyberspace. This is done in the name of national interest and national security, invoking values such as social stability, harmony, and morality. The Chinese government also deploys facial recognition and other digital technologies for the surveillance of Chinese citizens. This allows the state to dissuade dissent and reduce destabilizing behavior. Restricting online freedoms and deploying technology as a tool for social control contribute to the all-important goal of preserving the survival of the CCP.

These digital authoritarian practices represent a stark departure from the American market-driven regulatory model where the internet is seen as key to promoting individual liberty and advancing freedom in society. But it also represents a stark departure from the European rights-driven regulatory model where the government steps in with the goal of expanding, not curtailing, the digital rights and freedoms of its citizens vis-à-vis their government, not just vis-à-vis tech companies. This authoritarian control is the defining feature of the Chinese state-driven model, which causes the greatest fear and resentment in much of the democratic world. The fears relating to the curtailment of rights and freedoms also explain the efforts by the US, the EU, and their democratic allies to restrict China's ability to export its regulatory model to other countries, as discussed in Chapter 8.

How Censorship and Propaganda Entrench State Control

Controlling citizens' online communications and shaping those communications through government propaganda are essential elements in China's broader censorship and surveillance regime. These tactics illustrate how the state-driven regulatory model elevates social harmony and party control above the rights of Chinese citizens. Although the methods of censorship have changed over time and digital communications in particular have become a key target of state control over the past few decades, China has a long history of restriction of information and control over citizens' communications.[48] Chinese rulers have, since imperial times, feared political dissent that could undermine their rule. Even if there have been periods of more open debate, this persistent fear of political dissent and regime instability have entrenched censorship and propaganda deep into the Chinese governance model.

This culture of suspicion and political control extended to the online space when China opened internet service to the general public in 1995. Soon thereafter, the Chinese government developed what is known as the Great Firewall. The Great Firewall consists of a set of technologies and legal rules aimed at restricting Chinese internet users' access to certain harmful information. It deploys technologies that block access to selected websites, censoring content that the Chinese government finds undesirable. For example, Chinese internet users searching for terms such as "Tiananmen Square" will not be able to access any information on the People's Liberation Army's violent crackdown of the pro-democracy student protests that took place in Tiananmen Square in 1989. Similarly, any references to Tibetan independence or the political status of Taiwan that could endanger the unity and sovereignty of China are filtered out by the Chinese online censorship apparatus. In addition, many foreign sites like Amnesty International, the *New York Times*, Facebook, and Twitter remain entirely inaccessible to Chinese citizens trying to log in to the internet from China unless they use a virtual private network (VPN) that allows them to bypass the Great Firewall. However, even this channel to foreign information is more restricted today. China is increasingly taking measures to limit access to a VPN by, for example, ordering Apple to remove all VPNs from its Chinese app store, further restricting Chinese citizens' access to unwanted information.[49]

These technological filters sustaining the Great Firewall have been complemented with a set of regulations that limit the content that websites and platforms can host, that remove anonymity of internet users, and that entrench a culture of self-censorship. For example, websites are required to check the identities of users when they register their accounts, discouraging the more liberal online engagement these users might pursue if their anonymity was protected.[50] Internet users in China also have several reasons to exercise self-censorship. Under President Xi, the Chinese government has targeted individuals with a large social media following, as these individuals can exert significant influence over public opinion. In a 2013 government crackdown, some of these internet influencers were attacked in the Chinese media, required to "confess" their crimes to the press, or even detained for spreading rumors.[51] These measures have been effective, leading to fewer social media posts and a shift to less sensitive topics on online platforms.

Since President Xi assumed power in 2013, the government has further tightened its reins over citizens' online behavior and institutionalized its digital authoritarian vision through a series of legislative enactments. Some of the most prominent of these include the 2015 National Security Law,[52] the 2016 Cybersecurity Law,[53] and the 2021 Data Security Law.[54] The National Security Law entrenches the government's authoritarian control over Chinese society, both online and offline. It provides that "the state shall prevent, frustrate, and legally punish any conduct that betrays the country, splits the country, incites rebellion, subverts or incites the subversion of the people's democratic dictatorship."[55] The Cybersecurity Law, which specifically targets online behavior, provides that "any individual or organization using the network" must abide by "public order and respect social morality."[56] They must also refrain from any online activity that "endangers national security, honor and interest, incites to subvert the state power or overthrow the socialist system, incites to split the country or undermine national unity."[57] The Data Security Law imposes obligations on mandatory data security reviews and further restricts data transfers overseas. It vests the state with the power to carry out national security reviews relating to data processing and mandates relevant parties to cooperate "where a public security organ or national security organ needs to obtain data for the sake of national security or for investigating crimes in accordance with the law."[58] These laws—together with several other legislative, regulatory, and administrative documents released since the publication of the 2010 white paper—ensure that, under China's regulatory model, technology is first and foremost harnessed "in service of the state."[59]

The Chinese government also exercises control over individual citizens' online communications. Following a 2013 interpretation by the Supreme People's Court and China's highest prosecution agency, the Supreme People's Procuratorate, individuals face penalties, including possible imprisonment, if they spread online defamatory rumors or lies that are seen over 5,000 times or shared over 500 times.[60] The sharing of fabricated information online is also punished as "the crime of picking fights and troubles" in instances where such conduct causes "serious disorder."[61] These are not empty threats. The government has imprisoned numerous individuals over their social media activities, even internet users with very little actual influence over social media. In 2021, the *Wall Street Journal* reported that over fifty individuals were jailed in China over the past three years for using Twitter or other social media. This reflects the government's escalating effort to strangle criticism that disrupts public order or undermines Party rule.[62] Individuals have been jailed following social media posts that criticize the government or contain undesirable remarks about Hong Kong, Taiwan, or Xinjiang.[63] For instance, Sun Jiandong, who only had twenty-seven Twitter followers when he was detained in 2019, had replied to a Chinese state media tweet by tweeting: "Glory to Hong Kong, shame on Communist bandits."[64] This and other controversial tweets by Mr. Sun generated 168 likes, retweets from ten users, and comments from ninety-five users. Mr. Sun—hardly a social media influencer by numbers—completed a thirteen-month prison sentence.

The Chinese leadership faces a delicate balancing act in its efforts to censor the internet, which has led it to pursue optimal, as opposed to absolute, censorship. The government wants to harness the benefits associated with a free internet yet remains aware of the risks associated with such openness.[65] One benefit of maintaining a freer internet and media environment is that those channels can provide the government with valuable information that helps it govern the country more effectively. By allowing online communications to take place, Chinese leadership can better monitor the actions of lower-level and local government officials, in addition to learning and preempting various societal problems before they lead to wider resentment and popular unrest. This benefit was recognized in a 2016 research report published by the Central Party School, which argued that by monitoring internet users, authorities are able to "unearth hidden negative opinions, predict their development, intervene in advance, and effectively resolve public opinion problems to reduce the risk of societal safety incidents."[66] However, the government also acknowledges that an uncensored internet presents the "most potent media threat" to CCP rule, capable of fueling political opposition, and thus undermining government control.[67] In seeking to balance these competing interests and find an "optimal" level of censorship, the Chinese government typically allows some sensitive information to spread online. However, when this type of information exceeds a certain limit or risks triggering political unrest, the censorship apparatus is deployed to block access to such content. Thus, the goal is to use the information acquired from digital citizens to govern more effectively while reducing the risk of collective action.[68]

The state-driven model can be effective in attaining its censorship goals even when the government falls short of exercising complete control over the information environment. Margaret Roberts has shown how the Chinese government deliberately relies on "porous censorship" as part of its overall strategy to control the internet in China.[69] Whereas a strict censorship regime could cause a popular backlash among Chinese citizens, the government's more selective censorship strategy can yield a similar result without triggering such resentment. Roberts' research reveals how the Chinese leadership deploys a combination of fear, friction, and flooding in censoring the internet.[70] First, the government utilizes threats of punishment associated with spreading or accessing prohibited information to instill a sense of fear and cultivate self-censorship. Next, friction refers to the government's practice of increasing the costs of accessing prohibited information—such as slowing down websites or reordering search results—as a way of making such information less likely to spread. Finally, flooding refers to disseminating desirable information, such as government propaganda, that crowds out the undesirable information or distracts or confuses internet users. Government flooding thereby dilutes the ability of the undesirable information to influence public opinion. While under this porous censorship regime some individuals are still able to access objectionable information, the information will not reach the masses and is thus unlikely to spark any collective action that could destabilize the Chinese regime.

Recent experimental research by Yuyu Chen and David Y. Yang similarly shows that the prevailing political environment sustains a culture of censorship even if the regime was not strictly enforced.[71] The researchers carried out a field experiment where they provided some Chinese university students with access to an uncensored internet and tracked these citizens' behavior over eighteen months. One of their primary findings was that free access alone does not lead Chinese citizens to acquire politically sensitive information. Being accustomed to censorship, the demand for such information remains low, absent additional inducements. However, once offered some modest incentives to consume Western news, the subjects of the study began to acquire such politically sensitive information more persistently. Such a change in behavior also brought about a change in these students' attitudes. For example, after consuming foreign content that is normally censored, the subjects of the study became more critical of the Chinese government and less optimistic about China's economic growth or stock market. They also communicated some of their newly acquired knowledge to their peers but such information spillovers were ultimately limited. Thus, overall, the study suggests that the censorship regime in China is effective not only because of technical and legal restrictions that the government has implemented but also because of the broader political and cultural environment in which the demand for such information—absent some encouragement—is generally limited.

Propaganda is another important component of the state-driven regulatory model, and the Chinese government increasingly deploys the internet for this purpose. The COVID-19 pandemic serves as an example of an extensive propaganda campaign by the government to shape the narrative over the origins and management of the pandemic. The state-orchestrated social media commentary of the pandemic advances a narrative that casts China in a good light, both by suppressing news about the origins of the pandemic and by deflecting blame that China initially failed to notify its citizens and international health authorities about the outbreak of the virus. The propaganda messaging also highlights the Chinese leadership's competence in handling the pandemic response while systematically posting about foreign leaders' failures.[72] These government posts have been amplified by thousands of social media accounts—many of them reportedly fake—specifically set up to like, retweet, and repost the government's crafted narrative.[73] A particularly egregious example features a spokesman for the Chinese Ministry of Foreign

Affairs, Zhao Lijian, who accused the US of originating the pandemic: "CDC was caught on the spot. When did patient zero begin in US? How many people are infected? What are the names of the hospitals? It might be US army who brought the epidemic to Wuhan. Be transparent! Make public your data! US owe us an explanation!"[74] The tweet received over 13,000 likes after it was posted in March 2020. Twitter applied a fact check tag to the post, urging the reader to "Get the facts about COVID-19."[75] Li Yang, another official of the Ministry of Foreign Affairs with over 30,000 Twitter followers at the time, posted in July 2021: "The US won the first place in the fight against the pandemic with more than 30 million COVID-19 infections and more than 600 thousand COVID-19 deaths!!!"[76] These examples illustrate how Chinese government officials actively deploy social media to advance pro-government messages as part of their carefully orchestrated propaganda effort.

In addition to deploying elaborate technology to police online communications, the Chinese leadership has employed human monitors to censor harmful content and to carry out propaganda.[77] These human censors— estimated to be as many as 100,000—manually review and delete undesirable posts.[78] At the same time, a different group of internet commentators—known as the "50 Cent Army," due to the fact that these commentators are reportedly paid ¥0.50 for every post they write—blanket the internet with ideologically suitable posts, thereby crowding out politically incorrect or otherwise harmful content. This is confirmed by a 2017 study by Gary King, Jennifer Pan, and Margaret E. Roberts, who analyzed over 43,000 leaked posts linked to the Chinese Internet Propaganda Office's account. The researchers estimated that the Chinese government posts approximately 448 million fabricated social media entries annually.[79] They also show that the government propaganda is less focused on directly rebutting controversial comments and more focused on distracting the public by changing the subject. These posts seek to feed positive information about the government, cheerleading the regime and the accomplishments of the Communist Party. This study garnered significant media attention, including in China, and even prompted the government-affiliated newspaper, the *Global Times*, to respond. In its editorial, the paper acknowledged the government's engagement in "public opinion guidance," explaining that such control was needed to prevent instability in the country.[80] The paper also alleged that this practice had the backing of the Chinese citizens who, the paper claimed, recognized the "necessity" of such guidance.[81] However, contrary to this government's claim, when King and his coauthors analyzed Weibo posts discussing *The Global Times* article, only about 30 percent of those Chinese Weibo users appeared to support the articulated censorship policy.[82]

Chinese state-controlled media is frequently harnessed to amplify the government's censorship and propaganda efforts. In 2016, President Xi spoke at the News and Public Opinion Work Conference, stressing how "the media run by the Party and government are the propaganda battlefields of the Party and government, and must be surnamed Party. All the work of the Party's news and public opinion media must embody the Party's will, reflect the Party's standpoint, safeguard the authority of the Party Centre, safeguard Party unity, and must love the Party, uphold the Party and be [for] the sake of the Party."[83] The government owns or controls most of the leading media outlets, including Xinhua News, China Daily, and People's Daily and exerts additional control through the accreditation of journalists and by issuing daily directives to guide these outlets' news coverage.[84] Chinese internet companies must also sign the "Public Pledge on Self-Regulation and Professional Ethics for China Internet Industry."[85] In signing the pledge, they commit to "[refrain] from producing, posting or disseminating pernicious information that may jeopardize state security and disrupt social stability, contravene laws and regulations and spread superstition and obscenity" and to "monitor the information publicized by users on websites according to law and remove the harmful information promptly."[86] This ensures that any online media coverage is tightly controlled by the CCP, assisting in propaganda and thus serving the political agenda of the state.

Although China has woven internet propaganda deeply into its regulatory model, it is not clear that this propaganda is always effective in pushing the government's narrative. Chinese leaders can reinforce the chosen message by ordering multiple forms of media, including television, newspapers, and internet sites, to publish similar content. This uniformity across different information sources contributes to the effectiveness of propaganda.[87] However, Chinese people are conscious of tight state control over mass media and increasingly suspicious about the lack of conflicting sources of information. As a result, they may question the credibility of media information, especially if they hear conflicting narratives from their friends and colleagues who may have first-hand knowledge about certain events or are able to access different sources of media.[88] Chinese propaganda has also been distinctly unsuccessful in shaping the global narrative about China. For example, the government tried, but failed, to bury a scandal involving Peng Shuai, a Chinese tennis star who largely disappeared from public view in 2021 after accusing one of China's former leaders of having sexually assaulted her and publishing her accusations on the Chinese social media platform Weibo.[89] The government was able to swiftly delete the posting by Peng Shuai on Weibo, and took extensive measures to control the narrative of the scandal within China. However, it could not stem the international uproar about the incident, as Chinese state media's messaging about the incident was never seen as credible abroad.[90] Thus, while President Xi has aspired to shape a global narrative about China in a way that reflects the country's rising status in the world, the Chinese government has struggled to create "a credible, lovable and respectable image of China" abroad.[91]

How Pervasive Digital Surveillance Enhances State Control

Digital technologies provide the Chinese government with powerful tools for monitoring its citizens, making political control a pervasive feature of the state-driven regulatory model. Artificial intelligence, including facial recognition, has in particular become a central tool for Chinese state surveillance. China is home to several leading AI surveillance companies, including Huawei, Hikvision, Dahua, and ZTE, which develop, among other things, smart city technologies; and SenseTime, Megvii, CloudWalk, and Yitu, which are leading AI startups developing facial recognition technologies.[92] Many of these companies have helped the Chinese government build, sustain, and operate the present surveillance state. China has over one billion internet users transacting and communicating online,[93] giving these companies access to a vast pool of data, which they can leverage toward intricate surveillance.[94]

The Chinese government justifies its surveillance efforts as necessary for citizens' safety and efficient governance. For example, an oft-cited benefit is the technologies' contribution to public order and crime reduction, which makes society "more harmonious and orderly."[95] Local officials also often tout the benefits of surveillance technologies, citing examples of how those technologies have reduced crime across the country. One such example comes from a village in Sichuan province, where—according to a local CCP secretary—common crimes, including petty thefts and occasional assaults, had dropped to zero within two years because of the surveillance cameras.[96] Companies developing surveillance technologies are also eager to highlight the ways those technologies contribute to law enforcement. According to Sensetime, its facial recognition technology allowed the Guangzhou police to arrest 800 suspects and to solve over 100 crimes within a year.[97] Surveillance technologies have also been prominently—even if controversially[98]—deployed during the pandemic, with color-based health codes and tracking systems controlling people's movements and thus quickly reducing the spread of COVID-19.[99]

Chinese officials also point to surveillance technologies' contribution to more efficient management of cities, including alleviating traffic congestion, optimizing energy use, or combating pollution.[100] For example, these technologies reportedly helped reduce traffic jams by 15 percent in a district in Hangzhou.[101] The Chinese government sees the benefits associated with these technologies as directly contributing to the country's economic growth. Economic growth in China is tied to rapid urbanization, which has made the better management of cities a central issue for the government. Another economic benefit is the growth potential of the surveillance industry where Chinese companies can take advantage of the increased demand of those technologies,[102] both at home and abroad.[103]

However, the critical voices dismiss such stated motives and maintain that the real goal is not safety and efficiency but installment of authoritarian control. With the help of sophisticated AI, the Chinese government is building a surveillance society with the means to exercise unprecedented social control over the entire population. In detailed reporting in The Atlantic, Ross Andersen offers a grim glance into the realities of the Chinese surveillance state, describing ways that the government is leveraging AI to "achieve an unprecedented political stranglehold on more than one billion people."[104] Hundreds of millions of surveillance cameras are already installed across China, with the goal to soon achieve "full video coverage of key public areas."[105] AI technologies allow the government to match the video footage to personal data collected elsewhere, identifying individuals in real time and predicting impending political resistance. The Chinese government has rolled out various overlapping surveillance programs, such as smart cities or "Sharp Eyes."[106] The goal of the Sharp Eyes initiative is to create an "omnipresent, fully integrated, always working and fully controllable" nationwide surveillance system.[107] The high-tech surveillance state is constantly evolving, allowing the government to invade almost every aspect of its citizens' lives. The next frontier is likely to be digital currency, with a pilot program already underway.[108] Were Chinese citizens to switch to digital currency in large numbers, the Chinese government would gain an unprecedented ability to track their financial transactions.[109]

While China is also exporting its surveillance technologies, as discussed in Chapter 8, much of the surveillance technology today is deployed domestically. Indeed, eight out of the ten most surveilled cities in the world are in China.[110] Out of the roughly 1,000 smart cities that are being built worldwide, around 500 can be found in China.[111] While the government has emphasized the benevolent deployment of smart city technologies, such as smart traffic management or better management of power grids, little evidence supports the claim that those smart cities have to date significantly improved the lives of Chinese citizens. Instead, the smart city initiatives serve the governmental goal of installing an expansive surveillance system used to monitor and control the citizens. For the past decade, the Chinese government has spent more on smart cities and other technologies aimed at improving the country's internal security than it has spent to guard against foreign security threats.[112]

This high-tech surveillance is taken furthest in Xinjiang, the western region of China that is home to the country's Muslim Uyghur minority group. The Chinese government has blanketed Xinjiang with surveillance cameras, sensors, and other technologies designed to track every movement of its population, making Uyghurs "the most intensely surveilled population on Earth."[113] The government has required the Uyghurs to install mobile apps that allow more precise tracking of their online activity, revealing any religious or political activity of which the government disapproves. Chinese tech companies have been crucial partners in implementing Xinjiang's surveillance regime. For example, the telecom giant Huawei is reported to have partnered with a facial recognition startup Megvii to develop and test an AI facial recognition system that can trigger an "Uighur alarm" every time the system recognizes a person that belongs to the targeted ethnic group.[114] In addition to suppressing the dissenting voices in Xinjiang, this large-scale surveillance effort is believed to serve a broader goal: the Chinese government can use Xinjiang as a testing laboratory to perfect its surveillance technologies before their large-scale rollout elsewhere in China or in the rest of the world.

The Chinese authorities have also launched a controversial "social credit system," which rates citizens for their trustworthiness.[115] Some commentators describe this scheme as a highly invasive "Orwellian" surveillance system that aggregates information such as police, court, medical, and tax records, as well as political files and information on online activity.[116] This information is then used to produce an individual score that can lead to various economic and societal rewards or punishments. For example, a high social credit score can help a person gain employment opportunities, better access to a loan, or faster processing of government documents, while a low credit score can prevent an individual from purchasing an airline ticket, owning a house, or studying at a university.[117] The government is not hiding its intention that the social credit system is designed to come with consequences, noting how the system will "allow the trustworthy to roam everywhere under the heaven while making it hard for the discredited to take a single step."[118] However, the effectiveness of the social credit system, and its pervasiveness in ordering the lives of individuals in China, is debated. Some commentators suggest that its lofty goals in ordering Chinese society remain largely aspirational and its implementation is still fragmented.[119] As a result, despite raising legitimate fears about the ever-encroaching surveillance state, it appears to grant less control to the state than what is often assumed.[120]

The Role of Tech Companies and Chinese Citizens

A close partnership between the state and private companies is central to the successful implementation of the Chinese regulatory model. To operate a large-scale censorship regime, the Chinese government needs the help of its tech companies, and employs both rewards and threats of punishment to secure their cooperation. These companies were initially rewarded with lax regulation to help them grow and flourish. They have also been shielded from foreign competition, with the government imposing extensive restrictions on foreign tech companies, as discussed earlier. Noncompliance with government demands would not only risk removing this type of favorable treatment but would also expose these companies to various sanctions, including shutting down their service as the ultimate remedy.[121] This privatized censorship regime in the digital domain is not new, but rather an extension of the government's prevailing censorship system more generally. Commercialized media, for example, can compete for profit in the marketplace but must moderate their content according to strict government requirements.

These obligations targeting online platforms are entrenched in various laws. For example, the 2011 Administrative Measures for Internet Information Services mandates Chinese internet companies to delete content that would be "detrimental to State honour and interests," or content that counts as "disseminating rumours, disrupting social order and stability."[122] A 2019 regulation issued by the Cyberspace Administration of China (CAC) clarifies that online platforms are required to refrain from disseminating illegal content while "encouraged" to disseminate content that promotes socialist theories set out by President Xi Jinping.[123] Another 2019 regulation aimed specifically at audio and video platforms—including Douyin, which is the Chinese version of TikTok—requires that these companies shall "insist on the correct political direction, guidance of public opinions and value orientation, carry forward the core socialist values, and promote the formation of positive cyber culture toward kindness."[124] They are also required to monitor that their users do not carry out prohibited activities, including those that "endanger national security, undermine social stability, [or] disrupt social order."[125] Laws such as these make abundantly clear that these companies' ability to operate their business hinges on their submission to government demands for cooperation.

These laws are supplemented with continuing government direction and active monitoring. In a 2021 interview given under the pseudonym "Li An," an employee at ByteDance—the creator of TikTok and its Chinese version Douyin—shed light on how ByteDance's censorship machine works and how connected it is to the CAC.[126] Li An, who helped develop content moderation tools for the company, recounted how the CAC would issue recurrent directives—at times over a hundred a day—to ByteDance's Content Quality Center, which then ensured that these instructions were followed. The biggest fear for ByteDance was that it fails to delete politically sensitive content that triggers government scrutiny, which can be a "life-and-death matter" for the company without strong government relationships.[127] Troubled by the role she was playing in the Chinese censorship machine, Li An described her role in erasing the nation's "collective memories" of historical events, removing unwanted conversations, and amplifying narratives that the Chinese government approves. ByteDance's close compliance with government demands is not surprising given that the Chinese government actively monitors compliance and enforces its regulations.[128] In July 2021, it was revealed that the government had blocked new app registrations for the ByteDance-owned Jinri Toutiao, one of China's biggest mobile news sites, since September 2020. While no reason was given for this halt on registrations, the company's app had previously been taken off app stores, and Jinri Toutiao was summoned to meet with the regulators regarding the app's "vulgar content."[129] The State Administration of Radio and Television regulators also ordered Neihan Duanzi, another popular ByteDance app specializing in jokes and comedy sketches, to be shut down in 2018.[130]

If the tech companies submit to the government's demands, what has been the reaction of Chinese citizens to government censorship and surveillance? Chinese citizens are particularly active internet users. Recent analyses have shown that as of 2021, over one billion Chinese people were connected to the internet and they spent an average over four hours online every day.[131] Some commentaries portray Chinese internet users as defiant in the face of government controls while others describe them as more submissive. For example, while the social credit system is strongly condemned abroad, many Chinese citizens find it socially acceptable.[132] Its supporters believe that the social credit system can help address the trust deficit in China and gladly use the scoring in their own private lives, for example, to screen trustworthy dates on dating platforms. Others welcome scoring as it has allowed them to enjoy benefits such as discounted heating bills as a reward for their good behavior.[133] Some citizens note how they like surveillance cameras because they make them feel safe.[134] There are likely a myriad of reasons why Chinese citizens may generally be less alarmed by such a surveillance system—one being that they are accustomed to the government already maintaining a "dossier" of each citizen, tracking personal information, such as individuals' political liabilities.[135] In other words, the baseline expectation of privacy and freedom among Chinese citizens is lower.

At the same time, there are countless examples of Chinese citizens using the internet for resistance and activism, directly challenging public norms and authorities. Elizabeth Economy recounts several examples of Chinese citizens resorting to social media to call out local governments' mismanagement of policy issues or advocate for reform. A 2015 incident involving women's rights is illustrative. A group of five women's rights activists, known as "Feminist Five," protested against domestic violence and sexual harassment.[136] Their protests involved wearing blood-stained wedding dresses designed to attract public attention to their advocacy. In March 2015, the police detained them and held them for over a month without filing any formal charges. Public outrage followed. Digital campaigns were launched and an online petition advocating their release was circulated. The government sought to silence the campaign by censoring key terms used to advocate the women's release. Yet government censors could not stem the online activity calling for #FreeTheFive. Instead, the activity taking place online spilled into the streets of China and beyond, with people marching and calling for the release of the detained women. In the face of growing domestic and international pressure, the government relented and finally released the women. This is one of numerous stories showing how Chinese citizens are deploying the internet to raise awareness, to advocate for rights and reform, and to hold the government accountable. It may not translate into broader democratic reform in China but it has become a meaningful tool for issue-specific advocacy or social change locally.

In the years preceding Xi's ascension to power in 2013, the Chinese censorship regime was less absolutist, tolerating some degree of dissenting voices online.[137] Back then, Chinese citizens, eager to access foreign content, logged in using VPNs without the government restraining them. Activists were also able to advocate for social change without being immediately silenced by the government censorship machine. However, these voices have been dimming as President Xi has decisively restricted online engagement by the civil society. Many activists have lost their faith in the internet offering a vibrant political space capable of facilitating reform in the country.[138] Voices for political reform have been silenced, and posts on important platforms such as Weibo have fallen dramatically. Others remain more optimistic, arguing that the internet remains an important tool for social change and human rights. They recount how Chinese netizens have always been resourceful, discovering new and creative ways to circumvent censorship rules. However, few can ignore the shift under President Xi that has further entrenched digital authoritarianism as not merely an endorsed ideology but as a strictly enforced practice that rigidly demarcates citizens' online communications in China.[139]

How the Chinese Regulatory Model Overlaps with the American and European Models

The Chinese state-driven regulatory model has many features that are unique to its digital authoritarian governance regime. At the same time, the Chinese model embraces some elements of the European rights-driven and the American market-driven regulatory models as well. The government cannot survive only by limiting the rights of its citizens through censorship and surveillance—even if such restrictive policies were pursued in the name of protecting Chinese citizens from online harms or societal instability. The Chinese regulators are also genuinely concerned about the commercialization of internet users' data privacy and seek to promote certain consumer protection rights traditionally associated with the European rights-driven regulatory model. For example, China's new data privacy law, revised anti-monopoly law, and official guidance on the development of the platform economy all enhance the rights that Chinese internet users have vis-à-vis tech companies.

China's new data privacy law, the Personal Information Protection Law (PIPL), emulates many provisions of the EU's General Data Protection Regulation (GDPR), as discussed in Chapter 9. It states unambiguously that "the personal information of natural persons shall be protected by law. No organization or individual may infringe upon natural persons' rights and interests relating to personal information."[140] In preparing the law, the government acknowledged the importance of data privacy in this era where companies and other entities "arbitrarily collect, unlawfully obtain, overexploit, and illegally trade personal information" to advance their commercial interests.[141] The companies' data handling is a central concern that penetrates other legislative initiatives as well. In their official guidance on the platform economy in 2022, the Chinese authorities reiterated their commitment to curtailing platform companies' data abuses, including "trading of data on black markets" or deployment of big data toward price discrimination.[142] In addition to citizens' data privacy, the Chinese government is concerned with unfair business practices by dominant tech companies. In particular, Chinese legislators have curtailed practices such as price discrimination—often fueled by data and algorithms—that allow these companies to exploit consumers.[143] Also, the PIPL bans companies from using personal information to facilitate "differential treatment to individuals in terms of trading price or other trading conditions."[144] The recent crackdown on the tech industry in the name of common prosperity has also sought to introduce greater fairness in the marketplace, distributing power away from tech companies, not only toward the state, but also toward internet users and digital consumers.

As expected, these rights-driven policies have certain limitations in the Chinese context. First, the Chinese government seeks to enhance the rights of Chinese internet users vis-à-vis tech companies but not vis-à-vis the state itself. For example, the PIPL provides for extensive data protection rights, yet contains a public security exception that allows the government to carry out digital surveillance, unconstrained by these rights protections.[145] Second, while the Chinese government embraces a strong rights rhetoric in describing its digital policies, that rhetoric can at times be difficult to reconcile with the reality of rights' implementation in practice. For example, various Chinese AI regulations and policy statements read like they could have been drafted by European legislators in Brussels. In 2019, the Chinese Ministry of Science and Technology published *Governance Principles for a New Generation of Artificial Intelligence*, which describes "enhancing the common well-being of humanity" as the overarching goal of AI development.[146] According to these principles, AI should enhance fairness and justice and avoid bias, discrimination, and the infringement of data privacy. These lofty goals paint a very different reality from that exhibited by the several examples of the Chinese government's deployment of facial recognition technologies discussed earlier in this chapter. Despite these important limitations, some resemblance with the European rights-driven regulatory model is both real and significant, including the Chinese regulatory model's commitment to greater fairness and redistribution, as well as its preparedness to place limits on tech companies' ability to exploit their users' data for commercial gain.

The Chinese regulatory model also incorporates elements of the American market-driven model. The relatively hands-off approach toward the tech industry that the Chinese government embraced in the early years of the internet resembles a US-style, techno-libertarian approach where the government's role is to step aside and let companies innovate, unencumbered by regulation. Chinese government policy, including its industrial strategy, played a trivial role in cultivating China's tech success at that time. Instead, as Sebastian Mallaby has vividly described, the birth of China's tech industry owes much to the financial model created by the US venture capital (VC) industry.[147] Mallaby dispels any notion that the Chinese tech companies would have grown solely, or even predominantly, with the help of state subsidies. Instead,

American investors were important early backers of most successful Chinese tech companies. Even Chinese VCs that provided capital to those firms were "quasi-American," led by individuals who were largely educated in the US, had worked in US financial firms, and who embraced a US approach to venture investing.[148] In shaping the early years of the Chinese tech industry, these US-linked VCs structured deals the "U.S. way," using Silicon Valley lawyers to draft legal documents.[149] US investors thus not only provided the capital but also imported Silicon Valley's "equity culture" into China.[150] US lawyers also came up with creative ways to ensure that Chinese tech firms were able to tap into US capital by incorporating the firms in the Cayman Islands, thus allowing them to accept foreign capital and to list in foreign stock exchanges. These legal workarounds opened Chinese tech startups to opportunities that were not permissible under Chinese law or envisioned by the Chinese state-driven regulatory model.

Specific examples of American capital behind China's largest tech companies include Goldman Sachs, which invested $3.3 million into Alibaba back in 1999, helping Jack Ma start his company while enhancing Alibaba's credibility in subsequent funding rounds[151]—even though the US bank exited from Alibaba prematurely, forgoing tremendous financial gains that ensued for other investors.[152] As of October 2020, ByteDance's largest outside investor was reportedly a US high-speed trading firm, Susquehanna, which had invested in the company in 2012.[153] Qualcomm Ventures counts itself among the early investors of the phone maker Xiaomi.[154] Tencent started in 1998 with the backing of a US-based VC fund called IDG, and Baidu benefited from another American VC fund, DFJ.[155] American venture capital similarly contributed to the growth of JD.com,[156] which also secured a $550 million investment from Google in 2018.[157]

The importance of US VC in growing China's tech sector is hard to overstate even though over the years China's own VC culture has matured away from the US. According to research conducted by Rhodium Group and the National Committee on US–China Relations, American VC has fueled the growth of most of the leading tech firms in China, including Alibaba, Baidu, and Tencent.[158] Their research estimates that nearly a third of all Chinese tech companies that benefited from VC funding between 2000 and early 2019 raised money from American VCs, amounting to $47 billion (or 16 percent) of the total venture capital raised by Chinese startups over that period. In addition, the Chinese tech sector has benefited from VC raised from various other funds, through which various US limited partners have participated. This illustrates that the Chinese state-driven regulatory model rests on a solid capitalist foundation—akin to the American market-driven regulatory model—and that the initial fortunes of Chinese tech companies can be traced to investors in Silicon Valley and not to political leaders in Beijing.

The Government's Recent Tech Crackdown

Since late 2020, the Chinese regulatory model has taken a turn toward even greater state control of the country's tech industry. While governments around the globe are now inserting themselves more forcefully into the marketplace in an effort to rein in the outsized power of the tech industry, the Chinese government has shown particular resolve in this regard. This unfolding shift in China's regulatory approach suggests that the Chinese government is now fundamentally reevaluating the bargain that it initially struck with its tech companies, determined to curtail the influence of large tech companies whose growth it has been nurturing all these years. Its wide-reaching regulatory crackdown of the tech sector started with the suspension of the fintech company Ant Group's planned $37 billion initial public offering—the largest IPO in history—in November 2020,[159] followed by a $2.8 billion antitrust fine for the e-commerce giant Alibaba in April 2021.[160] Two days after fining Alibaba, Chinese regulators ordered Ant Group to restructure its operations and become a financial holding company subject to central bank supervision.[161] Next in line was the ride-hailing service DiDi Chuxing, whose data practices triggered a government investigation just days after the company's $4.4 billion IPO on the New York Stock Exchange.[162] Citing cybersecurity risks that the company posed to its customers, Chinese regulators ordered DiDi's app to be removed from app stores in July 2021—within a week following the IPO—sending the company's stock price tumbling,[163] and resulting in a record high $1.2 billion fine imposed on the company in July 2022.[164] In July 2021, the government blocked the proposed $5.3 billion Tencent-backed merger between DouYu with Huya, China's two leading streaming operators.[165] Another antitrust action followed in October 2021, with a $530 million fine imposed on Meituan, the food delivery giant, for its monopolistic practices.[166]

In parallel with targeting specific companies with enforcement actions, the government enacted a flurry of legislative measures between February and August 2021 to further assert control over the tech industry. It first released new, stringent Anti-Monopoly Guidelines, sending a chill through global markets.[167] Beijing also issued new rules restricting the collection of personal information by mobile internet apps.[168] Next, the regulators unveiled rules affecting online live-streamed marketing, which is a major trend in Chinese e-commerce.[169] Under these new measures, live streamers must provide their real names and tax information. As a major piece of legislation,

China's legislature, the Standing Committee of China's National People's Congress, issued a monumental Data Security Law, setting out stringent data security requirements across broad categories of data, which limits cross-border transfer of such data.[170] This law was complemented by the revised Cybersecurity Review Measures, imposing further cybersecurity obligations for companies seeking to list abroad.[171] Shortly thereafter, the government issued regulations to protect critical information infrastructure as an implementation measure of the 2016 Cybersecurity Law.[172] That same month, the Standing Committee of China's National People's Congress issued another major piece of legislation, the PILP, which is China's first comprehensive, national-level data protection law.[173] The next target was the online gaming industry, with the government setting a three-hour limit of online gameplaying per week on minors and banning gaming companies from providing minors with online game services outside these hours.[174]

The amount of sweeping regulatory activity that took place within a short few months in 2021 was dizzying, especially when contrasted to the US Congress' futile efforts to agree on any meaningful tech legislation, or compared to the years it takes for various EU institutions to prepare and debate legislation. While the crackdown has been wide-ranging, affecting many domains of the digital economy, certain sectors have emerged as primary targets. These include fintech, e-commerce, private education, and online gaming and entertainment. The target companies share two key features: first, they are mostly large firms, and second, they are almost exclusively software as opposed to hardware companies.[175] Among the 238 tech firms listed on Hurun China 500 Most Valuable Private Companies 2020, a total of 62 have faced regulatory actions, such as fines, bans, restructuring, or regulatory mandates. Among the targeted firms, 93 percent were classified as platform companies. In addition, the targets were predominantly large tech companies. This is not surprising given the Chinese government's emphasis on anti-monopoly actions and fair competition, a stance that targets large platform companies that are able to maintain a dominant market position due to the extensive network effects inherent in their business models.[176]

The government's assault on the tech industry likely stems from multiple motivations. In part, the newfound regulatory scrutiny reflects Beijing's growing attention to wealth redistribution and the pressing need to pursue "common prosperity" in the face of social divisions and inequalities found in Chinese society.[177] In his August 2021 speech at the meeting of the CCP's Central Committee for Financial and Economic Affairs, President Xi emphasized that "China must make resolute efforts to prevent polarization and promote common prosperity in order to safeguard social harmony and stability."[178] As part of this new policy orientation, the Chinese leadership is pushing wealthy tech entrepreneurs to share more of their wealth with the rest of society.[179] The government is also responding to public outrage related to the business practices of large tech companies. In particular, Chinese people feel that they are manipulated by tech companies through algorithms or otherwise exploited by tech monopolies.[180]

However, alleviating public concerns about inequality or exploitative business practices is unlikely to be the sole motivation behind the recent regulatory onslaught. The Chinese government also wants to restore its own control over an industry that has grown so large that it threatens the power and influence of the state. While Chinese regulators initially encouraged growth of the country's tech companies, they are now growing wary of the size and power of these tech behemoths. In particular, the government is concerned that these companies control a trove of data that the government itself would want to control in order to better manage the society.[181] Therefore, by reining in the power of the private tech companies, the government is also looking to claw back control over data these companies collect. Relatedly, the government is looking to protect the traditional state-owned financial sector. Companies such as Alibaba have disrupted the conventional financial services industry, with Alibaba's Ant dominating more than 50 percent of China's mobile payments market.[182] This suggests that a significant number of financial transactions are now moving onto a platform that is not state-owned and that falls outside financial regulation, posing a risk to Chinese consumers and undermining state control of a key industry.[183]

The crackdown may also be viewed as a response to regulatory developments elsewhere, including the measures the US government has taken as part of the US–China tech war. Chinese leadership is seeking to decouple some of the financial linkages between China's private sector and Wall Street even while trying to avoid the costs associated with complete financial decoupling. Pursuant to the 2020 US Holding Foreign Companies Accountable Act, all foreign firms listed on US stock exchanges—including Chinese tech companies—need to comply with the audit review process overseen by the Public Company Accounting Oversight Board (PCAOB). China is reluctant to have its companies cooperate with US auditing regulations, which is why Chinese regulators' enforcement action against DiDi may be viewed as "a preemptive strike" against the PCAOB and Congress.[184]

Finally, Chinese regulators' focus on software as opposed to hardware companies suggests that the Chinese government is eager to steer its tech industry toward more strategically relevant sectors that can support the country's long-term economic growth. The US–China tech war has made China conscious of its vulnerabilities and technological dependencies in the face of sanctions and supply chain disruptions. Therefore, China wants its economy to be leading innovations in so-called hard tech, such as manufacturing, semiconductors, new energy vehicles, and biotech, which requires a proactive shifting of resources away from less strategic industries such as online gaming and social media.[185] This also explains why hardware companies such as the telecom giant Xiaomi, alongside emerging industries in fields such as electric vehicles, have largely been spared in the regulatory crackdown.[186]

Already to date, the repercussions of the Chinese government's regulatory salvo have been severe. According to reporting from November 2021, the tech crackdown had "wiped out more than $1 trillion worldwide from the market value of Chinese companies."[187] DiDi alone lost $38 billion in market value from its peak on the day of its IPO to four weeks after its listing.[188] Holding back the industry may further drag down the Chinese economy, which is already facing multiple challenges, including the aftermath of extensive COVID-19 lockdowns, the US–China trade war and related sanctions, and the debt crisis in real estate. The heavy-handed regulation of the tech sector is now further destabilizing the wider economy and endangering the prospects of the country's future economic growth.[189] How this recent turn in Chinese tech regulation will affect the country's digital economy in the long term remains to be seen. Among the uncertain questions is whether the Chinese government is able to pursue its ambitions for global technological and economic leadership while simultaneously weakening the very companies that are the engine of the country's technological progress and innovation. The Chinese government is already seemingly alarmed by the sharp sell-off of Chinese tech company stocks, large-scale layoffs of tech workers, and other market reactions to its harsh policy measures. As a result, the government has pledged to introduce policies that reassure investors and increase the transparency of its policymaking toward the tech industry.[190] These promises suggest that its crackdown on the industry might be easing.[191] However, significant uncertainty is likely to linger concerning the future of the Chinese state-driven regulatory model and what its next phase will look like in the coming years.

The wisdom behind the recent tech crackdown has been heavily debated. Foreign news commentary has described the aggressive regulatory measures as "a strategic mistake," warning that the efforts to quash the most vibrant sector of the Chinese economy may compromise the country's efforts to become a technological superpower and achieve economic parity with the West.[192] Restricting Chinese tech companies' foreign listings is also likely to be self-defeating, as it will raise the cost of capital for Chinese firms and increase the "China discount" in their valuations as investors are pricing in the regulatory risk associated with investing in these companies. This will ultimately also undermine China's geopolitical aspirations to become a more important player in the global financial system.[193] However, some foreign commentary is more favorable in that it emphasizes how the Chinese government harbors many of the same concerns as the regulators and legislators in the US and the EU, including harms relating to market dominance and data privacy.[194] Without the need to adhere to the democratic process, the Chinese government simply faces fewer political hurdles to actually enact legislation or effectively enforce it. Within China, the official analysis has been largely positive, which is to be expected in a censored digital environment where unfavorable views on government policies, including the tech crackdown, would rarely be voiced in the public domain. For example, Chinese scholars emphasize the necessity of more stringent antitrust policy to address problems that have followed from the "barbaric growth" of the tech industry, including big tech companies bullying small companies or using algorithms to infringe consumer rights.[195] New laws are thus needed to "purify" competition in the tech sector,[196] and to ensure that platform companies face enough competition so as not to lose their drive to innovate.[197]

Chinese tech companies have responded to the government's crackdown of the industry with acquiescence rather than defiance, which reveals a stark contrast to US tech companies challenging government regulations in the US and the EU. None of the affected Chinese tech companies have contested the measures taken against them. For instance, on the same day that Alibaba was fined the record $2.8 billion, the company made a public statement conveying that it "accept[ed] the penalty with sincerity and will ensure [its] compliance with determination."[198] A similar statement was posted by Meituan after the company was fined $530 million.[199] Several tech executives have also stepped down, and several more have pledged to donate their shares or money to the government or government-backed public causes following the crackdown.[200] For example, in March 2021, Colin Huang, founder of the e-commerce giant Pinduoduo, resigned as chairman and promised to channel $100 million from his foundation to support scientific research.[201] In June 2021, Wang Xing, the founder of Meituan, donated over $2 billion worth of his company's shares to his philanthropic foundation.[202] In May 2021, Zhang Yiming announced he would step down as ByteDance's CEO and made a $77 million donation toward education in his native Fujian Province in June.[203] In August 2021, Tencent doubled the amount of money it sets aside for social responsibility programs to $15.4

billion.[204] In September 2021, Alibaba followed, vowing to invest \$15.5 billion into the country's common prosperity initiatives.[205]

This new era of tech regulation in China may well reflect a new settlement between tech companies and the Chinese government, rewriting some of the principles underlying the existing regulatory philosophy. Today, tech companies are increasingly expected to contribute to a fairer Chinese society— as defined by the CCP—and ensure that they do not grow more powerful than the state itself. The Chinese regulatory model may be seen as moving somewhat closer to the European regulatory model that emphasizes fairness and redistribution, yet it does so by adhering to some distinctly Chinese characteristics. Thus, even with this unfolding shift, the core tenet of the Chinese state-driven regulatory model is not only maintained but reinforced: the Chinese government reigns over the digital economy and, still today, remains very much in charge.

Criticism of the State-Driven Regulatory Model

From an American or European perspective, there is much to criticize in the Chinese state-driven regulatory model. Anyone subscribing to values of liberal democracy and individual freedom is pained to witness how China deploys the internet as a tool to entrench autocracy as opposed to advance democracy. Digital authoritarianism infringes on individual rights and deprives Chinese citizens of key civil liberties. It contributes to the political oppression of minorities through the surveillance of these groups by the government and deprives Chinese society of the benefits of free speech and diverse voices.

Governments, private actors, and civil society organizations have strongly criticized China's regulatory model. For example, the 2021 *Final Report* by the US National Security Commission on Artificial Intelligence describes China's domestic use of AI as "a chilling precedent for anyone around the world who cherishes individual liberty."[206] In a US Senate Committee on Foreign Relations' Democratic Staff report titled *The New Big Brother— China and Digital Authoritarianism*, Senator Robert Menendez described how China views new technologies "as a means of surveilling and controlling populations, stifling the free flow of information, ensuring the survival of their governments, and as tools for malign influence campaigns worldwide."[207] European political leadership shares these concerns. For example, in its 2020 Resolution on Forced Labour and the Situation of the Uyghurs in the Xinjiang Uyghur Autonomous Region, the European Parliament "strongly condemns the extensive use of digital surveillance technologies to monitor and control the population in Xinjiang."[208] Already back in 2008, European

Commissioner Viviane Reding emphasized the importance of freedom of information: "We say, for instance, to the Chinese very clearly that their blocking of certain Internet content is absolutely unacceptable to us."[209]

Of the US tech companies, Meta has been most vocal in its criticism of China's internet policies. In a 2019 speech, Facebook's Mark Zuckerberg criticized authoritarian regimes' laws and regulations that undermine free speech and other human rights, singling out China as a country that is "building its own internet focused on very different values, and is now exporting their vision of the internet to other countries."[210] He also drew a contrast between Chinese-owned TikTok and WhatsApp, noting how the latter is being used in protests by activists who rely on the app's strong encryption, whereas TikTok does not allow these protests to be mentioned. In 2021, the Freedom House, a US-based NGO researching and advocating for democracy, summarized its research on internet freedoms around the world by noting that "conditions for internet users in China remained profoundly oppressive, and confirmed the country's status as the world's worst abuser of internet freedom for the seventh consecutive year."[211]

The Chinese government is quick to retort any such criticism. It points to the many examples of the societal ills that free speech online can generate, be it hate speech, unsettling rumors and disinformation, or even terrorist or violent content.[212] The government defends the benefits of protecting its citizens from those ills and, with that, emphasizes its commitment to nurturing a more stable, safe, healthy, and harmonious society. Unsurprisingly, the Chinese leaders cherished the opportunity to portray the January 6, 2021, Capitol riots as revealing the ruinous state of democracy in the US, while providing an example of how uncensored speech online can destabilize societies. The Chinese state-controlled news outlet, *The Global Times*, reported on the Capitol riots, describing how the "bubbles of 'democracy and freedom' have burst" in the US.[213] The reporting focused on Chinese internet users' reactions to the incident, recounting how they saw the social media–fueled chaos in the US as "revenge" after the US had incited so much chaos around the world "under the pretext of 'freedom and democracy.' "[214]

China frequently accuses the US of hypocrisy in these areas, alleging that the US—often falsely—blames China for practices the US itself engages in. In one such instance in June 2022, China's Ministry of Foreign Affairs issued a "comprehensive, systematic, and elaborate response" to the US's China policy, rebutting "falsehoods" in the US perceptions of China, and dismissing the US's commitment to democracy and human rights as faulty, describing how "the human rights of the Chinese people are guaranteed like never before" while detailing rampant human rights violations in the US and by the US.[215]

According to the Chinese response, there are no human rights violations in Xinjiang. Allegations of a genocide in Xinjiang are a "lie of the century" and stem from disinformation transmitted by the US. The Chinese Ministry of Foreign Affairs also denied that the Chinese government spreads disinformation and accused the US instead of being the "biggest source of spreading disinformation."[216]

Similarly, China has defended its surveillance practices by stressing how the US government itself engages in similar activity.[217] It is well documented that the US National Security Agency (NSA) engages in extensive surveillance operations, often in collaboration with US tech companies.[218] Even if the NSA targets foreign individuals, including terrorists or others posing a threat to US national security, it also collects extensive incidental data on its own citizens in the process. In a 2019 article in *The Atlantic*, Derek Thomson tells "A Tale of Two Surveillance States," comparing surveillance practices in China and the US.[219] After discussing the brutality of the Chinese oppression of the Uyghurs in Xinjiang, including the mass surveillance program that sustains it, Thomson unambiguously writes that "nothing in the United States compares."[220] Yet he continues: "The use of novel surveillance tools to monitor, terrify, and even oppress minority citizens is not a foreign concept," revealing, for example, how minorities in low-income housing in the US are being surveilled by landlords in the name of providing a "safer environment for tenants."[221] While China is reported for having installed over 500 million surveillance cameras across the country by 2021, when adjusted to the population, the US has almost the same ratio of cameras to citizens installed. However, in China the cameras mainly monitor public spaces whereas in the US they are commonly deployed in private sector commercial spaces such as hotels, restaurants, and offices.[222]

Many Chinese companies producing surveillance technologies also seek to distance themselves from the ways their technologies are deployed in practice, denying that they should be held accountable for their complicit role in surveillance. For example, Huang Yongzhen, CEO of Watrix, recently defended his company's gait-recognition software, which uses AI to identify people from a distance based on the way they walk. This technology has already been deployed by security services given its ability to recognize people whose faces are not visible to the camera. Yet Yongzhen did not anguish about privacy concerns, noting how "from our perspective, we just provide the technology," even while he recognized that the technology may be used in ways that can make it a "double-edged sword."[223]

Even while the Chinese leadership refutes the external criticism of its control and surveillance efforts, the state-driven regulatory model contains

weaknesses and inconsistencies that may over time pose a challenge to
the Chinese government. Political goals underlying the country's internet
policy may ultimately compromise its economic goals, even if the Chinese
government may not presently acknowledge any such tensions. Several
commentators point out that innovation and economic growth require the
internet to be relatively free, while political control over online communications requires the curtailment of a free internet.[224] Chinese scientists have
expressed concern that blocking access to important sites such as Google
Scholar impedes their access to important research and hinders collaboration
with other researchers.[225] For China to meet its goal to become a dominant
cyberpower and a technological leader, it needs the free flow of information
both within China and with the outside world.

Foreign governments' discomfort with Chinese surveillance practices has
also led to an international pushback, including the imposition of sanctions
against Chinese firms. For example, the US recently imposed sanctions on
Chinese AI companies including Megvii that was involved in creating the
"Uyghur alarm" that was discussed earlier. The US government accused Megvii
and other Chinese AI companies of committing "human rights violations and
abuses in the implementation of China's campaign of repression, mass arbitrary detention, and high-tech surveillance" targeting Uyghurs and other
Muslim minorities.[226] Hangzhou-based surveillance company Hikvision has
also come under scrutiny in both the US and the EU due to its past claims that
its facial recognition technology could distinguish between the majority Han
Chinese and Uyghur ethnicities.[227] The US House of Representatives banned
Hikvision from government contracts in 2018, and the company was placed
on the Entity List in 2019,[228] which restricts American companies from doing
business with them without a government license.[229] Some European leaders
are now also cautioning against the use of the company's surveillance equipment in Europe after news surfaced that Hikvision landed a contract in July
2021 to supply several European airports with surveillance cameras, including
Madrid-Barajas and Barcelona's El Prat airports.[230]

Chinese censorship and surveillance practices are also complicating the
efforts of Chinese tech companies to expand abroad. In 2020, US President
Trump signed executive orders to ban WeChat and TikTok in the US within
forty-five days on the grounds that these companies' data collection allowed the
CCP to access Americans' personal information and to keep tabs on overseas
Chinese citizens.[231] These threats to ban Chinese tech companies, discussed
in more detail in Chapter 4, illustrate the concrete political risks and economic
costs these companies pay for the government's insistence on its authoritarian control over the digital economy. In the wake of these measures against

Chinese tech companies, some Chinese tech entrepreneurs have urged the government to ease internet controls in China.[232] Angela Zhang has further argued that the Chinese government ought to open its home market more to foreign companies in order to alleviate the problems that Chinese tech firms face abroad.[233] Tim Wu has argued, rather forcefully, for greater reciprocity in the treatment of tech companies: "If China refuses to follow the rules of the open internet, why continue to give it access to internet markets around the world?" According to Wu, the existing "unfair" asymmetry "ought no longer be tolerated."[234]

Huawei has been one of the main targets of US sanctions. For example, under their respective executive orders, both Presidents Trump and Biden have restricted US persons' investments in Chinese firms with ties to the Chinese military or firms that are producing surveillance technologies for the Chinese government.[235] Huawei is one of the companies subject to this restriction, among other reasons, due to its alleged role in facilitating the Chinese government's surveillance activities overseas.[236] The US government views Huawei as an extension of the CCP, thus posing a threat to America's cybersecurity and national security. Huawei is also accused of intellectual property theft[237] and was investigated for a possible violation of US trade sanctions, including selling technology to Iran and North Korea.[238] The US has also cajoled many of its allies to restrict Huawei's operations on their market, as discussed in Chapter 5, further restricting the commercial opportunities available to the company and adding to the costs of Chinese digital authoritarianism that the Chinese tech companies have to bear. Huawei is certainly feeling the adverse impact of sanctions, having lost access to critical components and experiencing the "biggest-ever decline" in revenues after the US sanctions took effect.[239] However, while some economic opportunities are closing for the Chinese tech companies caught in the middle of the US–China tech war, other opportunities are opening up. Several foreign governments readily welcome Chinese surveillance technologies, eager to replicate the Chinese government's success in silencing its opposition and bolstering their own law enforcement capabilities, as discussed in Chapter 8. The growing global turn toward authoritarianism is likely to accelerate this trend, mitigating the costs that Chinese tech companies need to bear as a result of US-led sanctions.

While the Chinese state-driven regulatory model is often criticized in the West, its influence as a counterpoint to the American market-driven regulatory model is hard to deny. In many ways, China's example has proven false many of the assumptions that underlie the US model. First, it has proven wrong the assumption that freedom is somehow inherent in the character of the internet. Instead, internet freedoms are subject to political choice by governments who are vested with the power to suppress those freedoms. Second, China has shown how restrictive policies can coexist with a culture of dynamic innovation. Contrary to a common view in democracies, a state-driven, authoritarian regulatory model can demonstrably sustain a dynamic culture of private entrepreneurship that is capable of fueling technological progress and economic growth. It is these apparent features that make it difficult for the West to counter the growing appeal of the Chinese regulatory model around the world, as will be discussed in Chapter 8.

3

The European Rights-Driven Regulatory Model

WITHIN MOMENTS AFTER completing his purchase of Twitter on October 27, 2022, Elon Musk tweeted "the bird is free,"[1] in an apparent reference to closing the contested deal and thereby gaining the authority to reinstate his favored techno-libertarian free speech norms on the platform. The European Union did not hesitate to respond. Within hours, the European Commissioner Thierry Breton retorted to Musk on Twitter: "In Europe, the bird will fly by our rules."[2] This exchange between an American tech entrepreneur and a European regulator captures the core sentiment underlying the European regulatory model: tech companies need rules and those rules are established by governments. Furthermore, in the EU, those rules are drafted to specifically reflect European values that call for, for example, restricting online content on platforms such as Twitter, if such restrictions are needed to protect human dignity, data privacy, democratic discourse, or other core rights of European digital citizens.

Unlike the United States, whose market-driven regulatory model leaves tech companies in charge, or China, whose state-driven model is aimed at regulating its tech industry to preserve the political power of the state, the EU has pursued a third path by adopting its own human-centric and rights-driven approach to digital regulation. This approach focuses on enhancing the individual and collective rights of European citizens in a digital society and demonstrates the EU's unwillingness to align itself with either the US or China. This distinctly European way of regulating the digital economy views governments as having a central role in both steering the digital economy and in using regulatory intervention to uphold the fundamental rights of individuals, preserve the democratic structures of society, and ensure a fair distribution of benefits in the digital economy.[3]

The EU has promulgated these values in various high-level political statements and declarations that further illustrate the core principles underlying the European regulatory model. The European Declaration on Digital Rights and Principles for the Digital Decade,[4] jointly adopted by the European Parliament, Council, and Commission in December 2022, proclaims that "people [are] at the centre of the digital transformation," and emphasizes the importance of "democratic functioning of the digital society and economy." It also asserts how the digital transformation should "benefi[t] everyone and improv[e] the lives of all people living in the EU." Technological solutions, according to the Declaration, should also "respect people's rights, enable their exercise and promote solidarity and inclusion." This political statement identifies democracy, fairness, and fundamental rights as key values guiding EU policymaking. These values, while not unique to the EU, are directly engrained in the EU's regulatory instruments with the goal of ushering in a human-centric, democracy-enhancing, rights-preserving, and redistributive digital economy where technology is harnessed for human empowerment.

The European rights-driven model has important similarities and differences with both the American market-driven model and the Chinese state-driven model. For example, the US model is also motivated by safeguarding fundamental rights and democracy. However, in the US, the rights discourse more commonly centers on protecting free speech as *the* fundamental right implicated by the digital transformation whereas the EU is looking to balance the right to free speech with a host of other fundamental rights, including human dignity, nondiscrimination, and the right to data privacy. The US and the EU also differ in how they seek to advance democracy through digital regulation. To protect the democratic foundations of the internet, the US government is less prepared to intervene in platform autonomy for fear of curtailing free speech. American regulators, who often evince techno-libertarian instincts, fear overdoing the content moderation rather than underdoing it. Thus, while the EU at times restricts online speech in the name of democratic discourse, the US frequently invokes this very same principle to allow such speech to remain online. European regulators' concern over fairness and redistribution is also in line with the EU's commitment to the social market economy and the pursuit of more equal wealth distribution in general. Conversely, the US has traditionally been more comfortable with income inequality, seeking to preserve equality of opportunities as opposed to equality of outcomes.

The EU's pro-regulation stance is not limited to the technology sector but reflects a broader view of how markets operate and what the optimal role of government is. Compared to the US, the state enjoys greater public trust in the EU and can therefore assume a more prominent role in regulating markets.[5] In contrast, Americans tend to embrace a pro-business, free market–oriented version of capitalism. Under this view, government intervention should be limited to avoid curtailing the innovative zeal of tech companies. In terms of the influential literature on "varieties of capitalism," most European countries exhibit features of a "coordinated market economy" as opposed to a "liberal market economy," meaning they reserve a greater role for government regulation and nonmarket institutions.[6]

By insisting that its vision for the digital economy must be engrained in laws—which are written and enforced by democratic institutions—the EU rejects the techno-libertarian idea of a "lawless" internet, advancing instead a view that the digital transformation needs to be firmly anchored in the rule of law.[7] This interventionist regulatory approach reflects the European view that governments play a key role in safeguarding competition in the digital marketplace. Whereas the American market-driven model frequently emphasizes how the government does not understand technology and should hence refrain from regulating it, the European rights-driven model is more concerned that technology companies do not understand how technology implicates constitutional democracy and fundamental rights, which their products and services are frequently undermining.[8]

The EU's rights-driven regulatory agenda has strong backing from the European citizenry, and several large public opinion surveys have shown important support for more extensive digital regulation.[9] This public support lends both political momentum and democratic legitimacy to the EU's regulatory agenda. The political environment in the EU has similarly been conducive to extensive rule-making. European political elites are ideologically less divided than their US counterparts and are consequently more responsive to public demand for more stringent regulations. Parties across the ideological spectrum in Europe may differ in the extent of their support for regulation, but they share a fundamental commitment to a regulated market economy.[10] The EU's Digital Markets Act (DMA) illustrates this political consensus particularly well. The DMA is a major piece of digital regulation, which aims to enhance market competition by restricting certain business practices by "digital gatekeepers" that are deemed anticompetitive.[11] The law was adopted in the European Parliament in 2022 with 588 votes in favor, 11 against, and 31 abstentions, with parties across the political spectrum lending resounding support.[12] This degree of consensus stands in stark contrast to the highly partisan US Congress that remains deadlocked on most important policy issues, including digital regulation.

The European rights-driven regulatory model also has some similarities with the Chinese state-driven regulatory model. For example, both models acknowledge the central role of government as a steward of the digital economy. Yet the European model clearly departs from the Chinese model in its key objective: in the EU, the goal is to strengthen digital citizens' rights vis-à-vis not only technology companies, but also the state.[13] While the Chinese state-driven model views government intervention as necessary to preserve social harmony and entrench government control, the European rights-driven model justifies government intervention in the name of safeguarding individual rights and the political autonomy of its citizens. Of course, the Chinese government can also argue that it acts in its citizens' best interests by, for instance, protecting them from harmful online content through a tight censorship regime. However, the European model is distinctly different in that it involves citizens and their elected representatives engaging in a democratic debate, which determines what citizens' "best interests" are and what form the regulatory intervention should take.

In addition to notable differences in the objectives of digital regulation, there are significant differences in the actual size of the tech industries in the three jurisdictions. Unlike in China and the US, for example, large tech companies have not emerged out of Europe. Compared to the US tech behemoths—including Amazon, Apple, Google, Meta, and Microsoft— or the Chinese tech giants—including Alibaba, Baidu, Huawei, JD.com, Tencent, and Xiaomi—the EU has nurtured few leading tech companies. In 2021, Germany's SAP, a leading enterprise software vendor, was the largest European tech company and the only European Fortune 500 tech company.[14] With the exception of perhaps Spotify, few European companies are embraced (or even known) by global internet users, which raises questions of why the EU has not been able to replicate the US's and China's success on this front.

This dearth of European tech companies has at times been attributed to extensive digital regulation across the continent. Critics of the rights-driven regulatory model often assume that stringent regulation hinders innovation and therefore explains why the EU has fallen behind the US and China in nurturing a thriving tech industry.[15] Whether extensive regulation has, indeed, dampened tech innovation in Europe can be debated, but the fact that the EU has engaged in wide-ranging regulatory activity in this domain is not in question. These digital regulations have had a significant impact on the daily operation of tech companies, including constraining the way they collect, process, or share data, design their products, or interact with internet users or other businesses in the marketplace. What these diverse regulations have in common is their focus on enhancing rights—be it the fundamental rights of internet users, the democratic rights of digital citizens, the social rights of platform workers, or various economic rights of smaller market actors. These regulations also reflect a deep-seated belief that markets will not, left to their own devices, yield optimal outcomes and that government intervention is needed to preserve and strengthen these rights.

The EU's affinity with regulation is well known, in particular among the tech companies that are frequent targets of EU regulations. Yet many people do not have a strong understanding of what exactly is driving European digital regulation. One narrative, often invoked by US tech companies and US policymakers alike, is that of European regulatory protectionism. These critical voices portray EU tech regulation as specifically targeting US companies, motivated by envy-driven protectionist zeal designed to give European tech companies a helping hand so that they can better compete against their more successful US rivals.[16] The US's dominance of the tech sector has been described as a "source of resentment in Europe,"[17] and the EU has been viewed as responding to such resentment by targeting US tech companies with the only tool the EU has at its disposal: regulation.

This argument focusing on digital protectionism, which will be addressed in detail in Chapter 6, is plausible yet overly simplistic. It is true that it is politically less costly for the EU to leverage regulation against leading tech companies when those companies are, in large part, foreign rather than European. It is also true that the EU has not been spared from a recent nativist shift in trade and technology policy around the world. Like the US and China, the EU has become more conscious of its need to build its technological capabilities and to reduce its dependencies in a more contested geopolitical environment. Such policy goals often veer governments toward greater techno-nationalism. But singling out protectionism as the key driver of the EU's digital regulation either mischaracterizes the EU's regulatory impulses or, at the very least, provides a highly incomplete account of the EU's motivations. There are a host of other values beyond digital protectionism that are genuine drivers of European digital regulation, and consistent with the ethos of the broader European economic and political project. As this chapter explains, the EU's digital agenda reflects its deep commitment to fundamental rights, democracy, fairness, and redistribution, as well as its respect for the rule of law.

Bringing into view how the European regulatory model has taken shape around this rights-driven agenda, this chapter outlines how the EU has ingrained these core values in its ambitious regulatory instruments. The focus is on EU-level regulation, even though there have also been significant legislative developments on the individual EU member state level, which have shaped the broader European approach toward the digital economy. The EU's commitment to fundamental rights manifests, in particular, in its regulatory approach to data protection, artificial intelligence, and online content regulation—all policy areas that have become central pillars of the European regulatory model. The EU has also developed regulatory instruments to preserve and strengthen democracy in the digital age, including by curtailing online disinformation and promoting a free and pluralistic media. The EU has further woven a commitment to fairness and redistribution into its regulatory model, as exemplified by its regulation of market competition, digital taxation, and social protections extended to platform workers. This chapter also explains how the European rights-driven model relies on regulation as a tool to advance European market integration. This chapter ends with a critical examination of the European rights-driven regulatory model. It asks whether extensive regulation impedes technological progress, possibly explaining the EU's struggles to keep up with American and Chinese technological leadership. Another concern is that while the EU has been successful in articulating its rights-driven vision of the digital economy and entrenching that vision in a number of regulations, it has been less successful in ushering in a digital economy that is, in practice, rights-preserving, democratic, and fair. In addition to these enforcement challenges, internal disagreements within the EU may be viewed as weakening the coherence, effectiveness, and legitimacy of the European rights-driven regulatory model.

Using Digital Regulation to Safeguard Fundamental Rights

Fundamental rights are deeply entrenched in the ethos of the EU, forming a value-based constitutional foundation for European integration and guiding the EU's legislative activity as well as its engagement with the world in all policy areas. This political ethos also provides the basis of the European rights-driven regulatory model. According to Article 2 of the Treaty of the European Union: "The Union is founded on the values of respect for human dignity, freedom, democracy, equality, the rule of law and respect for human rights, including the rights of persons belonging to minorities."[18] The 2000 Charter of Fundamental Rights of the European Union (the EU Charter), which gained legally binding force in 2009, further enshrines fundamental rights embedded in the Treaties. This European "Bill of Rights"[19] protects key rights implicated by the recent digital transformation of economies and societies, including the protection of privacy and personal data, the freedom of expression, and nondiscrimination principles.[20]

European political leaders frequently embrace fundamental rights as the cornerstone of the EU's digital policy in their public statements. The Commission's Executive Vice President, Margrethe Vestager, and the EU's High Representative, Josep Borrell, recently wrote how "the 1948 Universal Declaration of Human Rights established the dignity of the individual, the right to privacy and to nondiscrimination, and the freedoms of speech and belief. It is our common duty to make sure that the digital revolution lives up to that promise."[21] This sentiment has been echoed by the President of the European Court of Justice (CJEU), Koen Lenaerts, who has described the EU Charter as having enabled the EU legal order to evolve into "a globally-renowned beacon of fundamental rights protection."[22] In discussing the CJEU's decision to annul the EU's Safe Harbor data transfer agreement with the US based on fundamental rights concerns, President Lenaerts noted how "the rule of law is not up for sale. It is a matter of upholding the requirements in the European Union, of the rule of law, of fundamental rights. If this is also affecting some dealings internationally, why would Europe not be proud to contribute its requiring standards of respect of fundamental rights to the world in general?"[23]

Digital transformation has altered the ways in which businesses operate and societies function, implicating a number of fundamental rights in the process. As the demand for data multiplies, so does the potential for its misuse—by public and private actors alike. As a result, the EU is seeking to limit both government surveillance and the exploitation of internet users' personal data by technology companies. The EU is also looking to protect internet users from nondiscrimination, for instance by regulating the ways algorithms operate and AI systems are developed and deployed. EU regulators are further committed to safeguarding freedom of expression, which they see as under threat when internet platforms moderate content online, but at the same time recognize the need to balance that freedom against other fundamental rights such as human dignity, which can be undermined by illegal and harmful content online. Together, these specific issues—outlined below—drive the EU's digital agenda today, placing the protection of fundamental rights at the center of the European regulatory model.

The Right to Privacy and Protection of Personal Data

The right to privacy, and the related right to the protection of personal data, are at the heart of the EU's rights-based approach to digital regulation. Championing these rights as "fundamental" distinguishes the European regulatory model from the American market-driven and the Chinese state-driven regulatory models. The philosophy behind the EU's fundamental rights approach to data privacy is to foster self-determination of individuals by granting them enhanced control over their personal data.[24] In European rights discourse, the right to data privacy is also closely related to human dignity, which the EU Charter considers inviolable.[25] Europeans' concern about data privacy can be traced back to World War II and the atrocities committed by the Nazis, who systematically abused personal data to identify Jews and other minority groups the Nazi regime oppressed.[26] The infringement of privacy rights continued under the postwar socialist dictatorship in East Germany, where the Ministry for State Security, known as Stasi, continued the surveillance of its citizens.[27] These experiences have left Europeans suspicious of government data collection practices. These suspicions, combined with a mistrust that corporations would act in the public interest when handling user data, paved the way for a robust privacy rights regime in Germany, and later across Europe.

The rights to privacy and data protection have since been codified into European legal instruments, anchoring the EU's regulatory model even more firmly into those fundamental rights. The 1950 European Convention of Human Rights—to which all EU member states are party—recognizes the right to privacy as a fundamental right.[28] The EU Charter further guarantees individuals the right to privacy, including the right to the protection of their personal data.[29] In addition to these constitutional protections, the EU sets out detailed privacy protections in the General Data Protection Regulation (GDPR) that entered into force in 2018.[30] The GDPR is the EU's ambitious data protection law that has become a global "gold standard" on how to protect individuals' personal data from exploitation by governments or private companies alike. The GDPR calls for lawfulness, fairness, and transparency in processing personal data,[31] in addition to limiting the quantity and purpose for which data can be collected.[32] The Regulation also adds new obligations, such as the "right to be forgotten," that gives the data subject the right to ask for erasure of certain data,[33] and "privacy by design," which requires manufacturers to design their products and services with GDPR obligations in mind.[34] It mandates member states to establish independent data protection authorities that guarantee the enforcement of GDPR protections, in addition to establishing a European Data Protection Board.[35] The GDPR also provides for heavy sanctions: noncompliance may result in fines of up to €20 million or up to 4 percent of a company's total worldwide annual turnover of the preceding financial year, whichever is higher.[36]

The EU's judiciary has played a key role in shaping the European rights-driven model, expanding the scope of European citizens' data privacy rights in multiple landmark pro-privacy rulings, including in *Google Spain*—better known as the "right to be forgotten" case.[37] The "right to be forgotten" refers to the internet users' right to demand data on them to be permanently deleted. In this case, Mario Costeja González, a Spanish citizen, requested Google to remove from its search engine results that linked him to old newspaper articles detailing his financial troubles. According to Mr. González, the information, while accurate, was no longer relevant since all his debts were resolved. Google initially refused to delink the information. However, the CJEU ruled that Google was obliged to honor requests to make certain content, which is not adequate, relevant, or current, no longer searchable. The ruling has led to significant delisting of content, in part because of the asymmetrical incentives it imposes on search engines. While these companies retain the authority to decide whether to erase the requested information, any borderline case is likely to result in removal because a failure to do so can lead to heavy fines, whereas excessive delinking carries no penalty, incentivizing erasure.[38] As evidence of its responsiveness to delinking requests, by August 2022, Google had removed about 49 percent of the 5.1 million URLs that it had been asked to delist since the May 2014 ruling, according to the company's transparency report.[39]

While offering steadfast privacy protections, the GDPR acknowledges that "the right to the protection of personal data is not an absolute right; it must be considered in relation to its function in society and be balanced against other fundamental rights, in accordance with the principle of proportionality."[40] The CJEU has frequently been called on to weigh the right to data privacy against other pressing societal imperatives, such as national security and law enforcement, as discussed in more detail in Chapter 6 in the context of US–EU regulatory battles. Nevertheless, in carrying out its proportionality analysis, the CJEU has shown itself to be a staunch defender of data protection, actively shaping the EU's digital governance in ways that elevate the right to data privacy even when that right conflicts with these other important societal imperatives.[41] The court's expansive approach to data protection rights leaves no doubt that data privacy is a pivotal right that goes to the heart of the European rights-driven regulatory model.

Protections Against Harmful Applications of Artificial Intelligence

A second area where fundamental rights concerns have shaped the EU's regulatory model, and made it distinct from both the US and Chinese models, is artificial intelligence. AI is an area of the digital economy with significant implications for fundamental rights, prompting the EU to develop new regulatory instruments to ensure that those rights are protected. Increasingly, AI-driven algorithms are utilized in critical decisions across multiple sectors of society, including in screening candidates for education or employment, or in determining individuals' eligibility for credit or public benefits. Despite its growing prevalence and touted promise as a tool for better decision-making, companies' use of AI has frequently been controversial. For example, Amazon abandoned its AI-based recruiting tool after it was shown to discriminate against women. The reason for the gender bias was simple: the algorithm used in vetting job candidates was trained with the existing resumes submitted to the company over a ten-year period, most of which came from men.[42] These built-in biases can have life-altering consequences. In one case involving the Netherlands, it was discovered in 2019 that the Dutch tax authorities had used a biased algorithm to help identify individuals who are likely to engage in childcare benefits fraud.[43] The system relied on risk indicators that often singled out low-income families or families belonging to ethnic minorities as potential fraudsters. The reliance on algorithms in this case led to dire consequences, pushing families into poverty while sending thousands of children to foster care. The Dutch data protection agency fined the tax authorities, citing the violation of an affected individual's data privacy.[44] This and other similar scandals serve as a vivid reminder of the risks associated with relying on AI in governing societies.

Conscious of both the opportunities and risks that AI entails, the EU has moved to regulate this space by promoting the development and deployment of AI while seeking to mitigate the risks associated with it, including those implicating fundamental rights. In April 2021, the Commission unveiled a new proposal for a regulation laying down harmonized rules on AI.[45] The AI Act seeks to promote ethical, trustworthy, and human-centric AI development, ensuring a high level of protection of fundamental rights. For example, it acknowledges that algorithmic decision-making may reproduce existing biases, which can lead to large-scale discrimination. Moreover, the requisite collection of personal data for training AI threatens citizens' fundamental right to data privacy—a concern that is magnified when AI technologies, such as facial recognition, are deployed for mass surveillance of citizens. Thus, according to the proposed regulation, any AI must be free of harmful bias, respectful of citizens' right to privacy, and otherwise consistent with fundamental rights embedded in the EU Charter and Treaties.

To ensure that its regulatory model will not hinder the development of new AI systems while protecting the fundamental rights implicated in using AI, the proposed AI Act takes a risk-based approach to regulation. It divides

AI applications into four categories depending on the level of risk they pose—unacceptable risk, high risk, limited risk, and minimal risk—and adjusts the regulatory obligations accordingly. The category of "unacceptable risk" includes AI systems that manipulate human behavior and undermine their free will by using subliminal techniques. AI systems that deploy social scoring by governments—akin to China's "social credit system" discussed in Chapter 2—are also prohibited, as is the government's deployment of real-time facial recognition for law enforcement purposes. In these settings, AI is used for "manipulative, exploitative and social control practices," contradicting the EU's commitment to fundamental rights, including the right to nondiscrimination and data privacy.[46] A real-time remote biometric identification of individuals for law enforcement purposes is considered particularly invasive of fundamental rights and freedoms, as it places large parts of the population under constant surveillance.[47] AI involving "high-risk" applications is not prohibited but tightly regulated, with a set of risk managements obligations applying to developers, providers, users, distributors, and importers of AI systems.

The EU also maintains that AI technologies exist for the benefit of humans and must also be overseen by humans. The EU's 2019 "The Ethics Guidelines for Trustworthy AI,"[48] which paved the way for the proposed AI Act, emphasize the human-centric approach to AI, noting how "AI systems should not unjustifiably subordinate, coerce, deceive, manipulate, condition or herd humans." The Commission's 2020 White Paper similarly stresses the importance of a human-centric AI that improves the lives of individuals while respecting their rights and preserving their human dignity.[49] This policy imperative, according to the EU, also necessitates that AI is overseen by natural persons who can override algorithms, when needed, and help ensure that risks to fundamental rights are mitigated.[50]

The EU's proposed AI regulation is the first of its kind globally. It reflects the EU's commitment to ethics, trust, fundamental rights, and dignity as key principles guiding AI development. While many tech companies have adopted various ethics codes to mitigate risks associated with AI,[51] the European regulatory approach views these market-driven tools of self-regulation as ultimately insufficient. While such ethics codes can lead to better corporate practices, they cannot substitute or delay legally binding obligations that are generated through a democratic process to ensure that those obligations reflect the public interest more broadly.[52] Thus, by pursuing binding rules on AI, the EU affirms the primacy of the rule of law and democracy as the foundation of its regulatory model, while empowering EU citizens to exercise a countervailing power to tech companies and their AI-powered business models.[53]

Moderating Online Content While Preserving Freedom of Expression

Another key area of focus within the EU's effort to protect fundamental rights online relates to content moderation. Digital technologies have revolutionized the opportunities for communication, expanding individuals' freedom of expression. However, this vast opportunity for online engagement has also increased the dissemination of harmful content online. The tools that democratic governments and digital platforms have for addressing this complex issue are imperfect. Both the governments and the platforms know that freedom of expression is under threat when the platforms are permitted to moderate content. Yet the absence of such moderation practices would allow hate speech, disinformation, terrorist propaganda, and other harmful content to run rampant online. The line-drawing between permissible and impermissible speech is therefore complicated, and the key question thus becomes who gets to draw that line.

Fundamental rights, including the freedom of expression and the protection of human dignity, are central to the EU's efforts to regulate online speech. According to Article 11 of the EU Charter, "Everyone has the right to freedom of expression." Notwithstanding its staunch commitment to free speech, the EU is prepared to curtail free speech in instances of harmful speech, including hate speech. Compared to the US, the EU takes a harder line on hate speech, which is not considered a valuable part of public discourse and hence worthy of protection in Europe—whether such speech takes place online or offline.[54] Like its approach to data privacy, the EU's firm stand against hate speech is best understood in light of Europe's history of racist and xenophobic violence, including most prominently the incitement of hatred by the Nazis against the Jews. The burden of this history continues to define the European regulatory approach today, heightening its sense of a "duty of remembrance, vigilance and combat" against racist and xenophobic speech.[55] Today, the rise of populist parties with anti-migrant views is contributing to an increase of incidents of hate speech within the EU, particularly on social media, strengthening the EU's resolve to tackle this challenge with regulation.[56]

Until recently, the EU has relied on voluntary regulation of online hate speech. In 2016, the European Commission signed a nonbinding Code of Conduct on Countering Illegal Hate Speech Online (Hate Speech Code) with four US technology companies: Facebook, Twitter, YouTube, and Microsoft.[57] Additional companies have joined since, including Instagram and Snapchat in 2018 and TikTok in 2020.[58] These signatories agree to "prohibit the promotion of incitement to violence and hateful conduct on their platforms," and commit to reviewing any request to remove such content from their platform within 24 hours. Despite its voluntary nature, the Hate Speech Code has had a notable impact. Data from 2021 show that the signatories now remove, on average, 63 percent of all illegal hate speech that is notified to them.[59]

Another category of problematic content available online is terrorist propaganda. Such content presents a direct security challenge to the EU—a concern that has been magnified through recent terrorist attacks on European soil. The EU acknowledges that acts of terrorism amount to some of the most serious violations of individuals' right to life, liberty, and security.[60] However, efforts to combat the dissemination of terrorist content online touches many other fundamental rights as well, including the freedom of expression or nondiscrimination.[61] Consequently, there is a fear that platforms may deploy discriminatory proxies to screen terrorist content without respecting the individual rights of internet users. In 2021, the EU adopted a binding Regulation on Preventing the Dissemination of Terrorist Content Online, which seeks to strike a balance between the fundamental rights of all affected parties.[62] The Regulation mandates platforms to remove terrorist content within one hour following a removal order issued by an EU member state authority.[63] To safeguard due process and alleviate concerns of restricting free speech, platforms and content providers retain the right to challenge any removal order.[64]

To complement these existing codes and regulations, the EU adopted the Digital Services Act (DSA) in 2022.[65] The DSA adds legal force and considerable political momentum to the EU's rights-driven regulatory agenda by establishing a comprehensive and legally binding transparency and accountability regime for online platforms regarding the content they host. The DSA lays out various due diligence obligations as well as procedural safeguards that platforms must abide by when moderating online content. Very large platforms, including US tech giants that have a disproportionate impact on internet users in the EU, face additional obligations under the DSA.[66] For example, the DSA mandates them to carry out annual assessments identifying and mitigating systemic risks, and subjects them to an independent auditing regime. To promote algorithmic transparency, these large platforms must also share data with researchers and authorities on their content moderation decisions.

The DSA reflects the EU's commitment to the freedom of expression. It refrains from introducing a general monitoring obligation on platforms, preserving their immunity as currently provided under the 2000 e-commerce Directive. Fundamental rights considerations explain the DSA's regulatory restraint across a number of provisions. For example, in discussing the objectives of the DSA, the Commission refers to the liability shield as being "instrumental to the protection of fundamental rights online."[67] The DSA also underscores the importance of nondiscrimination as a core fundamental right affected online. In particular, the DSA acknowledges how user notices or content removal algorithms may reflect unconscious or conscious biases that disproportionally affect certain user groups, and prohibits such discriminatory practices.[68] Very large platforms must additionally evaluate and report on systemic risks that may compromise fundamental rights.[69] These provisions illustrate how the DSA, while seen as imposing considerable regulatory burdens on online platforms, is concerned with establishing a strong rights foundation for those content moderation decisions and processes at the same time.

Using Digital Regulation to Preserve and Strengthen Democracy

The Treaty of the European Union emphasizes "freedom" and "democracy" as the EU's founding principles.[70] Democracy is also a precondition for EU membership.[71] However, in recent years, democracy has come under threat, in Europe and elsewhere. Freedom House, an American NGO that conducts research and advocacy on democracy and political freedom, documented a fifteenth consecutive year of decline in global freedom in 2021. According to its "Freedom in the World 2021" report, less than 20 percent of the world's population now lives in what is categorized to be a "free" country.[72] Such democratic decay has not spared Europe. While in the 1990s, two-thirds of European citizens were satisfied with the functioning of their countries' democratic systems, today a majority feels dissatisfied.[73] Voter turnout in many European countries has also declined, as has membership in political parties.[74] At the same time, populist parties have gained ground, ascending into power in several EU member states. EU countries, such as Poland and Hungary, have experienced severe democratic backsliding as a result of these power shifts from the ideological center toward more authoritarian leaders, shaking faith in democracy as an inalienable foundation of the EU.

Against these broader economic, cultural, and political trends, there is a growing concern that technology may adversely affect democracy. For techno-optimists, technology can amplify individual freedoms and revitalize democracies.[75] At its best, the internet can preserve and strengthen democracy by providing an inclusive platform for diverse voices to participate in society. Yet critical voices point to a myriad of ways for technology to undermine democracy. Online communication channels have not only cultivated civic engagement; they have also facilitated the spread of disinformation, undermining public debate and the legitimacy of democratic elections.[76] Apart from producing freedom and enhancing democracy, online platforms have also sowed discord and deepened societal divisions.[77] In light of this, the internet's potential to amplify freedom and usher in a revitalized democracy has been, at best, only partially realized, and, at worst, proven to be a false promise.

Aware of these dangers, the EU has sought to harness the democracy-enhancing potential of technology while guarding itself against the dangers that digital technologies present. Reflecting its belief in the role of regulation to preserve democratic processes, the EU has adopted a number of regulatory instruments, including measures aimed at countering disinformation and strengthening free and pluralistic media, both of which the EU sees as crucial for sustaining democratic discourse. Through these efforts, the EU is elevating the preservation and strengthening of democracy as a central tenet of its rights-driven regulatory model.

Fighting Disinformation and Other Harmful Content Online

The European rights-driven regulatory agenda is anchored in the conviction that protecting citizens' ability to express themselves freely online is essential for a democratic society. In the 2018 European Democracy Action Plan, the Commission emphasizes how democracy cannot thrive without "engaged, informed, and empowered citizens."[78] To meaningfully participate in democratic processes, citizens must be able to form their own opinions, including to make electoral choices in a public space that exposes them to a plurality of viewpoints that are expressed freely.[79] According to the Commission, this requires both protecting the freedom of speech online and eliminating online disinformation that can undermine political processes.[80] Without the freedom of expression, individuals' political rights are compromised. At the same time, disinformation polarizes the public discourse and undermines citizens' trust in democracy.[81]

Given the prevalence and severity of disinformation, as well as its manifested adverse effect on democracy, the EU is steadfast in its commitment to limit the dissemination of such information online. However, crafting a rights-preserving regulatory approach toward the removal of disinformation is complicated given the EU's equally steadfast commitment to the freedom of expression online. The EU recognizes that freedom of expression is a fundamental right on which a democratic society is built. The European regulatory model thus reflects the belief that excessive content removal can lead to harmful censorship that is inconsistent with the EU's commitment to democracy and individual freedom.[82] Unlike hate speech or terrorist content, disinformation is not illegal, which makes it even harder to target through regulation. The EU regulation is therefore not mandating the removal of disinformation, but predominantly geared at alerting internet users of alternative information sources and educating them to more critically evaluate the information they encounter online.

As part of its regulatory efforts, the Commission developed a nonbinding Disinformation Code, which, in its updated 2022 version, has been signed by leading platforms including Google, Meta, Microsoft, TikTok, and Twitter.[83] These companies voluntarily commit to measures, including increasing transparency in political advertising, closing fake accounts, facilitating fact-checking, demonetizing the dissemination of disinformation, and granting researchers access to the data to facilitate research on disinformation.[84] While the voluntary Code has led to progress, disinformation remains prevalent online.[85] Acknowledging this, the Commission announced in 2020 that it was time to move from self-regulation to binding regulation.[86] This paved the way for the adoption of the DSA, which regulates illegal content such as hate speech, as discussed earlier, but also acknowledges how online disinformation can pose "systemic risks on society and democracy."[87]

Under the DSA, platforms identified as "very large online platforms," such as Google and Meta, are obliged to assess such systemic risks, and adopt "reasonable, proportionate and effective" measures to mitigate them.[88] These platforms must also subject themselves to an independent auditing regime.[89] To promote algorithmic transparency, they must further share data with researchers and authorities on their content moderation decisions.[90] The DSA is backed by notable sanctions. Very large platforms infringing the DSA can be fined up to 6 percent of their global turnover.[91] For example, if Meta were to be fined the maximum 6 percent under the DSA, it could cost the social network $7.1 billion, based on its 2021 revenue.[92] By resorting to binding rules and heavy fines, the DSA underscores the EU's view that government intervention is needed for preserving democracy in a digital society—an approach that stands in stark contrast to the US government, which has been reluctant to intervene for the fear that any such limits on free speech present ultimately an even greater threat for democracy.

The EU's efforts to fight online disinformation through digital regulation are particularly relevant in its quest to protect the integrity of political elections. Politically motivated disinformation campaigns, including interference by foreign governments, present a serious threat to democracy.[93] One particularly disturbing example of such election meddling is Russia's disinformation campaign orchestrated to influence the outcome of the 2016 Brexit referendum,[94] which further contributed to the EU's resolve to address the problem with more robust regulation. A related concern for the EU is the manipulation of voter behavior, which can compromise citizens' privacy, personal autonomy, and freedom to exercise free will in a political process.[95] The infamous Cambridge Analytica scandal revealed how various actors can deploy psychometrics—often obtained without the target's consent and hence infringing personal privacy—to engage in intricate micro-targeting of individuals aimed at influencing their electoral choices.[96] As a result, citizens' ability to partake in free and fair elections by exercising their full and autonomous political choice has become a central concern for the EU's regulatory model.

In an attempt to curtail malicious actors' ability to manipulate the electorate and undermine their political freedom, the Commission proposed a new regulation geared at enhancing transparency in political advertising and communication in 2021.[97] The proposed rules mandate labeling of political advertisements, which reveal the identities of individuals or entities paying for various ads. The proposed regulation also restricts various targeting and amplification techniques in the context of political advertising. These measures illustrate the common belief among EU leaders—supported by the European public at large—that democracy cannot be sustained by relying on free speech and platforms' self-regulation alone. Instead, the government must step in and help uphold citizens' political rights in a democratic society.

Strengthening Free and Pluralistic Media

The EU has been particularly active in using digital regulation to protect the news media, a regulatory effort that the EU sees as necessary for defending democracy and, more broadly, advancing its rights-driven regulatory agenda. Large online platforms increasingly threaten the viability of traditional media, which plays an essential role in democracy. In its 2020 European Democracy Action Plan, the Commission describes a free and pluralistic media as "key to hold[ing] power to account and to help[ing] citizens make informed decisions."[98] The plan also holds that "by providing the public with reliable information, independent media play an important role in the fight against disinformation and the manipulation of democratic debate."[99] This view provides a policy rationale for the EU to leverage regulation with the goal of enhancing the role of traditional media companies, including their ability to compete with large digital platforms, in the new digital landscape.

A techno-optimist approach to digital regulation emphasizes how online platforms have democratized the production of news by enabling new voices to emerge in public debates. Individuals can now more easily disseminate information to mass audiences and hence directly contribute to the public debate.[100] Under this approach, there is no need for a regulatory intervention as platforms, left to their own devices, act as information intermediaries capable of fostering media pluralism and public debate. However, it is not clear that the digital revolution has, in practice, contributed to media pluralism, given the extensive power a few large online platforms hold over the media industry. The EU has assumed a more skeptical view and stepped in with regulation to bolster traditional media in order to foster more informed public debate in a democratic society.

As part of its effort to promote a free and pluralistic media, the EU adopted a landmark Copyright Directive in 2019.[101] This Directive seeks to rebalance the relationship between online platforms (that display news content) and the news industry (that generates news content). This rebalancing advances ideas of fairness and redistribution that are central tenets of the European rights-driven regulatory model and that are discussed later in this chapter.[102] In addition to advancing this notion of fairness, the Directive highlights the relationship between a free and pluralist media and the state of democracy, noting how "a free and pluralist press is essential to ensur[ing] quality journalism and citizens' access to information. It provides a fundamental contribution to public debate and the proper functioning of a democratic society."[103] In supporting journalists and press publications, the EU seeks to ensure its citizens will have access to reliable news and other journalistic content, which enhances public debate and, with that, strengthens democracy. By adopting the Directive, the EU also revealed its belief that the best route to ensure such access to news content is through government action, rather than through reliance on the markets and tech companies' self-regulation.

The Copyright Directive takes direct aim at the sustainability of the press sector by seeking to ensure that journalists receive a fair share of the revenue generated by viewers accessing their news stories through online intermediaries.[104] Under the Directive, search engines, social networks, and news aggregators are required to obtain a license from publishers before displaying content these publishers create. This bargaining process is expected to lead to revenue sharing between the platforms and the publishers.

However, it is unclear whether the Copyright Directive will, in practice, support the news industry that remains dependent on traffic that these platforms offer.[105] This was illustrated in 2014 when Spain passed a law that obliged news aggregators to compensate publishers of news content.[106] Google responded by withdrawing Google News from the Spanish market, impairing the news publishers who were no longer able to benefit from the traffic Google generated for them.[107] This incident underscores the power that online platforms hold over the news media, and raises the question of whether the Copyright Directive will accomplish its aim to bolster high-quality journalism in practice.

Media outlets are acutely aware that, if they were to exercise their right to demand for revenue sharing under the Copyright Directive, Google could replicate what it did in Spain. This has led several publishers to waive their right to collect fees and to allow Google to link their content free of charge. For example, some German publishers acknowledged that they were forced to do so given the "overwhelming market power of Google."[108] However, a recent licensing agreement Google reached with APIG, an organization representing the French news media, suggests that Google intends to comply with the Copyright Directive.[109] Interestingly, however, Google agreed to negotiate individual licenses with the French publishers only after the French competition authority ruled that Google's refusal to negotiate with them amounted to an abuse of its dominant position and hence a violation of French competition law.[110] This, again, shows how the European regulatory model places its faith in government intervention to ensure that tech companies do not abuse their market power in ways that undermine news production and democratic institutions.

In addition to seeking to reduce the supply of disinformation, the EU has tried to wield its regulatory power to reduce demand for it. The EU has repeatedly emphasized the importance of promoting citizens' digital literacy as a way to counter disinformation and to empower citizens to critically consume and evaluate media content they encounter.[111] In this effort, the EU has adopted several soft law initiatives to advance digital literacy in Europe.[112] But the EU has issued binding obligations as well. The revised Audiovisual Media Services Directive from 2018 obliges video-sharing platforms to provide effective media literacy measures and tools.[113] A failure to comply with these obligations can lead to fines. This further illustrates how the EU's efforts to protect democracy have evolved into a multifaceted regulatory agenda geared toward ensuring that tech companies' actions enhance, and do not undermine, democracy as a foundation of a digital society.

Digital Regulation as an Instrument to Promote Fairness and Redistribution

Values relating to "social fairness" and "solidarity" are defining features of European economic policy. The EU's commitment to fairness and redistribution is consistent with the European social market economy model, which seeks to combine a free-market capitalist economy with social progress and a welfare state. In a 2020 Report, the Commission notes how "economic growth can be deemed fair when it is inclusive, benefiting all income groups, particularly the poorest."[114] Consistent with this statement, the EU seeks to integrate specific ideas about solidarity and fairness into its policymaking. This reflects a view that societies perceived as more equal and fair are associated with higher levels of life satisfaction and better social outcomes, whereas rising inequalities cultivate a sense of discontent within the public.[115] Various surveys among EU citizens further demonstrate that inequality at the bottom of the distribution elicits a particularly strong sense of injustice among Europeans— even more than inequality at the top of the distribution.[116] This view of societal fairness, embraced by political leaders and the public alike, has been integral in shaping the European rights-driven regulatory model.

The EU model is geared at mitigating existing power asymmetries with the goal of cultivating a fairer digital economy. European leaders are conscious that digital transformation has led to an exceedingly concentrated economy where few powerful companies control economic wealth and political power, accentuating inequalities and widening the gap between winners and losers. EU regulations are therefore aimed at reducing this power imbalance as a way of distributing the gains from the digital economy more equally. The EU integrates fairness into its digital policy both as *ex ante* fairness—such as by creating contestable markets where all players, big and small, are given the opportunity to compete on a level playing field—and as *ex post* fairness, where gains from the digital transformation are distributed more evenly.

These commitments around greater fairness have led the EU to adopt policies that shift power away from platforms to workers, internet users, smaller businesses and other economic actors, and to the public at large. In recent years, the EU's focus to fairness and redistribution has manifested itself, in particular, in three different areas of digital regulation, each discussed in detail below: first, the EU has deployed its antitrust laws to rein in the power of large tech companies, with the goal of empowering smaller firms and consumers; second, EU member states have led the quest toward a fairer digital tax regime in an effort to share gains from the digital economy with the general public; third, the EU has sought to improve the working conditions of platform workers, enhancing their social protections. Each of these three policy areas illustrates how the EU views government regulation as an essential tool for redistributing economic wealth and opportunities in a digital society.

Antitrust Law

Antitrust law offers an important policy tool for the EU in its efforts to promote a digital marketplace where all companies can compete fairly. Antitrust law, in Europe and elsewhere, is traditionally deployed to promote efficiency rather than fairness. The primary goal of EU antitrust law—or, using the European terminology, EU competition law—is the maximization of consumer welfare. Consequently, conventional thinking suggests that it cannot directly be leveraged to advance broader fairness considerations. However, Commissioner Margrethe Vestager, who is responsible for competition policy, has described how "competition policy contributes to shaping a *fairer society*, where all economic players—large and small—abide by the same rules."[117] In the competition law context, this entails creating a more equal playing field where even small rivals can contest powerful incumbents. In his 2016 State of the Union speech, the former Commission President Jean-Claude Juncker also emphasized how EU competition policy contributes toward "a fair playing field" and protects consumers against abuses by powerful companies. According to President Juncker, "The Commission watches over this fairness. This is the social side of competition law. And this is what Europe stands for."[118]

Some of the recent Commission decisions illustrate how this concept of fairness informs EU antitrust enforcement action in practice, both reflecting and furthering the EU's rights-driven regulatory model. In 2017, the Commission issued a decision against Google in a so-called *Google Shopping* case, finding that Google had given an unfair advantage to its own comparison-shopping service and hence engaged in self-preferencing and discrimination in breach of EU competition rules.[119] In this case, Google was accused of unfairly displaying its rivals' comparison-shopping services lower down in search results, which reduced traffic to these other sites and, according to the Commission, thereby denied these other companies the chance to compete and innovate. Google was ordered to grant equal treatment to its rivals. The EU's General Court upheld the Commission's decision in 2021,[120] thus endorsing these fairness-driven nondiscrimination obligations for large online platforms as a cornerstone of EU competition law.

The EU's adoption of the DMA in 2022 illustrates how antitrust regulation can be harnessed to advance the notion of fairness. There is a growing consensus that the EU's existing enforcement toolkit that relies on *ex post* enforcement of antitrust law is insufficient. These investigations are time-consuming and often fail to unlock competition. Smaller rivals cannot survive in the marketplace for the decade that it can take for the Commission to collect evidence and to build a case against a dominant company. Partly in response to these concerns, the EU adopted a new *ex ante* regulation on competition—the DMA—in 2022.[121] The DMA targets so-called digital gatekeepers, which are the largest online platforms that have the greatest ability to shape competitive conditions in the marketplace, thus bringing the large US tech giants under its fold. The DMA invokes the notion of fairness multiple times. In describing the goals of the legislation, the Commission emphasizes that "the DMA proposal is concerned with economic imbalances, unfair business practices by gatekeepers and their negative consequences, such as weakened contestability of platform markets."[122] By seeking to create "fairer and more equitable conditions for all players in the digital sector,"[123] the DMA thus directly contributes to the EU's fairness-driven digital policy.

Digital Taxation

The EU acknowledges that there is a limit to how much fairness and wealth redistribution can be accomplished through the enforcement of antitrust law alone. Taxation is commonly viewed as a more effective policy instrument than antitrust policy to transfer wealth in the economy, making it an essential policy tool for the European governments to promote fairness in the digital economy.[124] Acknowledging this, nearly half of all EU member states have either announced, proposed, or enacted a domestic Digital Services Tax (DST).[125] These DSTs reflect a belief that the country where digital companies create economic value—for instance, by offering digital services to users located in that country—should have taxing rights over that digital company. France was the first EU jurisdiction to enact a DST in 2019, imposing a 3 percent tax on digital services provided to French users.[126] Digital services such as online advertising, online platforms, or online marketplaces fall under the law's definition of digital services. The French DST applies to approximately thirty companies, including the large US tech firms, such as Amazon, Apple, Google, and Meta.[127] In announcing the new law, the French Minister for the Economy and Finance Bruno Le Maire emphasized that with the DST, France is "merely re-establishing fiscal justice," by creating "taxation for the 21st century that is fair and efficient."[128] European countries that have already implemented a DST include Austria, France, Hungary, Italy, Poland, Portugal, and Spain, in addition to the UK outside of the EU.[129]

The wide adoption of the DSTs at the EU member state level reflects an emerging European consensus that tax legislation offers an important policy instrument to promote a fair digital economy. In 2018, the Commission sought to implement a European-wide solution on digital taxation, incorporating this notion of fair digital taxation into the EU's regulatory model while also seeking to prevent the emergence of multiple DSTs at the member state level.[130] The Commission's regulatory effort subsequently evolved into a 2020 proposal for a digital levy.[131] The suggested levy consists of a 0.3 percent tax on goods and services sold online by companies with an annual turnover of €50 million or more in the EU.[132] With this levy, the Commission is seeking to ensure that "digital companies contribute their fair share to society, since a prolonged unequal distribution of rights and responsibilities undermines the social contract."[133] Highlighting key differences in the two regulatory models, national DSTs and the Commission's digital levy became a source of controversy in US–EU relations, bringing the parties to the brink of a trade war over the issue, and ultimately paving the way for a multilateral agreement within the OECD, as discussed in Chapter 6.[134]

While the developments discussed above are significant, to date the EU has had limited ability to shape the digital economy through taxation, as tax policy remains a competence of individual member states. But there are other related policies that intersect with taxation and that fall within the EU's competences, thus providing the EU an avenue to advance its rights-driven agenda. For example, the EU has often resorted to another policy tool—state aid control—in challenging what it considers unfair corporate tax planning. State aid refers to a selective advantage, such as a tax benefit, which a member state government grants to a company, and which may provide the recipient with an unfair competitive advantage over its rivals. Such aid can be considered a violation of EU competition law as it can distort fair competition in the marketplace.

The EU state aid rules formed the basis for the recent, controversial ruling involving the Irish government and Apple.[135] In 2016, the Commission ordered Ireland to reclaim €13 billion in unpaid tax revenue from Apple. According to the Commission, Apple had benefited from an "unfair advantage" over its competitors by paying a conspicuously low tax rate of 4 percent on nearly $200 billion in profits it earned outside the US over the past decade. To justify its low tax rate, Apple had relied on a 1991 tax ruling by Irish tax authorities, which the Commission found to violate EU state aid rules. As a result, the Commission ordered Ireland to claw back the unpaid taxes from Apple. In 2020, the EU's General Court overturned the Commission decision.[136] The

Commission is now appealing that decision to the CJEU, signaling the Commission's continuing resolve to assert its view of fairness over the tax treatment of large tech companies.[137]

Employment Protections for Platform Workers

The EU's attention to fairness in the context of the digital economy is also reflected in its increasing concern about the working conditions of platform workers or "gig workers."[138] Platform work encompasses services such as food-delivery or ride-hailing services where workers perform services on demand while being connected to their customers via a platform. This type of work can enhance fairness by offering new opportunities for individuals to engage in the labor market under flexible conditions, thus benefiting workers, businesses, and customers alike.[139] However, it can also undermine fairness, giving impetus for regulatory action. The EU institutions have expressed concern about the precarious nature of platform work, including insufficient social protections available for these workers.[140] For example, Nicolas Schmit, Commissioner for Jobs and Social Rights, has stressed that online platforms must offer platform workers social protections to ensure that "the digital transition is fair and sustainable."[141] The European Parliament has also called for legislative action. In its 2020 Report, the Parliament called for the benefits of digitalization to be shared broadly and equitably while stressing how "workers in the digital sector must enjoy the same rights and working conditions as those in other sectors."[142]

In December 2021, the Commission proposed a Directive aimed at improving working conditions for platform work.[143] The proposed Directive, which is now pending before the Council of Ministers and the European Parliament, seeks to ensure that platform workers are classified as employees when the nature of their work calls for such a designation. By setting out the criteria that determine when the platform is considered an "employer," the Directive is expected to lead to a significant reclassification of platform workers—such as Uber drivers—as employees.[144] This would extend various labor and social rights to these workers that traditional employees are entitled to under the national laws of each EU member state. In practice, platform companies would be required to respect laws on minimum wage, collective bargaining, working time, unemployment, sickness benefits, and more.[145] The Directive also calls for greater transparency in algorithmic management of platform workers, vesting workers with the right to contest automated decisions and mandating platforms to complement algorithms with human monitoring.[146]

This EU-level measure was, in part, motivated by the EU's growing awareness of the inadequate employment protections available to platform workers.

But the Commission was also spurred to action because of the growing legislative activity on platform work within individual member states—a development that often motivates Commission action, as it fears fragmentation of the single market with conflicting laws across member states. Some member states have already taken—or are considering—action, whether by introducing a rebuttable presumption of employment for platform workers (e.g., the Netherlands, Spain) or by placing the burden on the platform to show that an employment relationship does not exist (e.g., Germany).[147] Some no longer draw a binary distinction between workers and self-employed individuals in their legislation but have introduced a third status for platform workers (e.g., Germany, France, Italy, Spain, and Portugal).[148] The highest national courts across Europe—including in France, Spain, and the former EU member state UK—have also recognized platform workers as employees,[149] with significant consequences for ride hailing companies, such as Uber, and food delivery services, such as Deliveroo. In Italy, Uber was put into "judiciary administration" in 2020 after the company's executives were accused of "exploitation and modern slavery."[150] In the following year, the Tribunal of Milan lifted the restriction following commitments made by Uber.[151] This spate of legislative activity and court rulings at the member state level further illustrate the European governments' commitment to a redistributive, fairness-driven, and inclusive digital policy that is designed to "benefi[t] all income groups, particularly the poorest."[152]

These efforts by the EU to pursue greater fairness through its proposed regulation of platform work—along with those efforts discussed above in the context of antitrust law and digital taxation—reflect the EU's view that government intervention is needed to ensure that the digital economy benefits large segments of society. Realizing this policy objective requires the EU to deploy multiple and diverse regulatory instruments. If successful, their goal is to ensure that powerful platforms cannot harness their economic, political, and informational power simply to their own benefit; smaller businesses will have a fair chance to compete with them in the marketplace; public revenues grow through contributions of the digital giants; and platform workers' core social rights are protected.

Regulating Digital Markets While Advancing European Integration

Since the early days of the EU, regulation has served the fundamental goal of European integration. Developing harmonized EU regulations is critical for the operation of the common European market. As a result, the EU's regulatory agenda for the digital economy is also directly woven into that overarching governing objective: advancing European integration by creating a digital single market. A well-functioning digital single market calls for harmonized EU regulations as inconsistent regulatory standards hinder cross-border trade. For example, if each of the twenty-seven individual member states adopted a different national standard to safeguard personal data, the single market could not function efficiently, as companies would face a different regulatory environment in each country. Most EU regulations therefore advance a dual objective, one being the better functioning of the single market. For example, the GDPR seeks to enhance the fundamental right to privacy but also to facilitate data flows across member states. Similarly, the Copyright Directive seeks to introduce a fairer marketplace while also removing barriers from within the EU by creating a digital single market for copyrighted works online. The DSA was likewise motivated by the need to enhance transparency and accountability over tech companies' content moderation decisions, but also to prevent fragmentation that was emerging as individual member states began adopting conflicting hate speech laws and enforcing them extraterritorially, thus undermining the functioning of the single European market.[153] This dual objective has often allowed the EU to harness broad political support for its regulatory acts, offering pro-regulation and pro-trade coalitions alike a reason to advocate for common European rules.

The creation of a digital single market as a central policy goal also provides a sound legal basis for the EU's regulatory action, allowing the EU to regulate in domains over which it otherwise has no powers to act. For example, the EU does not have the legal authority to regulate copyright matters, which remain within member state powers. However, in adopting the Copyright Directive, the EU relied on its existing powers to pursue harmonization measures that are necessary for the establishment and functioning of the internal market.[154] The single market imperative provides a legal basis for many other EU tech regulations as well, including the AI Regulation, the DSA, and the DMA. Many of the EU's far-reaching regulatory initiatives—however controversial—have thus benefited from being supported by a less controversial policy goal that has an uncontested legal basis: the completion of the digital single market and hence the advancement of the process of European integration. Digital transformation can also be viewed as providing European institutions with a unique constitutional opportunity to advance European integration.[155] Digital policies affect numerous industries, implicating almost all aspects of today's economy and society. By regulating this space, the EU can achieve extensive harmonization of EU member state laws, thereby advancing European integration in the process.

To a large extent, the Commission's tendency to "govern through regulation" is also a result of the EU's small budget. The EU's budget amounts to only around 1 percent of its Gross National Income and consists primarily of transfers from member states.[156] To put this figure in perspective, US federal government spending regularly exceeds 20 percent of GDP.[157] These tight budgetary constraints restrict the Commission's ability to pursue direct-expenditure programs, such as large-scale industrial policy, innovation policy, or job creation programs at the EU level. In contrast, there is no "regulatory budget" to limit the number of regulations and directives the Commission can promulgate.[158] The Commission does not even need significant funds to enforce its regulations—it can leverage member state funds by often delegating the actual implementation and enforcement to them, as was done with the GDPR. Thus, the only way for the Commission to expand the EU's influence without extensive financial resources is to engage in regulatory activity, as regulations do not depend on tax revenue available to EU institutions. Consequently, digital regulation offers EU institutions the best avenue to promote its policy agenda with respect to digital transformation and its impact on broader European integration more generally.

How the European Regulatory Model Overlaps with the American and Chinese Models

The discussion thus far has shown how the European rights-driven regulatory model reflects many political, historical, and ideological commitments that are distinctly European and thus set the EU model apart from both the US and Chinese models. However, alongside these differences exist many similarities as well. European regulators are no strangers to market-driven principles, and many of the EU's digital regulations can be viewed as having a neoliberal undertone, hence resembling the American market-driven model. After all, the EU's digital regulation seeks to integrate the common European market and hence foster free trade across member states. At the same time, the EU's digital regulation also resembles some elements of the Chinese state-driven regulatory model. Especially more recently, the EU's digital policies are geared at proactively building greater technological capabilities in the name of technological self-sufficiency or strategic autonomy, mimicking an industrial policy approach traditionally associated with the Chinese model.

To foster an integrated, European single market, the EU has relied on several market-driven policies geared at eradicating tariffs and other trade barriers, while restricting various member state regulations capable of hindering market integration. Given these commitments, the EU has been described as "the leading exponent of neo-liberal regulation in Europe."[159] The EU's central goal with these policies has been to foster competition, especially across member state borders. Trade liberalization measures and antitrust law have contributed to this goal, as have various measures aimed at constraining member state governments from adopting regulations that distort the single market. Thus, even the regulations the EU has adopted across numerous policy domains have typically had a pro-competitive, market-creating character.

The EU's focus on creating a digital single market has also given the EU's digital regulations a neoliberal foundation. In particular, the early EU digital regulations, including the 1995 Data Protection Directive and the 2000 e-commerce Directive reflect "digital liberalism," and elevate the market-driven ideals above strong rights protections.[160] Those legislations had the flow of personal data across the EU and the creation of a European market for e-commerce as their primary motivation. Protection of fundamental rights and individual freedoms of the users of digital services were secondary considerations to the more prominent goal of advancing economic freedoms of the providers of those new services. For instance, the 2000 e-commerce Directive resembles Section 230 of the Communications Decency Act in the US, similarly shielding online platforms from liability with the goal of protecting internet service companies' incentives to innovate and develop new business models. Similarly, the 1995 Data Protection Directive focuses more on free movement of data, relegating fundamental rights considerations to a more modest role than the one they acquire in the 2016 GDPR. Over the past decade, however, the EU's digital policymaking has become more protective of rights, introducing more market-correcting policies alongside market-creating policies.[161] This ideological shift can be traced to the growing dominance of platform companies, and the revelation of new economic and societal harms associated with that dominance. Other external events, such as the 2013 Snowden revelations, have also revealed the limits of the market-driven model, explaining the more recent shift toward rights-driven digital policies in the EU. Yet this new approach has not replaced the strengthening of the single market as a key raison d'être of the EU. For example, even the rights-driven DSA retains the online platforms' liability shield that they benefited from under the 2000 e-commerce Directive. Thus, the EU's enduring single market imperative checks and balances its rights-driven regulatory model, ensuring that it accommodates many market-driven features even today.

In recent years, however, the EU's market-driven instinct has been complemented with a growing proclivity toward more state-driven economic policy, exhibiting some features of the Chinese regulatory model. The EU institutions are assuming an increasingly dirigiste role in steering the digital economy with the goal of asserting the EU's "digital sovereignty," which can be seen as a move toward a state-driven regulatory model. In today's tense geopolitical environment, European political leadership is stressing the EU's need to increase its technological self-sufficiency and boost its own strategic and industrial capabilities. In the digital economy domain, this entails bolstering the EU's "technological sovereignty" or digital sovereignty, including assuming control of European data and digital infrastructure, as well as nurturing European tech champions. "We must have mastery and ownership of key technologies in Europe," declared Ursula von der Leyen, President of the European Commission, in her inaugural speech at the European Parliament in November 2019.[162] This is one of many recent statements by European leaders that emphasize the importance of Europe's "strategic autonomy," including its digital sovereignty. In its 2020 Communication, the Commission emphasizes "the integrity and resilience of our data-infrastructure, networks and communications" as a foundation of European technological sovereignty. Only by developing and deploying Europe's own capacities can the EU reduce its dependency on others for the most crucial technologies. These capacities, according to the Commission, will also reinforce Europe's ability to "define its own rules and values in the digital age."[163]

The EU's recent push for strategic autonomy and digital sovereignty remains a contested policy goal for its regulatory policies. Some associate these terms with a desirable goal to bolster European capabilities while others see them as an undesirable attempt to build a "fortress Europe" through protectionist measures. At its core, digital sovereignty emphasizes the need for the EU to retain—or to regain—the freedom to make its own choices in the digital age, to reduce its dependencies on large US tech companies, and to avoid being at the mercy of the US–China tech war. The EU fears that it has become too dependent on digital services provided by foreign companies, leaving European governments, businesses, and citizens vulnerable to decisions made by others. Europeans navigate the internet using a search engine powered by algorithms created by Google, engage in online conversations moderated by Facebook or Twitter, remain connected using iPhones built by Apple, and store their data in clouds managed by Amazon and Microsoft. The EU's reliance on US technologies today exceeds its dependency on technologies emanating from China.[164] Nonetheless, China's rising influence in the digital realm adds to the European sense of vulnerability. Europeans are growing increasingly concerned that reliance on China's Huawei as a provider for their 5G network technology exposes them to Chinese government surveillance, as Beijing may gain access to any data Huawei obtains while operating critical infrastructure

in Europe. This—together with the pressure exerted by the US government—
has led some European governments to reverse their earlier decisions to rely
on Huawei as a 5G network provider.[165]

Europe's concern over its supply-chain dependencies is well founded.
Approximately 80 percent of the world's semiconductors are manufactured
in Asia today. By comparison, Europe used to be a leading producer of computer chips, contributing 44 percent to global production in the 1990s.[166] That
market share has dwindled to 10 percent today, leaving the EU dependent on
the US for the general chip design capacity and Asia for chip manufacturing.[167]
According to Commissioner Thierry Breton, Europe was "naïve" to outsource
much of its semiconductor capabilities abroad and now needs to "redress the
balance."[168] Batteries are another sector where the US and the EU remain
dependent on Asian producers. Currently, Chinese, Japanese, and Korean
companies combined account for 90 percent of global production of battery
cells.[169] In addition, lithium—a key component for many types of batteries—
is heavily concentrated in Asia, with only 3 percent of the global capacity
residing in Europe.[170] Similarly, 93 percent of the EU's magnesium comes
from China.[171]

The EU has pursued both a defensive and an offensive strategy to reduce
its dependencies from foreign technologies, while developing greater digital capabilities on its own. The Huawei controversy has ignited a broader
conversation in Europe about the need to protect strategic technology assets
from foreign acquirers, resulting in a more careful screening of foreign direct investment in such technologies.[172] The EU has also moved to combat
unfair foreign subsidies, including the Chinese government's practice of
funding Chinese companies' acquisitions of EU companies or their bids
for government contracts in the EU.[173] It has further strengthened its export
control regime, restricting the outflow of dual-use technologies, including
cybersurveillance tools, advanced computing, and AI,[174] and adopted new
laws aimed at enhancing Europe's cyber resilience and cyber defenses.[175]
Recently, the EU has introduced actual sanctions in response to cyberattacks
orchestrated by China, North Korea, and Russia.[176]

European governments are also resorting to new industrial policy measures, including the granting of government subsidies—a practice commonly
associated with the Chinese state-driven regulatory model. Subsidy races are
unfolding in cloud computing, batteries, and semiconductors where the EU,
alongside the US, China, and several other governments, is looking to shore
up its capabilities and to shed its dependency on foreign technologies. In 2021,
the Commission announced that the EU's goal was to produce 20 percent of
world semiconductors by 2030. The EU has also set a target to gain a 30 percent

market share in battery cell production by 2030.[177] To accomplish this latter goal, the Commission launched a European Battery Alliance in October 2017, which is a large-scale industrial policy initiative that benefits from significant public funding that member states are leveraging to stimulate private investment.[178] In its Coordinated AI Plan, the Commission further pledged to invest 1 billion euros per year on AI, while mobilizing additional investments from the private sector and member states, so as to reach investments of 20 billion euros per year within the next decade.[179] The European Recovery and Resilience Facility (RRF), created in 2020 to facilitate Europe's economic recovery postpandemic, provides another source of funding that can help boost European technological capabilities. The RRF makes nearly 700 billion euros in grants and loans available to the member state, with 20 percent of those funds earmarked for reforms and investments that foster digital transition across the EU.[180]

While most commentators likely agree that an EU with more capabilities and fewer strategic dependencies is a goal worth pursuing, it remains disputed how such a goal is to be achieved. The underlying debate raises hard questions of whether and how the EU can reconcile its commitment to economic openness and international cooperation with ensuring self-sufficiency around key technologies. Another question is whether an unintended consequence of the EU's digital sovereignty agenda is that it may even lend legitimacy to more extreme variants of digital sovereignty that authoritarian governments, including most prominently China and Russia, are pursuing. As such, the digital sovereignty narrative can be invoked to justify many forms of government control over the internet, offering a blueprint for autocracies to engage in extensive surveillance of their citizens. For example, China deploys the notion of digital sovereignty to justify the extensive government control of the digital sphere that goes beyond protectionism and competitiveness concerns and severely limits individual freedoms. The more the EU—or the US and other Western governments—step in to actively shape the digital economy, the less convincing their criticism becomes when they ask China to loosen its reins over the Chinese digital economy.

Ultimately, the EU will likely undertake this quest for digital sovereignty mindful of its core values that have been discussed earlier in this chapter—fundamental rights, democracy, and fairness—which set limits to how the EU can go about achieving greater strategic autonomy. For example, it is not clear Europeans actually want a "European Google" if that requires submitting to the company's "surveillance capitalism" in ways that compromises individuals' fundamental rights to data privacy. Europeans are also not prepared to adopt the Chinese model of surveillance even if that model has given

China an advantage in the tech race due to the amount of data its government and companies have harnessed. Thus, even in its newfound pursuit for digital sovereignty, the EU is expected to be committed to a digital order that is rooted in respect for fundamental rights, the defense of democracy, and the promotion of fairness. At the same time, how this rights-driven model evolves in today's challenging geopolitical environment will be a crucial test of the model's continuing appeal and resilience.

The Criticism of the European Regulatory Model

The European rights-driven regulatory model has been criticized on several fronts. Three of the most common lines of this criticism, which are discussed in more detail below, relate to compliance costs, enforcement deficits, and internal conflicts among the EU member states. First, the EU's heavy-handed regulatory approach is often thought to increase the operating costs of companies and to deter innovation, casting a shadow over the EU's technology sector and leaving the EU behind the US and China in the unfolding tech race. Second, EU regulation is often failing in its implementation, as manifested by the timid record of enforcing the GDPR or the failure to restore a competitive marketplace through antitrust enforcement to date. In addition, the EU's efforts to regulate online content have been criticized as insufficient and contrary to its ideas of democracy and the rule of law in that they leave it for tech companies to draw lines between permitted and prohibited speech. Third, the European rights-driven model is undermined by contradictions across the EU member states, raising the question of whether there even is a single European model for digital regulation. In addition to these three lines of criticism, the EU model is also commonly criticized as protectionist, targeting, in particular, US tech companies—a form of criticism that is discussed in Chapter 6 when examining closely the US–EU regulatory battles.

Raising Costs and Impeding Innovation

There are few leading tech companies emanating from Europe today, which some critics view as a reflection of the EU's overly stringent regulatory regime. A look at any key tech indicator reveals the extent to which the EU is currently lagging behind the technology prowess of the US or China.[181] On *The Forbes* 2021 list of "The World's Largest Technology Companies," only two EU-based companies, SAP and Accenture, make it to the top twenty. At the same time, there are 13 US companies on that list.[182] Other statistics portray an equally sobering picture. When focusing on the world's top 100 unicorns, only 12 European companies made the list in September 2021, with seven of those hailing from the UK as opposed to the EU.[183] European companies contribute less than 4 percent of the market capitalization of the world's 70 largest platforms.[184] These statistics paint a clear picture of the EU's relative weakness in this space, and raise the question whether Europe's relative lack of competitiveness can, indeed, be attributed to its alleged overregulation.

Several academics, tech entrepreneurs, and industry analysts trace EU tech companies' relative lack of success to the level of tech regulation they face. Some scholars describe the EU's regulatory approach toward platforms as "too blunt, with the risk of constraining value creation" while producing "stifling unintended consequences."[185] Andrew McAfee, cofounder of the MIT initiative on the Digital Economy, suggests that "more upstream governance translates to less downstream innovation" in the EU, and predicts that the "expensive and time-consuming requirements" in the EU's proposed AI rules "will generate less tech innovation."[186] Jack Ma, the cofounder of Alibaba Group, has also suggested that the EU's "tighter regulation could hamper its ability to innovate," noting that China's "lack of regulation around the internet in the early days allowed China's mobile internet to flourish and for Alibaba to thrive."[187] One tech industry association representative points out that Spotify is one of the few successful European tech companies, and to change that, the EU ought to "rethink its approach to regulation."[188] A 2020 study, conducted by Oxera but commissioned by Amazon, strikes a similar tone, warning that the EU's DMA "risk[s] reducing innovation overall."[189] These statements capture a common sentiment that assumes a direct link between the EU's stringent tech regulations and its lackluster technological progress.

However, it is not clear that more regulation always means less innovation. Looking back, the digital economy was not heavily regulated in Europe before 2010 (when the Commission opened its first antitrust investigation into Google), or even before 2018 (when the GDPR entered into force). The EU's 2000 e-commerce Directive—the predecessor to the DSA—closely resembles Section 230 of the US Communications Decency Act, shielding platforms from any general monitoring obligation.[190] The only other notable EU tech regulation in force before 2010 was the 1995 Data Protection Directive, which was considerably less protective of fundamental rights than the EU's 2016 GDPR. Thus, even though there was no substantial tech regulation in the EU during the years when companies such as Google and Facebook were founded—1998 and 2004, respectively—comparable companies were not founded in Europe. Similarly, European AI startups trail those hailing from the US and China even though there is currently no AI regulation in force in the EU. Furthermore, the main target of the EU's digital regulation to date has been large US tech companies; however, few would suggest that the stringent EU regulations have discouraged those companies from innovating. There are different views on whether these regulations are protectionist and hence problematic, as explored in Chapter 6, but it is difficult to see how these regulations would supposedly have held back the technological progress and innovative potential of these companies.

The EU's digital regulations can also generate economic benefits for companies. Common EU rules harmonize discordant regulations across member states. From this perspective, they often reduce companies' operating costs by streamlining the regulatory environment while contributing to greater predictability and legal certainty. Regulation can enhance consumers and organizational customers' confidence in tech firms' conduct and their products. For example, Microsoft's president, Brad Smith, recently called for regulation of facial recognition technology in the US.[191] He stressed the importance of clear rules in this area of technology precisely because, if left unregulated, it can be used "for ill as well as good" and unsettle consumers. Amazon similarly called on governments to "weigh in" after discovering an embarrassing mistake in its facial recognition technology.[192] Seen this way, stringent EU regulation can help firms obtain reputational gains and win over consumers. For example, in the global AI race, the EU competes by setting a higher standard for the AI's trustworthiness and ethics. According to the Commission, this not only allows the EU to defend its normative vision and guard against risks associated with AI, but also makes it possible for the EU to capture a commercial advantage if consumers prefer AI applications that adhere to high regulatory standards and are hence easier to trust.[193]

While one can debate how large of a net cost EU regulations impose on companies, and whether and how those costs also dampen innovation, it seems less disputed that those costs have a distributional effect. The cost of compliance with EU regulations, such as the GDPR, is relatively high for small and-medium-sized enterprises, while the large multinationals arguably have the resources to meet almost any standard that the EU sets. Thus, if anything, the concern ought to be how high regulatory barriers in the EU have the potential to protect and further entrench the power of the largest tech companies.[194] In the end, while big multinationals, such as Google or Meta, make the headlines, the real hidden cost of EU regulation is borne by small market players, which do not have the same capacity to engineer their products and services to meet the EU's regulatory demands. The EU is increasingly aware of this, which explains why the DMA only targets the largest tech giants capable of acting as digital gatekeepers and the DSA imposes more regulatory demands on very large platforms and search engines that have the greatest potential to cause harm—but also more resources to preempt any harm from occurring.

Inadequate Enforcement of Digital Regulation

The European rights-driven regulatory model has not only been criticized for its excessive stringency, but paradoxically also for being too lenient—at least with respect to its implementation. The EU's stringent digital regulations often fail to translate into effective enforcement, thus compromising the goals of the EU model in practice. Of course, this is not to say that the EU's regulatory model has not had any impact. There is likely more competition, more data privacy, and less harmful speech online, thanks to existing EU regulations. Yet it is fair to concede the European rights-driven regulatory model was designed to do more.

As an example of weak implementation, the lackluster enforcement of the GDPR has often left individuals' data vulnerable to exploitation. Particular criticism has been leveled against the Irish Data Protection Commission (DPC), which is in charge of enforcing the GDPR against large tech companies that have their European headquarters in Dublin, including Apple, Google, Meta, and Microsoft. The DPC has been overwhelmed by this task, bringing only a small number of cases under the GDPR, which to date have resulted in relatively modest fines.[195] In September 2021, reports surfaced that 98 percent of the 164 significant complaints submitted to the Irish DPC were still unresolved at that time.[196] The European Parliament has expressed concern over the Irish DPC's ability to discharge its obligations under the GDPR.[197] The Irish Parliament has similarly called for enhanced enforcement, noting how the current system "fails to adequately protect the fundamental rights of citizens."[198] Some other EU member states have enforced the GDPR more frequently, but even then, the average fines remain modest.[199] Even the US government, which has not adopted a federal privacy law, seems to be outdoing Europeans on the enforcement front. In 2019, the US Federal Trade Commission (FTC) imposed a historic high $5 billion fine on Facebook, after the company was found to have deceived users about their ability to control the privacy of their personal information.[200]

There is notable evidence that companies around the world have changed their privacy practices in light of the GDPR.[201] However, unless these companies observe effective enforcement, the GDPR's deterrent effect may wane over the years. At the same time, it is not clear that even high fines will be sufficient to change all tech companies' data privacy practices, raising the question on what "effective enforcement" would look like in practice. Even the FTC's $5 billion fine on Meta seems modest when compared to the revenues or valuations of these companies. The day this landmark fine was imposed, Meta's stock rose by 1.8 percent, adding $10 billion to its market value.[202] This suggests that the largest tech companies may treat fines as the price of doing business, and as something they can easily offset by other gains—so long as they are not forced to fundamentally overhaul their business models that rely on the exploitation of user data.

The EU's antitrust enforcement record suggests that high fines alone may not be sufficient to effectively discipline the tech giants. Even though the EU has fined Google over 8 billion euros across three antitrust cases in the past decade, critics note that these fines have hardly made a dent in Google's market dominance.[203] Despite high-profile cases resulting in high-profile fines, markets remain dominated by a few large tech behemoths, with few opportunities for rivals to effectively compete against them. In its November 2020 report, the European Court of Auditors criticized the EU's antitrust investigations as being too slow and delayed, intervening only after competition has already been "wiped out."[204] The report acknowledged that the Commission has no legal tools to intervene before competition problems occur, and is forced to rely on the slow process of gathering evidence of consumer harm. The Commission itself has seized on this argument, stating that it needs new enforcement tools. This very concern motivated the EU to create the DMA, which was adopted in 2022 and which bestows the Commission with new powers to regulate the marketplace with strong *ex ante* competition rules. This regulation, together with the DSA, presents the EU with the opportunity to show that it is not merely capable of regulating on paper, but actually able to transform the digital marketplace toward its values.

The EU's enforcement of its regulation targeting online content can also be seen as suffering from critical weaknesses. Some critics maintain that the EU errs too far on the side of protecting civility and dignity, leading to overly aggressive content removal.[205] A different, yet particularly damning, criticism relates to how other countries perceive—and, at worst, misconstrue—these European regulations. Some critics have argued that by forcing the platforms to police the internet, the EU and its member states are providing a cover for authoritarian governments to restrict speech as well, thus legitimizing their censorship policies. When Germany adopted the NetzDG, its law mandating removal of hate speech and other unlawful content, several authoritarian governments followed suit, citing the German law as an example for the need to curtail speech online.[206] For example, two weeks after the adoption of the NetzDG, Russia adopted its own copy-paste version of it, explicitly referring to the German law in the legislative process.[207] Yet Russia has deployed the law to silence government critics, exploiting the vagueness of many provisions copied from the NetzDG.[208] Some critics fear that the EU's DSA could provide a similar tool for repressive governments to legitimize their internet censorship regimes, using the EU's law as their cover.[209]

However, one can also make the opposite claim and assert that the EU has been too lenient in tolerating harmful content online. While such regulation has led tech companies to take down considerable amounts of hate speech, disinformation, and terrorist content in the name of dignity, safety, and democracy, this kind of speech remains rampant online. Major platforms such as Facebook, YouTube, and Twitter are overflowing with content that is harmful, dangerous, and often illegal. Few can dispute that these platforms have become go-to destinations for the spread of disinformation and the manipulation of public opinion on critical issues ranging from global pandemics to vaccines, and from migration to democratic elections. The role of social media in the January 6 Capitol attack vividly brought this reality home to Americans; however, one can argue that this is just the culmination of a trend that has been building for a long time—precisely because there has been too little, and not too much, content removal.

Drawing lines between permissible and impermissible speech is difficult and prone to errors in both directions. A critical question, therefore, becomes who should be vested with the responsibility to draw such difficult lines. Here, the European rights-driven regulatory model can be criticized as yielding in practice to the American market-driven model. While the EU has gradually developed content moderation rules, it relies on platforms themselves to implement those rules. It is the tech companies that retain the ultimate power to decide which content to disseminate, amplify, demote, label, and censor— replacing democratic governments as "custodians of the internet."[210] This increases, rather than curtails, platforms' power.[211]

Of course, there is no regulatory model under which EU institutions could be left to screen the trove of content posted online every second of every day. In the absence of direct democratic oversight over the platforms' content removal policies and practices, transparency and accountability therefore become key to enhancing the platforms' public accountability.[212] With the newly adopted DSA, the Commission requires platforms to disclose to users their detailed content moderation policies while also providing various safeguards, such as avenues for users to contest any removal decisions. Such transparency is designed to help ensure that the platforms are not engaging in overremoval of permissible content, while remaining responsive to legitimate removal requests. Whether the DSA will ultimately succeed in pushing platforms toward a more democratic, transparent, and accountable governance model will therefore be one of the biggest tests of the European rights-driven model, revealing whether the EU is capable of translating its stated values into actual market outcomes.

Internal Divisions Across the EU Undermining the Efficacy of EU Regulations

While all EU member states are thought to share certain common European values, clashes within the EU itself are also frequent, potentially undermining the coherence, effectiveness, and legitimacy of the European rights-driven regulatory model. While this chapter has focused on EU-level regulation and common values underlying it, it is well known that such regulation emanates from a contested political process that is characterized by notable intra-EU differences. Often, EU regulation is motivated by the desire to overcome such national differences, preventing legislative fragmentation that is inevitable if member states are left in charge to govern the digital economy on their own.

The sources of intra-EU differences are manifold. At times, they stem from notable disparities in the robustness of national technology ecosystems. Some member states are more digitally advanced while others have limited innovation capabilities on their own. The more advanced member states typically endorse a liberal approach on digital issues, such as the promotion of free flow of data or measures designed to enhance growth and competitiveness.[213] For example, Belgium, Finland, Denmark, Estonia, Ireland, Luxembourg, Sweden, the Netherlands, and the former member state UK have coordinated policy positions as "digitally advanced EU countries (D9)" group,[214] at times joined by the Czech Republic, Poland, Portugal, and Spain in what became known as a "D9+" group.[215] In 2020, these D9+ countries, together with France and Latvia, signed a position paper on the forthcoming AI regulation, calling for a well-calibrated, proportionate, and innovation-friendly AI regulation geared at fostering economic growth and European competitiveness.[216] The EU member states are also split in their support for digital sovereignty, with France leading the more dirigiste, industrial policy–oriented camp whereas the Northern European countries, in particular, emphasize the need to retain Europe's commitment to economic openness—a split that has even led to clashes among the key European Commissioners in charge of digital regulation.[217]

Another dividing line stems from differences in national tax regimes, explaining why a consensus on DSTs was difficult to forge across the EU. Only a few member states, such as Ireland, Luxembourg, and the Netherlands, host large global tech companies, making them more conscious of retaining favorable regulatory environments for those companies that benefit their national economies. The local tax regime is, no doubt, an important reason why the European headquarters of Apple, Google, Microsoft, and Twitter are in Dublin; the headquarters of Cisco, Netflix, and Tesla in Amsterdam; and the headquarters of Amazon and PayPal in Luxembourg. These three countries, in addition to other low-tax jurisdictions, such as Cyprus, Hungary, and Malta, have traditionally opposed any attempt to curtail their ability to set their own tax rates and hence undermine their ability to attract international companies.[218] Ultimately, these countries were brought onboard to the global OECD tax reform deal, even if initially reluctantly or in return for concessions.

Perhaps the hardest intra-EU conflicts are those that reflect a clash of fundamental values, as opposed to economic interests. For example, while all EU member states are committed to the fundamental right to data privacy, privacy cultures differ among them. Germany, in large part for historical reasons, tends to be more absolutist in its commitment to data privacy, whereas France, for example, has been more willing to make compromises on data privacy for reasons of public security. This is, in part, explained by repeated terrorist attacks, foreign election interference, industrial spying, and other threats France has endured.[219] According to the French government, the CJEU's pro-privacy rulings threaten member states' exercise of their key sovereign functions to protect national security and public order.[220] In 2020, the CJEU ruled that France's surveillance laws violated fundamental rights and freedoms and were hence contrary to EU law.[221] Rather defiantly, the French high administrative court issued a decision in 2021 that creatively interpreted the CJEU ruling in ways that allowed the French government to continue to indiscriminately and indefinitely retain data, effectively undermining the CJEU and the EU's fundamental rights regime.[222] Yet France is not alone in pressing the EU to rebalance its commitment to data protection with other fundamental public interests. A number of EU member states also joined together to challenge the strict pro-privacy approach before the CJEU in the *Dwyer* case, arguing that the EU's strict stance on data privacy curtails national law enforcement authorities' ability to fight crime.[223]

Recent revelations about the extensive use of spyware by Greek, Hungarian, Polish, and Spanish governments further expose intra-EU divisions in the privacy culture. These governments have allegedly carried out espionage operations by hacking phones of activists, journalists, and opposition politicians, prompting an investigation by the European parliament into surveillance practices that likely contravene EU law.[224] These disturbing discoveries cast a shadow over the EU's ostensibly inviolable commitment to a fundamental right to data privacy and thus compromise the core values underlying the EU's rights-driven model. These scandals further expose the EU model to criticism about the hypocrisy and double standards when it comes to the EU's demands for other governments, including China and the US, to curtail their surveillance practices in order to protect European citizens' data.[225]

Perhaps the most troubling divisions relate to the EU's commitment to democracy and the rule of law, including press freedoms and a pluralistic media. Poland and Hungary have taken extensive measures to curtail those freedoms, while the rule of law also remains a challenge in other member states, such as Bulgaria and Romania. In the digital realm, these divisions became palpable recently when the illiberal, conservative, and nationalist governments of Poland and Hungary wanted to curtail tech companies' ability to "limit the visibility of Christian, conservative, rightwing opinions."[226] Resembling the views of many Republicans in the US Congress, the Polish and Hungarian governments accused the tech companies of liberal bias and engagement in censorship. The Polish government even proposed a law banning social media companies from deleting content that was not contrary to Polish law.[227] This proposed law has raised concerns, especially as hate speech, in particular content that targets LGBTQ+ communities or Muslims and refugees, is prevalent in Poland.[228] These Polish and Hungarian measures are a direct challenge to the European rights-driven regulatory model. While Hungary and Poland lack the power to veto most EU digital regulation, they can still undermine the European regulatory model, at home and around the world. Their overt illiberalism invites criticism of the EU's hypocrisy and questions the EU's moral legitimacy when it seeks to defend and export its vision of a digital society grounded in fundamental rights, democracy, and human dignity.[229]

However, in some other instances, intra-EU differences can also be the EU's strength, and may help the European rights-driven model gain legitimacy and credibility. Inconsistencies and disagreements are an inevitable part of democratic lawmaking. Different member state positions check and balance one another, forcing the EU toward compromises, which often suppress more extreme policy positions—in any direction. For example, the EU's strong commitment to data privacy accommodates more exceptions for national security because of the position France has articulated. The EU's robust rights-driven AI Act is likely to be more innovation-friendly because of the pressures from the digitally advanced EU countries. What further balances EU regulation is the pursuit of dual goals, one being protective of rights and fairness, while the other being mindful of free trade. The end result is a more balanced regulatory model than what would have been absent such internal contradictions. In this respect, compared to the EU model, the American market-driven and the Chinese state-driven regulatory models may seem more unyielding in their ideological commitments. The EU's digital regulations are, by design, drafted to work in twenty-seven different jurisdictions that each harbor political, economic, ideological, and cultural differences. The EU model's ability to accommodate intra-EU conflicts also explains, in part, why the model resonates in many parts of the world, as will be shown in Chapter 9. These internal conflicts and contradictions have not managed to eradicate the core commitments underlying the European rights-driven regulatory model that give the European tech regulations their distinct character and that continue to set the EU apart from both the US and China. This European consensus—in all its diversity—has helped the EU carve its own path forward and avoid becoming a casualty in the US–China tech war, a topic that will be discussed in the next part of the book.

PART II

Imperial Rivalries

4

Between Freedom and Control

NAVIGATING COMPETING REGULATORY MODELS

"PRIVACY IS A fundamental human right. It's also one of our core values. Which is why we design our products and services to protect it," declares Apple, prominently and unequivocally, on its website.[1] A vocal advocate of data privacy and civil liberties, Apple frequently boasts of its unyielding commitment to data protection and human rights in the United States and Europe. However, the company's practices do not always match its lofty rhetoric. A closer look at Apple's business practices in China, for example, reveals that the company has systematically undermined those rights in return for permission to operate in the country.[2] To accommodate authorities in Beijing, Apple has agreed to store the data belonging to its Chinese users locally in a datacenter in Guiyang, where the data is kept on Chinese servers and managed by Chinese state employees. Apple has also compromised on its encryption technology used to guarantee the confidentiality of the data the company obtains, bowing to the Chinese government's demand to store the keys needed to unlock encryptions locally in China. There is genuine concern that these practices facilitate the Chinese government's access to the emails, photos, contacts, locations, and other personal information of Chinese users. To avoid violating the US law that prohibits the handing over of data to the Chinese government, Apple has granted the ownership of its Chinese customers' data to a Chinese state-owned company, Guizhou-Cloud Big Data.[3] Under this arrangement, Apple itself cannot be accused of handing data to the Chinese authorities—as any such request is channeled through the company's Chinese affiliate—allowing Apple to formally claim compliance with US law.[4] Yet it is difficult to avoid the conclusion that Apple has knowingly risked the integrity of its Chinese customers' data—its core values or its belief in privacy as a fundamental human right notwithstanding.

Apple's data practices in China represent only one of many examples of the compromises US tech companies make to take advantage of one of most lucrative and dynamic consumer markets in the world, while trying to avoid violating US law in doing so. This is part of a broader challenge faced by tech companies that operate globally, navigating different demands of American, Chinese, and European regulatory models. When these models collide, they can fuel horizontal battles between governments, as shown in Chapters 5 and 6. But they also fuel vertical battles featuring tech companies on one side and governments on the other. These battles are particularly intricate when multiple governments simultaneously impose competing regulatory demands on these companies. In these instances, different vertical battles intersect, thrusting tech companies into the midst of conflicting regulatory regimes and presenting them with increasingly irresolvable regulatory dilemmas. At worst, these dilemmas force tech companies to choose which of the conflicting regulatory models they comply with—while knowing that their compliance with one regulatory model inevitably violates another.

This chapter turns to examine the role of these intersecting vertical battles in the broader evolution of the digital economy, showing how tech companies navigate different regulatory models as they seek to maintain access to various markets. Here, the focus is on instances where tech companies confront conflicting obligations and expectations under American and Chinese regulatory models. Those vertical battles are particularly controversial and consequential as tech companies straddle between the US's demands for freedom and China's demands for state control. As tech companies encounter these different regulatory environments, they are often required to acquiesce to rules that contradict their own values and commitments made to other governments. In the process, these companies risk triggering a backlash in another jurisdiction—such as what happens when, for example, US tech companies capitulate to the Chinese government's demands to censor online content in China. These intersecting vertical conflicts also force tech companies to confront hard questions of what their own values are and how much those values can be compromised when operating in a market that embraces a different political or ideological vision for the digital economy. When navigating these battles over values, tech companies are often unable to appease all of their own customers and other key stakeholders, just as they are unable to satisfy all government regulators in different jurisdictions. Google, for example, discovered this when it decided to acquiesce to Chinese censorship rules in order to operate its search engine in China. Following this controversial decision, Google's US-based customers, employees, and shareholders revolted at the idea that Google would compromise its liberal values and capitulate to Chinese government demands, which eventually led the company to withdraw its search engine business from China entirely. This incident illustrates how a clash of values operates at many levels, amplifying the vertical battles and further complicating the strategies for tech companies involved in those battles.

In addition to being highly controversial, these vertical battles are consequential, with the potential to remake the global digital economy. Tech companies' inability to navigate mutually incompatible government rules is leading to a growing risk of technological and economic decoupling between China, the US, and the EU. Such decoupling occurs if tech companies conclude that they are no longer able to operate across the conflicting regulatory regimes and, consequently, must choose one over the other. This prospect of a broader decoupling is challenging the notion of a global internet and fragmenting the deeply connected digital economy. It is also undermining the remaining efforts at global cooperation and contributing to the existing forces that are driving deglobalization—thereby also aggravating the horizontal battles that are discussed in the following chapters. While it is unclear how far such decoupling will ultimately proceed given the costs associated with such a development, the decoupling of the tech economy remains one of the key challenges facing the global digital order in the coming years.

Vertical battles are not, of course, limited to clashes between the American and Chinese regulatory models. The American and European regulatory models also force tech companies to navigate differences between the two, as shown in Chapter 6. Those vertical conflicts, too, can be controversial. But they are different in that they are nested within a less contested US–EU horizontal conflict, which offers more pathways for mitigating or even resolving those vertical conflicts. In contrast, value conflicts are particularly stark for US tech companies who confront censorship obligations and other controversial demands of the state-driven regulatory model in China. This puts US tech companies on a direct collision course with the American market-driven regulatory model, including its underlying values centered around free speech and a free internet. Given the realities of the Chinese regulatory environment, US tech companies have few options but to either submit to the local laws, as companies like Apple have done or, alternatively, forgo the economic opportunities and abandon the Chinese market, as companies such as Google have largely chosen to do.

In contrast to the challenges faced by US tech companies doing business in China, Chinese tech companies have traditionally faced fewer obstacles when operating in the US, as the American market-driven regulatory model has embraced economic openness and welcomed foreign companies. However, since the onset of the US–China tech war, the US government is now exercising closer scrutiny over Chinese companies' US operations, fearing that they pose a threat to its national security. This has complicated Chinese tech companies' expansion in the US. The US government's central fear is that companies such as TikTok—a Chinese-owned video-sharing app featuring user-generated content—are not independent of the Chinese government. The data that TikTok collects from American internet users may therefore be passed on to the Chinese government and deployed toward extortion or other ill-motivated ends. Another fear is that the Chinese government may infiltrate TikTok's algorithms and thereby channel Communist Party propaganda to the company's US-based users. As a result, Chinese social media and messaging apps, including TikTok and WeChat, have faced the threat of government bans in the US. These bans—while addressing valid concerns relating to data security—are highly contested. After all, banning Chinese companies from the US market undermines the very values of the American market-driven model, including economic openness and a free internet, and emboldens the Chinese state-driven model, under which the government meddles with the ownership and content of tech companies' apps.

This chapter looks at several examples of these kinds of vertical conflicts between tech companies and governments, both to show their prominence in today's global digital economy and to assess their ability to fragment that economy. To illustrate the profound dilemmas companies can face in these conflicts, this chapter explains what it has meant for US-based tech companies to navigate the demands of the Chinese state-driven regulatory model, whose censorship requirements pose both commercial and ethical considerations for them. It documents how US companies have repeatedly submitted to the local censorship rules in China while facing criticism over such acquiescence at home. On the other hand, the chapter also highlights the challenges Chinese tech companies have recently encountered when attempting to operate in the US, seeking to assuage national security concerns that both US and Chinese regulators have expressed over their US expansion. Finally, this chapter highlights many of the significant implications of these intersecting vertical conflicts, including the growing risk of a further decoupling of the global digital economy.

US Tech Companies' Vertical Battle in China: Caught Between the Demands for Control and Freedom

Tech companies straddling the American market-driven model and the Chinese state-driven model tread a precarious terrain. The rift between the two warring technology powers, two conflicting sets of rules, and two opposing ideologies presents a challenge for private actors seeking to operate globally. For tech companies, complying with the demands of the Chinese government while adhering to the rules set by the US government—in addition to respecting the values and expectations of their US-based users, employees, and shareholders—can constitute a difficult, even impossible, balancing act. These companies are acutely aware that noncompliance with local rules comes with severe consequences: several US tech companies have either been banned from China or have withdrawn from the Chinese market after deciding that they are unwilling to submit to the government's authoritarian demands.[5] Others have stayed and are forced to make difficult compromises that subject them to criticism back home. Regardless of whether they leave or stay, these companies are compelled to confront the reality that today's digital economy is far from free or global.

US Tech Companies' Presence in China: A Brief Overview

Among US tech companies, Apple is by far the most heavily invested in the Chinese market. A 2021 *New York Times* investigation of Apple's China ties concluded that "Chinese workers assemble nearly every iPhone, iPad and Mac. Apple brings in $55 billion a year from the region, far more than any other American company makes in China."[6] As of 2021, Apple's sales in China contributed approximately 20 percent to the company's global sales,[7] and the Chinese App Store generated more revenue for the company than its US App Store in four of the past five years.[8] This level of market penetration has required Apple to invest heavily in the Chinese technology ecosystem.[9] For example, Apple moved its Chinese iCloud operations to Guizhou, China, in response to Beijing's passage of a new cybersecurity law in 2017.[10] It also contracted with the Chinese manufacturer Luxshare Precision Industry to assist in the production of the iPhone 13. In addition, Apple collaborates with Chinese software companies and trains Chinese technology workers, further contributing to local technological development. In return for Apple's local investments, the Chinese government has offered its "necessary support and assistance," including helping ensure that Apple's services such as the App Store, Apple Pay, and iCloud are able to continue to grow in China.[11]

Other US tech companies have a significantly more limited presence in China. These include Google, whose search engine is blocked in mainland China, but as of 2022, still remains operational in Hong Kong. Before abandoning China in 2010, Google held a 30 percent share of the Chinese search engine market, trailing the leading Chinese search engine, Baidu.[12]

When it was still operational in China, Google-owned YouTube had been blocked multiple times, including in the aftermath of the 2008 riots in Tibet. YouTube has not been accessible to Chinese internet users since 2009.[13] The Chinese government has also banned several other Google products, including Gmail, Google Maps, and Google Scholar.[14] Even though many of the company's flagship products are banned in China, some less prominent Google products are available. For example, Google's file management app and translation app can still be downloaded in China.[15] In March 2021, Google's Android was reported to be the most popular operating system among Chinese smartphone users.[16] Google's parent company Alphabet and its subsidiaries, such as Alphabet's driverless-car company Waymo, also continue to invest in Chinese partnerships and projects.[17] Google backed the Chinese e-commerce giant JD.com with a $550 million investment in the company in 2018,[18] and in 2017, Google announced that it would open a new AI research center in China.[19] These continuing investments suggest that Google recognizes the importance of the Chinese market yet remains limited in its ability to fully take advantage of operating in the country.

Microsoft also operates in China, offering a range of products, but ultimately has a small market presence in the country. In 2021, China contributed only 2 percent to Microsoft's global revenue.[20] Microsoft's Windows operating system remains dominant in China, but its Bing search engine—the only major foreign search engine available in China—accounts for less than 4 percent of the search market.[21] Microsoft's videoconferencing platform, Teams, also trails the Chinese tech giants, Tencent and Alibaba, with a similarly modest 4 percent market share.[22] Microsoft's cloud-computing service Azure is also a small player in China with a 2 percent market share, far behind local players Alibaba, Huawei, and Tencent, which are the three largest cloud-computing providers in the country.[23] Microsoft's Office 365 applications suite and Azure are both offered through a partnership with an internet data center services provider, 21Vianet Group—a strategic partnership backed by the Shanghai municipal government.[24] Microsoft is looking to grow its cloud service operations in China with 21Vianet and announced the establishment of a new data center in Hebei, China, scheduled to begin operations in 2022.[25] Yet Microsoft is at the same time retreating from other areas. In October 2021, Microsoft was forced to all but shut down its professional networking site LinkedIn in China after it became increasingly difficult to navigate China's censorship regime.[26] Before the withdrawal, China had been LinkedIn's third-largest market after the US and India, serving over 50 million users.[27]

Meta's Facebook is not accessible in China. The Chinese government first blocked Facebook in 2009 after protesters used the platform to communicate in the wake of riots in China's Xinjiang region.[28] In Facebook's absence, the Chinese social media market is dominated by the large Chinese companies Weibo and WeChat. Facebook has explored ways to comply with Chinese censorship demands in order to regain entry to the Chinese market, but to date these efforts have been unsuccessful.[29] Meta-owned Instagram and WhatsApp are similarly banned in China. Instagram was blocked in 2014 in the wake of pro-democracy protests in Hong Kong,[30] and WhatsApp was blocked in 2017 in preparation for that year's politically sensitive Communist Party congress.[31] However, China remains an important advertising market for Facebook. The company has made a conscious effort to "becom[e] the best marketing platform for Chinese companies going abroad," and this effort appears to be paying off: in 2020 alone, Facebook sold over $5 billion worth of advertising space to private and public Chinese entities.[32]

Amazon is another US tech company that maintains close economic ties in China without offering its e-commerce services there. Amazon closed its e-commerce operations in China in 2019 after concluding it could not compete with local companies Alibaba and Pinduoduo.[33] But even today, many of the most popular products sold on Amazon's US-based e-commerce site come from China.[34] For example, in 2019, a third of the approximately 1,500 suppliers who made Amazon's private-label products were Chinese.[35] Being a marketplace for Chinese products has been at times challenging for Amazon. Following a 2021 crackdown on fake reviews and other banned practices, Amazon removed over 50,000 Chinese shops from its site.[36] Beyond selling Chinese products on Amazon.com, the company's other China-related activities include Amazon Web Services (AWS), which is one of the largest cloud service providers to Chinese companies globally,[37] though in China, AWS still only makes up around 5 percent of the domestic market, in line with Microsoft Azure's market share.[38] In 2021, AWS announced that it was expanding its data centers in Beijing and Ningxia.[39] Some years ago, China was Amazon-owned Kindle's largest market, accounting for roughly 40 percent of the company's global device sales in 2017, though more recent reporting suggests that Kindle is scaling down its operations in China.[40] Yet even this limited presence of Amazon and other US tech giants in China has entailed several compromises, as discussed below.

Capitulate or Leave the Market: US Tech Companies' Acquiescence to China's Demands

Leading US tech giants all face a difficult choice with respect to operating their businesses in China, yet they have generally all made some efforts to acquiesce to the Chinese government's demands. In some instances, through these capitulations, the US companies have chosen to maintain major business operations in China; in others, these companies have faced blowback in the US, leading them to abandon the Chinese market. The choice is particularly fraught as the Chinese market is fast-growing and highly profitable, making it distinctly attractive for any tech company looking to tap into China's nearly one billion internet users.[41] However, operating in China carries a hefty price, as foreign tech companies need to subscribe to local laws that are integral to the Chinese state-driven model but often in tension with the companies' own core values or commitments back home. Most disturbingly, obeying the Chinese government's censorship rules or relinquishing control over user data compromise these foreign companies' commitment to free speech and data privacy. For US tech companies that espouse these principles elsewhere, adherence to local laws sets them on an inevitable collision course with their own governments, global customers, and even employees. Capitulating to authoritarian governments' demands for surveillance and censorship can therefore become a liability for these companies back home. Thus, too often, the choice these companies face is to abandon the values they champion elsewhere in favor of pursuing profits in China or—when that strategy becomes untenable—abandon the Chinese market altogether.

Despite the risk of a backlash in their home countries, the leading US tech companies have all made efforts to adhere to China's demands. To protect Apple's massive investment in China, the company has been forced to make significant compromises on the principles it has championed elsewhere. In addition to acceding to heavy concessions on its data privacy commitments, as described earlier, Apple also proactively censors its Chinese App Store with the help of algorithms and employees who flag and block apps that do not have the approval of the Chinese political leadership.[42] Such censored apps include foreign news services or gay dating services, as well as apps featuring sensitive topics, such as the Dalai Lama and the independence of Taiwan or Tibet, or apps that are used to organize pro-democracy protests. For example, as pro-democracy protests intensified in Hong Kong in 2019, Apple removed an app that helped the protesters track police activity.[43] Apple's app removal decisions in China are often difficult to reconcile with the company's human rights rhetoric in the West. In 2021, Apple removed the Quran app in China.[44] The app is used by millions of Muslims around the world but had to be removed according to Chinese censorship rules because it was "hosting illegal religious texts."[45] The removal of the Quran app stands in stark contrast to Apple's vocal defense of the rights of Muslims in the US, including Apple CEO Tim Cook's criticism of former president

Trump's 2017 decision to restrict the entry of individuals from several Muslim-majority countries to the US.[46] In addition to having its App Store censored, Apple has also acceded to the Chinese government's demands in operating Apple Maps.[47] In 2015, China's State Bureau of Surveying and Mapping ordered Apple Maps to make the contested Diaoyu Islands—or, as the Japanese call them, Senkaku Islands—look bigger on Apple Maps so that they seem more prominent to Chinese users. Apple was thereby thrust in the middle of a longstanding geopolitical dispute between China and Japan. And what did Apple get in return for complying? The Chinese government approved the Apple Watch for domestic sales.[48]

Google has also engaged in repeated efforts to appease the Chinese leadership but ultimately decided that it was untenable for the company to operate its search engine in China. Google first entered China in 2006 with a modified version of its search engine, which excluded from its search results any content censored by the government.[49] Google conceded that it was troubled by its own acquiescence to the Chinese censorship regime but felt that it was ultimately the right thing to do. In a 2006 blogpost, the company noted that "filtering . . . search results clearly compromises [Google's] mission. Failing to offer Google search at all to a fifth of the world's population, however, does so far more severely."[50] Google's decision to capitulate to Chinese censorship laws was not well received back home: the company's executives were questioned before Congress, where the lawmakers compared them to "Nazi collaborators."[51] There was also a popular backlash, with protesters gathering outside the company's California headquarters. Even investors were unsettled, causing the company's stock price to fall.[52]

Google did not have a smooth ride in China, facing repeated cyberattacks in addition to troubling censorship demands. As a result, the company announced in 2010 that it was withdrawing from mainland China, citing its unwillingness to continue to censor its search results.[53] Initially, Google tried to negotiate with the Chinese leadership, conveying its desire to operate an unfiltered search engine. After all, the Chinese government had been somewhat accommodating at first, allowing Google to display a notice acknowledging censorship every time an internet user searched for censored content using Google.cn.[54] However, the Chinese government subsequently tightened its reins and rebuked Google's demands for greater operating freedom. By 2010, the Chinese government had developed its own technology sector to the point that it no longer depended on Silicon Valley for talent or knowledge and felt no need to make compromises.[55] As a result, Google shut down Google.cn and exited the Chinese market. The reversal of Google's China policy was widely acclaimed in the US—the political left and right, business groups, and human

rights advocacy groups all welcomed the company's decision to finally prioritize human rights and free speech concerns over profits in China.[56]

However, the Chinese market remained tempting for Google. In August
2018, reports surfaced that Google was working on a search engine that
would comply with China's censorship laws.[57] By that time, this effort—
internally known as "Project Dragonfly"—had already proceeded to the
stage of discussions between Chinese officials and Google CEO Sundar
Pichai, with the new search engine apparently ready to be launched within
six to nine months. After the news about Project Dragonfly broke, the backlash was fierce. Human rights activists decried Google's effort, as did the
company's own employees. Some Google employees expressed their dismay
on internal messaging platforms, and others declined to work on the project.[58] Hundreds of Google employees also signed a letter, demanding
more transparency regarding work that "raise[s] urgent moral and ethical issues."[59] Given that Project Dragonfly was developed in secret, some
employees wanted to know whether they had unknowingly contributed to
China's censorship regime.[60] Google's own privacy team also raised alarms
after finding out about the project not from internal sources but from the
news media.[61] Congress weighed in, with lawmakers from both parties accusing the company of aiding the Chinese government in its efforts to crack
down on free speech and dissent.[62] At first, Google's leadership was evasive
in responding to questioning by Congress on the company's plans to reenter
China.[63] However, in July 2019, Google's vice president of public policy,
Karan Bhatia, confirmed at a congressional hearing that Project Dragonfly
had been abandoned.[64]

Meta's Facebook has also had to balance the lure of the Chinese market
with the ultimately insurmountable challenges associated with operating in
that market. The company has sought to reenter China numerous times after
being blocked in 2009. In 2016, Facebook was reportedly developing software
that would selectively suppress posts in ways that made the platform compatible with Chinese censorship rules.[65] However, this effort faced both opposition from Facebook employees and concerns from company executives, who
feared backlash among Facebook's international userbase.[66] While Facebook
has not since resumed its social media platform in the country, in 2017 it
launched a photo-sharing application, "Colorful Balloons," in China—without
publicly disclosing the app's affiliation with Facebook.[67] The app was released
by a Chinese company called Youge Internet Technology, and users accessed
it through the Chinese messaging app WeChat. Colorful Balloons provides
Facebook with valuable intelligence on how Chinese users engage online,
including how they share information with their friends.[68] However, it is

unclear if Facebook can ever leverage this information to reenter the Chinese market with its own social media platform.

Meta itself continues to insist that it is not entering the Chinese market due to a misalignment of values, with the company's CEO Mark Zuckerberg noting in 2018 that Facebook "need[s] to figure out a solution that is in line with [its] principles and what [it] want[s] to do, and in line with the laws [in China], or else it's not going to happen. Right now, there isn't an intersection."[69] In recent years, Meta has become one of the most vocal China critics among the large US tech companies, pledging in 2019 not to build data centers in countries with "a track record of violating human rights like privacy or freedom of expression" and noting that the company "could never come to agreement on what it would take" for Facebook to operate in China.[70] However, critics are quick to point out that the Chinese government makes extensive use of Facebook's platform outside of China to spread its propaganda.[71] It deploys Facebook to advance its policy positions and shape the global narrative about China. The government has also used Facebook to track down individuals who have voiced critical opinions about China abroad, including tracing those individuals' connections to China. This suggests that Facebook may not be able to completely avoid the obvious "values misalignment" by choosing not to operate in China.

The examples of Apple, Google, and Facebook outlined above all point to the same pattern: acts of defiance by US tech companies are rare, and acquiescence to the Chinese government's demands is common. Amazon is another company whose approach fits this pattern. Like Facebook, Amazon has a modest presence in China but has still been accused of submitting to demands from the Chinese government. The company has acknowledged that its core challenge in China is Beijing's desire for "ideological control and propaganda."[72] To navigate this challenge, Amazon has pursued a policy of acquiescence coupled with some resistance. In 2018, Amazon reportedly tried to "win favor in Beijing" in an effort to grow its cloud computing and e-commerce business, a part of which involved securing a license to sell Kindle devices and e-books in the country.[73] As a concession to the Chinese government, Amazon agreed to create a so-called China Books selling portal on the company's US-based Amazon.com e-commerce site, featuring 90,000 publications for sale.[74] While many titles were apolitical, some amplified government propaganda, featuring titles such as "Incredible Xinjiang: Stories of Passion and Heritage" or "Stories of Courage and Determination: Wuhan in Coronavirus Lockdown." The deal can be described as a classic win-win collaboration: the China Books project helped Amazon resolve the licensing problems it had encountered when selling e-books in China and, at the same time, gave the Chinese government the kind of visibility it was seeking in the US. To fend off criticism of its collaboration with China's propaganda apparatus on the China Books project, Amazon emphasized how the company, as a bookseller, ought to provide access to "diverse perspectives," including books that "some may find objectionable."[75]

Like most other US tech companies, Amazon has sought to navigate the Chinese regulatory environment by partnering with local companies and thus shielding itself from direct contact with the country's censorship and propaganda apparatus. For the China Books project, Amazon partnered with a state-owned company, China International Book Trading Corp.[76] To operate Amazon Web Services (AWS), Amazon handed off the content moderation task to a local company called Beijing Sinnet Technology, which dealt with the Chinese authorities' compliance requests.[77] For example, it was Beijing Sinnet Technology that instructed local AWS users to cease using circumvention software that had allowed them to bypass some of the content prohibited by Chinese censors.[78] Amazon also pushed back on some censorship demands. In February 2018, for instance, China's Ministry of Public Security threatened to retaliate against the company unless it blocked a US-based website for Guo Wengui, a Chinese dissident. Apparently, AWS initially refused, stressing that the Chinese government should not issue requests relating to data stored abroad. However, Amazon reportedly provided the Chinese authorities with Guo Wengui's IP address as a sign of partial accommodation of the regulators' demands. When Amazon was asked about this specific incident, it confirmed that the company had received the Chinese government's request, but said it "did not provide any non-public information or any other customer information."[79] In another 2019 incident, Amazon was asked to remove any negative reviews of President Xi's books on Amazon.cn, leaving only five-star reviews. Amazon complied, yet did so by disabling all reviews, ratings, and comments—not only negative ones—relating to that title.[80] As with the other tech companies, for Amazon, the choice has been either to acquiesce to the Chinese state's demands or leave the market.

Microsoft, the last of the big five US tech companies, has also encountered Chinese censorship demands, putting the company at odds with its core values. Despite evident ethical conflicts, Microsoft has acquiesced to China's censorship demands in order to maintain access to its markets, both historically and more recently. In 2005, Microsoft agreed to the Chinese government's request to shut down the MSN Spaces site of Chinese journalist Zhao Jing after he endorsed a boycott of Beijing News in one of his MSN blogs.[81] MSN Spaces was Microsoft's blogging platform and social network service that operated from 2004 to 2011. Microsoft's Bing and LinkedIn have also had to navigate the Chinese government's censorship rules. For example, if a Chinese user searches for the name "Dalai Lama" using the Bing search engine, the user will not be directed to the Wikipedia page of the spiritual leader and former head of state of Tibet, but to a state-controlled media site that accuses the Dalai Lama of inciting hatred and separatism.[82] Microsoft's professional networking site LinkedIn was also forced to censor content that was politically sensitive in order to operate in China.[83] The company acknowledged that it was compromising on its commitment to free speech, yet justified this because of its "belief that the creation of economic opportunity can have a profound impact on the lives of Chinese individuals, much as it has elsewhere in the world."[84] Despite LinkedIn's efforts to comply, in March 2021, the Chinese authorities reproached the company for "failing to control political content."[85] LinkedIn's position became even more untenable as it was simultaneously being criticized by US lawmakers for "gross appeasement and an act of submission to Communist China."[86] In late 2021, LinkedIn announced that it was shutting down its professional networking service in China, citing "a significantly more challenging operating environment and greater compliance requirements," and offering a new, considerably more limited app focused solely on job postings.[87]

As these examples of the decisions by Apple, Google, Facebook, Amazon, and Microsoft make clear, US tech companies repeatedly acquiesce to the Chinese government's demands in an effort to operate in China's large and dynamic tech market. The choice for these companies is simple: to capitulate or leave. Despite the companies' past willingness to prioritize commercial considerations and capitulate, the pressure to leave is increasing with the growing anti-China sentiment in the US. When accused of submitting to authoritarian demands, US tech companies offer a predictable response and simply retort that they follow the local law. For example, Apple has defended its practices in China by emphasizing its commitment to offer the best possible user experience "without violating the rules [it is] obligated to follow."[88] Before pulling out of China, Microsoft's LinkedIn justified its compliance with the Chinese government's demands by issuing a statement: "We're a global platform with an obligation to respect the laws that apply to us, including adhering to Chinese government regulations for our localized version of LinkedIn in China."[89] In response to the criticism of its China policies, Amazon gave a similar statement, stressing that the company "complies with all applicable laws and regulations . . . and China is no exception."[90]

While most of the US tech companies' struggles in China relate to Chinese authorities' censorship demands, some US tech firms have been accused of assisting the Chinese surveillance state by providing relevant hardware or software to the Chinese authorities. For example, the US semiconductor companies Intel and Nvidia have supplied products to a Chinese supercomputing center in Urumqi, Xinjiang, that is accused of tracking minorities, thereby contributing to their repression in the region.[91] The US companies have defended their conduct by arguing that they have limited ability to control where their products ultimately end up or how they are being used. In this particular instance concerning the Urumqi supercomputing center, Intel and Nvidia had not sold their semiconductors to the Chinese government, but to a Chinese company Sugon, which also supplies various ordinary Chinese companies with no relationship to the Chinese security services. A leading US software company Oracle has also faced accusations that its technologies are deployed by Chinese law enforcement authorities in criminal analysis and prediction.[92] In 2021, Oracle was reported to have marketed its data analytics software to the Chinese police. The company's leaked marketing materials explained how the Oracle technologies could assist the Chinese police to combine information from social media, DNA databases, and government records. When asked to comment on the marketing materials, the Oracle spokesperson referred to them as "aspirational business development ideas" as opposed to intended or targeted sales materials.[93]

This kind of criticism where US tech companies are accused of breaching US values—or even US law—to facilitate China's authoritarian practices often places these companies in untenable positions. In 2021, Intel was scolded for sourcing products from Xinjiang, which is subject to US sanctions due to human rights violations in the region.[94] Given the public pressure and Western sanctions—including the US Senate passing the Uyghur Forced Labor Prevention Act—Intel published a letter instructing its suppliers to discontinue sourcing supplies from the region. However, Intel's letter caused an uproar in the Chinese state media and across social media platforms in the country, forcing Intel to issue an apology to its Chinese customers and the general public. Intel's apology clarified that the company's ban on Xinjiang supplies was aimed at compliance with US law without representing the company's own position on controversies surrounding Xinjiang. Intel's decision to issue an apology is not surprising given that the Chinese market accounts for one-quarter of its global revenue.[95] Intel's balancing act with respect to Xinjiang further illustrates the difficulty for any US tech company to navigate the demands of both Washington and Beijing—demands that are increasingly difficult to reconcile.

The conflict of values that US tech companies face when operating in China is particularly notable given the economic importance of the Chinese market and the geopolitical salience of US–China relationships. However,

China is hardly the only country where US companies face this kind of conflict. There are other authoritarian countries that require American platforms to moderate content in ways that force them to engage in censorship and thus compromise their commitment to free speech. For example, Facebook has been accused of "bending to the will of Arab despots" in removing the accounts of hundreds of activists or deleting "hundreds of thousands" of their posts in the Middle East, even while claiming that it is giving "free expression maximum possible range" in the region.[96] In 2020, Amnesty International accused Facebook and YouTube of complicity in "industrial-scale repression" in Vietnam, acceding to the Vietnamese government's demand to censor posts critical of the government.[97]

In Russia, President Putin has tightened his grip over the Russian internet sphere, forcing US tech companies into increasingly troubling compromises. For example, Apple and Google agreed in 2021 to delete the Smart Voting app, which was used by the party of the opposition leader, Aleksei Navalny, to organize an election campaign against President Putin.[98] After Russia's invasion of Ukraine, US tech companies have found themselves caught in the middle of a high-stakes information war.[99] To comply with the EU's sanctions against Russia, US platforms such as Facebook, Microsoft, Netflix, Twitter, and YouTube blocked or limited access to Russian state-sponsored media to limit the reach of Russian propaganda about the war.[100] In response, Russia has blocked certain platforms, including Facebook, Instagram, and Twitter, though hundreds of thousands of Russians still seek to use virtual private networks to circumvent the ban.[101] Even if US tech companies no longer operate in Russia, they continue to face difficult content moderation decisions surrounding the war on a daily basis. While these markets pose an enduring challenge to US tech companies, abandoning a market like Russia is not nearly as costly as forgoing access to China and its one billion internet users. As a result, the decision of whether or not to abandon the Chinese market remains the most consequential one for most leading US tech companies.

When left with the choice of capitulating to the Chinese government or leaving the country, US tech companies feel there is no obvious answer as to what the right strategy is. In the early days of the internet, there might have been a stronger argument for submitting to China's demands. Back then, the provision of even censored access to information may have been better than ceding the market to local companies that have few incentives to test the boundaries of the Chinese censorship regime. Engagement through presence was also seen as valuable, coupled with hopes that a change toward a free internet and free society in China was eventually forthcoming. However, there are few illusions left that these companies are making inroads toward bringing democracy to or changing human rights practices in China. If anything, the regulatory demands are tightening and the operating space for these companies is narrowing. The economic rewards for staying are also questionable given the Chinese government's provision of subsidies to domestic companies, which makes it difficult for American tech companies to compete against local tech giants. Also, any concessions are even harder to justify today with growing anti-China sentiment back home, including in the US Congress. There are increasing pressures in the US for tech companies to decouple their business relations from China, and the companies have come to realize that the conflicting demands they face can, in the end, be impossible to reconcile.

In their battle against the Chinese government, few believe that US companies will prevail. Back home in the West, US tech companies may occasionally feel that they are more powerful than the national governments trying to regulate them—but it is doubtful that they can outmuscle the Chinese state. As one commentator recently concluded: "I know people in Silicon Valley are really smart, and they're really successful because they can overcome any problem they face," but "I don't think they've ever faced a problem like the Chinese Communist Party."[102]

Chinese Tech Companies' Vertical Battles in the US: Caught Between American and Chinese National Security Concerns

The previous section illustrated difficult decisions US tech companies encounter when they operate in China and face the conflicting demands of the Chinese state-driven regulatory model and the American market-driven regulatory model. Traditionally, Chinese tech companies have not encountered similar challenges in the US. The American market-driven regulatory model has kept the US market open to all foreign, including Chinese, companies. The two sets of vertical battles have therefore been highly asymmetrical to date, with Beijing imposing restrictions on American companies operating in China, yet Washington historically declining to reciprocate with similar restrictions on Chinese companies operating in the US. However, the intensifying US–China tech war is now causing the US to reassess this existing asymmetry. The US government is increasingly retreating from its market-driven principles and allowing national security considerations to dominate its policymaking. This is complicating Chinese tech companies' efforts to gain access to, and succeed in, the US market.

Chinese Tech Companies' Presence in the US:
A Brief Overview

Few Chinese tech companies have established a significant footprint in the US to date. Despite their rapid growth over the past decade, most Chinese companies have focused on their protected home market. The lack of US expansion, however, has not been due to US government restrictions—at least until recently. Despite the relative openness of the US market, only a few Chinese tech companies have gained traction in the US. TikTok has been the most successful Chinese tech company abroad to date, surpassing Facebook and Google in 2021 as the world's most popular web domain.[103] TikTok straddles the geopolitical divide: it is owned by its Chinese parent company ByteDance, which offers essentially the same short video app in China, known there as Douyin.[104] The Chinese fast fashion e-commerce company Shein is another example of a globally successful Chinese tech company. By 2022, the Shein shopping app had been downloaded more times in the US than Amazon.[105] The company comprised 28 percent of US fast fashion sales, ahead of popular brands such as H&M and Zara.[106] Shein's staggering growth over the past years has made it the biggest online fashion brand in the world. While the company is wildly successful abroad, interestingly, it is hardly known in China.

Shein and TikTok are rare examples of Chinese tech companies prospering in the US market. Most others have struggled to win market share in the US. Kuaishou, Douyin's rival in China, tried to launch a US app called Zine, but admitted a failure after it could not put a dent in TikTok's American market share.[107] Similarly, bilibili, a Chinese video platform roughly comparable to YouTube, has not gained popularity in the US.[108] Baidu and DiDi—which have clear US analogues in Google and Uber or Lyft, respectively—have likewise not been able to challenge the US incumbents in their home market.[109] In the past, these Chinese companies' struggles could have been explained by reasons such as the absence of a well-executed international expansion strategy, as the American regulatory model itself imposed few restrictions on them; going forward, however, their struggles may increasingly be attributed to US government measures as the US is moving away from its commitment to open markets and other principles that have defined its regulatory model to date.

Banning Chinese Apps in the US: TikTok and WeChat

Since the onset of the more active phase of the US–China tech war over the last few years, the US government has rapidly accelerated its regulatory shift toward a more stringent oversight of Chinese tech companies. For example, the Chinese communications technology giant Huawei—perhaps the most high-profile casualty of the US–China tech war—has endured crippling US export and investment restrictions since 2018. These restrictions have limited the company's access to essential supplies from US tech companies while also closing it off from 5G infrastructure projects across the US, as discussed in Chapter 5. But the sanctions against Huawei can be seen as merely the beginning of a new era of a tightly managed digital economy. In some instances, conflicts between the Chinese and American regulatory models have become intractable, making them exceedingly difficult to resolve. Intractable conflicts can be defined as those where a company cannot comply with the laws of one government without violating those of another. Tech companies are thus caught between two sets of irreconcilable legal obligations, forced to do what they always try to avoid doing: choosing sides. This inability by companies to resolve the regulatory conflicts will have significant consequences, setting in motion the decoupling of the digital economy and thus contributing to the existing trend toward "deglobalization" as a defining force shaping international economic and political relations.

Following sanctions on Huawei and other Chinese hardware companies, Chinese social media companies—including the popular video-sharing app TikTok—have now also become a target of US government restrictions.[110] This may not be surprising given that TikTok is the first large Chinese tech company that has managed to break into the US (and global) markets, challenging its US rivals and thus embodying China's ascendant technological power. As of 2020, TikTok has been downloaded 165 million times in the US alone.[111] Beyond those commercial considerations, TikTok's prominence has raised national security concerns. The company has unparalleled access to the data of over 100 million American internet users,[112] which gives it unprecedented influence over the American public. The US government fears that this influence will ultimately be wielded not just by TikTok but by the Chinese Communist Party (CCP). As a Chinese corporation, TikTok's parent company ByteDance must obey Chinese law, including the Chinese government's potential requests for the data that the company accumulates. For example, Republican Senator Josh Hawley has called TikTok "a surveillance apparatus for Beijing" and "a Trojan horse on people's phones."[113] President Trump warned in 2020 that TikTok posed a national security threat as its data collection could facilitate corporate espionage or be used for blackmailing individuals.[114] In essence, the US concern about TikTok is twofold. First, Chinese authorities may access American users' personal data. Second, the Chinese leadership may influence TikTok's content moderation policies, potentially exposing US users to the CCP's propaganda. Thus, TikTok poses a concern both in terms of the information it collects and the information it disseminates—with either activity potentially serving the interests of Beijing.[115]

ByteDance has sought to alleviate these concerns by separating its Chinese and US businesses. The company operates TikTok in the US and a separate (yet near-identical) app called Douyin in China. TikTok's management is based in the US, and the company insists that its content moderation decisions are made in the US. US-based users' data is further stored in the US and in Singapore, not in China.[116] However, it is not evident that such data localization prevents Beijing from requesting the data of American users and ultimately obtaining it.[117] It remains unclear—either as a matter of law or in practice—how the company would handle such a request from Beijing for foreign data.[118]

These concerns prompted the US government to take exceptional measures against TikTok in 2020. In August 2020, President Trump announced that TikTok would be shut down in the US if it was not bought by a US company by September 15.[119] Three days later, President Trump signed an executive order to ban TikTok in the US in forty-five days, alleging that TikTok's data collection practices allowed the CCP to access Americans' personal information, including those of overseas Chinese citizens.[120] President Trump then followed with a separate executive order giving ByteDance ninety days to divest its American assets and destroy any data that TikTok had gathered in the United States.[121] After a frantic search for a suitable buyer, a month later TikTok had reached a proposed deal under which Texas-headquartered Oracle would acquire the company.[122]

The executive order alone placed TikTok in a perilous position, imperiling its ability to continue to operate in the US. But what further deepened the company's travails was the Chinese government's reaction to the US measure. After the US government ordered the sale of the company to a US buyer, the Chinese government responded by extending its export control regime to "technology based on data analysis for personalized information recommendation services," thus making the export of any such technology conditional on obtaining a government license.[123] This definition likely covers TikTok since the company's app relies on algorithms that deploy user data to generate personalized content for app users. As a result, the Chinese government's amended export control regime risked making the sale required under US law an illegal action under Chinese law. This move by Beijing transformed the battle over the fate of TikTok into an intractable conflict where it is impossible for TikTok to comply with orders from both the US and Chinese governments. As a result, TikTok knew that it would likely need to pull out of the US market or find itself in violation of either US or Chinese law.

However, what came to TikTok's rescue, at least temporarily, was the US courts. In parallel with negotiating the forced sale, TikTok filed a motion for a preliminary injunction before the US District Court for the District of Columbia (DDC) in September 2020.[124] The District Court ruled in favor of TikTok later that month, reasoning that the ban would cause irreparable commercial harm to the company, while adding that the government's action likely exceeded the bounds of its lawful authority.[125] In December 2020, the court preliminarily blocked all provisions of the government's request to ban TikTok in the US, ruling that President Trump's emergency economic powers did not suffice to operate an arbitrary ban on a mobile app.[126] After his election, President Biden revoked his predecessor's order and requested a Commerce Department review of the security concerns posed by TikTok.[127] As of August 2022, the review is still pending, which has frustrated some US lawmakers.[128] The Biden administration's slow progress on the issue led a group of House Republicans to write a letter to Commerce Secretary Gina Raimondo, expressing their concern that the administration was doing nothing to protect Americans' data from being accessed by Chinese entities.[129]

The Trump administration's attempt to force a sale of WeChat to a US company reveals similar dynamics. WeChat is a ubiquitous social media app used by Chinese citizens both within China and overseas.[130] In the US, the app is particularly popular among Chinese Americans who use it to keep in touch with their family and friends in China.[131] The Trump administration grew concerned about WeChat's data collection practices, fearing that the CCP could access Americans' personal information while also using WeChat to keep tabs on overseas Chinese citizens.[132] As a result, in August 2020, President Trump signed an executive order to ban WeChat in the US within forty-five days.[133] The following month, the US Department of Commerce announced a plan to ban WeChat transactions in the US by September 20, 2020.[134] Like TikTok, WeChat also challenged the government order before US courts and won some notable victories. The District Court of the Northern District of California held that "certainly the government's overarching national-security interest is significant. But on this record—while the government has established that China's activities raise significant national security concerns—it has put in scant little evidence that its effective ban of WeChat for all U.S. users addresses those concerns."[135] The court also pointed out the availability of less restrictive alternatives to a complete ban, including barring WeChat from government devices, akin to what Australia had recently done.[136] Consistent with his policy toward TikTok, President Biden revoked President Trump's

executive order in June 2021, yet ordered the Commerce Department to review the security concerns posed by WeChat.[137]

The TikTok and WeChat battles represent a significant shift in the US
government's policy toward Chinese tech companies. But those two regulatory
battles are also remarkable in revealing how Chinese tech companies can successfully deploy the US legal system to defend themselves. A similar strategy
is rarely available in China where courts are not independent from the CCP's
influence. As a result, tech companies, whether domestic or foreign, seldom
challenge the Chinese government orders before courts. However, while these
court victories in the US will likely embolden other Chinese tech companies
to contest any subsequent government restrictions, the US legal system may
not always safeguard those companies' interests. As a result, Chinese tech
companies will likely continue to face regulatory challenges in the US. For
example, in the WeChat litigation, the Northern District of California acknowledged in principle that Chinese companies and technologies threatened
US national security—in this particular case, however, the government had
simply failed to marshal the requisite evidence to prevail.[138] The WeChat case
also reveals that even communications by ordinary citizens can be viewed by
the court as related to "national security."[139] While the December 2020 court
ruling helped TikTok secure a short-term victory, the DDC suggested in its
opinion that alternative US government actions short of a complete ban can
still be legal.[140] For example, the government could still use the CFIUS process to require ByteDance to divest its stake in TikTok.[141] And despite TikTok's
court victories, Republicans in Congress continue to pressure the company on
data privacy concerns,[142] with some members still calling for the app to completely sever its ties with its Chinese parent company.[143]

The battle that the US government has waged against TikTok is not
without its critics, even among American commentators. In deliberating
its next steps against the social media company, the US government thus
needs to weigh both the growing resentment against China and TikTok's
operations on the one hand, and the criticism of any hardline strategy on
the other. Some voices call for restraint and warn that, by banning Chinese
tech companies, the US is deviating too far from the core principles underlying its own American market-driven regulatory model. At the same
time, others urge the US government to maintain its heightened regulatory scrutiny and, if anything, escalate its regulatory measures toward
Chinese tech companies. The proponents of a more assertive approach can
also point to other governments' growing efforts to restrict TikTok's operations, suggesting that the US concerns are legitimate and extend beyond
US–China strategic competition. For example, India recently banned TikTok

and WeChat, together with over fifty other Chinese apps, arguing that they pose a national security threat to the country.[144] The security threat posed by TikTok is also a source of contention in other Western countries. For example, the UK Parliament quickly shut down its new TikTok account after some members objected to the Chinese government's access to user data.[145] The EU will also likely apply its recently adopted Digital Services Act, discussed in Chapter 3, to require TikTok to reveal more information about how its algorithms moderate content.[146] These mounting vertical battles that TikTok is now facing in different parts of the world may give the US additional impetus to press ahead with its own battle, while adding legitimacy to any measures the US takes against the company.

American political leadership and the general public are, no doubt, increasingly concerned about China's growing global influence. This concern about Chinese governmental influence also directly extends to a concern about the role of Chinese companies operating in the US, not least because of the closely intertwined relationship between Chinese companies and the CCP. In addition to being distrustful of China, Americans have grown increasingly suspicious of tech companies' digital surveillance practices. It is thus not surprising that the unease about the combination of the two concerns—a company that is both *Chinese-owned* and that is engaging in *digital surveillance*—is widespread, intensifying the US government's resolve to press ahead with its battle against a company like TikTok. Some US tech companies have also actively pushed the narrative that Chinese companies are untrustworthy, with the goal of keeping these China-focused vertical battles alive. For example, Meta reportedly hired a consulting firm to run a nationwide public relations campaign against TikTok, with the goal of portraying the Chinese-owned company as "a danger to American children and society."[147] Meta's Mark Zuckerberg also publicly criticized Chinese companies' censorship practices in a 2019 Georgetown speech on free expression: "If another nation's platforms set the rules, our discourse will be defined by a completely different set of values . . . We should also be proactive and write policy that helps the values of voice and expression triumph around the world."[148]

It is expected that a company like Meta will urge the US government to go after TikTok—after all, TikTok arguably poses the gravest competitive threat to Meta's own social media platforms. But several other prominent US voices with no such commercial incentives also support a tough line against companies such as TikTok. These include Professor Tim Wu—a former advisor to President Biden on antitrust and technology policy—who has argued that the "TikTok ban is overdue."[149] Wu's argument revolves around reciprocity.

While conceding that threats to ban Chinese apps can be seen as a "belligerent" departure from the US's commitment to the open internet, Wu argues that such a departure is a justifiable, tit-for-tat reciprocity strategy toward a China that promotes "net nationalism" and blocks foreign content from its domestic markets. The Chinese government has closed off its own internet economy while Chinese tech companies have benefited from open markets in the US and elsewhere in the world. "The asymmetry," according to Wu, "is unfair and ought no longer be tolerated."[150] Instead, "the privilege of full internet access—the open internet—should be extended only to companies from countries that respect that openness themselves."[151]

The banning of TikTok in the name of reciprocity would, indeed, accomplish the goal of greater symmetry in US–China relations. But critics caution that this symmetry would come at a price. In banning Chinese apps, the US can be accused of playing Beijing's game and giving up on the values underlying its own market-driven regulatory model, which cherishes freedom of commerce and the open internet. Consider the WeChat ban that the Trump administration announced. Chinese Americans have few alternatives to using WeChat to communicate with family and friends in China since US-based apps such as WhatsApp and Facebook Messenger are prohibited there.[152] When the ban was announced, some US-based WeChat users indicated that they were planning to do what their Chinese friends had done for a long time: use a virtual private network (VPN) to "circumvent the new great firewall of America."[153] Similarly, by banning TikTok, the US can be seen as endorsing—even if unwittingly—the Chinese state-driven regulatory model that lets the government determine what internet users can and cannot see.[154] With these bans, the US can be accused of contributing to the global trend of fragmenting the internet. Some commentators have adopted this view, arguing that "the United States, like China, no longer believes in [the] global internet" and pointing out how the US is now "promoting a fundamentally Chinese view of internet security."[155] In this way, the US government is faced with a quandary of whether it is "defending [its] values by undermining them."[156] Thus, the battle over TikTok's future in the US is also likely to shape the broader global battle over the values that govern the digital economy. If the US—as the most vocal champion of an open and free internet—abandons those principles and realigns instead with Chinese state-driven policies for the sake of reciprocity, those American values around openness and freedom are unlikely to guide or inspire other governments' digital policies going forward.

This realignment of the American regulatory model in order to force the sale of TikTok to a US company may be even more questionable if it fails to resolve the national security concerns motivating the sale. Storing TikTok's data locally in the US would not necessarily ensure its security, as various incidents of Chinese cyberespionage targeting data located in the US reveal.[157] An additional concern is that the forced sale of the company does little to mitigate the other security concern—namely, the manipulation of the content that Americans consume. This concern has less to do with who owns the company and more to do with who writes the algorithms that empower the app. It was not clear that Oracle—the winning bidder in TikTok's forced sale—intended to replace TikTok's Chinese engineers or assume control over the algorithms moderating the content. In contrast, Microsoft—a competing bidder for TikTok—had indicated that it was going to take over the source code and the algorithms immediately, and move the product development to the US.[158] Furthermore, putting a US company in charge might also not protect the data from the Chinese government. Oracle has been accused of having forged close links with the Chinese government, as discussed earlier.[159] The likely ineffectiveness of the TikTok divestment therefore raises the question of whether it is truly motivated by national security concerns or whether the decision is driven by commercial considerations—making the attempted ban resemble the economic protectionism typically associated with the Chinese state-driven regulatory model.

Whether the US bans Chinese tech companies like TikTok or WeChat from its market or not, it is evident that the ongoing struggle with China is fostering a shift in the American market-driven regulatory model. Some commentators have suggested that instead of emulating the Chinese state-driven model as a solution to its concerns about TikTok, the US could emulate the European rights-driven model and adopt its own version of the General Data Protection Regulation (GDPR). Under such a regime, the US would have a solid legal foundation to address broader concerns relating to data protection, which would be superior to its haphazard attempts to ban certain foreign apps.[160] Such a comprehensive regulatory scheme would establish overarching rules for data collection, use, and storage, and formalize the process according to which individuals and public authorities can protect their privacy and security interests. Instead, the bans on individual apps may only distract the US from the task of developing comprehensive solutions to protect data privacy and national security—both of which are under threat and lacking effective policy solutions.[161] An all-encompassing data privacy regime could also help the US in its dealings with the Chinese and Europeans alike: in addition to allowing the US to respond to the threat of Chinese tech companies' data collection, it would also help resolve the regulatory battles over data privacy with the Europeans, as discussed in Chapter 6.

Restricting Chinese Listings in the US: DiDi Chuxing

TikTok is not the only Chinese tech company finding itself caught between irreconcilable demands of American and Chinese regulators. Such intractable conflicts now also threaten Chinese tech companies listed on US stock exchanges. The stock market has become an increasingly heated battlefield as of late, raising the risks of a financial decoupling of the US and China. The 2021 New York Stock Exchange (NYSE) listing of DiDi Chuxing, a Chinese ride-hailing company comparable to Uber or Lyft, illustrates this evolution well. In June 2021, DiDi rushed ahead to publicly list itself on the NYSE before it had received full clearance from Chinese regulators on their cybersecurity concerns.[162] The backlash from regulators was swift: two days after the company's IPO, the Cyberspace Administration of China (CAC) announced that it was initiating a cybersecurity review of DiDi, and DiDi's app was soon taken off app stores in China.[163] According to the CAC, the app violated laws on collecting and using personal information.[164] DiDi was also banned from enlisting any new drivers.[165] DiDi's overseas listing raised particular red flags for Chinese regulators because, as a ride-hailing provider, the company had access to sensitive troves of location and map data. When the government initiated its probe, DiDi was reported as having 377 million annual active users, allowing it to amass data on over 25 million daily rides and thus granting the company access to the world's largest repository of real-world traffic data.[166] This data could be used to track rides to and from the Ministry of Public Security and other government departments, thus raising potential national security concerns.[167] Given these concerns, the Chinese government sent inspection teams from at least seven cybersecurity-related agencies to the company's offices for on-site review.[168] While cybersecurity reviews in China typically last for sixty days, DiDi's review finally wrapped up in July 2022, a full year after it was initiated.[169] In the end, Chinese regulators issued a $1.2 billion fine against DiDi—the largest fine issued by the Chinese government in any data protection breach case.[170]

The effects of the CAC decision for DiDi and the company's investors have been dire. The unanticipatedly harsh cybersecurity review sent the company's newly listed stock into a tailspin, plummeting investor value while casting uncertainty over DiDi's—and any other Chinese company's—ability to remain listed on US stock exchanges. In February 2022, the company announced that it would be laying off 20 percent of its staff.[171] By that time, DiDi shares had lost 70 percent of their value since their IPO price.[172] In December 2021, DiDi announced that it was going to delist from the NYSE[173] and offered US stockholders the option to transfer their shares over to the Hong Kong Stock

Exchange, where the company now intends to list.[174] DiDi is also facing at least two class action lawsuits from US stockholders, alleging that the company failed to accurately disclose its communications with the Chinese government.[175]

While DiDi's fall from grace has been especially dramatic, the saga is part of an ongoing, heightened regulatory scrutiny of US-listed Chinese companies on both sides of the Pacific. Both the US and China are intensifying their scrutiny of Chinese companies but their respective measures pull these companies in different directions: the US is seeking greater disclosure from Chinese companies listed in the US while China is focused on limiting any such disclosure to foreign authorities. This heightened scrutiny may encourage a broader decoupling of global digital and financial markets, especially when companies cannot simultaneously comply with different regulators' conflicting demands.

For its part, the US has been particularly concerned that American investors do not have the full picture of regulatory risks facing Chinese companies, exposing them to unanticipated losses such as those that materialized in the case of DiDi. The US Securities and Exchange Commission (SEC) and Nasdaq have already noted that Chinese companies may pose unique financial risks because of their lack of auditing transparency.[176] At the end of 2020, the US Congress passed the Holding Foreign Companies Accountable Act, which increases US regulators' rights to inspect audits of foreign public companies.[177] The legislation prohibits trading of a company's shares in the US if its auditors fail to comply with the auditing transparency requirements for three consecutive years.[178] In December 2021, the SEC finalized a rule implementing the legislation, which forces Chinese companies listed on US stock exchanges to "disclose whether they are owned or controlled by a government entity, and provide evidence of their auditing inspections."[179]

The new SEC rules also require Chinese companies to provide more information about the variable interest entity (VIE) structure that is common among US-listed Chinese companies. Indeed, 79 percent of the 241 Chinese companies listed in New York in 2021 rely on VIEs, including tech giants such as Alibaba, Pinduoduo, JD.com, NIO, and Baidu.[180] The VIE structure is an arrangement that allows Chinese companies to evade restrictive Chinese laws on foreign ownership by creating a shell company, often in the Cayman Islands or another similar jurisdiction, which contracts with the China-based operating company. The VIE can then issue shares on a foreign stock exchange.[181] In the wake of the developments surrounding DiDi's IPO, SEC Chair Gary Gensler issued a letter saying he was worried that "average investors may not realize that they hold stock in a shell company rather than a China-based operating company."[182] The SEC has since laid out the type of disclosures it expects from

Chinese companies operating under the VIE structure, given their increased complexity and potential financial risk.[183]

Meanwhile, China has pushed its companies to share less, not more, information with US regulators, setting the stage for a direct clash between the two regulatory regimes. First, China passed its Cybersecurity Law in 2017, which required companies that qualify as "critical information infrastructure operators" to store Chinese data locally and undergo a security assessment before being cleared to transfer any of that data overseas.[184] After the DiDi incident, the CAC announced in July 2021 that it was further tightening regulatory requirements; the regulator mandated that Chinese tech companies possessing the personal data of at least one million Chinese users must submit to a cybersecurity review before proceeding with an IPO in a foreign market.[185] The government further strengthened restrictions on data flows by adopting the Personal Information Protection Law (PIPL),[186] which focuses on personal data, and the Data Security Law (DSL),[187] which focuses on data processing.[188] Both laws came into effect in fall 2021.[189] The PIPL limits private companies' collection of personal information and restricts cross-border transfers of such information.[190] The DSL targets data that has a "potential impact on Chinese national security" and regulates the processing, storage, and transfer of such data.[191] Under the DSL, such data cannot be transferred to foreign authorities absent the requisite government authorization. The cumulative effect of these regulations is to make it considerably more difficult for Chinese multinational companies to comply with foreign regulators' requests for information.[192]

These competing rules enacted by the US and China have placed US-listed Chinese companies in an unenviable position. But they have also presented these Chinese companies' American auditing firms with difficult regulatory dilemmas. One investor in the industry noted how a direct clash now exists between Chinese and American law: "It's the Chinese regulators who are preventing the U.S. regulators from inspecting the audits . . . These companies are all audited by the Big Four accounting firms, but under Chinese law regulators are not allowing those audits to be sent to US regulators."[193] The large US auditors—Deloitte, EY, PwC, and KPMG—dominate the auditing market in China and are in charge of audits for around 140 Chinese companies listed in the US, even as these auditing companies must operate through local Chinese partnerships.[194] These firms now face the risk of either running afoul of Chinese regulators who do not want them to share financial records with US regulators or US regulators who demand they do exactly that. This illustrates how even the auditing firms are now being caught in the middle of the China–US regulatory clash.

This clash can have wide-reaching implications. At worst, it may lead to the decoupling of the US and Chinese stock markets, with approximately 2 trillion dollars of Chinese company stock listed on US stock exchanges at stake.[195] This is an unsettling prospect for many entities on both sides. Chinese companies like DiDi, ByteDance, and Ant Group could lose access to US capital markets.[196] Some smaller Chinese tech companies can also be adversely affected. For example, audiobook and podcast platform Ximalaya recently cancelled its planned US IPO in favor of a Hong Kong listing because of the new, onerous regulatory requirements.[197] Listing in New York has traditionally had advantages over a listing in Hong Kong: New York has deeper and more liquid financial markets and avoids Hong Kong's cumbersome regulatory requirements, including high profitability thresholds.[198] Foreign investors and other entities that stood to make money off of Chinese tech IPOs are also worse off in this new regulatory environment, including underwriters like Goldman Sachs[199] and investors like Softbank, which had poured money into DiDi.[200] Chinese tech companies that proceed with a US listing may also face a "China penalty" as investors and investment banks price in the legal and regulatory risks associated with such a listing.[201] The SEC also stands to lose from this conflict, as the Chinese government has blocked its regulatory access to, and leverage over, some of the world's biggest tech firms. While the winners of this regulatory battle are still unclear, some may include the emboldened Chinese agencies tasked with cybersecurity review powers, certain smaller Chinese tech companies, and China's domestic stock exchanges. For example, Beijing recently opened its own stock exchange. A crackdown on foreign listings may bolster its ability to attract the best Chinese companies to list locally, increasing the prestige and credibility of the Chinese stock market while showing the world that China no longer needs Wall Street.[202]

However, even the Chinese government is sensitive to the costs involved in total stock market decoupling. As a result, the seemingly irresolvable US–China conflicts are also marked by pressures toward restraint. In December 2021, the China Securities Regulatory Commission (CSRC) released new rules on the VIE structure that continue to allow Chinese companies to list on stock exchanges overseas, albeit with greater government oversight of national security concerns,[203] thus signaling a middle-of-the-road approach.[204] For now, neither the US nor China have taken the most drastic moves toward decoupling as both the CSRC and SEC still permit Chinese listings in the US using the VIE structure. The Chinese government has also recently made significant concessions in an effort to avoid a mass delisting of Chinese companies from US stock exchanges. In April 2022, the CSRC revised its 2009 audit secrecy rules that prohibited Chinese companies listed overseas from sharing sensitive financial information with foreign entities.[205] In July 2022, the Chinese authorities disclosed that they were considering a three-tier system whereby US-listed Chinese companies would be treated differently based on the sensitivity of the data they possess.[206] Only companies that hold "secretive" data would face delisting whereas companies holding "non-sensitive data" or "sensitive data" would be allowed to comply with US auditing transparency requirements.[207] For companies with sensitive data, however, compliance with Chinese laws might require changes to their data management practices, such as "outsourcing the information to a third party."[208]

As a further sign that the US and China are both seeking to defuse existing tensions, Chinese and American regulators announced in August 2022 that they had reached a landmark agreement that would allow for the sharing of audits of Chinese companies listed on US stock exchanges.[209] By giving US regulators the ability to inspect audits and investigate Chinese companies, the deal could prevent the delisting of the two hundred or so Chinese companies that issue stock in the US.[210] However, SEC Chairman Gary Gensler struck a cautious tone in celebrating the announcement: "Make no mistake, though: The proof will be in the pudding. While important, this framework is merely a step in the process. This agreement will be meaningful only if the [US's Public Company Accounting and Oversight Board] [PCAOB] actually can inspect and investigate completely audit firms in China."[211] In September 2022, inspectors from the PCAOB started vetting auditors' work on Chinese companies, beginning with Alibaba and fast-food company Yum China.[212]

Despite these tentative signs of progress, the threat of further financial decoupling remains real in today's tense geopolitical environment, where neither party can afford to be seen as capitulating to the demands of the other. The Chinese government remains adamant in calling for tighter control of personal data and greater recognition of the national security implications associated with data transfers. This suggests that the Chinese government will have a hard time accepting full disclosure of such data to US regulators. At the same time, the US government remains determined to prevent the exposure of American investors to unreasonable risks, undoubtedly keen to avoid a repeat of the now-infamous DiDi listing. The SEC thus has an incentive to demand greater disclosure of Chinese companies' ownership structures, links to the CCP, and full audit records. The PCAOB has been clear that it "must have complete access to audit work papers of any firm it chooses to inspect or investigate—no loopholes and no exceptions."[213] This conflict is already playing out in the details of the new landmark deal. Despite both countries' tentative commitments and incentives to cooperate in this new experiment in financial regulation, the countries already disagree on the role that Chinese regulators should play in the PCAOB's inspection process.[214] This suggests that, despite the costs involved, further decoupling of the US and Chinese financial markets remains possible, even probable. Under the most extreme scenario, such escalation could lead to a complete decoupling of the global stock market. Such a scenario—which may be unlikely, even if no longer impossible to imagine—would open a whole new era both in US–China relations and in deglobalization more generally, fragmenting the global economy in ways that were once unthinkable.

Will the Intersecting Vertical Battles Lead to Technological Decoupling?

The conflicts discussed in this chapter reveal the complex reality of today's digital economy where global tech companies are caught between different regulatory models, confronting hard choices or, even worse, irreconcilable demands from different governments. It is rarely possible for global tech companies to pledge their commitment to free speech in the US, to government censorship in China, and to users' data privacy in Europe, without being criticized for trading their values for profit or violating one country's law in seeking compliance with that of another. Yet these conflicts are inevitable for any tech company that operates globally—after all, governments set the rules for their markets, not tech companies. Google learned firsthand that it cannot operate its search engine in China while insisting that it believes in free speech instead of censorship. DiDi also learned—as did its investors—that it cannot list itself on the US stock exchange while disclosing only the data that Beijing allows it to disclose. When these choices become too costly or difficult, the decoupling of the global digital economy follows: Facebook is blocked in China, Google abandons its Project Dragonfly, and DiDi delists from the New York Stock Exchange. Yet others hold on, illustrating the benefits of the global digital marketplace: American teenagers can still dance to the tunes of TikTok, at least for now, thanks in part to the US judiciary. Apple still thrives in China, insisting elsewhere that "privacy is a fundamental human right"[215] while being prepared to look the other way in China. After all, Apple only "follows the law" in China—a law that is tied to one billion internet users and $55 billion in annual revenue.[216]

The intersecting vertical conflicts have several implications. First, they reveal the intricate balancing act US tech companies face in deciding whether and how to operate in China. These decisions entangle questions of commercial opportunities and profits with questions of national security, corporate values, and conflicting loyalties. How the US tech companies go about navigating these choices is closely scrutinized by political leaders, users, shareholders, and employees—and there are no choices that will leave all stakeholders satisfied. The Chinese state-driven model is also unyielding in that it leaves little space for US companies to exercise choice beyond total acquiescence or abandonment of the Chinese market. The way the leading US tech companies have gone about this choice in recent years suggests that they are willing to stay in China as long as the Chinese government allows them to stay, and as long as their core business activity—for example, freely searching for information online—is not in irreconcilable tension with the censorship requirement that lies at the heart of the Chinese state-driven regulatory model. In the face of such a complete conflict of values, staying in China would be even costlier for them than abandoning China.

The dynamics of the conflicts that Chinese tech companies face in the US display a different logic from those their American counterparts face in China. The American market-driven regulatory model presents few challenges to these companies. After all, the US model valorizes economic openness, which traditionally has meant welcoming Chinese companies to the US. Even as political attitudes in the US have recently hardened and geopolitical considerations have started to drive policy, Chinese tech companies have been able to challenge US government restrictions by turning to the American courts, invoking the US legal regime in their defense. In several instances, courts across the country have remained true to the American regulatory model, upholding the US's longstanding commitment to commercial freedom and the rule of law. However, a critical question is whether the US government is now making a conscious decision to move away from this commitment to economic openness, either in the name of national security or greater fairness and reciprocity. Such a policy shift may successfully keep Chinese tech companies at bay, but it also risks reinforcing the trend that the US–China tech war has already set in motion—namely, the abandonment of key tenets of the US's own market-driven regulatory model and, inadvertently, the bolstering of China's state-driven regulatory model as the lodestar for the digital economy.

Therefore, the key question in the midst of these tensions becomes how far the decoupling of the digital economy will go. In addition to the risks facing the global stock market that were discussed earlier, the internet and the broader digital economy are now heading toward greater balkanization. Chapter 5 shows how the ongoing US–China tech war, including the export and investment restrictions, is already fragmenting the global tech ecosystem as the US and China are fighting a horizontal battle for technological supremacy. Additional decoupling will follow if and when tech companies themselves conclude that they no longer find it feasible to operate across the different regulatory regimes and consequently choose one over the other. As one dimension of such decoupling, some predict that the global internet will fragment into a "splinternet"—a term understood to mean a world of "parallel internets that would be run as distinct, private, and autonomous universes."[217] In practice, this would entail the division of the global internet into different realms that would be controlled by different governments or tech companies. In this balkanized digital world, companies and individuals would need to choose one system or face the costs and complexities of operating across two internet architectures and two sets of devices—using, for example, one phone to send a WeChat message and another to use Gmail.[218]

Some argue that such decoupling has already taken place and the internet is already splitting into two—an American internet and a Chinese one—or even three, as Europeans create and globalize their own standards as well. A 2022 report by the Council on Foreign Relations, an American foreign policy think tank, declared that "the era of the global internet is over,"[219] capturing a sentiment shared by many. It is, indeed, already harder today for companies controlling sensitive technologies to operate in the US and China simultaneously. They may well need to choose their market, as many already have done, and abandon the idea of having a truly worldwide presence—sustained by what was once thought to be an inherently and inevitably global internet. What the past few years have shown is that the internet is not "inherently" or "inevitably" global. Its open and global character remains at the mercy of governments' political decisions to continue to let the internet emerge and evolve in that direction. Meta CEO Mark Zuckerberg acknowledged this back in 2019 by noting how "China is building its own internet focused on very different values, and is now exporting their vision of the internet to other countries."[220] US government representatives in China have made similar observations, with one diplomat acknowledging in 2021 that China has sought to decouple its internet from that of the West for a decade already, with the goal of ultimately creating two digital ecosystems.[221]

It is possible to view China as being well on its way in creating a separate digital architecture that includes a sovereign digital authoritarian internet. It does not need Facebook, Amazon, Google, or Apple because it has WeChat, Alibaba, Baidu, Huawei, and Xiaomi. China is also not dependent on others in terms of its AI capabilities, developing its own self-driving cars, smart cities, smart medicine, and health applications—in addition to perfecting its already robust AI-powered regime of state surveillance. Beijing will be one step closer to a sovereign Chinese tech ecosystem once it has rolled out its own digital currency, internationalized it, and thereby created an alternative financial universe that is less reliant on the US dollar or the SWIFT international payment system. However, if decoupling global semiconductor supply chains is difficult, as discussed in Chapter 5, so is the idea of creating a complete splinternet. It is true that the Chinese Firewall has already built borders on the internet, creating a separate content universe defined by the censorship policies of the Chinese government. Similar content controls are imposed by countries such as Iran and North Korea and, increasingly, by Russia. Yet completely cutting a country off from the global internet is costly and difficult, as Russia is now experiencing as it seeks to detangle itself from the global internet infrastructure in the wake of its invasion of Ukraine. Compared to Russia, China is in a better position to operationalize a splinternet, as the Chinese government has built the entire internet infrastructure from the outset as a controlled space.[222] China has also been willing to muster the considerable resources needed to create and maintain its "sovereign internet."[223] Yet it is not clear that even China will end up with a completely sovereign Chinese internet.

Even if content controls can partially fragment the internet, the fundamental technological infrastructure sustaining the internet is less likely to splinter. For example, the Internet Corporation for Assigned Names and Numbers (ICANN), which controls the domain name systems, recently declined Ukraine's request to suspend Russia's access to internet domain systems. In doing so, the regulatory body emphasized how the internet is a decentralized system that is designed so that no single authority has the ability to control or shut down the system.[224] A genuine splinternet would require making internet protocols technically incompatible in such a way that, for example, the internet in China would no longer be interoperable with that in the US. However, some experts have expressed doubt as to whether such a separation could be maintained as technologists could soon find a way to bridge those protocols. Countries could also create a splinternet by setting up different governance bodies to manage different realms of the internet, even if those realms still use technically compatible protocols. For example, China could seek to manage its own IP addresses and domain name systems. However, even if China had the technical capability to create a splinternet in some form, it is unclear that it would be willing to pursue such a strategy given the costs and complexities involved.[225]

The coming years will reveal how far digital decoupling will go, and the particular manifestations it will take. Escalating geopolitical tensions, discussed next in Chapter 5, may further fragment the global digital economy as the leading digital jurisdictions continue to restrict the transfer of data, technology, and information across global networks. Tech companies continue to be thrust in the middle of such conflicts, increasingly being forced to choose sides when faced with irreconcilable regulatory demands by different governments. At the same time, tech companies persist in advocating for the benefits of an open and interconnected digital economy, showing their willingness to take political and economic risks in order to reap the benefits of a global digital marketplace. Governments know that a world dominated by widespread data localization, a balkanized internet, decoupled stock markets, and segregated digital citizens may deliver greater control and a sense of security—but they also know that achieving such control and security would be, at best, a Pyrrhic victory that would be extremely costly to implement and maintain. It would impoverish their economies, societies, and individuals. Perhaps most consequentially, if extreme decoupling occurs, it would compromise the important technological progress and economic prosperity that all digital regimes depend on, and eliminate the prospect of future détente and coexistence—however uneasy and contested—between the three leading digital empires.

5

The Battle
for Technological Supremacy

THE US–CHINA TECH WAR

IN TODAY'S DIGITAL economy, few regulatory battles remain stagnant but instead evolve: some battles defuse over time as parties' interests change or converge whereas others morph into more intractable and multifaceted conflicts. In battles involving the United States and China, the direction of this evolution has been clear in recent years: both sides are escalating their battle strategies and resolutely moving toward an increasingly unyielding conflict. Consequently, the individual vertical battles, discussed in Chapter 4, are now evolving into a broader horizontal conflict between these two digital empires. Those earlier vertical battles have already set in motion the process of gradual decoupling of the global digital economy—a process that is now being accelerated as the US and China are fighting over technological supremacy, with strong ideological undertones and potentially grave geopolitical consequences. This new battlefront goes beyond Facebook deciding whether to pull out of China or acquiesce to the Chinese Communist Party's (CCP) demands for censorship; or the Chinese ride-hailing company DiDi choosing whether it will disclose sensitive data to the US regulators when doing so violates Chinese law. Tech companies themselves are still the main tools and casualties in this horizontal battle but the US government is no longer only fighting a few individual Chinese companies. Instead, the US is targeting the entire Chinese tech ecosystem, the Chinese state, and China's future economic, technological, and geopolitical prowess—the same way the Chinese government is now fighting a defining battle not only against the leading US tech companies but against the US as its main rival in the intensifying great power contest. Given this escalation in the US–China conflict, what may have been characterized as a "battle" in the past has now evolved into a "war" between two tech superpowers. This superpower conflict, many would argue, is also the main theatre of war where the highest-stakes battles for the future of the global digital economy are being fought.

The US–China tech war is casting a lengthening shadow over the global digital economy. This unfolding rivalry between the two economic and geopolitical superpowers is unraveling global supply chains, battering tech companies, frightening financial markets, and unsettling international relations far beyond the bilateral US–China relationship. This new era of a great power contest has replaced the more optimistic era of globalization where China was seen as integrating into the global economy—in particular, in the years after it joined the World Trade Organization (WTO) in 2001. In the two decades that followed, exports fueled China's record-high growth rates. Western companies were able to tap into China's vast and dynamic consumer market, while Western consumers benefited from having access to cheap Chinese imports. However, China's market opening was always incomplete, and foreign companies continued to face restrictions, including strict censorship requirements that were discussed in the previous chapter. But there was hope that, over time, China was moving toward greater economic integration with the rest of the world. That economic integration was viewed as an opportunity for closer political engagement with the West, which—under the most optimistic scenario—some observers believed would pave the way for the country's political easing and opening. This optimism has since faded as China's relationship with the US and its allies has deteriorated. International institutions, including the WTO, have struggled to integrate China's state-driven economy into their structures, all of which were established before China's accession. China's increasingly prominent role in the global economy and its unwillingness to play by the prevailing rules of the international economic order has fueled resentment in the West. These tensions—which rest on fundamental disagreements—appear irreconcilable in the short term and will likely sustain continuing conflicts between the US and China.

Over the past few years, this already contentious US–China relationship has escalated, with the digital economy emerging as the primary battlefield. Since President Trump took office in 2017, the conflict between the two countries has evolved into a full-blown trade and technology war, leaving companies and other governments to navigate the uneasy terrain between them. The US and China both view technological supremacy as a key to economic and political dominance and regard each other as strategic rivals with whom they are locked in a geopolitical conflict. This dynamic has converted the digital economy into a zero-sum game between the two countries with little space for collaboration and compromise and hastened the decoupling of Chinese and US technology assets. It has also galvanized an increasingly techno-nationalist response in other jurisdictions, including in the European Union (EU), as trust in global technology supply chains has eroded and governments around the world are hastening their efforts to safeguard access to key technologies in the midst of growing US–China tensions.

The US and China maintain different narratives about the origins of the tech war. For the US, the trade and tech war is a long-overdue response to the Chinese government's persistent pursuit of unfair economic policies, including systemic infringement of intellectual property rights, suppression of the value of Chinese currency, engagement in cybertheft and industrial espionage, subsidization of Chinese companies, preferential treatment for Chinese state-owned enterprises, as well as various market access restrictions targeting foreign companies seeking to operate in China.[1] In addition to China's market-distorting economic policies, the US government has referred to the Chinese government's oppressive human rights practices, including its recent crackdown on democracy protests in Hong Kong and mass detention of Muslim Uyghurs in Xinjiang as justifications for trade sanctions.[2] While these concerns have been brewing for over a decade, they began to dominate US policymaking after the election of President Trump in 2016. Under his presidency, the US initiated and escalated a trade war against China—a war that President Biden has continued. Several other governments, including the EU, share the US's concerns about China's market-distortive policies and suppression of human rights, but have traditionally preferred to address these trade disputes within the confines of the WTO.[3] The US, however, largely lost its patience with the WTO under the Trump administration and turned to unilateral trade sanctions instead. This bilateral US–China trade war has now evolved into a broader trade and technology war, where technological assets are seen as key to economic and geopolitical rivalries. As a result, the technology sector became the prime target of export controls and various market access and investment restrictions on both sides.

While the US justifies the trade and tech war by citing China's unfair economic policies, the Chinese leadership views the US's restrictive measures as an attempt to contain China's rise and preserve the US-dominated economic and political order.[4] The US's trade sanctions target China's "Made in China 2025" industrial strategy, which seeks to make China a leading global power in high-tech manufacturing.[5] For example, the US has imposed tariffs on industries such as aviation and electric vehicles, which are some of the key priorities indicated in China's industrial strategy. According to the Chinese view, these tariffs and other US policies—including sanctions against the

Chinese information and communications technology (ICT) giant Huawei, visa denials to Chinese scholars and students, and the demands for China to end its state subsidies to the tech industry—all suggest that the US's trade and tech war is motivated by the American "intention to suppress Chinese high-tech enterprises."[6] The two sides may never agree on whether the unfolding tech war is driven by the US's legitimate concerns about China's illegitimate market behavior or the US's illegitimate attempt to suppress China's legitimate challenge to the American technological dominance. But the reality is that the tech war has now morphed into a multifront battle that is gradually decoupling US and Chinese technology assets from one another while severely destabilizing the foundations of the global digital economy.

Most commentators would agree that trade and tech wars are costly to fight and that, ultimately, there are no winners in this US–China conflict. To the dismay of the Americans, the only clear winner of the unfolding tech war might be China's state-driven regulatory model, which is gaining prominence worldwide. The tech war is ushering in a strong state-led response in the US where the government is now emulating aspects of the Chinese regulatory model by restricting exports and shielding its technology industry from foreign investors. Like China, the US is also engaged in a relentless state-led capacity-building effort in order to gain new technological capabilities while reducing its foreign dependencies in the era of unraveling global supply chains. Other jurisdictions, including the EU, find themselves in the middle of this US–China rivalry, forced to navigate the costly conflict or even choose sides. To avoid being at the mercy of the warring rivals, the EU is now pursuing greater technological self-sufficiency—or, as the EU calls it, "strategic autonomy"[7] or "digital sovereignty"[8]—in the tense geopolitical environment. The EU response shows how the US–China tech war is fueling broader distrust in digital trade and international cooperation. Inadvertently, the tech war is also therefore pushing the US and the EU to integrate aspects of China's state-driven regulatory model, thus risking entrenchment of techno-nationalism as a global norm.

This chapter builds on the discussion in Chapter 4 to explain how the US and China have entered a new phase in their mutual conflict that moves them beyond individual vertical battles against selected tech companies. As the tensions have built up, the two leading tech powers are now embroiled in a broader horizontal battle for technological supremacy. In this tech war, the battlefield is the entire tech ecosystem, and the ultimate goal is economic and technological supremacy and, ultimately, geopolitical primacy. The chapter outlines key measures that the US has recently pursued against Chinese tech companies in this tech war—including limiting outflows of US technologies to China and restricting inflows of Chinese tech investments into the US. As part of its effort to further curtail Chinese firms' export opportunities, the US has also been pressuring its allies to limit the presence of Chinese tech companies in their markets. This chapter brings these measures into view and discusses some of the consequences that are likely to materialize in both the short and long term. The chapter also outlines the Chinese government's policies targeting US tech companies, including constraining US tech companies' ability to operate in China and preventing the outflow of critical technology assets from China. As this chapter explains, both American and Chinese policy measures reveal a mix of an intense economic, technological, and political rivalry, but also an attempt to avoid a full-blown escalation of the conflict and hence a complete decoupling of the global digital order. This chapter points to several examples of how the existing, deep economic interdependencies push both the US and China toward a strategy of restraint even in the midst of a great power conflict. The chapter also examines another frontier of the tech war—the technological arms race unfolding in fields such as artificial intelligence (AI), revealing how the US and Chinese governments are stepping deeper into the planning and management of the digital economy. As this chapter demonstrates, this US–China tech war is already having significant consequences, including the partial decoupling of technology assets and growing digital protectionism everywhere. The escalating conflict is fueling grave uncertainty around the globe, accelerating the unraveling of complex global supply chains and exposing the seismic, spillover effects that this US–China tech war is having on the world's digital order.

US Measures Against China: Countering Risks Associated with China's Rising Technological Dominance

The US government has pursued several legislative and executive measures against Chinese tech companies, citing the need to protect its commercial, foreign policy, and national security interests. First, it has limited the outflows of technology to Chinese companies by restricting exports of critical technology assets. In practice, this means that US tech companies are prevented from supplying certain technologies or components to designated Chinese tech companies and other entities. Second, the US government has limited inflows of Chinese technologies to the US, such as by curtailing the ability of Chinese companies to build fifth-generation (5G) telecommunications network infrastructures in the US. The US government has also pursued the controversial strategy of human decoupling by restricting the entry and stay of Chinese scientists and students in the US. Finally, the US has recently imposed sanctions in response to Chinese hackers' alleged involvement in major cyberespionage operations. These measures, taken together, have significantly limited Chinese tech companies' capabilities and commercial opportunities while escalating US–China political tensions.

Limiting Exports of Critical Technologies

Limiting technology exports to China is one of the key US government strategies in the US–China tech war. Export controls are designed to restrict China's access to strategic technology assets that have the potential to compromise the US's economic or geopolitical interests. The US's practice of deploying export controls to promote its foreign policy objectives and safeguard its national security interests is not new, but this policy tool has taken on new significance in the ongoing US–China tech war. In 2018, the US Congress strengthened the existing US export control regime, largely in response to growing efforts by Chinese entities to gain access to sensitive US technologies.[9] It adopted the Export Control Reform Act of 2018 (ECRA), which authorizes the US government to restrict the exportation of critical items to China or other foreign countries on the grounds that such exports may undermine US national security or foreign policy interests.[10] The Bureau of Industry and Security (BIS) of the Department of Commerce enforces these controls through the maintenance of a Commerce Control List and a licensing system, which sets licensing requirements for exports to specific destinations and end uses. For example, the BIS has had a longstanding policy to prevent exports of any national security–controlled items to China whenever those items "would make a direct and significant contribution to the [People's Republic of China]'s military capability."[11]

The ECRA marks a further escalation in the already heated trade and tech war between the US and China. In addition to vesting the BIS with permanent authority to implement and enforce the export control regime, the ECRA expands the US government's ability to restrict the transfer of "emerging and foundational technologies" to entities abroad whenever those technologies are "essential to the national security of the United States."[12] While the list of such technologies has not yet been finalized, it is expected to include technologies such as artificial intelligence (AI) and machine learning technology, microprocessor technology, quantum computing, data analytics, brain-computer interfaces, additive manufacturing, and robotics.[13] The Department of Commerce has been criticized for the delay in finalizing the list of affected technologies, which allows for the unfettered export of these technologies in the meantime—potentially undermining US national security interests.[14] For example, while the existing Commerce Control List already mentions "surveillance hardware," it is silent on facial and voice recognition technologies that are common forms of modern surveillance.[15] Such technologies are deployed, for instance, by the Chinese government in Xinjiang as part of the mass surveillance and detention of the Uyghur minority.

In practice, the ECRA has affected only a small number of US tech exports, which may seem surprising given the considerable political appetite in the US to adopt a resolute enforcement regime that effectively limits China's access to key technologies.[16] Before gaining new powers in 2018, the BIS had removed the export licensing requirement for many technologies that had become more widely available, in part in response to growing pressure to let businesses take advantage of market opportunities in China. However, as concerns about China's technological rise and geopolitical ambitions mounted, the 2018 reform presented an opportunity to revisit this lax enforcement policy. Yet the US government did not seize on that opportunity: it was reported in 2022 that US companies continue to sell sensitive technologies, such as semiconductors, AI, and aerospace components, to China.[17] Critics decry this as a "significant policy failure," suggesting that the US government is "improperly giving priority to U.S. commercial interests over national security."[18] Others are more understanding of the government's policy of restraint, stressing how US export controls would be ineffective in the absence of American allies implementing similar controls. They argue that, absent such a coordinated approach, other foreign exporters would simply step in to fill the void left by the US, thus directly undermining the US's sanctions regime.

Although the BIS has not taken full advantage of the authority given in the ECRA to ban or require licensing for entire technologies or end uses, the Bureau has frequently used a narrower export control instrument to block the transfer of certain technologies to China. This instrument, known as the Entity List, derives its authority from Export Administration Regulations (EAR) and targets specific recipients of technologies as opposed to technologies themselves. It allows the BIS to restrict exports aimed at certain entities, such as designated companies or research institutions that are involved in "activities contrary to US national security and/or foreign policy interests."[19] As of August 2022, the US government has targeted 260 Chinese tech companies using this more tailored Entity List instrument,[20] including leading AI and facial recognition companies Dahua, Hikvision, Megvii, Sense Time, and CloudWalk, and the ICT giant Huawei.[21] These restrictions have led to major constraints on US tech companies—Qualcomm, for example, is no longer permitted to supply 5G chips to Huawei, and Google's Android operating system can no longer be installed on Huawei phones.[22] Other entities, including Chinese universities, have also been placed on the Entity List, further expanding the reach of US export controls.[23]

Prior to the major escalation in US export controls in late 2022—a development that will be discussed later in this chapter—the US government's single most potent export control measure was its May 2020 decision to ban Huawei's access to semiconductors that are made using American technologies.[24] The decision brought numerous non-US chipmakers into the US export control regime's fold as the restrictions were extended to all foreign companies that use US chipmaking equipment or software tools.[25] Semiconductors are critical components in Huawei's smartphones and telecom equipment, and the US sanctions targeted the entire global supply chain that Huawei depends on. These sanctions, together with additional measures discussed below, have had a debilitating effect on the company.[26] After losing access to US-linked semiconductors, Huawei's smartphones and telecom network infrastructure businesses took a serious hit. In the fourth quarter of 2020, the company's phone sales declined 41 percent, and its revenues fell by 29 percent from 2020 to 2021.[27] These sanctions have forced Huawei to reinvent its business model and seek growth from new areas such as cloud services and smart cars, which are less dependent on access to foreign components.

Until 2021, the US export control regime was more narrowly focused on limiting China's access to technologies that are intended for a "military-intelligence end use," or destined for Chinese firms or entities that are "aiding [People's Liberation Army] weapons development."[28] Yet US officials continue to face growing pressures to do more on this front. In October 2021, House Republicans sent a letter urging US Commerce Secretary Gina Raimondo to extend export controls further, citing the threat posed by China's testing of a nuclear-capable hypersonic missile. The letter forcefully states: "It is likely that U.S. software and tools contributed to the creation of this weapons system, because of our country's permissive export controls and licensing policies with China. If this is not the clarion call to overhaul export controls and our technology and research collaboration with the PRC and its Military-Civil Fusion strategy, liberal democracies may cede more ground to a genocidal, authoritarian regime."[29] The US government has also been looking for ways to leverage export controls to limit China's human rights abuses. In June 2021, the US Senate passed the United States Innovation and Competition Act of 2021.[30] One component of the bill—the Meeting the China Challenge Act of 2021—extends export controls to items "with critical capabilities that enable human rights abuses."[31] All of these measures limit Chinese commercial and government entities' access to sensitive or strategically important tech assets, with the aim of curtailing China's quest for technological dominance and its effort to entrench its digital authoritarian rule in China and abroad.

The US recently escalated this tit-for-tat export control war to the next level. In October 2022, the US government unveiled a drastic new set of export restrictions aimed at cutting off Chinese access to advanced semiconductor chips and chip production tools, which are necessary for powering supercomputing and AI capabilities.[32] Additionally, the new rules published by BIS impose further licensing requirements on selling technology to twenty-eight Chinese firms already on the Entity List.[33] The rules aim to address US national security concerns and to prevent China from utilizing advanced technologies to crack the US's encrypted messaging or improve Chinese weapons systems.[34] Crucially, these controls incorporate a "foreign direct product rule," which extend those restrictions to companies operating anywhere in the world that manufacture chips with US technology and equipment, including major suppliers like the Taiwan Semiconductor Manufacturing Company.[35]

The new controls reflect the Biden administration's view that past export restrictions such as the Entity List have not done enough to hamper China's technological advances. In August 2022, it was reported that China's top chipmaker, the Semiconductor Manufacturing International Corporation (SMIC), had successfully made a seven-nanometer semiconductor despite being on the US Entity List.[36] This major breakthrough in China's semiconductor technology caused alarm in the Biden administration, which had already been seeking to persuade allies to impose tougher restrictions on China.[37] The new export controls therefore take a more drastic approach: they seek to utilize American-made technology as a "chokepoint" to prevent further Chinese technological advancement—starving China's AI industry with a lack of US chips, for example, and cutting off China's ability to build its own chips by withholding US chipmaking software.[38] Instead of targeting a particular Chinese company or technology, these restrictions take aim at the entire Chinese tech industry—civilian and military. The new controls will undoubtedly hurt Chinese chip manufacturers and tech companies in the short run; a wide swath of companies will struggle to access American-made hardware used for AI algorithms, affecting numerous industries such as medical imaging and autonomous vehicles.[39] However, as is the case with economic sanctions, US companies will be hurt too—Applied Materials and Lam Research, two major American chip equipment makers, each derived about a third of their sales from China prior to the new controls.[40]

It remains to be seen how effective the US will be in totally cutting off Chinese access to these technologies as the US could not persuade its allies to join the sanctions regime. News reports indicate that the US engaged in talks with the British, Dutch, Japanese, and other governments, seeking for those countries to also restrict exports to China.[41] But some allies were afraid to join the effort because they risked hurting their economic relationships with China.[42] In the past, China has sometimes pursued a "divide and conquer" strategy with the US and its allies—economically punishing those countries that go along with US measures while rewarding those that do not.[43] While China's reaction to the measures is still uncertain, it will likely involve seeking alternatives to American technology and building up its own domestic tech capabilities over the long term.[44]

In the short term, these controls will further push the decoupling of the US and Chinese tech ecosystems. Under the new restrictions, individuals who hold US passports can no longer work for Chinese chip companies, leading some top executives to step down.[45] Apple is exploring using Chinese-made chips for Chinese iPhones and separating that supply chain from the one used for Western iPhones.[46] Perhaps most importantly, the measures demonstrate consistent intent from the US—across political parties and successive administrations—to fully commit to halting China's technological rise. From President Trump's crackdown on Huawei to the CHIPS Act to the new export controls, the US has signaled it is no longer willing to play by the usual rules when it comes to China—it will instead view Chinese technological advancement as a matter of national security and through the lens of strategic competition for geopolitical primacy.

Limiting Investments in Critical Tech Assets or Infrastructures

In addition to limiting the outflow of strategic technologies from the US to China, the US has sought to restrict Chinese companies' access to critical tech assets and infrastructures inside the US. The US government's restrictions on Chinese companies' involvement in building US 5G networks are an especially prominent example of this phenomenon. Today, the 5G market is a major battleground in the US and China's broader fight for digital sovereignty. In the US, like elsewhere in the world, the 5G network forms a vital backbone to essential societal services and economic activities—ranging from electricity and transportation to banking and healthcare. As the world's leading vendor of 5G technology, China's Huawei has found itself in the crosshairs of the US–China tech war. The US government is concerned that any reliance on Huawei-built 5G networks in the US will expose data flowing through such networks to potential espionage by the Chinese government, given the company's close ties to Beijing. Consequently, the US government has banned Huawei from 5G networks in the US, while cajoling its allies around the world to do the same. In May 2019, President Trump signed an executive order prohibiting the use of telecom equipment manufactured by foreign companies that are deemed to pose a national security risk—thereby implicitly, if not explicitly, taking aim at Huawei.[47] The US State Department further described Huawei as "an arm of the Chinese Communist Party's (CCP's) surveillance state," which justified "measures to protect U.S. national security, our citizens' privacy, and the integrity of our 5G infrastructure from Beijing's malign influence."[48] Members of the US Congress supported the Huawei ban, citing similar concerns. Senator Ben Sasse noted how "China's main export is espionage, and the distinction between the Chinese Communist Party and Chinese 'private-sector' businesses like Huawei is imaginary."[49] Senator Tom Cotton struck a similar tone, warning that using Huawei for 5G networks "would be as if we had relied on adversarial nations in the cold war to build our submarines, or to build our tanks."[50]

President Biden has doubled down on these Trump-era policies, further pushing Huawei and other Chinese digital infrastructure companies, including ZTE, away from the US market. In 2021, President Biden signed the Secure Equipment Act of 2021. The bipartisan bill requires the US Federal Communications Commission (FCC) to enact rules clarifying that it will no longer issue licenses for any telecom equipment that "poses an unacceptable risk to national security."[51] Consequently, Huawei equipment can no longer be inserted into US communications networks.[52] Rather strikingly, the FCC is also undertaking a $1.9 billion "rip and replace" program to reimburse rural telecom carriers for their removal of Huawei and ZTE equipment from their networks.[53] This illustrates the lengths to which the US government is willing to go to disable Huawei's ability to retain any operations in the US. However, China is also willing to go far in defending Huawei. For example, when Canada detained Huawei executive Meng Wanzhou on fraud charges following a request from the US government, the Chinese government engaged in "hostage diplomacy" and detained two Canadian citizens in response.[54] Yet China's strong defense of Huawei only serves to deepen the US suspicion that the company's and the Chinese government's interests are deeply intertwined, thus escalating as opposed to alleviating the tensions around the company.

Notwithstanding its determination to oust Huawei from the US, the US government has been less successful in convincing the rest of the world of the dangers associated with using Chinese telecom technology.[55] According to a March 2021 study conducted by the Council on Foreign Relations, a total of eight countries have banned Huawei from their 5G markets either completely or with some limited exceptions.[56] These include traditional US allies, such as Australia, the United Kingdom (UK), Japan, and more recently, Canada.[57] Some other countries—including France, Italy, India, Vietnam, and Spain—have chosen not to take an official stand against Huawei but have de facto excluded or limited its market presence. These countries have gradually phased out contracts with the company, delayed the approval of new Huawei contracts, or simply chosen alternative vendors. Yet several US allies continue to allow Huawei to build their networks, including NATO members Hungary, Iceland, and Turkey, and close US allies in the Middle East such as the United Arab Emirates and Saudi Arabia. India has been on the fence in its approach toward Huawei, choosing to exclude Huawei from its 5G trials in 2021 without officially banning the company.[58] This comes as a surprise, as India has otherwise not hesitated in sanctioning Chinese tech companies. In June 2020, the country banned almost sixty Chinese apps—including TikTok and WeChat—due to concerns about China stealing user data and thereby infringing on India's sovereignty and integrity.[59]

Governments' hesitation to ban Huawei from their markets can, at least in part, be explained by the limited number of alternative suppliers of 5G technology. US companies have a trivial presence in the telecom equipment industry. In 2020, Huawei controlled 32 percent of the global telecom equipment market, while its closest competitors, the Swedish Eriksson and the Finnish Nokia, each held a 16 percent market share.[60] However, Eriksson and Nokia struggle to compete with Huawei due to the better financing conditions Huawei can offer, thanks to the extensive state support the company benefits from. For example, the Export-Import Bank of China lent Pakistan $124.7 million and waived most of the interest on the loan in return for Pakistan choosing Huawei as its 5G supplier—which Pakistan did without even conducting a competitive bidding process for the project.[61] The China Development Bank gave India's second-largest mobile operator, Reliance Communications Ltd. (RCom), a $750 million loan, which allowed RCom to cheaply finance a digital cellular network equipment contract with Huawei when building a second mobile network.[62] According to an investigation by the *Wall Street Journal*, Huawei has benefited from a total of $75 billion in state support over the years, which allows it to regularly underbid its rivals by up to 30 percent.[63] Huawei itself cites its high R&D expenditures and resulting technological expertise—both of which, indeed, are considerable—as reasons for its ability to offer competitive prices. Yet experts maintain that Huawei's prices would not even cover the company's production costs absent government subsidies.[64]

Many developing countries also do not share the US's data privacy and security concerns or, alternatively, are willing to overlook those concerns when faced with the opportunity to gain access to telecom and other digital infrastructures that they otherwise cannot afford. After all, these countries need a path toward digital development and they favor those goals over protecting fundamental data privacy. To illustrate how security concerns often play a secondary role, Malaysian former prime minister Mahathir Mohamad dismissed the US's concerns about Huawei's presence in the country by retorting, "What is there to spy on in Malaysia?"[65] Given this view, it is perhaps not surprising that the Malaysian government signed a Memorandum of Understanding in 2017 with Huawei concerning public security and smart cities solutions.[66] US allies have faced similar obstacles in trying to counter Chinese influence in their own regions. When Australia—with American and Japanese backing—tried to convince Papua New Guinea to forgo Huawei Marine's offer to build fiber-optic cables in the country in favor of an alternative project built by Australia, Papua New Guinea proceeded with the Huawei contract despite these warnings.[67]

Limiting Huawei's presence in the US has been one of the most prominent battles in the US–China tech war. But the US government's efforts to limit Chinese companies' presence in the US extend beyond Huawei. The US also scrutinizes Chinese investment in critical US technologies through the so-called CFIUS process, which screens foreign direct investment (FDI) on national security grounds.[68] The interagency Committee on Foreign Investment in the United States, known as CFIUS, conducts the screening process and can request that the president prohibit an investment or order a divestiture of a completed transaction. CFIUS's jurisdiction was expanded in August 2018 with the passing of the Foreign Investment Risk Review Modernization Act of 2018 (FIRRMA).[69] Among other changes, FIRRMA broadens the coverage of the CFIUS review and introduces mandatory filing requirements for certain transactions involving critical technologies.[70] It also vests CFIUS with jurisdiction to screen even noncontrolling investments in certain US businesses that involve critical technology, critical infrastructure, or sensitive personal data.[71]

These investment controls have recently targeted, predictably, Chinese companies and investors in particular. For example, a Chinese state-backed investment fund's proposed acquisition of Xcerra Corporation, a US-based semiconductor testing equipment firm, could not secure CFIUS approval and was consequently abandoned in 2018.[72] In May 2020, CFIUS review led to the unraveling of a joint venture between California-based Ekso Bionics and Chinese investors. The decision was motivated by concerns that the company's robotic mechanical suits, designed for medical and other health and safety settings, could also have military applications.[73] Chinese investors also seem to be retreating preemptively in anticipation of negative CFIUS reviews. Over the last few years, there has been a drop in Chinese investment in the US tech sector. Chinese investors were involved in only 17 CFIUS notices in 2020, which is a notable decline from 25 notices submitted in 2019 and 55 submitted in 2018.[74] This suggests that the US government's heightened scrutiny of Chinese tech investments is, indeed, having a chilling effect on Chinese investments in the US market—even if the US government has fallen short in persuading the rest of the world to do the same.

Human Decoupling as the New Frontier of the Tech War

US accusations of Chinese espionage have also had a notable human cost. In 2018, the Trump administration launched the "China Initiative," which facilitated the prosecution of individuals who were thought to have engaged in "trade secret theft, hacking, and economic espionage."[75] In practice, this Initiative often targeted Chinese-born researchers at US universities.[76] Massachusetts Institute of Technology professor Gang Chen, for example, was charged with "wire fraud, failing to report a foreign bank account and a false statement on a tax return."[77] While the charges were dismissed, Professor Chen said he remained hesitant to apply for US government research funds again because "in the end, you're treated like a spy."[78] Professor Anming Hu, who researches nanotechnology at the University of Tennessee, was charged with six felonies but was acquitted after a judge found that the Department of Justice (DOJ) "offered little evidence of anything other than a paperwork misunderstanding."[79] The Initiative was not limited to only a few individual cases. In June 2020, the US Federal Bureau of Investigation disclosed that it had over 2,000 active investigations linked to the China Initiative pending.[80] In February 2022, the Biden administration abandoned the Initiative, citing the potential for harmful bias against researchers "with racial, ethnic or familial ties to China,"[81] as opposed to effectively catching spies conducting espionage operations at the behest of the Chinese government.[82]

However, the end of the China Initiative is far from the end of the human decoupling that is underway. In 2020, the Trump administration abruptly canceled visas for over 1,000 Chinese students and researchers because of their alleged ties to "China's military fusion strategy" and out of fear that they could "[appropriate] sensitive research."[83] While the canceled visas represented a small fraction of the over 360,000 Chinese students who study in the US, the policy sends an unwelcoming message to Chinese students, who may be deterred from coming to the US to study if they know that their visas can be revoked at any time.[84] Some Republican members of Congress have also demanded the reestablishment of the China Initiative. In March 2022, Senator Marco Rubio, joined by five other Republican senators, proposed to reinstate the Initiative, citing the CCP as "the single greatest threat to our national security" and arguing that "it was a foolish decision to divert resources from confronting this threat."[85] Some members of Congress want to go even further. Three Republican members of Congress introduced the Secure Campus Act in May 2020, which "would bar all citizens of mainland China from receiving student or research visas to the United States for graduate or postgraduate studies in STEM fields."[86] Another 2022 bill, sponsored by a Republican congresswoman, seeks to ban any official of the CCP or their family members from attending US universities.[87]

The wisdom of targeting Chinese students and researchers is highly questionable given how much these individuals have contributed to the US's technological leadership. In STEM fields alone, 16 percent of US graduate students come from China, many of whom stay in the US and thus benefit the US innovation base upon graduation.[88] In addition, almost 30 percent of all top-tier AI researchers in the US were educated in China.[89] The crackdown on Chinese students and researchers can thus be self-defeating for the US if these individuals now decide to take their expertise back to China, rather than to stay and contribute to the American economy and society. For example, Steven Chu, a Nobel Prize–winning physicist, was one of nearly 2,000 academics who signed a letter protesting the China Initiative, emphasizing how much of the American "intellectual technological power" stems from immigrants.[90] The letter noted that the openness of the US innovation ecosystem has always been the "hallmark of [the US's] scientific endeavor," and abandoning that principle may undermine the very strength on which the American technological advancement and innovation culture is built.[91] Of course, some bad actors may abuse that openness, and some degree of IP theft may very well occur. However, as emphasized by Professor Rody Truex of Princeton University, this philosophy of openness "has propelled U.S. science ahead of the rest of the world," and "if Americans cordon off our scientific communities in the name of security, we will be sacrificing our greatest advantage, and the core of who we are."[92]

Using Sanctions to Deter Malicious Cyber Activity

The US government also increasingly views China as a cybersecurity threat, and it has developed a number of measures to try to combat this threat. The

US has been a major victim of cyberespionage in recent years, including enduring a Russian cyberattack targeting the Democratic Party during Hillary Clinton's 2016 presidential election campaign.[93] The US has also been the first mover in implementing unilateral cyber sanctions—first against North Korea in 2015[94] and against Russia in 2021.[95] In July 2021, the Biden administration turned up the heat on China, accusing the Chinese government of planning and carrying out cyberattacks worldwide.[96] The US alleged that China was involved in a major cyberespionage operation from 2011 to 2018 that targeted dozens of companies, universities, and government entities in the US and elsewhere.[97] In addition, the US accused China of infiltrating the Microsoft email systems widely used by companies, businesses, and governments around the world in a major espionage operation. To add to the gravity of the charge, US allies—including NATO, the EU, the UK, Australia, Canada, New Zealand, and Japan—joined the US in attributing the Microsoft hack to Chinese actors.[98] While Europeans took a more careful line, accusing China of allowing its territory to be used by hackers, the US directed the blame in no uncertain terms at China's Ministry of State Security, which is in charge of China's intelligence operations. The hard line adopted by the US reflects its realization that, over the past decade, China has transformed from a relatively low-level cyber threat into a sophisticated digital adversary—one that deploys elite hackers who conduct operations under the direction of the Ministry of State Security.[99]

This recent row over cyber hacks has further elevated the tensions between the US and China. The US Secretary of State, Antony Blinken, has accused China of "[compromising] global network security" and collaborating with criminals.[100] He has further characterized China's actions as "a major threat" to economic and national security.[101] China's rebuttal has been equally fierce. Zhao Lijian, a spokesperson for China's Ministry of Foreign Affairs, dismissed the accusations of the US and its allies, noting how the views expressed by a few countries do not represent the consensus of the international community.[102] Liu Pengyu, the spokesperson for the Chinese Embassy in the US, called the US accusations "groundless attacks" while alleging that the US itself engages in "large-scale, organized and indiscriminate cyberintrusion," as evidenced by the 2013 Snowden revelations, which exposed to the world the surveillance practices of the US National Security Agency (NSA).[103] The NSA documents revealed that Huawei computer systems were among the US's numerous surveillance targets, allowing China to paint the US as a perpetrator, as opposed to a mere target, of cyberespionage.[104] The threat of cyberattacks is growing worldwide in today's tense geopolitical environment—whether deployed by Russians as part of the Ukrainian war effort or by China in the midst of escalating tensions over Taiwan—suggesting that this particular frontier of the tech war may intensify in the years ahead.

The new American cybersecurity measures are designed to defend the country's core economic and national security interests against Chinese espionage. When seen alongside its tightening export controls and investment restrictions, these policies reveal a concerted effort by the US government to restrict Chinese access to strategic technology and infrastructure. The US views China as a strategic competitor and a growing threat in economic, geopolitical, and—increasingly—military terms. Until recently, the economic opportunities associated with preserving US tech companies' access to the Chinese market have instilled a sense of restraint in US policymakers, discouraging the government from pursuing a full decoupling of the two digital economies even in the midst of fighting the tech war. But the stifling export control restrictions imposed in 2022 suggest that the US government is now increasingly prepared to allow its foreign policy imperatives to dominate over those economic opportunities. With this shift toward greater government oversight, the US is also abandoning the core of the market-driven principles that have underpinned its regulatory approach toward the digital economy since the 1990s. The US government no longer views economic openness as justified in instances where Chinese inbound investment in critical technologies is seen as a national security threat. Additionally, the US is no longer willing to allow US tech companies to supply Chinese entities with strategic technologies that can enhance China's technologies capabilities—particularly if those capabilities could one day be deployed against the US's geopolitical interests. Thus, the tech war has the inadvertent effect of pushing the US closer to a Chinese-style state-driven regulatory model, where technology is increasingly seen as a strategic asset in need of government oversight and protection.

China's Measures Against the US: Responding to US Sanctions and Striving for Technological Self-Sufficiency

Recent US measures against China have prompted the Chinese government to implement its own set of market restrictions targeting US tech companies. Some may view these measures as a direct response to specific US policies, but others likely see them as simply exemplifying a continued protectionist policy orientation inherent in China's state-driven regulatory model. Regardless, few doubt that the US–China tech war has added to China's existing resolve

to shield its market from foreign players; it has also propelled the government to continue supporting the development of a powerful tech sector capable of enhancing China's technological self-sufficiency. Thus, while the
US–China tech war has led to a notable reorientation of digital regulation in
the US, for the Chinese government, this new era has reinforced—rather than
undermined—China's preexisting tendency to harness the digital economy
to serve the broader economic and geopolitical interests of the Chinese state.

China's strategies in the US–China trade and tech war have been three-
fold. First, the Chinese government has responded to the US measures in
kind by implementing its own export control restrictions. These include
Export Control Law and Unreliable Entities List, which were adopted in
2020 to restrict the outflow of critical tech assets from China. At the same
time, China has adopted various regulatory instruments designed to limit
Chinese companies' exposure to US sanctions, including the Blocking
Rules and the Anti-Sanctions Law, both of which were promulgated in 2021.
Second, China has also emulated the US's CFIUS regime by creating a legal
basis for screening incoming FDI on national security grounds, while also
leveraging its antitrust laws to further restrict foreign acquisitions in the tech
sector. Third, the tech war has reinforced the Chinese government's resolve
to pursue technological self-sufficiency so as to avoid supply chain dependencies that the US government can strategically exploit to the detriment of
Chinese tech companies.[105] Each of these Chinese responses to the tech war
further strengthens the role of the Chinese state as the guardian of the digital
economy—an approach motivated by the overarching goal to ensure that the
Chinese tech sector serves the political goals of the Party and, ultimately, helps
China achieve its economic and geopolitical ambitions.

Using Export Controls to Protect Chinese Tech Assets While Shielding Chinese Tech Companies From US Sanctions

Like the US, China has instituted a number of measures in recent years to
exercise greater control over exports, limiting the outflows of certain strategic
technologies and sensitive datasets. The Chinese government consolidated
its previously diffuse export control review process into a single legislative
framework under the Export Control Law (ECL), which entered into effect in
2020.[106] The new law applies to "controlled items" such as military products,
nuclear-related items, and dual-use technologies.[107] China has also emulated
the US government's Entity List approach to export controls.[108] After the
Trump administration announced that it was adding Huawei to the US Entity

List, China's Ministry of Commerce (MOFCOM) announced its intention to create a similar list—known as the Unreliable Entities List (UEL)—in May 2019. The Chinese government issued the UEL in September 2020, shortly after the US government announced a ban on US transactions on the Chinese apps WeChat and TikTok—again indicating that the Chinese government was determined to respond in kind.[109] The Chinese list targets foreign companies operating in China who "[endanger the] national sovereignty, security or development interests of China" or, in suspending normal transactions with Chinese business entities, "[violate] normal market transaction principles and [cause] serious damage to the legitimate rights and interests of the enterprise, other organization, or individual of China."[110] Penalties for entities placed on the UEL include losing the ability to invest, work, or engage in import or export activities in China.[111]

To date, China has yet to place any companies on the UEL.[112] But the list has already had economic effects; the mere speculation that HSBC would be placed on the list led its shares to crash to a twenty-five-year low in the days after the list's announcement.[113] This happened after Chinese news reports had indicated that HSBC could be targeted because the bank had provided financial information on Meng Wanzhou, the Huawei executive who was detained on fraud charges in 2018.[114] At the same time, China's UEL may not have a powerful effect on US companies, as many large US tech companies are already banned in China. US companies are thus far less vulnerable to such a designation as compared to Huawei, whose business was heavily reliant on operating in the US and on sourcing inputs from US tech companies.[115] China may also not ultimately be willing to designate many US companies as "unreliable," as restricting transactions with those companies would cause direct harm to the Chinese companies that remain reliant on access to many US high-tech supplies.[116]

To complement the ECL and the UEL, the Chinese government adopted the Data Security Law (DSL) in June 2021.[117] In practice, the DSL has been more impactful than the ECL and the Entity List. China views data security and national security as inseparable; China's legislator, the National People's Congress, described in a background document to the DSL how "data is a basic strategic resource of a nation. Without data security, there is no national security."[118] The DSL not only tightens government control over the data that private companies accumulate, but also limits the conditions under which such data can be transferred abroad. This suggests that the Chinese government is tightening its reins on cybersecurity and data security, likely in an effort to fend off foreign cyberespionage but also to set limits on how the country's large private tech companies handle the data they accumulate. The

Cybersecurity Law of 2016 had already imposed requirements on data local-ization, promulgating that "critical information infrastructure operators" are subject to data localization requirements, which requires companies to store personal information and important business data in China.[119] The new DSL further entrenches data localization as the norm in China. The Chinese gov-ernment has also shown its willingness to enforce its norms on data secu-rity, as evidenced by its recent interference with the US listing of a Chinese ride-hailing company DiDi Chuxing, discussed in Chapter 4. The conflict over DiDi's data—and how much of it was handed over to US regulators—demonstrated the serious national security concerns the Chinese government now associates with formerly routine tech transactions and data practices.

In parallel to its efforts to limit exports of sensitive data or strategic technologies out of China, the Chinese government has also engaged in efforts to shield its own companies from US sanctions. In January 2021, MOFCOM promulgated the Rules on Counteracting Unjustified Extra-territorial Application of Foreign Legislation and Other Measures, commonly known as the "Blocking Rules."[120] These measures target any foreign law which "unjustifiably prohibits or restricts the citizens, legal persons or other organizations of China from engaging in normal economic, trade and related activities" with a third-party country and its businesses.[121] Rather than aiming at primary sanctions—such as US companies obeying US sanctions against Chinese companies—these Blocking Rules seek to prevent non-US companies from following any secondary sanctions that they may be subjected to under US law.[122] For example, if a South Korean semiconductor company refused to sell chips to a Chinese telecom company placed on the US Entity List, such refusal could be "blocked" by the Chinese law if the Chinese government found the US law "unjustified." It would also provide a legal basis for the Chinese company to sue the Korean company for damages in China. In prac-tice, the Blocking Rules would thus force the Korean company to choose be-tween complying with US or Chinese laws. Blocking statutes are not unique to China, and even the EU has deployed them when faced with US secondary sanctions.[123] However, a key difference is that the EU's blocking statute lists the particular laws that are affected in an annex to its statute,[124] while the Chinese Blocking Rules leave significant discretion to the Chinese govern-ment. Currently, no specific foreign laws have been identified as subject to the Blocking Rules,[125] which, again, may be explained by the Chinese government being conscious of the costs associated with such countermeasures.[126]

To complement the Blocking Rules, the Chinese legislature also enacted the Anti-Foreign Sanctions Law (AFSL) in June 2021.[127] The AFSL authorizes the use of countermeasures against individuals and entities that assist in creating or implementing anti-China sanctions. The AFSL measures could hence target foreign government officials, individuals, and companies alike.[128] Countermeasures may include being denied entry to China, freezing of assets in China, and blocking of transactions with entities in China. The law also provides a statutory basis for China's sanctions against individual US and European politicians, including the former US Secretary of State Mike Pompeo[129] and the former US Speaker of the House of Representatives Nancy Pelosi, as well as her immediate family members.[130] However, as with the Blocking Rules, it is unclear how willing China is to authorize such countermeasures due to the possibility of collateral damage on the Chinese economy. Therefore, it is likely that the Chinese government is hoping that the threat of these countermeasures alone would, in most instances, deter companies from complying with foreign sanctions.[131]

Limiting Foreign Investment and Operations in China

Similar to the US, China has also recently stepped up its screening of FDI on national security grounds. It has formalized this process with a new law on Measures for the Security Review of Foreign Investments (FISR Measures), which was adopted in December 2020 and entered into force in January 2021.[132] The process introduced by the FISR Measures resembles that of the CFIUS review process in the US.[133] The Chinese investment screening is conducted jointly by the National Development and Reform Commission (NDRC) and MOFCOM.[134] The new law states that foreign investments are automatically subject to a review when the FDI involves "critical information technology and Internet products and services" or "key technologies."[135] Should national security concerns arise, the government may impose conditions on the investment to mitigate those concerns or even prohibit the investment altogether.[136]

Even before the adoption of FISR Measures, foreign investment in China was subject to uncertainty as the Chinese government has oscillated between encouraging foreign investment and seeking to impose limits on it. For example, the government publishes a *Negative List*,[137] in which it designates industries for which foreign investment in China is restricted, but has also removed sectors from that list in recent years following concessions made in trade talks with the US.[138] The government has also at times allowed foreign companies to invest in sectors that are normally tightly regulated. For example, the authorities recently allowed foreign companies to hold a 50 percent stake in joint ventures that provide virtual private networks (VPNs) to foreign businesses in Beijing, even though the average Chinese consumer is still banned from using VPNs to leap over the Great Firewall.[139] In contrast, China has continued to ban foreign investment in the rare earth mineral sector, retaining domestic control over this critical resource.[140] The US has complained about China's rare earth investment restrictions for years, with a group of senators writing in 2011 that "the United States should not sit passively while China's investment policies hamstring U.S. companies and undermine our national and economic security needs."[141] Despite foreign objections, China continues to list rare earth minerals as a sector prohibited for foreign investment in its 2021 *Negative List*.[142] This example illustrates how unpredictability surrounding the Chinese government's regulatory policies may create its own barrier to ongoing foreign investment in Chinese companies. These developments—asserting tighter control over FDI while at the same time agreeing to open up additional sectors for foreign investors—indicate that China's approach toward foreign investment has followed two parallel trends: on the one hand, the government has sought to ease trade tensions and communicate that China remains open for foreign investment, while on the other, it keeps a tight rein on those investments.

Another important policy tool that the Chinese government uses to protect its strategic technologies is antitrust law. When the Chinese government wants to block a specific high-profile transaction, whether domestic or international, it often turns to its antitrust powers to do so. By blurring the line between an antitrust review and a national security review of foreign acquisitions, the Chinese government compounds foreign investors' risks and uncertainty. For years, Chinese antitrust regulators faced accusations that they utilized merger review to further protectionist industrial policy objectives that favored domestic companies over foreign ones—a practice that can be viewed as consistent with its state-driven regulatory model.[143] In 2008, China adopted its Anti-Monopoly Law, and in the years following this law's adoption, Chinese regulators were seen as arbitrary, holding up mergers that had already been reviewed by the US and EU.[144] But even today, the Chinese merger control regime remains unpredictable. For example, when the US private equity firm Blackstone sought to acquire Soho China, one of China's biggest real estate firms, the State Administration for Market Regulation (SAMR) failed to grant timely approval, leading Blackstone to withdraw its takeover bid in 2021.[145] While the reasons behind the failed merger approval remained unclear, SAMR's inaction was expected to deter any other foreign buyer from attempting to acquire the company after Blackstone's failure.[146]

In the tech sector, a failure to get Chinese antitrust approvals has doomed, or nearly doomed, some major deals, illustrating how China has been able to restrict tech investments even outside China. The Chinese regulators failed to approve Qualcomm's proposed acquisition of a Dutch chipmaking company NXP, reviewing the deal for twenty months without reaching a decision until the deal expired in 2018.[147] A US chipmaking equipment supplier, Applied Materials, similarly abandoned its attempt to acquire another chipmaking equipment company, Japanese Kokusai Electric, because it could not secure a timely approval of the deal from Chinese regulators in 2021. At that time, Chinese approval had been pending for almost nine months, a period during which antitrust authorities in Japan, the US, and Europe had approved the transaction.[148] In other instances, Chinese approval was ultimately obtained— but at a cost. The SAMR eventually approved Cisco's acquisition of a US-based optical networking manufacturer Acacia in January 2021, eighteen months after the deal was initially announced.[149] The delay in securing Chinese antitrust approval almost led to the collapse of the deal, as Acacia announced it was going to terminate the agreement due to Cisco's failure to secure a timely approval from Chinese authorities. Ultimately, Cisco's acquisition was completed at an elevated purchase price.[150] While the difficulty of securing Chinese antitrust approvals can affect deals with little nexus to China, they may, in particular, deter foreign investors from acquiring Chinese companies due to the heightened regulatory scrutiny associated with such deals. These examples illustrate how antitrust law can be an effective tool in the broader US–China tech war. Antitrust reviews allow the Chinese government to assert greater control over the country's critical tech assets, shielding them from foreign ownership. This way, Beijing can ensure that those technologies continue to benefit China's technological development and, ultimately, serve its national interests.

Even beyond facing unpredictable FDI screening and antitrust scrutiny, foreign investment in China is often limited because foreign firms know that the conditions for accessing and operating in the Chinese market are onerous, as discussed in Chapters 2 and 4. Many US tech companies, including Google, had already largely withdrawn from the Chinese market years prior to the recent conflicts. The business environment is also getting harder to navigate for those that have stayed—for example, Microsoft's LinkedIn abandoned its professional networking service in China in 2021, leaving behind only a limited job posting feature.[151] Many US tech companies have found Chinese government requirements too costly and risky and have chosen to forgo the Chinese market, while others, including Apple, have submitted to heavy concessions as the price for operating there. Regardless, it is indisputable that access to the Chinese market comes at a price, and that price has recently gone up with the more tightly controlled business environment created by the US–China tech war.

The Pursuit of Technological Self-Sufficiency
in Response to Sanctions

Beyond adopting various measures designed to counter US sanctions, China's overarching strategy has been to ensure that it achieves technological self-sufficiency and hence becomes less dependent on access to US and other foreign technologies going forward. While this strategy dates back to before the onset of the US–China tech war, the tech war has served as an additional "Sputnik moment" for China, further escalating China's relentless pursuit of technological self-sufficiency so as to lessen the country's dependence on US technologies and its companies' vulnerabilities to US-imposed sanctions.[152] This policy goal has culminated in the implementation of the "dual circulation" strategy. Dual circulation refers to an economic strategy aimed at retaining the benefits of the international trade and financial systems as long as possible while simultaneously preparing an internally resilient China for the day when China might be cut off from global markets.[153] The idea of dual circulation was first publicly introduced by President Xi Jinping at a CCP conference in May 2020[154] and has since appeared in China's 14th Five-Year Plan and other implementing documents.[155] The strategy was formulated in response to the shock of COVID-19 and the US–China trade war, two events that revealed how China may well lose access to critical foreign supplies and accentuated the need for China to build its own technological capabilities.[156]

A key tenet of the dual circulation strategy is the need to enhance China's own technological capabilities and reduce its dependence on foreign technologies. President Xi Jinping and other Chinese leaders have emphasized the need to improve the country's "indigenous innovation" and to gain control over "chokepoint technologies."[157] In addition to shoring up domestic supply, the dual circulation strategy aims to cultivate domestic demand and thereby reduce China's reliance on access to foreign consumers.[158] However, in parallel with those efforts to make the domestic market a more robust source of supply and demand, the dual circulation strategy seeks to maintain China's connections to the outside world through programs like the Belt and Road Initiative—the Chinese government's foreign policy initiative aimed at fostering Chinese companies' infrastructure investments abroad.[159] Thus, the dual circulation strategy envisions China becoming a fully integrated and self-reliant domestic market that is not dependent on other countries, while continuing to benefit from access to some export markets, including those along the Belt and Road.[160]

As part of the Chinese government's drive toward technological self-sufficiency, the government is also nudging Chinese firms to invest in "deep tech." Here, the Chinese leadership draws a distinction between "nice to have" and "need to have" technologies.[161] Consumer internet companies such as social media, e-commerce, and ride-sharing belong to the first category. Semiconductors, electric vehicle batteries, and telecom equipment belong to the second category and are thus seen as central to China's technological ambitions. This also explains why consumer internet companies have been the target of the recent regulatory crackdown whereas investments in deep tech continue to benefit from strong state backing. Shanghai-based technology analyst Dan Wang has further argued that US sanctions have provided a major impetus for China's quest for technological self-sufficiency.[162] When faced with costly sanctions and loss of access to US technologies, China is responding by cultivating domestic alternatives. Thus, by imposing trade sanctions, "the U.S. government has inadvertently done more than any party directive to incentivize private investment in China's domestic technology ecosystem"[163]—thereby potentially strengthening China's relative position in the ongoing tech race.

An Arms Race to Bolster Technological Self-Sufficiency

The US–China rivalry and the resulting mutual distrust are pushing both technology powers toward greater technological self-sufficiency in an effort to shed any dependencies that have become, or will likely become, vulnerabilities in the tech war. In parallel with decoupling their respective tech ecosystems from one another, both countries are racing to build their capabilities in critical industries such as AI, semiconductors, cloud computing, and batteries. This battle to dominate these new frontiers of technological development is elevating the role of the state in the digital economy, with both the US and Chinese governments vying to grant heavy state subsidies to support technologies viewed as key toward technological supremacy. While the US government has had a nontrivial role in funding American digital innovations in the past, as discussed earlier in Chapter 1, the practical effect of this ongoing subsidy race is that it is reinforcing the Chinese regulatory approach under which the state plays a dominant role in directing the digital economy.

AI is one of the primary battlefields in the ongoing tech race. The Washington, DC–based think tank Brookings declared in a 2020 paper that "whoever leads in artificial intelligence in 2030 will rule the world until 2100."[164] The significance of AI is supported by various studies predicting how AI will affect the global economy. While projections regarding the gains from AI innovations differ somewhat, the McKinsey Global Institute predicts that by 2030, AI could add $13 trillion to the global economy, delivering an additional 1.2 percent of annual GDP growth.[165] The World Bank similarly predicts "significant gains in overall productivity and economic growth" globally from AI-related products and improved supply chains. It relies on a 2019 Deloitte study, which estimates that the global AI market will be worth $6.4 trillion by 2025, and a 2017 PwC study, which estimates that global GDP will have grown 14 percent by 2030 due to AI adoption.[166] To put these numbers in context, the PwC study notes how "AI could contribute up to $15.7 trillion to the global economy in 2030, more than the current output of China and India combined."[167] Given these projections, it is therefore not surprising that the global tech race is particularly intense in AI, with every major player eager to claim its share of that projected growth.

Both China and the US are determined to win the AI race. In 2017, the Chinese government released a Plan for Development of the New Generation of Artificial Intelligence ("2017 AI Development Plan")[168] that articulated a goal of making China "the front-runner and global innovation center in AI" by 2030.[169] China's State Council announced that AI development should exist "everywhere and at every moment."[170] The US has responded with equal resolve to maintain its AI leadership—a goal that has gained unremitting urgency with the rise in China's AI capabilities. In 2019, President Trump issued an executive order stating that the US policy is to "sustain and enhance the scientific, technological, and economic leadership position of the United States in AI" and instructing government agencies to develop plans and policies geared at maximizing the US's strength in AI.[171] The US National Security Commission on AI, appointed by President Trump in 2018 and led by ex-Google CEO Eric Schmidt, set a similar tone in its 2021 report to the US Congress.[172] The Final Report spans over 700 pages, and delivers a stark warning that China will soon replace the US as the world's AI superpower. Mentioning China 699 times,[173] the report emphasizes the importance of the US maintaining its technological advantage over China and urges the US government to double its annual AI R&D spending to $32 billion by 2026.[174]

The US is aware that China engages in the AI race from a unique position of strength. Chinese AI companies are able to harness an unparalleled amount of data generated by the country's vast consumer market, which is both digitally connected and subject to extensive online surveillance.[175] China also benefits from its fiercely effective culture of copying, which may not generate AI breakthroughs but gives China a leg up in refining new commercial applications from existing AI technologies.[176] The Chinese private sector's AI development also benefits from extensive government support.[177] Riding on these enabling features of the Chinese AI environment, the big Chinese tech companies are already today leading in AI developments, with Baidu excelling in automated driving, Alibaba in AI cities, and Tencent in smart medicine and health. And more is expected: China's 2017 AI Development Plan highlights several industries that China will "forcefully develop," ranging from smart robots and vehicles to virtual and augmented reality.[178]

The AI race is consequential because of the economic stakes involved. But the stakes are also high for political and ideological reasons. China is known for developing AI applications to pursue authoritarian surveillance, thus compromising individual rights and freedoms. In 2021, White House National Security Advisor Jake Sullivan emphasized this tendency, stating that "the US and its allies must continue to lead in AI . . . and other emerging tech to ensure that these technologies are safe, secure, and beneficial to free societies."[179] Yet a third reason the US cares deeply about the AI race is the contributions that AI can make to military power. Both the US and China are keenly aware of this, further intensifying the AI arms race. China's 2017 AI Development Plan calls for strengthening military-civilian integration in the AI domain so that AI can support "command and decision-making, military deduction, defense equipment, and other applications."[180] The Chinese government views AI as vital not only for the country's economic competitiveness but also for its national security,[181] thus envisioning AI-driven military technologies as critical in challenging the US in military supremacy.[182] The 2021 Report by the US National Security Commission on AI strikes a similar tone, warning that the US is unprepared in the face of AI-enabled threats, with grave consequences to the country's national security. As a result, the report urges the US government to make investments that will help it to "achieve a state of military AI readiness by 2025."[183] The US Defense Advanced Research Projects Agency (DARPA) shares this view, announcing back in 2018 that it had committed to investing up to $2 billion over the next five years in new AI programs.[184] This announcement was followed by a 2021 commitment made by Secretary of Defense Lloyd Austin to invest $1.5 billion into the US Department of Defense's Joint Artificial Intelligence Center.[185]

It is difficult to predict whether the US or China will ultimately fare better in the AI race, as each has somewhat different strengths in this domain. In terms of funding and investment, both countries record impressive numbers, with the US benefiting from extensive private funding and China from large-scale government funding. According to a 2021 OECD study analyzing trends in VC investment in AI companies, US and China-based startups were recipients of more than 80 percent of VC funding in 2020, followed by the EU with 4 percent and the UK and Israel with 3 percent each.[186] According to the same study, total VC investment in US AI firms reached $42 billion in 2020, representing 57 percent of the global total. In contrast, VC funding channeled into Chinese AI companies peaked in 2018, but slowed down after that, reaching $17 billion in 2020 and contributing 24 percent of the global total.

The US produces the most AI startups and attracts the most innovative talent, while China has an edge in AI-related patent applications. According to a 2018 study, the US remains the home of the most AI startups (40 percent), followed by China (11 percent).[187] An article in the *Harvard Business Review* cited a 2019 Global Artificial Intelligence Industry Data Report, which found that China had 1,189 AI firms, compared to over 2,000 active AI firms in the US.[188] Chinese AI firms are particularly active in speech, image, and video recognition. Even though the US still surpasses China in terms of the number of startups, China is filing more AI patents than any other country.[189] This is confirmed by a Stanford University study, which reported that China is today responsible for over half of the world's AI patent filings, even though only a small percentage of those patents are actually being granted.[190]

Most studies suggest that the US leads the AI race in terms of producing (or hosting) the most AI talent, even though China is catching up quickly. According to the China AI Development Report mentioned above, China's global share of research papers in the field of AI was approximately 4 percent in 1997 but reached almost 28 percent in 2017. This jump reveals a staggering growth in China's AI research activity and shows China surpassing all other countries, including the US.[191] On the other hand, another 2020 study that examines the distribution of top AI talent by analyzing the contributions to one of the largest and most selective AI conferences for deep learning indicates the US has far more of the world's top AI talent than any other country. This Neural Information Processing Systems 2019 conference saw a record-high 15,920 AI researchers submit 6,614 papers. Out of those submissions, 21.6 percent were accepted, which the researchers used as a proxy to identify the top 20 percent of global AI research talent. Among this group, the US retains a commanding lead over other countries, with nearly 60 percent of the top AI talent representing US universities and companies—Google ranking first and Stanford University second—followed by Chinese (11 percent) and European (10 percent) institutions. The US also maintains a significant lead over the EU and China in its ability to attract the best AI researchers into the country. The same study revealed that while the largest number of top-tier AI researchers today work in the US, the majority of those researchers are immigrants or foreign nationals, with 29 percent of them having received their undergraduate degree from China, 20 percent from the US, and 18 percent from Europe.[192] These various studies show how both the US and China are already deeply invested in AI development—creating and funding startups, producing research, and nurturing talent. Yet both countries are determined to do more—the US to stay ahead of China, and China to surpass the US.

While AI is one of the primary battlefields in the US–China tech war, there are other technologies that both governments view as important, even existential. Semiconductors, for example, are seen as key to any country's technological self-sufficiency as they power most of the devices and services consumers use daily. Everything digital runs on semiconductors, making semiconductors a critical component for mobile phones, computers, healthcare equipment, kitchen appliances, aircrafts, and cars alike. Even before the onset of the COVID-19 pandemic, China was known to flood the industry with subsidies. The *China Securities Journal* reported that local governments and the private sector in China have fueled the Chinese semiconductor industry with $170 billion worth of subsidies and investment since 2014.[193] The Chinese government renewed its support for the industry by setting up a $28.9 billion national semiconductor fund in 2019 and was spending a record $33 billion on semiconductor industry subsidies in 2020.[194] In the meantime, however, the US has also entered the subsidy race. Congress recently passed the CHIPS and Science Act of 2022, which allocates $52.7 billion for "American semiconductor research, development, manufacturing, and workforce development."[195] The CHIPS and Science Act is designed to help the US mitigate supply chain disruptions, achieve greater technological self-sufficiency, and better compete against China.[196] The EU, South Korea, Japan, and Taiwan are also extending extensive state support to the sector, turning the arms race over key technologies into a global one and further setting the world on a path toward state-driven "techno-nationalism."[197] Despite this massive investment, however, ultimately it is unclear if the subsidy race supercharges innovation and leads to technological progress around the world, or if it leads to wasteful competition that does little to enhance proclaimed goals around technological self-sufficiency, national security, and economic growth.

Implications of the US–China Tech War

While the ultimate outcome of the US–China tech war is difficult to predict, certain developments in the near term seem more likely than others. First, the prolonged tech war will continue to fuel uncertainty and undermine trust in global supply chains, making the pursuit of technological self-sufficiency a key policy objective not just for the US and China, but for other governments as well. Such spillover effects risk entrenching techno-protectionism as a global norm, thus shifting countries away from the American market-driven regulatory model toward the Chinese state-driven regulatory model. Second, the US–China conflict is likely to continue, even intensify, as trust between the two countries remains low. Neither party is seeking a pathway toward reconciliation; instead, both are determined to display resolve and view the conflict as a defining battle over technological, economic, and geopolitical power. The conflict has also acquired strong ideological undertones and features robust domestic support for hardline approaches—making it difficult for either side to back down.[198] However, despite these continuing tensions, deeply intertwined supply chains and commercial pressures in both the US and China are likely to prevent an all-out tech war that would lead to a full decoupling of US and Chinese technological assets. These countries, at some deeply pragmatic level, understand the economic damage that would result from going it alone. This suggests that the conflict will likely remain costly, yet will also continue to feature elements of restraint.

Toward Global Techno-Nationalism?

There may not be any winners in this tech war. Like trade wars, tech wars are costly to fight for all parties involved. Market restrictions and subsidy races also rarely cultivate merit-based competition or spur innovation, which are the actual drivers of technological progress. Instead, one of the more predictable consequences of the unfolding US–China tech war is that it will trigger a worldwide shift toward techno-protectionism. By closing their markets off from foreign technologies and pouring subsidies into their domestic ones, the US and China risk cementing techno-nationalism as the norm across jurisdictions. Such development presents a significant setback for proponents of open trade, technological progress, and the global internet, which have always been central to the American market-driven regulatory model. At the same time, China's sovereignty-centric vision of the global digital order and the values underlying its state-driven regulatory model triumph in this increasingly protectionist world.

The political environment today offers fertile ground for this kind of techno-protectionism or digital nationalism. Even before the onset of the pandemic, economic nationalism was gaining ground, undermining institutions that sustain market openness and rule-based international cooperation. Governments around the world are now increasingly trading economic openness for industrial policy with strong nationalist undertones.[199] They are limiting foreign investment, restricting exports, and subsidizing domestic production in pursuit of a broader structural change in the economy. The outbreak of the COVID-19 pandemic further reinforced these underlying trends by closing borders, hobbling supply chains, and leaving countries to fight over critical medical supplies. Every nation realized that they cannot count on mutual solidarity in times of crises, when critical goods such as masks are in short supply. As a result, governments are now adjusting their trade and technology policies to the shifting global economic and political reality where uncertainty among governments runs high and trust low. This dynamic is difficult to reverse as that forgone trust will take a long time to rebuild, particularly with the feeble efforts to do so currently underway.

The US has recently been leading the world away from economic openness, ushering in this protectionist trend during the Trump presidency.[200] After taking office, President Trump moved immediately and decisively to implement the nativist, anti-trade platform that was central to his election campaign. The US withdrew its support from international cooperation and institutions, undermined the WTO by refusing to appoint members to its Appellate Body, and abandoned regional trade agreements such as the Trans-Pacific Partnership. This protectionist tirade culminated in the US waging trade wars not only against China, but even against its closest allies and trade partners, including Canada, the EU, and Mexico. President Trump also took a decisive turn toward techno-nationalism, actively seeking to decouple the US from Chinese technology supply chains. President Trump's "America First" policies seem to outlive his presidency. President Biden's trade and technology policy aims to, first and foremost, empower the American middle class and preserve American jobs, as opposed to defending free trade and economic openness. It is illustrative that President Biden, when introducing his ambitious $2 trillion infrastructure bill, emphasized how "not a contract will go out" to a company that is not an "American company with American products, all the way down the line, and American workers."[201] In this sense, both Presidents Trump and Biden can be described as "fundamentally mercantilist" in their approach to international trade.[202]

President Biden has not only continued his predecessor's trade and tech war against China, but also ushered in a new era of big government. He has injected unprecedented amounts of funds into the domestic economy in the name of increasing the US's technological self-reliance, rebuilding the country's infrastructure, and remaking the US economy. This new era of industrial policy is gaining notable bipartisan political support in Congress, especially when deployed as a tool to counter China's rise—even while it is shifting the US away from the core values underlying its market-driven regulatory model. At the same time, this new policy orientation also has its critics. Nikki Haley, the former US ambassador to the UN, recently accused the US government of embracing "their own versions of central planning," thus emulating China's state-centric economic model. She argued that "economic freedom is the proven path to beat communist China. If Washington keeps trying to pick winners and losers, America will lose."[203]

While the US's turn inward may surprise some observers, China's engagement in blatant digital protectionism is hardly unforeseen. China's economy has always been characterized by extensive state intervention and discriminatory treatment of foreign investment. This is particularly true in the domain of the digital economy. Its policies have forced transfers of technology and kept out foreign tech firms, all while shoring up national champions who have been able to grow in a large domestic market shielded from foreign rivals. The pursuit of a path toward "self-reliance" has dominated China's economic policy under President Xi long before the Europeans introduced concepts such as "strategic autonomy" and digital sovereignty into policy conversations. China's ambitious Made in China 2025 agenda only reinforces this existing trend. Not unlike the US and the EU, the key objective behind China's digital sovereignty agenda is to reduce China's dependence on foreign technologies and enhance China's standing in the global tech race. Yet China has to date been prepared to go furthest in enmeshing the state into the operation of the marketplace, and has actively engineered China's path toward technological sovereignty while restricting foreign tech companies' abilities to operate in its domestic market.[204]

These developments in the US and China have also hardened the digital sovereignty narrative in Europe, illustrating how the US–China conflict is having global implications. Many Europeans continue to urge the EU to defend the open internet and open trade, reasoning that there is otherwise little hope for reviving international cooperation and reversing the zero-sum mentality that is governing the ongoing tech race. At the same time, other Europeans retort that the EU would be naïve in letting others take advantage of Europe's openness while not extending that same openness to Europeans. The tech war has laid bare the limits of the global and open digital economy, while also exposing vulnerabilities in the deeply integrated tech ecosystem that was built to maximize efficiency and that—erroneously, many would claim—relied on the political stability of the international system. As a result, the EU must be prepared to stand on its own and protect its interests in an increasingly unfair world dominated by America First or Made in China 2025 ideologies.[205] According to this view, relying on open markets and international cooperation in a world where others do not play along can be seen as detrimental, futile, and even dangerous. The current situation thus leaves the EU with few options but to defend and bolster its own technological sovereignty, even when that contributes toward techno-protectionism elsewhere as well. And the EU is far from being alone in this effort. The pursuit of digital sovereignty has become a defining feature of national digital strategies around the world. Scott Malcomson goes as far as characterizing the "mission for self-sufficiency" as "the most striking geopolitical feature" of the current era, as major economies are retreating from globalization and ushering in "the New Age of Autarky."[206]

If the US and the EU refashion their economies around a technological self-sufficiency and digital sovereignty agenda, they risk diminishing their ability to convince the rest of the world of the merits of an open digital economy and their respective regulatory models. Governments around the world are starting to deploy this concept of digital sovereignty as a veneer to legitimize measures such as data localization and industrial policies designed to favor domestic technologies over foreign ones. The EU's emphasis on digital sovereignty as a central policy objective in the EU may even lend legitimacy to the more extreme variants of digital sovereignty that authoritarian governments such as China and Russia are pursuing. The digital sovereignty narrative can be invoked to justify many forms of government control over the internet, offering a blueprint for autocracies to engage in extensive surveillance of the digital space. For example, China deploys the notion of digital sovereignty to justify extensive government control of the digital sphere that extends beyond protectionism and competitiveness concerns into intruding on free speech and other individual freedoms. Consequently, the more that the US and the EU step in to actively shape their national digital economies, the less convincing their criticism becomes when they ask China to loosen the reins on its digital economy or try to persuade other countries not to emulate China's state-driven regulatory model.

Next Phase of the Tech War: Between Rivalry and Restraint

Nobody can predict the outcome of the ongoing US–China tech war with certainty. But most likely, neither the US nor China will in the end be able to declare victory or claim the status of a sole "tech superpower." There may be no unipolar tech world awaiting on the other side of this conflict. Examining different fields of technology today suggests that China is pulling ahead in some of them while the US is, at least for now, still holding an advantage in others.[207] For example, Apple may be the most well-known smartphone brand in many parts of the world, but Chinese companies lead in global smartphone sales, capturing over 50 percent of the sales among the top fifteen brands globally. In particular, across Asia and Africa, Chinese smartphones are more popular than Apple's iPhone. Even though US sanctions have slashed Huawei's market share, Huawei's retreat has created a windfall for other Chinese brands such as Xiaomi, which is now selling more smartphones than Apple globally, trailing only Korea's Samsung. China also dominates the US in the sales of telecom network equipment, an area from which the US is largely absent, and in battery cell production. Perhaps most surprisingly, China is now making important gains in the software industry, including in social media, which is a field that US tech companies have long dominated. In 2019, the Chinese social media company TikTok overtook Facebook as the most popular social media app among US users. In contrast, the US still today leads in several other fields such as mobile gaming and sales of semiconductors (even if not in their manufacture). The US can also claim, for the moment, to be the home of the top electric vehicle brand, Tesla, even while being closely challenged by European and Chinese electric vehicles.[208]

Yet even in the absence of a clear winner emerging from the conflict, the US–China rivalry is almost certain to continue. There is likely no truce in sight anytime soon, as both parties remain steadfast in the pursuit of their economic and geopolitical goals. If anything, the superpower conflict is likely to only accelerate. A key question then becomes whether the nature of the rivalry will change in the near future. Under the worst scenario, US–China relations will further deteriorate and trade and tech wars will intensify, heightening the risk of exploding into an even larger and more dangerous military conflict. Graham Allison has argued that the US and China may be heading toward what he calls a "Thucydides Trap," which refers to the tendency of a military conflict to occur when a rising power threatens to topple a ruling power as an international hegemon—just like the Peloponnesian War ensued when Sparta feared the rising power of Athens.[209] Over the past five hundred years, a war ensued in twelve out of sixteen cases where an emerging power challenged an existing power. This historical phenomenon leads Allison to argue that a war between the US and China in the coming decades is "more likely than not,"[210] while hastening to add that such a development is not inevitable if the US–China relationship is carefully managed. While Allison's thesis is controversial, several foreign policy experts point to escalating US–China tensions, including an increasingly real threat that China might seek to take over Taiwan by force and thus potentially trigger a US military response.[211] Given the challenges associated with indigenous innovation in semiconductors—one of the key frontiers of the US–China tech rivalry—some commentators have gone so far as to suggest that Taiwan's prominence in the semiconductor industry may provide an impetus for China to invade the island, while others remain doubtful that would happen.[212] These fears of a looming military confrontation intensified in 2022 following US House of Representatives Speaker Nancy Pelosi's visit to Taiwan, which the Chinese government viewed as a provocation, and responded by conducting military exercises encircling Taiwan. Thus, the prospect of the ongoing tech war morphing into something even more dangerous, including a US–China military conflict, cannot be excluded.

However, even if a military conflict is avoided, contestation in the economic realm is likely to persist. Most likely, the US and China will continue to decouple their technological assets by implementing further export and investment restrictions and continuing their buildup of domestic capabilities in strategic technologies. This will have an adverse effect on tech companies, governments, and consumers. However, any such technological decoupling is likely to have its limits, not least because of the high costs involved. Trade and tech wars are costly for all parties fighting them, offering a strong argument for de-escalation, or even a truce, over time. A recent Deutsche Bank report estimates the costs of the ongoing tech war to exceed $3.5 trillion over the next five years.[213] In addition to being costly, decoupling is also a difficult strategy to implement in practice, as illustrated by the examples discussed in Chapter 4, and as shown by the effects of the US–China trade war to date. Even though exports and imports have dropped since the onset of the trade war, the supply chains between the two have not been meaningfully delinked.[214]

Technological self-sufficiency may also not even be a realistic strategy for any country, including the US and China, given how integrated the digital economy is today. The US–China tech war is unlike the Cold War between the US and Russia; those two economies were not closely connected from the beginning, making it less costly to sever economic and political ties between the two.[215] For example, despite its determination to achieve technological self-sufficiency, there are certain complex products that China is not capable of manufacturing today, including large aircraft and advanced semiconductors.[216] Semiconductors pose perhaps the biggest challenge as they rely on complex supply chains across multiple jurisdictions. Despite large investments in self-reliance, China has not been able to produce high-end semiconductors and remains reliant on importing them.[217] The semiconductor industry is among the most R&D-intensive, and companies need access to global markets to recoup those R&D costs.[218] The Chinese government is painfully aware of the challenge and has poured state funding into upgrading its local industry, but to date, little progress has been made toward self-sufficiency.[219] The US is following a similar strategy, flooding the semiconductor industry with generous government subsidies without any guarantee that genuine self-sufficiency will ensue from the costly effort.[220] The leading tech powers may thus ultimately come to concede that decoupling their deeply intertwined economies is not only costly, but may not even be feasible to execute in practice. These interdependencies push both the US and China toward a strategy of restraint even in the midst of a great power conflict.

Tech companies also urge their governments to exercise restraint. US tech companies want to take advantage of market opportunities in China the same way that many Chinese tech companies want to retain access to US suppliers, consumers, and investors. Several US tech firms are keen to see the US–China conflict wane, freeing them to exploit commercial opportunities in a valuable market. Existing government restrictions such as US export controls directly undermine their market opportunities. For example, President Trump pointed to the Chinese IP theft targeting Idaho-based semiconductor company Micron as an example of why the trade and tech war against China was justified. But according to Micron's CEO Sanjay Mehrotra, export restrictions, including the company's inability to supply Huawei, were hurting Micron's business.[221] Other US tech companies such as Cadence, Lam Research, and Teradyne have similarly expressed their opposition to potentially expansive export controls on foundational and emerging technologies.[222] Cadence warned that such controls would adversely affect US companies and their workers while only having a modest effect on China, which could turn to alternative sources of supply. Export controls would also reduce the funding available for Cadence to innovate and cause the company to potentially lose Chinese engineers who may take their expertise to Chinese companies.[223] Intel has also emphasized how the US export controls impose costs on the US tech industry and urged the US government to forgo unilateral measures and instead coordinate sanctions with other countries.[224] The US Semiconductor Industry Association also issued a statement opposing the new export controls announced by the US government in 2020, stressing how "sales of non-sensitive, commercial products to China drive semiconductor research and innovation here in the U.S., which is critical to America's economic strength and national security."[225]

The US government cannot afford to be indifferent to these business interests—the US does need its tech companies to thrive after all. Ultimately, US companies' profits in China help fund their innovations, which are critical to the US's ability to stay ahead in the tech race and prevail in its horizontal battle against China.[226] This guides the US government toward greater restraint in managing existing political tensions. Already today, the tech war reflects this difficult balancing act between commercial and geopolitical interests and explains why neither country has pursued an unmitigated attempt to decouple the two economies. For example, while US sanctions have been both severe and effective against Huawei, the US has often opted for a more subdued strategy toward most other Chinese tech firms.[227] The US government has also chosen an export licensing regime as opposed to a complete export ban on most technologies. The US government has further kept granting such export licenses in many instances as it has sought to balance its national security interests with its companies' economic interests. As a result, while Huawei's revenues have been in free fall, many other Chinese companies have not faced any adverse consequences. For example, Hikvision, a manufacturer of surveillance technologies that was placed on the US's Entity List in 2019 due to its involvement in repression in Xinjiang, reported a 40 percent increase in its operating income in the first half of 2021.[228] Similarly, as mentioned earlier, the Chinese government has to date refrained from deploying its new Entities List to designate any US companies as unreliable, as such a decision would inflict harm on Chinese companies that need access to US high-tech supplies. Thus, in the near future, the US–China tech war is likely to feature only partial technological decoupling. Periods of escalation will alternate with periods of de-escalation, making the conflict protracted and costly, but ultimately manageable.

In fighting their tech war, the US knows that it needs to balance its geopolitical interests and values—such as addressing China as a growing military threat or condemning China's treatment of the Uyghur minority in Xinjiang—with its desire to maintain commercial opportunities with the world's soon-to-be-largest economy. But there are also ideological and political reasons for the US to de-escalate the tensions. Jessica Chen Weiss has described the "Perilous Logic of Zero-Sum Competition" characterizing the US–China relationship today.[229] While acknowledging that China has become increasingly authoritarian, coercive, and intolerant—and hence legitimately a central concern for US policymakers—she criticizes the US policy response as stemming from "what it fears" rather than "what it wants."[230] Consequently, the US risks losing sight of its affirmative interests; the country's own values no longer underpin the US government's foreign policy strategy toward China. In trying to "out-China China," the US is allowing the strategic competition to become an end goal in itself. In the process, the US may forgo its own strengths and obscure its vision for the world, moving away from its commitment to core values underlying its market-driven regulatory model, such as openness and nondiscrimination. Chen Weiss suggests that if the US becomes more faithful again to its own core values—human progress, peace, and prosperity—it will realize that "the United States does not need to beat China in order to win."[231]

As this chapter has revealed, there is no doubt considerable political momentum to escalate the US–China conflict. Despite the costs of fighting the tech war and decoupling the two digital ecosystems, a partial technological decoupling is likely to continue due to the persisting sentiment that the only thing costlier than fighting a tech war is losing a tech war. Even then, there are limits to any such technological decoupling given the deeply entangled US-economic relationship in today's digital economy. Both the US and China, straddling the competing needs of ideology and pragmatism, must therefore carefully balance their desire to cut economic ties while ensuring the viability of their tech industries, which still continue to rely on those ties. However, even in the absence of all-out war or full technological decoupling, the US–China tech war will continue to cast a long and dark shadow over the once-optimistic vision of a global, integrated digital economy that spans across jurisdictions and connects the world as opposed to risks breaking it apart.

6

When Rights, Markets, and Security Collide

THE US–EU REGULATORY BATTLES

THE HIGH-STAKES BATTLE that the United States and China are fighting over technological supremacy, discussed in the prior chapter, is transforming the global economic and geopolitical landscape. Much of the scholarly literature and news commentary to date focuses on this very visible US–China contest, seeing it as a classic clash of superpowers between an existing dominant hegemon and a rising power. To many, understanding which of these two superpowers or their respective regulatory models will dominate—or if they will somehow be able to coexist—is the only important determinant of the fate of the world's digital order.

But that unfolding superpower contest is not, by itself, the only rivalry shaping the global digital economy, and may ultimately not be the one that most determines outcomes. In fact, over the past decade, US tech companies have been fighting a two-front battle, as they have not only encountered the demands of the state-driven regulatory model in China but also the demands of the rights-driven regulatory model in the European Union. The EU's assertive digital regulations have become a major constraint for US tech companies, frequently drawing them into protracted vertical battles with European regulators over issues surrounding data privacy, digital taxation, anticompetitive conduct, and content moderation, to name a few. These vertical battles have at times morphed into contested horizontal battles between the US and the EU as the US government has sought to come to the rescue of its companies, challenging what it considers European regulators' overreach. In some instances, the US government has alleged that the European regulatory model compromises not just the interests of its tech companies but also those of the US government, including its ability to engage in effective law enforcement or to maintain national security.

The EU's vertical battles against US tech companies rarely bring the European and American regulatory models into a direct clash. More often, the EU model simply imposes on these companies regulatory constraints that they do not face in the US. However, the US and the EU regulatory regimes occasionally conflict in ways that leave tech companies with competing mandates and the choice of violating either one law or the other. Microsoft found itself in such a bind in 2013 when US prosecutors served a warrant to the company, requesting it to hand over data in the context of an ongoing drug-trafficking investigation in the US.[1] However, the relevant data was stored on Microsoft servers in Ireland and hence subject to European data protection laws, which prohibited the requested data transfer. A contested court battle ensued. In 2014, a District Court in New York held that Microsoft was forced to produce the requested information to the US government, regardless of where the information was stored.[2] Microsoft appealed the case and prevailed before the Second Circuit Court of Appeals, which overturned the lower court's ruling.[3] But this victory for digital privacy rights in the Second Circuit was not final. In 2017, the US government appealed the decision to the US Supreme Court. In petitioning the Supreme Court to review the case, Acting Solicitor General Jeffrey B. Wall emphasized that "the [Second Circuit] decision is causing immediate, grave, and ongoing harm to public safety, national security, and the enforcement of our laws."[4] The US government's position was clear: the EU's rights-driven model should yield to the US's fundamental law enforcement and national security interests.

The Supreme Court never had the opportunity to rule on the issue, as it was rendered moot after the US Congress stepped in and passed the Clarifying Lawful Overseas Use of Data Act (CLOUD Act) in March 2018.[5] The CLOUD Act authorizes the US government to enter into bilateral data-sharing agreements with countries that are certified as having adequate protections for privacy and civil liberties in place.[6] Under these bilateral agreements, governments can issue orders directly to communications-service providers, such as Microsoft, requesting information that these providers store abroad.[7] The passing of the CLOUD Act was welcomed by Microsoft, whose main concern all along had been the conflicting legal obligations that the company was facing.[8] However, it is uncertain that the conflicts such as the one Microsoft faced will completely fade with the passing of the CLOUD Act. The US and the EU are now negotiating a bilateral agreement that would provide a legal basis for future data requests in the cross-border law enforcement context.[9] However, progress in the negotiations has been slow due to persisting disagreements.[10] EU regulators have also warned the US government that some EU member states have adopted so-called blocking statutes that prevent EU companies—or European branches of US companies—from disclosing information to a third-country government. The CLOUD Act may therefore come into conflict with those statutes.[11] This suggests that existing regulatory differences can be obstinate and hard to overcome—even in the context of US–EU battles that are politically considerably less charged than the ongoing US–China battles.

Microsoft's protracted legal fight over data transfers reveals how the US–EU regulatory battles can be consequential, affecting tech companies, governments, and digital citizens alike. At the same time, the US's battles involving the EU differ from those involving China. In contrast to the major clash of ideologies that amplifies the ongoing US–China conflict, the US shares many values—including commitments to human rights, individual freedom, democracy, and the rule of law—with the EU. However, the US and the EU often disagree on how best to uphold those shared values. Whereas the EU often views government intervention as necessary to protect these values, the US remains reluctant to interfere in the digital marketplace. Thus, at the heart of these transatlantic battles lies a difference in philosophy about the relative roles of markets and the government in shaping the digital economy and digital society. The US and the EU also frequently disagree on how to resolve some inevitable trade-offs when various policy imperatives come into conflict. As a result, these horizontal battles between the EU and the US often pit the fundamental rights of internet users against the commercial freedoms of tech companies; government intervention in the name of consumer welfare against private sector innovation in the name of technological progress; the pursuit of fairness against the pursuit of freedom; civility and human dignity against free speech and individual liberty; and the fundamental right to privacy against the fundamental need to uphold national security.

Over the last decade, the EU and the US have engaged in a number of distinct battles that have highlighted important differences in their respective regulatory agendas. Some of the most notable transatlantic conflicts have centered on data protection, digital taxation, and antitrust law. These battles illustrate a fundamental tension between the European and the American regulatory models: the EU distrusts tech companies, whereas the US distrusts regulators. On the EU's side, Europeans worry that the business practices of dominant US tech companies undermine the EU's attempts to safeguard the fundamental rights of European citizens and deprive European consumers of the benefits of a competitive and fair marketplace. Not only is the personal data of European internet users extracted for tech companies' commercial gain, but even worse, the transfer of European data to the US risks the extraction of this data for the US government's surveillance purposes. Whether Europeans' personal data is compromised by either private or public surveillance in the US, the EU maintains that it has the sovereign right, even an obligation, to step in and protect the fundamental rights of all Europeans. In the same vein, the EU is determined to leverage its antitrust laws against the US tech companies that exploit their market power and extract the surplus that is supposed to flow to European consumers, alleging that American tech companies undermine a competitive marketplace and deprive smaller players from a fair chance to compete. Finally, the European governments' efforts to extend their tax authority to the digital services provided by large US tech companies in Europe reflects the view that these companies must do their share and contribute to the public purse the same way other economic operators in Europe do. In other words, the largest US tech companies take too much and give too little. These concerns have given European regulators the impetus to step in and protect European data, safeguard the competitive marketplace, and assert their tax authority to reclaim some of the revenue that stems from digital business conducted in Europe.

If Europeans are concerned about US tech firms' alleged overreach, Americans are concerned about European regulators' alleged overreach. The US often views the EU's regulatory efforts as both excessive and protectionist, unfairly targeting European companies' more successful American rivals. These concerns were expressed particularly starkly by Charlene Barshefsky, the former US Trade Representative, who recently accused the EU of digital protectionism and called for an end to its "techno-nationalism."[12] She refers to EU antitrust enforcement as consisting of "aggressive action against US technology companies," including Intel, Microsoft, Meta, Google, Qualcomm, and Amazon, while characterizing the EU's recently adopted Digital Services Act and Digital Markets Act as "rigged" in that they unfairly target US companies' business models. Digital service taxes that France and some other EU member states have enacted or proposed are, according to Barshefsky, "discriminatory" and designed to weaken US tech platforms. Efforts to develop a European cloud and the proposed European rules for artificial intelligence are similarly driven by a protectionist motive. Instead of "demonizing US technology companies," Europe should work together with the US to counter Chinese digital protectionism, Barshefsky concludes, while adding that if the EU continues on the path of techno-nationalism, the US has "no choice but to treat it as a strategic threat."[13]

However, on many of these contested issues, the transatlantic battles seem to be gradually waning, painting a stark contrast with the escalation of the US–China conflicts examined in Chapter 5. The US–EU disagreement on digital taxation gave way in 2021 to a historic international agreement on global tax reform, negotiated to replace the unilateral digital services taxes imposed by several EU member states. The US and EU also reached an agreement in 2022 to address the European Court's concerns over the safety of Europeans' data, which is expected to restore unhindered data flows between the two jurisdictions. The US is further softening its market-driven ideals and increasingly conceding that antitrust laws are needed to mitigate the unprecedented power of large tech companies. As the US and the EU are moving toward greater convergence, it is notable that the two regulatory models are not compromising in the middle. Instead, the US is clearly moving closer to the European rights-driven regulatory model. That said, the US is neither able nor willing to embrace the EU model in its entirety; but it is acknowledging that political momentum is shifting toward more extensive regulation of tech companies—along the lines that the EU has advocated for years. What gives an even greater impetus for bridging the remaining US–EU differences is the two jurisdictions' shared concern regarding China's rise and the impact of that rise on the future of liberal democracy. Both the US and the EU acknowledge that their mutual differences seem manageable compared to the AI-powered mass surveillance, internet censorship, and relentless online propaganda practiced by the Chinese government. These practices are antithetical to the values of democracy and freedom that both the EU and the US have long embraced at home and championed abroad.

This chapter brings the larger evolution of the transatlantic regulatory conflicts and subsequent rapprochement between the EU and the US into view. It outlines the key issues underlying the US–EU regulatory battle over data transfers, with a particular focus on the parties' different views on the relationship between data privacy and national security. The chapter also looks closely at the EU–US conflict over digital taxation, explaining European efforts to tax some of the revenue that American tech companies generate in Europe and showing how that conflict ultimately paved the way for a global agreement on taxation. The chapter further examines the US–EU disagreement over EU antitrust enforcement, which the US government has described as a manifestation of European protectionism. These individual regulatory battles have strained the transatlantic commercial and diplomatic relationship over the past decade, often pitting US tech companies against European governments. They have also complicated US–EU governmental relations in instances where the US government has sought to defend its tech companies by directly confronting EU policies. This chapter concludes with a closer look at the forces that are now contributing toward greater transatlantic regulatory alignment and discusses the prospects of enhanced US–EU cooperation in digital policy going forward.

Transatlantic Data Transfers: Between Privacy and Surveillance

One of the most contested regulatory battles between the EU and the US—and one with particularly significant consequences for the broader transatlantic digital economy—revolves around data privacy. The EU views data protection as a fundamental right, anchored in the EU's Charter of Fundamental Rights and the pathbreaking General Data Protection Regulation (GDPR), as discussed in Chapter 3. This European rights-driven approach has often clashed with the American market-driven approach that views data as a commodity that can be monetized by tech companies with few restrictions. The US government, companies, and policy experts have often been skeptical about the EU's regulatory approach, asserting that the EU's data protection laws are protectionist and costly, unnecessarily restricting trade and curtailing American companies' commercial freedom.[14] At the time the GDPR entered into force in 2018, the former US Commerce Secretary Wilbur Ross warned that the regulation could "significantly interrupt transatlantic cooperation and create unnecessary barriers to trade."[15] Other commentators have equated the GDPR to tariffs, describing how that regulation could push smaller US companies out of Europe while increasing the operating costs for larger US companies, thereby providing "assistance to native European tech companies that have thus far failed to get traction in internet markets."[16] Several US tech companies have similarly criticized the high compliance costs involved, with Google commenting on having spent "hundreds of years of human time" to achieve GDPR compliance.[17] These criticisms reveal how the European rights-driven approach toward personal data collides with the American market-driven approach, pitting individuals' fundamental right to data privacy against private companies' freedom to conduct business.

The US–EU differences regarding data privacy are not limited to how private companies are allowed to extract and monetize personal data. The US and the EU also disagree on how to balance their citizens' data privacy rights with governments' need to carry out digital surveillance for law enforcement or national security purposes, further elevating the stakes in the transatlantic regulatory battle. The individuals' right to data privacy often yields to national security authorities in the US. The government's extensive authority to engage in digital surveillance reflects the importance of national security interests in US policy making. The primacy of national security is also built into the American regulatory model, which—its steadfast commitment to free markets notwithstanding—recognizes that government intervention in digital markets is warranted to protect national security. As a result, the US government has often struck a different balance than the EU in reconciling conflicting demands for national security and data privacy, especially in the post-9/11 environment where the war on terror entrenched surveillance deeper into US intelligence policy.[18] After 2013, when former National Security Agency contractor Edward Snowden exposed the extent of the US surveillance state to Americans and the wider world, US government surveillance activities were curtailed and additional privacy safeguards were instituted.[19] However, even after these safeguards were put into place, US courts have generally been less prepared to second-guess the country's national security interests compared to their European counterparts.[20] Consequently, from the vantage point of Europeans, the balance in US policymaking remains tilted toward national security at the expense of individual privacy.

In marked contrast to the American approach, the EU has adopted extensive privacy protections to constrain similar activity by European governments. The European Court of Justice (CJEU) has defended these privacy protections in its distinctly rights-driven rulings, which repeatedly display the Court's proclivity to elevate the fundamental right to privacy above the needs of law enforcement and, many would argue, even above EU member states' core national security interests. For example, in its 2014 judgment in *Digital Rights Ireland*, the CJEU declared the EU's 2006 Data Retention Directive to be invalid on the basis that it required indiscriminate and disproportionate retention of personal metadata contained in electronic communications.[21] The Court rejected the argument that such data retention was necessary to fight serious crime, emphasizing how extensive data retention interferes "with the fundamental rights of practically the entire European population."[22] In 2020, the CJEU was asked to rule directly on whether and how the EU's data protection rules limit European intelligence services' data collection and retention programs in two linked cases, known as *Privacy International* and *La Quadrature du Net* (LQDN).[23] In its judgment, the Court distinguished between indiscriminate data retention for the purpose of combating serious crime and for the purpose of protecting national security. It ruled that bulk data collection for crime control purposes exceeded the limits of what is "strictly necessary," and could not hence be justified within a democratic society. However, such bulk collection may be justified in instances of "a serious threat . . . to national security which is shown to be genuine and present or foreseeable."[24] Even then, however, the Court ruled surveillance shall not be systematic and must be limited in time, in addition to being subject to effective review mechanisms.[25] Although this ruling illustrates how the right to data privacy is not absolute in the EU and still needs to be balanced against legitimate national security imperatives, it nevertheless demonstrates a central difference with recent US court decisions, which have shown deference toward government surveillance. This case and other CJEU judgments reveal that when faced with a trade-off between privacy and surveillance, the Court's instinct is, ultimately, to lean toward privacy.

Several national security experts in both the EU and the US argue that the EU is striking the wrong balance between data privacy and national security. With its unyielding defense of the fundamental right to data protection, these critics claim that the EU is curtailing governments' ability to engage in effective protection against national security threats, be it military action by a hostile foreign state or an act of terrorism committed by nonstate actors on European soil.[26] Some European governments, most notably France, have been vocal in criticizing the restrictions on its surveillance programs stemming from CJEU rulings.[27] The US government has also repeatedly expressed concerns about the national security implications of the GDPR, in particular as it also restricts data transfers between the EU and the US. Former US Attorney General Loretta Lynch noted how "terrorists, like other criminals, count on the difficulties law enforcement agencies have in sharing information across borders," while adding that it was "highly concerning" that the GDPR could further restrict sharing data across the Atlantic.[28] Cybersecurity officials in the Trump administration similarly expressed that the GDPR's "overly restrictive implications for public safety and law enforcement" were a grave concern for them.[29] The private sector has shared these concerns. Companies like CrowdStrike, a Texas-headquartered cybersecurity firm, highlighted that "modern technologies designed to stop personal data breaches are dependent upon dynamic, real-time cross-border data flows."[30] An additional concern relates to the EU's alleged hypocrisy. While the CJEU has also frequently curtailed EU member states' surveillance operations, critical voices in the US point out how the EU takes a harder line against US surveillance practices while frequently tolerating similar practices by European governments or even other trade partners,[31] adding to the concerns about the anti-American bias that EU regulations are often seen as harboring.

How EU Court Battles Have Disrupted Transatlantic Data Transfers

This US–EU divergence has not simply been a philosophical battle between the EU and the US on how to balance citizens' fundamental rights with the government's critical national security interests. Instead, this battle has had far-reaching economic, legal, and policy consequences, complicating the transfer of data from the EU to the US. At the heart of this conflict today is the GDPR provision that bans the transfer of European data to any non-EU country that fails to offer "equivalent" data privacy protections.[32] To determine whether such equivalent protections exist, the EU maintains an "adequacy regime" that allows the EU to reach a formal determination on whether data can be safely transferred from the EU to a non-EU country. The adequacy regime predates the GDPR and was already used to assess the equivalency of foreign data privacy laws in light of the GDPR's predecessor, the EU's 1995 Data Privacy Directive. However, it has always been clear that the US was not going to benefit from such an adequacy decision given its weak data privacy laws. At the same time, finding a legal solution to transatlantic data transfers has been particularly important for both the US and the EU, given the significance of data flows that underpin the US–EU $7 trillion trade and investment relationship.[33] As of 2018, the value of annual digital services trade between the US and the EU was $412 billion, up from $260 billion in 2016.[34] Unhindered data flows are crucial not just for large tech companies, such as Google and Meta, but also for banks, law firms, and many other commercial entities that obtain personal data when they sell products to European customers. As a result, both the US and the EU have been determined to find a way to keep data flowing across the Atlantic.

To create a legal basis for transatlantic data transfers, the US and the EU had to find an alternative to the EU's adequacy regime, which led them to conclude the Safe Harbor agreement in July 2000.[35] The EU-US Safe Harbor Agreement consisted of a set of negotiated principles, which the EU considered to meet European adequacy standards. The US companies that voluntarily subscribed to these principles were allowed to transfer data concerning European data subjects. Over 5,000 US companies entered the Safe Harbor agreement, including Amazon, Apple, Facebook, Google, and Microsoft.[36] However, this agreement was struck down by the CJEU in 2015.[37] The CJEU judgment took place in the aftermath of the Snowden revelations, which exposed how the US National Security Agency had engaged in a mass surveillance campaign by harvesting Facebook data, in the US and abroad. These revelations gave the Court a strong rationale to reevaluate the adequacy of the EU-US Safe Harbor Agreement. In invalidating the Safe Harbor agreement, the CJEU interpreted the European Data Protection Directive—the valid EU data protection law at the time—in ways that few had predicted, setting an exacting standard for data transfers to third countries to be lawful. According to the Court, the adequacy standard required that a non-EU country guaranteed "a level of protection of fundamental rights and freedoms that

[was] *essentially equivalent* to that guaranteed within the European Union."[38] The EU-US 2000 Safe Harbor agreement that had governed EU data flows across the Atlantic for fifteen years did not meet that standard.

The origins of this dramatic Court decision can be traced to an Austrian lawyer and data protection activist, Max Schrems, who launched a case against Facebook in 2011 as a twenty-three-year-old law student, requesting Facebook to hand over any personal data the company had collected on him.[39] After learning that Facebook had amassed 1,200 pages of data on him, Schrems filed multiple complaints before the Irish Data Protection Commission (DPC), which had jurisdiction over Facebook, accusing the company of violating his right to data privacy. His case gained additional momentum in 2013 when the Snowden revelations surfaced. This led Schrems to file his twenty-third complaint before the DPC, this time alleging that his personal data was being exposed to US surveillance. The DPC declined to investigate Schrems's complaint, noting that Facebook's transatlantic data transfers were protected by a then-valid Safe Harbor agreement. Undeterred, Schrems filed a lawsuit before Irish courts, seeking judicial review of the DPC's refusal to investigate his complaint on its merits.[40] The Irish High Court ultimately referred the case to the CJEU, which in its monumental 2015 judgment struck down the EU-US Safe Harbor Agreement.[41]

This setback before the European judiciary led the US and the EU to negotiate a new agreement to govern transatlantic data transfers: the EU-US Privacy Shield.[42] This new agreement, which entered into force in August 2016, had 5,380 corporate signatories in July 2020.[43] To withstand any new legal challenge, the Privacy Shield was negotiated to embody significantly stronger privacy protections, enhanced enforcement mechanisms, and new safeguards related to US government's access to personal data.[44] For example, it required the US to appoint an independent ombudsman, who would respond to individuals' complaints regarding potential misuse of personal data by US national security agencies.[45] Despite these improvements, the future of the Privacy Shield remained uncertain. The Commission, the European Parliament, and the European Data Protection Board all expressed concerns about the US's implementation of the Privacy Shield in their 2017 and 2019 reviews of the agreement.[46] The fate of the Privacy Shield was finally sealed in July 2020 when the European Court struck again, invalidating the Privacy Shield, following another challenge initiated by Max Schrems.[47] The US surveillance laws remained the main concern of the Court in *Schrems II*, which found that the extensive US surveillance practices failed the "proportionality test," and hence did not guarantee the fundamental rights of persons whose data are transferred to the US.[48] The Court was particularly concerned that

US surveillance laws allow for bulk collection of intelligence data overseas, including in the EU, without that collection being subject to judicial oversight.[49] The Court also took issue with inadequate redress mechanisms available for foreign targets of American intelligence operations who cannot challenge surveillance operations involving them before US courts. Even though these foreign individuals could raise their concerns before a designated privacy Ombudsperson within the US State Department, this mechanism did not provide data subjects a cause of action that would be considered "essentially equivalent" to that required by EU law. For example, any decisions by the Ombudsperson are nonbinding on the American intelligence services.[50] These inadequacies in the US legal system led the European Court to issue its far-reaching ruling, which for the second time removed the legal foundation from much of the transatlantic digital commerce, delivering a major blow to the thousands of companies that had relied on the Privacy Shield for their data transfers.

The Future of Transatlantic Data Flows

The fateful CJEU ruling left companies relying on data transfers with few alternatives. Since the Privacy Shield was struck down, these companies have been primarily relying on standard contractual clauses (SCCs) as a basis for transatlantic data transfers. While undoing the Privacy Shield, the Court upheld the validity of these SCCs, at least in principle, in the same *Schrems II* judgment.[51] The SCCs are a set of terms and conditions used in commercial contracts that the European Commission regards as providing adequate safeguards for data transfers. However, SCCs are considered an inferior mechanism to transfer data as companies that rely on these standard clauses are left with the daunting task of verifying that foreign countries' surveillance regimes do not undermine the EU's privacy concerns, using the high benchmark set by the Court. Alternatively, corporations may continue to transfer data across the Atlantic within a corporate group under approved Binding Corporate Rules that incorporate adequate data protections. Yet even these rules require verification that they meet the high privacy standards set by the Court. Companies adversely affected by this persisting uncertainty have urged the importance of finding a solution to the impasse. In its 2022 annual report to the US Securities and Exchange Commission, Meta even warned that it may need to pull out its key services—such as Facebook and Instagram—from the EU if no solution to the transatlantic data transfers is found.[52] After Meta's threat of exit was reported in the press, the company hastened to clarify that it had "no desire to withdraw from Europe" but was simply disclosing a material risk that the uncertainty around international data transfers poses to the company.[53]

While SCCs and Binding Corporate Rules hardly offer a satisfactory long-term basis for data transfers for companies such as Meta, most other proposed solutions are either politically unlikely or commercially unappealing. Privacy advocates endorse a view that data flows can be reinstated and legal challenges avoided if the US agrees to rewrite its national laws on surveillance. Max Schrems, whose legal complaint led to the unraveling of the Privacy Shield and the Safe Harbor agreement, commented after the *Schrems II* ruling that "it is clear that the U.S. will have to seriously change their surveillance laws, if U.S. companies want to continue to play a major role on the EU market."[54] The Center for Democracy & Technology (CDT), a Washington and Brussels–based NGO focused on promoting fundamental rights and democratic values in tech policy, similarly called for reforms to US surveillance law and practice in the wake of the ruling.[55] Among the proposed reforms, the CDT urged for greater transparency about surveillance operations conducted; limits to purposes and targets of surveillance; more timely deletion of information collected unnecessarily through surveillance; and establishment of court-ordered redress for unlawful surveillance. The US Congressional Research Service has also presented potential solutions to consider in the aftermath of the decision. These include, for example, legislation or executive orders limiting bulk intelligence collection or offering additional redress mechanisms as pathways to resolve the European Court's concerns.[56]

Henry Farrell and Abraham Newman have similarly argued that *Schrems II* presents the US with an opportunity to rethink its national security interests and surveillance practices in today's interconnected world.[57] According to them, America's problem isn't "European imperialism" but "America's own imperialism." The US cannot assume that it can unilaterally impose its national security policies on its allies without incorporating into its policies enhanced civil rights for the citizens of those allies. Engagement in cross-national surveillance calls for the recognition of cross-national legal rights. To safeguard its own core national security interests, the US needs more extensive intelligence sharing and closer collaboration with its democratic allies, which will not be possible without the US revisiting its understanding of how national security intersects with the individuals' right to data privacy. Others have similarly emphasized the importance of deeper US–EU collaboration on both surveillance and privacy, advocating for an agreement between the US and EU member states on digital surveillance that seeks to balance the US views on surveillance with the European concerns for data privacy.[58]

However, others reject the idea that the US should change its approach toward surveillance, let alone allow the European Court to dictate US surveillance laws. Some members of the US Congress called the CJEU decision "a significant setback to the safety of American and European consumers."[59] Adam Klein, the Chair of the US Privacy and Civil Liberties Oversight Board, recalled how US intelligence agencies frequently share valuable intelligence generated under US surveillance laws with their European counterparts, allowing the EU to free ride on, and thus directly benefit from, US surveillance efforts.[60] Stewart Baker, former Assistant Secretary for Policy at the US Department of Homeland Security and a former General Counsel of the National Security Agency, took a starker tone, accusing the EU of "judicial imperialism and Eurocentric hypocrisy," and noting how it was "astonishing that a European court would assume it has authority to kill or cripple critical American intelligence programs by raising the threat of massive sanctions on American companies."[61] He urged the US government to respond to the ruling by imposing trade sanctions on European goods, in addition to withdrawing any pro-privacy concessions the US had made to the EU in negotiating the Privacy Shield. Others have adopted a more measured tone yet still called into question what they see as a discrepancy or outright hypocrisy between the absolutist standard the European Court takes against foreign surveillance operations while at the same time recognizing national security exemptions for EU member state governments' surveillance practices.[62] They also point out how European governments do not extend equivalent due process rights for Americans in Europe, calling into question why European citizens should be entitled to challenge US intelligence operations before US courts.[63]

There are few signs that the US is prepared to change its approach to national security, in particular in today's tense geopolitical environment where China is growing more assertive and Russia has launched the largest military conflict in Europe since World War II by invading Ukraine. Any legislative reform restricting US surveillance capabilities is unlikely in the midst of these developments. Indeed, it is suddenly more likely that Europeans will now be reevaluating their relationship toward national security and surveillance following the Russian invasion of Ukraine, acutely aware of the new security threats facing the continent. European governments are already moving to rebuild their security architecture, with national security issues gaining new salience in policy agendas and budgetary expenditures alike. At the same time, it is difficult to predict whether and how the European judiciary would factor in the transformed geopolitical reality should it be asked to review any new US–EU data transfer deal. For now, these complexities will only translate into prolonging the uncertainty and legal risks undermining the transatlantic data flows.

Some have suggested that the only feasible, risk-free solution to this impasse is for companies to store all European personal data in the EU and agree not to export it. Such calls for data localization have been mounting since the *Schrems II* ruling. In the immediate aftermath of that judgment, a German data protection authority in Berlin called for data controllers based in Berlin to transfer any personal data they were currently storing in the US to Europe, while also ensuring that data was not transferred out of the EU to the US until the legal framework for transatlantic data transfers was reformed.[64] European Commissioner Thierry Breton—who is in charge of the many key digital initiatives such as the EU's technological sovereignty agenda—has also forcefully argued that "European data should stay in Europe,"[65] effectively suggesting that data localization should become a norm in Europe. Some commentators have argued that *Schrems II* already imposes a "soft data localization" mandate by leaving companies with few practical options but to store their data in Europe.[66]

Data localization hardly presents a satisfactory solution for either the US or the EU.[67] First, it would be unlikely to end American surveillance given that the US already engages in extensive espionage operations within the EU. There is no guarantee that keeping the data in Europe can therefore insulate it from US surveillance practices. Second, data localization would be commercially costly, impeding trade in digital and nondigital goods and services alike. The costs would be even greater for smaller companies who cannot afford to set up different data processing and storage systems for each jurisdiction. Finally, European leaders have often criticized the data localization practices of other countries, such as China, India, and Russia. For example, in commenting on the Indian draft Privacy bill in 2018, the European Commission noted how the bill's proposed data localization provisions are "both unnecessary and potentially harmful as they would create unnecessary costs, difficulties and uncertainties that could hamper business and investments."[68] If the EU were to embrace data localization as a solution to *Schrems II* at home, it would legitimize this practice in other countries as well, likely paving the way for data localization to emerge as a globally accepted norm.

This suggests that the US–EU regulatory conflict over data transfers has been one of the most intractable transatlantic regulatory battles with no permanent resolution seemingly in sight. The EU has remained adamant in protecting European data from invasive US surveillance practices. At the same time, the US has not been prepared to go further in rebalancing privacy and surveillance interests under its domestic laws to alleviate the EU's concerns.

This regulatory battle has not only been a major disruption for US–EU commercial relations but has also complicated both parties' efforts to influence the data practices of other countries, including those of China. The US is unyielding in condemning the Chinese digital surveillance while defending its own surveillance efforts in the transatlantic context. Similarly, while the EU has objected to the Chinese government's data localization practices, it insists that it can limit transfer of data outside the EU—whether to the US or, on similar grounds, to China.

Yet even this obstinate battle now seems to be heading toward a resolution. Ever since the US–EU agreement sustaining transatlantic data flows was struck down—not once, but twice—by the European Court, efforts have been underway to negotiate yet another US–EU data transfer agreement that would eventually withstand the Court's exacting judicial review. The European Commission and the US government have a strong interest in restoring transatlantic data flows that are vital to companies on both sides.[69] In March 2022, President Biden and European Commission President von der Leyen issued a joint statement to indicate that the US and the EU had reached a preliminary deal on an EU-US Data Privacy Framework to restore data flows from the EU to the US.[70] Shortly thereafter, in October 2022, President Biden signed an Executive Order on Enhancing Safeguards for United States Signals Intelligence Activities.[71] The Executive Order mandates that intelligence activities will be conducted "only when necessary to advance a validated intelligence priority and . . . proportionate to that priority."[72] This incorporation of the "necessary" and "proportionate" language from EU jurisprudence can be read as part of an American effort to assure the EU that any intelligence collection by US authorities will be limited and reflective of European values of respect for civil liberties and privacy.[73] The Order also sets up a new mechanism for European citizens "to obtain independent and binding review and redress" if they believe their personal information has been handled illegally under US law.[74] Their claims will first be heard by a Civil Liberties Protection Officer in the Executive branch, then potentially reviewed by a Data Protection Review Court comprising non–US government judges.[75]

Now, the ball is back in the EU's court. The European Commission will draft a decision assessing the new US commitments and send that decision for review to EU member states and the European Data Protection Board.[76] While it is still unknown whether the Executive Order will be judged as satisfactory under EU law, the European Commission has struck an optimistic tone, suggesting that the new redress mechanism and the incorporation of the necessity and proportionality language in particular were likely to address the CJEU's concerns.[77] But, unsurprisingly, not all European voices were satisfied. Notably, Max Schrems has already signaled his discontent, pointing out that the redress mechanism "is simply not a court" that complies with the European Charter's requirement for "judicial redress,"[78] and accusing the Commission, once again, of "allowing the continued surveillance of Europeans."[79] Given that "the core issues were not solved," he predicted that these issues "will be back to the CJEU sooner or later."[80]

On the US side, there are also concerns that the deal will remain vulnerable to a legal challenge. Former Senator Patrick Toomey, writing with Ashley Gorski of the ACLU, pointed to a March 2022 Supreme Court decision in *FBI v. Fazaga*,[81] which makes it easier for the US government to invoke the "state secrets privilege" in surveillance cases, thereby making it harder for individuals to pursue surveillance cases against the government. According to Toomey and Gorski, rulings such as this are undercutting the US government's efforts to show Europeans that it takes privacy seriously.[82] In response to Biden's new executive order, Gorski also wrote that "although the executive order is a step in the right direction, it does not meet basic legal requirements in the EU, leaving EU-US data transfers in jeopardy going forward."[83] Instead, she called for "Congress [to] enact meaningful surveillance reform."[84] Thus, any truce in this battle may hence ultimately be short-lived—yet these developments also show how even multiple setbacks in the midst of deeply held disagreements have not dissuaded the US and the EU from seeking compromise.

Digital Services Taxes Fueling a Transatlantic Trade War

The taxation of tech companies is another domain of transatlantic regulatory disagreement that has contributed to the broader regulatory battle between the US and the EU. The largest US tech companies generate tremendous revenue from their activities in Europe yet pay trivial taxes there. For example, in the financial year 2021, Apple's sales in Europe exceeded $89 billion.[85] These large revenues generated in Europe have been contrasted with the company's negligible tax payments there. As part of its investigation into the tax arrangement that Apple had struck with Ireland, the European Commission noted in 2016 that Apple paid "an effective corporate tax rate of 1 percent on its European profits in 2003 down to 0.005 percent in 2014."[86] Revelations such as this have become a source of public resentment across Europe over the recent years, and led to efforts to increase these companies' tax liability, in addition to ensuring that part of this tax is collected by European tax authorities. This resentment has not been limited to Europe, and calls for updating antiquated international tax rules have been mounting across jurisdictions.[87]

The concern about digital companies not paying enough taxes is two-fold. First, there is a concern that these companies are exploiting various loopholes in different countries' tax laws and thereby shielding themselves from tax liability altogether. The Commission's recent investigation into Apple's tax rate reflects this concern. What explains Apple's meager tax payments is that the company has taken advantage of the different definitions of tax residence under US and Irish law, creating subsidiaries that reside nowhere for tax purposes.[88] This is just one example of how companies can exploit the weaknesses in the current international tax regime in order to diminish their overall tax liability.[89] A second concern relates to *where* digital companies pay their taxes. Here, the EU and individual member state governments have questioned the existing tax laws and agreements, arguing that they fail to fairly allocate revenue across jurisdictions. This has led some European countries to introduce new forms of digital tax to better reach companies' profits. These efforts to increase American tech companies' tax liability in Europe have been met with fierce resistance in the US, elevating political tensions between the US and the EU.

This discrepancy between the significant digital presence and the trivial tax contributions of the largest tech firms in Europe has led numerous EU member states to either propose or implement national digital services taxes (DSTs), as discussed in Chapter 3.[90] The DSTs are designed to create a link between where digital companies make profit and where they are being taxed. By creating new taxing rights to the market jurisdiction where digital companies have substantial economic presence, the DSTs challenge the fundamental principles of international tax law, according to which only the source country—the place of production—or the country of residence have the taxing authority.[91] The DSTs depart from existing international tax norms by granting new taxing rights to market jurisdictions, thereby bringing many US tech companies under the EU member states' taxing authority. France was the first EU member state to implement a DST in 2019, followed soon thereafter by several others.[92] The European Commission, in seeking a more harmonized European approach, had previously sought to implement an EU-wide tax reform in March 2018, proposing a DST and a digital profits tax.[93] Since then, however, as France and other states moved ahead with their DSTs, the Commission refocused its efforts in this domain, and proposed instead a new EU-level digital levy.[94] The proposed digital levy differs from the DSTs in that it was designed to be a sales tax on all firms that sell goods and services online in the EU whose annual turnover exceeds €50 million.[95] However, the Commission agreed to put on hold its preparations for a digital levy in July 2021 to focus on efforts to find a compromise in concurrent OECD negotiations on international tax reform.[96]

The EU member state governments justify their DSTs by emphasizing how the traditional permanent establishment-driven taxing authority is outdated and ill-suited for the globalized and digitalized world.[97] Today, users of digital services provide value to digital companies, for example, by disclosing their personal data that is then deployed by these companies in targeted advertising. Tax scholars have also advanced various conceptual arguments that recast the conventional thinking of how value is created in today's digital economy, and how taxing rights ought to be reallocated as a result.[98] Yet the US has insisted that digital companies should not be treated differently from other companies for tax purposes. The US government has rejected the rationales offered by the EU and its member state governments, describing the DSTs instead as protectionist, and accusing the European governments for unfairly targeting large American tech companies. The US government position echoes the views of the critics who have called the EU's focus on digital users' value creation as "conceptually bold and fiscally convenient."[99] These disagreements fueled transatlantic tensions and set the stage for a major horizontal battle.

How the US–EU Conflict Over DSTs Brought Parties to the Brink of a Trade War

The US has consistently opposed the European DSTs at the EU and member state levels. The US government views these measures as discriminatory, alleging that they largely target American companies. Steven Mnuchin, US Treasury Secretary in 2017–2021, criticized the EU's proposed 2018 DST initiative as "unfair," arguing that there "should not be a two-tiered system where internet companies are taxed under a different standard."[100] Other commentators have similarly disparaged the DSTs as unfairly targeting "nearly exclusively" American firms, attributing the European taxes to "the short-term goal of grabbing revenue and the long-term goal of disadvantaging U.S. tech firms."[101] This commentary typically suggests that a European protectionist intent is baked into the DSTs by applying high revenue thresholds that catch mainly large US tech firms, and by excluding certain revenue categories that are often earned by European firms, including subscription fees charged by firms such as the Swedish streaming company Spotify.[102]

These concerns led the US to threaten the EU countries with trade sanctions. As the first EU country implementing a domestic DST, France was also the first target of the US ire. Former President Trump decried the French tax, stating, "France just put a digital tax on our great American technology companies. If anybody taxes them, it should be their home Country, the USA. We will announce a substantial reciprocal action on Macron's foolishness shortly," before adding to his tweet that he had always thought that American wine is better than French wine.[103] The US response was not confined to Twitter. The Office of the United States Trade Representative (USTR) announced a formal investigation into France's DST in July 2019.[104] Under Section 301 of the 1974 Trade Act, the US is entitled to restrict foreign imports if the USTR concludes that certain policy or practice is unreasonable or discriminatory and burdens or restricts US commerce. Following the investigation in July 2019, the USTR concluded that the French DST was discriminatory in that it deliberately targets Google, Apple, Facebook, and Amazon while excluding digital services in domains where French companies are more successful.[105] The US also announced a 25 percent tariff on certain French-origin luxury products. The US, however, suspended the tariff in January 2021 pending the result of the USTR's investigation into DSTs in other European countries.[106]

The USTR opened additional Section 301 investigations in June 2020. In announcing the investigations, then US Trade Representative Robert Lighthizer noted that "President Trump is concerned that many of our trading partners are adopting tax schemes designed to unfairly target our companies. We are prepared to take all appropriate action to defend our businesses and workers against any such discrimination."[107] In June 2021, the USTR concluded its year-long investigations and found that the digital services taxes imposed by Austria, Spain, Italy, and the United Kingdom discriminated against US companies and were inconsistent with international tax principles.[108] For example, the USTR found that Italy's DST discriminates against US digital companies in terms of the services it covers and the revenue thresholds it applies. The tax also violated principles of international taxation due to its extraterritorial nature and its application to revenue rather than income as the basis of tax liability.[109] The USTR further found that Italy's DST "burdens or restricts U.S. commerce."[110] After its findings, the USTR announced 25 percent tariffs on over $2 billion worth of imports from these designated countries, while suspending the tariffs for up to 180 days in order to complete the negotiations at the OECD level.[111]

It is not perhaps surprising that the US responded to the DSTs with retaliatory trade measures. In today's economic and political environment, trade wars and protectionism have become common. Some tax scholars and trade experts have also argued, rather convincingly, that some elements of the DSTs are rightly seen as discriminatory, justifying US retaliation.[112] These elements include carve-outs of specific revenue categories that have the effect of shielding European companies from the scope of the DST. At the same time, other tax scholars in the US have argued that "the claim that DSTs represent discrimination against U.S. Tech giants is baseless, even ironic."[113] These scholars argue, also convincingly, that there is nothing discriminatory when France treats digital advertising and traditional advertising differently when the very goal of the DST is to reach revenue not tied to the physical presence of a company.[114] They also point to various DSTs that have been implemented or proposed at the subnational level in the US, such as Maryland's Digital Advertising Tax or the Data Mining Tax in New York. The existence of subnational DSTs in the US undermines the US government's argument that market jurisdictions should not be taxing digital revenue. In light of these different views, no consensus exists on whether the DSTs are protectionist and retaliatory tariffs justified. But few would argue that unilateral DSTs and a resulting trade war present the best path forward. Consequently, despite the escalation of the transatlantic conflict, both parties have strong economic incentives to continue to alleviate tensions and back off from the brink of a trade war—a dynamic that stands in stark contrast to the US–China trade and tech war where, despite the costliness of that war, neither party has shown willingness to back down or seek negotiated compromise.

Toward a Truce by Way of a Global Tax Deal

Throughout the time when the European governments were implementing their DSTs and the USTR was pursuing investigations into those DSTs, multilateral negotiations at the OECD level attempted to find a consensus on a global tax reform. While the tech sector was never the sole focus of the global tax reform, identifying solutions to the tax challenges arising from the digitalization of the economy has been one of reform priorities. However, as the progress within the OECD was slow until recently, EU member states began to announce their own DSTs as a temporary measure until an agreement was reached at the OECD level.[115] The US had consistently opposed countries passing their own domestic digital taxes, but supported the OECD-led global tax reform.[116] In a letter to José Ángel Gurría, the OECD Secretary-General at the time, former US Treasury Secretary Mnuchin affirmed the US's support for the OECD-level discussions while registering the US's firm opposition to DSTs because of their discriminatory impact on US-based businesses and their inconsistency with the architecture of existing international tax rules.[117] US tech companies have also favored a multilateral tax reform. For example, Meta's CEO Mark Zuckerberg said he welcomed OECD efforts, even though it would increase his company's overall tax bill, because it would create a "stable and reliable system going forward."[118]

The EU's unilateral DSTs added to the urgency of finding a solution within the OECD. Even the US government recognized that the alternative to the OECD deal was a persistent threat of unilateral tax measures and "a world that threatens chaos."[119] While some progress was made during the negotiations, continuing US–EU disagreements and tensions kept a final deal at bay throughout the Trump presidency. The Biden administration provided a critical push toward concluding OECD negotiations by unveiling a set of compromise proposals in April 2021. Under these proposals, large tech companies and other big corporations would need to pay taxes based on the sales they generate in each country, regardless of where they are based. In addition, the US proposals advocated a global tax floor at the level of 21 percent.[120] José Ángel Gurría, the OECD Secretary General at the time, called the US proposals a "once in a lifetime opportunity to achieve a complete overhaul of the international tax system, to both provide more tax certainty for businesses, as well as ensure everyone pays their fair share of taxes."[121] European leaders concurred, with Bruno Le Maire, French Minister of Economy and Finance, noting how an agreement was now within reach "especially now that the United States have confirmed they are dropping the safe harbor principle,"[122] a provision critics viewed as allowing some multinational companies to opt out of global digital tax rules.

Following this breakthrough in negotiations, the OECD announced in October 2021 that 136 countries had finally reached an agreement on global tax reform, and committed to implementing it by the end of 2023.[123] The agreement has two pillars. Under Pillar One of the Agreement, a portion of any multinational company's profits will be allocated to market countries even if the company does not have a physical presence there. These companies will pay corporate tax under the existing international tax rules on profits up to a certain threshold, while the income exceeding that threshold will be divided between countries where the company's users and customers are located.[124] Pillar One is not limited to digital companies but applies generally to firms that meet specified revenue thresholds.[125] The final compromise in this respect reflects the US position, which had always been that the digital economy should not be treated separately from the rest of the economy. Yet it also reflects the EU's demand that market jurisdictions gain a taxing authority in recognition of the value created in those jurisdictions. In addition to these reforms, Pillar Two of the Agreement introduces a global minimal corporate tax rate of 15 percent for companies that meet stated revenue thresholds, which is designed to mitigate harmful tax competition, level the playing field, and thus promote fair competition.[126]

After the OECD deal was reached, the US agreed not to impose the punitive tariffs it had announced, and temporarily suspended, against European countries in June 2021.[127] In addition, France, Italy, Spain, Austria, and the UK agreed to repeal their domestic DSTs once Pillar One of the OECD reform is implemented. If a new global tax regime is in force by the end of 2023, these European countries will credit the companies any taxes collected in excess of what the companies would pay under the global tax deal during the transition period.[128] The OECD deal was heralded as a rare and precious victory for US–EU relations and international economic relations more broadly. Should the deal be implemented as planned, it would convert this obstinate US–EU horizontal battle into one of the rare victories for international cooperation in today's conflict-ridden world. However, critical voices warn that it remains unclear whether the US Congress will actually be able to pass the legislation required to implement the OECD deal domestically.[129] Recently, the EU has indicated that it will resume the preparations for a digital levy if the implementation of the OECD deal fails.[130] This leaves some uncertainty as to whether this landmark agreement, in the end, provides a permanent victory and a lasting truce to US–EU relations or merely a fleeting moment of reconciliation and optimism.

The EU's Antitrust Policy and the US's Allegations of Digital Protectionism

Antitrust law has been another major battlefield for transatlantic digital policy, illuminating meaningful US–EU regulatory differences and causing resentment on both sides. The reason for the friction is that the battle lines in antitrust regulation have been highly asymmetrical: US companies dominate the European market across almost all aspects of digital services while European regulators repeatedly challenge these companies' alleged abuse of their dominant position. While EU regulators lament US tech companies' anticompetitive behavior that distorts the EU market and harms European consumers, American firms and the US government lament the European stringent antitrust enforcement that, according to their view, is protectionist in its deliberate targeting of innovative US tech companies that outcompete their weaker European rivals.

The EU has earned a reputation, quite deservingly, as the most aggressive antitrust enforcer in the world. Many of the EU's high-profile antitrust cases today are further targeting the tech industry or, as many US commentators would point out, the *American* tech industry. It is telling that, as of this writing, the European Commission is simultaneously challenging the business practices of Google, Apple, and Meta. The EU is concerned about the way Google collects user data and favors its own online display advertising tech services,[131] how Apple imposes the mandatory use of its own in-app purchase mechanism on App developers,[132] and how Meta uses the data it gathers from advertisers to compete against them in the market of classified ads.[133] The EU similarly alleged that Amazon was misappropriating the data it gathers of third-party sellers to compete against them on the marketplace it both operates and participates in—a case that Amazon settled in 2022.[134] In addition to these EU-level antitrust probes, several EU member states are in parallel leveraging their national antitrust laws to investigate these tech giants, adding to the regulatory challenges US tech companies face across Europe.[135]

The EU and its member states also have a track record of successfully completing their antitrust investigations and imposing significant remedies against US tech companies in the recent past. The European Commission has fined Google three times, resulting in almost $10 billion in fines across those three cases. In 2019, the Commission fined Google $1.7 billion in a case involving the company's AdSense online advertising program.[136] That fine came on the heels of a $5 billion fine in 2018, this time targeting Google's operating system Android.[137] At that time, the Commission had already fined Google $2.3 billion in 2017, after concluding that Google had engaged in self-preferencing by favoring its own comparison shopping service to the detriment of its rivals.[138] While Google has recently been the Commission's primary target, there have been others, including an adverse antitrust decision against Qualcomm in 2018.[139] These cases are also not a new phenomenon. They build on a series of earlier high-profile antitrust decisions against leading US tech firms—including Intel,[140] Microsoft,[141] and General Electric[142]—over the past two decades. A few large EU member states have further added to this Commission's enforcement record, most prominently with Italy fining Amazon $1.2 billion in 2021.[143]

While most of the EU antitrust cases have consisted of allegations of the abuse of a dominant position, the EU has also wielded its antitrust powers to control anticompetitive state aid granted to companies. State aid refers to a selective advantage, such as tax benefit, which a member state government gives to a company, and which may provide the recipient company with an unfair competitive edge over its commercial rivals. Such aid can be considered a violation of EU antitrust law as it can distort the level playing field and fair competition on the marketplace. The Commission's most significant and controversial state aid case to date also had a US target, namely Apple.[144] In its

2016 decision, briefly mentioned earlier, the Commission ordered Ireland to reclaim $15 billion in unpaid tax revenue from Apple.[145] According to the Commission, Apple had benefited from an "unfair advantage" over its competitors by relying on a tax ruling issued by Irish tax authorities back in 1991, and paying a conspicuously low tax rate, which distorted competition. In 2020, the EU's General Court issued a judgment overturning the Commission decision,[146] which the Commission is now appealing to the CJEU,[147] demonstrating its resolve to carry on the regulatory battle it initiated against the company.

Yet the EU wants more. Frustrated by its ability to unlock competition with one enforcement case at the time, the Commission sought new enforcement powers through a Digital Markets Act (DMA), which it gained in 2022 when the European Parliament and the Council adopted the regulation.[148] The DMA targets so-called digital gatekeepers, which are the largest digital platforms that have the greatest ability to influence market competition. Given the high revenue thresholds associated with the designation of a company as a gatekeeper, the regulation will mainly apply to the largest US tech companies, including Amazon, Apple, Google, Meta, and Microsoft. The DMA will vest the EU with the authority to regulate the business conduct of these gatekeepers *ex ante*, prohibiting them from engaging in certain business practices—such as self-preferencing—while at the same time demanding them to engage in other practices—such as ensuring interoperability of their technologies with those developed by their rivals.[149] Most importantly, under the DMA, the Commission does not need to marshal evidence to show that any such practice harms consumers, as such specified practices are presumed illegal and hence prohibited.

The EU's antitrust enforcement record against the leading tech companies would seem ambitious even standing on its own. But it seems all the more startling when contrasted with the enforcement record of US antitrust agencies. The US antitrust policy for the past half a century or so—ever since the influential Chicago school entrenched pro-market ideas into US antitrust policy in the 1970s—has been shaped by the US's market-driven instincts. US antitrust enforcers have refrained from challenging these powerful tech companies even when these firms' market position and conduct in the US have resembled those repeatedly challenged by their European counterparts. What has caused perhaps the greatest resentment is that the European regulatory choices have spilled over to the US, shaping the business practices of American companies and imposing costs on them. US regulators have largely watched from the sidelines when the EU has taken the lead and pursued antitrust enforcement against these American companies, directly undermining the laissez-faire policy that these companies were enjoying on their home market. This way, the European rights-driven regulatory model has often prevailed over the American market-driven model, as the US government's deliberate decision to forgo antitrust enforcement has repeatedly been offset by decisive regulatory action in the EU.

The US View That EU Antitrust Policy Is Protectionist

The primary concern of the US government and the business community is that the EU's mounting antitrust investigations of American tech companies are motivated by protectionism, making them both harmful and unfair. Critical voices in the US trace the EU's antitrust investigations targeting of the most successful American tech companies to Europe's desperate, envy-driven attempt to offset the US companies' technological edge by tilting the market in favor of their weaker European rivals.[150] Apple's lawyer, for example, has accused the Commission of choosing Apple as a "convenient target for an EU antitrust chief driven by headlines."[151] The political leadership in the US has advanced similar arguments. In 2015, President Obama described the EU's competition investigations into Google and Facebook as reflecting European service providers' inability to compete with their US counterparts. He stated, "We have owned the internet. Our companies have created it, expanded it, perfected it in ways that they can't compete," further alleging that EU investigations were motivated by the EU's need to "carve out some of their commercial interests."[152] In 2016, the US Treasury Department issued a White Paper in which it rebuked the Commission's state aid investigations, including the one targeting Apple's tax payments to Ireland.[153] In 2018, President Trump reacted to the $5 billion EU competition fine on Google by complaining how "American businesses were at a disadvantage in Europe"[154] and how "[Europeans] truly have taken advantage of the U.S., but not for long!"[155]

Recently, American concerns about the EU's antitrust protectionism have centered on the DMA in particular as the regulation is seen as narrowly targeting only the largest US tech firms that the DMA designates as digital gatekeepers. For example, in a June 2021 letter, the staff of the US National Security Council wrote to the staff of the EU diplomatic delegation, conveying their concern that some members of the European Parliament sought to specifically target the five biggest American tech companies with the DMA, and that the Commission was not interested in engaging with the US "in good faith." The letter further warned that "such policies will also hinder our ability to work together to harmonize our regulatory systems."[156] The US Commerce Secretary, Gina Raimondo, has also acknowledged that "we have a great many concerns of the DMA. I hear [this] from the tech industry all the time." Despite these concerns, she has also called for a dialogue and respect for the European legal system and values given that "there's fundamentally so much more about which we agree than disagree."[157] Some members of the US Congress similarly expressed concern about the EU's "digital sovereignty campaign" and the DMA's adverse effect on US companies in a letter addressed to President Biden in June 2021.[158] The DMA also became a target of relentless lobbying by the US tech companies which, however, accomplished little in terms of reining in the EU's regulatory ambitions.[159] The final text of the DMA, adopted in 2022, was hailed as transformative by EU institutions yet strongly criticized by digital gatekeepers, including Apple and Google.[160]

Other US legislators and business leaders have pointed out that the EU's antitrust protectionism is consistent with the European broader digital agenda that rests on its pursuit of digital sovereignty and is marked by anti-American bias. Commenting on the EU's $5 billion antitrust fine imposed on Google, Republican Senator Orrin Hatch tweeted in 2018: "The EU has a history of engaging in regulatory, tax & competition actions & proposals that disproportionately hit U.S. tech companies. This decision calls into question whether these actions are anything more than a series of discriminatory revenue grabs."[161] Head of the US Chamber of Commerce, Myron Brilliant, echoed this sentiment, noting how "unfortunately, some EU officials seem to think the best way to boost the fortunes of European tech firms is by discriminating against their U.S. competitors."[162] Nick Clegg, Meta's head of global affairs, commented on the proposed Digital Services Act in October 2020, warning the EU that "a shift toward digital protectionism would be self-defeating. Far from putting Europe at the cutting edge, it could accelerate the splintering of the internet, leaving Europe a bystander as US and Chinese companies dominate,"[163] while reminding the EU that its "mission is to tear down walls, not to build new ones."[164] This commentary captures the prevailing sentiment among the US political leadership and the business community, which assumes that the EU's antitrust policy is part of the broader European regulatory agenda that is guided by digital protectionism and displays a distinct anti-American bias. This sentiment has deepened the broader US–EU regulatory conflict, fueling resentment and mistrust between the parties while complicating the pursuit of a joint transatlantic digital policy agenda.

Is the EU Engaged in Antitrust Protectionism?

Whether the EU is engaged in antitrust protectionism or broader techno-nationalism can be difficult to verify. As discussed earlier in Chapter 3, the EU's antitrust enforcement reflects its concern about consumer welfare and the "fairness" of the marketplace. Yet there is admittedly a fine line between the protection of the consumer interest and protectionism, and the true motivations of regulators are at times hard to detect. It is undeniable that US tech companies have been a frequent target of EU competition enforcement. And it is, indeed, politically less costly for the EU to wield its antitrust laws against leading tech companies when those companies are not European. At the same time, it is not evident that the EU is targeting these companies be-cause of their nationality as opposed to their sheer market dominance and alleged abusive practices.[165] There is no European search engine that the Commission is seeking to protect when challenging Google's practices. Also, the original complaint behind the enforcement actions against Google came from another US company, Microsoft, and not from a European competitor.[166] Many other EU antitrust challenges against US tech firms similarly have other US firms as primary complainants or beneficiaries. Epic Games, a US-based video game and software developer, complained to the Commission about Apple, and would be one of the main beneficiaries of an adverse EU decision in its pending antitrust case against Apple.[167] Yelp has been a frequent critic of Google, urging the EU to challenge Google's anticompetitive practices.[168] Similarly, the EU's antitrust ruling against Intel originated from a complaint by the company's US rival, AMD.[169] A closer look at the European antitrust battles thus reveals that they often have US companies on both sides of the dispute, making it harder to sustain a claim that these battles reflect simply an anti-American bias.[170]

Recent empirical research into EU merger control suggests that the EU is not challenging acquisitions of European companies by foreign parties more vigorously, or adopting a more lenient approach vis-à-vis European companies seeking to merge, as those accusing the EU of protectionism might assume.[171] This study, which examined the entire universe of over 5,000 mergers notified to the Commission between 1990 and 2014, reveals no evidence that the Commission has systematically used its authority to protectionist ends. If anything, the results indicate that the Commission is less likely to challenge transactions involving foreign acquirers, and more likely to chal-lenge acquisition attempts by European companies. This suggests that the Commission is not seeking to build European champions or protect EU firms from being acquired by foreign companies through its merger review powers, thereby casting doubt on the narrative of European antitrust protectionism. Nevertheless, it remains uncertain if these findings can be extended into other areas of EU antitrust policy, including the Commission's state aid decisions or its investigations into the behavior of dominant companies. Those areas of enforcement are harder to test empirically as every disbursement of state aid or the total number of the unilateral conduct cases, including those cases that the Commission does not pursue, are not known. However, it is the very same institution within the Commission—the Directorate General for Competition—that engages in investigations across mergers, abuse of dominance, cartels, and state aid cases alike. If protectionism were indeed permeating into other areas of EU antitrust policy, there would need to be some reason why the Commission would rein in its protectionist tendencies in the merger area while engaging in biased enforcement elsewhere—and it is not obvious what such a reason would be.

Even if the EU's antitrust enforcement record to date may not reflect protectionism, it is noticeable that the tone of the conversation today across the EU is changing.[172] This change in rhetoric can be traced to the Commission's 2019 decision prohibiting the proposed *Siemens/Alstom* merger.[173] The acquisition would have combined German and French industrial giants and created a European high-speed rail champion. The critics of the Commission decision decried it as a lost opportunity to boost European companies facing competition from their bigger Chinese rival, China Railway Rolling Stock Corporation.[174] The Commission stood firm, reminding the critics that "we are not supposed to be political," but rather "loyal to our mandate" to protect European consumers from higher prices.[175] This prohibition decision triggered heavy criticism of the absence of industrial policy guiding the EU's antitrust policy, coupled with mounting calls to change that policy orientation. Aggrieved by the *Siemens/Alstom* decision, France and Germany published a "Franco-German Manifesto for a European industrial policy fit for the 21st Century" in February 2019.[176] The Manifesto advocated for several reforms designed to revitalize European industrial strategy and make it "fit for tough global competition." Among them, it called for a political oversight of EU merger control in an effort to inject industrial policy considerations into merger decisions. This would allow the Council consisting of member state governments to override the Commission merger decisions in certain instances, paving the way for the creation of European champions. France and Germany, joined by Poland, have since softened this demand of a political veto over merger review in a subsequent manifesto, yet continue to insist that member states should be able to "provide input" into the Commission's merger decisions in light of international competitiveness considerations.[177]

The Franco-German Manifesto and the criticism of the *Alstrom/Siemens* decision can be viewed as blunt endorsements of European protectionism and techno-nationalism. The EU's recent quest for digital sovereignty is also moving the EU toward more actively managed industrial policy, which risks crossing the line from protection to protectionism. The techno-nationalist rhetoric across the EU is growing more assertive, with mounting calls toward a proactive industrial policy as a foundation of Europe's technological sovereignty. Now, the industrial policy is moving from political statements to actual policy initiatives, with the EU announcing new industrial policy projects that extend government support to the development of technologies from semiconductors to batteries and from artificial intelligence to cloud services. France is among the countries that is more receptive to interventionist economic policy. It is now advocating this dirigisme with renewed vigor, with President Macron noting how "the battle we're fighting is one of sovereignty," continuing that, "If we don't build our own champions in all new areas . . . our choices . . . will be dictated by others."[178]

Yet politicized merger control or other protectionist antitrust reforms do not have a uniform backing across Europe.[179] Several prominent voices in Brussels are pushing back against the idea of digital protectionism. Margrethe Vestager, the Commission's Executive Vice-President responsible for Europe's digital transformation, has denied that the EU tech policy was motivated by anti-American bias, repeatedly emphasizing that "the [DMA] is not directed toward certain businesses or toward certain nationalities of businesses."[180] Some key European legislators have conceded that the DMA is narrowly targeting large US tech companies but that the EU is doing so for entirely legitimate, not protectionist, reasons. Andreas Schwab, an influential member of European Parliament in charge of steering the DMA through the legislative process, kept arguing that the DMA should indeed focus on the top five tech companies—Amazon, Apple, Google, Meta, and Microsoft—which according to Schwab were the "biggest problems" for competition, adding that there is no need to "include a European gatekeeper just to please [US President Joe] Biden."[181] Other European legislators concede that the DMA is targeting US companies yet remain uneasy on whether that constitutes good policy. For example, Dita Charanzovà, Vice President of the European Parliament, commented on the then-pending Digital Services Act and DMA legislation, noting that "we must state the truth: these proposals target US companies."[182] Charanzovà also warned against the EU following China's path and "turning Europe's internet to a walled garden," urging for close transatlantic cooperation in digital regulation instead.[183]

Although these statements reveal there is no uniform European view on how to balance the EU's commitment to openness with its need for greater digital sovereignty, the general political environment today is nevertheless conducive to a more nationalist economic policy orientation in Europe. The combination of populist governments in several EU member states, China's growing economic heft and assertiveness, the removal of the UK's free-market voice from the EU legislative process following Brexit, and the heightened sense of insecurity in a volatile geopolitical environment may have a cascading effect that will pave the way toward a new economic settlement between the state and the markets, ushering in some industrial policy–driven reforms in the process. Protectionism is also becoming increasingly common across the world, as reflected in more nativist policy orientation in China and the US alike, and discussed in more detail in Chapter 5. Consequently, several European leaders are now calling for the EU to rethink and adjust its policies to better navigate the increasingly unpredictable and hostile world, or else be left dependent on the policy choices made by others. This view emphasizes that the EU would be naïve to forgo defending its national interest in today's closed world dominated by protectionist strategies of other leading economies.[184] Thus, the EU knows that it is making choices about its antitrust policy and the broader digital agenda in a world that is turning inward, with concerns for technological sovereignty increasingly prevailing over concerns for economic openness.

Toward Transatlantic Rapprochement in Digital Policy

As the many disagreements between the US and EU highlighted in this chapter reveal, the American market-driven regulatory model and the European rights-driven regulatory model frequently clash, fueling transatlantic conflicts over digital regulation. The vertical and horizontal battles over data privacy, digital taxation, and antitrust are particularly prevalent examples of these conflicts, yet one could also point to others, including a disagreement over content moderation. Europeans remain concerned about the ways US tech companies are shaping the European public discourse, often for worse, by allowing hate speech and disinformation to run rampant on their platforms. As a result, the EU has adopted regulations aimed at restricting illegal and harmful content online. In response, the US has expressed concern that the EU's regulatory efforts risk replacing undesirable content with even more undesirable censorship. This particular battle illustrates how the American regulatory model is focused more narrowly on protecting one fundamental right—that of free speech—while the European rights-driven model seeks to balance the freedom of expression with various other fundamental rights, such as human dignity.

However, the transatlantic divide in digital policy might be gradually closing. Two developments are paving the way for this new era of potential rapprochement. First, the domestic conversation in the US is becoming more critical of the tech industry. The US may therefore be moving closer to the European rights-driven regulatory model, mitigating frictions or perhaps even allowing for greater regulatory alignment. Second, the US and the EU increasingly share a concern that China's digital authoritarian overtures threaten the US and EU's shared commitment to liberal democracy, individual freedom and a global, open internet. This mutual concern about the rise of digital authoritarianism may further pave the way for transatlantic alignment and cooperation.

There is an ongoing shift taking place in the American public conversation about the role of tech companies in shaping the digital economy and digital society, as was acknowledged in Chapter 1. Following repeated scandals—be it Cambridge Analytica, the January 6 US Capitol riots, or Facebook whistleblower Frances Haugen's revelations on the platform's inner workings—the American public is now turning against the tech industry as these scandals are becoming too hard to ignore.[185] Scholars, journalists, policy advocates, small businesses, and more recently, the legislators and the Executive branch in the US are also raising concerns about the unmitigated power of the biggest tech companies. Fewer voices today believe that self-regulation by tech companies themselves is sufficient, which has led to calls for the government to step in—resembling the ways that the European legislators and regulators have stepped in for several years already. This shift is potentially paving the way for greater regulatory alignment with the EU. In particular, it may influence the US's approach toward antitrust and privacy regulation, mitigating the ongoing battles discussed in this chapter.

There are even signs that some future battles over digital policy may be averted in this new policy environment. For example, the US seems to be moving toward greater acknowledgment of the EU's concerns regarding the regulation of AI. When the European Commission published its White Paper on AI in 2020, the White House expressed its concern that overregulation may lead Western nations to fall behind the rest of the world in the AI race, making it harder to counter authoritarian uses of AI.[186] However, the tone changed soon thereafter. When the European Commission published its draft AI Regulation in April 2021, President Biden's national security advisor Jake Sullivan praised the EU's Regulation on Twitter, conveying how the US "will work with our friends and allies to foster trustworthy AI that reflects our shared values and commitment to protecting the rights and dignity of all our citizens."[187]

More skeptical voices are likely to caution the optimists by pointing out that the new policy rhetoric may never translate into concrete legislative or executive action in the US. The global tax deal may still unravel in Congress. And even though there may be a (rare) bipartisan consensus between the Democrats and Republicans that tech companies need to be regulated, there is little agreement on *how* that ought to be done. The bipartisan anti-tech crusade may therefore never amount to a genuine shift in US policy, maintaining the US–EU regulatory differences in place. There is also grave uncertainty as to whether US courts will buy into the new "antitrust revolution" or whether the revived agency action targeting tech companies will end up faltering in courts that remain guided by the Chicago school orthodoxy and entrenched techno-libertarian ideals. Yet even if no significant regulatory alignment will occur in practice, there is reason to think that the US's criticism of the EU's digital policy will be toned down given its own attempts to reevaluate the market-driven foundations of the American regulatory model.[188]

To institutionalize their commitment to closer cooperation, the US and the EU established a Trade and Technology Council (TTC) in June 2021.[189] The purpose of the TTC is both to mitigate the US–EU horizontal regulatory conflict and to strengthen the Transatlantic alliance to jointly counter China's market-distortive policies and the use of technology toward illiberal ends. The TTC addresses a host of trade and technology issues of mutual concern, including cooperation in technology standards; supply chain resilience; data security, data governance, and cyber security; as well as foreign investment screening and export controls. The US's support for closer transatlantic cooperation was summarized by US national security advisor Jake Sullivan, who remarked, "With Europe, we can no longer let sibling rivalries turn into a larger family feud. That's why we're proud to partner with our European allies in a new U.S.-EU Trade and Technology Council."[190] Commissioner Vestager struck a similar tone, emphasizing the EU's and US's "common democratic values" and praising the TTC as "a great step for our renewed partnership" that allows the US and the EU to translate their shared values into "tangible action on both sides of the Atlantic."[191]

What gives perhaps an even greater impetus for bridging the remaining transatlantic differences is the EU's and US's shared concern about the growing influence of China and the diffusion of the digital authoritarian values that it espouses—including the impact of that rise and those values to the future of liberal democracy. The TTC's founding document does not explicitly single out China, yet its agenda is informed by a shared understanding that China's technological advancement poses a strategic threat that calls for a coordinated transatlantic response.[192] The Joint Statement issued by the US and the EU following their inaugural TTC meeting in September 2021 emphasizes, for example, the parties' shared commitment to developing AI technologies that "respect universal human rights and shared democratic values."[193] Similarly, the US and the EU reaffirm their commitment to maintaining foreign investment screening mechanisms to address "risks to national security." Without mentioning Chinese tech company Huawei's role in building 5G infrastructure, the statement embodies a shared concern that China is actively acquiring strategic tech infrastructures and other assets around the world.

The US has been particularly vocal about the need to counter China, and views the TTC as an important instrument to harness the EU's cooperation in that endeavor.[194] The US government has emphasized that the TTC "will focus on aligning our approaches in trade and technology so that democracies and not anyone else, not China or other autocracies, are writing the rules for trade and technology for the 21st century."[195] European leaders, however, have until recently been more cautious. They have been careful not to flame tensions with China, emphasizing that the TTC "is not aimed at any single country,"[196] while underscoring how the EU and the US "have common democratic values," which allows them to "work for a human centered digitization and open and competitive markets."[197] This different approach stems from the deeper economic ties that the EU has with China. Focusing on trade in goods, China overtook the US as the EU's most important trade partner in 2020.[198] The EU has tried to navigate the heating US–China tech war by hedging its bets and collaborating with both parties. Germany, in particular, has been careful not to antagonize China given that China is a major destination for its automobile and other industrial exports.[199] However, recent geopolitical developments, including China's refusal to condemn Russia's invasion of Ukraine and its potential to undermine Western sanctions against Russia, are elevating tensions in EU–China relations and hardening the EU's stance against China. The EU's External Action Service is now calling for the EU to recalibrate its relationship with China, describing EU–China relations today as one following the logic of "all-out competition," both economically and politically.[200] This new policy orientation is likely to limit the EU's engagement with Beijing across most policy areas and thereby move the EU's China policy closer to that of the US.

For the TTC to be effective, the US and the EU likely need to meet in the middle, with the US acknowledging that the TTC is not just a venue for the transatlantic powers to gang up against China, and the EU granting that the transatlantic digital agenda must also provide a strategic response to China's increasing assertiveness.[201] This kind of compromise is likely needed for the TTC to form a foundation for broader cooperation among techno-democracies, as will be discussed in Chapter 8 in the context of examining China's efforts to export its state-driven regulatory model, and the US and other democracies' attempts to counter those efforts. While neither the US nor the EU trusts China—both invoking their "systemic rivalry" with China[202]—it remains unclear whether the TTC will bridge the transatlantic divisions to the extent that the EU and the US will be able to act as genuine partners that trust one another. Europeans are still struggling to gain trust that "America is back" after the transatlantic relationship reached a low point during the four years of combative and erratic foreign policy under the Trump presidency.[203] The recent history of transatlantic cooperation has a mixed record at best, with the negotiations over the Transatlantic Trade and Investment Partnership being abandoned in 2019, and the efforts such as the Transatlantic Economic Council, established in 2007, fading into irrelevance over time.[204] The EU remains internally divided on many questions pertaining to technology, as it does on the question of how the EU ought to engage with China. At the same time, as the US is moving closer to the EU's approach to tech regulation and the EU is growing more assertive on China, it is possible that a joint transatlantic agenda on the digital economy is beginning to emerge around the TTC. This might pave the way for a new era in transatlantic digital policy where the US and the EU are prepared to put aside their mutual regulatory battles in order to focus on the battle that many argue matters the most: the joint battle to defeat digital authoritarian norms embedded in the Chinese state-driven regulatory model and to defend liberal democracy as a foundation of the digital economy.

PART III

The Expansion of Empires

The Waning Global Influence
of American Techno-Libertarianism

TODAY'S GLOBAL DIGITAL economy rests on a foundation built by the United States and its leading tech companies. For more than two decades, the American market-driven regulatory model enabled large US tech companies' international expansion. Since the early days of the internet in the 1990s, the US government has maximized opportunities associated with the technological revolution by advocating for an open, unregulated, and private sector–led digital economy—both at home and abroad. Across the Clinton, Bush, and Obama administrations, the US not only championed its values around a free market and free internet domestically, but also proactively exported those values to other countries, emphasizing the importance of those values for economic growth and societal progress everywhere. The US has sought to globalize its market-driven regulatory model most prominently through its promotion of an "internet freedom agenda," according to which innovation must be free from government regulation or censorship, or else economic and political progress will be compromised.[1] This policy agenda has, in practice, meant relying on *private power* to shape the global digital economy— private power in the form of large US technology companies exerting often unconstrained economic, political, and cultural influence in foreign societies.

This American private power is today seen everywhere. Citizens around the world communicate using US online platforms—they send WhatsApp messages, Google information, share life stories via Facebook, upload and watch YouTube videos, post pictures on Instagram, and comment on world news using Twitter. These US tech companies foster global connections and conversations in ways that most people find beneficial, even essential, for their daily lives. Few individuals would want to go back to the world without these tools that enable humans to interact and share information with each other with remarkable ease. At the same time, digital citizens are increasingly concerned about the vast influence these digital companies wield over their everyday lives. Today, the algorithms of a handful of large US tech companies determine the content that digital citizens everywhere are exposed to on-line. This way, these American companies shape what people across Africa, Asia, Australia, Europe, and Latin America think, want, and buy. These companies are often more resourceful and powerful than actual states, which allows them to exert penetrating economic, political, and cultural influence, thereby shaping the lives of foreign internet users and foreign societies in profound ways. Despite their multifaceted global influence, the ethos of these US companies is far from global. These companies continue to reflect the "Californian ideology" and the American techno-libertarian instincts, ex-porting within their products and services the values of the US market-driven regulatory model.

Building on the discussion of the American, Chinese, and European reg-ulatory models in Part I, and the conflicts among those models in Part II, the book now turns to examine these models' relative global influence. This last part shows how the digital empires have not only engaged in regulatory battles with each other, but also competed for global prominence. By exporting their regulatory models, the US, China, and the EU are each seeking to expand their respective spheres of influence, thus attempting to shift the rest of the world closer to the norms and values inherent in their market-driven, state-driven, and rights-driven models. In reaching across all continents, these chapters show how each digital empire relies on different forms of influence, with the US leveraging its private power; China, its infrastructure power; and the EU, its regulatory power.

This last part begins by first looking closely at the global influence of the American market-driven regulatory model. This chapter documents the rise and fall of the American digital empire and its regulatory model as the lodestar for the global digital order. Revealing the early success of the US government's internet freedom agenda in promoting US tech companies' pri-vate power abroad, it highlights how these leading tech companies have come to influence foreign societies in a myriad of ways. The chapter also looks at the way the US government has facilitated its tech companies' global pres-ence and often-unconstrained influence by promoting its internet freedom agenda abroad as part of US foreign policy. As this chapter explains, the in-ternet freedom agenda has focused on exporting two core principles: a com-mercial nonregulation principle and anti-censorship principle.[2] Since the Clinton presidency, the US government has sought to globalize both princi-ples through extensive diplomatic efforts. These efforts have in most instances been supported by US tech companies that benefit from an unregulated and uncensored global internet, leaving them free to shape the global digital marketplace toward their interests and values. But this accumulation of power among US tech companies has also raised significant concerns among foreign governments. This chapter details these concerns, highlighting the criticism that has recently been leveled at US tech companies' global power, and the US government's efforts to enable and entrench that power. It also shows how, in recent years, a growing backlash against US tech companies has eroded the global influence of the American market-driven regulatory model, thus creating space for the European rights-driven model and the Chinese state-driven regulatory model to gain in influence.

A Brief Look at the Rise of US Tech Companies' Global Influence

The American market-driven regulatory model is externalized primarily through the worldwide presence of its tech companies, which have fueled technological progress and shaped foreign societies economically, politically, and culturally. As there was little to no digital regulation when several of today's large tech companies were founded in the 1990s and 2000s, these companies were able to grow and accumulate power everywhere, largely unconstrained by governments. As a result, these companies' private power provided a "private ordering" for the global digital economy.[3] In this privatized legal order, tech companies, not governments, largely set the rules of engagement and thus act as institutions of governance. These companies' business practices, community norms, terms of service, and other forms of self-regulation thus replace the governments as rule-setters. Kate Klonick describes tech companies as "new governors,"[4] often exerting more power and influence than actual governments. Ian Bremmer refers to a "technopolar" world, which may more accurately describe today's world order than traditional references to a state-centric—be it unipolar, bipolar, or multipolar—world order.[5] With this kind of power, it is relevant to wonder whether these companies will ultimately prevail over governments—a question that will be addressed in the concluding chapter. Regardless of how that vertical battle between governments and tech companies unfolds, it is undisputed that these companies' power is real, extensive—and *global*. It is telling that the four most valuable brands in the world in 2021 were Apple, Amazon, Microsoft, and Google.[6] While these companies shape the entire world, they hardly reflect the diversity of the values that characterize their global user base. Instead, these companies all hail from the US, which explains why their global power also reflects many quintessentially American values embedded in the market-driven regulatory model.

Although Meta-owned Facebook is not among those top four companies featuring the highest brand value, the footprint that Facebook has made across the world since it was founded in 2004 powerfully captures the global presence that these US companies have today. Facebook is the most popular social network worldwide, followed by YouTube, WhatsApp, Instagram, and Facebook Messenger.[7] Even though the popularity of TikTok is growing, the Chinese-owned social media app still trails behind Facebook in global user numbers.[8] Of these leading networks, all but YouTube and TikTok are owned by Meta. Facebook has around two billion active daily users and three billion active monthly users worldwide.[9] In 2021, 36 percent of the world's population had a Facebook account,[10] and over 70 percent of daily social media users globally were Facebook users.[11] Facebook's user base is also spread around the globe, India being the company's number-one market in January 2022 with 417 million users.[12] Overall, Southeastern Asia comprises 21 percent of Facebook's total registered users; Southern Asia, 18 percent; and North America, 13 percent.[13] These statistics reveal how the US market constitutes only a fraction of the company's total user base. However, Facebook's advertising revenue is still anchored within North America. On a user level, each North American user generated $160 of advertising revenue in 2021 for Facebook, while each European user generated $51, and each Asian user generated $13.[14] Thus, even though North America accounts for only 13 percent of Facebook users, the region generates close to 50 percent of Facebook's revenue.[15] The market penetration of Meta-owned messaging and video-calling platform WhatsApp is also relatively greater outside the US. More than 2 billion people in over 180 countries are using WhatsApp.[16] India leads in WhatsApp use, recording 488 million users in 2021, followed by Brazil and Indonesia.[17] Only 30 percent of American phone users are using WhatsApp,[18] whereas 93 percent of Brazilian, 84 percent of Argentinian, and 81 percent of Italian phone users are using the service. These statistics leave in no doubt Meta's remarkable global reach.

Google is another US tech giant whose worldwide footprint has come to define key aspects of daily life and work for much of the planet's population. In 2021, Google had over 86 percent of search engine market share worldwide[19]—a figure that is all the more staggering considering that Google is banned in China, which entails that only internet users in Hong Kong or those who access Google from mainland China using a VPN connection can contribute toward Google's global market share. In North America, Google had an 89 percent market share in 2021. Its market share is even higher in other regions, including 92 percent in Europe, 93 percent in Asia, and 94 percent in Australia.[20] Google's market share has grown quickly in Asia due to the rapid growth of internet users there.[21] This growth has been particularly striking in India, where Google had a 94 percent market share as of July 2022.[22] China and Russia form exceptions to Google's global market dominance: Baidu is the most popular search engine in China; Yandex the most popular in Russia. However, even in Russia—where Google is not banned—Google still accounted for over 45 percent of search engine traffic in 2021.[23] Similar to Facebook, Google's advertising revenue is still today predominantly generated in the US and Europe despite the company's global user base. However, the relative contribution of the rest of the word to the company's revenues is likely to increase with the expected growth of incomes in those markets.

Similarly, Apple has built a staggering global presence since it was first founded back in the 1970s. Apple's revenue, which stood at over $365 billion in 2021—is currently anchored in the United States and Europe, but the company also has a strong and constantly growing presence outside those regions.[24] Apple also stands out among US tech giants in its strong presence in the Chinese market. In 2021, 42 percent of Apple's global revenue originated from North and South America, 24 percent from EMEA (defined as including European countries, India, the Middle East, and Africa), 19 percent from Greater China (including China, Hong Kong, and Taiwan), 8 percent from Japan, and 7 percent from the rest of the Asia Pacific (including Australia).[25] Apple's non-US revenue is rapidly expanding, especially in Asia. Through 2021, Apple's ten-year average annual revenue growth was 23 percent in the US, 30 percent in Europe, 69 percent in China, 33 percent in Japan, and 34 percent in the rest of Asia.[26] The sale of iPhones—Apple's most valuable product—is also growing faster in Europe and China than in the US. From 2020 to 2021, iPhone sales grew by 15 percent in the US, 50 percent in Europe, and 23 percent in China.[27] However, Apple continues to have a modest 13 percent market share of the mobile phone market in Africa as of August 2022, with Korean Samsung and multiple lower-cost China-based phone companies controlling the rest of the market.[28] Apple's recent diversification of offerings, such as AirPods, the Apple Watch, and its services have also contributed to the growth of Apple's revenue, especially in China. Remarkably, Apple has seen a 243 percent growth in its wearable, home, and accessories revenue, predominately focused in Asia.[29]

Microsoft's expansive global presence has the longest history among the US tech giants. Since 2011, Microsoft has generated approximately 50 percent of its annual revenue outside the United States.[30] The company's revenue is divided almost evenly into three streams: cloud systems; personal computing; and productivity, including Office 365, LinkedIn subscriptions, and Microsoft Teams.[31] Microsoft's cloud systems are sold globally, its top three clients being the US-based Verizon, Taiwanese MSI Computer, and South Korean LG electronics.[32] Microsoft Teams is heavily used all around the globe. The popularity of the videoconferencing platform soared during the pandemic, with 2.7 billion minutes in meetings being recorded in one day (March 31, 2020) by all Teams users in early days of the pandemic.[33] There are 270 million total Teams users, including 145 million daily active users in 181 countries around the world.[34] In contrast, Microsoft's Office365 subscriptions are heavily skewed toward the US and Europe.[35]

Amazon, despite earning most of its revenue today in the US, is also expanding internationally. Even with the US generating 68 percent of Amazon's revenue in 2020,[36] the e-commerce giant has increased its influence in a number of important foreign markets. In 2018, Amazon's largest market outside the US was Germany, but since the boom of Amazon Warehouse Services, Amazon's most important export market today is India.[37] In the US, Amazon has 45 percent of market share in the US e-commerce market. Within European countries, Amazon faces tougher competition but remains an important player in some key markets: in the UK, Amazon has 30 percent of the e-commerce market, while in Germany Amazon's share is 27 percent. In India, Amazon has a market share of 31 percent, trailing Indian e-commerce company Flipkart.[38] However, Amazon is growing relatively faster outside the US, which may increase the company's global footprint in the coming years.[39]

It is also notable that, despite the staggering growth of the Chinese tech industry over the last decade, the global digital private ordering is still very American at its core. While several Chinese tech giants have grown even larger than their US counterparts, they have not been as significant in shaping the lives of internet users outside China. The reason is that while the US tech companies' have long focused on developing their global presence, their Chinese equivalents have, until recently, mainly focused on their vast and protected home market. For example, Alibaba dwarfs Amazon in terms of global sales due to the massive size of the Chinese market—according to data published in 2021, Amazon generated $239bn in global sales in 2019 compared to Alibaba's $765bn[40]—but only about 7 percent of Alibaba's total revenue that year came from international business.[41] Most of Tencent's income also comes from mainland China, with international revenues similarly contributing only 7 percent to the company's total sales in 2020.[42] At the time when DiDi submitted its prospectus in preparation for its IPO in New York, only 12 percent of its users were outside China.[43] Telecommunications giant

Huawei used to generate more international than domestic revenue, but following the crippling effect of the US sanctions over the past years, the company has had to retreat from several overseas markets.[44] As a result of this retreat, 65 percent of its revenues came from China in 2021.[45] However, Chinese tech companies' international presence may grow in the coming years. Following the recent, significant regulatory crackdown on the tech industry by the Chinese government and the restrictions imposed by the US government, several Chinese tech companies are now diversifying their business opportunities and investing heavily in overseas expansion—focusing on markets outside of both China and the US.[46]

The US tech companies, while at times reviled for their excessive market power and extractive data practices, are often admired for their success. There are numerous examples of countries attempting to replicate the success of US tech companies by emulating California's startup haven, the Silicon Valley. Examples of Silicon Valley replicas include "Silicon Wadi" in Tel-Aviv, Israel; "Silicon Roundabout" in London, UK; "Chilecon Valley" in Santiago, Chile; "Silicon Allee" in Berlin, Germany; "Silicon Lagoon" in Lagos, Nigeria; and "Silicon Savannah" in Nairobi, Kenya. One of the earliest examples is the United Arab Emirates' "Internet City" in Dubai, which was established around the same time as California's Silicon Valley. It tried to emulate the US techno-libertarian approach of eliminating taxes and other barriers to growth, leaving the industry largely unregulated.[47] As a departure from standard business regulation in the country, foreign companies are also permitted to have 100 percent ownership in their businesses based there. In part for this reason, the Internet City has attracted some of the world's leading tech companies to Dubai, including Microsoft, Oracle, Dell, Cisco, HP, IBM, Canon, Siemens, Logica, Sony Ericsson, and Compaq. Sheik Mohammed bin Rashid Al Maktoum, Dubai's ruler and Prime Minister of the UAE, has proudly stated that "Dubai has become the 'Silicon Valley' of the Middle East."[48] African governments have also increased their investments in the vibrant tech scene. Kenya's "Silicon Savannah" was one of the first attempts by Africa to establish itself in the tech field, emerging between 2007 and 2010.[49] The Minister of Communications and Digital Economy for Nigeria, Isa Pantami, has further claimed that Ogun, a city in Nigeria, will be the next Silicon Valley of Africa.[50] Despite the many efforts to establish these other tech centers around the world, the US's Silicon Valley remains the largest and most influential ecosystem of digital development in the world today—while also providing an inspiration for governments around the world.

In foreign countries where US tech companies have significant market presence, these companies' products and services influence internet users' access to information, professional habits, commercial transactions, the consumption of news, private conversations, and more. This puts US tech companies in a position to influence what these foreign users think and want. In the absence of effective government regulation, these companies—driven by their own commercial interests—have been left free to remake foreign societies and shape foreign internet users' lives. In the process of exercising their private power, these American tech companies are also extending the values embedded in the US's regulatory model across continents. US tech companies' mainly US-based engineers, steeped in American values, write the algorithms and build the products that are driving a profound global change—despite these engineers' limited understanding of vast cultural and societal differences that exist around the world. This dynamic explains why the private ordering that exists today is global, while at the same time fundamentally American.

During the decades after the internet was first commercialized in the 1990s, US tech companies' globalization was largely welcomed by foreign governments, which often endorsed the US government's view of free markets and a free internet as cornerstones of the digital economy. However, in recent years, as these companies' power and societal influence have grown beyond what any government had been able to imagine, attempts to regulate these companies have grown. A number of countries are now looking for ways to tame these companies' private power and impose local laws on them, including demanding them to store data locally or adhere to certain cultural, political, or religious norms in moderating content on their platforms. Despite these recent efforts, the largest tech companies' private power often overwhelms that of the governments who struggle to regulate them. These US tech companies' continuing influence is further sustained by the popularity of their products and services among the local citizens using them, further entrenching their global private power and complicating any foreign government's efforts to limit that power.

Understanding this rise of the US tech companies' private power, and the largely unconstrained globalization of that power, explains why the American market-driven regulatory model has been so influential in shaping the global digital order over the past two decades. However, as discussed later in this chapter, the extent of that private power—and the harmful manifestations of that power—has recently become a growing source of concern among governments around the world, providing a reason for them to now constrain that power. Thus, while the formidable private power vested in the leading US tech companies drove the ascent of the American market-driven regulatory model as the hallmark of digital globalization, that private power is now also paving the way for the global decline of that model.

Globalizing the American Regulatory Model Through the Internet Freedom Agenda

The global expansion of US tech companies benefited from a strong backing of the US government. The US government's foreign policy agenda—centered around the concept of internet freedom—facilitated the global diffusion of the American market-driven regulatory model and, with that, enabled US tech companies' ascent to global dominance. While there may not be a single definition of the internet freedom agenda, Jack Goldsmith has reduced it to two core principles that are at the heart of the US's regulatory model: the commercial nonregulation principle and the anti-censorship principle.[51] Since the early days of the internet in the 1990s, the US government has cultivated an enabling domestic regulatory environment, thus contributing to the unhindered growth of its tech companies. It has also sought to export this regulatory environment abroad, paving the way for these companies to take over the world. Yet the internet freedom agenda extends beyond furthering commercial opportunities for US tech companies. It has also been a deeply ideological, value-driven political project, designed to promote democracy, freedom, and other Western values as part of a larger US foreign policy agenda in the post–Cold War era. After the fall of the Berlin Wall and the dissolution of the Soviet Union, the US's fear was that the promise of a new era of political freedom could be compromised if the countries around the world started building new "virtual walls" to divide the world by censoring the internet and targeting dissidents online. For example, in 2010, Secretary of State Hillary Clinton drew a comparison to the Berlin Wall and Soviet-style restrictions on press freedom, warning that with growing censorship efforts by authoritarian governments, "a new information curtain is descending across much of the world."[52] The US government was determined to prevent that from happening.

Exporting Nonregulation Principle

The 1993–2001 Bill Clinton presidency coincided with the early days of the commercialization of the internet. His administration was keenly aware of the economic opportunity that the internet presented and was eager to seize that opportunity for the benefit of US tech companies. This required that the global internet be allowed to develop without regulatory intervention.

The US Congress codified this nonregulation principle in 1996 by adopting the Communications Decency Act, including its famous Section 230 that shields tech companies from liability in terms of the content they host.[53] The Executive branch then took on the task of globalizing this principle. It made concerted efforts to shape the global narrative on digital governance, urging foreign governments to follow the US lead and embrace a nonregulatory, market-oriented approach to e-commerce.[54]

In a 1994 speech at the World Telecommunication Development Conference in Buenos Aires, Vice President Al Gore urged countries around the world to facilitate the creation of a "Global Information Infrastructure" and commit to a market-driven, private sector–led internet governance. Gore argued that this approach would connect the global community, facilitate information sharing and communication, and promote economic growth and democracy around the world.[55] In 1997, the Clinton administration released "A Framework for Global Electronic Commerce" (Framework), outlining a new US policy on promoting internet freedom around the world.[56] The main architect of the Framework was President Clinton's Chief Policy Advisor Ira Magaziner, who led the endeavor to globalize the US digital policy, including the nonregulation principle. Magaziner emphasized how "markets maximize individual freedom and individual choice, and competition maximizes the choices that people have. So competition and individual choice should be the watchwords of the new digital economy."[57] He also stressed the importance of the Framework being "global in nature," and the need for the US to pursue discussions with other countries to ensure that the digital revolution everywhere unfolds in a predictable legal and political environment.[58]

In the early years of promoting its internet freedom agenda, the US government targeted its closest trading partners and political allies. In the late 1990s and early 2000s, the US was successful in obtaining commitments from several of its allies, who agreed to promote the nonregulatory, market-driven global e-commerce model. In a series of joint declarations and trade agreements between 1997 and 2001, countries such as Australia, Chile, France, Japan, Jordan, the Netherlands, the Philippines, Singapore, and the United Kingdom, as well as the EU and the Asia-Pacific Economic Group all agreed to the principles outlined in the 1997 Framework.[59] For example, the Clinton administration secured an agreement in 1998 with Japan, where the two countries agreed to "move forward together, with a market-oriented private sector–led approach to enhance privacy, protect intellectual property, and encourage the free flow of information and commerce on the Internet."[60] According to a US–Japan Joint Statement, "both governments should avoid imposing unnecessary regulations or restrictions on electronic commerce." The joint statement also emphasized the importance of being able to transfer data freely across borders and stressed that "governments should not impose stronger restrictions on content on the Internet than exist in the real world."[61] In announcing the political agreement with Japan, the White House applauded Japan's endorsement of the US's market-driven and tax-free approach to regulating e-commerce, which included Japan taking a "stance against privacy regulations like those favored by the European Union."[62]

Already in those early years of the internet's adoption, the US sensed that the EU was more prone to regulate new technologies and feared that this European regulatory proclivity could compromise the US's vision of a free, un-regulated digital economy. The EU had taken steps to regulate data flows with its 1995 Data Protection Directive, adopted shortly before the US pronounced its Framework.[63] In that regulation, the US foresaw potential impediments for digital trade and data flows resulting from conflicting regulatory approaches. Likely in part to fend off further regulation stemming from Europe, the US negotiated and issued separate Joint Statements with the EU and the UK to-ward the end of the Clinton presidency. In a 2000 US–EU Joint Statement, the US and the EU agreed that "the expansion of electronic commerce will be essentially market-led and driven by private initiative."[64] Both governments also pledged their support "for the development, preferably on a global basis, of self-regulatory codes of conduct and technologies to gain consumer confi-dence in electronic commerce." This mutual commitment to market-driven governance of e-commerce was echoed in the 1999 US–UK Joint Statement.[65]

Other countries signed on to the US's policy agenda as well. In a 1998 Joint Statement with Australia, the US and Australia agreed to both the nonregulation and anti-censorship principles.[66] The statement stresses the importance of the private sector's leadership in ensuring the growth of e-commerce, while affirming how "governments should avoid imposing un-necessary regulations. When regulation is necessary, they should rely on a 'light touch' regulatory environment." While most of the commitments that the US secured for its nonregulation principle were given in the form of political declarations—such as the one with Australia—occasionally these commitments were incorporated in binding agreements. Shortly after Jordan's accession to the World Trade Organization (WTO), the US and Jordan signed the "Jordan Free Trade Agreement" in 2000, marking the US's first free trade agreement (FTA) with an Arab country.[67] The US–Jordan FTA included sub-stantive provisions on e-commerce, which was seen as an important way to advance export opportunities for the US technology sector. In the FTA, both countries agreed to "seek to avoid" imposing unnecessary market access barriers for digitized products, recognizing how such barriers would impede e-commerce.[68]

The US government also sought to convince a number of developing countries to embrace a market-oriented regulatory model through its Development Initiative: a policy effort launched in 1999 to provide regulatory assistance to support adoption of policies aimed at creating an information society in targeted countries.[69] As part of the Development Initiative, the US government helped countries in Africa, Asia, Central Europe, Latin America, and the Caribbean to establish independent regulatory agencies to oversee the digital economy. The goal of the US was to ensure that these agencies provide universal access to telecommunications infrastructure in the country, in line with principles of "competition, liberalization, privatization, and transparency."[70] During the Clinton administration, the US and other G-8 leaders—consisting of today's G-7 countries and then-member Russia—also established a Digital Opportunity Task Force, which formed one of the first efforts to "bridge the international digital divide and create digital opportunity."[71] To further that goal, President Clinton urged the private sector to assist the US government in its efforts to expand the internet and relevant technologies in developing countries. Several companies signed on to this effort, including Cisco Systems, which committed to expanding its Cisco Networking Academies to 24 of the Least Developed Nations, and Microsoft, which agreed to support Digital Divide projects in Colombia, India, Korea, and Russia. To help finance these efforts, the Export-Import Bank of the United States offered to accept credit of many emerging market governments. The US Overseas Private Investment Corporation also committed to establishing a $200 million line of credit for US companies seeking to support e-commerce projects or digital development projects in developing countries.[72]

The US's efforts to export its internet freedom agenda also extended to international institutions, including the WTO, where the US took an active role in leading early discussions on digital policies. In his remarks at the WTO Ministerial meeting in Geneva in 1998, President Clinton described the internet's "unimagined, revolutionary potential to empower billions of people around the world."[73] He then urged WTO members to adopt policies similar to the US, calling for "the nations of the world to join the United States in a standstill on any tariffs to electronic transmissions sent across borders" so as to ensure the growth of "the most promising new economic opportunity in decades." These discussions led to trade agreements addressing e-commerce that reflected a nonregulatory approach in close alignment with the Clinton administration's policy goals. The WTO members agreed to eliminate and refrain from imposing tariffs or other trade barriers on information technology and e-commerce in the 1996 WTO Information Technology Agreement (ITA).[74] The ITA is a plurilateral, as opposed to a multilateral, agreement, and it was initially signed by 29 WTO member countries consisting primarily of wealthy developed nations.[75] The WTO members also recommitted to these market-driven principles in the subsequent 1998 Declaration on Global Electronic Commerce.[76]

The US government also sought to ensure that any multilateral governance frameworks for the digital economy would follow a multistakeholder model where the private sector played a dominant role. Instead of vesting existing state-driven institutions such as the United Nations with the authority over digital policy issues, as China has advocated, the US has endorsed a multistakeholder approach to the global governance of the internet. The Internet Corporation for Assigned Names and Numbers (ICANN) is an example of this approach. ICANN is a nongovernmental organization that administers the internet's domain name system or its "address book," which is critical in ensuring that internet users are routed to the correct website each time they enter a website name on their browser. In 1998, the US government established the ICANN and tasked the organization with administering the internet, including managing the domain name system. Although it was set up as a nongovernmental organization and became more autonomous over time, initially ICANN operated under a contract issued by the US Department of Commerce and included US government oversight. However, the US government granted the group gradually more autonomy over time, before relinquishing the US's control entirely in 2014, in line with the US's initial goal to give the private sector control over internet governance. There were multiple occasions since the ICANN's establishment when other governments sought to wrestle more control over the operation of ICANN, but the US successfully fended off those challenges. As a result, the US view that favored a market-driven governance model prevailed.[77]

While the US's efforts to promote the nonregulation principle were particularly active during the Clinton presidency, the US government maintained this same posture toward the regulation of the digital economy until recently. Throughout the 1990s and 2000s, the US seemed to have succeeded in its efforts to globalize the nonregulation principle as very few digital regulations were adopted around the world—a development that only began to reverse after 2010, as discussed further below. As a result of this success, the US government's policy agenda shifted toward the goal of fending off government censorship as the remaining, pertinent threat to a free internet. Despite its focus on democracy promotion and its anti-censorship principle, the US government continued to resist all efforts to regulate the digital economy, in particular after 2010 when regulatory activity picked up in Europe and elsewhere.

Exporting the Anti-Censorship Principle

The American market-driven regulatory model—and the internet freedom agenda designed to export that model—was never only about economic freedom; it was also about political freedom. In addition to promoting the nonregulation principle, the US government has endorsed and exported the anti-censorship principle as a cornerstone of global internet governance. The efforts to globalize the anti-censorship principle helped the US to disseminate its regulatory model abroad which, in turn, advanced both the US government's economic and political agenda. First, it furthered the US's economic agenda by shielding its tech companies from foreign censorship, thus allowing these companies to expand their private power across global markets without foreign governments' interference in the content disseminated on their platforms. Second, it contributed to the US government's political agenda by seeking to promote freedom and democracy as organizing principles for political life. Thus, both US tech companies and the US government had a keen interest in globalizing the internet freedom agenda's noncensorship principle and, with that, exporting one of the defining features of the American regulatory model.

This determination to export the anti-censorship principle can be viewed as part of the US's longstanding democracy promotion agenda that has characterized the American foreign policy over several administrations— both during and after the Cold War. During the Cold War, the US viewed the "information war" as critical to its democracy promotion, causing it to invest in projects such as Radio Free Europe and Radio Liberty (RFE/RL). RFE/RL is a US government–funded news organization that broadcasted news aimed at the Soviet Union and Eastern Europe during the Cold War. It still today airs news in 27 languages to 23 countries, including Afghanistan, Iran, Russia, and Pakistan.[78] Projects such as RFE/RL were designed to counter Communist propaganda and expose people living under Communism to reform ideas with greater knowledge of the everyday freedoms that Western citizens enjoyed.[79] Thus, even before the internet era, the US view was that access to free information offered a path toward democracy around the world.

The US's efforts to globalize the anti-censorship aspect of its regulatory model builds on these other democracy promotion initiatives. Starting in the early 2000s in the aftermath of the 9/11 terrorist attacks, there were efforts in Congress to promote American internet freedoms abroad. In 2001–2003, several bipartisan bills were introduced with the goal of exporting democracy, including a bill calling for a global strategy to "defeat Internet jamming and censorship."[80] Members of Congress repeatedly expressed their view that the internet was a tool for promoting individual rights and democracy abroad, and that the US government should increase its funding dedicated to supporting internet freedoms abroad. One bipartisan Senate bill, for example, referred to the internet as becoming "the most powerful engine for democratization and the free exchange of ideas ever invented," while emphasizing the importance of an uncensored internet as a "check on repressive rule by authoritarian regimes around the world."[81] The bill singled out Burma, Cuba, Laos, North Korea, the People's Republic of China, Saudi Arabia, Syria, and Vietnam as countries where governments are actively restricting access and online content, while lamenting the US government's meager efforts to defeat internet censorship abroad.[82] Members of Congress were particularly concerned about the absence of internet freedoms in China. They sponsored legislation, formed caucuses, funded programs, and held hearings on this topic.[83] However, these efforts did not yield significant results.

In 2006, under the Bush administration, then–Secretary of State Condoleezza Rice identified internet freedom as a US policy priority and established the Global Internet Freedom Task Force (GIFT) to advance this policy abroad. GIFT, which operated within the State Department, was dedicated to maximizing freedom of expression and the free flow of information and ideas online, while hindering the efforts of repressive regimes in censoring and silencing legitimate debate.[84] GIFT laid the groundwork for the future US efforts in combating suppression of online speech by foreign governments— efforts that intensified under Secretary of State Hillary Clinton, who expanded on the work of GIFT.[85] In 2006, the Bush administration also started to monitor more systematically the extent to which foreign governments were protecting internet freedoms and human rights online, including tracking those policies as part of the US State Department's annual Country Reports on Human Rights Practices.[86] While internet freedom was, no doubt, part of the Bush administration's democracy promotion agenda, that aspect was overshadowed by controversial efforts to deploy military power to export democracy abroad. These efforts culminated in the Iraq War, launched in 2003, which was geared at overthrowing the government of Saddam Hussein. The Iraq War was widely denounced as a reckless and ill-conceived manifestation of American interventionism. The legacy of that war also explains why part of the world has always been apprehensive whenever the US has sought to export its values, including democracy and freedom, to countries around the world.

Internet freedom became an even more prominent foreign policy goal during the Obama presidency. Secretary Clinton launched internet freedom as a US foreign policy agenda in a famous speech in January 2010.[87] She elaborated that agenda in other notable speeches delivered in 2010 and 2011, advocating for a unified, open, and global internet. Secretary Clinton pledged necessary resources—whether diplomatic, economic, or technological—to advance these freedoms abroad, while committing the US to support "the development of new tools that enable citizens to exercise their rights of free expression by circumventing politically motivated censorship."[88] Under President Obama, the US government directly supported freedom of expression and the free flow of information online in repressive countries through funding the development of new technologies and the training of journalists and democracy activists. The State Department's NetFreedom Task Force, which was established to succeed GIFT, oversaw efforts geared at circumventing government censorship in over forty countries with new technologies, coupled with training to deploy those technologies.[89] These efforts reveal how the US government was adamant in its belief that exporting its regulatory model—in particular the commitment to a free internet as a core tenet of that model—had the potential to ignite and sustain democratic transitions across the world.

During President Obama's first term, the US government's internet freedom agenda gained even greater salience in the wake of the Arab Spring—an uprising that started in 2010 with social media-empowered protests in Tunisia and that spread across North Africa and the Middle East—sparking hope that the internet was going to unleash a wave of democratization across the region.[90] Social media and digital technologies supported these uprisings, with dissidents using American internet platforms such as Facebook and Twitter to organize protests.[91] The US government also played a role in assisting the dissidents. The International Republican Institute and the National Democratic Institute provided social media training and financing to grass-roots activists organizing the protests. Both Institutes—loosely affiliated with the Republican and Democratic Parties—were created by Congress and were financed through the National Endowment for Democracy.[92]

The US had some eager partners in its efforts to promote internet freedoms, in particular in Europe. Following Secretary Clinton's 2010 speech, several European countries developed their own internet freedom initiatives, in part responding to the same external events as the US, including the 2009 suppression of mass public protests in Iran following a contested presidential election in the country.[93] Sweden and the Netherlands, in particular, collaborated on multiple occasions with the US State Department to advance internet freedoms abroad, thus helping the US to export its regulatory model. Collaborating with these countries made it easier for the US to spread its internet freedom narrative while also alleviating some degree of suspicion and opposition that several countries felt toward the US's foreign policy agenda in general, and democracy promotion in particular.[94]

Together with its allies, the US government advanced its internet freedom agenda in bilateral and multilateral fora, including the United Nations.[95] An important victory for the US's internet freedom agenda came in 2012, when the UN Human Rights Council (UNHRC) unanimously adopted a resolution urging all states to "promote and facilitate access to the Internet."[96] It was the first UN resolution that recognized the right to digital freedoms, and a victory for Secretary Clinton who had pledged in her 2010 internet freedom speech to propose such a resolution at the UN.[97] Around the time the UNHRC Resolution was adopted, many more countries started participating in discussions around internet freedoms. In September 2012, Kenya took the lead in organizing the Second Freedom Online Coalition conference, extending conversations about internet freedom to Africa under the leadership of an African country.[98] Tunisia was another African country to join the Coalition, followed by Ghana.[99] The US State Department's support for dissidents in authoritarian countries or countries that underwent democratic transitions, such as Tunisia, may have helped to expand the internet freedom narrative in those countries. With these developments, the US regulatory model—in particular its central commitment to advance internet freedoms—seemed to have reached a new height of its global influence.

In addition to sponsoring resolutions, signing declarations, and championing the freedom agenda in conferences and diplomatic conversations, the US government engaged in various initiatives in support of dissidents in authoritarian countries. This reflected a belief that without directly supporting these political activists on the ground, the values underlying the American regulatory model were not going to diffuse and spark democratic reforms in those countries. Between 2008 and 2012, Congress allocated nearly $100 million in funding to support various internet freedom efforts outside the US.[100] The State Department provided internet freedom grants to nonprofit organizations and tech developers to invent new technologies that would allow individuals in repressive countries to access information and communicate freely online.[101] Additionally, funding was given to initiatives that provided training for activists on the use of such technologies. New tools developed by these state-funded groups included technologies and software that helped individuals circumvent censored content, prevent cyberattacks, remain anonymous, and prevent government tracking or collection of data.

Some of the funding provided activists with hardware, such as satellite phones, laptops, or mobile networks, so that they could remain connected even when governments shut down the internet. A reporting from 2012 noted that with the help of the State Department's Internet Freedom Grants, "more than 10,000 bloggers, journalists and activists have been trained in 10 languages through 50 programs, and hundreds of thousands more have accessed materials and guides published by the groups."[102] Most government-funded projects were carried out by NGOs, although in some instances these NGOs outsourced the technological development to private companies.[103]

The State Department's efforts were generally aimed at oppressive regimes with a history of internet censorship and suppression of political rights. In Secretary Clinton's 2010 speech, she noted that "the State Department is already working in more than 40 countries to help individuals silenced by oppressive governments."[104] She identified several countries, including China, Egypt, Iran, Tunisia, Uzbekistan, and Vietnam, where government censorship was prevalent, free flow of information online was under threat, or bloggers and activists were detained. In the Middle East, the State Department supported internet freedom projects in Afghanistan, Iran, and Syria, among others. For example, the State Department and Pentagon jointly spent over $50 million to create an independent cellphone network in Afghanistan in an effort to offset the Taliban's ability to shut down official services in the country.[105] In Iran, the State Department developed programs focusing on developing anti-censorship tools, securing activists' communications and platforms, and providing digital safety training for local activists.[106] During the civil war in Syria, the State Department led several programs that assisted the opposition, including providing media-technology training to the rebels and equipping them with circumvention technology and communications tools, such as satellite phones and laptops.[107] These examples illustrate how the US government viewed internet freedoms as central to its foreign policy agenda and held a belief that these freedoms were essential to fostering political reforms around the world.

A core tenet of the State Department's strategy for advancing its internet freedom agenda was to coopt the private sector.[108] By endorsing a market-driven regulatory model, the US government had helped cultivate tech companies' private power and was now keen to leverage that power toward the US's broader political goals. In her 2010 speech, Secretary Clinton warned tech companies against "being complacent with the rules of oppressive governments to reap the benefits of their markets," while invoking these companies' "shared responsibility to help safeguard free expression."[109] The US tech companies were, in most instances, active supporters of the government's internet freedom agenda.[110] After all, their business models were intrinsically tied to the global internet. Google even engaged in its own diplomatic missions, with its chairman Eric Schmidt urging the Burmese government in 2013 to harness the private sector's help to establish a free internet, noting how "a free Internet and more widespread Web access will help cement ongoing political reform."[111] That same year, Schmidt travelled to North Korea, pressing Pyongyang to open up the internet as well. Cisco similarly lent its support. It feared that a breakup of the global internet into separate national internets would have severe consequences for its hardware business.[112] The State Department also called on tech companies to collaborate on a one-off basis when needed. For example, the government requested Twitter to delay its scheduled network maintenance during the 2009 Iran protests surrounding the country's presidential election, as the State Department feared that the maintenance might interfere with the Iranian protesters' ability to exchange information and inform the outside world about the events that were unfolding in their country.[113] By turning to Twitter with this request, the US government indicated that it expected its tech companies to share the government's political goals—an expectation that may be seen as reflecting the broader ethos of the American regulatory model that often treats the government and tech companies as partners.

However, the US's reliance on the private sector as integral to exporting its regulatory model poses clear dilemmas for the US government whenever those tech companies' commercial agenda does not align with the government's political agenda. For example, there have been instances where the US government had been spending millions in trying to circumvent a specific technology that its own companies had provided to authoritarian governments. Some US tech companies were accused of selling technologies to repressive regimes that aided those regimes in their conduct of surveillance and restriction of individual freedoms. For example, Narus, a California-based company that is owned by Boeing, supplied technology that was deployed by oppressive governments in the Middle East and North Africa against democracy activists. After the 2011 protests in Egypt that resulted in the overthrow of Egyptian President Hosni Mubarak's regime, it was discovered that the Mubarak regime had used the deep packet inspection technology from Narus to collect and analyze vast amounts of data about Egyptian citizens.[114] Juniper Networks and Cisco were similarly reported for aiding foreign governments' surveillance and censorship efforts. Juniper was criticized for its role in upgrading China's CN2 network, which enabled China's Great Firewall, while Cisco Systems provided hardware that the Chinese government used to monitor and censor the internet. Cisco denied allegations of its role in aiding Chinese censorship efforts. However, leaked documents revealed that the company had pitched its technology to the Chinese by flaunting how it could help the government in its aims to suppress political dissent.[115] These and other similar conflicts, explored in Chapter 4, illustrate how the US government's freedom agenda has occasionally been undermined by its own tech companies that are eager to pursue profits in foreign markets—even when those pursuits put them at odds with the US government's foreign policy objectives.

Some members of the US Congress were outspoken critics of US tech companies' role in assisting repressive regimes. Republican Congressman Christopher Smith led the charge, spearheading legislation that would hold US companies accountable for such conduct.[116] In his 2006 remarks, Representative Smith scolded US tech companies for their "sickening collaboration" that was "decapitating the voice of the dissidents" and "crush[ing] human rights . . . for the sake of market share and profits." He singled out Google, Yahoo!, Cisco, and Microsoft for their role in aiding the Chinese regime's surveillance effort, thereby contributing to the "massive crackdown on its citizens." Congress also repeatedly sought to hold tech companies accountable for their activities in China but was ultimately unable to enact legislation.[117] These developments suggest that embracing a regulatory model that serves to maximize tech companies' private power may ultimately undermine the US government's policy objectives as these companies deploy their private power predominantly toward their commercial ends. These conflicts also illustrate how the interests of the US government and its tech companies have sometimes been difficult to align, leading to tensions that have only grown recently.

Recent Evolution of the Internet Freedom Agenda

Despite some clashes between the US government and tech companies in the earlier years, the US government largely treated tech companies as its partners during the Clinton, Bush, and Obama presidencies. Their administrations were committed to paving the way for these companies' global expansion and viewed the internet freedom agenda as a joint effort to shape the global digital order toward the values embedded in the American regulatory model. However, this policy orientation changed under President Trump. The US's foreign policy became more narrowly focused on fighting the trade and tech war with China and disentangling the US from its international alliances and engagements.

As part of this policy shift, the US government largely abandoned its efforts to promote internet freedoms abroad during the Trump administration. The administration still nominally included the promotion of internet freedom in the 2018 US cyber security strategy,[118] but deprioritized this policy by allowing existing programs to falter and by downgrading the stature of the cybersecurity office within the State Department. For example, in 2020, the Trump administration withheld $20 million of congressionally approved funding for the US's Open Technology Fund—a nongovernmental organization that fights digital censorship and surveillance worldwide—which forced the Fund to halt forty-nine of its sixty internet freedom projects.[119] According to the Head of the Open Technology Fund, withholding the funds "affects about 80 percent of the group's work helping human rights and pro-democracy advocates, journalists and others in 200 countries." The Trump administration also sought to weaken an organization called Voice of America—a US government–sponsored international radio broadcaster that was established in 1942 to counter Nazi propaganda with free and accurate information. Today, its task is to deliver trusted news content in forty-seven languages and to protect digital speech worldwide. Like the Open Technology Fund, Voice of America is also overseen by the US Agency for Global Media. However, the Trump-nominated head of the Agency engaged in extensive efforts to undermine the agency by firing its staff, including refusing to approve visa extensions for the organization's foreign journalists who risked facing repercussions if forced to return to their home countries.[120] By pulling back from global leadership in this area, the US was criticized for creating a vacuum, which authoritarian governments were eager to step in to fill.[121] This policy stand thus directly contradicted the Trump administration's extensive efforts to curtail China's global influence.

President Trump also sought to undermine the US's internet freedom agenda by actively threatening to institute policies at home that resembled those deployed by authoritarian regimes—marking a notable departure from the American market-driven regulatory approach. After Twitter added fact checks to his tweets, President Trump suggested that he had the power to shut down social media companies,[122] or even switch off the entire internet in order to protect US national security.[123] Some of the Republican members of Congress lent their support to President Trump's salvo. For example, Republican members of the House Judiciary Committee released a report in October 2020 calling for legislative action to combat tech companies' censorship of conservative voices.[124] In September 2020, three Republican Congress members introduced a bill titled the "Online Freedom and Viewpoint Diversity Act,"[125] aimed at holding tech companies accountable when they abuse their Section 230 protections and suppress free speech.

These examples reveal how much of the US government's focus has recently shifted from tackling authoritarian governments' censorship practices abroad to allegations that the US tech companies harbor a liberal bias and engage in censorship practices at home. Despite these allegations, recent research shows no evidence of this anti-conservative bias in social media.[126] Instead of censoring conservative views, the right-wing media in the US often features conservative propaganda, cultivates conspiracy theories, and disseminates disinformation in the news media.[127] This suggests that US news outlets have engaged in the kind of propaganda that the US government's internet freedom agenda for years sought to tackle abroad. The online disinformation surrounding the stolen 2020 presidential election—propagated most prominently by President Trump himself—provides perhaps the starkest evidence of how the US government has leveraged the internet at home to weaken, as opposed to strengthen, democracy. While President Trump was not successful in dethroning the tech companies, his actions contradicted—and hence directly undermined—the key principles underlying the American regulatory model. They also further compromised the US government's attempts to defend internet freedoms abroad.

President Biden has reversed many of the Trump-era policies, even while maintaining a more adversarial relationship with the tech industry. In particular, he has emphasized the need to adjust the American regulatory model away from the nonregulation principle. At the same time, the Biden administration has restored the US's commitment to internet freedoms at the center of US foreign policy.[128] This renewed focus on internet freedoms comes at a time when China and Russia have become more assertively authoritarian and deployed digital tools to entrench their authoritarian rules. In his 2021 remarks, Secretary of State Anthony Blinken stressed how the US was working to ensure that "the technology works for democracy, fighting back against disinformation, standing up for internet freedom, reducing the misuse of surveillance technology."[129] In April 2022, President Biden announced the establishment of the Bureau of Cyberspace and Digital Policy within the US State Department,[130] which complements the existing efforts of the State Department's Bureau of Democracy, Human Rights, and Labor to combat the rise of digital authoritarianism around the world.[131] In describing the motivation behind the new Bureau, Secretary Blinken noted how the US is "in a contest over the rules, infrastructure, and standards that will define our digital future," while urging the democracies of the world to defend universal rights and democratic values as the foundation of that digital future.[132] Thus, this new phase of the US government's internet freedom agenda is predominantly focused on China's rising ambition and capabilities as well as, more recently, on Russia's military aggression that is also seen as an assault on freedom.

While President Biden has been committed to restoring the American internet freedom agenda, he has moved away from advocating the principle of nonregulation as a cornerstone of the digital economy. Although still at times criticizing foreign regulations, including some of the ambitious EU regulations that the US viewed as targeting US tech companies,[133] the Biden administration and Congress are increasingly of the view that tech companies have become too powerful and must be regulated—a stark shift from the past US approach that held government intervention as an obstacle to technological, economic, and political progress. In July 2021, President Biden issued an executive order, calling for enhanced antitrust regulation of the tech sector.[134] Several bills are pending in Congress, calling for greater antitrust regulation over tech companies, enhanced data privacy protections, and liability for content published on internet platforms. Thus, even the US government itself is no longer endorsing the nonregulation principle as a foundation for today's digital economy. This has left the US government in a position where its recent foreign policy agenda has been primarily focused on countering China's digital authoritarian vision—without, however, offering an affirmative and coherent alternative vision of its own.

Criticism of the US's Global Influence and a Shift Away from the Market-Driven Regulatory Model

The vast global influence of US tech companies is facing growing criticism abroad, creating a backlash against these companies' private power while casting a shadow over the US's efforts to promote its market-driven regulatory model abroad. While these companies have shaped the lives of foreign citizens in countless beneficial ways, these citizens and their governments are also increasingly conscious of a myriad of societal harms that can be attributed to US tech companies and their business models. In addition, the US government's promotion of its internet freedom agenda is often met with suspicion as citizens' faith in the market-driven regulatory model is waning. Consequently, governments around the world are now turning against US tech giants, reining in their business practices with stronger regulations and thereby asserting greater control over their domestic digital economies. In the global contest for influence, the American market-driven regulatory model is losing its allure and retreating. This decline is most consequential in its relative contribution to the growing appeal of the European rights-driven regulatory model and the Chinese state-driven regulatory model as alternatives for governments distressed by the inherent problems of the US model.

Criticism of the US Tech Companies' Global Role

Despite the genuine admiration—perhaps even jealousy—of the success of US tech companies among foreign companies and governments, these US companies have also become a subject of growing criticism around the world. The harmful effects of these tech giants' business practices on foreign economies and societies are increasingly felt abroad, fueling discontent and accelerating demands to curtail their power and influence across jurisdictions. Several examples have been discussed earlier in this book, including Facebook providing a platform for racist attacks and thus facilitating ethnic cleansing of the Rohingya minority in Myanmar.[135] In a prominent legal action, Rohingya is now suing Meta for £150bn over its role in enabling genocide.[136] As recounted in earlier chapters, Facebook and other American social media platforms also served as a platform for foreign election interference and manipulation, influencing the 2015 Brexit campaign in the UK.[137] Not only did the algorithms of Twitter, Facebook, Instagram, and YouTube amplify the more emotional and divisive Leave-campaign messaging at the expense of the Remain-campaign, but they also allowed more than 150,000 Russian social media accounts' to post pro-Brexit messages close to the day of the referendum.[138] This reveals how US tech companies' business practices can compromise the integrity of democratic elections abroad.

While Facebook's complicity in the genocide in Myanmar is a particularly abhorrent example, instances of US social media companies hosting messages of hatred and disinformation blanket the global internet. In one such example, the unbridled spread of false stories in social media led to mass violence in Europe in 2019, amplifying anti-gypsy tropes and claiming that the Roma people were snatching children in France.[139] These rumors spread quickly on Snapchat, Twitter, and Facebook, and escalated into mob violence—an angry group of 50–70 people attacked two Roma groups in the suburbs of Paris.[140] The European Parliament's Special Committee found that the Roma people have been a target of multiple disinformation campaigns in Europe, and that online platforms led to the escalation of rumors and to the 2019 mob attack.[141] Another prominent fake news story was peddled by a Facebook group called Anonymous.Kollektiv in 2016, falsely claiming that a thirteen-year old Russian-German girl was raped by refugees in Germany.[142] Strategically, the story was timed to spread soon after former Chancellor Angela Merkel's controversial decision to admit one million refugees into Germany, undermining the already challenging policy task of integrating refugees into German society.[143]

"The Facebook Papers"—referring to a set of documents disclosed by Frances Haugen, a former Facebook employee and a whistleblower, in 2021—further revealed a large cache of hate speech on the company's platforms.[144] One startling example comes from India, which is Facebook's largest market, with 417 million users by the end of 2021. There, a Facebook researcher created a new user account to see what it was like to experience the social media site as a person living in Kerala. The researcher accepted all recommendations generated by Facebook's algorithms on which accounts to follow. The researcher then reported seeing "more images of dead people in the past three weeks than I've seen in my entire life in total."[145] After a suicide bombing in Kashmir,[146] anti-Pakistan content began to circulate in the Facebook-recommended groups that the researcher had joined. Many of the groups have tens of thousands of users, with the country's median group size being 140,000 members. In the "Adversarial Harmful Networks: India Case Study" report, over 40 percent of top views in the Indian state of West Bengal were marked as "fake/inauthentic." One inauthentic account had amassed more than 30 million impressions. The content was not only fabricated but also racist and hateful, comparing Muslims to "pigs" and "dogs," and claiming that the Quran calls for men to rape their female family members.[147] This example shows the adverse effects when a US social media company expands its business in a foreign country without fully understanding the local culture or politics, or without devoting adequate resources to preempt and address various societal harms fueled by its platforms.[148]

The criticism of these companies' influence abroad has also focused on how US internet platforms are all too frequently deployed to facilitate terrorism or other criminal activity. A tragic example, discussed earlier, involved the live broadcasting of a terrorist attack in 2019 in Christchurch, New Zealand, where a gunman killed fifty people at two mosques.[149] Another egregious incident took place in 2020 in France where Samuel Paty, a schoolteacher, was beheaded in a terrorist attack after he had shown cartoons of the Prophet Muhammad to his students in a class on the freedom of expression. The killing followed harassment on social media, which helped the perpetrator to identify and to target Paty in an act of domestic terrorism.[150] Critics have also pointed out how these platforms have been deployed to recruit terrorists or to plot terrorist attacks. For example, Meta's WhatsApp platform was used to plan the London Bridge Terror Attack that took place in June 2017 and that led to the killing of four people in Westminster.[151] The attack was planned between three perpetrators on a WhatsApp group across several weeks. WhatsApp uses end-to-end encryption to hide the users' messages even from the company it-self. Amber Rudd, the UK Home Secretary at the time, called upon technology firms to open up encrypted data for high-risk individuals or for messages that trigger a terrorism alert.[152] Still today, the police are unable to access the group chat.[153]

Even when the platforms try, they often fail to adequately remove the harmful content. Social media companies struggled to remove the footage of the Christchurch shootings as the content kept being reposted on dif-ferent websites and platforms. Likewise, Meta and Google have repeatedly failed to enforce bans against the Taliban being able to create accounts on their platforms. As the Taliban took control of the Afghan capital of Kabul in August 2021, a spokesperson of the group uploaded five videos to his official YouTube page.[154] Between August 9 and 18 of that year, more than a hundred new social media accounts and pages, either claiming to belong to the Taliban or supporting the Taliban mission, were created despite the social media platforms' bans. Within ten days, the accounts had over 49,000 followers and over half a million views. The inability of US platforms to prevent Taliban propaganda on their platforms has also allowed the Taliban to deploy US so-cial media companies as a powerful tool to silence their opposition and mask their violent proclivities with images of peace and stability.[155] This way, US platforms have contributed to the Taliban's ability to cement their power in the country, deepening the criticism of these platforms' global role today.

Foreign governments also deploy US platforms for their propaganda, adding to the resentment of these platforms' societal role. For example, the Chinese leadership has been found to manipulate search results on Google and Bing, even though these platforms are banned in China.[156] A US-based think tank, Brookings, found that Chinese state media have influenced the content returned for the search term "Xinjiang"—region where the Chinese government is accused of engaging in grave human rights violations—with at least one Chinese state-backed news outlet appearing in the top-10 results in 88 percent of searches.[157] Removing such propaganda or disinfor-mation presents a thorny challenge for the US platforms. According to re-search by the Oxford Internet Institute, governments in over 80 countries are pursuing disinformation campaigns.[158] In 2021, Meta deactivated more than 20 Facebook accounts linked to Ugandan President Yoweri Museveni's ruling National Resistance Movement party. The Ugandan president had been using fake accounts to make his government seem more popular and stronger than it actually was.[159] In Tanzania, Twitter removed 268 accounts for spreading "malicious reports" directed at members of the Tanzanian human rights or-ganization Fichua Tanzania and its founder.[160] However, these deactivations catch only a fraction of the accounts that are deployed for disinformation or government propaganda. For example, Twitter reportedly deactivated only 11 percent of over 3,500 total accounts spreading pro-government propaganda worldwide.[161]

US platforms are also criticized for their inability to effectively moderate content in foreign languages. Documents leaked by Frances Haugen reveal Facebook's inability to curtail inflammatory hate speech in Ethiopia, where the platform was deployed to call for killings and mass internment of the country's ethnic Tigrayans as part of the ongoing civil war.[162] Timnit Gebru, a data scientist who used to lead Google's ethical AI team and who is fluent in the Amharic language used in Facebook posts in Ethiopia, described the content circulating as "the most terrifying I've ever seen anywhere," likening it to the language used in the context of the earlier Rwanda genocide. In the leaked documents, Facebook acknowledged that it lacked the capabilities to moderate content in Amharic. Frances Haugen further confirmed this in her testimony to Congress while drawing a comparison to the role that Facebook played in facilitating genocide in Myanmar.[163] Facebook faces similar problems in India where the company has reportedly struggled to efficiently remove hate speech against Muslims in 17 out of the 22 languages in the country.[164]

One may question whether US platforms are even making a genuine effort to address various societal harms that they cause outside the US. It is striking that even though only 10 percent of Facebook's active users are in North America, Facebook devotes 87 percent of its budget dedicated for policing misinformation to the US and only 13 percent for the rest of the world.[165] Frances Haugen emphasized this discrepancy in her remarks to the European Parliament in 2021. She noted how this was a pertinent concern for Europe given the number of languages spoken there, warning, "I guarantee you there are a lot of languages in Europe with no safety systems, or minimal safety systems."[166] In addition to the pervasive linguistic bias, the US companies' products and services offered overseas are marked by a cultural and ideological bias that reflects the worldview of Silicon Valley engineers. Danielle Citron has highlighted how the architectural choices that US tech companies bake into their products reproduce largely the values held by white and Asian men steeped in the Silicon Valley mentality, with all their personal and environmental cognitive biases. As a result, their life experiences shape technologies deployed by people who are very far removed from those experiences.[167] This further adds to the mounting criticism—originating from all corners of the world—that US tech companies are either ill-motivated or ill-equipped to handle the global power they have accumulated. This criticism is now directly contributing to a larger policy shift away from the American market-driven regulatory model, which is seen as having enabled the ascent of the US tech behemoths to global dominance—with all the adverse consequences that flow from that global dominance.

Criticism of the Internet Freedom Agenda

The world has not just grown distrustful of US tech companies. The US government's active promotion of its internet freedom agenda has also been met with suspicion in many countries. Targeting authoritarian countries and emerging powers can be perceived as controversial since it aims to influence foreign political structures, even to foster a regime change.[168] For example, when the US State Department requested Twitter during the 2009 Iranian protests to delay its scheduled network maintenance in order to aid the protesters, it reinforced the view already held by the Iranian leadership that "the Internet is an instrument of Western power and that its ultimate end is to foster regime change in Iran."[169] China has also viewed the US's internet freedom agenda as being geared at "regime destabilization."[170] Some critics further see the internet freedom agenda as a selective tool of US foreign policy rather than a global principle that applies to all countries.[171] For example, the US did not speak out against the arrest of Ali Abdulemam, a blogger and activist in Bahrain, seemingly because of the US's allegiance with Bahrain, the presence of the US Navy's Fifth Fleet in the country, and the US's need to carefully manage its relationships with the members of the Gulf Cooperation Council who were backing Bahrain's actions.[172] Even countries that were not necessarily the direct targets of the US government's early freedom-promotion efforts were concerned about the way the US was deploying its policy agenda. For example, Russia, whose internet was relatively free at the time, began looking into social media restrictions in 2011. Russian officials were suspicious that "the West" was using social media to encourage and coordinate uprisings around the world, and started to view tech companies, such as Facebook and Twitter, as "agents of cyberterrorism."[173]

Authoritarian leaders were not the only ones concerned about the American internet freedom agenda. Several democratic countries turned against the US's efforts to promote internet freedoms, in particular in the aftermath of the Snowden revelations. The Snowden revelations exposed the extent to which the US government itself was engaged in extensive global surveillance operations, deploying the internet for its national security objectives and thus violating the central tenet of its regulatory model that calls for the internet to be free of government interference. Human rights advocates called out the hypocrisy and decried the US practices, condemning how the former champion for internet freedom "has now provided a roadmap for mass surveillance, including with the knowing and unwitting assistance of global Internet companies."[174] Even the Europeans that had generally supported the US's internet freedom agenda felt threatened by the US surveillance apparatus—all the more so after learning that those surveillance operations were targeted not only at authoritarian countries but also at the US's friends and allies, including European leaders, companies, and citizens.[175] The Snowden revelations therefore severely and unquestionably damaged the US's credibility to advocate for its internet freedom agenda, which directly undermined the global appeal of its market-driven regulatory model.

The internet freedom agenda has also lost its credibility because of its ineffectiveness in meeting its stated goals in practice. Perhaps the biggest testament for the failure of the US's internet freedom agenda is the lack of those freedoms in many parts of the world today. That failure was not obvious at the outset. The internet freedom agenda gained some traction initially, with several countries adopting principles endorsing an open and interconnected internet in response to the US's promotion efforts. In a 2012 speech to the UN General Assembly, President Obama defended the US's record in supporting democratic transitions, including the Arab Spring movement, while praising the peaceful transitions of power in Malawi and Senegal and the steps toward opening Burma.[176] It is true that the Arab Spring initially sparked hope that the internet was going to unleash a wave of democratization in the region.[177] However, the Arab Spring's hope of the democratic dawn has largely faded since, with totalitarian governments suppressing democracy movements and regaining control across the region.[178] In another example, President Alexander Lukashenko has thus far remained in power in Belarus despite the heroic efforts of the country's protest movement that had been empowered by the messaging app Telegram.[179] These and many other examples reveal how celebrated, internet-fueled democratic transitions have largely reversed course and authoritarian governments have gained ground in many parts of the world. They also cast a shadow on the US government's efforts to tout the digital technologies' revolutionary potential. While digital technologies have armed freedom fighters and democracy activists with new tools for change, authoritarian leaders themselves have also shown to be skillful in exploiting digital technologies to entrench their rule. A 2021 report by Freedom House, a nonprofit organization researching and advocating for democracy and political freedom, documents how global internet freedom had declined every year since 2010, with governments around the world curtailing online speech, arresting internet users, suspending access to social media platforms, or ordering internet shutdowns.[180] This suggests that the US's internet freedom agenda only gained fleeting traction internationally, never fully succeeding in its goal to leverage digital technologies to strengthen democracy and freedom in the world.

The US has also largely lost legitimacy as the champion of internet freedoms and democracy abroad, given the many examples of its tech companies becoming platforms for disinformation and other harmful content that reveal in no uncertain terms what a "free internet" looks like today. While censorship has a bad name in the democratic world, there is a growing consensus that an unregulated internet harms individuals and societies and undermines freedom and democracy in the process. The US's internet freedom agenda is further challenged by the troubled state of democracy in the US. It is difficult to watch the video footage of the chaotic January 6, 2021, US Capitol insurrection—fueled by online disinformation about a stolen election—and argue that the internet advances freedom and democracy, or that the US ought to be the country that leads the world in telling that tale.

The nonregulation principle has experienced a similar fate. After gaining traction initially, the principle has largely been discredited today as numerous governments are looking to assert their regulatory powers over these companies. But it was not always that way. The US's early efforts in the 1990s to influence the global narrative on e-commerce and internet governance more broadly were quite successful.[181] President Clinton's policy advisor Ira Magaziner recalls several governments contemplating regulation at the time, including imposing custom duties on internet transactions or granting powers for telecommunications authorities to regulate internet services. For example, Europeans were considering imposing a "bit tax" on all transmissions through the internet. However, after the US published its Framework, Magaziner observed a change in foreign governments' approaches. He credits the US Framework, and the US government's diplomatic efforts to globalize that Framework, for changing the momentum with respect to tariffs and taxation, including the European governments' decision to abandon the bit tax they first contemplated. At that time, it seemed that the US had successfully convinced the world of the merits of companies' self-regulation as the organizing principle for the digital economy.

Consistent with the US's policy agenda, the digital economy remained largely unregulated until around 2010. As a result, today's digital economy is in many ways the product of those early years when many governments adhered to the US-endorsed principle of commercial nonregulation. The EU's 1995 Data Protection Directive, which was the predecessor to the 2016 General Data Protection Regulation (GDPR), represents a rare attempt to regulate the digital economy—and even that was a relatively feeble attempt to do so when compared to the GDPR. In many ways, the EU's early approach toward content moderation was in line with the US's nonregulation principle. The EU's 2000 e-commerce Directive largely resembles the US's Section 230 of the Communications Decency Act, codifying a liability shield and hence exempting platforms from obligations regarding content moderation.[182] However, this commitment to nonregulation has changed since 2010 with numerous regulations being enacted first in Europe and, over the past years, increasingly around the world, as discussed in Chapters 3 and 9. The EU and many other governments have reversed their previous policies, and are now actively targeting the tech industry. Indeed, there is a near global consensus today that the largest tech companies have grown too powerful and must be reined in with regulation—a stark contrast to the nonregulation principle once so heavily promoted by the US. It is telling that this consensus may soon include the US itself. As mentioned earlier, the Biden administration is now increasingly admitting that self-regulation is no longer sufficient and that governments need to step in and assert their powers over the digital economy. As a result, as the US is witnessing the declining influence of its regulatory model, it needs to ask whether it even ought to try to reverse that decline or simply concede that its market-driven model no longer serves the US—or the world—well.

The Dwindling Influence of the American Regulatory Model and the Rise of the Alternatives

Today, the US's internet freedom agenda has become a victim of its own, early success, triggering a backlash around the world. The free-for-all regulatory landscape nurtured tech giants that expanded globally, and that grew perhaps too influential in the process. Over time, they began to overpower even governments in terms of their economic, political, and cultural power, sparking significant concern among political leaders as these platforms continued to abuse their market power, infringe on user privacy, and circulate hate speech, disinformation, and other harmful content. In response, a countermovement to rein in these companies emerged, and foreign governments began to engage in efforts to repeal the private ordering these tech giants created under the protective shadow of the US government's internet freedom agenda.

The EU's response was to unleash a wave of regulation. Over the past few years, the EU and its member states have promulgated new laws on antitrust, data privacy, online copyright, artificial intelligence, digital taxation, content moderation, platform work, and more.[183] As Jack Goldsmith describes, the

Europeans "have come to see the hegemony of U.S. internet firms as nothing less than a danger to the European way of life," citing the Snowden revelations but also attributing the EU's resentment to the way "U.S. internet firms wield their enormous power to shape morals, politics, news, consumer choice, and much more in ways that many European officials abhor."[184] The EU-style digital regulation is now further becoming global, as shown in Chapter 9, with a number of countries emulating the European regulatory model in an effort to mitigate the power of tech companies and protect their digital citizens. The wave of tech regulation proliferating around the world can thus be seen as a reaction to the American regulatory model and the exportation of US tech companies' private power beyond what was seen as acceptable for these foreign societies.

Understood this way, the US government's internet freedom agenda sowed the seeds of its demise, causing it to subsequently wane in policy agendas around the world. Uncensored platforms did not simply produce freedom as the early American techno-optimist view had predicted—they also cultivated an online public square littered with hatred, violence, and disinformation. Societal harms associated with free speech online, as illustrated by many of the examples cited earlier in this chapter, cast doubt on the idea that free speech absolutism offers a path toward democracy and freedom. Even democratic governments that are committed to the freedom of expression—such as the EU—have moved away from the internet freedom narrative and sought to balance free speech norms with rules restricting hate speech, disinformation, and other harmful content online. For these governments, the US's internet freedom agenda is best seen as a reflection of a different era of techno-optimism that had its moment in the early years of the internet revolution but that has since proven ill-suited for the modern digital economy where internet freedoms are often abused or leveraged toward societal harms.

The backlash to the US's internet freedoms has been even starker in the authoritarian world. Fearful of US companies' outsized influence, China started to push its narrative on "internet sovereignty" to articulate an alternative view to the US's market-driven, private sector–led, global freedom agenda. Among other criticisms, China advocated a view that global digital governance should move away from private sector–led institutions, such as ICANN, to state-driven organizations, such as the UN, where China could exert greater influence. Determined to engage in extensive censorship of the internet in the name of social stability at home, China always resisted the US's internet freedom agenda. But over the past years, China has also provided an alternative vision for the world, showing how innovation and technological progress are not dependent on those freedoms that the US advocated; instead, they can coexist with an authoritarian government that tightly controls the internet. This way, China has not only responded by criticizing the American market-driven regulatory model and the US's attempts to globalize it; it has also provided an alternative narrative for any state or entity that is resentful of US tech companies' power and the US government's efforts to amplify that power through its internet freedom agenda.

At the same time as the US model is losing its legitimacy, China, as shown in the next chapter, has been gaining global influence by exporting its authoritarian, state-driven regulatory model, directly undermining the US's internet freedom agenda and, in particular, its anti-censorship principle. The EU has also been exporting its regulatory power—discussed in detail in Chapter 9—as part of promoting its rights-driven regulatory model, thereby directly undermining the other facet of the internet freedom agenda: the commercial nonregulation principle. These developments point to an evolution whereby the exportation of the American market-driven regulatory model has powerfully shaped today's digital economy but has also triggered a significant backlash in recent years. This backlash has paved the way for the European rights-driven model and the Chinese state-driven model to gain greater global traction as governments around the world come to realize that the digital economy—as conceived by the US—was too free and too dominated by US interests and companies. The adjustment away from the American regulatory model is now clearly underway.

8

Exporting China's Digital Authoritarianism through Infrastructure

THROUGHOUT THE PAST two decades, China was not idle as US tech companies expanded their global footprint and the US government promoted its internet freedom agenda abroad. Instead, the Chinese government spent those years cultivating a domestic tech industry that today rivals that of the United States and helped that industry expand internationally through generous state support. China also refined its alternative regulatory model that advances a profoundly different vision for the digital economy from that promoted by the US or the European Union. As the American market-driven model has largely lost its legitimacy among countries around the world in recent years, the global influence of the Chinese state-driven model has grown significantly. Gradually but decisively, China has harnessed the power of its tech companies to shape the global digital economy toward its digital authoritarian norms, extending the reach of the Chinese digital empire.

Over the past decade, China has expanded its global influence primarily by supplying digital infrastructures to countries across the world. Chinese tech companies are exporting physical components to build several countries' digital regimes, including 5G networks, fiber-optic cables, data centers, and other key technologies that establish connectivity and allow data to flow within, across, and throughout countries. Increasingly, Chinese tech companies are also providing surveillance technologies and other digital products and services that shape the way foreign digital societies are built and governed. China's global influence manifests itself in particular through a so-called Digital Silk Road (DSR)[1] initiative that seeks to connect large swaths of Africa, Asia, and

Latin America to Chinese digital networks, pulling these countries more tightly into China's orbit in the process. As a result, China can be described as exerting digital "infrastructure power" and thus shaping the global digital economy predominantly by providing digital infrastructure and foundational technologies for many societies around the world.

This infrastructure power has enabled Chinese tech companies to extend their influence deep into foreign markets. By providing the backbone for these countries' digital ecosystems, Chinese companies establish a foundation for digital development that is more likely to steer these countries toward the adoption of Chinese technologies, standards, and norms down the road. Once a recipient country is first powered with Chinese networks, cables, and data centers, its future technology investments are also likely to favor Chinese companies, making them more dependent on Chinese supply chains.[2] After all, the foundational Chinese digital infrastructure is designed to be interoperable with subsequent Chinese technology and can typically be maintained by Chinese vendors, nurturing path dependency. As a result, these countries can become more reliant on the Chinese tech ecosystem going forward, tying them closer to the Chinese sphere of digital influence and potentially exposing them to greater influence by, and dependency on, the Chinese government.

Moreover, as a growing number of countries are choosing Chinese technology, Chinese technical standards associated with those technologies are also becoming more common—ultimately reaching the point of becoming default standards around which other technologies must be built. This helps China gain greater leverage over international standard setting and technological development. To further solidify its national standards as global standards, China has made a concerted effort to place its nationals into leadership positions in many of the key international standard-setting organizations, giving Chinese firms—and, indirectly, the Chinese government—increasing sway over the standards that govern new technologies.

The Chinese state-driven regulatory model may also spread along the Digital Silk Road with the growth in "smart cities"[3] and the mounting use of surveillance technologies in those cities. Those technologies hand governments the capabilities for greater control over their citizens, which may normalize digital surveillance and cause it to seep deeper into those societies.[4] However, while such infrastructural path dependencies exist, they are not inevitable. Every country that acquires Chinese digital infrastructures or technologies is not destined to adopt digital authoritarian norms and practices in the process. But even the mere prospect of such adoption is already shaping the global horizontal battles among the US, China, and the EU over the norms that govern the digital economy, and fueling a backlash against the Chinese infrastructure power.

A number of push and pull factors contribute to the global adoption of Chinese technologies and, indirectly, the diffusion of its state-driven regulatory model.[5] On the one hand, the Chinese government is engaged in a deliberate effort to export Chinese digital technologies, extending generous state support to facilitate foreign infrastructure investments that favor Chinese tech companies. On the other hand, many jurisdictions exhibit a genuine demand for Chinese technologies, which represent an affordable path toward digital development for these mostly developing countries. The Chinese government's emphasis on digital sovereignty[6] as a cornerstone of the Chinese regulatory model also resonates in many parts of the world, further paving the way for Chinese influence to take hold in those foreign markets. At the same time, several other countries, including the US, have warned developing nations about the dangers associated with Chinese infrastructure investments, including the possibility that such investments could expose the recipient countries to Chinese government surveillance. As a result, the US shuns Chinese tech vendors—while cajoling other countries to do the same.

This chapter highlights the origins and implications behind the Digital Silk Road, examining projects such as AI-driven "smart cities" or "safe cities"[7] that are quickly proliferating around the world. It also discusses the growing role that China has assumed in international organizations involved in standard-setting over digital technologies, helping Chinese tech standards gain greater prominence internationally. China's approach to regulating the digital economy relies on many tools of authoritarian governance, tools that are not unique to China. To show this, the chapter illustrates how China's state-driven model compares with that of Russia, another authoritarian regime whose regulatory approach has similarities to but also important differences with China's model. This comparison reveals that while China is not the lone world power embracing digital authoritarian norms, it remains in a unique position to implement the state-driven regulatory model and hence is rightly seen as the unquestionable leader of the world's "techno-autocracies." But as China's digital infrastructures extend around the globe and the international influence of its state-driven regulatory model grows, the US and its allies have become concerned over China's escalating influence over the global digital economy—even if finding effective ways to counter that influence remains elusive.

Globalizing China's Infrastructure Power

China has spread its influence over the global digital economy primarily through its tech companies that build core digital infrastructures in different jurisdictions. Much of the Chinese tech exports underpinning this infrastructure power consist of hardware, such as Huawei's and ZTE's telecom equipment. But this kind of influence has also spread through Chinese companies that provide other kinds of digital infrastructure: cloud services, e-commerce platforms, and more recently, social media platforms as companies such as Alibaba, Tencent, and ByteDance globalize their operations. Thus, the term "infrastructure power," as used in this chapter, broadly describes Chinese companies' growing global role in building not only physical digital infrastructures (such as 5G telecom networks and undersea cables) but also other types of foundational digital ecosystems (such as cloud systems and AI-driven surveillance capabilities) that countries, cities, and other governing entities procure to build and manage their digital societies.

This increasingly vast global influence of Chinese companies has raised concerns among governments, particularly among the US and its close allies. Although the US tech companies' private power has also become a source of concern around the world, as discussed in the last chapter, in the case of China this concern is magnified because the private power of Chinese tech companies is understood to be deeply intertwined with China's state power. Chinese companies are commonly believed to be beholden to Beijing and hence influenced by the Chinese government's political objectives.[8] It is already known, for example, that these companies are expected to assist the Chinese government in its censorship and surveillance efforts, as documented in Chapter 2. When these companies provide digital infrastructures to foreign markets, critics of China's influence question whether, in fact, it is the Chinese government that is encroaching deeper into those foreign societies. If that were true, the Chinese government might, for instance, gain access to the data that flows through Huawei-built 5G infrastructures, or influence foreign societies by spreading Chinese propaganda through the ByteDance-owned TikTok app that is rapidly gaining popularity abroad.[9] Consequently, the Chinese infrastructure power not only entrenches Chinese tech companies' global influence but possibly also increases the Chinese government's global influence—albeit in ways that can be difficult to verify or measure. If that happens, these foreign societies risk falling within the purview of Chinese government surveillance and influence. Thus, while these foreign countries may not consciously adopt or emulate the Chinese state-driven regulatory model, that model may reach them indirectly through their adoption of Chinese digital infrastructures.

The Digital Silk Road and China's Expanding Influence Through Infrastructure Building

China is leveraging its norms and values most notably in building a Digital Silk Road. The DSR forms a component of the Chinese government's Belt and Road Initiative (BRI), which is a global infrastructure-driven development strategy and a centerpiece of China's foreign policy. Since its introduction in 2013, the BRI has provided an umbrella framework for Chinese investment in over a hundred countries.[10] The goal underlying the BRI is to connect Asia with other continents via land, rail, and maritime networks in an effort to deepen trade relations and contribute toward China's economic growth. The DSR, which the Chinese government unveiled in a 2015 white paper, adds a digital connectivity element to the BRI.[11] The DSR comprises a range of projects, including building telecom networks, laying submarine data cables, establishing data centers, installing global satellite navigation systems, and exporting technologies for smart cities and other cyber infrastructure across Africa, Asia, Europe, Latin America, and the Caribbean.

According to some estimates, over a third of the 138 countries participating in the BRI in 2019 were involved in some DSR projects with Chinese companies.[12] But given the somewhat amorphous character of the DSR, it is difficult to assess the initiative's true scope. The DSR is less of a monolithic, top-down initiative tightly orchestrated by the Chinese government and more of a loose initiative or a branding effort linking various overseas digital projects pursued by private Chinese tech companies. That said, many of these private companies, even if not all, benefit from different forms and levels of support from the Chinese government. Even in instances where the government's role is more remote, Chinese tech companies tend to label their international activities as part of the DSR to signal their alignment with the government's digital strategy and thereby ensuring Beijing's support of their activities.[13]

The DSR serves the interests of the Chinese government and the private sector alike. It expands economic opportunities for Chinese tech giants including Huawei, ZTE, Alibaba, and Tencent but also supports many other companies seeking to grow their operations overseas as part of the DSR umbrella. Once these companies have built the foundational digital infrastructure in a foreign country, they can often lock the DSR recipient country into using Chinese technologies, which are designed to operate with such infrastructure and built according to these companies' standards and specifications. This helps Chinese companies gain a foothold over future contracts for technology acquisitions, maintenance, and upgrades. The further the DSR reaches, the more common Chinese standards thus become in different parts of the world, lending China greater leverage over international standard setting.[14] This, again, presents an advantage to Chinese companies, who can now reap significant royalties and licensing profits from other tech companies relying on the international standards that reflect Chinese technologies.

While Chinese companies are the direct beneficiaries of the DSR as they gain new export markets for their technologies, the Chinese government also has a keen interest in promoting the DSR for economic and broader geopolitical reasons. The Chinese government is invested in developing a thriving tech industry to boost the country's economic growth and to reach its stated goal of becoming a global technological leader. This quest entails building a stronger presence for Chinese companies on export markets. The government is therefore willing to support Chinese companies' international expansion both politically and financially, including by granting export credits to its companies and guaranteeing loans for countries buying Chinese technologies. For example, the Export-Import Bank of China financed 85 percent of the Pakistan-China Fiber Optic Project and gave Nigeria a loan for the 5G network that Huawei built in the country.[15] At a time when the unfolding US–China tech war has triggered a process toward greater decoupling of the US and Chinese digital economies, the Chinese government also knows that it cannot rely on having unhindered access to the US market—or to the markets of US allies that may also be increasingly shunning Chinese technology. As a result, China needs to cultivate relationships across the developing world with countries that are still likely to allow Chinese companies to manifest their global ambitions.

This strong government presence in DSR projects has raised fears that China might also be leveraging the DSR toward geopolitical ends. With the DSR, China can gain more influence over standards for key technologies such as artificial intelligence, robotics, the Internet of Things, and blockchain.[16] This gives the Chinese government not just an economic advantage but also a strategic advantage over the US and other geopolitical rivals. The DSR further grants Chinese companies access to large pools of data around the world, including, in some instances, to data that is politically sensitive or geostrategically valuable. A common fear among the US and many of its allies is that this data may also become accessible to the Chinese government, as Chinese espionage and national security laws require companies to share the data they obtain with the government when requested to do so.[17] Finally, by providing technology and training that help foreign governments exert greater control over their digital societies, China is exporting its notion of digital sovereignty and state control abroad. This way, the DSR also paves the way for the Chinese government to externalize its state-driven regulatory model abroad—one DSR project at a time.

While DSR projects come in many forms, so-called smart cities or safe cities can be highlighted as common yet contested examples of China's global influence over digital infrastructures. While these two terms are often used interchangeably, including in this book, smart city initiatives typically refer to improving municipal operations such as automating traffic control or power distribution, whereas safe city initiatives typically refer to improving public safety by automating policing to detect criminal and other harmful behavior.[18] What these initiatives have in common is their reliance on AI-powered technologies such as surveillance cameras, metering devices, sensors, and other similar monitoring technologies, combined with processing of data that these systems acquire. These technologies, according to the Chinese companies that design them, allow for important efficiency gains, streamlined governance, and better everyday lives for city residents. To export these smart city initiatives, Chinese companies, including Huawei, ZTE, Hikvision, and Alibaba, typically partner directly with foreign cities that purchase these technologies.[19] Yet the Chinese government is often in the background, subsidizing loans to fund these initiatives or giving its political backing to them. In addition—and this is what critics fear the most—the Chinese government is potentially also gaining access to the data that flows through these AI systems empowering smart cities, given the closely intertwined relationship between the Chinese tech companies and the Chinese Communist Party (CCP).[20]

It is difficult to gain information about the precise scope of the smart city projects. According to a 2020 report by the US–China Economic and Security Review Commission, which was created by the US Congress to monitor the national security implications of US–China economic relations, Chinese companies have installed smart city technologies in 398 identified projects. Those projects span across 106 countries and involve 34 different Chinese firms, Huawei being the leading vendor.[21] While the greatest demand for smart city contracts comes from authoritarian countries, liberal countries are also deploying Chinese technologies to optimize their governance. According to a 2021 study, 41 out of 64 countries that had installed Chinese safe and smart city technologies were designated as "not free" or "partly free" by the US-based nongovernmental organization Freedom House, while the remainder were classified as "free."[22] For example, several European countries have embraced Chinese smart city technologies, with Huawei reporting on its website that it has supplied technologies to cities in Germany, Italy, the Netherlands, and

Spain.[23] Among these is also the French city of Marseille, which entered into a partnership with ZTE in 2016 to implement a Big Data of Public Tranquility Project, which relies on an intelligence operations center and closed-circuit television cameras that are deployed for crime-prevention purposes.[24] In Germany, Chinese companies have partnered with local governments to build smart city platforms and to establish joint research centers with local companies.[25] This suggests that the Chinese sphere of influence is expansive, and not limited to countries that share an ideological commitment to digital authoritarian norms.

China's Growing Sphere of Digital Influence

The Chinese digital infrastructure power is felt throughout Africa, Asia, Latin America, and Europe. This influence has been most palpable in the developing world, even though many developed countries have also imported certain Chinese technologies and, with that, contributed to the global expansion of Chinese technology standards. The reasons driving demand for Chinese digital infrastructures are far from uniform. Several jurisdictions that have embraced Chinese technologies do not necessarily subscribe to the Chinese government's ideology. Many developing countries, for example, view Chinese infrastructures as the most affordable path toward digital development, which is key to their economic growth. Some of these governments are also likely drawn to the promise of "data sovereignty," which gives them greater control of data flows. However, no doubt, some governments also share the ideological underpinnings of the Chinese regulatory model. They cherish the idea that Chinese-built technology can also allow them to replicate some of the key features of the state-driven regulatory model, including enhanced surveillance of their citizens and content controls for suppressing dissent, both of which allow them to cement their power over the society. These authoritarian-leaning countries have at times also complemented their importation of Chinese tech infrastructure with the adoption of certain Chinese-style legislative norms that have further entrenched the state-driven regulatory model as a foundation for their digital societies.

Chinese tech companies have made particularly important inroads in many parts of Africa. In 2018, ZTE was reported to be installing mobile networks and other digital infrastructures, providing data storage and analysis services, and supplying surveillance technologies to cities in Ethiopia, Nigeria, and Sudan.[26] Huawei is another company that plays a dominant role across Africa. By 2019, the company had already installed telecom networks in approximately forty African countries.[27] For example, Huawei has signed a Memorandum of

Understanding with Egypt's Minister of Telecommunications, according to which Huawei will build cloud computing and AI centers in the country.[28] Chinese financial institutions also provided $200 million of financing on "favorable payment terms" to Egypt's telecom sector to support its deployment of Huawei's 4G network.[29] The Chinese state-owned firm Hikvision, which manufactures surveillance equipment, also provides mobile video surveillance systems for buses in the Suez Governorate in northeast Egypt.[30]

Huawei has similarly launched important smart city projects in Kenya, including in the country's capital city, Nairobi.[31] Nairobi has a high crime rate, which has made the city an opportune destination for Chinese surveillance technologies. As part of this project Huawei has installed 116 LTE base stations, 1,800 cameras, 200 traffic surveillance systems, and two data centers in the city. Huawei is not trying to hide the power of its surveillance equipment, boasting on its website how "Big Brother monitors their goings-on from miles away" in Nairobi.[32] The local authorities in Kenya reinforce this message, with the superintendent of the Nairobi police force noting that "anybody who does anything is being watched."[33] In addition to this extensive surveillance system, Huawei provides the platform for Kenya's mobile payment systems, M-PESA, further entrenching the presence of Chinese technology in a country where over half of the population uses mobile payment systems to transfer money.[34]

Zimbabwe is another African country that has embraced Chinese surveillance technologies. In 2018, its government announced a partnership with Hikvision, which entails using the company's surveillance technology for border security.[35] Hikvision has also provided smart city technologies in the country's fourth largest city, Mutare. The government has further collaborated closely with CloudWalk Technology, a Chinese AI company that donated facial recognition terminals to the country in 2019. After Zimbabwe's President Emmerson Mnangagwa visited China in 2019, the Zimbabwean government entered into an agreement with CloudWalk whereby CloudWalk provides facial recognition technology for the country's financial sector, as well as security applications for airports and railway and bus stations. Christopher Mutsvangwa, former Zimbabwean Ambassador to China, welcomed the Chinese presence in the country, noting how "China has proved to be our all-weather friend and this time around, we have approached them to spearhead our AI revolution in Zimbabwe."[36]

Chinese tech firms, of course, welcome such economic opportunities. But they gain an additional benefit when providing technologies to countries such as Zimbabwe. CloudWalk likely did not donate facial recognition technologies for altruistic reasons or deepen its partnership with the country only to gain a monetary benefit. Zimbabwe offered CloudWalk a particularly attractive market—or a laboratory—for testing and improving the company's facial recognition technologies.[37] Through its presence in Zimbabwe, CloudWalk gained access to a population that represents a very different racial mix than that in China, which gives the company an important advantage in retraining its facial recognition algorithms to remove existing racial biases—a problem that notably limits the AI systems available today. The CEO of CloudWalk, Yao Zhiqiang, recognizes this benefit, noting in an interview how "the differences between technologies tailored to an Asian face and those to a black one are relatively large, not only in terms of color, but also facial bones and features."[38] According to a 2018 study conducted by MIT Media Lab and Microsoft Research, error rates in facial recognition techniques were considerably higher for darker-skinned individuals.[39] While the error rate for lighter-skinned men was below 1 percent, the error rate was almost 35 percent for darker-skinned women. What explains the error rate is that the algorithms have been trained predominantly on male and white faces, illustrating also how access to extensive data from Zimbabwe can give CloudWalk an edge in global competition for AI technologies. While few people would condemn efforts by tech companies to develop bias-free algorithms, a different question is whether these companies should be using the data of an entire population to do this without seeking the affected individuals' consent or putting other privacy safeguards in place.

In addition to deploying Chinese digital technologies, some African governments have taken conscious steps to replicate the Chinese digital governance model in their domestic legislation, especially on the content moderation front. Tanzania passed a cybersecurity law in 2015 that is described as being "heavily influenced by the Chinese model."[40] The law prohibits "false" content, which resembles China's prohibition of "falsehoods."[41] Another 2018 Tanzanian law regulating online content also contains a vague provision banning content that "causes annoyance,"[42] which resembles in its elusiveness the Chinese government ban on content that "disrupts social order."[43] One of the goals of the law is to root out "moral decadence," just like the Chinese regulation bans "decadent" material from social media.[44] Egypt similarly adopted a 2018 cybercrime law with digital authoritarian characteristics. The law resembles Chinese cybersecurity legislation in that it expands the government authority to censor the internet and punish individuals who either publish or access such restricted information.[45]

It is, of course, plausible that these countries would have pursued this type of content regulation regardless of China's example given their intrinsic authoritarian tendencies. But even then, these laws contribute to China's growing sphere of influence by making state-driven digital regulation the norm in a growing number of countries. There are also examples that reveal more directly how these countries benefit from China's advice. For example, China has offered training on cyberspace management to government officials in developing countries, including in Africa.[46] Chinese officials trained the Ethiopian People's Revolutionary Democratic Front on ways to monitor and manage public opinion online through technology, legislation, and engagement with the media. Similar internet management guidance was provided to senior media staff from North Africa and the broader Arab region, including Egypt, Jordan, Lebanon, Libya, Morocco, Saudi Arabia, and the United Arab Emirates.[47]

Chinese influence is also deeply felt across China's own backyard in Asia, perhaps nowhere as extensively as in Pakistan, a fast-growing digital market of over 220 million people. Huawei Marine has helped the Pakistani government construct the Pakistan East Africa Cable Express, which connects Pakistan to Kenya and Djibouti.[48] Pakistan has also adopted the BeiDou Navigation Satellite System, which is the Chinese rival to the US Global Positioning System (GPS). Huawei has supplied surveillance equipment for safe cities in Pakistan, including for the Lahore Safe City project, which Huawei described back in 2016 as "the largest comprehensive Safe City architecture in the world."[49] Chinese companies also dominate the e-commerce and fintech markets in the country. Chinese e-commerce giant Alibaba has helped build Pakistani e-commerce infrastructure following a Memorandum of Understanding that the company signed with the Pakistan Trade Development Authority in 2017. With its affiliate Ant Group, Alibaba has also pursued e-commerce and fintech acquisitions in Pakistan, further entrenching Chinese tech companies' control over the local digital economy.

Chinese companies have made similarly significant inroads into other parts of South and Southeast Asia. For example, the Philippines' "Safe Philippines" project is an extensive surveillance project, launched in 2019, that focuses on improving public safety in the metro Manila region.[50] It features over 12,000 surveillance cameras that public authorities deploy alongside facial recognition technologies. Huawei and China International Telecommunications and Construction Corporation (CITCC) provide the technology for the project, which also benefits from close to $400 million of Chinese loans. Huawei and ZTE also have a strong presence in constructing digital infrastructure such as fiber optic cables across the region.[51] In addition, Huawei Marine has undertaken several undersea cable projects in the Philippines and elsewhere in Southeast Asia, further illustrating the pervasive influence that Chinese tech companies have exercised in the region.

The Chinese sphere of influence also reaches into Latin America, which has traditionally been politically more connected to the US by geographic proximity and the deep economic relationships the US has cultivated in the region. Ecuador is an example of a South American country that has participated in the DSR in various ways. It has acquired safe city and other surveillance technologies from Chinese companies with the goal of reducing crime in the country. The *New York Times'* investigative reporting from 2019 reveals an extensive surveillance regime—known as ECU-911—that is set up with the help of Chinese technologies and Chinese funding, and that has transformed the country into what the reporting calls a "voyeur's paradise."[52] Ecuador's main partners in ECU-911 are Huawei and the state-controlled China National Electronics Import & Export Corporation (CEIEC). The CEIEC technicians are also reported to work in the ECU-911 headquarters in Quito, alongside Ecuadorian personnel.[53] The project is financed by Chinese loans, and as part of this funding deal, Ecuador has committed much of its oil reserves for China's use. The ECU-911 system feeds footage primarily for the Ecuadorian police. However, the investigation also uncovered that Ecuador's domestic intelligence agency has access to the data harnessed by ECU-911.[54] This access has been of particular concern to human rights activists, who point to the intelligence agency's record of intimidating and attacking political dissidents under the country's past president Rafael Correa. At the same time, given Ecuador's high crime rates, many segments of the population are reportedly willing to accept the trade-off in their privacy and submit to mass surveillance in exchange for promises of greater public safety.

While the Chinese influence is most deeply felt across authoritarian countries and in developing countries in need of digital development, the Chinese influence also extends to the US and Europe. In the US, at least a hundred municipalities have procured surveillance technology from Chinese tech companies, even after the US government added those companies, including Hikvision and Dahua, to the government's economic blacklist in 2019.[55] In Europe, the Serbian government and Huawei have cooperated closely since 2019 through the implementation of the Safe City project, which involves the installation of thousands of smart surveillance cameras in the country.[56] The Serbian government has classified the project as confidential and disallowed public debate on the issue.[57] While Serbia can be viewed as a "flawed democracy,"[58] established Western European democracies have also turned to China as a supplier of these technologies. For example, Chinese companies have built 5G networks in or sold surveillance technologies to France, Germany, the UK, and other European countries.[59]

However, China's strategy toward the US and Europe differs from its strategy toward developing markets. Chinese tech firms view developed countries not only as a destination, but also as a source, for new technologies. The Chinese government actively supports Chinese companies' efforts to acquire foreign technologies. According to a 2021 study, Chinese embassies in over fifty countries host a cadre of "science and technology diplomats" whose task is to identify investment opportunities for Chinese firms in the countries where these diplomats are stationed.[60] This effort is coordinated through China's Ministry of Science and Technology, and the diplomats' task is to monitor technological breakthroughs and assess whether the sources of those breakthrough technologies—be they firms, research institutions, or individuals—would be likely to share their IP, establish joint ventures, or otherwise collaborate with Chinese firms. The targeted partnerships often reflect specific needs that Beijing has identified as bottlenecks in China's technological development or that otherwise align with priorities articulated by the CCP. These diplomats also help Chinese companies sign investment deals, licensing and production agreements, or hire foreign researchers to work in China. To date, tech diplomacy has been particularly common in Japan, Russia, the UK, and the US. The Chinese consulate in Houston, Texas, was reported to be the most active in this type of diplomacy prior to July 2020, when the US government forced its closure.[61] At the time, US Secretary of State Mike Pompeo linked the closure of the Houston consulate to China's practice of stealing American and European IP, referring to the consulate as "a hub of spying and intellectual property theft."[62]

The closure of China's Houston consulate is but one example of how the growing global influence of the Chinese state-driven regulatory model is becoming an increasing source of concern among the US, the EU, and their allies, as will be discussed in detail toward the end of this chapter. Those concerns are now being magnified as China is complementing its DSR-driven influence by assuming a more prominent role in global standard-setting institutions, as explained below.

The Role of International Standard Setting in China's Broader Influence Strategy

By exporting digital infrastructures, Chinese tech companies are also exporting Chinese technical and industrial standards, as those standards are embedded in the networks and equipment that rely on Chinese-built technology.[63] This way, Chinese standards are increasingly governing technological development around the world. In addition, China has sought to further amplify those standards by leveraging Chinese influence over international standard setting in relevant organizations. China has also tried to amend the broader international governance model for the digital economy in ways that reflect its state-driven regulatory approach. China's strategy has been twofold. First, the Chinese government has advocated a shift in global digital governance away from the US- and EU-backed multistakeholder institutions toward state-centric institutions such as the United Nations. Second, China has also sought to ensure that to the extent that such a shift will not take place, Chinese influence will be channeled more effectively in existing multistakeholder governance bodies. Thus far, the second strategy has been more successful.

At the heart of the Chinese state-driven regulatory model is the idea that sovereign states should be in charge of how the internet and the broader digital economy are governed. As a result, the Chinese government has consistently advocated for a state-centric international internet governance model that would reserve a prominent role for the UN—a forum where states play a dominant role.[64] For example, in 2011, China—together with Russia—called for the UN General Assembly to adopt an "international code of conduct for information security."[65] The proposed code focused on norms deterring cyberattacks while also affirming the sovereign right of states across all internet-related public policy issues. The Code was updated and resubmitted to the UN in 2015 by the Shanghai Cooperation Organization, which is a Eurasian political, economic, and security alliance composed of China, Kazakhstan, Kyrgyzstan, Russia, Tajikistan, and Uzbekistan (at the time). Even though the proposed Code was never adopted by the UN, China has continued to advocate similar policies since.[66] In 2017, China issued a BRICS Leaders Declaration together with Brazil, Russia, India, and South Africa, emphasizing how "all states should participate on an equal footing in the evolution and functioning of the Internet and its governance."[67] That same year, China released a position paper on the UN's role in internet governance, reaffirming its view that the UN should be the main actor in developing international rules for cyberspace.[68] China has advocated for a greater role for the UN as it would enhance the role of governments at the expense of private-sector and civil-society actors that have been central players in the US-led and EU-supported multistakeholder governance model. Another advantage for China in the UN-centric internet governance model is the presence of developing countries in the UN governance bodies, which gives China the opportunity to mobilize these countries behind its vision for state-led digital governance.

In parallel with its efforts to enhance the UN's role in global internet governance, China has launched a World Internet Conference, which takes place annually in Wuzhen, and which serves as a high-profile international platform to advance China's vision of internet sovereignty.[69] In the inaugural conference in 2014, General Secretary and President Xi Jinping gave a monumental speech that emphasized China's commitment to international cooperation in a spirit that respects state sovereignty. The Wuzhen Declaration that was circulated to the participants at the end of the conference reaffirmed this vision by stating that "we should respect each country's rights to the development, use and governance of the internet, [and] refrain from abusing resources and technological strengths to violate other countries' internet sovereignty."[70] This Declaration was never formally adopted in Wuzhen, but its tenets were subsequently incorporated into China's 2017 International Strategy for Cooperation on Cyberspace,[71] which similarly emphasizes all countries' "right to choose their own path of cyber development, model of cyber regulation and internet public policies." This can be read as a rebuke of the market-driven model that emphasizes the internet's open, free, and universal character.

By seeking to embolden the UN, China has sought to weaken the multistakeholder organizations such as the Internet Corporation for Assigned Names and Numbers (ICANN) or other private sector–led governance bodies such as the Internet Engineering Task Force (IETF), which have endowed tech companies with an important voice over digital governance, including technical standards. Yet in the absence of the power to render these multistakeholder organizations irrelevant, China has also pursued a strategy to gradually transform these organizations to better reflect Chinese interests. In 2021, China adopted a "China Standards 2035" plan,[72] which lays out the blueprint for China's growing role over international standard setting. This goal was also emphasized by Dai Hong, a member of China's National Standardization Management Committee, who noted that "global technical standards are still in the process of being formed," which "gives China's industry and standards the opportunity to surpass the world."[73]

Who gets to define key technical standards is one of the major global battlefields of the digital economy, as these standards can become the default standards around which subsequent technologies are built. Power over these industrial standards and protocols entails influence over present and future technologies, ranging from hardware pieces such as lithium batteries, USB plugs, satellites, electricity transmission, and broadband cellular networks to software, internet protocols, AI, and the Internet of Things, to name a few. The Chinese government understands the significance of these standards, emphasizing how "third-tier companies make products. Second-tier companies make technology. Top-tier companies set standards."[74] One concrete advantage of defining these technical standards is that the developers of patented technologies that become the international standard can collect licensing fees from everyone using their technologies.[75] If China became the source of these industrial standards, the licensing fees would flow to Chinese companies. Today, influence over international standards may also entail greater geopolitical power as many of the technologies over which standards are being debated—such as AI—have geostrategic significance. The competition for setting standards for technologies like AI plays a prominent role in technological rivalry, especially as these technologies developed for civilian use are increasingly also deployed toward military aims.

Until recently, American and European technical experts have primarily set these standards given their outsized influence in the leading standard-setting organizations. Yet China's efforts to gain greater influence over these standards are starting to pay off. Chinese individuals have assumed leadership roles within international standard-setting organizations and their key working groups. Zhao Houlin was the Secretary General of the International Telecommunications Union (ITU) from 2014 to 2022.[76] The ITU plays an important role in setting standards for phone and internet connectivity. Zhang Xiaogang became the first Chinese president of the International Organization for Standardization (ISO), serving in this role from 2015 to 2018.[77] The ISO is the world's largest organization developing worldwide technical, industrial, and commercial standards. China has similarly ascended into the leadership of the International Electrotechnical Commission (IEC), which develops standards for all electronic items, with Shu Yinbiao being elected as the IEC president in 2020.[78] In the 3rd Generation Partnership Project (3GPP), which is a coalition of several 5G standard-setting organizations, Chinese companies were reported in 2018 to have claimed 10 of the 57 available chair and vice-chair positions.[79] China is also seeking more influence in discussions about technical standards applicable to smart cities. In the Joint Technical Commission of the ISO and IEC, 28 countries are represented in the working group on smart cities, yet the working group's five former and current officers all hail from China, and many of the meetings have taken place in China.[80]

Some statements by Chinese leaders suggest that the individuals who have risen to leadership positions in these organizations are also using these positions to advance China's national interests. Zhao Houlin, the former head of the ITU, unabashedly promoted China's landmark Belt and Road Initiative during his tenure, defended Huawei against US accusations of espionage, and praised China's growing presence in standard setting in the telecom and internet industries.[81] These public statements can be difficult to reconcile with the pledge Mr. Zhao took when swearing in as the Secretary General of the ITU to avoid being influenced by any single ITU member state and to act "with the interest of the union only in view."[82]

Chinese companies are also frequently submitting their standards for consideration within these organizations. For example, ZTE, Huawei, and Hikvision have all proposed standards governing the surveillance technologies they have developed to the ITU with the goal that the ITU would endorse them.[83] The future standards for AI systems form a particularly important battleground. In preparation for that battle, China has developed domestic standards on AI, which it is now seeking to impose internationally through its participation in the AI Committee of the ISO, a group that is developing standards for the AI industry on data quality, risk management, and big data analytics.[84] To cite another example, Huawei—the world's leader in patents for 5G technology—has proposed over 35,000 standards to the 3GPP, one quarter of which have been approved.[85]

In one of the most controversial efforts to leverage China's influence within these standard-setting organizations, Chinese telecom companies Huawei, China Unicom, and China Telecom, together with the Chinese Ministry of Industry and Information Technology (MIIT), proposed a new standard for core network technology—"New IP"—at the ITU.[86] The Chinese proposal sought to shift power over IP standardization away from nongovernmental organizations IETF and ICANN to the ITU, which is part of the UN system and hence controlled by governments.[87] The fear is that this proposed standard, if adopted, would replace the existing IP system that transmits information across the world from one IP address to another IP, connecting all individual computers and internet users. Thus, this new standard would limit interoperability across different networks, undermining its global character. According to Huawei, the New IP protocol would be superior to the existing "unstable" internet infrastructure as devices within the same network would communicate directly with each other and thus obviate the need to send or receive information across the broader internet. But the proposal's critics warn that it would radically transform the open internet into a closed one where state-run internet service providers would exert control over citizens' internet use due to "tracking features" required to authenticate and add new IP addresses to the closed network.[88] In presenting the new standard to the ITU, Huawei also explained that it would come with a "shut up command" that could cut off a particular IP address from the network.[89] Russia, Saudi Arabia, and Iran have supported China's proposed standard, while the US and several European countries have vehemently opposed it.[90]

Some Western commentators have agreed with Chinese tech companies that concerns about the New IP protocol are overblown, while others have pointed out that the existing IP system's technical problems can be solved without embracing the Chinese approach. Milton Mueller, a professor at

Georgia Tech, accused journalists of fanning fears of New IP beyond what the nascent proposal justifies.[91] He characterizes New IP as not a standard, but a policy white paper and argues that "since there are no real technical specifications here, it is impossible to know whether the 'New IP' direction proposed by Huawei would make global data communications more or less authoritarian."[92] On the other hand, Alissa Cooper, a technology policy executive at the US telecom company Cisco, articulated the Internet Engineering Task Force's opposition to New IP: "We believe the creation of a top-down design effort to replace the existing IP protocol stack wholesale would be harmful. . . . We see no evidence that the challenges described in the proposals cannot be met by continuing to evolve the existing IP protocol suite."[93]

In the years since its introduction, the New IP proposal continues to be cited as a source of concern in Western policymaking. In February 2022, European Commission Executive Vice-President Margrethe Vestager announced a new initiative to counter China's standard-setting influence in cutting-edge technological sectors. In explaining the need for the initiative, Commissioner Vestager pointed to the New IP proposal and argued that global standards should instead be "set in a vibrant, democratic market economy."[94] At the June 2022 ITU conference on telecom development, the Chinese government and Huawei jointly touted a new proposal called IPv6+.[95] Once again, Chinese voices made the case that this new system would improve upon the current internet, leading to "more efficient allocation of information across the network" and the "integration of other technologies."[96] A human rights advocate observing the conference, however, warned that "IPv6+ and [N]ew IP are the same song, different verse."[97] The battle over IP standards thus continues to play out as part of the battle between those who support China's digital authoritarian model and those who are wary of its spread around the world.

With the ascent of the Chinese influence over international standard setting, the existing multistakeholder governance model is challenged by a governance model that is considerably more state-centric and hence consistent with the Chinese state-driven regulatory model. Both the US and the EU have embraced a strong role for the private industry in standard setting. With the growing Chinese influence in organizations such as the ICANN, IEC, ISO, and ITU, the voices of European and American industry will not merely be diluted by those of the Chinese industry but also by that of the Chinese state. Many Chinese standard-setting organizations that send representatives to these organizations have close ties to the Chinese government.[98] The Chinese government gives informal guidance to these organizations, ensuring that any standards they promote remain aligned with the Chinese national interest. Chinese state-owned enterprises also participate actively in standard setting, and the Chinese government is involved in coordinating the positions of various Chinese participants in these organizations, especially when important national priorities such as 5G standards are at stake.[99] Thus, while failing to elevate the role of the UN as the central decision-making body for internet governance, China is entrenching its vision for digital sovereignty by gradually transforming multistakeholder organizations into more state-controlled institutions where digital authoritarian norms can better challenge the ideals of the free, open, and global internet.

Digital Authoritarianism Beyond China

While the Chinese state-driven regulatory model is spreading globally, all authoritarian measures toward internet controls and state surveillance observed around the world can hardly be attributed to China's direct influence. Regardless of the policies China has pursued, it is unlikely that the leaders of countries such as Iran, North Korea, Russia, or Saudi Arabia would have ever embraced the US's internet freedom agenda or emulated the EU's commitment to citizens' rights as a cornerstone of digital governance. For example, the Russian government has over the past decade moved from a Western-style regulatory model that featured few internet restrictions to a tightly controlled state-driven regulatory model. Today, Russia increasingly shares China's vision that the digital economy is a domain of state sovereignty and that the internet should be subject to political control. Following its invasion of Ukraine, Russia is moving even more forcefully to deploy the internet as a tool for state control and propaganda. By asserting authoritarian control over the digital economy, Russia is thus contributing to the spread of a state-driven, digital authoritarian vision while directly undermining the influence of the American market-driven model and the European rights-driven model. Russia is, no doubt, inspired by China's example and could be seen as aspiring to replicate part of the Chinese model. However, a closer look at the Russian government's efforts to gain control over the country's digital economy also reveals a vast gap between its aspirations and capabilities. This suggests that China remains in a globally unique position to implement the state-driven model toward authoritarian ends and that most attempts to emulate China—including Russia's—will fall short of the ways that China has perfected the state-driven regulatory model. In other words, adopting a state-driven regulatory model requires not just political will but also tremendous resources and technological capability.

Russia is an interesting country to examine when assessing the global reach of China's digital authoritarian norms, not least because Russia has transitioned over the years toward a Chinese-style, state-driven regulatory model. In 2019, Russia adopted a "Sovereign Internet Law," which closely mirrors China's digital authoritarian principles.[100] The law establishes a legal framework that allows the state to exert increasing control over the internet in the country. Some commentators draw a parallel to the Great Firewall of China, as the Sovereign Internet Law aims to similarly restrict internet users' access to content that the government deems harmful.[101] It further vests the Russian government with the power to shut down the network and to isolate Russia from the global internet.[102] The Russian government claims that the country now has the technology to operate an autonomous Russian internet— "sovereign RuNet"—that runs entirely on Russian servers.[103] The government justifies this to the public as necessary to protect Russian interests if Western powers seek to cut the country off from the global internet. But Russian activists claim that the efforts to create a sovereign internet are instead driven by the Kremlin's desire to have the option to cut Russia off from the world.[104]

In 2021, the Russian government further tightened its sovereign control over the internet by passing a new law that requires social media giants and other large operators of foreign websites to open local offices in Russia.[105] This law builds on an earlier 2014 law that mandates data localization.[106] Data localization requires foreign companies operating in Russia to collect, store, and process any Russian citizens' personal data in databases that are located within Russia, further tightening Russian sovereign control over data. Russian authorities have also shown that they are prepared to enforce these laws. In 2016, Roskomnadzor, Russia's agency responsible for monitoring, controlling, and censoring Russian mass media, blocked Microsoft's LinkedIn in the country after the company was found to have violated data localization laws.[107] In 2020, Roskomnadzor fined Facebook and Twitter for the violation of the data localization law, while also threatening the companies with additional fines if they failed to establish databases on Russian territory by July 2021.[108] Google was the next to be targeted on similar grounds, with Roskomnadzor opening a case against the company in June 2021[109] and a district court in Moscow issuing a fine against Google in August 2021.[110] The 2016 "Yarovaya law" and its 2018 amendments have further added to these demands. The laws require tech companies to retain user communications (including images and text and voice messages),[111] to store this data locally, and to hand this information over to Russian authorities on demand.[112]

Russia is also increasingly adopting the Chinese approach toward content moderation. Over the past few years, the Russian government has implemented several new laws and pursued numerous actions against social media companies to gain greater state control over public discourse. It has punished online platforms both for censoring content that promotes the pro-Russia narrative, and for failing to censor content that contradicts this narrative or gives voice to the opposition. Meta, YouTube, and Twitter have been the main targets of this legislation. A 2020 federal law orders social media companies to remove content that is considered "illegal" under Russian law and imposes fines for noncompliance.[113] This law has also been strictly enforced in practice, with the Russian authorities imposing fines in 2021 on Google, Facebook, Twitter, and TikTok for these companies' failure to delete content related to the January 2021 anti-government protests in Russia.[114] Another 2020 federal law introduces sanctions for any internet platform that censors Russian media.[115] Relying on this law, an arbitration court in Moscow ordered Google to reinstate the YouTube channel Tsargrad TV, which is owned by Russian oligarch Konstantin Malofeev,[116] ruling that Google had unfairly discriminated against Malofeev. Malofeev has been targeted by US and EU financial sanctions since 2014 for his role in funding pro-Russian separatists fighting in Ukraine. Malofeev boasted of his court victory as a win for Russian internet sovereignty, noting how "people from California can't set the rules in Russia."[117] He also wrote to former President Trump, who has been banned by Twitter and Facebook, urging him to sue US tech companies before Russian courts.[118]

This Russian turn toward a state-driven model has taken place over the past decade, and can be traced to events surrounding the reelection of President Putin in 2012.[119] Mass street protests taking place in 2011 and 2012, fueled by social media, were a key development that drove Russia's shift toward digital authoritarianism. These events turned the Putin regime's attention to the threat that social media can pose to the regime and political stability in the country. President Putin has been hardening his rhetoric ever since, noting in March 2021 that Russian society would "collapse from the inside" if the internet did not "submit to formal legal rules and the moral laws of society."[120] The Russian government is further tightening its grip over online speech with a new 2020 law that makes online libel punishable by up to two years in prison.[121] This can be an arbitrary and effective tool to deter news and any other commentary that could undermine the Putin regime.

Russia's turn to digital authoritarianism has also paved way for greater cooperation with China. With shared goals, China and Russia have collaborated on a joint internet governance agenda. They share a resentment of the US's role in global digital governance. Olga Melnikova, the head of the Department of International Information Security of the Ministry of Foreign Affairs of Russia, expressed these sentiments in her July 2021 comments, noting how "both Moscow and Beijing oppose Washington's global domination, including in the digital space."[122] The two countries signed a bilateral cooperation treaty on cybersecurity in 2015.[123] There have also been media reports that the two countries planned to sign an international treaty on managing illegal online content in 2019. However, the treaty text is not publicly available, and it is not clear if the agreement between the two countries was ever concluded.[124] Both China and Russia also actively promote the notion of "cyber sovereignty" in fora such as the UN,[125] as discussed earlier, which can be viewed as another shared attempt to legitimize the state-driven regulatory model internationally. Despite their shared values and occasional collaboration, Russia and China also have some differences, both in terms of priorities and capabilities.[126] China pursues global technological dominance, which is not a feasible goal for Russia, as it lags behind China in technological capabilities. Russia has also been more focused on harnessing the internet to leverage its relatively greater military and intelligence capabilities, including toward destabilizing other regimes.

Notwithstanding Russia's efforts to imitate several features of Chinese internet governance, it has not managed to replicate China's state-driven model as successfully in practice. One challenge is that the Russian digital society was not initially built on digital authoritarian foundations, and those foundations have been harder to establish retroactively. Before the authoritarian turn that took place a decade ago, the Russian internet was largely free of state involvement and reflective of Western values. This history of internet freedom in the country has made it politically difficult for the government to establish a tight censorship regime, as the Russian population is accustomed to online engagement. For example, Western social networks, such as Instagram and YouTube, remained extremely popular until they were blocked in response to Western sanctions following the Ukrainian invasion.[127] This set limits to the government's ability to censor the internet—until the war provided a forceful reason for the government to implement an even tighter censorship regime.

Russia also lacks the capacity possessed by the Chinese government to monitor and censor the internet.[128] This suggests that Russia may have embraced the spirit of China's state-driven model but it has not to date invested the resources China has to actually entrench that model as an effective regime of state control. For example, Russia's internet censor Roskomnadzor has 3,000 employees, which pales in comparison to the estimated 100,000 people China has deployed for this task.[129] Russia also lags behind in the technological capabilities needed to engage in effective censorship. To illustrate this, in June 2020, Russia reversed a two-year ban on the popular messaging platform Telegram after its repeated failures to block the site also caused collateral damage to unrelated sites.[130] When Russian censors attempted to ban

Telegram in 2018, they accidentally took out over 16 million unrelated sites, including the site of the internet censorship agency itself, while Telegram remained easily accessible and increased its audience from 10 to 30 million.[131] In 2021, when the government tried to punish Twitter by slowing down its operations, the unintended side effect was that the websites of the Kremlin, the Russian Parliament, and several government agencies went offline.[132] These incidents highlight Russia's dependence on foreign internet infrastructure and the resulting difficulties it faces in fencing itself off from the global internet, engaging in mass surveillance, or otherwise replicating the Chinese state-driven model in practice. China is actively helping Russia to build better technological capabilities through talent exchanges and joint technology development projects,[133] but a vast gap continues to exist between Russian digital authoritarian aspirations and the country's actual capabilities.

Russia knows that it remains dependent on foreign digital technologies and that it must rely either on China or the West for many of its technological needs. In choosing to collaborate closely with China, including by embracing Huawei's technologies, Russia has shown that it is more comfortable with dependence on China than on the US or the West more broadly. As one government official noted, "We're either going to be bugged by the US or by China, so we need to choose the lesser evil."[134] However, as a sign that Russia also harbors mistrust against China, the Russian government allowed Huawei in to construct the 5G network in the country under the condition that only Russian telecom equipment would be used. Due to this requirement, the 5G project is currently stalled in Russia as no local equipment exists.[135] Additionally, Russia is not solely relying on Chinese surveillance technologies; it has, until recently, also bought advanced technology from the West, especially when it is perceived as superior in quality. For example, Moscow's smart city surveillance systems rely primarily on equipment bought from US companies including Cisco, Dell, HP, and Nvidia.[136] This suggests that Russia is not simply importing the Chinese state-driven model but is looking to entrench its own Russian variant of it. Russia is also seeking ways to promote its own technologies and to reduce its dependence on all foreign platforms. A new law from 2021, colloquially known as "the law against Apple," mandates that device manufacturers preinstall Russian apps on smart devices such as smartphones, tablets, and laptops[137]—a law Apple initially opposed, but ultimately agreed to comply with it.[138]

With the 2022 Russian invasion of Ukraine, the dynamics in Russia are changing toward greater authoritarianism, amplified by rapidly growing hostility toward the US and the EU and a resulting decoupling of the country from Western technologies. In an attempt to control the narrative about the war,

Russia has turned even more authoritarian, leveraging the internet as a tool for state propaganda. The Russian government has blocked access to several US digital platforms, including Facebook, Instagram, and Twitter. According to a Moscow court decision in March 2022, Facebook and Instagram had to be banned because their parent company, Meta, was "carrying out extremist activities" relating to the war. The Russian Federal Security Service has also accused Meta of "creating an 'alternative reality'" in which "hatred for the Russians was kindled."[139] The Russian ban followed the Western sanctions, which required these companies to limit carrying Russian propaganda— including content by Russian state-controlled media outlets Russia Today and Sputnik—on their platforms.[140] The US and the EU have sought to isolate Russia through banning the export of Western technologies to the country, hoping to pressure the Kremlin into ending the aggression and withdrawing from Ukraine. China, on the other hand, has not condemned the Russian invasion and has tolerated, even amplified, Russian narratives about the war on Chinese online platforms.[141] As a result, Russia is thus likely to align itself even more closely with China in the coming years.

The ongoing war in Ukraine also heightens the broader conflict between democracies and autocracies, shaping not only how the US and the EU are responding to the threat posed by Russia—but also to the threat posed by the most capable digital authoritarian nation, namely China. While digital authoritarianism in countries such as Russia presents grave concerns, China remains the main digital adversary of the US and its allies, given the superior influence and global clout of the Chinese state-driven model.

Concerns With China's Global Influence

Critics point to several concerns about the expansion of Chinese digital infrastructures and influence over the global digital economy. One prominent concern is that by allowing Chinese companies to build smart cities, those partnering cities also risk becoming more authoritarian. The same surveillance cameras that can be deployed to reduce traffic congestion and optimize energy use can also be used to monitor citizens' every movement in real time. This way, the Chinese digital authoritarian culture can spread around the world as foreign governments gain new tools of state control. Another concern is that reliance on Chinese technologies risks exposing these countries to Chinese government surveillance, as Chinese tech companies are widely believed to hand over any data they gather to their government upon request. While some of these concerns have been difficult to verify in practice, they have prompted the US and its allies to seek to curtail China's influence.

Concern Over Globalizing Chinese Surveillance

In assessing China's growing influence through the DSR, it is important to keep in mind that while the DSR is sometimes characterized as the Chinese government's masterplan to proactively export its digital authoritarian norms, the DSR is also often demand-driven as several governments actively seek to acquire Chinese technologies.[142] Many foreign governments in countries with high crime rates welcome surveillance infrastructure as a tool for law enforcement—often with the full backing of their citizens, who worry about their physical safety more than their data privacy. These governments can point to numerous examples of digital technologies reducing crime effectively, thus justifying the decision to invest in greater digital surveillance. Local governments in China have been eager to tout the benefits of surveillance technologies. For example, it was reported that in a village in Sichuan province, crime rates dropped to zero in two years because of the surveillance cameras.[143] Foreign governments are sharing similar examples, emphasizing how digital surveillance is having a beneficial effect on other societies as well. For example, in New Delhi, facial recognition software was reported to have helped police recognize 3,000 missing children in the span of only four days.[144]

Smart cities are powered by technologies that can, indeed, be deployed toward multiple ends, some beneficial, others more sinister. There is nothing unlawful or disturbing in deploying modern technology to make cities run more efficiently in light of the information that these technologies can collect. Fighting crime is also a government responsibility, and carrying out that task can thus legitimately include utilizing technologies that improve citizens' safety.[145] However, alongside these entirely benevolent uses of surveillance technologies exists the possibility of leveraging these technologies to entrench authoritarian control in violation of individual rights. Facial recognition and other similar technologies can help governments monitor their citizens, including tracking dissidents and other activists who pose a risk to reigning governments—akin to what the Chinese government is doing domestically to curtail dissent and maintain social order. The key concern thus stems not from the fact that these technologies exist, but from how they are being deployed.

Chinese companies have been quick to emphasize the distinction between manufacturing a certain technology and making a policy decision on how to deploy it. When asked about the potential malicious uses of its technology, Huawei has commented that the company "provides technology to support smart city and safe city programs across the world. In each case, Huawei does not get involved in setting public policy in terms of how that technology is used."[146] Chinese facial recognition company CloudWalk, which has been sanctioned by the US government, justifies its exports of surveillance technology to countries such as Zimbabwe by emphasizing that it is not the company, but the Zimbabwean government, that decides how the technology is deployed. Fu Xiaolong, a company spokesperson, drew a parallel to US arms sales: "Just as the United States sells arms around the world—it does not care whether other governments use American weapons to kill people."[147]

Whether or not one subscribes to the view that the entities supplying technologies bear no responsibility for the actual deployment of those technologies, it is reasonable to assume that smart city technologies provided by Chinese tech companies are being leveraged to entrench state control in many parts of the world. The growing authoritarianism across countries further ensures that there is a steady, even growing, demand for rights-invasive, control-enhancing surveillance technologies. According to the rankings published by Freedom House, internet freedom across the world is declining. Their *Freedom on the Net 2021* report measures countries' internet freedom across indicators such as obstacles to internet access, limits on content, and violations of user rights, and found that global internet freedom had declined for an eleventh consecutive year.[148] The same report documents that the procurement of spyware is proliferating, with a growing number of governments gaining access to sophisticated surveillance technology.[149] This suggests that numerous authoritarian governments are eagerly embracing surveillance technologies in their efforts to control their societies—and China provides them the tools to do so.

The COVID-19 pandemic may further increase demand for digital surveillance technologies around the world. All governments were scrambling to prevent the spread of the pandemic, and many quickly deployed digital technology to introduce new contact-tracing measures. Digital surveillance proved helpful in tracking potential infections and alerting individuals who could have been exposed to the virus. China's relatively more successful control of the COVID-19 pandemic during its early stages can, in part, be attributed to its societal willingness to tolerate highly invasive digital surveillance measures alongside with harsh lockdowns—even if those invasive measures have since been heavily criticized. China's color-based health codes and tracking systems were rightly described as far-reaching, yet many commentators concede that they were effective in preventing people from traveling and thus reducing early COVID-19 cases quickly.[150] However, this type of essential public health measure can also provide an excuse for governments to infringe on individual freedoms and collect personal data on individuals. The pandemic can also be used as a justification to monitor the movements and contacts of citizens, enforce quarantines, or otherwise keep cities "safe."[151] There is also a legitimate fear that these measures will not be lifted after the pandemic but will instead be used to carry out government surveillance for less pressing purposes in the future.

Chinese-supplied surveillance technologies provide governments with the tools to pursue digital surveillance of their citizens—however, China is not the only country to offer these kinds of technologies. According to a 2019 Carnegie Endowment for International Peace study that examines AI surveillance in 176 countries, Chinese companies are indeed the largest source of those technologies, supplying them to 63 countries. Huawei alone has sold surveillance technologies to at least 50 countries.[152] At the same time, governments eager to monitor their citizens can also acquire Western surveillance technology and deploy those systems toward illiberal ends. For example, French, German, Israeli, Japanese, and US companies are also active in this domain. Surveillance technologies supplied by US firms, such as IBM, Palantir, and Cisco, can be found in 32 countries. An Israeli company called NSO Group has developed spyware called "Pegasus," which has been described as the "World's Most Powerful Cyberweapon," and which the company has sold to governments around the world.[153] Reports have subsequently surfaced documenting widespread abuse of the spyware by democratic and authoritarian countries alike.[154] NSO Group also became a target of US sanctions in 2021 after it was discovered that the company supplied its Pegasus spyware to foreign governments that used it to target political activists, politicians, business leaders, and journalists.[155]

It is also not the case that Chinese tech companies are supplying AI surveillance technologies to other authoritarian states, while tech companies from liberal democracies are servicing liberal democracies.[156] Chinese companies are active in democracies and autocracies alike, and similarly, companies based in liberal democracies are supplying technologies to markets with dismal human right records. For example, Saudi Arabia is procuring safe city technology from Huawei. But Google is establishing cloud servers there, and the Japanese company NEC is supplying facial recognition cameras to the country. In addition, while the US government has criticized and sanctioned Chinese companies that have facilitated surveillance of the Uyghur minority in Xinjiang, it was revealed in 2019 that US tech company Hewlett Packard also contributed to the effort.[157] Thus, China is by no means the only source of technologies that power global surveillance efforts.

Critics of Chinese surveillance technologies, however, highlight an additional reason for concern over technologies supplied by Chinese companies.

This concern relates to the amorphous relationship that Chinese firms have with the Chinese government, including the entanglements that come with the Chinese government often supplying loans to fund foreign governments' acquisitions of surveillance technologies. Chinese companies are expected to hand over data they acquire to the Chinese government, and few believe that they can credibly commit to refusing to do so. The most potent concern is therefore that the Chinese government itself could access the data that Chinese companies gather by exporting, installing, or managing technologies in foreign jurisdictions. In other words, Chinese infrastructure in foreign markets may not only facilitate digital surveillance by foreign governments but also surveillance by the Chinese government. Should Beijing deploy its access to data in DSR-recipient countries toward espionage operations, these countries' core national security interests could be compromised. Some countries, including the US, are already shunning Chinese technology precisely for the fear of being exposed to Chinese espionage operations, as discussed in Chapter 5. This concern was also articulated by former Japanese trade minister Akira Amari, who recently warned that China's efforts to set standards on smart cities is a "trap"; the surveillance systems ultimately allow China to mine data from high-tech-powered cities around the world and feed it back to Beijing.[158]

Some commentators have also warned that by allowing Chinese companies to build smart city infrastructure, cities hand those companies the tools to "flick a 'kill switch'" to shut down city operations.[159] The Chinese government could also resort to coercion or blackmailing of foreign political elites using its access to politically sensitive data, thus gaining political leverage over foreign governments.[160] Others emphasize that while the DSR to date has been less tightly controlled by the Chinese government, that may well change as geopolitical conflicts over technology intensify. The DSR plants an infrastructure channel that the Chinese leadership may start deploying more strategically to challenge the US-led technology order, pulling more countries closer into its orbit both technologically and geopolitically.[161] If this occurs, the Chinese government's much-touted idea of data sovereignty will be illusory as these DSR recipients will ultimately be subject to the control of the CCP.[162]

To date, there is limited evidence on which to judge whether these potential fears will actually materialize. In 2019, the *Wall Street Journal* reported that Huawei employees had assisted the Ugandan and Zambian governments in spying on their political opponents.[163] This assistance entailed intercepting those individuals' encrypted communications and social media accounts and using cellular data to track their movements. The investigation did not uncover evidence showing that this assistance was done at the behest of

the Chinese government or that the executives in China directed the operations or even knew about them. But the investigation did show that Huawei
employees in those countries were directly involved in these surveillance
operations. Local security officials shared copies of intercepted WhatsApp
messages with the *Journal* and explained that Huawei technicians' help was
essential for the operation.[164] This direct, on-the-ground assistance came on
top of the general technical training that Huawei employees had provided to
African officials in Beijing. Huawei executives had also recommended that
the Ugandan government study Huawei surveillance systems in Algeria,
where the Algerian government deployed mass surveillance technologies and
engaged in hacking of members of the opposition who were seen as threats to
national security. However, while this type of general training has been well
documented, Huawei's involvement in day-to-day government surveillance
operations in countries deploying the company's technology has been more
difficult to prove.

The data breach scandal involving Huawei and the African Union (AU),
which was discussed earlier in the introduction, is another event that raised
significant international concern after it was uncovered that the Chinese-built
AU headquarters had been a target of a major hacking operation that exposed
the AU's data to Chinese surveillance.[165] Unsurprisingly, the Chinese government denied allegations of its involvement.[166] Despite efforts to address the
problem, including putting out new tenders and awarding new contracts for
the building's ICT systems,[167] the Chinese influence over the AU's operations
has been hard to shed. In 2020, Japanese cyber researchers alerted the AU
of another cyberhack after discovering that a group of Chinese hackers was
suspected of having rigged AU servers, allowing them to siphon off surveillance videos from across the AU building complex.[168] The Chinese mission
to the AU again denied the allegations, stating that "we never interfere in
Africa's internal affairs," and emphasizing that Africa and China are "good
friends, partners and brothers."[169] The AU's dependence on Chinese support complicates the AU's options for responding to the Chinese hacking
operations—which also explains why the AU was hesitant to validate and condemn the breach in the first place. China plays a key role in providing technical support, capacity building, and technology to combat security concerns,
and also contributes to broader peacekeeping missions throughout the region.[170] This likely explains why the AU has not taken drastic measures to
disentangle its partnership with China.

Others may argue that it is not fair to single out China as several
governments, including democratic governments, conduct extensive surveillance operations around the world. While it is doubtful that comprehensive

data on global digital surveillance practices can be assembled, some attempts to do so exist. For example, the 2019 Carnegie Endowment for International Peace study cited above confirms that AI surveillance technologies are used by liberal and illiberal regimes alike.[171] This also became evident with the so-called Snowden revelations that exposed the extensive surveillance practices of the US National Security Agency (NSA), including how the US government had Huawei among its many surveillance targets.[172] The US government does not deny that it conducts wide-ranging surveillance operations. But it is keen to draw a distinction between surveillance conducted by democracies and by autocracies. When faced with accusations that their surveillance programs violate civil liberties, the US intelligence agencies defend their programs as being essential to fend off terrorist attacks and other national security threats,[173] in addition to being constitutional and subject to rigorous congressional and judicial oversight.[174] In line with the US argument, the Carnegie study acknowledges that greater concerns exist when surveillance technologies are deployed by authoritarian rather than liberal governments. Liberal democracies are expected to have better governance mechanisms in place to protect individuals' fundamental rights, whereas authoritarian governments are more likely to abuse these technologies because they face fewer legal constraints and political checks in doing so.[175] However, the Snowden revelations have undoubtedly undermined the US government's ability to criticize China for its surveillance practices. The Chinese government, for example, has been quick to fend off any US criticism by pointing out how invasive the US's own intelligence operations are, with the Chinese Ministry of Foreign Affairs Spokesperson Zhao Lijian referring to the US as "the No. 1 empire of hacking, surveillance and theft of secrets."[176]

In addition to highlighting the US surveillance in an effort to call out Western hypocrisy, China is also actively pushing back on any efforts to paint the country as an enemy in need of a counter force. After Sweden banned Huawei from its domestic networks, China threatened to retaliate by banning the Swedish company Ericsson from China's own 5G building efforts.[177] In a curious twist of events, these Chinese threats led Ericsson to lobby its own government against a Huawei ban—fiercely advocating for its rival in an effort to preserve its own access to Chinese markets.[178] These retaliatory threats are just one example of the ways China seeks to inflict economic pain on those who join initiatives to resist Chinese influence. In 2020, Australia sparked China's ire by imposing restrictions on Huawei, criticizing the national security law in Hong Kong, and advocating for an investigation into China's early coronavirus pandemic missteps.[179] China responded by imposing high tariffs on Australian barley exports, suspending some Australian beef imports, and placing antidumping duties on Australian wine.[180] In a press briefing after the wine duties were announced, Chinese Ministry of Foreign Affairs spokesman Zhao Lijian said that Australia should "do more things conducive to mutual trust and cooperation."[181] In addition to penalizing countries that have stood up to China, China also promises countries better relations and corresponding economic benefits for going along with the Chinese agenda. In recent years, a number of countries have switched from recognizing and maintaining diplomatic ties with Taiwan to partnering with mainland China.[182] When Nicaragua made the switch in 2021, foreign observers noted that Chinese investment behind the Nicaraguan government's plans to build a $50 billion canal may have been a significant factor driving the decision.[183] These examples reveal that China's common strategy of deploying rewards and punishments can be effective in toning down any criticism that would otherwise be voiced against China's global influence.

The Difficulty of Countering China's Growing Global Influence

There have recently been several calls and proposals for deeper cooperation among liberal democracies to counter China's influence.[184] These proposals call for a coalition of "techno-democracies" to counter China and other "techno-autocracies" in an increasingly ideological battle over fundamental norms that govern the global digital economy. These proposals, which will be discussed in the concluding chapter, build on an acknowledgment that too little has been done to counter the rise of the Chinese state-driven regulatory model and that no country can effectively respond to this challenge alone. To date, democratic countries have been unable to provide an alternative to China's DSR, make real progress in defending themselves against cyberattacks, or successfully coordinate on tech standards that reflect their shared values.

While these proposals have not yet led to a steady alliance of techno-democracies or a comprehensive strategy to counter China's digital authoritarianism, some initiatives, pledges, and institutions have been put in place or are being prepared. The Trump administration initiated a program in August 2020 known as the "Clean Network."[185] The Network is described as a "comprehensive approach to safeguarding the nation's assets including citizens' privacy and companies' most sensitive information from aggressive intrusions by malign actors, such as the Chinese Communist Party."[186] In establishing this Network, former Secretary of State Michael Pompeo called on "all freedom-loving nations and companies" to participate in the initiative and help address threats to "data privacy, security [and] human rights."[187] The Network has developed "digital trust standards" to assess the trustworthiness of telecom equipment suppliers as they construct and operate their 5G infrastructures. This includes designating some 5G providers as trustworthy "Clean Telcos," a labeling effort that is designed to halt Huawei's ability to offer its services to the members of the Network.[188] The Clean Network builds on the so-called Prague Proposals, which refer to a common position reached in negotiations among 30 countries on 5G security in a conference hosted in May 2019 in the Czech Republic.[189] This conference brought together security officials across Europe, North America, Australia, Japan, and South Korea in addition to representatives of the EU and NATO.[190] Without naming Huawei, the Prague Proposals consist of a set of nonbinding principles that warn governments of relying on suppliers of 5G networks that could be subject to state influence or that are based in countries that are not signatories to international agreements on cybersecurity or data protection.

As of December 2020, over 50 countries have signed up to the Clean Network, together with 180 "Clean Telcos" and numerous other "Clean Companies" such as Oracle, Fujitsu, Cisco, Siemens, and HP.[191] Almost all EU member states—26 out of 27—have joined the Network; Germany is the one country that has not made a decision to join, likely because of its deeper economic ties with China and the desire not to antagonize its key trading partner.[192] Other democracies and large economies, including Australia, Canada, India, and Japan, are also among the members of the Network. It is unclear how President Biden plans on building onto this particular Trump-era effort, but his administration is facing continued pressure from Congress to do more to counter China's growing influence.[193] To date, his administration has shown its determination to keep the pressure against Chinese tech companies, including sanctions, in place. In addition to countering China's technological ambitions,[194] the Biden administration is focused on strengthening the US's own capabilities in order to preserve the American lead in technologies that are vital to the US's long-term economic and military power, as discussed in Chapter 5.[195]

The group of advanced economies known as the G7 is another forum for fostering cooperation among techno-democracies and countering China's DSR. This political forum consists of Canada, France, Germany, Italy, Japan, the UK, and the US. In the group's June 2021 meeting, the G7 launched an initiative known as the "Build Back Better World" (B3W).[196] Through this initiative, the G7 members pledge to mobilize private capital to help "narrow the $40+ trillion infrastructure need in the developing world."[197] The B3W is depicted as an alternative to China's BRI and DSR, consistent with the democratic values embraced by the G7 members. Other democracies outside of the G7 are also invited to join the initiative.[198] A senior official in the Biden administration denies that the B3W is just about "confronting or taking on China," and claims that the initiative is instead designed as a "positive alternative that reflects our values, our standards and our way of doing business."[199] In 2021, the EU also pledged to invest up to 300 billion euros by 2027 to fund critical infrastructure projects around the world as part of a "Global Gateway" initiative, which has been described as the EU's response to China's BRI.[200] However, it remains unclear how effective any initiative such as B3W or Global Gateway will be, including whether the pledged funding will ultimately materialize.[201] In contrast, the BRI has the solid financial and political backing of the Chinese government, which allows Chinese companies to take on more ambitious and riskier projects across the developing world.[202]

In addition to these initiatives with an intended global reach, the US has also sought to counter China's digital infrastructure power through regional efforts in Asia. For example, the US is considering a digital trade agreement with Indo-Pacific economies as a way to restrain China's influence in the region.[203] This proposed digital trade deal would include countries such as Australia, Canada, Chile, Japan, Malaysia, New Zealand, and Singapore. It would be narrowly confined to digital issues and aim to reach agreement on cross-border data flows, data protection, and various regulatory standards, including those for artificial intelligence. The deal could build on existing agreements such as the 2019 US–Japan Digital Trade Agreement and the 2020 Singapore–New Zealand–Chile Digital Economy Partnership Agreement.[204] Other efforts to align the Asian nations with the US include an agreement between the US, Japan, India, and Australia—known as "the Quad"—to collaborate on creating a safe supply chain for semiconductors and ensuring the development of secure communications networks.[205] After its September 2021 meeting, the four-way alliance issued a joint statement on common principles on tech development, emphasizing their shared commitment to "democratic values and respect for universal human rights" as a foundation for the governance and use of technology.[206] While not explicitly framing the effort as a counter to China, the Quad approach affirms its view that "technology should not be misused or abused for malicious activities such as authoritarian surveillance and oppression."[207]

Harnessing a cohesive anti-China coalition to counter China's infrastructure power is not easy. The US cannot halt China's economic rise and technological prowess, nor can it easily cajole other nations into forgoing the opportunities that China's dynamic and growing economy present. Already today, China is the largest trade partner for almost twice as many countries as the US is.[208] If these countries are forced to choose between the US and China, they may well choose China. The US is facing some challenges in particular in its efforts to pull Asian economies into any digital agreement geared at countering China, as China is the leading trade partner for every country in the region.[209] China has already registered its opposition to the proposed digital trade deal between the US and Indo-Pacific economies.[210] As a result, several Asian economies may not join any deal with the US over China's opposition.

In recent years, the US government has intensified its efforts to counter China's growing global influence by depicting the battle against China as one being fought over the future of liberal democracy. In the digital domain, this battle has consisted of an attempt to harness a coalition of techno-democracies to fight China and other techno-autocracies. This contest between two warring ideologies and political systems, which will be discussed in the concluding chapter, further elevates the stakes in the US and other Western efforts to halt China's growing global influence and limit the reach of the digital regulatory model it espouses. By framing the battle as one between digital democracy and digital autocracy, the US presents a stark choice to the countries around the world, appealing to their political convictions and fundamental values that organize digital societies. However, despite these sustained efforts, there are few signs to date that the Chinese state-driven regulatory model—or its global influence—will wane anytime soon.

9

Globalizing European Digital Rights through Regulatory Power

WHEN THE EUROPEAN UNION adopted its landmark data privacy regulation—the General Data Protection Regulation or the GDPR—in 2016,[1] it was soon embraced as a global data privacy standard by many of the leading American tech firms, including Meta, Google, Apple, and Microsoft. In anticipation of its entry into force, Meta chose to extend GDPR protections to the company's then 2.2 billion users—now nearly 3 billion users—worldwide.[2] Google similarly updated its privacy policy globally in response to the GDPR, sending its users a notice saying that "We're making these updates as new data protection regulations come into effect in the European Union, and we're taking the opportunity to make improvements for Google users around the world."[3] Apple carries out GDPR-mandated privacy impact assessments across all its products and rolls out updates required by the GDPR on its operating systems worldwide.[4] Microsoft implements the GDPR's "privacy by design" concept, designing its products at the outset to incorporate the EU's data privacy standards and thereby globalizing those standards through its inherent product features.[5]

Why would these powerful US companies comply with the GDPR even outside the EU, instead of taking advantage of more lenient data privacy laws elsewhere? The answer lies in a phenomenon known as the "Brussels Effect,"[6] which describes the EU's unilateral power to regulate the global marketplace. Because of the size and the attractiveness of the EU market, most large tech companies want to access that market, which requires them to comply with the European regulatory standards. While these tech companies could, of course, adopt one data privacy standard for the EU market and various other standards for the rest of the world, scale economies and other benefits of uniform business practices often make such a customization strategy unappealing. Instead, these companies frequently choose the most stringent regulatory standard—which typically is the EU standard—as their global standard to ensure regulatory compliance worldwide. In this way, market forces and companies' business incentives alone are often sufficient to convert the EU's data privacy regulation into a global regulation.

In addition to this type of de facto Brussels Effect, which explains how large tech companies adjust their global conduct to the EU regulations, those regulations are often entrenched globally through the so-called de jure Brussels Effect, which refers to the adoption of EU-style regulations by foreign governments. To date, nearly 150 countries have adopted domestic privacy laws, most of them resembling the EU data protection regime.[7] According to Paul Schwartz and Karl-Nikolaus Peifer, "EU data protection has been stunningly influential: most of the rest of the world follows it."[8] Another privacy expert, Graham Greenleaf, notes that "something reasonably described as 'European standard' data privacy laws are becoming the norm in most parts of the world with data privacy laws."[9] Many governments emulate GDPR because they perceive it to be the "gold standard," providing the highest and most widely accepted standard to follow.[10] After a certain tipping point, there is such widespread convergence behind the EU norm that it is harder for any government enacting data privacy laws to justify a deviation from that global norm.

These two variants of the Brussels Effect, de facto and de jure, reveal how the EU has been able to extend its influence across the global markets by leveraging its vast regulatory power to shape foreign tech companies' and governments' data privacy policies. The EU's vast regulatory power is the primary source of its global influence and the defining feature of the European digital empire. Whereas the US exports its private power and China its infrastructure power, the EU's primary export in the digital sphere is, no doubt, its regulatory power—a form of power that neither foreign tech companies nor other governments, including the US and China, can fully evade. This regulatory power externalizes the European rights-driven regulatory model around the world, enabling the EU to play a leading role alongside the US and China in shaping the global digital economy.

This chapter explains why the EU—as opposed to the US, China, or any other jurisdiction—has become the primary source of legal norms that shape the digital economy across jurisdictions. It begins by examining this phenomenon in the domain of data privacy. The GDPR is often heralded as the prime example of an EU law with a global impact, affecting foreign companies, governments, and digital citizens alike. But the Brussels Effect can also be observed in other areas of the digital economy where the EU's influence has been, or is becoming, pertinent. The discussion reveals how the EU's antitrust rules and content regulations, including norms covering online hate speech and disinformation, can similarly be externalized through the Brussels Effect, and how artificial intelligence (AI) is likely to be the next frontier of the EU's global regulatory influence. These policy fields further entrench the global footprint of the European rights-driven regulatory model. After illustrating the global reach of the EU's regulatory power, the discussion turns to examine accusations of European "regulatory imperialism" and various other criticisms leveled against this form of global influence.

How the Brussels Effect Shapes Data Privacy Policies Around the World

Over the past decade, the EU has asserted itself as the most powerful regulator of the digital economy, giving it unique leverage to determine how digital technologies are developed and deployed around the world. The Brussels Effect explains how the EU often sets the rules and standards according to which products are built and how business is conducted, in Europe and beyond. This has allowed the EU to transform global markets in a variety of policy fields—both digital and nondigital—toward its norms. In the digital space, the EU's global regulatory influence can be observed in both tech companies' business practices and in foreign governments' legislative activities, each phenomenon being significant in globalizing the European rights-driven regulatory model in several policy domains. The EU's regulation of data privacy provides perhaps the most pertinent example to illustrate this, as shown below.

The Impact of the De Facto Brussels Effect on Companies' Data Privacy Policies

The Brussels Effect is a form of regulatory influence that stems from the combination of the EU's large consumer market, its powerful regulatory institutions that adopt stringent regulations, and market forces that steer tech companies toward uniform rules generated by the EU as the leading regulatory jurisdiction. Most fundamentally, the EU's global regulatory influence is rooted in its large internal market, consisting of nearly 450 million relatively wealthy consumers. Few multinational companies today can afford to forgo access to those consumers. But the *market size* alone does not guarantee global regulatory influence, or else we would also witness the "Beijing Effect," the "Delhi Effect," the "Tokyo Effect," and the "Washington

Effect." Instead, the jurisdiction must have the *regulatory capacity* as well as the political will to generate *stringent rules* in order to be a unilateral global regulator. Today, the EU alone often meets these additional two criteria across several policy fields. China still cannot match the experience and the expertise of the EU regulators, thus trailing the EU in regulatory capacity. The US has extensive regulatory capacity but has to date lacked the political will to deploy it, trusting its market-driven instincts that view government regulation with suspicion. In contrast, the EU is known for its affinity for rules and regulations, as well as the extensive bureaucratic machinery based in Brussels, which is ready and able to generate them. However, even the EU cannot externalize all of its rules. The Brussels Effect only occurs when the EU regulates *inelastic targets*, such as consumer markets, as opposed to capital. Unlike capital, consumers will not flee to less regulated jurisdictions, compromising the EU's regulatory clout. Finally, EU standards become global only when companies' production or conduct is *nondivisible*—in other words, when the benefits of adhering to a single regulatory standard exceed the benefits of taking advantage of more lax standards in other markets. These five conditions, taken together, underpin the Brussels Effect and explain why the EU today is the only digital power that effectively wields unilateral regulatory influence across global markets.

To further unpack these conditions, consider the first condition: market size. The country's market size is a well-understood proxy for its ability to exercise regulatory authority over foreign corporations and individuals. The larger the market, the more valuable it is for companies to access that market. As a result, large, lucrative consumer markets can better force regulatory compliance with their rules due to the costs associated with forgoing access to such a market. A small market lacks this kind of power. For example, if Sweden alone—without the benefit of being part of a larger EU market—enacted stringent data protection rules that Google did not want to comply with, Google could simply pull out of the Swedish market. But Google cannot as easily abandon the vast EU market and its nearly half a billion wealthy consumers. Of course, focusing on market size alone, several other jurisdictions could also qualify as potential global standard setters. The EU is the second-largest economy in the world, with a gross domestic product (GDP) of over $17.1 trillion.[11] It is also arguably the world's most significant consumer market. With a high proportion of affluent consumers, a large number of producers depend on their ability to supply products and services to those consumers. The EU's population is nearly 450 million, and its GDP per capita is $44,024.[12] The US is relatively more affluent, but its consumer market is smaller. China, on the other hand, has a larger consumer market but its consumers are relatively less affluent. However, all three jurisdictions could, in principle, become global regulators due to the large size of their domestic markets.

There is little doubt that the EU has become an indispensable market for many tech companies, including Meta, Google, Apple, and Amazon. While most tech companies do not report separate user statistics for the EU alone, Meta recorded 407 million monthly active users in Europe in the second quarter of 2022.[13] Google's share of the search market is over 90 percent in most EU member states.[14] For Google's YouTube, four EU member states alone account for more than 9 percent of the company's global users.[15] Europe was also the second biggest market for Apple products in the second quarter of 2022, contributing approximately 24 percent to the company's global revenue.[16] Amazon's overall market share in Europe is around 10 percent, but goes as high as 28 percent in countries such as Germany and the Netherlands.[17] Abandoning the EU market is therefore hardly a commercially viable option for these companies.

But a large consumer market alone does not make any state or jurisdiction a global rule setter. The state must also commit to building legal institutions and vesting them with the requisite regulatory capacity, allowing it to translate the power of its large market into tangible regulatory influence.[18] Over the past six decades, the EU has consciously built a vast regulatory state. The EU member states have gradually bestowed European institutions with more regulatory powers, which today are deployed by a distinctly competent bureaucracy with both a deep expertise in rule making and a strong commitment to the EU. The European Commission—the EU's executive arm and source of most EU regulatory initiatives—consists of highly educated, cosmopolitan bureaucrats who share a mission for European integration.[19] This shared mission often allows the Commission to forgo political infighting and articulate a relatively coherent vision for deployment of its competences, paving the way for extensive regulations. Another key feature of the EU's regulatory capacity is its extensive sanctioning authority, which induces compliance with EU regulations. As the ultimate form of sanction, the EU has the authority to withhold market access for products or services that fail to meet the EU's regulatory requirements. It further has the power to impose significant fines on companies that fail to obey its regulations. For example, EU member state data protection authorities may impose a fine amounting to 4 percent of the company's global revenue in cases of noncompliance with the GDPR.[20] To illustrate the potential scale of such fines using Google's 2021 revenue, a data protection fine could amount to $10.3 billion.

In contrast to the EU, China still lacks the capacity or expertise for the kind of rulemaking—including extraterritorial rulemaking—that emanates from EU institutions. While China is in the process of building regulatory institutions, it is likely to be a while before any Beijing Effect would replace the Brussels Effect. The US, on the other hand, would certainly have the requisite regulatory capacity for a Washington Effect. It lacks, however, a sustained political will to deploy this regulatory capacity. Where Europeans support high levels of government regulation, Americans, in most instances, prefer companies' self-regulation. There are several reasons that explain the EU's willingness to enact stringent regulations, as discussed in Chapter 3. These include Europeans' lower trust in markets and their relatively greater trust in governments generating fair and efficient outcomes by stepping in to govern the markets with regulation. The GDPR also reflects this European distrust in market forces. Europeans do not have the confidence that tech companies protect consumer data when this very data fuels the companies' revenue models. Regulation also serves an important political goal in the EU as it is deployed as a tool for European integration. If each of the twenty-seven individual member states adopted a different national standard to safeguard personal data, the single market could not function efficiently, as companies would face a different regulatory environment in each country. Thus, every directive and regulation—including the GDPR—typically has a dual purpose: it not only serves to advance a specific policy goal, such as a fundamental right to privacy, but it also contributes toward an integrated single market where divergent national regulations are aligned to ensure a free movement of data across the EU. This integration goal has provided a vital impetus for regulation.

The EU's large internal market, coupled with its extensive regulatory capacity and the preference for stringent regulations, explains how it has become a global regulatory superpower. But even the EU cannot export all its regulations. The Brussels Effect only takes place when the EU regulates inelastic regulatory targets—that is, targets that cannot be moved to another jurisdiction in order to circumvent EU rules. In the domain of data privacy, for example, tech companies cannot circumvent the GDPR by moving their data processing activities outside the EU. The GDPR protects European data subjects regardless of where the data processing takes place, which makes the regulation both extraterritorial and highly inelastic. This feature, in part, explains why the GDPR has been so difficult for tech companies to escape, paving way for its adoption as a global standard by these companies.

The Brussels Effect is also able to shape multinational companies' business practices because these companies prefer to follow a uniform data privacy policy across their global conduct. In choosing which standard to follow globally, companies typically opt for the GDPR as the most stringent regulation that allows them to maintain compliance everywhere.[21] In other words, tech companies choose standardization as opposed to customization, extending the EU rule across all jurisdictions in which they operate. For example, while data privacy regulations themselves may differ from jurisdiction to jurisdiction, tech companies often streamline their global data management systems to reduce the cost of complying with multiple regulatory regimes.[22] The benefits associated with uniform standards explain why many multinational companies today have only one company-wide privacy policy, which is drafted to conform to the EU's stringent GDPR.[23]

The reasons why companies often treat data protection as nondivisible and hence opt for uniformity over customization are manifold. Historically, it has been technologically difficult for companies to separate data involving European and non-European citizens.[24] Today, it may often be feasible, but still too costly, to create special websites or data processing practices for the EU alone.[25] As a result, this technical or economic nondivisibility has prompted several US tech companies to opt for a uniform privacy policy.[26] Reputational and brand-related reasons may also push tech companies toward uniformity, as they find it hard to deny privacy protections for some users while allowing them for others in another jurisdiction. For instance, Sonos, a wireless speaker company in California, extended the GDPR protections to its customers worldwide, citing its belief that "all Sonos owners should have the right to these protections, [hence] we are implementing these updates globally."[27] One of the most powerful drivers for nondivisibility has been the GDPR's requirement for the companies to engage in "privacy by design" and "privacy by default" in developing their products.[28] These concepts oblige companies to design their products and services to comply with GDPR-consistent privacy rules by default, minimizing data collection through privacy-conscious design choices at the outset. As mentioned earlier, large tech giants such as Apple and Microsoft follow this concept,[29] further entrenching the Brussels Effect through their uniform product design.

Of course, the Brussels Effect cannot be observed every time and everywhere. At times, tech companies have the incentive to introduce divisibility and limit their policy changes to the EU only. For example, while Meta was ordered to stop collecting WhatsApp data in Europe after its acquisition of WhatsApp, the company continues to combine the data acquired through both platforms in the United States.[30] Meta also responded to the GDPR by changing its corporate structure. While the company chose to extend the GDPR protections to all its users worldwide, it proceeded to limit its legal liability by moving its users in Asia, Africa, Australia, and the Middle East away from the company's Irish corporate structure, placing them under its US legal structure instead.[31] This change was presumably motivated by Meta's desire to limit non-European users' ability to seek remedies under the GDPR. In addition, data localization requirements in some jurisdictions may limit companies' ability to opt for a single global privacy policy. Data localization forces companies to choose whether to create separate operations for a certain market, or cease operating there. Currently, for example, Russia and China require data localization.[32] Russia blocked the Russian operations of Microsoft's professional networking site, LinkedIn, due to the company's refusal to locate the data there.[33] In contrast to the strategy adopted in Russia, LinkedIn gave into China's demands for data localization for a long time and continued to operate there,[34] before finally pulling out in October 2021.[35] Data localization provisions are also on the rise globally. India has indicated its intention to include such a requirement in a data privacy legislation that the government is preparing.[36] Data localization laws may further limit the ability of companies to rely on EU privacy rules as their sole global policy.

Ultimately, whether the Brussels Effect allows the EU to transform the world toward its norms simply by regulating the European single market is an empirical question. In recent years, there has been a growing scholarly effort to measure the Brussels Effect. Some of this early work does, indeed, offer empirical support for the phenomenon. For example, a 2021 study on whether the GDPR affected multinational companies' data protection practices toward Canadian citizens shows that the GDPR did enhance the rights these companies extended to Canadians, even though they were not formally protected under the GDPR. The authors attribute this to the Brussels Effect.[37] Another 2019 study focusing on privacy policies shown to US consumers in the wake of the GDPR suggests that US consumer-facing privacy policies, on average, became longer and included more of the elements introduced by the GDPR.[38] Similarly, a 2021 study tracking over 110,000 websites over eighteen months shows that, after the GDPR became effective, websites reduced their connections to web technology providers in an effort to ensure GDPR compliance. This effect also holds for websites catering to non-EU audiences that are not formally bound by the GDPR.[39]

These examples reveal that while the Brussels Effect may be incomplete, it has become a powerful force in transmitting European data protection norms across the global marketplace. Like the exportation of the American market-driven regulatory model through US tech companies' private power or the exportation of the Chinese state-driven regulatory model through Chinese companies' infrastructure power, the EU also relies on private companies to export its regulatory model. However, the EU is different in that it does not need a strong domestic tech industry to exert global influence over digital policy. Instead, unlike the other digital empires, the EU is able to harness the power of *foreign* companies—including American tech companies—to export its rights-driven model through the Brussels Effect. Thus, it is often US tech companies that externalize the European market-driven regulatory model and help the EU to counter the global influence of the American market-driven regulatory model. What makes the Brussels Effect so potent is also the ease with which the EU has been able to expand its influence. All the EU has had to do is to regulate the single market; market forces and the business interests of the global companies then globalize the European data protection rules, giving the EU the kind of influence that few European bureaucrats dreamed of when setting themselves to the task to protect the data of Europeans.

The Impact of the De Jure Brussels Effect on Countries' Data Privacy Policies

In addition to influencing the worldwide market conduct of global companies, European digital regulations are also shaping the regulatory frameworks adopted by foreign governments, producing a de jure Brussels Effect. This phenomenon of legislative copying is nowhere more evident than in the domain of data privacy. It is driven by multiple reasons, including the EU's inherent ability to draft regulations that are designed to work in various different jurisdictions. After all, they reflect a compromise among twenty-seven different countries. In addition, all EU regulations, preparatory materials, and subsequent court interpretations are published in over twenty languages—including French, Portuguese, and Spanish in addition to English—which facilitate their copying in particular across Africa and Latin America.

But often the de jure Brussels Effect builds directly on the de facto Brussels Effect: after multinational companies have adjusted their global conduct to conform to EU rules, they have an incentive to lobby for EU-style regulations in their home jurisdictions. This ensures that they are not at a disadvantage when competing domestically against companies that do not export to the EU, and therefore have no incentive to comply with costly EU regulations. This dynamic was the focus of David Vogel's "California effect" theory, which showed how environmental regulations shift in the direction of the most stringent regulatory jurisdiction (i.e., California) as corporations subject to those stringent Californian rules advocated for similarly stringent rules in other US states.[40] In the global context, this same phenomenon can be observed where rules generated in Brussels are gradually adopted by governments around the world due to growing domestic corporate support for those rules.

The US market illustrates this dynamic with respect to data privacy, revealing how US tech companies affected by the EU's data privacy regulations subsequently become advocates of similar regulations in their home markets. In October 2018, Apple CEO Tim Cook urged the US government to adopt a comprehensive, federal, EU-style privacy law, noting that it was "time for the rest of the world" to follow the EU's lead.[41] Mark Zuckerberg, Meta's founder and chief executive, similarly called for the adoption of GDPR-style laws worldwide, writing in the *Washington Post* that "it would be good for the Internet if more countries adopted regulation such as GDPR as a common framework. New privacy regulation in the United States and around the world should build on the protections GDPR provides."[42] Meta's business model is more reliant on data collection than Apple's, making the stakes even higher for Meta and Zuckerberg's statement therefore all the more striking. Another reason these tech companies endorsed a federal US privacy law was the decision by California in 2018 to adopt its own variant of the GDPR, the California Consumer Privacy Act (CCPA), which was subsequently expanded (and further aligned with the GDPR) in 2020 with the California Privacy Rights Act (CPRA).[43] Tech companies resent the emergence of a complex patchwork of potentially conflicting state privacy laws, which complicates their compliance efforts.[44] When lobbying for a federal law, the GDPR presents an attractive template for companies such as Apple and Meta, given that these companies have already adjusted their business practices to conform to the EU regulation.

Another powerful reason for the proliferation of EU-style privacy regimes around the world is countries' desire to obtain an "adequacy decision" from the EU.[45] An adequacy decision refers to a formal determination by the EU that a country's data protection standards provide sufficient protections to safely allow data transfers from the EU to that country. The finding of adequacy opens the data flows between the EU and the country whose laws are deemed adequate, creating significant business opportunities for any foreign company active in Europe. To date, the EU has recognized fourteen non-EU countries as having adequate data protection laws. This includes Andorra, Argentina, Canada (for commercial organizations only), the Faroe Islands, Guernsey, Israel, the Isle of Man, Japan, Jersey, New Zealand, South Korea, Switzerland, the United Kingdom, and Uruguay.[46] Notably, the US does not benefit from an adequacy decision, and the legality of the data flows between the US and EU has been a subject of numerous legal disputes, as discussed in Chapter 6. Argentina obtained an adequacy decision in 2003 based on its data protection law from the year 2000, which closely resembles Spain's 1992 data privacy law and the GDPR's predecessor, the EU's 1995 data protection directive.[47] In 2016, Argentina established a working group to study legislative reforms that may be necessary to retain Argentina's adequacy status in the post-GDPR legal environment, showing the country's willingness to keep updating its laws to remain in conformity with the EU.[48] The EU and Japan reached an agreement on adequacy in 2018, which led each country to recognize the other's data protection systems as equivalent.[49] Before this agreement, Japan had amended its Act on the Protection of Personal Information in 2015,[50] in part to bring it in line with the GDPR.

Australia is in the process of reviewing its 1988 Privacy Act, which is expected to bring its legislation further into line with the GDPR.[51] Australia's law reform draws on a recent Digital Platforms Inquiry (DPI),[52] conducted by the Australian Competition and Consumer Commission (ACCC) at the direction of the government. The 2019 DPI Final Report contains a range of recommendations, including proposals regarding data privacy reform. It recommends that the Australian government will consider seeking to obtain an adequacy decision from the EU,[53] along with outlining several recommendations that would incorporate GDPR-inspired concepts into Australian law. For example, the ACCC recommends "strengthening consent requirements in a way that broadly aligns with the GDPR."[54] Another recommendation states that consumers ought to be able to require the erasure of their personal information, which "broadly aligns with the principles outlined in Article 17 of the GDPR"—that is, the GDPR's "right to be forgotten" provision.[55] The ACCC moreover calls for updating the definition of "personal information" in the Privacy Act, in part to align it with the way "personal data" is defined in the GDPR.[56] In general, while the DPI report does not propose the adoption of the GDPR wholesale, it endorses a view that "closer alignment of Australian privacy regulations with the GDPR's higher standards of protection could significantly increase the effectiveness of Australian privacy law and increase the accountability of entities processing the personal information of Australian consumers."[57] The Australian government has already expressed preliminary support for most of the privacy-related recommendations of the DPI Final Report.[58]

China adopted a Personal Information Protection Law (PIPL) in 2021[59] that includes many provisions that closely resemble the GDPR, illustrating how the EU has been able to export its rights-driven agenda via the Brussels Effect even to countries that embrace a different vision for the digital economy. Like the GDPR, the PIPL applies extraterritorially, defines personal data broadly, and requires covered entities to secure a legal basis for processing personal data.[60] It also replicates the GDPR's key principles for data processing, including lawfulness, transparency, purpose limitation, accuracy, security, and data minimization.[61] Although the law clearly reveals the EU's regulatory influence, at the same time, the law also reflects China's digital authoritarian tendencies: while the Chinese data protection law distinguishes several categories of "sensitive" personal data as requiring stronger protections, it fails to include some key categories defined as sensitive under the GDPR, including union membership, political opinions, and data related to sexual preferences.[62] The PIPL further contains a public security exception,[63] and expressly contemplates mass public surveillance.[64] Moreover, it includes strong data localization requirements, which enhances state control by requiring Chinese data to be processed and stored locally in China.[65] Despite these features that can be traced to China's own state-driven regulatory model, many aspects of the law described above indicate that China's data privacy law was also—partially but nontrivially—influenced by the EU's GDPR.

Several other countries across Asia, Africa, and Latin America have also emulated many features of the GDPR, even while retaining some distinct national features that depart from the text or spirit of the GDPR. India's draft Personal Data Protection Bill (PDPB), unveiled in 2019 yet withdrawn in 2022, was clearly inspired by the GDPR. Like the GDPR, the PDPB protected citizens' privacy rights by requiring covered entities to secure a legal basis for processing personal data,[66] and by distinguishing categories of "sensitive data" that are afforded stronger protection.[67] However, there were certain distinct features of the proposed Indian law that departed from the GDPR. For example, the bill did not include a right to be forgotten provision or grant rights against automated decision-making.[68] Privacy advocates also expressed concerns about the relatively weak protections against government surveillance.[69] In another departure from the GDPR, the PDPB contained provisions on "critical data," which cannot be taken out of the country, effectively requiring data localization in instances the government deemed appropriate.[70] In response to criticism from the industry and privacy advocates alike, the Indian government withdrew the bill in 2022, yet promised that "a new bill will be presented for public consultation" on data privacy.[71]

Africa's largest economy, Nigeria, has also emulated the GDPR in its privacy legislation. Following the passage of the GDPR, the Nigerian government issued the Nigerian Data Protection Regulation in 2019.[72] The law tracks closely the GDPR, often using even identical phrasing.[73] The law's enforcement provisions have been criticized, which has led the Nigerian government to consider reforming the law.[74] Some of the proposed changes, such as the establishment of a Data Protection Commission or the inclusion of a right against automated decision-making, would further align the Nigerian law with the GDPR. However, a broadly worded "public morality" and "public interest" exceptions to data privacy risk a deviation from the GDPR's strong rights-protection norm.[75] Finally, to highlight another example from Latin America—in addition to Argentina that was mentioned earlier—Brazil adopted a general data protection law in 2018.[76] The Brazilian Lei Geral de Proteção de Dados Pessoais resembles the GDPR, emulating its broad definition of personal data, as well as including the GDPR's six legal bases among those that justify data processing.[77]

Given this global trend toward adopting GDPR-style data protection laws, the US stands out in not having a comprehensive federal data privacy regime in place. In the face of inaction by the US Congress, individual states—led by California—are forging ahead with their own state-level data protection laws.[78] California's privacy law CCPA took effect in 2020, and its successor, the CPRA, will fully supersede the CCPA in 2023. Several of the CCPA provisions resemble the GDPR, including data collectors' mandate to provide notice of the categories of personal information collected,[79] the right for individuals to know all data that businesses collect on them,[80] and the right for citizens to request data pertaining to them to be deleted—the so-called right to be forgotten provision.[81] The CPRA aligns California's data protection law even more closely with the EU's GDPR, including by imposing a more stringent purpose limitation for data processing and limiting data retention.[82] However, both versions of the California laws remain more limited in scope than the GDPR in that they protect personal data vis-à-vis businesses whereas the GDPR applies to both public or private entities, as long as these entities qualify as "controllers" or "processors" of data under the GDPR.

Several other US states have followed California in introducing statewide data privacy laws, including Florida, Massachusetts, New Jersey, New York, Texas, and Virginia.[83] While most of these states closely emulate California's law, they also borrow concepts directly from the GDPR. For example, Virginia's Consumer Data Protection Act, as well as laws introduced in New Jersey and Minnesota, emulate the GDPR by distinguishing between data "controllers" and data "processors."[84] In New Jersey, legislators invoked the GDPR's fundamental principle that all data processing must be lawful, fair, and transparent.[85] A bill proposed in New York adopts almost word-for-word the GDPR's requirement that individuals should not be subject to a decision based solely on automated profiling that produces "legal effects."[86] These examples suggest that while the de jure Brussels Effect may fall short in reaching the US Congress, the European privacy protections have already landed on US shores, even if by way of legislative action at the state level.

The Impact of the Brussels Effect Beyond Privacy

The GDPR is the most prominent—but not the only—example of the EU's digital regulations having a global impact. The EU has also shaped global norms on content moderation, including hate speech and disinformation, as well as antitrust, both of which highlight how the European rights-driven regulatory model is able to influence the broader digital economy in ways that neither the US nor China are currently able to do. More recently, the EU is leading the way in regulating AI, which may also influence tech companies' development of AI applications as well as governments' AI legislation around the world. To illustrate this global regulatory power, the discussion below looks at several examples from Australia, Japan, South Korea, and the United Kingdom, jurisdictions that have often been closely associated with the US in their economic policies, political alliances, and ideological commitments. However, as the examples discussed below make clear, these jurisdictions turn more frequently to the European rights-driven model for inspiration in regulating their digital economies.

Content Moderation

The EU's regulation of online content through its codes on hate speech and disinformation, discussed earlier in Chapter 3, is shaping the global policies of tech companies such as Facebook, Twitter, and YouTube. When it comes to hate speech, these tech companies often follow the European definition of hate speech and ban content that would be protected under the First Amendment of the US Constitution. Whereas the US Constitution seeks to protect all ideas—even hateful ones—and permits the curtailment of inflammatory speech only when that speech is likely to provoke an imminent violent response,[87] the EU bans speech that incites hatred as such.[88] YouTube is among the US companies that have opted for the EU's definition of hate speech, defining hate speech in its global terms of service as "content promoting violence or hatred against individuals or groups," before listing various common attributes or categories for such prohibited hatred.[89] Thus, the company not only bans hate speech that incites violence, but also speech that incites hatred against individuals or certain groups. YouTube's policy illustrates how a leading US tech company helps the EU to shape the global digital economy—moving it away from the American regulatory model's steadfast commitment to free speech toward the European rights-driven regulatory model.

In moderating online content, tech companies' international user base presents them with a choice: they can either adopt universal rules that apply across all the markets where they operate, or they can choose country-specific rules tailored to each market.[90] A review of the leading tech companies' terms of service reveal that they tend to adopt the same definition globally after signing the EU's Hate Speech Code. Typically, the European-style prohibitions are reflected in these companies' *global* terms of service, thereby applying to their operations worldwide, even though the European Commission explicitly clarifies that its Hate Speech Code only regulates the companies' conduct in Europe.[91] Meta and Google adopted universal rules from early on. Twitter used to follow country-specific rules, but six months after signing the EU's Hate Speech Code, it moved toward adopting a universal standard, prohibiting "hateful conduct" in its global terms of service.

In principle, tech companies could customize their content moderation for each country by using geoblocking technology.[92] Geoblocking separates internet users according to their geography based on the location of the user's internet protocol (IP) address.[93] At times, tech companies deploy this technique as a way to tailor content moderation policies to some jurisdictions only. For example, Apple complied with Russian demands to show Crimea as Russian territory on Apple Maps and its Weather app when viewed from Russia during 2019–2022. However, when those apps were viewed outside of Russia, Crimea was not shown as part of any country. After the Russian invasion of Ukraine in 2022, Crimea is displayed as part of Ukrainian territory when viewed from outside of Russia.[94] Similarly, to avoid being banned in Turkey, Meta removed Turkish users' access to certain pages considered insulting to the Prophet Muhammad, though the content remained available elsewhere.[95] Geoblocking can also be implemented through country-specific domain names. For example, because Germany and France have made it illegal to deny the Holocaust, the internet user cannot find Holocaust-denial sites on German and French Google default search engines Google.de and Google.fr, even when those sites would be available on Google.com.[96]

In practice, tech companies often forgo geoblocking and follow globally uniform rules for reasons that can range from technical or economic to social and cultural. For example, it can at times be difficult to accurately isolate European-only data. Rachel Whetstone, Google's former director of Global Communications and Public Affairs in the Europe, the Middle East, and Africa region, acknowledged that legal differences between how governments regulate freedom of expression "create real technical challenges, for example, about how you restrict one type of content in one country but not another."[97] Further, internet users can circumvent geoblocking by changing the location settings of their accounts,[98] or by using encryption technology that allows them to hide their locations online, making it sometimes technically impossible to comply with jurisdiction-specific rules without removing content worldwide.

Today, tech companies are likely to be able to resolve many of these technical challenges, yet various practical compliance considerations often still push tech companies toward more uniform content moderation policies. In operationalizing their terms of service and community guidelines to police hate speech, tech companies have to translate them into detailed internal policy guidelines. These guidelines contain highly specific definitions, which hundreds of thousands of employees and contractors around the world must follow when reviewing the posts in a strict twenty-four-hour timeline. If all these content moderators applied different rules based on country-specific guidelines, their monitoring would become unwieldy, error-prone, and costly.[99] Various social or cultural brand-related reasons further incentivize these companies to maintain uniform standards. Platforms such as Meta view themselves as global operators fostering conversations across jurisdictional boundaries. Geoblocking directly undermines the company's social network model by hiding portions of the exchange from some participants.[100] Extensive geoblocking would be contrary to Meta's goal of ensuring that "people are able to communicate in a borderless way"[101] and that there is only "one Facebook."[102] Uniform content moderation rules, therefore, better support its core business model and explain why the company is often unwilling to remove speech in one region and not in another.

The challenges associated with isolating European-only data have led to court orders requiring tech companies to remove illegal content globally.[103] In October 2019, the European Court of Justice (CJEU) issued a ruling in a case relating to Meta's responsibility to remove hate speech postings on its platform.[104] The case stems from a complaint by a former leader of the Austrian Green Party, Eva Glawischnig, who had requested Meta remove what she considered defamatory postings implicating her on Facebook. The CJEU was asked to rule on whether Meta must remove access to the relevant content not just locally but globally, and whether this obligation extends to similar (but not identical) hate speech postings against the same person. In its ruling, the CJEU found that Meta can be ordered to identify all postings that are identical *or equivalent* to a defamatory comment that has been found illegal. The CJEU noted that the EU law does not have a territorial limitation, which means that it "does not preclude such an injunction from producing effects worldwide."[105] This ruling—which departs from a more cautious approach the CJEU has taken with respect to the obligation to remove content globally under the EU's "right to be forgotten" rule[106]—paves the way for the European hate speech norm to migrate across jurisdictions.

The EU's Digital Services Act (DSA), which was adopted in 2022, may further increase the EU's ability to shape tech companies' global business practices, and regulate the global digital economy in ways that the US and China are not able to do.[107] The DSA will not replace the EU's disinformation or hate speech codes, which continue to provide substantive benchmarks for what kind of speech must be removed. But it will provide binding procedural obligations that will require platforms to expeditiously remove or disable access to prohibited content. The DSA will also enhance platforms' transparency and accountability obligations, for example, by forcing them to disclose to the user why the user sees a certain advertisement or who is behind the advertisement. It also bans certain practices, including targeted advertising to minors or to other individuals based on some protected categories such as race, ethnicity, religion, political affiliation, or sexual orientation.[108] Very large online platforms will have to comply with additional obligations relating to annual risk assessments and external auditing, as well as share data with researchers and authorities on their content moderation decisions.[109] This enhanced access to platforms' data allows regulators to better verify platforms' claims regarding how their algorithms work and how they moderate content online.

There are several pathways for these obligations to extend beyond Europe. For example, in granting its European users the opportunity to influence and modify the content these users are shown on its platform, Meta will need to develop a new way of interacting with users in Europe, including adjusting its settings to accommodate greater user autonomy. For the same technical, economic, and reputational reasons that the company decided not to limit its new GDPR-induced privacy settings for Europe only, it may now extend these enhanced user rights around the world. In today's climate, when the company's every decision is publicly scrutinized, Meta will have an even harder time justifying a decision that extends lesser rights for non-European users—even if the company found it to be technically or economically feasible to make these settings country-specific. For example, as Meta will no longer be permitted to deliver targeted advertising to European teenagers on Instagram, it may struggle to justify its continuation of that same practice in the US or elsewhere. Such a strategy may lead to allegations that the company is prepared to protect European minors—but not American or other minors—from well-documented exploitation of these minors' vulnerabilities toward commercial ends. In addition, authorities' and researchers' increased access to information about platforms' business models and algorithms under the DSA will shed light on these platforms' global practices, to the extent that these companies do not develop and deploy separate algorithms for Europe. The results of those investigations will be made public worldwide, enhancing transparency and accountability in other markets as well. And, to the extent the DSA will successfully force large platforms to better prepare for systemic risks, such as election interference, these additional investments in risk mitigation measures are likely to affect these companies' global compliance and risk management strategies.

The DSA may also provide a template for other governments to pursue regulation in this space, leading to the de jure Brussels Effect, and underscoring the EU's ability to influence foreign legislation in this domain. Already, the EU's disinformation and hate speech codes have inspired foreign lawmakers, prompting legislative reforms. For example, Australia has closely emulated the EU's disinformation code, publishing an Australian Code of Practice on Disinformation and Misinformation in February 2021.[110] According to the drafters of the Code, it was developed while "drawing learnings from a similar code in the European Union."[111] The need for such a code in Australia was first acknowledged in the Digital Platforms Inquiry that was mentioned earlier.[112] In the DPI Final Report, the ACCC proposed that the code "would apply to 'disinformation' using a definition of this concept based on existing internationally-accepted models such as the EU Code of Practice On Disinformation."[113] In responding to the DPI Final Report, the Australian government affirmed this view, noting that the voluntary codes "will be informed by learnings of international examples, such as the European Union *Code of Practice on Disinformation*."[114] Tech companies Adobe, Apple, Google, Meta, Microsoft, Redbubble, TikTok, and Twitter have all signed the Australian Code of Practice on Disinformation and Misinformation, thereby committing to EU-inspired content moderation practices in Australia as well.[115]

Although the Australian and EU Codes reflect some differences, the extent of similarities highlights the impact the EU's regulatory policy has had on Australia. Among the differences is the Australian Code's application to both disinformation and misinformation,[116] while the EU Code only applies to disinformation, which requires intent to deceive the person receiving the information. The Australian Code also has a higher threshold for "harm" in that it requires platforms to intervene in instances where online content poses an "imminent and serious threat" to democratic, political, and policymaking processes, or public goods,[117] whereas the EU Code bans disinformation, which "may cause public harm."[118] In explaining the departure from the EU standard, the ACCC noted that a lower threshold might be appropriate in the EU, "in which multiple countries have already experienced harms including social media interference, and campaigns of disinformation and malinformation

from external countries seeking to affect domestic political processes."[119] The
Australian Communication and Media Authority will oversee the implementation of the Code. The Authority has stated that it anticipates greater compliance with the Code because of the EU's earlier efforts in this domain, noting
how "it would expect platforms will have learnt from the EU code experience
by including meaningful commitments to achieve outcomes that are carefully
defined and clearly linked to the objectives of the code."[120]

Another example of how the EU's rights-driven regulatory model resonates
abroad can be seen in the United Kingdom, which has taken a highly interventionist stand toward content moderation in its Online Safety Bill (OSB),
which the government published in May 2021, five months after the European
Commission had unveiled its proposal for the DSA.[121] In 2022, the OSB was
pending before the UK Parliament. It has a broad scope, regulating both illegal
as well as "legal but harmful" content, including hate speech, terrorist content,
fraud, and child sexual abuse. The UK government does not hide its ambition
about the bill, noting how the "Bill aim[s] to create the most progressive, fair and
accountable system in the world."[122] Rather than the UK copying the EU, or the
other way around, the parallel legislative efforts in the EU and the UK have been
marked by dialogue and close cooperation in pursuit of largely similar aims.[123]
The UK's bill has many similar features to the DSA, including various reporting
requirements, risk assessments, and procedural rights of appeal regarding content that is removed. It also strives to balance those prohibitions with strong
protections for freedom of expression.[124] On some dimensions, the OSB has an
even wider scope than the DSA. It prohibits content, such as romance scams,
where victims are tricked into sending money or personal information to a
fraudster after being made to believe that they are engaged in a relationship
through an online dating service. The bill further prohibits fraud, such as user-
generated fake investment opportunities posted by users on Facebook groups
or sent via Snapchat.[125] The OSB envisions heavy penalties, including imprisonment for tech executives under limited conditions, in addition to the more traditional remedies such as fines or blocking access to the site containing banned
content.[126] The UK's regulatory approach thus contributes to a growing trend in
many parts of the world to move away from the US-style market-driven regulatory model toward the EU-inspired rights-driven regulatory model in regulating
content moderation.

Antitrust Regulation

The EU has been at the forefront of deploying antitrust laws against the largest
tech companies, as discussed in Chapter 3. These enforcement decisions

have had a global impact in several ways. In some instances, the European Commission decisions have led tech companies to adopt the EU's remedies globally, generating a de facto Brussels Effect. In other cases, foreign antitrust authorities have followed the EU's lead and opened their own investigations against these companies on the same or similar grounds. Most recently, legislators and antitrust enforcers around the word are closely watching the EU roll out its Digital Markets Act (DMA), which can provide them with a template for introducing similar regulations at home, reinforcing the de jure Brussels Effect.

Whenever an antitrust remedy is imposed on a tech company, the company needs to decide whether to implement the remedy locally or globally. Only when the company opts for a global implementation does the Brussels Effect take place. The 2004 Microsoft case provides an early illustration of this concept.[127] After finding that Microsoft had abused its dominant position by illegally withholding interoperability information—that is, information necessary to exchange and mutually use information related to software products for work group server operating systems—from its rivals, the European Commission ordered the company to disclose that information. While the disclosure order was limited to Europe, Microsoft implemented it on a worldwide basis in order to maintain a single, worldwide licensing agreement. This is a classic illustration of a de facto Brussels Effect. It can be contrasted with the 2017 *Google Shopping* decision,[128] which failed to produce a Brussels Effect. In that case, Google was found to have violated EU antitrust rules by giving preference to Google's own shopping service over other similar online comparison-shopping platforms. The Commission fined Google and ordered the company to remove any algorithmic bias that favored its own platform—a decision that was upheld in 2021 by the EU's General Court.[129] To comply with the decision, Google established a separate business unit to operate Google Shopping in the EU, confining its compliance only to the EU market.[130] With the help of geolocation techniques, Google managed to ringfence its European shopping business and ensure that the users who access Google sites using a non-European IP address will continue to be governed by its previous business model for Google shopping.[131] Although dividing its operations across different markets this way can be appealing for the tech company in that it allows it to evade the Brussels Effect, this option is not always available either for economic, technological, or reputational reasons.

At times, tech companies have the incentive to extend their remedies worldwide because they know that should they fail to do so, foreign antitrust enforcers can open their own investigations and demand similar remedies in their respective jurisdictions. For example, the Australian Digital Platform

Inquiry emphasized the importance of consumer choice in selecting a default internet browser, recommending that "Google should provide Australian users of Android devices with the same options as those being rolled out to existing Android users in Europe," while adding that "If Google does not introduce similar options for Australian Android users by six months from the date of the Report, the ACCC will submit to the Government that it should consider compelling Google to offer this choice."[32] In its response to the DPI Final Report, the Australian government urged the ACCC to "monitor and report back on Google's rollout of options in Europe to allow consumers to choose their default internet browser and search engine before making a commitment to rollout in Australia."[33]

Antitrust regulators around the world are increasingly turning their sights on the tech industry, following the European Commission's lead in challenging the business practices of leading US tech companies. At times, but likely not always, these investigations can amount to so-called copycat litigation, where foreign agencies free ride on the EU's investigations, leveraging fines or imposing other remedies domestically without the need to develop their own competitive assessment. This can be valuable as antitrust investigations take time, technical expertise, and often substantial resources. Alternatively, an ongoing EU investigation or a negative EU decision against a tech company also generates an informational benefit, alerting the foreign agencies of possible anti-competitive conduct, and giving them an impetus to act. In practice, it can be difficult to show whether any given foreign antitrust case is prompted by an existing EU challenge or driven by independent concerns and investigations unrelated to the EU probe. However, it is likely that any foreign antitrust agency looking to go after a leading tech company is paying close attention to what the most active—and at this point, most experienced—regulator is doing.

For example, the EU's multiple investigations into Google since 2010 have paved the way for agencies in other jurisdictions to act. These EU investigations have received prominent attention worldwide, and several jurisdictions have pursued very similar cases against Google. To take one example, the European Commission's case relating to Google's operating system Android, which led to a $5 billion fine in the EU in 2018, has likely inspired several jurisdictions to act, including Russia, Brazil, Turkey, South Korea, and Japan. In February 2015, the Russian Antimonopoly Service (FAS) launched an investigation into Google's business practices regarding Android. The investigation followed a complaint of Google's biggest local competitor, search engine Yandex NV, which had also been one of the complainants in the EU's investigation against Google. At the time FAS opened its investigation, it was public knowledge that the Commission was investigating Google's practices regarding Android and preparing to initiate formal proceedings.[134] Turkey similarly opened an investigation into Android following a complaint lodged by Yandex, and fined Google shortly after the EU had issued its decision against Google.[135] Given the timing and the content of the decision, commentators suggested that "the TCA's decision shows once again that the TCA is still following the European Commission's footsteps to a significant extent in evaluating anti-competitiveness of a behavior, especially in complex matters."[136] Brazil's on-going investigation into Google's Android, which opened a year after the EU's decision,[137] is also likely inspired by the EU. After the Commission handed down its decision, the Brazilian antitrust agency CADE's then-President, Alexandre Barreto, indicated that "what we are doing now is analyzing the de-cision of the European Union to determine if we have grounds to act here."[138] To add to this increasingly global effort to restrict Google's anticompetitive practices following the EU's lead, Japan opened its investigation of Google in a case relating to Android in 2021,[139] and Korea fined Google in 2021 for abusing market dominance in the Android operating system market.[140]

Brazil, Japan, Russia, South Korea, and Turkey are not alone in joining the EU's quest to pursue antitrust enforcement against the leading tech companies. According to data collected by *The Information*, Apple, Amazon, Google, and Meta were facing over seventy antitrust investigations around the world in the summer of 2021.[141] Interestingly, over fifty of those cases were brought in the past two years, showing the growing momentum that has recently been building around the world as countries move away from the American market-driven model and embrace—if not directly imitate—the European rights-driven model. In addition to the EU and several individual EU member states (France, Germany, Italy, the Netherlands, and Spain), these four companies were facing antitrust investigations in Australia, Brazil, Canada, Israel, India, Japan, Russia, South Korea, Turkey, the UK, and the US. Google is the most common target, with twenty-five probes pending across fourteen jurisdictions, and fines already imposed by France, Italy, and Turkey—in addition to the nearly $10 billion in fines imposed by the EU. Apple is the second most common target, facing a total of nineteen antitrust probes across thirteen jurisdictions, followed by Meta (fourteen probes in seven jurisdictions), and Amazon (twelve probes in six jurisdictions).

In addition to inspiring other countries to ratchet up their enforcement against tech companies, the EU is now showing the way for governments looking to strengthen their regulatory instruments to better contain large tech companies' market power and the harmful conduct associated with that power. The EU's pathbreaking DMA, which was adopted in 2022, is being closely watched around the world, with several governments introducing or considering similar regulations. The UK's Competition and Markets Authority, led by its newly established Digital Markets Unit, issued its own regulatory proposal in December 2020—a week prior to the Commission's unveiling of the DMA.[142] The envisioned UK regulatory regime is very similar to the DMA. It is also a legally binding *ex ante* regulatory regime, which applies to the largest digital companies with "substantial" and "entrenched" market power that gives these companies a "strategic market status." Both EU and UK regulations target similar concerns, containing obligations such as interoperability requirements and enhanced consumer choice over default settings. They are also backed by similar penalties, including fines or behavioral or structural remedies. The main difference is that the UK regime tailors the obligations for each tech company—for example, Meta may face different obligations than Amazon—whereas the EU's DMA will apply the same rules of conduct for all digital "gatekeepers" even if the actual implementation of the DMA will result in more tailored obligations. The UK's regime also contains additional obligations for notifying mergers, which were not included in the DMA, suggesting that the UK may in some ways be taking the rights-driven, consumer-centric regulatory model even further than the EU.

Japan is another major US ally that is now gradually moving away from the American market-driven model toward the European rights-driven model. Over the last few years, Japan has initiated legislative reforms to regulate large digital platforms, albeit with a considerably lighter touch than the EU. In May 2020, the National Diet, the Japanese legislator, passed the Act on Improvement of Transparency and Fairness in Trading on Specified Digital Platforms (TFDPA), which entered into force in February 2021.[143] The law currently targets online mall operators and app store operators, yet its scope is expected to widen to cover digital advertising companies. Apple, Amazon, and Google have already been designated as "specific digital platform providers" that fall within the scope of the law.[144] The law imposes new disclosure obligations on these designated tech companies,[145] and requires them to conduct self-assessments and submit annual reports to the Japanese Ministry of Economy, Trade and Industry (METI) to further enhance transparency and accountability.[146] This self-reporting may lead to an antitrust investigation by the Japan Fair Trade Commission if METI finds that the designated platform impairs transparency and fairness.[147] The TFDPA reflects a coregulation approach, which combines the European rights-driven regulatory model in terms of the substantive goals it embodies, and the American market-driven model in trusting the companies to implement those goals.[148] The TFDPA falls short of the DMA, yet resembles the EU's 2019 Regulation on Platform-to-Business

Relations,[149] which similarly focuses on promoting fairness and transparency for business users of online intermediation services.

South Korea's regulatory efforts, comparatively bolder than Japan's, also point to the EU's influence. In August 2021, the government adopted a landmark amendment to the country's Telecommunications Business Act 31 that targets Google's and Apple's app stores.[150] The new law, dubbed the "Anti-Google Law," bans Google, Apple, and other app store operators from requiring their users to exclusively use their own in-app purchasing systems when paying for their apps. The law prohibits app stores from "inappropriately" removing apps from their app stores or delaying their approval or insisting on exclusivity with app developers.[151] The law echoes the EU's emphasis of fairness in its antitrust regulation, as evidenced by the law's use of the language of "gapjil," which refers to the practice being "unjust." It also resembles the pending European Commission investigation into Apple's app store practices, the language of the DMA, as well as the pending private lawsuit against Apple in California and the US government suit against Google on similar grounds. However, South Korea is the first country in the world to make this practice illegal, thereby not only following the EU but showing the way for the EU and the rest of the world.

Even China and the US are now increasingly sharing the EU's view that more robust antitrust enforcement is warranted to restore competition in the digital marketplace. Indeed, antitrust is the domain of the digital economy where all three powers—the EU, the US, and China—are now beginning to converge behind a similar regulatory approach. Over the past two years, China has initiated an unprecedented crackdown on its tech sector, as discussed in Chapter 2. In an effort to advance "common prosperity," the Chinese government has repeatedly leveraged its antitrust powers to distribute wealth away from its largest tech companies. In February 2021, China's market watchdog, the State Administration for Market Regulation (SAMR), released new Antimonopoly Guidelines,[152] marking the beginning of a new era in the country's antitrust enforcement. In April 2021, SAMR imposed a record 18.2 billion yuan ($2.8 billion) fine on China's e-commerce giant Alibaba because the company "had been behaving like a monopoly."[153] In July 2021, SAMR blocked the Tencent-driven $5.3 billion merger between China's top two streaming operators DouYu and Huya,[154] while in October 2021, it was food-delivery giant Meituan's turn, with SAMR imposing a $530 million fine on the company for its monopolistic practices.[155] While China's antitrust actions feature some distinctly Chinese procedural characteristics, they clearly indicate that China increasingly shares the EU's view that antitrust laws are well suited to promote a fairer marketplace. Thus, even while China and the EU remain far apart in

some policy domains, such as censorship and digital surveillance, in the antitrust domain, China is moving toward the regulatory approach that the EU
has pioneered over the last decade.

While the Chinese government's regulatory turn has been both swift and
decisive, a change in the US's regulatory approach toward that of the EU has
been harder to implement. As discussed in Chapter 1, criticism toward the
American market-driven regulatory model is growing. With dominant tech
companies exploiting the marketplace, pressures to revive, even rewrite, antitrust laws are increasing. Even Congress is now increasingly embracing a
view that more robust antitrust laws are needed, in particular vis-à-vis the tech
industry. It has held several antitrust hearings questioning tech executives,
drafted reports, and introduced bills that seek to strengthen existing antitrust
laws, with some proposed changes closely resembling those embedded in the
DMA.[156] The Executive branch has also been spurred into action, with the
Department of Justice and the Federal Trade Commission challenging the
business conduct of Google and Meta, respectively.[157] These developments
are bringing the US antitrust conversation close to the one the EU has been
having for a long time. However, it is unclear whether the changed US rhetoric will translate into new legislation, and whether US courts will ultimately
embrace the new theories of antitrust harm that are driving the ongoing enforcement actions against the largest tech companies.[158] However, it is obvious
that any regulatory alignment that we are witnessing in antitrust is clearly
moving toward the EU approach—even in the US, which has thus far been
one of the last frontiers untouched by the Brussels Effect.

Artificial Intelligence

Artificial intelligence may well be the next frontier of the Brussels Effect. The
EU is taking a lead in regulating artificial intelligence with its ambitious and
comprehensive regulatory proposal on AI unveiled in April 2001.[159] The EU's
goal is to ensure that AI is ethical and that the algorithms empowering AI
applications are free of harmful bias, as discussed in Chapter 3. This regulation has the potential to shape the development of AI globally for a number
of reasons. Any developer of AI systems who wants to include European
data in training the algorithms, or develop AI applications for the European
market, will be bound by the new EU regulation. If this developer then offers
this same AI application outside the EU, those algorithms would need to
be retrained based on different, non-European data, to escape the EU's regulatory constraints. Such divisibility may not be in the AI developer's economic interest as high-quality AI applications benefit from large datasets.

AI developers may therefore conclude that they prefer to include data on European data subjects even if that would extend the European norms across all markets where the AI application is deployed. Of course, there may be several AI applications developed for specific geographical settings where European data is less useful and customized algorithms hence preferable. Those settings would always remain outside the reach of the European rights-driven regulatory model.

There may also be other reasons for tech companies to use the European standard as their global standard in AI development. The proposed EU regulation requires AI developers to adopt several data governance measures that are likely to be implemented company-wide. For example, the measures taken to ensure the robustness, accuracy, and security of European data will likely be extended across the board. Once the company has invested in processes to manage risk and ensure high data quality for the EU, it has few incentives to develop less accurate AI systems for other markets. If a global company relies on AI in recruiting, it is similarly unlikely to develop bias-free hiring algorithms that it uses in Europe while resorting to lesser-quality algorithms for its hiring in other markets. Instead, the firm is likely to deploy a standardized algorithm across all its human resource practices. The EU's push for greater transparency of algorithms also exposes the AI developers globally as information about the quality of AI systems will be available outside the EU as well. Any information that the EU's transparency regime generates about the safety of AI could even be deployed in litigation in the US.[160] If self-driving cars powered by AI had been programmed to stop operating under certain conditions under EU rules, for example, would the developer turn off this feature in the US? If an accident happened in the US under those same conditions, the company would have a hard time arguing before US courts that such an accident was not reasonably foreseeable when the plaintiff can show that additional safety features were adopted for the European market. This is just one example to illustrate how legal risk and reputational concerns may push companies toward global compliance with EU rules.

The EU's AI regulation may also serve as a template for other jurisdictions, given the EU's role as the first mover in this space. There are currently no other comprehensive AI regulations for countries to use as a benchmark as they start developing their own regulatory frameworks. For example, in March 2019, the Japanese government released *Social Principles of Human-Centric AI* (Social Principles),[161] which closely replicate the values embedded in the EU's proposed AI regulation. The Social Principles emphasize dignity, diversity, and inclusion. They envision a society where "human dignity is respected" as opposed to building a society where "AI is used to control human behavior."

The Social Principles emulate the EU's strong fundamental rights language, noting how "utilization of AI must not infringe upon the fundamental rights guaranteed by the Constitution and international standards." To echo the European approach, the Social Principles call for strong privacy protection, fair competition, fairness, accountability, and transparency. However, Japan has thus far chosen to pursue these principles through voluntary norms, citing the need to keep up with the speed and complexity of AI development and deployment, as well as the risk that prescriptive regulation poses to innovation.[162] An expert group involved in preparing the legislation in Japan also adopts a techno-optimist tone, noting the possibility that certain risks associated with AI "may be eliminated due to the development of technologies."[163] Thus, as with the Japanese digital regulation TFDPA, discussed earlier, Japan seems to embrace values and goals that it shares with the EU yet opts for a more American-style implementation of those values through voluntary norms.

There are other countries that, like Japan, are preparing new regulations to govern AI and whose approaches are clearly influenced by the EU. Australia, for example, is contemplating a new regulation to govern AI, and its preparatory works in this domain reflect very similar principles to those embraced by the EU. In 2019, the Australian government published an AI Ethics Framework, which emphasizes the need to ensure "safe," "secure," "reliable," "fair," "inclusive," "ethical," and "trustworthy" AI that centers on fundamental rights.[164] The government notes that the Framework was developed while monitoring similar developments abroad, including the EU's 2019 Ethics Guidelines for Trustworthy AI.[165] The Australian government's 2021 AI Action Plan also emphasizes "trusted, secure and responsible AI,"[166] again echoing the EU's approach to regulating AI. As a further sign that Australia is likely to embrace the EU's rights-driven regulatory approach, the Australian Human Rights Commission (AHRC) issued a "Human Rights and Technology Final Report" in March 2021. Among its recommendations, the Report calls for the Australian government to undertake a human rights impact assessment before adopting a new AI-informed decision-making system to make administrative decisions. It states that "this approach aligns with the advice of expert authorities, such as that of the Council of Europe's Commissioner of Human Rights."[167] In relation to facial recognition, the AHRC also endorsed the risk-based approach taken by the Council of Europe's Directorate General of Human Rights and the Rule of Law's in their Guidelines of Facial Recognition.[168] Australia may further continue to develop its AI legislation in close cooperation with the EU after the two jurisdictions launched a digital economy and technology dialogue to promote mutual cooperation "based on shared values" in areas such as AI and blockchain.[169]

Until recently, the US has been focused on maintaining its lead over China in the AI race and warned the EU against overregulating AI. In January 2020, the White House stated that "Europe and our allies should avoid heavy handed innovation-killing models," while adding that "the best way to counter authoritarian uses of AI is to make sure America and our international partners remain the global hubs of innovation."[170] These statements underscore the US's view that emphasizes clear benefits of the American market-driven model over the European rights-driven model. However, the Biden administration has responded to the EU's AI proposal positively, with the White House National Security Advisor Jake Sullivan tweeting soon after the proposed regulation was issued that "The United States welcomes the EU's new initiatives on artificial intelligence. We will work with our friends and allies to foster trustworthy AI that reflects our shared values and commitment to protecting the rights and dignity of all our citizens."[171] This comment suggests that even the US may now be inching toward the European rights-driven approach on regulating AI. This shift in tone is likely explained by the US government's growing awareness of the ways in which the Chinese government deploys AI toward repressive ends, and the recognized need to ensure that Chinese AI-powered surveillance technologies will not become common around the world, as discussed in Chapter 8.

* * *

As these examples above highlight, the European rights-driven regulatory approach has influenced both tech companies' global business practices and the regulatory practices of foreign governments in domains ranging from data privacy to content moderation, and from antitrust to artificial intelligence. However, additional examples exist as well. These include the EU's pathbreaking 2019 Online Copyright Directive,[172] which provided an impetus for Australia to regulate the news industry—and even go beyond the EU— in its own pro-regulation approach toward internet platforms. In early 2021, the Australian government was poised to introduce a news media mandatory bargaining code designed to encourage digital platforms such as Google and Meta to pay news publishers for the content they display on their platforms.[173] The backlash was both immediate and drastic. As the law was about to pass, Meta blocked all Australian news outlets from posting on its platform globally, and prevented Australian Facebook users from viewing or sharing Australian or international news content.[174] This decision caused an even greater uproar, as the public could not use Facebook to access critical health and emer-gency information in the midst of the COVID-19 pandemic.[75] Google took a different approach—even if reluctantly, as it had also criticized the law and threatened to leave the Australian market—by striking a revenue sharing deal with media conglomerate NewsCorp.[76] Even Meta subsequently reversed its decision, following last-minute negotiations with the Australian government, which resulted in an amended version of the bargaining code passing into law in February 2021. Under this compromise, the Australian government agreed not to apply the mandatory bargaining code to a digital platform if the digital platform has made a "significant contribution" to the Australian news industry.[77] Meta and, by extension, Google are not mandated to negotiate with every news outlet but are expected to do so with those media companies whose content they feature. The EU may now follow Australia's example and tighten its own Copyright Directive, with some politicians already calling for the EU to incorporate stronger provisions on revenue sharing within its dig-ital regulation.[78]

The digital services tax (DST) is another policy area where several European countries' decisions to impose a DST—and the EU's proposals to replace those national DSTs with an EU-wide digital levy—have provided a template for other governments eager to claim their share of the profits generated by the large tech companies operating on their markets. Canada, for example, had vowed to move ahead with a national digital services tax, despite US opposition, if an agreement was not reached at the OECD level by 2023.[79] Pierre-Olivier Herbert, a spokesman for Canada's Minister of Finance, said that while the country was committed to OECD negotiations, "at the same time we will make sure that multinational tech giants pay corporate tax on the revenue they generate in Canada."[80] Similar to the EU proposal, Canada's national DST, if implemented, would impose a 3 percent tax on annual rev-enue earned over a certain amount by an individual entity or consolidated group with at least €750 million in global revenue.[81] In 2019, it was reported that the Israeli Tax Authority and the Ministry of Finance were preparing draft legislation to introduce a 3–5 percent DST, modeled on the French proposal.[82] Similarly, Turkey adopted a DST in 2019 that emulated key provisions of the EU digital levy. While Turkey's DST rate is set at 7.5 percent and is broader than the EU proposal, Turkey's DST contains many similarities in that it sets a global revenue threshold of €750 million; covers digital advertising serv-ices, digital platform services and data-related services; and applies to revenue rather than income.[83] For these reasons, the Office of the United States Trade Representative concluded that "the EU's 2018 proposal appears to have served as the model" for Turkey's DST.[84]

These examples suggest that the EU is hardly alone in looking to regulate the tech industry. Numerous governments around the world share the EU's concern that the largest tech companies have become too powerful and need to be governed through regulation. Even countries that are typically more closely aligned with the US in their approach to regulation and markets, such as Australia, are pursuing extensive digital regulation to advance values very similar to those underlying the European rights-driven regulatory model. The tech industry is feeling the pressure around it grow, as regulators around the world challenge their business models on multiple fronts, contesting the way they compete on the marketplace, manage content on their platforms, develop algorithms for AI applications, and handle consumer data. Combined, these regulatory efforts suggest that the European rights-driven regulatory model is no longer only guiding the EU and its member state governments, but a growing number of governments around the world, all of which seek to take back control from the tech companies and reassert their role in shaping the digital economy.

Foreign Tech Companies and Governments' Concern With the Brussels Effect

The Brussels Effect is neither universally celebrated nor derided outside the EU. While some foreign stakeholders welcome the global reach of the EU's rights-protective regulations, others condemn the EU's role as a global regulatory hegemon in either economic or political terms. There are several strands of common criticism that have been invoked in assessing the EU's growing, and increasingly global, regulatory influence. Some of this criticism, as outlined in Chapter 3, relates to the European rights-driven regulatory model in general. But there is also a specific concern among some companies and governments regarding the externalization of that regulatory model via the Brussels Effect. In some cases, this resentment of the Brussels Effect has caused foreign companies and foreign governments to look for ways to counter the EU's digital regulations that adversely affect them. But as described below, these efforts have achieved limited success to date.

Common Criticism of the Brussels Effect

The main criticism against the globalization of the European rights-driven regulatory model relates to the so-called multiplier effect, whereby the Brussels Effect globalizes not only the benefits but also any costs of the EU model. For example, if any given EU regulation is inefficient, those inefficiencies become entrenched in the global business practices of multinational companies, in addition to often being replicated in legislative frameworks around the world. In other words, if the EU gets it right, it may get it globally right; but if the EU gets it wrong, it may get it globally wrong. The EU's global regulatory influence also removes the benefit of experimentation and hedging, whereby different regulatory frameworks are tried out in different jurisdictions, allowing policy makers to learn from those differences and adjust their own domestic regulatory approaches accordingly.

The primary criticism of the EU's regulatory approach, discussed in Chapter 3, relates to the relationship between regulation, costs, and innovation. Critics often assert that the EU's heavy-handed approach toward the digital economy increases the costs of doing business and dampens innovation in the sector.[185] If this is right—and Chapter 3 argues that it might be, but does not have to be—these costs can be felt outside the EU as well. Another criticism relates to assertions that the EU regulation is motivated by protectionist impulses, targeting in particular US tech companies with its laws and enforcement actions.[186] This has raised a suspicion that the EU is using its tech regulation as a weapon against more successful US companies to enhance the relative position of their less innovative European counterparts. This allegation was examined closely in Chapter 6. That discussion suggested that protectionism has not been a major driver of the EU's digital regulation but also acknowledged that protectionist pressures are growing in the EU and around the world, as countries are seeking to enhance their "digital sovereignty" in a volatile world.

Another strand of criticism leveled against the Brussels Effect relates to its inherent ability to undermine democratic institutions in foreign countries. According to this view, the EU's global regulatory influence compromises the democratic prerogatives of foreign sovereigns and undermines the political autonomy of their citizens. The most pointed criticism invokes the language of "regulatory imperialism," accusing the EU of exporting its norms abroad without seeking the consent of foreign regulators, companies, or consumers.[187] For example, the EU has been accused of engaging in "data imperialism," deploying the GDPR to "conquer the world all over again," through its "legal juggernaut aimed at imposing ever tougher privacy rules on governments and companies from San Francisco to Seoul."[188] The EU can counter this criticism by arguing that it is simply regulating its own market, which it has the sovereign right to do. All the EU is doing is asking any company—domestic or foreign—doing business in Europe to play by European rules.[189] If tech companies' business considerations lead them to voluntarily extend EU regulations across their global operations, the EU can hardly be accused of "imperialism." For example, the EU is not compromising the foreign sovereign interests if Facebook chooses to adopt the EU's definition of hate speech to govern its global operations, or if Google decides to offer GDPR protections to internet users in the US or across Latin America.

However, even if the Brussels Effect does not amount to a new form of imperialism, in practice it does constrain foreign governments' regulatory freedom by often overriding their preferences. For instance, if the European Commission prohibits a merger between two US companies that the US regulators have cleared, it is the more stringent EU decision that prevails over the US decision. This dynamic reveals the logic whereby the European rights-driven regulatory model eclipses the American market-driven regulatory model simply by virtue of being more constraining on tech companies. Many Americans may be uneasy with unelected European civil servants ultimately deciding the fate of a transaction involving US companies. After all, American citizens cannot hold European politicians accountable for decisions they disagree with, compromising their political autonomy. This countermajoritarian element inherent in the Brussels Effect arguably undermines the ability of foreign governments to serve their citizens in accordance with their democratically established preferences. The US government may therefore argue that the Brussels Effect constrains its regulatory freedom, undermining US sovereignty in the process.

Even if one accepts that the Brussels Effect compromises foreign governments' regulatory autonomy, some may still argue that it does not compromise democracy. Many Americans worry that extensive business lobbying has distorted the American democratic process and legislative agenda, especially after the US Supreme Court's ruling in *Citizens United* paved the way for unlimited corporate spending to influence elections.[190] The EU's legislative process, while not flawless nor perfectly democratic,[191] is less susceptible to corporate influence when compared to the legislative process in the United States. In the EU, business interests are typically balanced with the influence that civil society groups exert over regulation.[192] Thus, an argument—even if potentially a controversial one—exists that the Brussels Effect may partially offset the overrepresentation of corporate interests in the US by restoring some of the consumer interests that have been overridden in the process.

Despite the occasional criticism, it is important to recognize that not all foreign actors view the EU's global regulatory influence as sovereignty-infringing. Some even welcome the Brussels Effect. Public opinion surveys indicate that most Americans (75 percent) think there should be more governmental regulation of what companies can do with personal data, and favor the use of better tools that would allow users to exercise greater control over their own personal data.[193] In a large-scale 2020 survey of American consumers, 93 percent of the respondents said they would switch to buying from a company that prioritizes data privacy, and another 91 percent said they would prefer to buy from a company "that always guarantees them access to their information."[194] EU regulations often help foreign advocacy groups raise awareness of a policy problem at home, and influence domestic debates on the issue.[195] For example, the American Civil Liberties Union has said that "the U.S. can learn from the approach being taken by the European Union" and that "Congress should look to this model and similarly enact comprehensive privacy legislation."[196] In advocating for stronger federal data privacy legislation, the US-based Council on Foreign Relations also cited the GDPR as an example of comprehensive data privacy legislation that "protects all people" in contrast to the "patchwork approach of the United States."[197] Linda Sherry, director of national priorities at US-based advocacy group Consumer Action, also described how US consumer rights are inadequately protected by state and federal laws. According to Sherry, "as global firms adapt to the EU's data protection law, we're hopeful that all consumers will benefit from stricter data security and gain a reasonable measure of control over their personal information that so many others prosper from the EU's strong regulation."[198] This suggests that any foreign criticism of the Brussels Effect is unlikely to be uniform, and examples of foreign stakeholders embracing the reach of the European rights-driven regulatory model abound as well.

How Tech Companies and Governments Are Seeking to Counter the Brussels Effect

Even when foreign companies or governments resent the EU's global regulatory power, it is difficult for them to do much about it, highlighting why the Brussels Effect has enabled the EU to become a major player alongside China and the US in shaping today's global digital economy. Being market-driven, the Brussels Effect is not subject to political negotiations. Foreign companies affected by EU rules have therefore realized that they need to influence those rules before they are adopted and enforced by EU institutions and EU member state governments. As a result, lobbying activity is particularly salient in Brussels. This is because the benefits available from the possible regulatory capture of the Commission or other EU institutions are particularly high: at best, being able to shape European regulatory response gives the successful lobbyist a say over not just European, but global, regulation.

The Brussels Effect has given foreign firms, including tech companies, an incentive to invest heavily in the EU regulatory process through lobbying, with the Commission and the Parliament being their primary targets. According to a 2021 study conducted by Corporate Europe Observatory, the digital economy is the biggest lobbying sector in the EU as measured by spending, ahead of industries such as finance, pharmaceuticals, and energy.[199] US tech companies in particular are increasing their lobbying presence in the EU: out of the top ten digital industry lobbyists, eight are US-based tech companies, with Google, Meta, Microsoft, and Apple spending the most on lobbying. These companies also benefit from active lobbying by industry associations. For example, the Information Technology Industry Council—a US-based lobbying group representing several tech companies—is increasing its staff in Brussels because they explicitly recognize that the EU is "driving and directing policy."[200]

The GDPR is one of the most lobbied pieces of EU legislation to date, pitting digital companies against consumer and data protection advocates. This contributed to a highly contentious legislative process. It is telling that over 4,000 amendments were introduced in the European Parliament's legislative process alone.[201] Foreign governments, companies, and business groups engaged in active lobbying to mitigate the costs of the GDPR on their businesses. Leading US companies such as Cisco, Intel, Microsoft, and NBC Universal, as well as organizations such as TechAmerica Europe, the American Chamber of Commerce, and the Japan Business Council in Europe submitted comments at the consultation stage.[202] On the civil society side, European nongovernmental organizations (NGOs) such as European Digital Rights received support from foreign NGOs such as the Australian Cyberspace Law and Policy Center and the American Center for Democracy & Technology.[203] Ultimately, while privacy advocates may not be able to declare a complete victory, what emerged from the legislative process was an unprecedentedly stringent data protection law, with extensive obligations imposed on data controllers, backed by severe penalties.

Despite their concerted efforts and growing lobbying budgets, foreign companies have not to date been able to substantially mitigate the Brussels Effect through lobbying. They may be able to win some concessions, but often their influence is offset by that of citizen groups and other nonbusiness actors. According to a 2019 study on lobbying in Europe, business interests are no more influential in shaping EU regulations than other interests.[204] The recent DMA was subject to relentless lobbying in Brussels, yet those lobbying efforts did little to rein in the European regulators. When the DMA was provisionally adopted in March 2022, policy commentary uniformly described how tech giants "lost the antitrust battle with Europe" and noted how the legal teams of these companies have started to focus on compliance with new rules, conceding that the regulators prevailed.[205] Even lobbyists hired to fight the DMA were hesitant to defend the tech sector in public, with one lobbyist noting how "it was a done deal from the start. It's been an artificial battle. The sector was always going to lose after fighting against the entire establishment."[206]

With political momentum behind the regulators in Brussels, tech companies have often had to concede that the EU will regulate them, and there is only so far they should go in fighting a losing battle. As a result, some of them have not only adopted regulations such as the GDPR as their global privacy norm, but have also become advocates of similar regulatory reforms at home—a dynamic discussed earlier. Occasionally, these companies also leverage the EU's regulatory prowess against their own competitors. Foreign tech companies are increasingly bringing their legal battles to Brussels, urging the Commission to challenge their competitors' practices. For example, Microsoft lodged an antitrust complaint before the European Commission against Google in 2011,[207] and even though Microsoft ultimately reached a settlement with Google in 2016, other US companies, including Oracle, Kayak, Expedia, and Trip Advisor, continued to press the Commission to reach a decision against the company.[208] In 2020, Meta and Microsoft voiced concerns before the Commission regarding the Apple App Store's restrictive rules.[209] Smaller US tech companies have been particularly active in urging the European Commission to leverage its antitrust powers against the US tech giants. In 2021, Epic Games filed a formal antitrust complaint before the Commission against Apple.[210] Yelp has repeatedly urged the EU to act against Google.[211] It was also among the group of US companies that sent a letter to the Commission in 2017, accusing "Google of destroying jobs and stifling innovation" while supporting "penalties against Google for 'anticompetitive conduct,' "[212] in addition to supporting the EU's proposed DMA.[213] These examples illustrate how some foreign firms are occasionally able to turn the Brussels Effect to their advantage—even if only by shifting the costs of European digital regulations to their competitors.

Tech companies are not alone in struggling to respond to the Brussels Effect. Foreign governments have equally few pathways available to limit the EU's regulatory reach. After all, the EU is regulating its own market, which is its sovereign prerogative. When US companies voluntarily adjust their global practices to the EU rules, the US government cannot easily blame the EU for impacts on the US market that arise as a byproduct of those private business decisions. As a result, the US government—like any other foreign government—is often left as a spectator, unable to influence the market forces pushing companies and governments toward EU regulations. International institutions, such as the World Trade Organization (WTO), also fail to provide a venue for foreign governments to challenge the EU regulations. To successfully challenge EU tech regulations before the WTO, foreign governments would need to show that the EU regulations are discriminatory, which is difficult to do given that EU companies are subject to the same rules. The WTO therefore offers, at best, a limited avenue for foreign governments to mitigate the costs they incur through the external effect of EU regulations. At times, the WTO may even facilitate the Brussels Effect by constraining the EU's trading partners' ability to respond with unilateral retaliation. Had the US, for instance, imposed trade sanctions on the EU when faced with the EU's data transfer ban, it would have violated the WTO rules and subjected itself to a WTO complaint by the EU. In this sense, the WTO can more often provide a shield for, rather than a weapon against, the Brussels Effect.[214]

Given the difficulties of evading the EU's regulatory influence, foreign governments' best strategy would seem to be regulatory cooperation with the EU. Such cooperation would offer them an opportunity to play a shared, rather than obsolete, role in shaping global digital regulation. It may therefore seem surprising that the US has deliberately turned its back on international trade deals with the EU, including the Transatlantic Trade and Investment Partnership.[215] The trade deal's potential to overcome US–EU regulatory disagreements presented the greatest opportunity for economic gains for both parties. Abandoning the negotiations in 2019, the US directly undermined its ability to influence global regulatory standards, inadvertently cementing the Brussels Effect. Now, the US and the EU are seeking to cooperate more closely on technology standards through the newly established Transatlantic Trade and Technology Council,[216] which may again present the US with an opportunity to counter the EU's unilateral regulatory influence. At the same time, it is less clear that the US even wants to counter the globalization of the European rights-driven regulatory model today, given the growing popular support and bipartisan backing of more stringent digital regulations in the US. Given the inability of the US Congress to enact many key laws—whether on data privacy, antitrust, or content moderation—the best hope of the US may indeed lie in the Brussels Effect and its ability to deliver to Americans the kind of digital regulatory model that they have increasingly come to support.

Conclusion

THIS BOOK HAS described the three digital empires and their models of regulating the digital economy, each organized around a different emphasis of the market, the state, or the rights of digital citizens. It has also shown how these respective American, Chinese, and European regulatory models reach across the deeply intertwined global digital economy, shaping societies and individuals' lives at home and abroad. The models have also frequently come into conflict with one another, fueling contested battles that have a profound impact on the future of our digital economies and societies. This discussion raises important predictive questions: Which regulatory model—or which aspects of various regulatory models—will ultimately dominate, and how will the ongoing digital rivalries reshape the global economic and political landscape?

This concluding chapter takes on these questions, asking which regulatory model will prevail in the horizontal battle between governments, while simultaneously examining whether the tech companies or governments will ultimately triumph in their various vertical battles. It looks closely at one of the most pressing questions relating to these battles: how the digital economy will be governed in the near future, and whether a regulatory model focused on markets, the state, or citizens' rights will gain the greatest traction worldwide, shaping our digital lives in line with the values embedded in that model. Similarly, it explores whether governments will continue to set the rules for tech companies—which today rival many states in size and influence—or whether it is the tech companies that will exert more influence than governments over societies' economic, political, and cultural destinies. These questions go to the heart of how we organize and govern every aspect of our societies. Gaining insight into their answers will help us envision a path forward and, hopefully, guide our decision-making along that path toward a vibrant digital economy and a thriving digital society.

The US Is Losing the Horizontal Battle to China and the EU

Much of the public conversation on the future of the digital economy to date has focused on the technological rivalry between the US and China. In this conversation, the EU is treated as a powerless bystander with no significant technology industry of its own, squeezed between two superpowers battling for technological supremacy.[1] Some commentators describe Europe as becoming a "casualty in the U.S.–China tech war" or "a colony caught between the U.S. and China," with "less bargaining power to determine its own digital fate," and thus forced to "make a choice" between the US and China.[2] What this narrative gets right is the indisputable lead that the US and China currently have over the EU in developing new digital technologies and nurturing national champions in the tech industry. However, this narrative is also incomplete in that it focuses on a single aspect of the global digital contest— technological dominance—while casting aside an equally significant, ongoing contest over the rules and norms that govern the digital economy. This more complete understanding of the ongoing superpower rivalry reveals that the EU is not a powerless bystander forced to choose between its two rivals, but retains considerable power and influence in advancing its own digital agenda.

This book has shown that the EU is adamant in asserting its own vision for the digital economy and explained how that vision is backed by a strong regulatory apparatus that resonates around the world. Thus, while the EU may not be the source of many of the leading technologies, it remains the primary source of the rules that govern those technologies. In many cases, the EU's regulatory rivals have little to no effective response to counter the influence that European regulations have on the conduct of tech companies, in Europe and around the world. As a number of countries accelerate their recent turn away from the American market-driven model, the EU's cascade of regulations provides both a normative vision and a legal foundation for the digital economy for the majority of the nonauthoritarian nations. As a result, when it comes to governing the digital economy, it is not the EU that will be forced to choose between China and the US, but rather the US that must choose between joining forces with the EU or allowing China's influence to further grow.

The Decline of the American Regulatory Model

One of the primary conclusions of the earlier chapters is that the American market-driven regulatory model is fading in its normative appeal and global influence. As the discussion in Chapter 7 made clear, the authority of the US model has been dwindling across jurisdictions. For years, the US actively promoted its internet freedom agenda abroad, urging countries to implement its market-driven regulatory model. This freedom agenda called for governments to refrain from regulating technology companies or censoring the internet. However, this agenda has largely failed, with digital regulations burgeoning and internet censorship increasing across the world.[3] In many ways, the tremendous success of the US tech companies may have sown the seeds of the demise of the US model, exposing the downsides of the freewheeling pro-market ethos that sustains it. The global presence of these companies—and what is often seen as the excessive power they wield around the world—has triggered backlash worldwide, prompting numerous jurisdictions to mobilize efforts to curtail the power of these corporations with mounting regulation.[4] As part of this regulatory response, many democratic countries have abandoned the American market-driven model in favor of the European rights-driven model. At the same time, in several more authoritarian countries, governments have shifted toward the Chinese state-driven regulatory model. At some level, this shift toward greater state control over the digital economy can also be understood as a response to the outsized influence of US tech companies, which many governments saw as a threat to their ability to maintain authoritarian rule. That gave these countries an additional reason to consolidate the power of the state over the digital realm.

Yet what provides perhaps the strongest evidence of the decline of the American regulatory model is that the US itself is now gradually turning away from it, as documented in Chapter 1. American internet users have started to question the benefits of the market-driven regulatory model, saying that they, too, want more digital regulation. For example, according to a 2020 survey, 72 percent of US adults believe social media companies have "too much power and influence in politics."[5] The American public is also rethinking the US model's traditionally inviolable commitment to free speech. Internet users are growing more concerned about harmful content online, including rife disinformation, terrorist propaganda, and foreign interference with elections. In recent years, the public has also become vehemently opposed to the misogyny and racism running rampant both offline and online. These attitudes are amplified through the #MeToo and #BlackLivesMatter movements, which have exposed the deep structural discrimination and abuse endured by women and people of color. These public campaigns have directed new attention to racism and hate speech appearing online and resulted in mounting calls for tech companies to remove such content from their platforms.[6] This popular criticism of the platforms' content moderation policies is increasing in parallel with a reinvigorated conversation about the need to revitalize antitrust laws in the US, particularly against the largest tech companies.

This shift in public opinion is increasingly reflected in the views of political leaders, who are starting to question the merits of the market-driven regulatory model. The US Congress is debating several bills seeking a reversal of the long-standing policy of nonregulation in areas such as antitrust, content moderation, and data privacy.[7] After a long hiatus, the US government is leveraging its antitrust powers, with the Department of Justice and the Federal Trade Commission challenging the business conduct of Google and Meta, respectively.[8] These developments are bringing the US policy discourse closer to the conversation that has been taking place in the EU for the past decade. Even tech companies themselves are increasingly conceding that regulation is needed. As the number of high-profile scandals increases, the tech industry has lost its credibility in arguing that, if technology is the problem, technology is the solution. And if anyone had any doubts left, the *Wall Street Journal*'s recent reporting on the "Facebook Files" showed how Facebook knew that its platform was causing serious societal harm but did not take measures to address those harms.[9] These public scandals have put the tech companies on the defensive, forcing them to acknowledge that the era of self-regulation is over. As a result, much of the tech industry's lobbying effort is now geared at shaping government regulation rather than resisting it—though a more cynical view suggests that while they are publicly endorsing regulation, they are privately counting on the US Congress's inability to ultimately agree on any meaningful legislation that would fundamentally rein in their existing commercial freedom.

Some commentators suggest that the January 6, 2021, attack on the US Capitol may have been a turning point in the US's approach toward regulating online content.[10] Emily Bazelon described the event as showing how the "American marketplace of ideas clearly failed," implying that American techno-libertarian beliefs about free speech were among the causes of the event.[11] The Capitol riots led to broad condemnation of the role that online platforms played in allowing harmful and dangerous speech to gather so much momentum that it ultimately led to violence. Given these developments, it is plausible that the US will come to embrace an EU-style regulatory model through a series of legislative reforms in the coming years. As shown in Chapter 6, the US–EU horizontal regulatory battles over data privacy, digital taxation, and antitrust are already being resolved largely in favor of the European model. Many stakeholders in the US are endorsing the EU-style regulatory model in its own right as the public becomes more skeptical of the role that tech companies play in our society. Others focus more on the rising threat of China's digital authoritarian norms, which provides an additional impetus for the US to seek greater alignment with the EU and other techno-democracies, discussed in more detail below.

At the same time, other commentators believe that any regulatory reform in the US is unlikely. There is no guarantee that the political dynamics in the Congress, including the different concerns that Democrats and Republicans have about Section 230 of the Communications Decency Act, will lead to any substantial legislative reform on content moderation.[12] For similar reasons, bills proposing a federal privacy law may also falter. While discontent about tech companies is strong, the political dysfunction of the US Congress might prove to be even stronger, preventing any meaningful legislation from being enacted. It is also unclear whether US courts are ready for an antitrust revolution, which could lead to judges rejecting the new theories of antitrust harm that are driving the pending enforcement actions against the leading tech giants.[13] In addition, there remains a genuine concern about the potential downsides of regulation, including that regulation might curtail future innovation by these companies whose products consumers desire and have come to depend on. There are many internet users who say that they value consumer choice and data privacy—but, at the end of the day, they may value daily conveniences such as Amazon's free shipping even more.[14] Americans are also torn on how to regulate online speech given that, as Bazelon notes, "we are uncomfortable with government doing it; we are uncomfortable with Silicon Valley doing it. But we are also uncomfortable with nobody doing it at all."[15] As a result, this shift in the American public discourse may not ultimately translate into regulatory reforms, or at least into ambitious ones. If this turns out to be the case, the EU may remain the primary source of regulatory constraints for the tech industry in the years to come, with US citizens and regulators watching from the sidelines—or even cheering the EU on and hoping that it will succeed.

Authoritarian Governments Are Turning to the Chinese Regulatory Model

While the American market-driven regulatory model is waning in popularity in both the US and abroad, the Chinese state-driven regulatory model is on the ascent worldwide, leading to growing concern in the US, the EU, and the rest of the democratic world about the implications of that ascent. The worry that China's regulatory model will prevail is real, both normatively and descriptively. China's technological development is impressive, but its way of harnessing that technology is often deeply oppressive. The Chinese government has converted the internet from a tool that advances democracy to an instrument that serves autocracy. China's digital authoritarian governance model infringes individual rights and deprives Chinese citizens of key civil liberties. It also contributes to the political oppression of minorities through far-reaching government surveillance. This shows that freedom is not inherent in the character of the internet, but rather subject to a political choice by those with the power to permit or suppress that freedom. China's success in exporting its norms and surveillance technologies abroad through the Digital Silk Road, discussed in Chapter 8, further suggests that the Chinese regulatory model presents a threat to liberal democracy and individual freedom not just in China, but around the world.

However, even if a strong normative case could be made against the Chinese regulatory model, it is harder to predict its demise in practice. The state-driven model is faring well, as indicated by several governments around the world emulating many of its key censorship and surveillance features. These governments do not share the US's and EU's concern about the future of liberal democracy. The number of countries embracing that view is also rising as the world is turning more authoritarian. According to research by the US-based NGO Freedom House, the year 2021 was the eleventh consecutive year of a decline in global internet freedom, as governments were increasingly curtailing online speech; arresting internet users for nonviolent political, social, or religious speech; and suspending access to various social media platforms, or the internet itself.[16] A growing number of governments are also obtaining spyware, facial recognition, and other data-extraction technologies from private vendors, vesting themselves with tools for authoritarian control in violation of individual rights. This trend bodes well for the global appeal of Chinese digital authoritarianism as an ideology, while increasing the demand for Chinese-made surveillance technologies or censorship techniques that help governments ingrain that ideology into the structures of their societies. The COVID-19 pandemic has provided an additional reason for many authoritarian-leaning governments to deploy emergency powers and engage in various forms of digital surveillance.[17] These measures may not be repealed even as the pandemic wanes, instead becoming permanent features of digital societies in many parts of the world.

The Chinese state-driven model also appeals to many developing, authoritarian countries in that it combines political control with tremendous technological success, which has fueled China's rapid economic growth. Although the US has traditionally been viewed as the technological superpower, China is quickly catching up, and even surpassing the US in several domains, as documented in Chapter 5.[18] For example, Chinese tech companies currently lead the world in sales of smartphone and telecommunications network equipment. China is also well on its way to become the world's premier AI superpower, potentially surpassing the US in the next decade.[19] For many developing countries hesitant to embrace the American market-driven model that is centered on economic and political freedom, these statistics offer a reassuring message. They show that political freedom is not necessary for technological and economic progress, which provides these countries with an additional reason to embrace the Chinese regulatory model.

The US government's assertive response to the US–China tech war may have further elevated the Chinese regulatory model in the horizontal battle, however unintentionally. As shown in Chapters 4 and 5, the intense US–China tech rivalry has led the US government to abandon many of the key principles—such as openness and nondiscrimination—underlying the American market-driven regulatory model. In an effort to limit China's access to strategic technologies that are central to the US–China geopolitical rivalry, the US has moved to restrict exports of such technologies, such as advanced semiconductors, to China. The US has also banned Chinese investment into critical digital infrastructures, such as 5G networks, in the US. To preserve its technological lead over China, the US is now shoring up its strategic capabilities by pouring unprecedented amounts of government funding into technologies such as AI and semiconductors, fueling a subsidy race that is leading to growing techno-nationalism around the world. Thus, instead of embracing and exporting its values around freedom or advocating a limited role for the government as it has traditionally done, the critics are now accusing the US government of playing Beijing's game. In doing so, the US is modeling elements of the state-driven model and thus, effectively even if inadvertently, leading the world away from the values underpinning the American market-driven model toward those that reinforce the Chinese state-driven model.

Democratic Governments Are Turning to the European Regulatory Model

The Chinese regulatory model is not the only one benefiting from the decline of the American regulatory model; the turn away from the techno-libertarian worldview has also elevated the EU's standing in the horizontal battle. While the authoritarian governments are turning toward the Chinese state-driven regulatory model, deepening discontent with the American model is pushing much of the democratic world toward the European model. For many democratic countries, the American market-driven regulatory model has proven to be too permissive, while the Chinese state-driven model is seen as too oppressive, leaving the European rights-driven model the most attractive one to follow. Chapter 3 argued that the European regulatory model rests on three pillars—fundamental rights, democracy, and fairness—all of which, according to the EU, require government oversight to be adequately protected in the modern digital era. These key elements of the European model are increasingly seen as necessary building blocks of a more equitable and human-centric digital economy. Each additional privacy scandal and online disinformation campaign further vindicates the European model while revealing the limits of the American model. Even the US itself is now growing aware of the limits of its regulatory approach, asking whether it also ought to implement several aspects of the European rights-driven regulatory model, including more robust antitrust laws or enhanced data privacy protections for its citizens.

Several normative arguments suggest that the US should, indeed, abandon elements of its market-driven regulatory model and emulate aspects of the European rights-driven model. There is growing consensus in the US that free markets and free speech as cornerstones of a digital economy no longer seem adequate to address the challenges of modern society. The US's hands-off approach toward regulation has allowed the leading tech companies to amass the kind of economic and political power they are no longer equipped to responsibly handle. As a result, the shortcomings of the US regulatory model have left many Americans searching for a different way of governing the digital economy, with the European rights-driven regulatory model emerging as an increasingly attractive alternative.

The European regulatory model is seen as appealing, in part, because it is associated with greater economic fairness and distributional justice. Its central goal is to foster a fairer digital economy that ensures that the gains from the digital economy are divided more equally. In practice, this has entailed leveraging European antitrust, employment, and tax laws to redistribute power away from platforms, vesting more power instead with internet users and consumers, platform workers, smaller businesses, and the public at large. This regulatory philosophy is more in line with today's political environment where the ideological underpinnings of neoliberalism, including any manifestations of capitalist excess, are increasingly criticized. As a result, there is a growing number of voices arguing that the European regulatory model facilitates greater economic success not because of its ability to maximize wealth through digital transformation, but because of its commitment to distribute that wealth more evenly across society.

Another normative argument in favor of the EU model stems from the growing discontent toward the US's uncompromising commitment to free speech, even when that speech harms individuals and destabilizes societies. One can be a staunch proponent of free speech yet still argue that the US government has gotten more than it bargained for with Section 230 of the CDA. That provision created an online world in which techno-libertarianism has gone wild, turning the American regulatory model against the country's own democratic institutions and wreaking havoc around the world. Many of the deeply disturbing examples described in this book—be it the disinformation-fueled US Capitol insurrection, the encouragement of illegal sex trafficking in the infamous *Backpage* case, or the hate speech–fueled genocide in Myanmar—have their roots in the digital economy created by Section 230, vividly illustrating the fallacies of the market-driven model, which placed its trust in internet platforms as the guardians and amplifiers of democracy.

Now this illusion has been shattered. The digital public space is frequently compromised by rampant disinformation, which interferes with elections and destabilizes democracies. America had a rude awakening on January 6, 2021, when President Trump's loyalists stormed the US Capitol, riled into action by social media–amplified lies about a stolen election. Platforms and their algorithms have also contributed to greater polarization by delivering each internet user a highly personalized online experience, thereby insulating citizens from alternative viewpoints and genuine societal debate, and undermining, as opposed to enhancing, democracy.[20] Similarly, harmful content online has too often trumped the decency, dignity, and safety of individuals, with Section 230 coming to the rescue of tech companies no matter how repulsive or harmful the content they host. Here, the contrast to the EU is again stark. Even though the EU shares the US's commitment to protecting free speech, it is prepared to restrict that fundamental right in the name of other fundamental rights and important public policies, be it human dignity, personal privacy, public safety, or democracy. The EU's willingness to intervene in internet freedoms by restricting hateful or dangerous content is increasingly seen as necessary in today's society, lending further support to the EU model.

The European regulatory model also protects internet users' privacy more than the extensive "surveillance capitalism" enabled by the American market-driven model, where tech companies track internet users' every move online and acquire a trove of personal data that they then monetize through targeted advertising.[21] But the perverse impact of this targeting on users can go even deeper. Disturbing revelations by a Facebook whistleblower, Frances Haugen, provide evidence of how Facebook's algorithms intentionally target the vulnerabilities of teenage users by, for example, displaying weight loss adds to a teen with an emerging eating disorder.[22] At worst, privacy-infringing data extraction can compromise users' "decisional privacy" by subverting individual choice, liberty, and self-governance.[23] Voter behavior can also be manipulated whenever someone gains access to internet users' personal data and deploys that data for psychographic profiling that enables microtargeted political advertising. This is exactly what happened in the infamous Cambridge Analytica scandal, where British political consulting firm Cambridge Analytica harvested data from 87 million Facebook profiles for use in political advertising. This data, which was obtained without user consent, was used to build psychological profiles of users, and then leveraged in political campaigns, including Donald Trump's 2016 presidential campaign. Meta admitted to mishandling user privacy and has pledged to make significant changes in securing user data going forward.[24] Regardless of this pledge, the scandal has been engrained in the memory of internet users and regulators alike, elevating the importance of data protection in their minds. In doing so, such scandals also lend support for the European regulatory model, which views safeguarding personal privacy and individual self-determination as a paramount concern, vigorously defended by European courts.

It is these types of normative concerns that are behind the evident dimming of the techno-optimist vision that marked the early days of the digital economy: a vision that came to define the American market-driven regulatory model. These concerns also explain why a growing number of governments and individuals around the democratic world are coalescing around a view that the European regulatory model best enhances public interest, checks corporate power, and preserves democratic structures of society, and are increasingly emulating that model as a result. This shift in public discourse also sheds light on why some degree of convergence between the American and European regulatory models is already occurring, and why the direction of that convergence comes from the US adjusting toward the EU model. Next, the discussion moves to examine potential concerns with the prevalence of the European regulatory model over that of the American regulatory model, assessing both the challenges and opportunities that such a shift is likely to entail.

The Convergence Around the EU Model Does Not Inevitably Compromise Innovation

Perhaps the biggest concern discouraging a potential shift away from the American market-driven model toward the European rights-driven model is the widely held belief that such a shift would necessitate that the US give up some of its fundamental values, such as economic freedom. It is almost an article of faith that innovation, technology leadership, competitiveness, and economic growth derive from an unregulated marketplace, explaining the dominance of US tech companies in the global digital landscape. Thus, a deep-rooted concern remains that, by abandoning its faith in the free market and moving toward a more regulated digital economy, the US would inevitably be forced to relinquish its role as a technological leader. This would leave the US, and the entire world, without many beneficial innovations that economic prosperity and social progress depend on.

However, this concern about a potential trade-off that the US would be making by adjusting its regulatory model toward that of the EU reflects several misunderstandings about both the American and European regulatory models. First, under the US model, a free market was never the end goal in itself, but rather the means to safeguard both economic and political freedom. Keeping the government at bay was seen as necessary to maximize economic progress and innovation, while also ensuring that democracy will thrive. However, today's concentrated digital marketplace dominated by a handful of tech giants is hardly a reflection of economic freedom as conceived by early techno-libertarians. Similarly, recent scandals, including those revealing how online disinformation campaigns can undermine democratic elections, have shown that strong democracy does not necessarily flow from an unregulated digital marketplace. Consequently, a more regulated digital economy in the US may be one where, in the end, greater political and economic freedom will prevail.

Second, this view that associates the European regulatory model—or the US's potential shift toward that model—with meager technological innovation reflects a limited understanding of the EU's strengths and weaknesses. It also relies on a simplistic view regarding the relationship between digital regulation and innovation. A common criticism associated with the European rights-driven regulatory model is that the EU model overdoes regulation—to the extent that it kills innovation and stifles economic progress. According to this view, while the EU may be more successful in safeguarding the fundamental rights of individuals and the democratic structures of the society, its regulatory approach will deprive societies of economic opportunities. This concern stems from a widely held belief that there is an inevitable trade-off between regulation and innovation. However, although it is true the EU has been less successful in producing leading tech companies to date, as discussed below, there are other reasons besides regulation that primarily explain this fact. There is much that Europe is not getting right in terms of nurturing innovation. But choosing to regulate the tech industry in the name of safeguarding individual rights and societal freedoms is not where the problem lies.

It is tempting to observe causality between the EU's stringent regulatory regime and the dearth of leading tech companies emanating from Europe. After all, there is no European Amazon, Apple, Meta, Google, or Microsoft. As Chapter 3 documented, various metrics all point to the same, unambiguous conclusion that the EU is currently lagging behind the US and China in technological prowess. However, as that chapter also pointed out, it is questionable whether EU tech companies' relative lack of success can be attributed to the level of tech regulation they face. After all, digital regulation in Europe is more recent, and there was no substantial tech regulation in place in the EU at the time when today's leading tech giants were founded—yet those companies were founded in the US and not in Europe. European tech regulations, once enacted, have also frequently targeted US tech companies, without compromising their ability to innovate. This suggests that the EU's lackluster performance as a developer of new technologies may not, at least in its entirety, be attributed to its pro-regulation instincts.

However, we are still left with the question of why the EU has not produced tech giants comparable to those in the US and China. If onerous regulation is not the main problem, what keeps EU tech companies from succeeding? Looking more closely, the EU's innovation gap can be largely explained by other factors, all discussed in detail below, including the fragmented digital single market (DSM), underdeveloped capital markets, punitive bankruptcy laws that deter risk-taking, and the absence of a proactive immigration policy that would allow the EU to harness foreign talent in the way the US has done over the past decades. Recognizing these reasons should offer solace to any American decision-maker—or any other foreign government—that harbors a view that embracing a European-style rights-driven regulatory model would inevitably hamper innovation and set back the country's economic and technological progress.

One significant impediment faced by EU tech companies is that they do not benefit from a fully integrated DSM that would allow them to seamlessly operate across the EU. This explains, in part, why European tech companies have struggled to build a market presence comparable to their American and Chinese rivals. Scaling is key to growth and competitiveness, yet such a growth strategy is harder to pursue when companies are operating across numerous national markets that possess different languages, cultures, and government regulations. It was naturally easier for Amazon to grow as an online bookseller in the US where the demand for English-language books was high across the country. In Europe, the publishing market is more fragmented because of linguistic diversity. Video-on-demand (VOD) services have similarly been difficult to scale in Europe because audience demand varies across member states.[25] As a result, providers of VOD services in Europe sometimes have to offer a different mix of content in different member states, which hinders their ability to market their services at scale. Legal barriers have further contributed to fragmentation of the DSM. Tech companies must often navigate a diverse set of national laws across Europe, which adds costs and complexity to their business operations.[26] This fragmentation forces European startups to internationalize earlier than their American counterparts, which are able to build scale domestically at first.[27]

European lawmakers acknowledge that the fragmented DSM hampers the European technology sector's growth. Back in 2010, the Commission recognized that, as a result of this fragmentation, few of Europe's innovative SMEs (small and medium-sized enterprises) grow into globally successful companies.[28] However, these barriers to growth and innovation have remained in place since 2010, despite the EU's efforts to pursue greater digital integration. In 2015, only 4 percent of all digital services consumed in the EU were sold cross-border.[29] A 2019 study conducted by the McKinsey Global Institute concluded that "fragmentation seems to put Europe at a structural disadvantage" when considering the innovation deficit between Europe and competing regions.[30] This fragmentation is costly for large tech companies but imposes even greater costs on the SMEs that form the majority of the European homegrown tech companies. Around 96 percent of the over 10,000 potentially high-growth platforms established in the EU are SMEs.[31] For them, the costs of fragmentation are prohibitively high as they cannot draw on economies of scale to grow beyond a certain size. In contrast, American and Chinese companies benefit from more homogenous home markets, which makes it relatively easier for their companies to scale in size.

The DSM is not the only domain where European integration is falling short and hindering the growth potential of the EU's tech sector. Another major impediment is the absence of deep and integrated capital markets that would allow European companies to fund their innovations in Europe. Instead, EU firms often need to rely on the US capital markets for growth opportunities. According to a study by the McKinsey Global Institute, the underdevelopment of equity finance in Europe poses a major challenge for startups seeking funding.[32] Analyzing the density of European AI startups, this study concludes that financing has a "significantly higher impact" on the density of AI startup networks than other factors such as the ability to build innovative business models. While European companies can often secure seed funding and succeed in early fundraising rounds, they struggle to raise capital in later rounds. The comparison to the US here is stark: when companies enter the later stage D and E funding rounds, the percentage of total European VC funding as a proportion of US VC funding falls by approximately 50 percent.[33] In the absence of large European VC funds that have the capital to support late-stage rounds, US companies with "similar success metrics" in comparable industries tend to raise significantly higher sums than their European rivals.[34]

Despite the fragmented and relatively underdeveloped capital markets in Europe, recent years offer a ray of optimism for the European tech industry. There are signs that American VC firms view Europe as an increasingly attractive investment destination, and their capital is now flowing into European startups at a greater rate than before. As evidence of this trend, investments made by American VC firms in European ventures tripled between 2020 and 2021, reaching $83 billion.[35] Several prominent US-based investment firms have also opened European offices, which may indicate the arrival of more American capital in the future. For instance, the storied Sequoia Capital— which had $85 billion in assets under management in 2022[36]—opened an office in London in early 2021.[37] These developments reflect an increasing conviction among some of Silicon Valley's most successful venture capitalists that the European tech ecosystem is on the cusp of exponential growth.[38] They also give hope that even if European sources of capital remain limited for the continent's startups, American and other foreign capital may be able to offset some of those deficiencies.

Despite this greater availability of US-based VC funding for promising European startups in recent years, few question the benefits that would ensue from more integrated and robust European capital markets. The EU has undertaken several initiatives aimed at improving the funding available for European startups and scale-ups. One landmark initiative is the Capital Markets Union (CMU), established in 2015. The CMU's goal is to reduce fragmentation in financial markets by creating a single market for capital in the EU. Deep and integrated European capital markets would help diversify financing sources, facilitate cross-border capital flows, and improve businesses' access to finance. The Commission has stated that the completion of the CMU is needed to strengthen the EU's global competitiveness.[39] Key leadership from the European Central Bank has similarly called for deeply integrated European capital markets. According to these individuals, boosting capital markets and progress toward the CMU would "support growth and innovation" as capital markets are "better at financing innovation and new sources of growth."[40] However, the implementation of the CMU has been slow. In practice, European capital markets remain far from integrated, hampering European tech companies' ability to access the kind of funding available to their American counterparts.

Another potential reason for the absence of European tech giants is Europe's legal and cultural barriers to risk-taking and entrepreneurship. Punitive bankruptcy laws across the EU have made failure so costly that European entrepreneurs often shy away from the kind of risk-taking required for ambitious technological ventures. In a report studying insolvency regimes across countries, the Organisation for Economic Co-operation and Development (OECD) found that the personal costs of entrepreneurship were the lowest in the US, Canada, and Turkey, and the highest in the Czech Republic, Sweden, Portugal, and several other European countries.[41] Aware of this problem, EU institutions have sought to pursue greater harmonization of national insolvency laws across member states, mindful that insolvency should not have to turn into a "life sentence."[42] In 2016, the European Commission proposed a Directive aimed at reducing the costs of failure for entrepreneurs, endorsing the "principle of second chance."[43] The Directive, which bears similarities to Chapter 11 of the US Bankruptcy Code, was formally adopted in 2019.[44] This and other legislative efforts to date have, nevertheless, been slow to harmonize and modernize EU bankruptcy laws across member states, prolonging the problem faced by European tech entrepreneurs.[45] Yet unforgiving bankruptcy laws are only part of the story behind European entrepreneurs' risk aversion. Cultural factors also play a role. Business failure carries a greater stigma in Europe, hampering risk-taking and consequently holding back innovation. In Europe, failure is viewed as a "personal tragedy," whereas in Silicon Valley failure is seen as a badge of honor or rite of passage, leading to the mantra of "fail fast, fail often."[46] Instead of celebrating—or even merely accepting—failure, Europeans value stability, which cultivates a mentality that is antithetical to disruptive innovation.[47]

Finally, the innovation deficit in Europe can be partly attributed to the EU's inability to attract the world's best innovative talent through a proactive migration policy. In comparison, the US technology sector relies heavily on its ability to attract immigrants. Looking at the founders of the most successful US tech companies reveals a powerful story of the role of immigration behind these tech companies. Steve Jobs of Apple was the son of a Syrian immigrant; Jeff Bezos of Amazon is a second-generation Cuban immigrant; Eduardo Saverin, the cofounder of Facebook, is Brazilian; Sergey Brin, the cofounder of Google, was born in Russia; and Elon Musk of Tesla was born in South Africa. And these famous individuals are not rare exceptions. According to a 2018 study by the National Foundation for American Policy, 55 percent of America's billion-dollar companies have an immigrant founder.[48] Looking at skilled migration more generally, Europe also fares worse than the US. According to a 2019 study, only 25 percent of immigrants to Europe are highly educated, compared to 36 percent of immigrants who migrate to other OECD countries.[49] The EU is not only struggling to attract migrants to its tech sector, but is also losing European talent to the US. This brain drain can be measured in several ways. One study focusing on the distribution of top AI talent around the world reveals that while top AI researchers overwhelmingly work in US institutions— 60 percent of the talent pool is US-based, as opposed to 11 percent in Europe—this US-based talent is only partially homegrown. Over half of the top-tier AI researchers in the US are immigrants or foreign nationals, with 29 percent of them having received their undergraduate degree in China, followed by 20 percent in the US and 18 percent in Europe.[50] This suggests that the world's top AI researchers, including top European AI researchers, are migrating to the US and rarely the other way around.

There are several reasons for why the global tech talent prefers the US to the EU, including the attractiveness of US universities that can act as a gateway to the US labor market.[51] According to the 2021 Times Higher Education World University Rankings, only six universities in the EU are listed among the top fifty universities in the world, with the highest ranked number thirty-two. In contrast, the same list features twenty-two universities in the US among the top fifty.[52] The US's world-class universities are a major draw for foreign talent. Many foreign students stay in the US after graduating, subsequently contributing to the US talent base in the labor market. A 2018 report by the National Science Foundation revealed that 70 percent of foreign-born, noncitizen science and engineering doctoral students in the US remain in the US after graduating.[53] Another reason that explains why foreign talent prefers the US is the financial rewards available in the US for tech entrepreneurs. A 2017 study by European VC firm Index Ventures found that more than 75 percent of the EU countries' stock-option rules lagged those in the US.[54] European tech startups are aware of this limitation. In 2019, five hundred chief executives from European startups, joined by European VC investors, signed an open letter to European policymakers, urging them to overhaul regulations governing employee stock options so that EU tech firms can attract better talent and thereby better compete with Silicon Valley.[55]

The examples noted above largely dispel the notion that the European rights-driven regulatory model would inevitably hinder innovation and curtail technological and economic progress. Instead, the EU's inability to produce digital giants can be traced to a variety of policies other than digital regulation that have, to date, thwarted European technological progress. This observation should alleviate the concerns of American policymakers and other stakeholders about the expected consequences of endorsing EU-style digital regulations. Any adjustment in the US toward the European rights-driven regulatory model—or the widespread emulation of that model across the world more generally—would not, as a rule, set the US back in terms of innovation. Protecting internet users' data privacy, regulating tech giants' anticompetitive behavior, or calling for more platform accountability over harmful online content would not dismantle the dynamic US capital markets, repeal its entrepreneurship-friendly bankruptcy laws, or discourage the global tech talent from migrating to the US. This suggests that when it comes to the regulation of the digital economy, the US would be well served by adopting some of the rights-protective regulatory policies promoted by the EU. However, when it comes to capital markets, insolvency laws, the entrepreneurial culture of risk-taking, and attracting global innovative talent, the EU should learn from the US. The two digital regimes should not be viewed as alternatives, but instead as complementary digital ecosystems whose best features can be emulated and pursued in tandem.

Governments Are Not Destined to Lose Their Vertical Battles Against Tech Companies

Rather than worrying that a victory for the European model would come with too much regulation, one should instead be concerned that it will not lead to effective enforcement of that regulation, with dire consequences for both the US and the EU. In many domains of digital regulation, the EU has been successful in articulating policy goals that resonate globally and adopting stringent regulations that are being replicated across jurisdictions, as evidenced by Chapter 9. However, as Chapter 3 showed, the EU has seen less success in translating those policy goals and regulations into concrete changes in the marketplace. Tech companies' market dominance remains undented, the internet continues to be flooded with hate speech and other harmful content, and internet users' personal data is still being exploited by companies and governments alike. The discussion below explores reasons for the deficiencies in the EU's enforcement record, showing how the horizontal and vertical battles are interconnected. For the EU to win the horizontal battle against the US—not just the battle of values, but also the battle of outcomes—it needs to first win the vertical battle against global tech companies. Were the EU to lose that vertical battle, the American market-driven model—through its tech giants—would govern the digital economy in practice, even if US regulators and users themselves had already lost faith in that model.

Why Large Tech Companies Are Difficult to Regulate

It has become increasingly obvious that the EU—like other democratic governments—is struggling to effectively govern tech companies that have grown to unprecedented scale and global reach. Today's largest tech companies rival some countries in their size and influence, and these companies' tremendous economic, political, and social influence make it difficult for governments to police their business practices. The tech industry also has almost unlimited resources to spend on lobbying against regulations and defending themselves in legal battles against the government, further strengthening their position vis-à-vis governments. For example, recall the discussion in Chapter 3 on how the Irish Data Protection Commission (DPC) has struggled to enforce its sprawling data privacy docket against Dublin-based US tech companies that fall within its jurisdiction. Ireland's limited enforcement activity likely has multiple causes but is at least in part explained by the DPC's inadequate resources. The DPC must take on some of the world's most powerful tech giants, whose resources dwarf its modest budget. When the GDPR entered into force, the Irish agency was bestowed a $9 million annual budget, which is equivalent to the revenue that the large US tech companies based in Dublin— including Apple, Facebook, Google, Twitter, and Microsoft—generate roughly every ten minutes.[56] It is therefore not surprising that we have not witnessed as many cases brought by the Irish regulator against these tech giants as we may have hoped.

The tech giants' size and resources are not the only reasons why governments' vertical battles against them are challenging. The digital economy is also difficult to regulate given the sheer volume of economic activity that would require regulatory oversight. In the EU's defense, one of the reasons why it has relegated so much power to the platforms to manage their own behavior is the unremitting amount of content that needs moderating and the unfeasibility of policing it at scale. In December 2021, Facebook had 1.93 billion daily users on average.[57] Every minute in 2020, Facebook users uploaded about 147,000 photos and shared 150,000 messages, Twitter gained 319 users, Instagram users posted 347,222 stories, and YouTube users uploaded 500 hours of video.[58] There is no realistic way that someone in Brussels, or anywhere else, could review this amount of content to ensure nothing illegal ends up online. *Ex ante* content review is rarely possible even for companies armed with unparalleled technological filtering tools. Apple is an exception, reviewing all submitted apps before making them available in the App Store. But compared to the scale of the content circulating on Facebook, YouTube, or Twitter, Apple's App Store review is manageable—the company reviews over 100,000 applications weekly.[59] Beyond this anomaly, platforms review the content posted on their platforms *ex post*—and even then, only do so when an algorithm, a platform user, or some other entity flags the content to them as potentially harmful.

Finally, some of the EU's enforcement challenges can be traced back to its commitment to democracy and fundamental rights, which entails a need to carefully balance numerous competing rights in enforcing its rights-driven model. Digital regulation poses difficult trade-offs that complicate any enforcement task. It is naturally easier for an authoritarian government to "effectively" enforce online content rules when they do not need to balance freedom of speech considerations with other grounds for content removal. In contrast, the EU's attempt to weigh its commitment to free speech against its desire to restrict illegal and other harmful speech calls for the kind of nuanced enforcement approach that is much harder to implement in practice. It is time-consuming, error-prone, and—in a democratic society—open to constant criticism.

The EU's commitment to the rule of law and due process also explains, at least in part, the deficiencies in its antitrust enforcement. The much-disparaged delays in the EU's enforcement of antitrust laws against tech companies stem from the EU's adherence to due process in its investigations. A dramatic and speedy crackdown on the tech industry, akin to what has recently taken place in China, is not feasible in Europe. Instead, proposed laws must go through a legislative process that consists of numerous democratic checks and balances across several institutions—the Commission, the Council of Ministers, the European Parliament, and the legislative institutions across all twenty-seven member states—to ensure that all interests are carefully considered before any regulations are enacted. Similarly, in enforcing those laws, the EU remains sensitive to the tech companies' right to be heard and offers two layers of appeals following any adverse decision the Commission makes against tech companies. Thus, it is the combination of these factors—regulating an unrelenting flow of complex economic activity with limited human and financial resources while adhering to a carefully crafted democratic process and observing the rule of law—that explains why the EU's vertical battle against the tech companies has been so challenging to date.

What Governments Can—and Must—Do to Win the Vertical Battle

These enforcement challenges are daunting yet do not mean that tech companies are destined to win the vertical battle against governments or that the European rights-driven regulatory model is doomed to fail in practice. It would be imprudent to write off governments and endorse a technological determinist view, according to which technologies developed by companies override governments and determine the future of our societies. While several commentators have argued—some convincingly—that tech firms are increasingly "new governors"[60] that "are exercising a form of sovereignty," even ushering in a world that will not be unipolar, bipolar, or multipolar but rather "technopolar,"[61] there are reasons to doubt that states will be powerless to govern these firms. Governments have always been the fundamental political unit around which societies are built. As aptly asked by Stephen Walt: "Which do you expect to be around in 100 years? Facebook or France?"[62]

Writing in 2006 against a tide of scholarship that envisioned the internet to be self-governing, Jack Goldsmith and Tim Wu reminded us why and how states continue to matter.[63] They argued that while the internet may be disruptive and transformative in shaping societies and human interaction, it will not replace the central role of governments. Governments retain the authority to exercise coercive force on firms. This authority to coerce can be, and frequently has been, deployed to change the way these firms operate. Tech companies today are more powerful than they were in 2006, but the basic argument still stands: the codes, community guidelines, and any other rules written by large tech companies ultimately remain subject to the laws written by governments possessing the coercive authority to enforce compliance with those laws. The US government may have set these companies free with Section 230 of the CDA but it retains the authority to repeal or rewrite that law. Tech companies cannot decouple themselves from governments, and while these companies may resist government regulations, they ultimately must comply with them. They cannot coerce their way into merger clearances, refuse to pay digital taxes, or restore content that the government has ordered them to take down. Neither can they engage in targeted advertising if governments ban such targeting, or treat gig workers as independent contractors if the government has legislated for these workers to be employees. The power of these companies—their ultimate sovereignty—is limited to not doing business in jurisdictions whose laws they do not like. However, that is a distinctly costly way for them to exercise sovereignty.

Acknowledging that tech companies remain subject to the coercive power of the state does not mean that regulating these companies is easy, or always effective. Noting the challenges associated with restraining today's tech giants, the literature regarding the relationship between states and tech companies has undergone an evolution. The early contributions to this line of scholarship in the 1990s claimed that the tech industry is self-governable and that states should stay on the sidelines.[64] The second wave of literature in the 2000s argued that states should, and can, assert power over tech companies.[65] However, if the first wave was overly optimistic about tech companies' ability to self-govern, the second wave might have at times been too optimistic about states' ability to govern these companies successfully. We are now moving into an era where there is an increasing consensus that tech companies' self-governance does not work and governments need to get involved, but there is increasing doubt about governments' ability to do so effectively. Thus, it is not that governments should not engage in a vertical battle against tech companies (because they should) or that they could not prevail in that battle (because they could). However, governments may need new tools to engage in that battle effectively.

For European regulators, this entails figuring out how to reclaim democratic control over the tech industry. If the EU fails in its vertical battle, it is indeed the tech companies, not democratically elected governments, that will build and run the digital society. In that society, democracy, rule of law, and individual and collective rights will only be as strong as is compatible with the profit-seeking business motives of tech companies. Thus, instead of reining in its regulatory instincts for fear of overregulating, the EU needs to double down on its commitment to regulation and follow through with more potent enforcement. However, this claim comes with a word of caution. In recommitting to regulation, the EU must remain true to the rights-driven values guiding that regulation, as it is those values which have gained traction around the world and have ultimately served the EU well in its horizontal battle against the US and China. Given that the EU is increasingly regulating the digital economy in the shadow of the US–China tech war, there is a risk that its regulatory instincts are veering it toward techno-nationalism in an effort to safeguard its digital sovereignty in a volatile and uncertain world, as recognized in Chapter 5. This could lead to regulations calling for data localization or industrial policy–driven antitrust enforcement. Yet if the EU starts embracing digital protectionism, there is a risk that techno-protectionism will become the global norm. After all, EU regulators should keep in mind that the Brussels Effect—the EU's ability to externalize its regulations—is a potent mechanism for exporting both good and bad regulations alike.

The EU has repeatedly acknowledged that its enforcement record to date leaves much to be desired and knows that it must find a way to translate its stated values and adopted laws into concrete progress on the ground. As a result, the EU has recently shown greater resolve by adopting new digital regulations that are designed to address some of the known shortcomings of its existing policies. To avoid lengthy delays associated with its past antitrust investigations focusing on the tech industry, the EU adopted the Digital Markets Act (DMA), discussed in Chapter 3, which will ban *ex ante* a set of anticompetitive practices by digital gatekeepers—including Amazon, Apple, Google, Meta, and Microsoft—without the need to show that these companies harm competition.[66] Prohibiting a set of business practices outright allows the Commission to bypass lengthy investigations, which have often hampered its efforts to intervene in digital markets in a timely fashion. Mandating a set of practices (such as interoperability or data portability) and banning a set of practices (such as self-preferencing or using data across different services) will strike at the heart of these companies' business models, giving European regulators stronger tools to enhance competition.

Similarly, the EU's recently adopted Digital Services Act (DSA), also discussed in Chapter 3, will introduce binding obligations on tech companies in relation to content that is hosted on their platforms.[67] The DSA calls for platform transparency and accountability, and strengthens those mandatory requirements with heavy sanctions. While it does not impose a general monitoring obligation on platforms in terms of the content they host, the DSA sets clear limits on platforms' freedoms by, for example, banning targeting advertising toward minors and forbidding manipulative designs that distort autonomous and informed decisions or choice.[68] These specific provisions accompany a host of general rules on algorithmic transparency and due process regarding the users' ability to contest any content moderation decisions. The largest platforms will be subject to additional rules, including independent audits and an obligation to grant access to authorities and researchers to investigate their business models. Whether these regulations will eventually push tech companies to govern in ways that are more democratic, more transparent, and more accountable will be one of the biggest tests of the EU's ability to translate its stated values into actual market outcomes—and, with that, prove the viability of its regulatory model as a template for other democracies to follow.

Harnessing the Power of the Large Tech Companies to Enforce Digital Regulations

The next several years will reveal whether the more assertive regulatory action by the EU will enhance its standing in the vertical battle against tech companies. These coming years will also tell if the US will join this battle by strengthening its own regulations against tech companies or whether Congress will remain deadlocked, leaving US citizens with heated congressional debates but ultimately failed bills that do little to overhaul the American market-driven regulatory model. Yet a transformed political environment that is increasingly hostile to tech companies may help these governments' regulatory efforts. Tech companies suffer from a deep reputational and trust deficit with policymakers and the general public, making it difficult for them to take a combative stand against the regulators without triggering an even harsher backlash. Afraid of antagonizing regulators even more, tech companies are likely to pick their vertical battles and fight only some of them, while conceding others.

The battlefield is also shifting in ways that might make the governments' failures to enforce their regulations against tech companies less consequential. Most strikingly, certain large tech companies are now leveraging their market power against other large tech companies, helping the governments' enforcement efforts in the process. These horizontal battles within the tech industry can transform the digital marketplace, while offsetting the enforcement deficit that has haunted the EU and other regulators to date. One of the most consequential horizontal battles over data privacy is now unfolding between Meta and Apple. Meta has the most to lose from stronger data privacy protections as the business model for Facebook is dependent on access to consumer data that fuels targeted advertising.[69] In contrast, Apple's revenue is primarily driven by selling hardware. Consequently, Apple can seize on the privacy narrative and leverage it strategically against companies like Meta. In April 2021, Apple rolled out an update on its iPhone that asks users whether they want apps, such as Facebook, to track them.[70] This change is seen as a tremendous boon for user privacy, but a devastating blow to companies like Meta.[71] Meta reacted with a fierce—and contested—argument outlining the economic benefits of unrestrained personal data collection, while claiming the mantle of the defender of small businesses that rely on Facebook's personalized advertising tools.[72]

Meta was right to fear Apple's new anti-tracking measures: users have overwhelmingly chosen not to be tracked. Early market research from July 2021 shows that users permit tracking only around 25 percent of the time.[73] Other market research suggests an even more drastic outcome. According to one analysis published in May 2021, 96 percent of the users in the US were found to be opting out of the app tracking since Apple introduced the option, while the percentage worldwide was 89 percent.[74] Despite some variance across these numbers, the general trend is undisputed: users are choosing privacy over surveillance. This, in part, explains the unprecedented 26 percent plunge in Meta's stock price in February 2022, following Meta's disclosure that Apple's privacy change will cost the company billions of dollars a year.[75] Meta stood to lose the most, yet several other tech firms, including Twitter,

Snap and YouTube, also saw their revenues evaporate following the introduction of Apple's App Tracking Transparency tool.[76]

In another example of a large tech company aligning itself with governments, Microsoft has urged regulators in Australia, the EU, and the US to mandate platforms displaying news to share revenue with media outlets that generate the news.[77] This breaks the united front that the tech industry typically assumes against governments while also helping Microsoft tilt the market toward its products and services at the expense of those of its rivals, including Google and Meta. This is not the first time Microsoft has advocated regulatory action against its rivals. After fighting the EU's antitrust regulators for years—largely unsuccessfully—Microsoft turned the tables and initiated an EU antitrust complaint against Google in 2011, accusing Google of entrenching its dominance in the markets for online search and search advertising.[78] News reporting acknowledged the shift in the regulatory landscape, noting how "Microsoft is relishing a second act in Brussels, playing the role of scold instead of victim."[79] While Microsoft entered into a temporary truce with Google in 2016,[80] Microsoft has recently again become more vocal in urging governments to act against Google and other tech giants. In 2021, Google's Senior Vice President Kent Walker accused Microsoft of "reverting to their familiar playbook of attacking rivals and lobbying for regulations that benefit their own interests,"[81] while accusing Microsoft of "naked corporate opportunism" in the wake of Microsoft's support for legislation that forces platforms to share revenue with media organizations.[82] These examples involving Microsoft and Google further reveal that leading tech companies can be seen as allies and enemies alike, at times working in unison to defend their common interests against governments eager to regulate them, while at other times engaging in bitter horizontal battles with one another and thus—directly or indirectly—assisting the regulators in their vertical battles against some of those same warring tech companies.

These horizontal battles within the tech industry can be highly consequential in transforming the regulatory landscape. A single decision made by a large tech company to curtail the business model of another large tech company can be a considerably more effective way to realize the goals of the GDPR than any effort by European privacy regulators. No doubt Meta would rather pay fines to European regulators than have Apple ask every user on its devices whether they want the Facebook app to track them. Now, some may argue that these horizontal battles are proof that the tech industry should be self-regulating. Some may go further and suggest that the American market-driven model is vindicated, since tech companies can, and do, keep one another in check. Why worry about vertical battles between governments and tech companies if those can be replaced by horizontal battles among the tech companies themselves? Yet anyone who takes democracy seriously is likely to be uncomfortable with the idea that digital citizens' privacy rights will be respected as long as the tech companies determine that this beneficial societal objective and their business interests are aligned.

Reliance on tech companies' horizontal battles as a tool for digital governance invites the question of what these companies' values are, and whether they could thus replace governments as regulators of the industry. There are, indeed, signs that tech companies are gradually shifting their corporate policies and actual business practices toward the values espoused by the EU, potentially alleviating governments' vertical battles against them. Numerous highly publicized scandals have left tech companies embattled, making their defense of the free-for-all techno-libertarianism untenable. Instead, they have joined the calls to reform Section 230 of the CDA and have urged Congress to adopt a GDPR-like federal privacy law in the US.[83] We see a shift not just in these companies' public relations rhetoric but also in some of their policies. Initially, tech companies were reluctant to moderate content on their platforms but now increasingly concede that they have a responsibility to do so more proactively. Until recently, Meta remained adamant that it is not "the arbiter of truth" and refused to remove some controversial speech, including hate speech.[84] The #StopHateForProfit boycott embodied the widespread criticism of Facebook's policy, with several advertisers withholding advertising on any social media platform that failed to condemn or remove racist content on their platforms.[85] The January 6 Capitol attack compelled Meta to take action, leading it to temporarily suspend President Trump from the Facebook platform. Most recently, the Russian invasion of Ukraine forced Meta to assume an active role in the information war to reduce the spread of significant state propaganda promoted by Russia.[86] These examples illustrate that even the tech companies themselves no longer believe in the techno-libertarian ethos that underlies the American market-driven regulatory model, which is now shaping vertical battles in favor of governments.

Tech companies also face increased pressure from their employees to adjust their business practices toward values embedded in the European regulatory model. Frances Haugen represents a rather extreme case of an employee turning on her former employer when she widely publicized Meta's harmful practices. However, discontent among tech employees is growing more broadly. Employees are more outspoken about hate speech on social media platforms. In 2020, Meta's employees were outraged by the company's decision not to remove President Trump's controversial post about the racial protests relating to the death of George Floyd, an African American who was brutally killed by a Minnesota police officer that May. Many viewed the post as glorifying violence. Twitter had decided to hide Trump's post from view, while Meta took no action. In protest, as many as 600 Meta employees staged a "virtual walkout."[87] Some employees tweeted that they were going to leave the company, and others circulated internal petitions calling for all employees to voice similar commitments.[88] At Twitter, employees took part in these virtual walkouts in solidarity with Meta employees,[89] reinforcing the message that the industry had to adjust its ways.

While these examples are encouraging for many, it is not clear that tech companies' true values are actually changing. In a world of shifting public consciousness and intensifying regulatory scrutiny, tech companies aim to strike a more conciliatory tone. Some tech companies, such as Microsoft, seem more consistent than some others in taking a stand in favor of regulation and endorsing a rights-driven regulatory model.[90] But for others, the conciliatory rhetoric often belies continuing attempts to shape the regulatory environment in ways that allow these companies to preserve their core business models. For example, most tech companies continue to resist antitrust reforms—the policy domain where an onslaught of regulation could, indeed, debilitate their core business models.[91] There, the best hope for these companies is the continuing deadlocks in Congress and the unwillingness of the US courts to abandon their entrenched, market-driven approach to antitrust regulation. It is unclear whether the pressure from employees or users is sufficient to push these companies to abandon their business models, such as targeted advertising. Even the consumers who lament the repeated failures of these companies are often too addicted to the convenience of using their products to abandon them—just like advertisers and investors are too addicted to the profits and returns these companies help them generate. The vertical battle thus remains one that governments need to continue fighting—and should do so with even greater intensity—to ensure that the European rights-driven regulatory model thrives in practice.

The Battle for the Soul of the Digital Economy

The forces, trends, and choices affecting the outcomes in important regulatory battles—both horizontal or vertical—outlined above are shaping the digital economy today and will continue to do so far into future. An enhanced understanding of these elements may not accurately predict what kind of world will emerge from these battles. But it will, hopefully, help guide our thinking on questions such as whether conflict or cooperation will characterize the digital economy in the coming years, whether technological decoupling across jurisdictions will abate or accelerate, and whether various regulatory models can or will continue to coexist in a digital economy that we can still call "global." Some battles will likely wane; others will intensify. Digital regulators and tech companies alike will increasingly pick their battles to win conflicts that matter the most—ones that truly shape the economic opportunities and political structures of digital societies. After all, tech companies and governments alike know that winning a battle is of little consolation if you lose the war.

A Bipolar World Marked by Continuing Conflict and Cooperation

There are multiple possible outcomes in the horizontal battles among the US, China, and the EU, some of which we now understand to be more likely than others. A *unipolar world* where one of the three models emerges as victor, defining the norms and values for the global digital economy, is unlikely. As shown in the discussion in Chapters 5 and 6 about key conflicts in these horizontal battles, economic, political, and technological power is too dispersed for any single jurisdiction to declare anything but a partial or fleeting victory. A *multipolar world* where different regulatory models harmoniously coexist, and where coordination and cooperation surpass existing differences and conflicts among the models, is equally improbable. The norms and values reflected in the three leading regulatory models are too distinct from each other for any such consensus or extensive cooperation to emerge. Although either scenario—a unipolar digital world based on domination or a multipolar digital world based on cooperation—would sustain a global internet and an integrated digital economy, these two developments are unlikely to occur in practice.

The most likely outcome for today's global digital economy is a *continuing conflict*. Horizontal battles are likely to endure, and even intensify, or extend to new policy areas or other jurisdictions. The aggravating geopolitical tensions lead governments to view digital regulation increasingly through the lens of national security. This outlook pushes governments to adopt policies that maximize their technological self-sufficiency, which in turn feeds techno-nationalist policies aimed at greater decoupling of digital regimes. In particular, a near-term resolution of the US–China tech war seems unlikely as tensions between the two powers persist. The US and China continue to view each other as economic and geopolitical rivals and approach their technological competition as a zero-sum game where an advantage for one side is a loss for the other.

In contrast, the horizontal conflict between the US and the EU shows signs of abating as the domestic preferences in the US are shifting toward those prevailing in the EU. The growing demand for China's state-driven regulatory model across the world further enhances the likelihood that the US will increasingly align itself with the EU—a trend that is already underway. This enhanced transatlantic alignment toward the European rights-driven model may pave the way for a *bipolar digital world order*. In this state of the world, the US and the EU would jointly lead the coalition of techno-democracies to challenge digital authoritarian norms and values embraced by China and its ideological allies, as discussed further below. Battle lines would be drawn around political ideology: on the one side, jurisdictions where digital technologies are harnessed to empower individuals to protect their rights; on the other, jurisdictions where those technologies are leveraged by authoritarian leaders as tools for political control.

Even in a bilateral digital world marked by continuing conflict, various stabilizing forces are likely to keep these conflicts under control—and the existing digital order functioning. For example, the US and China both want to retain market opportunities for their tech companies in each other's markets despite their simultaneous attempts to limit each other's access to key technologies or investment opportunities. After all, to win its tech race against China, US tech companies need to be able to fund their innovations, which they often do with the help of profits generated in China. The same way, China wants its tech companies to grow, which may require them to be able to tap into the US capital markets. The discussion in Part II has shown how these interdependencies across the key actors and key battles leave all parties more constrained in terms of the battle strategies they can deploy. In this world, the global digital economy will likely feature a managed conflict with alternating periods of escalation and de-escalation. The multiple entanglements across key players and battles will prevent an all-out war, yet the depth of the disagreements will simultaneously keep a lasting truce or permanent peace out of reach. Even so, it remains possible to reach limited areas of consensus or cooperation in the midst of the protracted conflict,[92] such as agreeing to auditing rules that allow Chinese tech companies to remain listed on US stock exchanges, or by permitting the exportation of some key technologies even while restricting others, as discussed in Chapters 4 and 5.

Another force driving de-escalation in these horizontal battles is that none of the entities in the conflicts are uniform or internally coherent; there are conflicting priorities within each of the US, China, and the EU. The pro-market voices within Europe often moderate the EU's regulatory impulses, making them more acceptable to the US. Similarly, the US's pro-market forces are tempered by growing internal dissent calling for tighter regulation, paving way for continuing transatlantic alignment. The Chinese government refrains from total censorship, choosing not to enforce a total ban on VPNs and hence letting Chinese internet users remain partially connected to the outer world. These balancing impulses within each jurisdiction moderate the extremes and pave the way for a world characterized by limited cooperation, managed conflict, or bearable coexistence.

These forces of restraint also explain why the continuing conflicts are unlikely to lead to full technological decoupling. Some commentators have predicted an emergence of a "splinternet,"[93] where the internet fragments into different national internets such as a "Chinese internet" and an "American internet," with the rest of the world opting into one or needing to navigate between the two. Already, in part, the internet has lost its global character: China is fencing off many foreign providers from its market and blocking access to numerous foreign websites. And the US is limiting the ability of some American companies' software—such as Google's apps—to operate in Chinese-built Huawei phones. However, any such technological decoupling is likely to be partial and incomplete, at best. As the discussion in Part III showed, the US, China, and the EU are all providing a different layer for the operation of the internet and the digital economy more broadly. As a result, the three regulatory models will continue to overlap in several—if not most—countries that continue to rely on Chinese digital infrastructure, American tech companies, and European regulations to govern that infrastructure and those companies. The complementary roles that each of the digital empires plays in the world's tech ecosystem will thus sustain at least a minimal foundation of a global, interconnected digital economy.

A Battle Between Techno-Democracies and Techno-Autocracies

As the US and the EU are pursuing greater alignment, the most consequential horizontal battle is now emerging between a US–EU–led coalition of techno-democracies that endorses some variant of the European rights-driven regulatory model and a group of techno-autocracies that adheres to a variant of the Chinese state-driven regulatory model.[94] There have recently been several calls and proposals for deeper cooperation over technology policy among liberal democracies.[95] These proposals build on an acknowledgment that too little has been done to counter the rise of China and the diffusion of its state-driven regulatory model, and that no country can effectively do this alone. To date, democratic countries have not provided an alternative to China's Digital

Silk Road or made real progress in defending themselves against cyberattacks, nor have they coordinated on technology standards that would reflect their shared values. For example, the Halifax International Security Forum, which focuses on the world's security challenges,[96] has warned that the failure of the techno-democracies to step up cooperation risks entrenching digital authoritarian norms globally. Absent a joint response, China has the ability to assume global dominance in AI applications, spy on much of the world, and deploy key international institutions to entrench its norms, thereby making "the world as a whole safe for authoritarianism."[97] A deeper cooperation among techno-democracies would require these countries to put aside their differences and acknowledge that they are all better off in a world that is founded on liberal democratic ideals rather than in a world that sustains authoritarian norms.

Any proposed collaboration among techno-democracies, however, begs the question as to who ought to be joining such a group and what the group's agenda should be. Jared Cohen and Richard Fontaine propose an informal coalition among a "T-12" group of techno-democracies,[98] initially consisting of the US, France, Germany, Japan, and the United Kingdom (which all have large economies and are important technology players); Australia, Canada, and South Korea (which all have smaller economies but are important technology players); Finland and Sweden (which are powerful players in technology and engineering); and Israel and India (which have notable technology and start-up sectors). Over time, the T-12 could expand to other techno-democracies, and also invite the participation of the private sector. Cohen and Fontaine envision the T-12 as a forum for information sharing, with participating countries comparing their assessments on the risks associated with China's 5G technology, as well as standard setting for emerging technologies like facial recognition. At a higher level, this group could "articulate a vision of the future based on innovation, freedom, democratic collaboration, and liberal values."[99]

Other similar proposals exist, including the "China Strategy Group" that is chaired by former Google CEO Eric Schmidt, the UK-led "Democracy-10," or the US-led "Tech-10."[100] While specifics across these and other proposals vary, Australia, Canada, Japan, South Korea, and the UK are often cited as leading techno-democracies alongside the EU and the US. China and Russia are viewed as the most prominent techno-autocracies but there are several others, including Iran, Pakistan, and Saudi Arabia, that suppress internet freedoms.[101] Though most major economies would naturally fall into one bloc or another, there is no clear delineation between techno-democracies and techno-autocracies—many countries are not perfect democracies or full autocracies but are often characterized as "hybrid regimes" or "flawed democracies." As a result, even in this bipolar, ideologically divided digital world order, spheres of influence would overlap and some nations would continue to straddle the divide between the Chinese authoritarian model and the US–EU–endorsed liberal democratic regulatory model.

The idea of a closer cooperation among techno-democracies is gaining momentum, in part because it benefits from strong political backing by the US government. President Biden often depicts the world as a contest between democracy and autocracy, and his foreign policy doctrine is geared at countering China's ambitions and global influence.[102] He has made cooperation with democracies a hallmark of his foreign policy, and even hosted a "Summit of Democracy" in December 2021, which sought to "set forth an affirmative agenda for democratic renewal."[103] In April 2022, these efforts culminated in the US government announcing a partnership with sixty countries who signed a "Declaration for the Future of the Internet," which pledges to harness digital technologies to "promote connectivity, democracy, peace, the rule of law, sustainable development, and the enjoyment of human rights and fundamental freedoms."[104] This political commitment seeks to send a message of unity among the nations that share a vision for the "internet that is an open, free, global, interoperable, reliable, and secure [one]" and that are committed to "respecting human rights online and across the digital ecosystem."[105]

Despite these efforts to build a more cohesive coalition of techno-democracies, it is unclear how effective such a coalition would be in shaping the global digital order toward the values articulated in the 2022 Declaration. The group of techno-democracies is heterogeneous, and existing disagreements may impede any meaningful collaboration among them. While the Declaration remains open for new signatories, the US and its democratic allies also face a dilemma on how puritan does a country's commitment to democratic values need to be in order to be included in such a coalition.[106] There are many important countries sitting between the democratic and authoritarian spheres of influence that often break liberal democratic norms. The question for the US and the EU is whether they refuse to accept countries such as India and Brazil to any alliance of democracies and thus risk pushing these countries closer to China. Techno-democracies may also struggle to persuade these swing states—the countries straddling the democratic and authoritarian divide—to abandon their collaboration with China. The US cannot halt China's economic rise and technological prowess while easily cajoling other nations to forgo the opportunities that China's growing economy presents. Already today, China is the largest trade partner for almost twice as many countries as the US.[107] When confronted with a choice between the US and China, these countries may end up choosing China. Finally, rallying the world around the cause for democracy is also a tall order at a time when the

US and EU are facing particularly stark challenges to their own democratic institutions at home. Notwithstanding these challenges, the need to preserve liberal democracy remains the most compelling battle cry for governments seeking an alternative to the Chinese state-driven regulatory model.

In this battle between techno-democracies and techno-autocracies, China and its state-driven regulatory model have certain advantages. First, China's regulatory model can be viewed as somehow more effective. While the US struggles to legislate and the EU struggles to enforce its digital regulations, the Chinese government can operationalize its regulatory model in the absence of the constraints of democratic rulemaking. Not only is China effective in passing regulations, but it faces little resistance in enforcing those regulations. It tolerates little dissent from tech companies, all of which know that compliance is their only option. This applies to Chinese and foreign companies alike. On the same day that the Chinese government fined Alibaba a record $2.8 billion, the company made a public statement saying that it "accept[ed] the penalty with sincerity and will ensure . . . compliance with determination."[108] To further show its commitment to the Chinese government's goal to spread wealth, Alibaba vowed in September 2021 to invest $15.5 billion into the country's common prosperity initiatives.[109] Other Chinese tech companies have followed a very similar script, submitting to the government's demands and pledging their commitment to the values espoused by the government.[110] The Chinese government expects similar, unequivocal compliance from foreign firms. Chapter 4 showed how the US tech companies active in China repeatedly capitulate to the demands of the Chinese government even when those demands are contrary to these companies' stated values. This relative success of the Chinese regulatory model in obtaining compliance from tech companies stands in stark contrast with the repeated difficulties faced by European and American regulators in holding tech companies accountable. In the EU and the US, regulators often face lengthy legal battles as tech companies contest, rather than acquiesce to, the regulatory actions targeting them. These features make the Chinese state-driven regulatory model attractive for governments that are reluctant at being drawn into the kind of vertical battles that the US and EU are struggling to win.

China has also been notably successful in exporting its state-driven model through the Digital Silk Road, which consists of building digital infrastructures around the world, as discussed in Chapter 8. The US and its allies have made few gains in their attempts to counter the global ascent of this particular avenue of Chinese influence, which leaves the door open for China to continue to export its norms surrounding political control and digital surveillance. One of the reasons for China's success is that it has not had to push its norms that aggressively. In many parts of the world, there has been a genuine ideological demand for a state-led regulatory model that harnesses the internet for government surveillance and provides tools for the control of political dissidents and minorities. On the other hand, a subset of countries has entered the Chinese fold for more practical than ideological reasons, choosing to import Chinese digital infrastructures simply because it offered them the most affordable path toward digital development. Unless the techno-democracies can offer these countries an alternative and similarly attractive path toward digital development, these countries are likely to welcome Chinese influence and, with that, risk allowing their societies to be shaped by digital authoritarian norms. Finally, China's success in generating prominent tech companies gives a boost to its regulatory model. By nurturing leading tech companies such as Alibaba, Huawei, JD.com, and Tencent, China has shown to the world that political freedom is not necessary for economic success. China's emergence as a technological superpower suggests to many that state control over the digital economy can coexist with a culture of dynamic innovation, technological progress, and economic growth. Techno-democracies therefore have a hard time arguing that by emulating China's state-driven regulatory model, countries would compromise their digital development. Instead, by looking at the Chinese model, some of these governments see the best of both worlds: effective political control and impressive economic success.

The stakes in this broader battle between techno-democracies and techno-autocracies go beyond being able to claim victory in strictly economic terms. This battle is a political and ideological fight that tests the strength of liberal democracy as a model of government. The battle also extends beyond the digital realm; it is nested within a larger battle pitting democracy and freedom on one side against autocracy and control on the other. The ongoing conflict surrounding Russia's invasion of Ukraine reinforces these divisions as liberal democracies have rallied to support Ukraine's fight for their freedom while many authoritarian leaders refuse to condemn the invasion, seeing it as part of the larger battle against Western dominance and its values around freedom and democracy. Interestingly, many countries that can be identified as battleground states, sitting between the different regulatory models in terms of digital governance, are the very same governments—including Brazil and India—that have declined to condemn Russia's invasion of Ukraine and instead chosen to remain neutral. This further shows how the spheres of influence between the digital empires are still being drawn, and how the unfolding battle over the future of the digital economy is embedded as part of a larger ideological conflict: a contest to crown democracy or autocracy as the defining current geopolitical order.

The stakes in this monumental battle could not be higher. The coalition-building among the world's techno-democracies has been motivated thus far by the understanding that this is the battle that truly defines the soul of the digital economy. The coalition's primary focus has been the horizontal battle against China in the name of saving democracy from the autocracy. But techno-democracies should bear in mind that democratic institutions can be weakened in two distinct ways: they can be weakened if the US and the EU lose their horizontal battle to China or, alternatively, if the US and the EU lose their vertical battle to tech companies. While the democratic governments are struggling to regulate tech companies, the Chinese government has launched a fierce crackdown on the tech industry in its home market, as discussed in Chapter 2. Few are betting against the Chinese government in that vertical battle. Conversely, it is not a given that the US and the EU will be able to win the various vertical conflicts in their home markets. The question surrounding vertical battles is therefore not whether governments, as a general matter, can control tech companies, but whether *democratic governments* can do so. China, as this book has shown, certainly has no problem reining them in. The most disturbing outcome of that battle would be an affirmation that only authoritarians have the tools to effectively fight vertical battles and govern the digital economy while democracies fail in that endeavor. This elevates the stakes further, making this a battle that neither the EU nor the US—or any liberal democracy—can afford to lose.

The digital society is at an inflection point. The cascade of regulation that is being drafted, and that will be drafted in the coming years, will be crucial in shaping the digital economy and digital society for years to come. Governments, tech companies, and digital citizens are making important choices that will shape the future ethos of the digital society and define the soul of the digital economy. The goal of this book has been to lay bare the choices we face as societies and individuals, explain the forces that shape those choices, and spell out the stakes involved in making those choices. The choices will define what kind of society we live in for years and decades to come, including whether we, as humans, control technology or whether technology and its providers control and exploit us—and whether surveillance capitalism, digital authoritarianism, or liberal democratic values will prevail as a foundation for human engagement and for our society as we advance further into the digital era.

Acknowledgments

Writing this book has left me indebted to many. Throughout the writing process, I relied on the generosity and intellect of a number of colleagues whose thoughtful feedback made this a much better book. I am particularly grateful to a brilliant group of individuals who read early drafts and participated in a manuscript conference held in January 2022: Elena Chachko, Adam Chilton, Danielle Citron, Katerina Linos, Paul Nemitz, Abe Newman, Marietje Schaake, Joris van Hoboken, and Angela Zhang. Putting aside your own important work to discuss mine is an act of tremendous collegiality that I will never take for granted. Your honest feedback was invaluable and gave me the roadmap to continue.

Many other colleagues read drafts, discussed ideas, or pointed me to relevant literature that helped me see further and think deeper. My warm thanks to Bill Alford, Yochai Benkler, Akeel Bilgrami, Kurt Björklund, Gabby Blum, Rachel Brewster, John Coates, Jonathan Cole, Alex de Streel, Einer Elhauge, Luca Enriques, Tom Ginsburg, Jack Goldsmith, Monica Hakimi, Howell Jackson, Suzanne Kingston, Ben Liebman, Tambiama Madiega, Florencia Marotta-Wurgler, Amanda Parsons, Nicolas Petit, Katharina Pistor, Christina Ponsa-Kraus, Eric Posner, Kal Raustiala, Gustavo Ribeiro, Dan Richman, Tim Rühlig, Paul Schwartz, Thomas Streinz, Holger Spamann, Cass Sunstein, and Salome Viljoen. Thank you for helping me see where I was advancing the conversation and where the argument needed more. Special thanks to the colleagues who helped me fill the many gaps in my knowledge. You taught me about US constitutional law, national security, espionage, empires, technical standards, fundamental rights, the Chinese Communist Party, digital taxation, venture capital, and more. I could have never written on such a wide range of topics without your expertise and guidance. My thanks also to the two anonymous reviewers at the Oxford University Press for distinctly thoughtful comments.

I leaned particularly heavily on a few trusted colleagues. I am especially grateful to Dave Pozen and Matt Waxman, my wonderful Columbia colleagues whose scholarly judgment I have come to rely on tremendously. Thank you, Dave and Matt, for availing yourselves for multiple reads and conversations on these topics. Angela Zhang, thank you for reading several versions of my manuscript. My confidence to write about the Chinese digital economy owes much to your terrific scholarship, encouragement, and patience to educate me. Finally, my deep gratitude goes to Adam Chilton and Katerina Linos, whose generosity as readers of my work knows no bounds. I cannot even begin to count the hours you invested in reading and discussing every version of this book with me. Thank you for your honesty, generosity, and brilliance.

I also benefited from the opportunity to present early drafts at various conferences and workshops, including at the Columbia Law School Faculty Workshop; Global Justice Workshop, Law & Economics Workshop, and the Faculty Workshop at Harvard Law School; the Legal Theory Workshop at the University of Michigan Law School; the Faculty Workshop at Vanderbilt Law School; the International Law Colloquium at the UC Berkeley Law School; and the Golem Project seminar series at the London School of Economics. My talks at the Brooklyn Law School, Oxford University, and Tilburg University presented valuable opportunities to clarify my thinking on these topics. I also acknowledge with gratitude the financial support by Columbia University's Jerome A. Chazen Institute for Global Business and Richard Paul Richman Center for Business, Law, and Public Policy. Thank you for believing in this research and making it possible.

I could have never written this book without my excellent team of research assistants. My warmest thanks to Fahad Al-Sadoon, Kelly Benguigui, Jan Brack, Sarah Clouston, Jerry Du, Iris Duan, Haley Flora, Lucas Forbes, Mara Hellendoorn, Jamie Herring, Victoria Jin, Britt Jordan, Anita Kapuyr, Aroosa Khokher, Eddie Kim, Susie Kim, David Leys, Eileen Li, Nicole Miller, Tatum Millet, Matan Neuman, Mario Palacios, Aita Seck, Aparna Sundaram, Greta Ulbrick, Alexandra Valas, and the additional Chinese students who were instrumental for this research but asked to remain anonymous. Your talent, resourcefulness, and dedication amaze me every day. Samantha Lim and Lena Rieke from the Columbia Law Library helped me stay on top of new developments across all these fields—no small task yet always impeccably done. Thank you both.

I also owe thanks to my talented development editor, Chris Lura, whose astute editing helped me weave the many stands of the argument together. I am also grateful to Dave McBride, my editor at OUP. Your interventions were selective but always spot on. Thank you for sharing my conviction that this book had to be written and your faith that I was the right person to write it.

Finally, my profound gratitude to my husband, Travis. You heard about *Digital Empires* every day for the past two years. You read every chapter and were asked to comment on every idea. And in the days when my arguments needed focus and when the writing process was at a crossroads, you helped me find the right direction. Thank you for your tireless support and for your partnership, in my intellectual journey and in life.

This book is dedicated to my children, Oliver, Sylvia, and Vivian. Being your mom is the greatest privilege and joy of my life. It gives deeper meaning to everything I do, including writing this book. I am keenly aware how much your personal interactions and life experiences are shaped by technology. My concern for your future gave me a keen sense of purpose to better understand the digital world in the making. We owe it to you to govern technology in ways that it serves you, protects you, empowers you, and never undermines you.

New York
December 2022

Notes

INTRODUCTION

1. Cass Sunstein, Is Social Media Good or Bad for Democracy?, SUR: INT'L J. ON HUM. RTS. 83, 84–87 (2018).
2. *See generally* Shoshana Zuboff, THE AGE OF SURVEILLANCE CAPITALISM: THE FIGHT FOR A HUMAN FUTURE AT THE NEW FRONTIER OF POWER (2019).
3. Alison Beard, Can Big Tech Be Disrupted?, HARV. BUS. REV., Jan.–Feb. 2022.
4. Leo Lewis, Tokyo Stock Market Eclipsed by the Four Tech Leviathans, FIN. TIMES (Sep. 1, 2021), https://www.ft.com/content/460747da-a410-41aa-a8a4-0c991 f264c06.
5. Naushad K. Cherrayil, Microsoft Acquires More Unicorns Among Big Five Technology Companies, TECHRADAR (June 27, 2020), https://global.techradar. com/en-ae/news/microsoft-acquires-more-unicorns-among-big-five-technol ogy-companies; discussed in Eileen Li, Note, Merger Review 2.0: Infusing CFIUS's "Critical Technologies" Approach into Antitrust Oversight of Nascent Tech Acquisitions, 122 COLUM. L. REV. 1691, 1694 (2022).
6. Justin Harper, Apple Buys a Company Every Three to Four Weeks, BBC NEWS (Feb. 24, 2021), https://www.bbc.com/news/business-56178792.
7. Paul Nemitz, Constitutional Democracy and Technology in the Age of Artificial Intelligence, 376 PHIL. TRANSACTIONS OF THE ROYAL SOC'Y A, 1, 2–4 (2018).
8. Christchurch Shooting Live Updates: 49 Are Dead After 2 Mosques Are Hit, N.Y. TIMES (Mar. 14, 2019), https://www.nytimes.com/2019/03/14/world/asia/ new-zealand-shooting-updates-christchurch.html.
9. David Kaye, SPEECH POLICE: THE GLOBAL STRUGGLE TO GOVERN THE INTERNET 23 (2019).
10. Burcu Gültekin Punsmann, Three Months in Hell: What I Learned From Three Months of Content Moderation for Facebook in Berlin, SÜDDEUTSCHE ZEITUNG

(Jan. 6, 2018), https://sz-magazin.sueddeutsche.de/internet/three-months-in-hell-84381.

11. Meta disputes this figure. *See* Kaye, SPEECH POLICE, *supra* note 9, at 59.

12. Reyhan Harmanci, Tech Confessional: The Googler Who Looked at the Worst of the Internet, BUZZFEED NEWS (Aug. 21, 2012), https://www.buzzfeednews.com/article/reyhan/tech-confessional-the-googler-who-looks-at-the-wo.

13. See Bobby Allyn, In Settlement, Facebook to Pay $52 Million to Content Moderators with PTSD, NPR (May 12, 2020), https://www.npr.org/2020/05/12/854998616/in-settlement-facebook-to-pay-52-million-to-content-moderators-with-ptsd.

14. John Perry Barlow, A Declaration of the Independence of Cyberspace, ELEC. FRONTIER FOUND. (Feb. 8, 1996), https://www.eff.org/cyberspace-independence.

15. *See* Zuboff, *supra* note 2.

16. Adrian Chen, Cambridge Analytica and Our Lives Inside the Surveillance Machine, THE N. YORKER (Mar. 21, 2018), https://www.newyorker.com/tech/annals-of-technology/cambridge-analytica-and-our-lives-inside-the-surveillance-machine.

17. Daniel Susser, Beate Roessler, and Helen Nissenbaum, Technology, Autonomy, and Manipulation, 8 INTERNET POL'Y REV. 1, 2–3 (2019).

18. Ross Andersen, The Panopticon Is Already Here, ATL. (Sep. 2020), https://www.theatlantic.com/magazine/archive/2020/09/china-ai-surveillance/614197/.

19. Dave Gershgorn, China's "Sharp Eyes" Program Aims to Surveil 100% of Public Space, ONEZERO (Mar. 2, 2021), https://onezero.medium.com/chinas-sharp-eyes-program-aims-to-surveil-100-of-public-space-ddc22d63e015; Robert Muggah & Greg Walton, "Smart" Cities Are Surveilled Cities, FOREIGN POL'Y (Apr. 17, 2021), https://foreignpolicy.com/2021/04/17/smart-cities-surveillance-privacy-digital-threats-internet-of-things-5g/.

20. *See* Orville Schell, Technology Has Abetted China's Surveillance State, FIN. TIMES (Sep. 2, 2020), https://www.ft.com/content/6b61aaaa-3325-44dc-8110-bf4a351185fb; *see also* Louise Lucas & Emily Feng, Inside China's Surveillance State, FIN. TIMES (July 19, 2018), https://www.ft.com/content/2182eebe-8a17-11e8-bf9e-8771d5404543. *See also* Guanyu Jiaqiang Gonggong Anquan Shipin Jiankong Jianshe Lianwang, Yingyong Gongzuo de Ruogan Yijian (关于加强公共安全视频监控建设联网, 应用工作的若干意) [Several Opinions on Strengthening the Construction, Connection and Application of Public Safety Video Surveillance Network], NAT'L REFORM AND DEV. COMM'N, 2015, https://web.archive.org/web/20181121120527/http://www.ndrc.gov.cn/zcfb/zcfbtz/201505/t20150513_691578.html (China) (laying out the goals of the surveillance system as "全域覆盖、全网共享、全时可用、全程可控") (unofficial translation).

21. *See Snowden Revelations*, LAWFARE, https://www.lawfareblog.com/snowden-revelations.

22. Paul Mozur et al., A Global Tipping Point for Reigning in Tech Has Arrived, N.Y. TIMES (Apr. 30, 2021), https://www.nytimes.com/2021/04/20/technology/global-tipping-point-tech.html.

23. Sam Schechner, Big Tech Braces for a Wave of Regulation, WALL ST. J. (Jan. 16, 2022), https://www.wsj.com/articles/big-tech-braces-for-wave-of-regulation-11642131732.

24. Silvia Amaro, How Europe Became the World's Top Tech Regulator, CNBC (Mar. 25, 2021), https://www.cnbc.com/2021/03/25/big-tech-how-europe-became-the-worlds-top-regulator.html.

25. Edward White & Mark Wembridge, Xi Jinping Defends Crackdowns in 'Common Prosperity' Drive at Davos, FIN. TIMES (Jan. 17, 2022), https://www.ft.com/content/8963b1ee-9ffb-4f2e-8648-472e641716ba.

26. Cecilia Kang, Lawmakers, Taking Aim at Big Tech, Push Sweeping Overhaul of Antitrust, N.Y. TIMES (JUNE 29, 2021), https://www.nytimes.com/2021/06/11/technology/big-tech-antitrust-bills.html; Müge Fazlioglu, Privacy Bills in the 117th Congress, INT'L ASS'N OF PRIV. PRO. (Aug. 24, 2021), https://iapp.org/news/a/privacy-bills-in-the-117th-congress/; Cristiano Lima, Can Congress Unite on Section 230 Reform? This Top Democrat Has Hope, WASH. POST (Dec. 1, 2021), https://www.washingtonpost.com/politics/2021/12/01/can-congress-unite-section-230-reform-this-top-democrat-has-hope/.

27. This term refers to the influential debate on "varieties of capitalism." *See* Peter A. Hall & David Soskice, VARIETIES OF CAPITALISM: THE INSTITUTIONAL FOUNDATIONS OF COMPARATIVE ADVANTAGE (2001).

28. See discussion in Chapter 1.

29. *See Read the Framework*, CLINTON WHITE HOUSE, https://clintonwhitehouse4.archives.gov/WH/New/Commerce/read.html.

30. Karl Manheim & Lyric Kaplan, Artificial Intelligence: Risks to Privacy and Democracy, 21 YALE J.L. & TECH 106, 129–130 (2019).

31. Mark Scott and Rebecca Kern, The Online World Still Can't Quit the "Big Lie," POLITICO (Jan. 6, 2022), https://www.politico.com/news/2022/01/06/social-media-donald-trump-jan-6-526562.

32. See discussion in Chapter 2.

33. *See* Zhongguo Hulianwang Zhuangkuang (中国互联网状况) [The Internet in China], ST. COUNCIL INFO. OFF., 2010, http://www.gov.cn/zhengce/2010-06/08/content_2615774.htm (China), *translated in* PKULAW, CLI.WP.3146(EN), http://en.pkulaw.cn/display.aspx?cgid=a4f57cb2f97d1776b633c6794f964662b dfb&lib=dbref#.

34. *See* Paige Leskin, Here Are All the Major US Tech Companies Blocked Behind China's "Great Firewall," BUS. INSIDER (Oct. 10, 2019), https://www.businessinsider.com/major-us-tech-companies-blocked-from-operating-in-china-2019-5.

35. *See* Staff of S. Comm. on Foreign Relations, 116TH CONG., THE NEW BIG BROTHER— CHINA & DIGITAL AUTHORITARIANISM: KEY FINDINGS & RECOMMENDATION, S.

PRT. 116–47, at 1–2 (2020), https://www.foreign.senate.gov/imo/media/doc/New%20Big%20Brother%20-%20Key%20Findings%20and%20Recommendations.pdf.

36. Elizabeth C. Economy, THE THIRD REVOLUTION: XI JINPING AND THE NEW CHINESE STATE 79–80 (2018); Rene Chun, China's New Frontiers in Dystopian Tech, ATL. (Apr. 2018), https://www.theatlantic.com/magazine/archive/2018/04/big-in-china-machines-that-scan-your-face/554075/.

37. See discussion in Chapter 3.

38. *Berlin Declaration on Digital Society and Value-Based Digital Government*, GERMAN PRESIDENCY OF THE COUNCIL OF THE E.U., at 2 (Dec. 8, 2020), https://ec.europa.eu/newsroom/dae/document.cfm?doc_id=75984.

39. Nemitz, *supra* note 7, at 5.

40. *See e.g.*, Carmelo Cennamo & D. Daniel Sokol, Can the EU Regulate Platforms Without Stifling Innovation?, HARV. BUS. REV. (Mar. 2021).

41. Case C-131/12, Google Spain SL v. Agencia Española de Protección de Datos, ECLI:EU:C:2014:317, ¶¶ 30–31 (June 25, 2013); Peter Fleischer, Implementing a European, Not Global, Right to Be Forgotten, GOOGLE EUROPE BLOG (July 30, 2015), https://europe.googleblog.com/2015/07/implementing-european-not-global-right.html; Farhad Manjoo, Google's Grand Plans: A Conversation With Larry Page and Sundar Pichai, N.Y. TIMES (June 26, 2014), https://bits.blogs.nytimes.com/2014/06/26/googles-grand-plans-a-conversation-with-googles-larry-page-and-sundar-pichai/.

42. *See generally* Kai Fu-Lee, AI SUPERPOWERS: CHINA, SILICON VALLEY, AND THE NEW WORLD ORDER (2018); Nigel Inkster, THE GREAT DECOUPLING: CHINA, AMERICA AND THE STRUGGLE FOR TECHNOLOGICAL SUPREMACY (2021); Bob Davis & Lingling Wei, SUPERPOWER SHOWDOWN: HOW THE BATTLE BETWEEN TRUMP AND XI THREATENS A NEW COLD WAR (2020).

43. Steven Erlanger and Adam Satariano, Europe Feels Squeeze as Tech Competition Heats Up Between U.S. and China, N.Y. TIMES (Sep. 11, 2020), https://www.nytimes.com/2020/09/11/world/europe/eu-us-china-technology.html; Tyson Barker, Europe Can't Win the Tech War It Just Started, FOREIGN POL'Y (Jan. 16 2020), https://foreignpolicy.com/2020/01/16/europe-technology-sovereignty-von-der-leyen/.

44. *See generally* Anu Bradford, THE BRUSSELS EFFECT: HOW THE EUROPEAN UNION RULES THE WORLD (2020).

45. Jack Goldsmith, The Failure of Internet Freedom, KNIGHT FIRST AMEND. INST. (June 13, 2018), https://knightcolumbia.org/content/failure-internet-freedom.

46. Zhongguo Hulianwang Zhuangkuang, *supra* note 33.

47. Bates Gill, China's Quest for Greater Technological Self-Reliance, ASIA SOC'Y AUSTL. (Mar. 23, 2021), https://asiasociety.org/australia/chinas-quest-greater-technological-self-reliance.

48. Case C-311/18, *Data Prot. Comm'r v. Facebook Ir. Ltd. (Schrems II)*, ECLI:EU:2020:559 (July 16, 2020).

49. Ursula von der Leyen, Pres., Eur. Comm'n, State of the Union Address (Sep. 15, 2021), https://ec.europa.eu/commission/presscorner/detail/en/SPE ECH_21_4701.

50. See discussion in Chapter 5.

51. Implementation of Additional Export Controls: Certain Advanced Computing and Semiconductor Manufacturing Items; Supercomputer and Semiconductor End Use; Entity List Modification, 87 Fed. Reg. 62186, 62189–62192 (Oct. 13, 2022) (to be codified at 15 C.F.R. pts. 734–774).

52. James K. Jackson, CONG. RSCH. SERV., RL33388, THE COMMITTEE ON FOREIGN INVESTMENT IN THE UNITED STATES (CFIUS) 11–12 (2020).

53. Shuju Anquan Fa (数据安全法) [Data Security Law] (promulgated by the Standing Comm. Nat'l People's Cong., June 10, 2021, effective Sep. 1, 2021), 2021 STANDING COMM. NAT'L PEOPLE'S CONG. GAZ. 951 (China), translated in Data Security Law of the People's Republic of China, NAT'L PEOPLE'S CONG. CHINA (June 10, 2021), http://www.npc.gov.cn/englishnpc/c23934/202112/1abd88297 88946ecab270e469b13c39c.shtml; Matt Haldane, What China's New Data Laws Are and Their Impact on Big Tech, S. CHINA MORNING POST (Sep. 1, 2021), https://www.scmp.com/tech/policy/article/3147040/what-chinas-new-data-laws-are-and-their-impact-big-tech.

54. Narayanan Somasundaram, Beijing's Didi Blast Shakes $2tn of China Stocks in US, NIKKEI ASIA (July 12, 2021), https://asia.nikkei.com/Spotlight/Market-Spotli ght/Beijing-s-Didi-blast-shakes-2tn-of-China-stocks-in-US.

55. See discussion in Chapter 6.

56. Case C-311/18, *supra* note 48.

57. Alan Rappeport et al., Europe's Planned Digital Tax Heightens Tensions With U.S., N.Y. TIMES (Mar. 19, 2018), https://www.nytimes.com/2018/03/19/us/polit ics/europe-digital-tax-trade.html.

58. *See, e.g.,* Commission Decision in Case No. AT.39740 (Google Search—Shopping), C(2017) 4444 final (June 27, 2017) *cited in* 2018 O.J. (C 9) 11.

59. Bernard-Henri Lévy, The New American Empire, ATL. (Jan. 24, 2019), https://www.theatlantic.com/ideas/archive/2019/01/internet-has-turned-us-silent-emp ire/579721/.

60. See discussion in Chapter 4.

61. Robert Barnes, Supreme Court to Consider Major Digital Privacy Case on Microsoft Email Storage, WASH. POST (Oct. 16, 2017), https://www.washingtonp ost.com/politics/courts_law/supreme-court-to-consider-major-digital-privacy-case-on-microsoft-email-storage/2017/10/16/b1e74936-b278-11e7-be94-fabb0f1 e9ffb_story.html.

62. *See* Anton Troianovski & Adam Satariano, Google and Apple, Under Pressure From Russia, Remove Voting App, N.Y. TIMES (Sep. 17, 2021), https://www.nyti mes.com/2021/09/17/world/europe/russia-navalny-app-election.html.

63. *See* Adam Satariano & Sheera Frenkel, Ukraine War Tests the Power of Tech Giants, N.Y. TIMES (Feb. 28, 2022), https://www.nytimes.com/2022/02/28/tec hnology/ukraine-russia-social-media.html.

64. Jack Nicas, Raymond Zhong & Daisuke Wakabayashi, Censorship, Surveillance and Profits: A Hard Bargain for Apple in China, N.Y. TIMES (May 17, 2021), https://www.nytimes.com/2021/05/17/technology/apple-china-censorship-data.html.

65. *See* Jeb Su, Confirmed: Google Terminated Project Dragonfly, Its Censored Chinese Search Engine, FORBES (July 19, 2019), https://www.forbes.com/sites/jeanbaptiste/2019/07/19/confirmed-google-terminated-project-dragonfly-its-censored-chinese-search-engine/?sh=5c83547c7e84.

66. *See* Tom Daly et al., China's New Tech Export Controls Could Give Beijing a Say in TikTok Sale, REUTERS (Aug. 30, 2020), https://www.reuters.com/article/us-usa-tiktok-china/chinas-new-tech-export-controls-could-give-beijing-a-say-in-tik tok-sale-idUSKBN25Q05Q.

67. *See* Hudson Lockett and Tabby Kinder, China's Crackdown on US Listings Threatens $2tn Market, FIN. TIMES (July 7, 2021), https://www.ft.com/content/299ba00b-dfef-4c53-88a2-e6725d14025d; *see also* DiDi Provides Notification to Delist Its ADSs from NYSE, DIDI (May 23, 2022), https://ir.didiglobal.com/news-and-events/news/news-details/2022/DiDi-Provides-Notification-to-Del ist-its-ADSs-from-NYSE/default.aspx.

68. Ian F. Fergusson & Karen M. Sutter, CONG. RSCH. SERV., IF11627, U.S. EXPORT CONTROL REFORMS AND CHINA: ISSUES FOR CONGRESS 4 (2021).

69. Patrick Wintor, Europe Divided on Huawei as US Pressure to Drop Company Grows, THE GUARDIAN (July 13, 2020), https://www.theguardian.com/technol ogy/2020/jul/13/europe-divided-on-huawei-as-us-pressure-to-drop-comp any-grows.

70. Nitasha Tiku, Big Tech: Breaking Us Up Will Only Help China, WIRED (May 23, 2019), https://www.wired.com/story/big-tech-breaking-will-only-help-china/;

71. *See* Meta Platforms, Annual Report (Form 10-K) (Feb. 2, 2022), https://d18rnop 25nwr6d.cloudfront.net/CIK-0001326801/14039b47-2e2f-4054-9dc5-71bcc7cf0 1ce.pdf.

72. Katrina Manson, US Has Already Lost AI Fight to China, Says Ex-Pentagon Software Chief, FIN. TIMES (Oct. 10, 2021), https://www.ft.com/content/f939d b9a-40af-4bd1-b67d-10492535f8e0; Carl Benedikt Frey & Michael Osborne, China Won't Win the Race for AI Dominance, FOREIGN AFF. (June 19, 2020), https://www.foreignaffairs.com/articles/united-states/2020-06-19/china-wont-win-race-ai-dominance.

73. Huileng Tan, If Forced to Take Sides, Most Countries Would Pick the US Over China, Says Author, CNBC (Dec. 26, 2018), https://www.cnbc.com/2018/12/26/if-forced-to-choose-most-countries-will-pick-us-over-china-expert.html; Uri Friedman, How to Choose Between the U.S. and China? It's Not That Easy, ATL. (July 26, 2019), https://www.theatlantic.com/politics/archive/2019/07/south-korea-china-united-states-dilemma/594850/.

74. Joseph S. Nye, Opinion, Internet or Splinternet?, AL JAZEERA (Aug. 12, 2016), https://www.aljazeera.com/opinions/2016/8/12/internet-or-splinternet.

75. Ian Bremmer, The Technopolar Moment: How Digital Powers Will Reshape the Global Order, FOREIGN AFF. (Oct. 19, 2021), https://www.foreignaffairs.com/artic les/world/2021-10-19/ian-bremmer-big-tech-global-order; Stephen M. Walt, Big Tech Won't Remake the Global Order, FOREIGN POL'Y (Nov. 8, 2021), https://foreignpolicy.com/2021/11/08/big-tech-wont-remake-the-global-order/.

76. *See generally* Mark Leonard, THE AGE OF UNPEACE: HOW CONNECTIVITY CAUSES CONFLICT (2021).

77. *See generally* Michael Kwet, Digital Colonialism Is Threatening the Global South, AL JAZEERA (Mar. 13, 2019), https://www.aljazeera.com/opinions/2019/3/13/digital-colonialism-is-threatening-the-global-south; Bill Wasik, Welcome to the Age of Digital Imperialism, N.Y. TIMES (June 4, 2015), https://www.nyti mes.com/2015/06/07/magazine/welcome-to-the-age-of-digital-imperialism. html; Matthew S. Erie and Thomas Streinz, The Beijing Effect: China's "Digital Silk Road" as Transnational Data Governance, 54 N.Y.U. INT'L L. & POL. 1 (2021); Cara Mannion, Data Imperialism: The GDPR's Disastrous Impact on Africa's E-Commerce Markets, 53 VANDERBILT L. REV. 685 (2021).

78. Brian Dean, WhatsApp 2022 User Statistics: How Many People Use WhatsApp?, BACKLINKO (Jan. 5, 2022), https://backlinko.com/whatsapp-users.

79. Deyan Georgiev, 111+ Google Statistics and Facts That Reveal Everything About the Tech Giant, REVIEW42 (Jan. 18, 2022), https://review42.com/resources/goo gle-statistics-and-facts/#:~:text=There%20are%20over%2070%2C000%20 Google,246%20million%20unique%20US%20visitors.

80. Lisa Maria Neudert & Nahema Marchal, Polarisation and the Use of Technology in Political Campaigns and Communication, at 19–20, PE 634.414 (March 2019), https://www.europarl.europa.eu/RegData/etudes/STUD/2019/634414/EPRS_STU(2019)634414_EN.pdf.

81. DIGITAL, CULTURE, MEDIA AND SPORT COMM., DISINFORMATION AND "FAKE NEWS," REPORT, 2017–2019, HC 1791, at § 6 (UK); Alexi Mostrous, Mark Bridge, & Kate Gibbons, Russia Used Twitter Bots and Trolls 'to Disrupt' Brexit Vote, TIMES (Nov. 15, 2017), https://www.thetimes.co.uk/article/russia-used-web-posts-to-disrupt-brexit-vote-h9nv5zg6c?region=global.

82. Steve Stecklow, Why Facebook Is Losing the War on Hate Speech in Myanmar, REUTERS (Aug. 15, 2018), https://www.reuters.com/investigates/special-report/myanmar-facebook-hate/.

83. Alexandra Stevenson, Facebook Admits It Was Used to Incite Violence in Myanmar, N.Y. TIMES (Nov. 6, 2018), https://www.nytimes.com/2018/11/06/tec hnology/myanmar-facebook.html.

84. Ross An Chen, The Panopticon Is Already Here, ATL. (Sep. 2020), https://www. theatlantic.com/magazine/archive/2020/09/china-ai-surveillance/614197/.

85. Nat'l Dev. & Reform Comm'n, Ministry of Foreign Affairs & Ministry of Commerce of China, Vision and Actions on Jointly Building Silk Road Economic Belt & 21st Century Maritime Silk Road, NAT'L DEV. & REFORM COMM'N (Mar. 28, 2015), https://web.archive.org/web/20210530173528/https://en.ndrc.gov.cn/ newsrelease_8232/201503/t20150330_1193900.html.

86. *See* Daniel Cave, The African Union Headquarters Hack & Australia's 5G Network, AUSTRALIAN STRATEGIC POLICY INST.: THE STRATEGIST (July 13, 2018), https://www.aspistrategist.org.au/the-african-union-headquarters-hack-and-australias-5g-network/.

87. *See* Ghalia Kadiri & Joan Tilouine, A Addis-Abeba, le Siège de l'Union Africaine Espionné par Pékin, LE MONDE (Jan. 26, 2018), https://www.lemonde.fr/afri que/article/2018/01/26/a-addis-abeba-le-siege-de-l-union-africaine-espionne-par-les-chinois_5247521_3212.html.

88. *See* Aaron Maasho, China Denies Report It Hacked African Union Headquarters, REUTERS (Jan. 29, 2019), https://www.reuters.com/article/ us-africanunion-summit-china/china-denies-report-it-hacked-african-union-headquarters-idUSKBN1FI2I5.

89. *See* Kathrin Hille, Eleanor Olcott, & James Kynge, US–China Business: The Necessary Reinvention of Huawei, FIN. TIMES (Sep. 28, 2021), https://www. ft.com/content/9e98a0db-8d0a-4f78-90d3-25bfebcf3ac9.

90. *The Clean Network*, U.S. DEP'T OF STATE (2020), https://2017-2021.state.gov/ the-clean-network/index.html; David Sacks, China's Huawei Is Winning the 5G Race. Here's What the United States Should Do to Respond, COUNCIL ON FOREIGN REL. (Mar. 29, 2021), https://www.cfr.org/blog/china-huawei-5g.

91. *See generally* Bradford, *supra* note 44.

92. *Id.*

93. Case C-311/18, *supra* note 48.

94. *See* Meta Platforms, Annual Report, *supra* note 71.

95. *See, e.g.*, Editorial, Regulatory Imperialism, WALL ST. J. (Oct. 26, 2007), https:// www.wsj.com/articles/SB119334720539572002.

96. See discussion in Chapter 7.

97. See discussion in Chapter 8.

98. See discussion in Chapter 9.

99. *See* Paul Kramer, Power and Connection: Imperial Histories of the United States in the World, 116 AMER. HISTORICAL REV. 1348, 1381–1382 (2011).

100. See discussion in Chapter 7.

101. See discussion in Chapter 8.

102. See discussion in Chapter 9.
103. See discussion in Chapter 8 and conclusion.

CHAPTER 1

1. *See generally* Margaret O'Mara, THE CODE: SILICON VALLEY AND THE REMAKING OF AMERICA (2019).
2. *See generally* Sebastian Mallaby, THE POWER LAW: VENTURE CAPITAL AND THE MAKING OF THE NEW FUTURE (2022).
3. *Id.* at ch. 1.
4. O'Mara, *supra* note 1, at ch. 2.
5. Richard Barbrook & Andy Cameron, The Californian Ideology, 6 SCI. AS CULTURE 44, 45, 49 (1996).
6. *Id.* at 44–45.
7. James A. Lewis, Sovereignty and the Role of Government in Cyberspace, 16 BROWN J. WORLD AFFS. 55, 56 (2010).
8. Amy Lynne Bomse, The Dependence of Cyberspace, 50 DUKE L.J. 1717, 1726 (2001).
9. *See, e.g.,* Yochai Benkler, THE WEALTH OF NETWORKS: HOW SOCIAL PRODUCTION TRANSFORMS MARKETS (2006); *About EFF*, Electronic Frontier Foundation, https://www.eff.org/about.
10. Barbrook & Cameron, *supra* note 5, at 52–53.
11. Bomse, *supra* note 8, at 1726.
12. Alistair S. Duff, Rating the Revolution: Silicon Valley in Normative Perspective, 19 INFO., COMMC'N & SOC'Y 1605, 1606 (2016).
13. *Id.* at 1615.
14. Kai Fu Lee, AI SUPERPOWERS: CHINA, SILICON VALLEY AND THE NEW WORLD ORDER 26–28 (2019).
15. Duff, *supra* note 12, at 1613.
16. John Perry Barlow, A Declaration of the Independence of Cyberspace, ELECTRONIC FRONTIER FOUNDATION (Feb. 8, 1996), https://www.eff.org/cyberspace-independence.
17. *See e.g., generally* David R. Johnson & David Post, Law and Borders: The Rise of Law in Cyberspace, 48 STAN. L. REV. 1367, 1376 (1996) [hereinafter: Johnson & Post, *Law and Borders*].
18. Ira Magaziner, Creating a Framework for Global Electronic Commerce, THE PROGRESS & FREEDOM FOUNDATION (July 1999), http://www.pff.org/issues-pubs/futureinsights/fi6.1globaleconomiccommerce.html [hereinafter: Magaziner, *Framework*].
19. Clinton's Words on China: Trade Is the Smart Thing, N.Y. TIMES (Mar. 9, 2000), https://www.nytimes.com/2000/03/09/world/clinton-s-words-on-china-trade-is-the-smart-thing.html, *discussed in* Jack L. Goldsmith,

The Failure of Internet Freedom, KNIGHT FIRST AMENDMENT INSTITUTE AT COLUMBIA UNIVERSITY (June 13, 2018) [hereinafter: Goldsmith, *Failure of Internet Freedom*].

20. Ira Magaziner, Democracy and Cyberspace: First Principles, MIT COMMC'NS F. (1998), https://web.mit.edu/comm-forum/legacy/papers/magaziner. html [hereinafter: Magaziner, *First Principles*]; Bradford L. Smith, The Third Industrial Revolution: Policymaking for the Internet, 3 COLUM. SCI. & TECH. L. REV. 1, 19 (2002).

21. Johnson & Post, *Law and Borders, supra* note 17, at 1367; Smith, *supra* note 20, at 26–27.

22. Johnson & Post, *Law and Borders, supra* note 17, at 1367.

23. *Id.* at 1374; Bomse, *supra* note 8, at 1731.

24. Lawrence Lessig, CODE: AND OTHER LAWS OF CYBERSPACE 6–7, 60, 207 (2nd ed., 2008).

25. Jack L. Goldsmith, Against Cyberanarchy, 65 U. CHI. L. REV. 1199 (1998) [hereinafter: Goldsmith, *Against Cyberanarchy*].

26. *Id.* at 1250.

27. *Id.* at 1242.

28. *Id.*

29. Justin Hughes, The Internet and the Persistence of the Law, 44 BOSTON COLL. L. REV. 359 (2003), https://core.ac.uk/download/pdf/71464363.pdf.

30. David R. Johnson & David Post, The New "Civic Virtue" of the Internet, 3 FIRST MONDAY 3, 44 (1998) *published in* 1998 ANNUAL REVIEW OF THE INSTITUTE FOR INFORMATION STUDIES (C. Firestone, ed. 1998) [hereinafter: Johnson & Post, *Civic Virtue*].

31. *Online Platforms and Market Power, Part 6: Examining the Dominance of Amazon, Apple, Facebook, and Google Before the Subcomm. on Antitrust, Commercial, and Admin. L. of the H. Comm. on the Judiciary,* 116th Cong. (2020).

32. *See, e.g.,* Smith, *supra* note 20, at 19–20.

33. Duff, *supra* note 12, at 1610.

34. Polly Sprenger, Sun on Privacy: "Get Over It," WIRED (Jan. 26, 1999), https:// www.wired.com/1999/01/sun-on-privacy-get-over-it/.

35. Duff, *supra* note 12, at 1611–1622.

36. Tarleton Gillespie, CUSTODIANS OF THE INTERNET 43 (2018).

37. Smith, *supra* note 20, at 2.

38. *Id.* at 27–33.

39. Madhumita Murgia & Tim Bradshaw, Apple Plans to Scan US iPhones for Child Abuse Imagery, FIN. TIMES, Aug. 5, 2021, https://www.ft.com/content/ 14440f81-d405-452f-97e2-a81458f541if.

40. Adi Robertson, Apple's Controversial New Child Protection Features Explained, VERGE (Aug. 10, 2021), https://www.theverge.com/2021/8/10/22613225/apple-csam-scanning-messages-child-safety-features-privacy-controversy-explained.

41. Press Release, European Commission, Fighting Child Sexual Abuse: Commission Proposes New Rules to Protect Children (May 11, 2021), https://ec.europa.eu/commission/presscorner/detail/en/ip_22_2976.

42. Barbrook & Cameron, *supra* note 5, at 48.

43. Magaziner, *Framework, supra* note 18.

44. Hillary Clinton, Secretary of State, Speech at The Newseum: Remarks on Internet Freedom (Jan. 21, 2010) (transcript available at https://2009-2017.state.gov/secretary/20092013clinton/rm/2010/01/135519.htm).

45. Nathaniel Persily, THE INTERNET'S CHALLENGE TO DEMOCRACY: FRAMING THE PROBLEM AND ASSESSING REFORMS 4–5 (2019).

46. Measuring the #MeToo Backlash, THE ECONOMIST (Oct. 20, 2018), https://www.economist.com/united-states/2018/10/20/measuring-the-metoo-backlash.

47. Alexandra Kelley, #BlackLivesMatter Hashtag Averages 3.7 Million Times Per Day Following George Floyd's Death, THE HILL (June 11, 2020), https://thehill.com/changing-america/respect/equality/502353-blacklivesmatter-hashtag-averages-37-million-times-per-day.

48. *See, e.g.,* Brian Miller, There's No Need to Compel Free Speech: The Marketplace of Ideas Is Working, FORBES (Dec. 4, 2017), https://www.forbes.com/sites/briankmiller/2017/12/04/theres-no-need-to-compel-speech-the-marketplace-of-ideas-is-working/.

49. *See generally* Anupam Chandler, How Law Made Silicon Valley, 63 EMORY L. J. 639 (2014).

50. 47 U.S.C. § 230 (2018).

51. Emily Bazelon, How to Unmask the Internet's Vilest Characters, N.Y. TIMES MAG. (Apr. 22, 2011), https://www.nytimes.com/2011/04/24/magazine/mag-24ledE-t.html.

52. CDA 230: The Most Important Law Protecting Internet Speech, ELECTRONIC FRONTIER FOUNDATION, https://www.eff.org/issues/cda230/legislative-history.

53. *Id.*

54. Communications Decency Act of 1996, Pub. L. No. 104-104, 110 Stat. 133–145 (1996) (codified as amended at 47 U.S.C. § 223 (1934)).

55. Lorraine Mercier, The Communications Decency Act: Congress' First Attempt to Censor Speech Over the Internet, 9 LOY. CONSUMER L. REV. 274, 275 n. 8 (1997); *see also* 141 Cong. Rec. §1953 (daily ed. Feb. 1, 1995).

56. Telecommunications Act of 1996, Pub. L. No. 104-104, 110 Stat. 56 (1996) (codified as amended at 47 U.S.C. §151 et seq. (1934)).

57. H.R. 1555, 104th Cong. (1995).

58. 141 CONG. REC. H.R. 8469 (daily ed. Aug. 4, 1995); Danielle K. Citron & Benjamin Wittes, The Problem Isn't Just Backpage: Revising Section 230 Immunity, 2 GEO. LAW TECH. REV. 453, 455 (2018).

59. *See* 141 CONG. REC. H.R. 8470 (daily ed. Aug. 4, 1995).

60. 41 CONG. REC. H.R. 8470 (daily ed. Aug 4, 1995).

61. 47 U.S.C § 230 (2018).

62. Mike Masnick, Authors of CDA 230 Do Some Serious 230 Mythbusting in Response to Comments Submitted to the FCC, TECHDIRT (Sep. 22, 2020), https://www.techdirt.com/2020/09/22/authors-cda-230-do-some-serious-230-mythbusting-response-to-comments-submitted-to-fcc/.

63. 47 U.S.C § 230 (2018).

64. 17 U.S.C. §§ 101, 104, 132 (2018).

65. Internet Protection Act of 1997, H.R. 2372, 105th Cong. 2 (1997). *See also* Bomse, *supra* note 8, at 1725.

66. Internet Regulatory Freedom Act of 1999, S. 1043 106th Cong. 231 (1999). *See also* Bomse, *supra* note 8, at 1725.

67. 15 U.S.C. §§ 6501–6506.

68. *Id.* at § 6503

69. *Zeran v. America Online, Inc.*, 129 F.3d 327 (1997); *see also* Kate Klonick, The New Governors: The People, Rules, and Processes Governing Online Speech, 131 HARV. L. REV. 1598, 1606–1609 (2018) (discussing the *Zeran* case).

70. *Zeran*, 129 F.3d at 330 (1997).

71. *Batzel v. Smith*, 333 F.3d 1018, 1027 (2018); *see also* Zeran, 129 F.3d at 330 (1997);Klonick, *supra* note 69, at 1606–1609.

72. Bomse, *supra* note 8, at 1724.

73. *Reno v. American Civil Liberties Union*, 521 U.S. 844, 871–872 (1997).

74. *Id.* at 872.

75. *Id.* at 873.

76. *Packingham v. North Carolina*, 137 S. Ct. 1730 (2017).

77. *Id.* at 1735.

78. *Id.* (quoting *Reno v. American Civil Liberties Union*, 521 U.S. 844, 868 (1997)).

79. *Id.* at 1737, *discussed in*, Danielle K. Citron & Neil Richards, Four Principles for Digital Expression (You Won't Believe #3!), 95 WASH. UNIV. LAW REV. 1353, 1353 (2018).

80. Citron & Richards, *supra* note 79, at 1353.

81. *Packingham v. North Carolina*, 137 S. Ct. 1730, 1737 (2017).

82. Goldsmith, *The Failure of Internet Freedom*, *supra* note 19; Bomse, *supra* note 8, at 1717–1718, 1725.

83. Steven Levy, Battle of the Clipper Chip, N.Y. TIMES MAG., June 12, 1994, https://www.nytimes.com/1994/06/12/magazine/battle-of-the-clipper-chip.html.

84. Press Release, President Clinton, A Framework for Glob. Elec. Com., https://clintonwhitehouse4.archives.gov/WH/New/Commerce/read.html, *discussed in* Goldsmith, *The Failure of Internet Freedom*, *supra* note 19.

85. Magaziner, *Framework*, *supra* note 18.

86. U.S. GOVERNMENT PUBLISHING OFFICE, PUBLIC PAPERS OF THE UNITED STATES: WILLIAM J. CLINTON 898–901 (1997, Book II), available at https://www.govinfo.gov/content/pkg/PPP-1997-book2/html/PPP-1997-book2-doc-pg898-2.htm.

87. James A. Lewis, Sovereignty and the Role of Government in Cyberspace, 16 BROWN J. WORLD AFFS. 55, 60–61 (2010).

88. THE WHITE HOUSE, NATIONAL STRATEGY TO SECURE CYBERSPACE xiii (Feb. 1, 2003), available at https://apps.dtic.mil/sti/citations/ADA413614.

89. *Id.* at xi.

90. The White House, INTERNATIONAL STRATEGY FOR CYBERSPACE: PROSPERITY, SECURITY, AND OPENNESS IN A NETWORKED WORLD, 17 (2011).

91. Victoria Espinel et al., Combating Online Piracy While Protecting an Open and Innovative Internet, THE WHITE HOUSE (Jan. 14, 2012), https://obamawhiteho use.archives.gov/blog/2012/01/14/obama-administration-responds-we-people-petitions-sopa-and-online-piracy.

92. INTERNATIONAL STRATEGY FOR CYBERSPACE, *supra* note 90, at 12.

93. Shannon Bond & Avie Schneider, Trump Threatens to Shut Down Social Media After Twitter Adds Warning to His Tweets, NPR (May 27, 2020), https://www.npr.org/2020/05/27/863011399/trump-threatens-to-shut-down-social-media-after-twitter-adds-warning-on-his-twee.

94. Tom Wheeler, Could Donald Trump Claim a National Security Threat to Shut Down the Internet?, BROOKINGS (June 25, 2020), https://www.brookings.edu/blog/techtank/2020/06/25/could-donald-trump-claim-a-national-security-thr eat-to-shut-down-the-internet/.

95. Exec. Order No. 13925, 85 Fed. Reg. 34,079 (May 28, 2020).

96. Adi Robertson, Let's Go Through Trump's Terrible Internet Censorship Order, Line by Line, THE VERGE (May 29, 2020), https://www.theverge.com/2020/5/29/21273191/trump-twitter-social-media-censorship-executive-order-analy sis-bias.

97. Jeremy K. Kessler & David E. Pozen, The Search for an Egalitarian First Amendment, 118 COLUM. L. REV. 1953 (2018), https://columbialawreview.org/wp-content/uploads/2018/11/Kessler-Pozen-THE_SEARCH_FOR_AN_EGAL ITARIAN_FIRST_AMENDMENT.pdf; Jack M. Balkin, Information Fiduciaries and the First Amendment, 49 UC DAVIS L. REV. 1183, 1185–1186 (2016), https://lawreview.law.ucdavis.edu/issues/49/4/Lecture/49-4_Balkin.pdf.

98. Klonick, *supra* note 69, at 1606.

99. *See generally* Jerrold Nadler, CHAIRMAN, COMM. ON THE JUDICIARY, INVESTIGATION OF COMPETITION IN DIGITAL MARKETS (2020); Microsoft Investor Relations, *Acquisition History*, https://www.microsoft.com/en-us/Investor/acquisition-hist ory.aspx; American Economic Liberties Project, *Big Tech Mergers*, https://www.economicliberties.us/big-tech-merger-tracker/. However, actual number of acquisitions is difficult to ascertain due to unreported transactions. *See generally* Fed. Trade Comm'n, NON-HSR REPORTED ACQUISITIONS BY SELECT TECHNOLOGY PLATFORMS, 2010–2019: AN FTC STUDY (2021), https://www.ftc.gov/system/files/documents/reports/non-hsr-reported-acquisitions-select-technology-platforms-2010-2019-ftc-study/p201201technologyplatformstudy2021.pdf.

100. *See generally United States v. Microsoft Corp.*, 253 F.3d 34 (2001).

101. Press Release, Dep't of Justice, Justice Department Sues Monopolist Google for Violating Antitrust Laws (Oct. 20, 2020), https://www.justice.gov/opa/ pr/justice-department-sues-monopolist-google-violating-antitrust-laws; Press Release, Fed. Trade Comm'n, FTC Sues Facebook for Illegal Monopolization (Dec. 9, 2020), https://www.ftc.gov/news-events/press-releases/2020/12/ftc-sues-facebook-illegal-monopolization.

102. Anu Bradford, THE BRUSSELS EFFECT: HOW THE EUROPEAN UNION RULES THE WORLD 147–155 (2020).

103. Press Release, The White House, Fact Sheet: Plan to Protect Privacy in the Internet Age by Adopting a Consumer Privacy Bill of Rights (Feb. 23, 2012), https://obamawhitehouse.archives.gov/the-press-office/2012/02/23/fact-sheet-plan-protect-privacy-internet-age-adopting-consumer-privacy-b; *White House: Consumer Bill of Rights*, ELEC. PRIV. INFO. CTR., https://archive.epic.org/ privacy/white_house_consumer_privacy_html.

104. Press Release, The White House, We Can't Wait: Obama Admin. Unveils Blueprint for a "Priv. Bill of Rights" to Protect Consumers Online (Feb. 23, 2012), https://obamawhitehouse.archives.gov/the-press-office/2012/02/23/ we-can-t-wait-obama-administration-unveils-blueprint-privacy-bill-rights.

105. *White House: Consumer Bill of Rights*, ELEC. PRIV. INFO. CTR., https://archive. epic.org/privacy/white_house_consumer_privacy_.html.

106. Brendan Sasso, Obama's "Privacy Bill of Rights" Gets Bashed from All Sides, THE ATLANTIC, Feb. 27, 2015, https://www.theatlantic.com/politics/archive/ 2015/02/obamas-privacy-bill-of-rights-gets-bashed-from-all-sides/456576/.

107. Kate Kaye, New Privacy Report Already Removed from White House Site, ADAGE, Jan. 20, 2017, https://adage.com/article/privacy-and-regulation/priv acy-report-removed-white-house-site/307632.

108. *Doe v. Backpage.com, LLC*, 817 F.3d 12, 15 (1st Cir. 2016), *cert. denied*.

109. Patrick J. Carome and Ari Holtzblatt, Congress Enacts Law Creating a Sex Trafficking Exception From the Immunity Provided by Section 230 of the Communications Decency Act, WILMERHALE, Apr. 16, 2018, https://www.wil merhale.com/en/insights/client-alerts/2018-04-16-congress-enacts-law-creat ing-a-sex-trafficking-exception-from-the-immunity-provided-by-section-230-of-the-communications-decency-act.

110. Allow States and Victims to Fight Online Sex Trafficking Act of 2017, Pub. L. No. 115-164, § 4, 132 Stat. 1253, 1254 (amending the Communications Act of 1934, 47 U.S.C. § 230(e) (2018)).

111. Danielle Blunt & Ariel Wolf, ERASED: THE IMPACT OF FOSTA-SESTA 9 (2020); Adi Robertson, Internet Sex Trafficking Law FOSTA-SESTA Is Almost Never Used, Says Government Report, THE VERGE (June 24, 2021), https://www.theverge. com/2021/6/24/22546984/fosta-sesta-section-230-carveout-gao-report-prose cutions.

112. Eric Goldman, The Complicated Story of FOSTA and Section 230, 17 FIRST AMEND. LAW REV. 279, 291–292 (2019).

113. Jack M. Balkin, Digital Speech and Democratic Culture: A Theory of Freedom of Expression for the Information Society, 79 N.Y.U. L. REV. 1, 42–46 (2004).

114. *See* Jack M. Balkin, Old-School/New-School Speech Regulation, 127 HARV. L. REV. 2296, 2301–2302 (2014).

115. *See* Danielle K. Citron, HATE CRIMES IN CYBERSPACE 126–128 (2014); Danielle K. Citron, Cyber Civil Rights, 89 B.U.L. REV. 61, 115–125 (2009).

116. *See* Allow States and Victims to Fight Online Sex Trafficking Act of 2017, Pub. L. No. 115-164, 132 Stat. 1253 (2018), *amending* Communications Decency Act of 1996, 47 U.S.C. § 230 (2018); *see also* Tom Jackman, House Passes Anti-Online Sex Trafficking Bill, Allows Targeting of Websites Like Backpage.com, WASH. POST (Feb. 27, 2018), https://www.washingtonpost.com/news/true-crime/wp/2018/02/27/house-passes-anti-online-sex-trafficking-bill-allows-targeting-of-websites-like-backpage-com/.

117. *See* Felix Gillette, Section 230 Was Supposed to Make the Internet a Better Place. It Failed, BLOOMBERG: BUSINESS WEEK (Aug. 7, 2019), https://www.bloomberg.com/news/features/2019-08-07/section-230-was-supposed-to-make-the-internet-a-better-place-it-failed; *see also* Eric Johnson, Nancy Pelosi Says Trump's Tweets "Cheapened the Presidency"—and the Media Encourages Him, VOX (Apr. 12, 2019), https://www.vox.com/2019/4/12/18307957/nancy-pelosi-donald-trump-twitter-tweet-cheap-freak-presidency-kara-swisher-decode-podcast-interview.

118. *See, e.g.,* Rachel Lerman, Social Media Liability Law Is Likely to Be Reviewed Under Biden, WASH. POST (Jan. 18, 2021), https://www.washingtonpost.com/politics/2021/01/18/biden-section-230/.

119. *See* Eric Johnson, Nancy Pelosi Says Trump's Tweets "Cheapened the Presidency"—and the Media Encourages Him, VOX (Apr. 12, 2019), https://www.vox.com/2019/4/12/18307957/nancy-pelosi-donald-trump-twitter-tweet-cheap-freak-presidency-kara-swisher-decode-podcast-interview (addressing Rep. Pelosi's perspective on Section 230).

120. *See* David Morar & Chris Riley, A Guide for Conceptualizing the Debate Over Section 230, BROOKINGS INST. (Apr. 9, 2021), https://www.brookings.edu/techstream/a-guide-for-conceptualizing-the-debate-over-section-230/.

121. Jerrold Nadler, Chairman, Comm. on the Judiciary, INVESTIGATION OF COMPETITION IN DIGITAL MARKETS 133 (2020).

122. Press Release, Jerrold Nadler, Chairman, H. Comm. on the Judiciary, Judiciary Antitrust Subcommittee Investigation Reveals Digital Economy Highly Concentrated, Impacted by Monopoly Power (Oct. 6, 2020), available at https://judiciary.house.gov/news/email/show.aspx?ID=RI72Q22K6GSKA7LMGT4TVF7EIE#:~:text=Cicilline%20(RI%2D01)%20in,roadmap%20for%20achieving%20that%20goal.%22.

123. American Innovation and Choice Online Act, S. 2992, 117th Cong. (2021) (as reported by S. Comm. on the Judiciary, Jan. 20, 2022).

124. Press Release, William Barr, Att'y Gen., Statement of the Att'y Gen. on the Announcement of Civil Antitrust Lawsuit Filed Against Google (Oct. 20, 2020), available at https://www.justice.gov/opa/pr/statement-attorney-gene ral-announcement-civil-antitrust-lawsuit-filed-against-google.

125. Kari Paul, Washington Crackdown on Google Is the Greatest Threat Yet to Big Tech, THE GUARDIAN (Oct. 20, 2020), https://www.theguardian.com/technol ogy/2020/oct/20/google-antitrust-charges-threat-big-tech.

126. *See generally* California Consumer Privacy Act of 2018, CAL. CIV. CODE § 1798.100 (2018) *amended by* Initiative Proposition 24, Sec. 4 (California Privacy Rights Act of 2020).

127. Press Release, Rep. Ro Khanna, Release: Rep. Khanna Releases "Internet Bill of Rights" Principles, Endorsed by Sir Tim Berners-Lee (Oct. 4, 2018), https:// khanna.house.gov/media/press-releases/release-rep-khanna-releases-inter net-bill-rights-principles-endorsed-sir-tim#:~:text=Set%20of%20Princip les%20for%20an,of%20personal%20data%20by%20companies%3B&text= (10)%20To%20have%20an%20entity,accountability%20to%20protect%20y our%20privacy.

128. H.R. 5815, 115th Cong. (2018), available at https://www.govinfo.gov/content/ pkg/BILLS-115hr5815ih/html/BILLS-115hr5815ih.htm.

129. Press Release, Sen. Ed Markey, As Facebook CEO Zuckerberg Testifies to Congress, Senators Markey and Blumenthal Introduce Privacy Bill of Rights (Apr. 10, 2018), https://www.markey.senate.gov/news/press-releases/as-faceb ook-ceo-zuckerberg-testifies-to-congress-senators-markey-and-blumenthal- introduce-privacy-bill-of-rights.

130. President Biden, State of the Union Address (Mar. 1, 2022), transcript available at https://www.whitehouse.gov/briefing-room/speeches-remarks/2022/03/ 01/remarks-of-president-joe-biden-state-of-the-union-address-as-delivered/.

131. FTC v. Facebook, Inc., No. 20-3590 (JEB), slip op. at 1 (D.D.C. June 28, 2021); *but see FTC v. Facebook, Inc. ("Facebook II")*, F. Supp. 3d, Case No. 1:20-cv-03590, ECF No. 90, 2022 WL 103308 at *5 (D.D.C., Jan. 11, 2022).

132. Dustin Volz, Facebook Zuckerberg Faces Senate Hearing but Little Hope for Action, REUTERS (Apr. 9, 2018), https://www.reuters.com/article/us-facebook- privacy-congress/facebooks-zuckerberg-faces-senate-hearing-but-little-hope- for-action-idUSKBN1HH08G.

133. Emily Birnbaum, Tech Spent Big on Lobbying Last Year, POLITICO (Jan. 24, 2022), https://www.politico.com/newsletters/morning-tech/2022/01/24/ tech-spent-big-on-lobbying-last-year-00001144.

134. Cat Zakrzewski, Tech Companies Spent Almost $70 Million Lobbying Washington in 2021 as Congress Sought to Rein in Their Power, WASH. POST

(Jan 21, 2022), https://www.washingtonpost.com/technology/2022/01/21/tech-lobbying-in-washington/.

135. *Lobbying Report*, Lobbying Disclosure Act of 1995 (Section 5), https://www.politico.com/f/?id=0000017e-7dc2-d1fc-ad7f-ffc269ad0000.

136. Msadiq Bidar, National Labor Relations Board Officer Recommends New Vote in Amazon Union Effort, CBS NEWS (Aug. 3, 2021), https://www.cbsnews.com/news/amazon-union-nlrb-recommends-new-vote/.

137. *Lobbying Report, supra* note 135.

138. Kent Walker, The Harmful Consequences of Congress's Anti-Tech Bills, GOOGLE: PUBLIC POLICY (Jan. 18, 2022), https://blog.google/outreach-initiatives/public-policy/the-harmful-consequences-of-congresss-anti-tech-bills/.

139. H.B. 20 § 120 (2022).

140. Balkin, *supra* note 97, at 1186.

141. Citron & Wittes, *supra* note 58.

142. James Whitman, The Two Western Cultures of Privacy: Dignity Versus Liberty, 113 YALE L.J. 1151, 1155–1156 (2004).

143. *See generally* California Consumer Privacy Act of 2018, CAL. CIV. CODE § 1798.100 (2018) *amended by* Initiative Proposition 24, Sec. 4 (California Privacy Rights Act of 2020).

144. *See generally* O'Mara, *supra* note 1.

145. *Id.* at 52.

146. Bomse, *supra* note 8, at 1721.

147. Mariana Mazzucato, Taxpayers Helped Apple, But Apple Won't Help Them, HARVARD BUS. REV. (Mar. 8, 2013), https://hbr.org/2013/03/taxpayers-helped-apple-but-app.

148. Mariana Mazzucato, The Innovative State: Governments Should Make Markets, Not Just Fix Them, FOREIGN AFFS. (Feb. 2015), https://www.foreignaffairs.com/articles/americas/2014-12-15/innovative-state [hereinafter: Mazzucato, *The Innovative State*].

149. *Id.*

150. Deborah Sweeney, Not Just for Small Businesses: How the SBA Helped Grow 3 Major Companies, FORBES (Sep. 4, 2018), https://www.forbes.com/sites/deborahsweeney/2018/09/04/not-just-for-small-businesses-how-the-sba-helped-grow-3-major-companies/?sh=443b0ab51b31.

151. Mazzucato, *The Innovative State, supra* note 147.

152. FACT SHEET: CHIPS and Science Act Will Lower Costs, Create Jobs, Strengthen Supply Chains, and Counter China, WHITE HOUSE BRIEFING ROOM (Aug. 9, 2022), https://www.whitehouse.gov/briefing-room/statements-releases/2022/08/09/fact-sheet-chips-and-science-act-will-lower-costs-create-jobs-strengthen-supply-chains-and-counter-china/.

153. President Barack Obama, Remarks by the President at the National Cybersecurity Communications Integration Center (Jan. 13, 2015) (transcript available at https://obamawhitehouse.archives.gov/the-press-office/2015/01/13/remarks-president-national-cybersecurity-communications-integration-cent).

154. Kristen Eichensehr, Public-Private Cybersecurity, 95 TEXAS LAW REV. 467, 467 (2017).

155. Saheed Oladimeji & Sean Michael Kerner, SolarWinds Hack Explained: Everything You Need to Know, WHATIS.COM (June 29, 2022), https://www.techtarget.com/whatis/feature/SolarWinds-hack-explained-Everything-you-need-to-know.

156. Ewen Macaskill & Gabriel Dance, NSA Files: Decoded: What the Revelations Mean for You, THE GUARDIAN (Nov. 1, 2013), https://www.theguardian.com/world/interactive/2013/nov/01/snowden-nsa-files-surveillance-revelations-decoded.

157. Jon Michaels, All the President's Spies: Private-Public Intelligence Partnerships in the War on Terror, 96 CALIF. LAW REV. 901, 927–928, 937–938 (2008).

158. Alan Rozenshtein, Surveillance Intermediaries, 70 STAN. LAW REV. 99, 99 (2018).

159. Lisa O. Monaco, Comprehensive Cyber Review, U.S. DEP'T OF JUST. (July 2022), https://www.justice.gov/dag/page/file/1520341/download.

160. Gillian Tett, Business Is at Last Collaborating on Cyber Security, FIN. TIMES, Mar. 17, 2022, https://www.ft.com/content/2d6ff4b2-21f5-4cd0-b2ed-4dec98f96dc9?shareType=nongift.

161. Ellen Nakashima & Reed Albergotti, The FBI Wanted to Unlock the San Bernardino Shooter's iPhone: It Turned to a Little-Known Australian Firm, WASH. POST (Apr. 14, 2021), https://www.washingtonpost.com/technology/2021/04/14/azimuth-san-bernardino-apple-iphone-fbi/.

162. A Message to Our Customers, Apple (Feb. 16, 2016), https://www.apple.com/customer-letter/.

163. Michaels, *supra* note 157, at 902.

164. Exec. Order No. 14028, 86 Fed. Reg. 26,633 (May 12, 2021); Jack Gillum & Katrina Manson, Biden Signs Law Requiring Firms to Report Hacks in 72 Hours, Mar. 16, 2022, https://www.bloomberg.com/news/articles/2022-03-16/biden-signs-law-requiring-firms-to-report-hacks-in-72-hours.

165. David Sanger et al., As Tanks Rolled Into Ukraine, So Did Malware: Then Microsoft Entered the War, N.Y. TIMES, Feb. 28, 2022, https://www.nytimes.com/2022/02/28/us/politics/ukraine-russia-microsoft.html.

166. Press Release, Brad Smith, President & Vice Chair, Digital Technology and the War in Ukraine, Microsoft (Feb. 28, 2022), https://blogs.microsoft.com/on-the-issues/2022/02/28/ukraine-russia-digital-war-cyberattacks/.

167. Gillian Tett, Business Is at Last Collaborating on Cyber Security, FIN. TIMES, Mar. 17, 2022, https://www.ft.com/content/2d6ff4b2-21f5-4cd0-b2ed-4dec9 8f96dc9?shareType=nongift.

168. *See generally* Tim Wu, THE CURSE OF BIGNESS: ANTITRUST IN THE NEW GILDED AGE (2018).

169. Carrie Goldberg, Herrick v. Grindr: Why Section 230 of the Communications Decency Act Must Be Fixed, LAWFARE (Aug. 14, 2019), https://www.lawf areblog.com/herrick-v-grindr-why-section-230-communications-dece ncy-act-must-be-fixed.

170. *Herrick v. Grindr LLC*, 306 F. Supp. 3d 579 (2d. Cir. 2019), *cert. denied*, 140 S. Ct. 221, 221 (2019); Carrie Goldberg, Herrick v. Grindr: Why Section 230 of the Communications Decency Act Must be Fixed, LAWFARE (Aug. 14, 2019), https://www.lawfareblog.com/herrick-v-grindr-why-section-230-communicati ons-decency-act-must-be-fixed.

171. *Doe v. Backpage.com, LLC*, 817 F.3d 12 (1st Cir. 2016), *cert. denied*, 2017 WL 69715 (No. 16-276).

172. Press Release, Xavier Becerra, Attorney General of California, Attorney General Becerra Announces Shutdown of World's Largest Online Sex Trafficking Website, Backpage.com (Apr. 9, 2018), https://oag.ca.gov/news/press-relea ses/attorney-general-becerra-announces-shutdown-world%E2%80%99s-larg est-online-sex.

173. Citron & Wittes, *supra* note 58, at 453.

174. Cass Sunstein, Is Social Media Good or Bad for Democracy?, 15 THE SUR FILE ON INTERNET AND DEMOCRACY 83, 83 (2018).

175. *Id.* at 84–87.

176. *Id.*

177. Lisa Maria Neudert & Nahema Marchal, POLARISATION AND THE USE OF TECHNOLOGY IN POLITICAL CAMPAIGNS AND COMMUNICATION 13 (2019), available at https://www.europarl.europa.eu/RegData/etudes/STUD/2019/634414/ EPRS_STU(2019)634414_EN.pdf.

178. *Id.* at 17.

179. Soroush Vosoughi et al., The Spread of True and False News Online, 359 SCI. 1146, 1146 (2018).

180. GROUPM, THIS YEAR NEXT YEAR: GLOBAL END-OF-YEAR FORECAST 11 (Dec. 2020), available at https://images.assettype.com/afaqs/2020-12/68dce78e-9b54- 4866-8f05-64aa4156f6ef/GroupM___This_Year_Next_Year_Global_End_of_ Year_Forecast.pdf.

181. Tucker Warns About "Ominous" Google Censorship of Political Content, FOX NEWS INSIDER (Sep. 7, 2017), https://insider.foxnews.com/2017/09/07/tucker- ominous-google-censorship-certain-political-content; Deepa Seetharaman, Facebook Rebuts Criticisms About a Bias Against Conservatives, WALL ST. J.

(May 10, 2016), https://www.wsj.com/articles/facebook-refutes-criticisms-about-a-bias-against-conservatives-1462890206.

182. Paul M. Barrett & J. Grant Sims, N.Y. Univ. Stern Ctr. Bus. Hum. Rts., FALSE ACCUSATION: THE UNFOUNDED CLAIM THAT SOCIAL MEDIA COMPANIES CENSOR CONSERVATIVES 1 (2021).

183. Jonathan Zittrain, Engineering an Election, 127 HARV. L. REV. F. 335 (2014).

184. Gilad Edelman, How Facebook's Political Ad System Is Designed to Polarize, WIRED (Dec. 13, 2019), https://www.wired.com/story/facebook-political-ad-system-designed-polarize/.

185. Josh Constine, Zuckerberg's Response to Cambridge Scandal Omits Why It Delayed Investigating, TECHCRUNCH (Mar. 21, 2018), https://techcrunch.com/2018/03/21/zuckerberg-cambridge-analytica/.

186. Shoshana Zuboff, THE AGE OF SURVEILLANCE CAPITALISM: THE FIGHT FOR A HUMAN FUTURE AT THE FRONTIER OF A NEW POWER 17 (2019).

187. Karl Manheim & Lyric Kaplan, Artificial Intelligence: Risks to Privacy and Democracy, 21 YALE J.L. & TECH. 106, 133–134 (2019).

188. Jack Goldsmith & Stuart Russell, *Strengths Become Vulnerabilities: How a Digital-World Disadvantages the United States in its International Relations*, Aegis Series Paper No. 1086, at 2–3 (2018), available at https://www.hoover.org/sites/default/files/research/docs/381100534-strengths-become-vulnerabilities.pdf.

189. Josh Rogin, NSA Chief: Cybercrime Constitutes the "Greatest Transfer of Wealth in History," THE CABLE (July 9, 2012), https://foreignpolicy.com/2012/07/09/nsa-chief-cybercrime-constitutes-the-greatest-transfer-of-wealth-in-history/.

190. Goldsmith & Russell, *supra* note 188, at 2–3, available at https://www.hoover.org/sites/default/files/research/docs/381100534-strengths-become-vulnerabilities.pdf.

CHAPTER 2

1. *See* Feng Chongyi, The Dilemma of Stability Preservation in China, J. CURRENT CHINESE AFFS., June, 1, 2013, at 3, 7, 10 (2013).

2. Bruce J. Dickson, The Survival Strategy of the Chinese Communist Party, WASH. Q., Winter 2017, 27, 33–35, 39 (2016); *see* Susan Trevaskes, Rationalising Stability Preservation Through Mao's Not So Invisible Hand, J. CURRENT CHINESE AFFS., June 2013, at 51 (2013).

3. Elizabeth C. Economy, THE THIRD REVOLUTION: XI JINPING AND THE NEW CHINESE STATE 58 (2018).

4. Xi Jinping: Tuidong Woguo Xinyidai Rengong Zhineng Jiankang Fazhan (习近平：推动我国新一代人工智能健康发展) [Xi Jinping: Advancing the Healthy Development of Our Nation's New Generation of Artificial Intelligence], XINHUA WANG (新华网) [XINHUANET] (Oct. 31, 2018), http://www.xinhuanet.com/politics/

leaders/2018-10/31/c_1123643321.htm (China), translated in Elsa Kania & Rogier Creemers, Xi Jinping Calls for "Healthy Development" of AI (Translation), NEW AMERICA (Nov. 5, 2018), https://www.newamerica.org/cybersecurity-initiative/digichina/blog/xi-jinping-calls-for-healthy-development-of-ai-translation/.

5. Carrie Gracie, The Thoughts of Chairman Xi, BBC (Oct. 13, 2017), https://www.bbc.co.uk/news/resources/idt-sh/Thoughts_Chairman_Xi.

6. *See* "Zhongguo Hulianwang Zhuangkuang" Baipishu (Yingwen Ban) (《中国互联网状况》白皮书（英文版）) ["The Internet in China" White Paper (English Version)]: Foreword, Guowuyuan Xinwen Bangongshi (国务院新闻办公室) [ST. COUNCIL INFO. OFF. CHINA] (June 8, 2010), http://www.scio.gov.cn/zxbd/nd/2010/Document/667385/667385.htm.

7. *Id.* at IV (Basic Principles and Practices of Internet Administration).

8. Andre Laliberte & Marc Lanteigne, The Issues of Challenges to the Legitimacy of the CCP Rules, in THE CHINESE PARTY-STATE IN THE 21ST CENTURY: ADAPTATION AND THE REINVENTION OF LEGITIMACY 1, 8–13 (Andre Laliberte & Marc Lanteigne eds., 2007), discussed in Angela Huyue Zhang, Agility Over Stability: China's Great Reversal in Regulating the Platform Economy, 63 HARV. INT'L L. J. 457, 464 (2022).

9. *See* Largest Internet Companies by Market Cap, COMPANIESMARKETCAP, https://companiesmarketcap.com/internet/largest-internet-companies-by-market-cap/ [https://perma.cc/Q4PC-X6BB] (last visited Aug. 22, 2022).

10. *See* Market Capitalization of the Largest Internet Companies Worldwide as of June 2022, STATISTA, https://www.statista.com/statistics/277483/market-value-of-the-largest-internet-companies-worldwide/.

11. Katharina Buchholz, China's Mobile Payment Adoption Beats All Others, STATISTA (July 8, 2022), https://www.statista.com/chart/17909/pos-mobile-payment-user-penetration-rates/; *see also* STATISTA, FINTECH REPORT 2021—DIGITAL PAYMENTS 4, 7 (2021), https://www.statista.com/study/41122/fintech-report-digital-payments/.

12. Jeanne Whalen & Chris Alcantara, Nine Charts to Show Who's Winning the US–China Tech Race, WASH. POST (Sep. 21, 2021), https://www.washingtonpost.com/technology/2021/09/21/us-china-tech-competition/.

13. *Id.*

14. *Id.*; Kalhan Rosenblatt, TikTok Surpasses Google as Most Popular Website of the Year, New Data Suggests, NBC NEWS, https://www.nbcnews.com/tech/tech-news/tiktok-surpasses-google-popular-website-year-new-data-suggests-rcna9648.

15. Xi Jinping (习近平), Zhashi Tuidong Gongtong Fuyu (扎实推动共同富裕) [Making Solid Progress Toward Common Prosperity], QSTHEORY.CN (求是网) (Oct. 15, 2021), http://www.qstheory.cn/dukan/qs/2021-10/15/c_1127959365.htm (China), translated in Making Solid Progress Toward Common Prosperity, QIUSHI, http://en.qstheory.cn/2022-01/18/c_699346.htm (Jan. 18, 2022).

16. Zhang, *supra* note 8, at 471–483.

17. *Id.* at 471.

18. Xinhua She (新华社) [Xinhua News Agency], Zhonggong Zhongyang Guowuyuan Yinfa "Guojia Chuangxin Qudong Fazhan Zhanlüe Gangyao" (中共中央 国务院印发《国家创新驱动发展战略纲要》) [Outline of the National Innovation-Driven Development Strategy Issued by the CPC Central Committee and the State Council], STATE COUNCIL GAZ., May 30, 2016, at 5 (China), translated in CTR. FOR SEC. AND EMERGING TECH, OUTLINE OF THE NATIONAL INNOVATION-DRIVEN DEVELOPMENT STRATEGY ISSUED BY THE CPC CENTRAL COMMITTEE AND THE STATE COUNCIL (2019), https://cset.georgetown.edu/publication/outline-of-the-national-innovation-driven-development-strategy/.

19. Zhang, *supra* note 8, at 476–480.

20. Arjun Kharpal, Alibaba's Jack Ma Has Been a Communist Party Member Since the 1980s, CNBC, https://www.cnbc.com/2018/11/27/alibabas-jack-ma-has-been-communist-party-member-since-1980s.html.

21. Zhang, *supra* note 8, at 476–477; Lianghui Jianyi | Ma Huateng Lianghui "Xiance" Xinjiuye yu Shuzi Zhili (两会建议 | 马化腾两会"献策"新就业与数字治理) [Proposals in the Two Sessions | Ma Huangteng Submitted Suggestions on New Form of Employment and Digital Regulation], Renmin Youdian Bao (人民邮电报) [PEOPLE'S PAPER ON MAILS AND TELECOMM.] (Mar. 4, 2021), https://mp.weixin.qq.com/s/UhD7GBQiU_FsBYZ-bA9sAg (China).

22. Zhang, *supra* note 8, at 477–480.

23. Xueguang Zhou, Organizational Response to COVID-19 Crisis: Reflections on the Chinese Bureaucracy and Its Resilience, 16 MGMT. AND ORG. REV. 473, 479–480 (2020).

24. Zhang, *supra* note 8, at 480–483.

25. *See* Guowuyuan Guanyu Yinfa Zhongguo Zhizao 2025 de Tongzhi (国务院关于印发《中国制造2025》的通知) [Notice of the State Council on the Publication of Made in China 2025] (promulgated by St. Council, May 8, 2015), ST. COUNCIL GAZ., June 10, 2015, at 10 (China), translated in CTR. FOR SEC. AND EMERGING TECH, NOTICE OF THE STATE COUNCIL ON THE PUBLICATION OF "MADE IN CHINA 2025" (2022).

26. James McBride & Andrew Chatzky, Is "Made in China 2025" a Threat to Global Trade?, COUNCIL ON FOREIGN REL., https://www.cfr.org/backgrounder/made-china-2025-threat-global-trade.

27. *Id.*

28. *Id.*

29. Institute for Sec. & Dev. Pol'y, MADE IN CHINA 2025 (2018), https://isdp.eu/content/uploads/2018/06/Made-in-China-Backgrounder.pdf; Notice of the State Council on the Publication of Made in China 2025, ST. COUNCIL GAZ. at 18 (China), translated in Ctr. for Sec. and Emerging Tech, *supra* note 25, at 15 (2022).

30. *Id.*

31. McBride & Chatzky, *supra* note 26.

32. Issaku Harada, Beijing Drops "Made in China 2025" from Government Report, NIKKEI ASIA (Mar. 6, 2019), https://asia.nikkei.com/Politics/China-People-s-Congress/Beijing-drops-Made-in-China-2025-from-government-report.

33. *See* Guowuyuan Guanyu Yinfa Xinyidai Rengong Zhineng Fazhan Guihua de Tongzhi (国务院关于印发新一代人工智能发展规划的通知) [State Council Notice on the Issuance of the Next Generation Artificial Intelligence Development Plan] (promulgated by St. Council, July 8, 2017), ST. COUNCIL GAZ., Aug. 10, 2017, at 7, 9 (China), translated in Rogier Creemers et al., New America, STATE COUNCIL NOTICE ON THE ISSUANCE OF THE NEXT GENERATION ARTIFICIAL INTELLIGENCE DEVELOPMENT PLAN (2017), https://d1y8sb8igg2f8e.cloudfront.net/documents/translation-fulltext-8.1.17.pdf.

34. Nat'l Sec. Comm'n on A. I., FINAL REPORT 25 (2021), https://www.nscai.gov/wp-content/uploads/2021/03/Full-Report-Digital-1.pdf.

35. Sam Shead, Eric Schmidt on AI: "Trust Me, These Chinese People Are Good," INSIDER (Nov. 1, 2017), https://www.businessinsider.com/eric-schmidt-on-artific ial-intelligence-china-2017-11.

36. Damien Ma, Getting to $30 Trillion: China Aims for Largest Economy by 2035, MACROPOLO (Mar. 1, 2021), https://macropolo.org/getting-to-30-trillion-china-aims-for-largest-economy-by-2035/?rp=m; *see also* Xi Focus: Xi Says China's Economy Has Hope, Potential to Maintain Long-Term Stable Development, XINHUANET (Nov. 3, 2020), http://www.xinhuanet.com/english/2020-11/03/c_139488075.htm; *see generally* Zhonghua Renmin Gongheguo Guomin Jingji He Shehui Fazhan Dishisige Wunian Guihua he 2035 Nian Yuanjing Mubiao Gangyao (中华人民共和国国民经济和社会发展第十四个五年规划和 2035 年远景目标纲要) [Outline of the People's Republic of China 14th Five-Year Plan for National Economic and Social Development and Long-Range Objectives for 2035] (promulgated by Nat'l. People's Cong., Mar. 12, 2021), 2021 STANDING COMM. NAT'L PEOPLE'S CONG. GAZ. 429 (China), translated in Ctr. for Sec. & Emerging Tech., OUTLINE OF THE PEOPLE'S REPUBLIC OF CHINA 14TH FIVE-YEAR PLAN FOR NATIONAL ECONOMIC AND SOCIAL DEVELOPMENT AND LONG-RANGE OBJECTIVES FOR 2035 (2021), https://cset.georgetown.edu/wp-content/uploads/t0284_14th_Five_Year_Plan_EN.pdf.

37. Agatha Kratz & Janka Oertel, Eur. Council on Foreign Rel., HOME ADVANTAGE: HOW CHINA'S PROTECTED MARKET THREATENS EUROPE'S ECONOMIC POWER 2–3, 6–7 (2021), https://ecfr.eu/wp-content/uploads/Home-advantage-How-Chinas-protected-market-threatens-Europes-economic-power.pdf.

38. Alan O. Sykes, The Law and Economics of "Forced" Technology Transfer (FTT) and Its Implications for Trade and Investment Policy (and the U.S.–China Trade War), 13 J. LEGAL ANALYSIS 127, 128–129 (2021).

39. Kratz & Oertel, Eur. Council on Foreign Rel., *supra* note 37, at 2–3.

40. David Wolf, Why Buy the Hardware When China Is Getting the IP for Free?, FOREIGN POL'Y (Apr. 24, 2015), https://foreignpolicy.com/2015/04/24/ibm-technology-transfer-china-virginia-rometty-strategy-lenovo-huawei-it/.

41. Paul Mozur, IBM Venture with China Stirs Concerns, N.Y. TIMES (Apr. 19, 2015), https://www.nytimes.com/2015/04/20/business/ibm-project-in-china-raises-us-concerns.html.

42. *E.g.*, Wangluo Anquan Fa (网络安全法) [Cybersecurity Law] (promulgated by the Standing Comm. Nat'l People's Cong., Nov. 7, 2016, effective June 1, 2017), arts. 24, 28, 47, 2016 STANDING COMM. NAT'L PEOPLE'S CONG. GAZ. 899, 901–902, 904 (China), translated in PKULaw, CLI.1.283838(EN).

43. Paige Leskin, Here Are All the Major US Tech Companies Blocked Behind China's "Great Firewall," INSIDER, https://www.businessinsider.com/major-us-tech-companies-blocked-from-operating-in-china-2019-5.

44. *Id.*

45. *See* A New Approach to China, GOOGLE BLOG (Jan. 12, 2010), https://googleblog.blogspot.com/2010/01/new-approach-to-china.html; *see also* Guoxinban Wangluoju Fuzeren jiu Guge Tuichu Zhongguo Neidi Fabiao Tanhua (国新办网络局负责人就谷歌退出中国内地发表谈话) [The Head of the Internet Bureau of the State Council Information Office Comments on Google's Withdrawal from Mainland China], Guowuyuan Xinwen Bangongshi (国务院新闻办公室) [ST. COUNCIL INFO. OFF. CHINA] (Mar. 23, 2010), http://www.scio.gov.cn/zxbd/nd/2010/Document/580801/580801.htm.

46. Alyssa Abkowitz, Deepa Seetharaman, & Eva Dou, Facebook Is Trying Everything to Re-Enter China—and It's Not Working, WALL ST. J. (Jan. 30, 2017), https://www.wsj.com/articles/mark-zuckerbergs-beijing-blues-1485791106.

47. Gracie, *supra* note 5.

48. Economy, *supra* note 3, at 60–62.

49. *See* Paul Mozur, Apple Removes Apps From China Store That Help Internet Users Evade Censorship, N.Y. TIMES (July 29, 2017), https://www.nytimes.com/2017/07/29/technology/china-apple-censorhip.html.

50. *E.g.*, Cybersecurity Law, *supra* note 42, art. 24; Hulianwang Yonghu Zhanghao Mingcheng Guanli Guiding (互联网用户账号名称管理规定) [Provisions on the Administration of Account Names of Internet Users] (promulgated by Cyberspace Admin. of China, Feb. 4, 2015, effective Mar. 1, 2015) art. 5, CLI.4.242696 (PKULaw) (China), translated in PKULaw, CLI.4.242696(EN).

51. Economy, *supra* note 3, at 78.

52. Guojia Anquan Fa (国家安全法) [National Security Law] (promulgated by the Standing Comm. Nat'l People's Cong., July 1, 2015, effective July 1, 2015), 2015 STANDING COMM. NAT'L PEOPLE'S CONG. GAZ. 701 (China), translated in PKULaw, CLI.1.250527(EN).

53. Cybersecurity Law, *supra* note 42.

54. Shuju Anquan Fa (数据安全法) [Data Security Law] (promulgated by the Standing Comm. Nat'l People's Cong., June 10, 2021, effective Sep. 1, 2021), 2021 STANDING COMM. NAT'L PEOPLE'S CONG. GAZ. 951 (China), translated in Data Security Law of the People's Republic of China, NAT'L PEOPLE'S CONG. CHINA (June 10, 2021), http://www.npc.gov.cn/englishnpc/c23934/202112/1abd88297 88946ecab270e469b13c39c.shtml.

55. National Security Law, *supra* note 52, art. 15.

56. Cybersecurity Law, *supra* note 42, art. 12.

57. *Id.*

58. Data Security Law, *supra* note 54, arts. 24, 35.

59. Adam Segal, When China Rules the Web: Technology in Service of the State, FOREIGN AFFS., Sep./Oct. 2018, at 10.

60. Zuigao Renmin Fayuan, Zuigao Renmin Jianchayuan Guanyu Banli Liyong Xinxi Wangluo Shishi Feibang deng Xingshi Anjian Shiyong Falü Ruogan Wenti de Jieshi (最高人民法院、最高人民检察院关于办理利用信息网络实施诽谤等刑事案件适用法律若干问题的解释) [Interpretation of the Supreme People's Court and the Supreme People's Procuratorate on Several Issues concerning the Specific Application of Law in the Handling of Defamation Through Information Networks and Other Criminal Cases] (promulgated by the Jud. Comm. Sup. People's Ct. & Procuratorial Comm., Supreme People's Procuratorate, Sep. 6, 2013, effective Sep. 10, 2013), art. 2, 2014(3) SUP. PEOPLE'S CT. GAZ. 9 (China), translated in PKULaw, CLI.3.209618(EN) [hereinafter *Handling of Defamation*], discussed in China Issues New Internet Rules That Include Jail Time, BBC (Sep. 9, 2013), https://www.bbc.com/news/world-asia-china-23990674.

61. *Handling of Defamation, supra* note 60, art. 5.

62. Chun Han Wong, China Is Now Sending Twitter Users to Prison for Posts Most Chinese Can't See, WALL ST. J. (Jan. 29, 2021), https://www.wsj.com/articles/ china-is-now-sending-twitter-users-to-prison-for-posts-most-chinese-cant-see-11611932917.

63. *Id.*

64. *Id.*

65. *See* Bei Qin, David Strömberg, & Yanhui Wu, Social Media and Collective Action in China (Ctr. Econ. Pol'y Resh. Working Paper, DP 16731, 2021); Susan Shirk, Changing Media, Changing China, in CHANGING MEDIA, CHANGING CHINA 1, 5–6, 13–15 (Susan Shirk ed., 2011).

66. Liu Jianfei (刘建飞), Zhonggong Zhongyang Dangxiao Guoji Zhanlüe Yanjiu Yuan (中共中央党校国际战略研究院) [Cent. Party School of the Communist Party of China Int'l Strategy Rsch. Inst.], Zhongguo Tese Guojia Anquan Zhanlüe Yanjiu (中国特色国家安全战略研究) [Research on National Security Strategy with Chinese Characteristics] 154 (2016) (China) (unofficial translation).

67. Shirk, *supra* note 65, at 13.

68. Qin, Strömberg, & Wu, *supra* note 65, at 27.

69. *See generally* Margaret Roberts, CENSORED: DISTRACTION AND DIVERSION INSIDE CHINA'S GREAT FIREWALL (2018).

70. *Id.* at 6, 8, 41–92.

71. Yuyu Chen & David Y. Yang, The Impact of Media Censorship: 1984 or Brave New World?, 109 AM. ECON. REV. 2294 (2019).

72. China Covid-19: How State Media and Censorship Took on Coronavirus, BBC (Dec. 29, 2020), https://www.bbc.com/news/world-asia-china-55355401; Vanessa Molter & Renee Diresta, Pandemics & Propaganda: How Chinese State Media Creates and Propagates CCP Coronavirus Narratives, MISINFORMATION REV. (June 8, 2020), https://misinforeview.hks.harvard.edu/article/pandemics-propaganda-how-chinese-state-media-creates-and-propagates-ccp-coronavirus-narratives/.

73. Raymond Zhong et al., Behind China's Twitter Campaign, a Murky Supporting Chorus, N.Y. TIMES (June 8, 2020), https://www.nytimes.com/2020/06/08/technology/china-twitter-disinformation.html.

74. Zhao Lijian (@zlj517), TWITTER (Mar. 12, 2020), https://twitter.com/zlj517/status/1238111898828066823?ref_src=twsrc%5Etfw%7Ctwcamp%5Etweetembed%7Ctwterm%5E1238111898828066823%7Ctwgr%5E%7Ctwcon%5Es1_&ref_url=https%3A%2F%2Ffortune.com%2F2020%2F05%2F28%2Ftwitter-fact-check-zhao-lijian-coronavirus-origin%2F.

75. Derek Wallbank, Twitter Fact-Checks China Spokesman's Tweets About Virus Origins, BLOOMBERG (May 28, 2020), https://www.bloomberg.com/news/articles/2020-05-28/twitter-fact-checks-china-spokesman-s-virus-origin-tweets.

76. Li Yang (@Li_Yang_China), TWITTER (July 13, 2021), https://twitter.com/Li_Yang_China/status/1414894373897216000.

77. Economy, *supra* note 3, at 82–83.

78. Cat and Mouse: How China Makes Sure Its Internet Abides by the Rules, ECONOMIST (Apr. 6, 2013), https://www.economist.com/special-report/2013/04/06/cat-and-mouse.

79. Gary King, Jennifer Pan, & Margaret E. Roberts, How the Chinese Government Fabricates Social Media Posts for Strategic Distraction, Not Engaged Argument, 111 AM. POL. SCI. R. 484 (2017).

80. *See* Lydialyle Gibson, China's Social-Media Smoke Screen, HARV. MAG. (May/June 2017), https://www.harvardmagazine.com/2017/05/chinas-social-media-smoke-screen; *see also* King, Pan, & Roberts, *supra* note 79, at 499–500 (2017); Huanqiu Shibao (环球时报) [Global Times], Sheping: Hafo Tuandui dui Suowei "Wumaodang" Yizhi Banjie (社评：哈佛团队对所谓"五毛党"一知半解) [Opinion: Harvard Team's Superficial Knowledge of the So-Called "50 Cent Party"], HUANQIU WANG (环球网) [HUANQIU.COM] (May 21, 2016), https://opinion.huanqiu.com/article/9CaKrnJVAx2 (China), translated in HOW THE CHINESE GOVERNMENT FABRICATES SOCIAL MEDIA POSTS FOR STRATEGIC DISTRACTION, NOT ENGAGED ARGUMENT: SUPPLEMENTARY APPENDIX, https://sta

tic.cambridge.org/content/id/urn:cambridge.org:id:article:S0003055417000 144/resource/name/S0003055417000144sup001.pdf.

81. *Id.*

82. King, Pan, & Roberts, *supra* note 79, at 499; Gary King, Gary King on Reverse Engineering Chinese Government Information Controls, 78 TAIWANESE J. POL. SCI. 1, 16 (transcribed and edited by Stephen B. Reynolds, 2018).

83. Xi Jinping: Jianchi Zhengque Fangxiang Chuangxin Fangfa Shouduan Tigao Xinwen Yulun Chuanboli Yindaoli (习近平：坚持正确方向创新方法手段 提高新闻舆论传播力引导力) [Xi Jinping: Persisting in the Correct Orientation, Innovating Methods and Means, and Raising the Dissemination Strength and Guidance Strength of News and Public Opinion], Renmin Wang (人民网) [PEOPLE.CN] (Feb. 19, 2016), http://politics.people.com.cn/n1/2016/0219/ c1024-28136159.html (China), translated in Speech at the News and Public Opinion Work Conference, CHINA COPYRIGHT AND MEDIA, https://chinaco pyrightandmedia.wordpress.com/2016/02/19/speech-at-the-news-and-public-opinion-work-conference/.

84. *See* Shannon Tiezzi, China's Quest to Build an "Influential and Credible" Media, DIPLOMAT (Aug. 20, 2014), https://thediplomat.com/2014/08/chinas-quest-to-build-an-influential-and-credible-media/; Freedom in the World 2021 China, FREEDOM HOUSE, https://freedomhouse.org/country/china/freedom-world/2021.

85. Beina Xu & Eleanor Albert, Media Censorship in China, COUNCIL ON FOREIGN REL. (Feb. 17, 2017), https://www.cfr.org/backgrounder/media-censors hip-china.

86. Zhongguo Hulianwang Hangye Zilü Gongyue (中国互联网行业自律公约) [Public Pledge of Self-Regulation and Professional Ethics for China Internet Industry], Zhongguo Hulianwang Xiehui (中国互联网协会) [INTERNET SOC'Y CHINA] (Aug 9, 2011), https://www.isc.org.cn/article/10677353062592512.html (China), translated in Public Pledge of Self-Regulation and Professional Ethics for China's Internet Industry (Chinese and English Text), CONG.-EXEC. COMM'N ON CHINA, https://www.cecc.gov/resources/legal-provisions/public-pledge-of-self-regulation-and-professional-ethics-for-chinas.

87. Daniela Stockmann & Mary E. Gallagher, Remote Control: How the Media Sustain Authoritarian Rule in China, 44 COMPARATIVE POL. STUD. 436, 436–437, 463 n.10, app. tbl. A11 (2011) (Table A11 available at ONLINE APPENDIX, 10–11, http://daniestockmann.net/wp-content/uploads/2013/02/RemoteControl CPS_OnlineAppendixFinal.pdf).

88. *See* Stockmann & Gallagher, *supra* note 87, at 458.

89. Gabriel Crossley & Yew Lun Tian, Analysis: In Peng Case, a Glimpse Into the Machinery of Beijing's Control, REUTERS (Nov. 23, 2021), https://www.reut ers.com/business/media-telecom/peng-case-glimpse-into-machinery-beiji ngs-control-2021-11-23/; Li Yuan, Why China Can't Bury Peng Shuai and Its

#MeToo Scandal, N.Y. TIMES (Nov. 23, 2021), https://www.nytimes.com/2021/11/23/business/china-peng-shuai-metoo.html.

90. Yuan, *supra* note 89.

91. Steven Lee Myers & Keith Bradsher, China's Leader Wants a "Lovable" Country. That Doesn't Mean He's Making Nice, N.Y. TIMES, https://www.nytimes.com/2021/06/08/world/asia/china-diplomacy.html (Nov. 11, 2021).

92. Kaan Sahin, The West, China, and AI Surveillance, ATL. COUNCIL (Dec. 18, 2020), www.atlanticcouncil.org/blogs/geotech-cues/the-west-china-and-ai-surveillance.

93. Lai Lin Thomala, Number of Internet Users in China from 2008 to 2021, STATISTA (May 12, 2022), https://www.statista.com/statistics/265140/number-of-internet-users-in-china/.

94. Ross Andersen, The Panopticon Is Already Here, ATLANTIC (Sep. 2020), https://www.theatlantic.com/magazine/archive/2020/09/china-ai-surveillance/614197/.

95. Katherine Atha et al., SOS Int'l LLC, CHINA'S SMART CITIES DEVELOPMENT. RESEARCH REPORT PREPARED ON BEHALF OF THE U.S.–CHINA ECONOMIC AND SECURITY REVIEW COMMISSION 46 (2020), https://www.uscc.gov/sites/default/files/China_Smart_Cities_Development.pdf; Xinhua She (新华社) [Xinhua News Agency], Zhonggong Zhongyang Bangongting, Guowuyuan Yinfa Guanyu Jiaqiang Shehui Zhi'an Fangkong Tixi Jianshe de Zhidao Yijian (中共中央办公厅、国务院办公厅印发《关于加强社会治安防控体系建设的意见》) [The General Office of the Central Committee of the CPC and the General Office of the State Council Print and Issue the Opinions on Strengthening the Building of the System for Crime Prevention and Control], ST. COUNCIL GAZ., Apr. 30, 2015, at 4 (China), translated in Ctr. for Strategic and Int'l Stud., THE GENERAL OFFICE OF THE CCP CENTRAL COMMITTEE AND THE GENERAL OFFICE OF THE STATE COUNCIL ISSUED THE OPINION REGARDING STRENGTHENING THE CONSTRUCTION OF A SOCIETAL SECURITY PREVENTION AND CONTROL SYSTEM 2–3, https://interpret.csis.org/translations/the-general-office-of-the-ccp-central-committee-and-the-general-office-of-the-state-council-issued-the-opinion-regarding-strengthening-the-construction-of-a-societal-security-prevention-and-control-sy/.

96. Robyn Dixon, China's New Surveillance Program Aims to Cut Crime. Some Fear It'll Do Much More, L.A. TIMES (Oct. 27, 2018), https://www.latimes.com/world/asia/la-fg-china-sharp-eyes-20181027-story.html.

97. *Id.*

98. Engen Tham, China Bank Protest Stopped by Health Codes Turning Red, Depositors Say, REUTERS (June 16, 2022), https://www.reuters.com/world/china/china-bank-protest-stopped-by-health-codes-turning-red-depositors-say-2022-06-14/.

99. Kai Kupferschmidt & Jon Cohen, China's Aggressive Measures Have Slowed the Coronavirus. They May Not Work in Other Countries, SCIENCE (Mar. 2,

2020), https://www.science.org/content/article/china-s-aggressive-measu res-have-slowed-coronavirus-they-may-not-work-other-countries; Paul Mozur, Raymond Zhong, & Aaron Krolik, In Coronavirus Fight, China Gives Citizens a Color Code, With Red Flags, N.Y. TIMES, https://www.nytimes.com/2020/03/ 01/business/china-coronavirus-surveillance.html (Jan. 26, 2021).

100. Katherine Atha et al., SOS Int'l LLC, *supra* note 95, at 9.

101. Abigail Beall, In China, Alibaba's Data-Hungry AI Is Controlling (and Watching) Cities, WIRED (May 30, 2018), https://www.wired.co.uk/article/alib aba-city-brain-artificial-intelligence-china-kuala-lumpur.

102. Emily Lin, China's Safe Cities Serve as Solutions and Opportunities for Growth, ASMAG.COM (Dec. 23, 2015), https://www.asmag.com/showpost/19628.aspx.

103. Ron Alalouff, The Spectacular Rise of the Chinese Video Surveillance Industry, IFSEC GLOBAL (Mar. 7, 2018), https://www.ifsecglobal.com/video-surveillance/ the-unstoppable-rise-of-hikvision-and-dahua-and-how-the/; Steven Feldstein, The Global Expansion of AI Surveillance 7–8 (Carnegie Endowment for Int'l Peace Working Paper, 2019), https://carnegieendowment.org/files/WP-Feldst ein-AISurveillance_final1.pdf.

104. Andersen, *supra* note 94.

105. *Id.*

106. Dave Gershgorn, China's "Sharp Eyes" Program Aims to Surveil 100% of Public Space, ONEZERO (Mar. 2, 2021), https://onezero.medium.com/chinas- sharp-eyes-program-aims-to-surveil-100-of-public-space-ddc22d63e015; Robert Muggah & Greg Walton, "Smart" Cities Are Surveilled Cities, FOREIGN POL'Y (Apr. 17, 2021), https://foreignpolicy.com/2021/04/17/smart-cities-surveilla nce-privacy-digital-threats-internet-of-things-5g/.

107. *See* Orville Schell, Technology Has Abetted China's Surveillance State, FIN. TIMES (Sep. 2, 2020), https://www.ft.com/content/6b61aaaa-3325-44dc-8110- bf4a351185fb; *see also* Louise Lucas & Emily Feng, Inside China's Surveillance State, FIN. TIMES (July 20, 2018), https://www.ft.com/content/2182eebe-8a17- 11e8-bf9e-8771d5404543; Guanyu Jiaqiang Gonggong Anquan Shiping Jiankong Jianshe Lianwang Gongzuo de Ruogan Yijian (关于加强公共安全视频监控 建设联网应用工作的若干意见) [Several Opinions on Increasing Efforts to Establish and Network Public Security Video Surveillance] (promulgated by Nat'l Dev. and Reform Comm'n, Office of the Cent'l Public Sec. Comprehensive Mgmt. Comm'n, Ministry of Science & Tech., Ministry of Indus. & Info. Tech., Ministry of Public Sec., Ministry of Fin., Ministry of Hum. Res. & Soc. Sec., Ministry of Hous. & Urb.-Rural Dev., Ministry of Transp., May 6, 2015), PKULaw, CLI.4.248342 (China), partly translated in Several Opinions on Increasing Efforts to Establish and Network Public Security Video Surveillance, CHINA L. TRANSLATE (May 17, 2015), https://www.chinalawtranslate.com/en/ cctv/?tpedit=1.

108. Yin Yeping, Digital Yuan Finds Root at the 5th Digital China Summit as the Nation Adopts Easy and Safe Transaction, GLOBAL TIMES (Jul. 25, 2022), https://www.globaltimes.cn/page/202207/1271339.shtml.

109. Schell, *supra* note 107.

110. Charlie Campbell, "The Entire System Is Designed to Suppress Us": What the Chinese Surveillance State Means for the Rest of the World, TIME (Nov. 21, 2019), https://time.com/5735411/china-surveillance-privacy-issues/.

111. Jamil Anderlini, How China's Smart-City Tech Focuses on Its Own Citizens, FIN. TIMES (June 4, 2019), https://www.ft.com/content/46bc137a-5d27-11e9-840c-530737425559.

112. *Id.*

113. Andersen, *supra* note 94.

114. Drew Harwell & Eva Dou, Huawei Tested AI Software That Could Recognize Uighur Minorities and Alert Police, Report Says, WASH. POST (Dec. 8, 2020), www.washingtonpost.com/technology/2020/12/08/huawei-tested-ai-software-that-could-recognize-uighur-minorities-alert-police-report-says.

115. Economy, *supra* note 3, at 79–80; Guowuyuan Guanyu Yinfa Shehui Xinyong Tixi Jianshe Guihua Gangyao (2014–2020 Nian) de Tongzhi (国务院关于印发社会信用体系建设规划纲要（2014—2020年）的通知) [State Council Notice Concerning Issuance of the Planning Outline for the Establishment of a Social Credit System (2014–2020)], Zhonghua Renmin Gongheguo Zhongyang Renmin Zhengfu (中华人民共和国中央人民政府) [ST. COUNCIL CHINA] (June 27, 2014), http://www.gov.cn/zhengce/content/2014-06/27/content_8913.htm (China), translated in Establishment of the Social Credit System, CHINA L. TRANSLATE (Apr. 27, 2015), https://www.chinalawtranslate.com/en/socialcreditsystem/.

116. Schell, *supra* note 107; Louise Matsakis, How the West Got China's Social Credit System Wrong, WIRED (July 29, 2019), https://www.wired.com/story/china-social-credit-score-system/.

117. Schell, *supra* note 107; Economy, *supra* note 3, at 79.

118. Rene Chun, China's New Frontiers in Dystopian Tech, ATLANTIC (Apr. 2018), https://www.theatlantic.com/magazine/archive/2018/04/big-in-china-machines-that-scan-your-face/554075/.

119. Vincent Brussee, China's Social Credit System Is Actually Quite Boring, FOREIGN POL'Y (Sep. 15, 2021), https://foreignpolicy.com/2021/09/15/china-social-credit-system-authoritarian/.

120. Jeremy Daum, Untrustworthy: Social Credit Isn't What You Think It Is, VERFASSUNGSBLOG (June 27, 2019), https://verfassungsblog.de/untrustworthy-social-credit-isnt-what-you-think-it-is/.

121. *See* Hulianwang Xinxi Fuwu Guanli Banfa (互联网信息服务管理办法) [Administrative Measures for Internet Information Services] (promulgated by the St. Council, Sep. 25, 2000, rev'd. Jan. 8, 2011), art. 20, http://www.

cac.gov.cn/2000-09/30/c_126193701.htm (China), translated in PKULaw, CLI.2.174868(EN).

122. *See id.* arts. 15, 16.

123. *See* Wangluo Xinxi Neirong Shengtai Zhili Guiding (网络信息内容生态治理规定) [Provisions on Ecological Governance of Network Information Content] (promulgated by Cyberspace Admin. of China, Dec. 15, 2019, effective Mar. 1, 2020), arts. 5–7, 10–11, http://www.cac.gov.cn/2019-12/20/c_1578375159509309.htm (China), translated in PKULaw, CLI.4.338029(EN).

124. Guanyu Yinfa "Wangluo Yinshiping Xinxi Fuwu Guanli Guiding" de Tongzhi (关于印发《网络音视频信息服务管理规定》的通知) [Notice of Issuing the Provisions on the Administration of Cyber Audio and Video Information Services] (promulgated by Cyberspace Admin. of China, Ministry of Culture and Tourism & Nat'l Radio and Television Admin., Nov. 18, 2019, effective Jan. 1, 2020), arts. 4, http://www.cac.gov.cn/2019-11/29/c_1576561820967678.htm (China), translated in PKULaw, CLI.4.337537(EN).

125. *Id.* arts. 9, 12.

126. Shen Lu, I Helped Build ByteDance's Vast Censorship Machine, PROTOCOL (Feb. 18, 2021), https://www.protocol.com/china/i-built-bytedance-censorship-machine.

127. *Id.*

128. *See* Segal, *supra* note 59.

129. ByteDance's Toutiao Ordered by China to Halt New Registrations Since Sept—Sources, REUTERS (July 16, 2021), https://www.reuters.com/technology/bytedances-toutiao-ordered-by-china-halt-new-registrations-since-sept-sources-2021-07-16/; Nicole Jao, China Is Serious About Cleaning Up Jinri Toutiao and Kuaishou This Time, TECHNODE (Apr. 4, 2018), https://technode.com/2018/04/04/china-is-serious-about-cleaning-up-jinri-toutiao-and-kuaishou-this-time/.

130. Raymond Zhong, It Built an Empire of GIFs, Buzzy News and Jokes. China Isn't Amused., N.Y. TIMES (Apr. 11, 2018), https://www.nytimes.com/2018/04/11/technology/china-toutiao-bytedance-censor.html.

131. Lai Lin Thomala, Average Online Time of Internet Users in China Per Week from 2011 to 2021, STATISTA (Mar. 14, 2022), https://www.statista.com/statistics/265176/average-online-time-of-users-in-china/.

132. Economy, *supra* note 3, at 80.

133. Campbell, *supra* note 110.

134. *Id.*

135. Economy, *supra* note 3, at 80.

136. *Id.* at 84–85.

137. *Id.* at 58.

138. *Id.* at 57.

139. *Id.*

140. Geren Xinxi Baohu Fa (个人信息保护法) [Personal Information Protection Law] (promulgated by Standing Comm. Nat'l People's Congress, Aug. 20, 2021, effective Nov. 1, 2021), art. 2, 2021 STANDING COMM. NAT'L PEOPLE'S CONG. GAZ. 1117, 1117 (China), translated in PKULaw, CLI.1.5055321(EN).

141. Liu Junchen (刘俊臣), Guanyu Zhonghua Renmin Gongheguo Geren Xinxi Baohu Fa (Cao'an) de Shuoming (关于《中华人民共和国个人信息保护法（草案）》的说明) [Explanation for the Personal Information Protection Law of People's Republic of China (Draft)], 2021 STANDING COMM. NAT'L PEOPLE'S CONG. GAZ. 1125, 1125–1126 (China) (unofficial translation).

142. China Issues Opinions on Regulating Platform Economy, NEWS.CN (Jan. 19, 2022), https://english.news.cn/20220119/49c58cb414524854b90b687e2 edd74e8/c.html (discussing Guojia Fazhan Gaigewei Deng Bumen Guanyu Tuidong Pingtai Jingji Guifan Jiankang Chixu Fazhan de Ruogan Yijian (国家发展改革委等部门关于推动平台经济规范健康持续发展的若干意见) [Several Opinions from National Development and Reform Commission and Other Departments on Promoting the Development of Lawful, Healthy, and Sustainable Development of Platform Economy] (promulgated by Nat'l Dev. and Reform Comm'n., St. Admin. for Mkt. Regul., Off. of Cent. Cyberspace Affs. Comm'n, Ministry of Indus. & Info. Tech., Ministry of Hum. Res. & Soc. Sec., Ministry of Agric. & Rural Affs., Ministry of Com., People's Bank of China, St. Admin. of Tax'n, Dec. 24, 2021), https://www.ndrc.gov.cn/xxgk/zcfb/tz/202201/t20220119_1312326.html?code=&state=123 (China)).

143. Fanlongduan Fa (反垄断法) [Anti-Monopoly Law] (promulgated by the Standing Comm. Nat'l People's Cong., Aug. 30, 2007, effective Aug. 1, 2008, revised June 24, 2022, effective Aug. 1, 2022), arts. 9, 24, 2022 STANDING COMM. NAT'L PEOPLE'S CONG. GAZ. 619, 620–622 (China), translated in PKULaw, CLI.1.5128034(EN), discussed in GIBSON DUNN, CHINA AMENDS ITS ANTI-MONOPOLY LAW (2022), https://www.gibsondunn.com/wp-content/uplo ads/2022/06/china-amends-its-anti-monopoly-law.pdf.

144. Personal Information Protection Law, *supra* note 140, art. 24.

145. *Id.* art. 26.

146. Fazhan Fuzeren de Rengong Zhineng: Xinyidai Rengong Zhineng Zhili Yuanze Fabu (发展负责任的人工智能：新一代人工智能治理原则发布) [Governance Principles for a New Generation of Artificial Intelligence: Develop Responsible Artificial Intelligence Issued], MINISTRY SCI. & TECH. CHINA (June 17, 2019), https://www.most.gov.cn/kjbgz/201906/t20190617_147107.html, translated in Graham Webster, Lorand Laskai, Translation: Chinese Expert Group Offers "Governance Principles" for "Responsible AI," DIGICHINA (June 17, 2019), https://digichina.stanford.edu/work/translation-chinese-expert-group-offers-governance-principles-for-responsible-ai/.

147. Sebastian Mallaby, THE POWER LAW: VENTURE CAPITAL AND THE MAKING OF THE NEW FUTURE 225 (2022).

148. *Id.* at 224.

149. *Id.* at 226.

150. *Id.* at 231–232.

151. James Kynge, For US Venture Funds, Next Jack Ma Is Outside China, NIKKEI ASIA (Mar. 5, 2020), https://asia.nikkei.com/Spotlight/Comment/For-US-vent ure-funds-next-Jack-Ma-is-outside-China.

152. MALLABY, *supra* note 147, 233 (2022).

153. Rolfe Winkler, Jing Yang, & Alexander Osipovich, Secretive High-Speed Trading Firm Hits Jackpot with TikTok, WALL ST. J. (Oct. 1, 2020), https://www.wsj.com/articles/secretive-high-speed-trading-firm-hits-jackpot-with-tiktok-11601544610?utm_campaign=The%20Interface&utm_medium=email&utm_source=Revue%20newsletter.

154. Qualcomm Ventures: Two Decades of Driving Innovation in Mobile, QUALCOMM VENTURES (Nov. 25, 2020), https://www.qualcommventures.com/insights/blog/qualcomm-ventures-two-decades-of-driving-innovation-in-mobile/.

155. Mallaby, *supra* note 147, at 231–232.

156. Wei Gu, "Amazon of China" Gets a Jolt from Venture Capital, GLOBE & MAIL (Nov. 20, 2012), https://www.theglobeandmail.com/globe-investor/amazon-of-china-gets-a-jolt-from-venture-capital/article5479388/.

157. Saheli Roy Choudhury, Google Places a $550 Million Bet on China's Second-Largest E-Commerce Player, CNBC, https://www.cnbc.com/2018/06/18/goo gle-to-invest-550-million-into-chinas-jd-com.html.

158. Adam Lysenko, Thilo Hanemann, & Daniel H. Rosen, DISRUPTION: US–CHINA VENTURE CAPITAL IN A NEW ERA OF STRATEGIC COMPETITION 20 (2020), https://publications-research.s3-us-west-2.amazonaws.com/RHG_Disruption_US+China+VC_January2020.pdf.

159. *See* Julie Zhu, Meg Shen, & Greg Roumeliotis, China Slams the Brakes on Ant Group's $37 Billion Listing, REUTERS (Nov. 3, 2020), https://www.reuters.com/article/us-ant-group-ipo-idUSKBN27J1OS.

160. Ryan McMorrow & Yuan Yang, Chinese Regulators Fine Alibaba Record $2.8bn, FIN. TIMES (Apr. 10, 2021), https://www.ft.com/content/bb251dcc-4bff-4883-9d81-061114fee87f.

161. Laura He, Ant Group Cut Down to Size in Latest Blow for Jack Ma's Business Empire, CNN (Apr. 13, 2021), https://www.cnn.com/2021/04/13/tech/ant-group-restructuring-intl-hnk/index.html.

162. Emily Cadman, Why Didi Shares Are Falling and Why China Is Cracking Down, BLOOMBERG, https://www.bloomberg.com/news/articles/2021-07-05/what-is-didi-and-why-is-china-cracking-down-on-it-quicktake (July 6, 2021).

163. Alexis Benveniste, China Bans Didi, Its Biggest Ride-Hailing Service, From App Stores, CNN (July 4, 2021), https://www.cnn.com/2021/07/04/tech/china-app-store-didi/index.html.

164. *See* Guojia Hulianwang Xinxi Bangongshi dui Didi Quanqiu Gufen Youxian Gongsi Yifa Zuochu Wangluo Anquan Shencha Xiangguan Xingzheng Chufa de Jueding (国家互联网信息办公室对滴滴全球股份有限公司依法作出网络安全审查相关行政处罚的决定) [Cyberspace Administration of China's Decision on Administrative Penalty According to the Law Against Didi Global Inc. Related to Cybersecurity Review], Zhonghua Renmin Gongheguo Guojia Hulianwang Xinxi Bangongshi (中华人民共和国国家互联网信息办公室) [CYBERSPACE ADMIN. CHINA], http://www.cac.gov.cn/2022-07/21/c_1660021534306352.htm (China); Paul Mozur & John Liu, China Fines Didi $1.2 Billion as Tech Sector Pressures Persist, N.Y. TIMES (July 21, 2022), https://www.nytimes.com/2022/07/21/business/china-fines-didi.html.

165. Chinese Streaming Firm DouYu Terminates $5.3 Bln Merger with Huya, REUTERS (July 12, 2021), https://www.reuters.com/world/china/chinese-live-streaming-firm-douyu-terminates-merger-deal-with-huya-2021-07-12/.

166. Raymond Zhong, China's Tech Antitrust Campaign Snares Meituan, a Food-Delivery Giant, N.Y. TIMES (Oct. 8, 2021), https://www.nytimes.com/2021/10/08/technology/china-meituan-antitrust-fine.html.

167. Guowuyuan Fanlongduan Weiyuanhui Guanyu Pingtai Jingji Lingyu de Fanlongduan Zhinan (国务院反垄断委员会关于平台经济领域的反垄断指南) [Guidelines of the Anti-Monopoly Commission of the State Council for Anti-Monopoly in the Field of Platform Economy] (promulgated by Anti-Monopoly Comm. of the St. Council, Feb.7, 2021, effective Feb.7, 2021), https://gkml.samr.gov.cn/nsjg/fldj/202102/t20210207_325967.html (China), translated in PKULaw, CLI.4.352590(EN).

168. Guanyu Yinfa, "Changjian Leixing Yidong Hulianwang Yingyong Chengxu Biyao Geren Xinxi Fanwei Guiding" de Tongzhi (关于印发《常见类型移动互联网应用程序必要个人信息范围规定》的通知) [Notice of Issuing the Provisions on the Scope of Necessary Personal Information for Common Types of Mobile Internet Applications] (promulgated by Sec'y Bureau of Cyberspace Admin. of China, General Off. of Ministry of Indus. & Info. Tech., General Off. of Ministry of Public Sec., General Office of St. Admin. for Mkt. Regul., Mar. 12, 2021, effective May 1, 2021), http://www.cac.gov.cn/2021-03/22/c_1617990997054277.htm (China), translated in Provisions on the Scope of Necessary Personal Information for Common Types of Mobile Internet Applications, CHINA L. TRANSLATE (Mar. 22, 2021), https://www.chinalawtranslate.com/en/necessary-app-info/.

169. Wangxinban Gong'an Bu Shangwu Bu Wenhua he Lüyou Bu Shuiwu Zongju Shichang Jianguan Zongju Guangdian Zongju Guanyu Yinfa, "Wangluo Zhibo Yingxiao Guanli Banfa (Shixing)" de Tongzhi (网信办 公安部 商务部 文化和旅游部 税务总局 市场监管总局 广电总局关于网络直播营销管理办法（试行）的通知) [Circular of the Office of the Central Cyberspace Affairs Commission, the Ministry of Public Security, the Ministry of Commerce,

the Ministry of Culture and Tourism, the State Administration of Taxation, the State Administration for Market Regulation and the National Radio and Television Administration on Printing and Issuing the Measures for the Administration of Live Streaming Marketing (for Trial Implementation)] (promulgated by Off. of Cent. Cyberspace Affs. Comm'n, Ministry of Public Sec., Ministry Com., Ministry of Culture & Tourism, St. Admin. of Tax'n, St. Admin. for Mkt. Regul., Nat'l Radio & Television Admin., Apr. 16, 2021, effective May 25, 2021), ST. COUNCIL GAZ., July 10, 2021, at 60 (China), translated in PKULaw, CLI.4.5012115(EN).

170. Data Security Law, *supra* note 54.

171. Wangluo Anquan Shencha Banfa (网络安全审查办法) [Measures for Cybersecurity Review] (promulgated by Cyberspace Admin. of China, Nat'l Dev. & Reform Comm'n., Ministry of Indus. & Info. Tech., Ministry of Public Sec., Ministry of St. Sec., Ministry of Fin., Ministry of Com., People's Bank of China, St. Admin. for Mkt. Regul., Nat'l Radio & Television Admin., China Sec. Regul. Comm'n, Nat'l Admin. of St. Secret Prot., St. Cryptography Admin., Apr. 13, 2020, effective June 1, 2020, revised Dec. 28, 2021, effective Feb. 28, 2022), ST. COUNCIL GAZ., Mar. 30, 2022 (China), translated in PKULaw, CLI.4.5113083(EN).

172. Guanjian Xinxi Jichu Sheshi Anquan Baohu Tiaoli (关键信息基础设施安全保护条例) [Regulation on Protecting the Security of Critical Information Infrastructure] (promulgated by St. Council, July 30, 2021, effective Sep. 1, 2021), St. Council Gaz., Sep. 10, 2021, at 5 (China), translated in PKULaw, CLI.2.5055187(EN).

173. Personal Information Protection Law, *supra* note 140.

174. Guojia Xinwen Chuban Shu Guanyu Jinyibu Yange Guanli Qieshi Fangzhi Weichengnianren Chenmi Wangluo Youxi de Tongzhi (国家新闻出版署关于进一步严格管理切实防止未成年人沉迷网络游戏的通知) [Notice by the National Press and Publication Administration of Further Imposing Strict Administrative Measures to Prevent Minors from Becoming Addicted to Online Games] (promulgated by Nat'l Press & Publ'n Admin., Aug. 30, 2021, effective Sep. 1, 2021), http://www.gov.cn/zhengce/zhengceku/2021-09/01/content_5634661.htm (China), translated in PKULaw, CLI.4.5055621(EN).

175. Ruihan Huang & Joshua Henderson, Is There a Method Behind China's Tech Crackdown Madness?, MACROPOLO (Oct. 21, 2021), https://macropolo.org/china-tech-crackdown-software-hardware/?rp=e.

176. *Id.*

177. Edward White, China's Top Court Takes Aim at "996" Overtime Culture in Blow to Tech Groups, FIN. TIMES (Aug. 27, 2021), https://www.ft.com/content/a794faf1-2ee9-4d19-abc6-72620227396c?shareType=nongift.

178. Xi Jinping (习近平), Zhashi Tuidong Gongtong Fuyu (扎实推动共同富裕) [Making Solid Progress Toward Common Prosperity], QIUSHI WANG (求是

㓉) [QSTHEORY.CN] (Oct. 15, 2021), http://www.qstheory.cn/dukan/qs/2021-10/15/c_1127959365.htm (China), translated in Making Solid Progress Toward Common Prosperity, QIUSHI, http://en.qstheory.cn/2022-01/18/c_699346.htm (Jan. 18, 2022).

179. Paul Mozur, The End of a "Gilded Age": China Is Bringing Business to Heel, N.Y. TIMES (Oct. 5, 2021), https://www.nytimes.com/2021/10/05/business/china-businesses.html.

180. Stephanie Yang, China's Tech Clampdown Is Spreading Like Wildfire, WALL ST. J., https://www.wsj.com/articles/chinas-tech-clampdown-is-spreading-like-wildfire-11622971802 (June 6, 2021).

181. *See* Laura He, Natalie Leung, Marco Chaco, & Carlotta Dotto, China's "Unprecedented" Crackdown Stunned Private Enterprise. One Year On, It May Have to Cut Business Some Slack, CNN (Nov. 3, 2021), https://www.cnn.com/2021/11/02/tech/china-economy-crackdown-private-companies-intl-hnk/index.html.

182. Do Alipay and Tenpay Misuse Their Market Power?, ECONOMIST (Aug. 6, 2020), https://www.economist.com/finance-and-economics/2020/08/06/do-alipay-and-tenpay-misuse-their-market-power.

183. *See* Canghao Chen, The Real Cause of China's Alibaba Crackdown, DIPLOMAT (Sep. 9, 2021), https://thediplomat.com/2021/09/the-real-cause-of-chinas-alibaba-crackdown/.

184. George Calhoun, DiDi Means War—A Financial Cold War with China, FORBES (July 19, 2021), https://www.forbes.com/sites/georgecalhoun/2021/07/19/didi-means-war--a-financial-cold-war-with-china/?sh=128603cd5ce7.

185. Chang Che & Jeremy Goldkorn, China's "Big Tech Crackdown": A Guide, SUPCHINA (Aug. 2, 2021), https://supchina.com/2021/08/02/chinas-big-tech-crackdown-a-guide/; Bo Zhuang, Loomis Sayles & Co., A Guide to Understanding China's Regulatory Crackdown, LOOMIS SAYLES (Sep. 21, 2021), https://blog.loomissayles.com/a-guide-to-understanding-chinas-regulatory-crackdown.

186. Huang & Henderson, *supra* note 175.

187. He et al., *supra* note 181.

188. Rich Karlgaard, The Bigger Picture Behind China's Tech Crackdown: Ambition to Achieve Tech Supremacy, FORBES (Aug. 31, 2021), https://www.forbes.com/sites/richkarlgaard/2021/08/15/the-bigger-picture-behind-chinas-tech-crackdown-ambition-to-achieve-tech-supremacy/?sh=665826adee77.

189. He et al., *supra* note 181.

190. Rebecca Feng & Clarence Leong, China Shares Soar After Beijing Signals Support; Alibaba Jumps 37%, WALL ST. J. (Mar. 16, 2022), https://www.wsj.com/articles/china-markets-rebound-on-supportive-government-comments-11647416023?mod=Searchresults_pos1&page=1.

191. Raffaele Huang & Cao Li, Chinese Internet Stocks Hit Three-Month High, WALL ST. J. (June 8, 2022), https://www.wsj.com/articles/chinese-internet-sto cks-hit-three-month-high-11654685396.

192. Calhoun, *supra* at 184.

193. *Id.*

194. Will Oremus, The Technology 202: China Is Doing What the U.S. Can't Seem to: Regulate Its Tech Giants, WASH. POST (July 28, 2021), https://www.washing tonpost.com/politics/2021/07/28/technology-202-china-is-doing-what-us-cant-seem-regulate-its-tech-giants/.

195. Lijiya Sitanqingke (莉季娅·斯坦钦科), Zhongguo Jiaqiang Hulianwang Longduan Jianguan Huidui Hulianwang Jutou Zaocheng Weixie Ma? (中国加强对互联网垄断监管会对互联网巨头造成威胁吗？) [Will China's Tightening Internet Monopoly Regulation Threaten Tech Giants?], Eluosi Weixing Tongxun She (俄罗斯卫星通讯社) [SPUTNIK], https://sputniknews. cn/20201111/1032510519.html (Jan. 26, 2022) (China) (unofficial translation).

196. *Id.*

197. Ding Yixin (丁亦鑫), Zhongyang Shengaiwei Jujiao Fanlongduan Shifang le Shenme Xinhao? (中央深改委聚焦反垄断 释放了什么信号？) [Central Commission for Comprehensively Deepening Reform Focused on Anti-Monopoly. What Signal Does It Send?], Renmin Wang (人民网) [PEOPLE.CN] (Sep. 3, 2021), http://www.people.com.cn/n1/2021/0903/c32306-32216236. html (China).

198. Alibaba Group, A Letter to Our Customers and to the Community, ALIZILA (Apr. 10, 2021), https://www.alizila.com/a-letter-to-our-customers-and-to-the-community/.

199. Gonggao (公告) [Statement], WEIXIN: MEITUAN (微信：美团) [WECHAT: MEITUAN] (Oct. 8, 2021), https://mp.weixin.qq.com/s/530n50AZb1aaCTaiOTCEHw (China).

200. Laura He, Pinduoduo's Founder Leaves as His Chinese E-Commerce Giant Grows Bigger Than Ever, CNN (Mar. 18, 2021), https://edition.cnn.com/2021/ 03/18/tech/pinduoduo-colin-huang-intl-hnk/index.html; Laura He, The Young CEO Who Helped Make TikTok a Global Hit Is Latest Chinese Tech Entrepreneur to Quit, CNN (May 20, 2021), https://edition.cnn.com/2021/05/ 20/tech/zhang-bytedance-ceo-resignation-intl-hnk/index.html.

201. Zhong, *supra* note 166.

202. Xie Yu, Founder of China's Meituan Donates $2.3 Billion Stake, WALL ST. J. (June 4, 2021), https://www.wsj.com/articles/founder-of-chinas-meituan-dona tes-2-3-billion-stake-11622804438.

203. Yingzhi Yang & Bhargav Acharya, ByteDance Founder Zhang Yiming Steps Down as Chairman—Source, REUTERS (Nov. 3, 2021), https://www.reuters. com/business/cop/bytedance-founder-zhang-step-down-chairman-bloomb erg-news-2021-11-03/; Zhong, *supra* note 166.

204. Yue Wang, Tencent Warns of More Regulations, Pledges Additional $7.7 Billion for Social Philanthropy Projects, FORBES (Aug. 19, 2021), https://www.forbes.com/sites/ywang/2021/08/19/tencent-warns-of-more-regulations-pledges-additional-77-billion-for-social-philanthropy-projects/?sh=5769c3972e9f.

205. Frances Yoon, Alibaba Pledges $15.5 Billion as Chinese Companies Extol Beijing's "Common Prosperity" Push, WALL ST. J. (Sep. 3, 2021), https://www.wsj.com/articles/alibaba-pledges-15-5-billion-as-chinese-companies-extol-beijings-common-prosperity-push-11630587923.

206. Nat'l Sec. Comm'n on A.I., *supra* note 34, at 2.

207. THE NEW BIG BROTHER—CHINA AND DIGITAL AUTHORITARIANISM 1 (2020) (United States Senate Committee on Foreign Relations Democratic Staff report), https://www.foreign.senate.gov/imo/media/doc/2020%20SFRC%20Minority%20Staff%20Report%20-%20The%20New%20Big%20Brother%20-%20%20China%20and%20Digital%20Authoritarianism.pdf.

208. Forced Labour and the Situation of the Uyghurs in the Xinjiang Uyghur Autonomous Region, EUR. PARL. DOC. P9_TA (2020)0375, https://www.europarl.europa.eu/doceo/document/TA-9-2020-0375_EN.pdf.

209. EU Finds China's Censorship of Web Unacceptable, REUTERS (June 20, 2008), https://www.reuters.com/article/oukin-uk-eu-china-censorship/eu-finds-chinas-censorship-of-web-unacceptable-idUKSIN30210920080620.

210. Mark Zuckerberg, Speech at Georgetown University (Oct. 17, 2019), in Tony Romm, Zuckerberg: Standing for Voice and Free Expression, WASH. POST (Oct. 17, 2019), https://www.washingtonpost.com/technology/2019/10/17/zuckerberg-standing-voice-free-expression/.

211. Freedom on the Net 2021: China, FREEDOM HOUSE, https://freedomhouse.org/country/china/freedom-net/2021.

212. Xi Jinping (习近平), Zai Wangluo Anquan he Xinxihua Gongzuo Zuotanhui shang de Jianghua (在网络安全和信息化工作座谈会上的讲话) [Speech at the Network Security and Informatization Work Conference], Renmin Wang (人民网) [PEOPLE.CN] (Apr. 26, 2016), http://politics.people.com.cn/n1/2016/0426/c1024-28303544.html (China), translated in Speech at the Work Conference for Cybersecurity and Informatization, CHINA COPYRIGHT AND MEDIA, https://chinacopyrightandmedia.wordpress.com/2016/04/19/speech-at-the-work-conference-for-cybersecurity-and-informatization/ (Rogier Creemers eds., Apr. 26, 2016).

213. Chinese Netizens Jeer Riot in US Capitol as "Karma," Say Bubbles of "Democracy and Freedom" Have Burst, GLOBAL TIMES (Jan 7, 2021), https://www.globaltimes.cn/page/202101/1212074.shtml.

214. *Id.*

215. Reality Check: Falsehoods in US Perceptions of China, MINISTRY FOREIGN AFFS. CHINA (June 19, 2022), https://www.mfa.gov.cn/eng/wjbxw/202206/t20220619_10706059.html.

216. *Id.*

217. *Foreign Ministry Spokesperson Zhao Lijian's Regular Press Conference on July 25, 2022*, MINISTRY FOREIGN AFFAIRS CHINA, https://www.fmprc.gov.cn/mfa_eng/xwfw_665399/s2510_665401/2511_665403/202207/t20220725_10727739.html .

218. Bruce Schneier, DATA AND GOLIATH: THE HIDDEN BATTLES TO COLLECT YOUR DATA AND CONTROL YOUR WORLD 62–87 (2015).

219. Derek Thompson, A Tale of Two Surveillance States, ATLANTIC (May 30, 2019), https://www.theatlantic.com/technology/archive/2019/05/the-us-and-china-a-tale-of-two-surveillance-states/590542/.

220. *Id.*

221. *Id.; see also* Lola Fadulu, Facial Recognition Technology in Public Housing Prompts Backlash, N.Y. TIMES (Sep. 24, 2019), https://www.nytimes.com/2019/09/24/us/politics/facial-recognition-technology-housing.html.

222. Irina Ivanova, Video Surveillance in U.S. Described as on Par with China, CBS NEWS (Dec. 10, 2019), https://www.cbsnews.com/news/the-u-s-uses-surveillance-cameras-just-as-much-as-china/.

223. Campbell, *supra* note 110.

224. *See, e.g.,* Economy, *supra* note 3, at 59.

225. Dennis Normile, Science Suffers as China's Internet Censors Plug Holes in Great Firewall, SCIENCE (Aug. 30, 2017), https://www.science.org/content/article/science-suffers-china-s-internet-censors-plug-holes-great-firewall.

226. Harwell & Dou, *supra* note 114; Addition of Certain Entities to the Entity List, 84 Fed. Reg. 54002, 54003 (Oct. 9, 2019) (amending 15 C.F.R. Part 744).

227. Charles Rollet, Hikvision Admits Minority Recognition, Now Claims Canceled, IPVM (July 23, 2020), https://ipvm.com/reports/hikvision-cancels.

228. Liv Klingert, China's Cameras Face Fresh Scrutiny in Europe, POLITICO (Oct. 6, 2021), https://www.politico.eu/article/hikvision-china-surveillance-chinese-tech-europe/; Addition of Certain Entities to the Entity List, 84 Fed. Reg. at 54004.

229. *See* Entity List, U.S. DEP'T OF COM., BUREAU INDUS. & SEC., https://www.bis.doc.gov/index.php/policy-guidance/lists-of-parties-of-concern/entity-list.

230. Liv Klingert, China's Cameras Face Fresh Scrutiny in Europe, POLITICO (Oct. 6, 2021), https://www.politico.eu/article/hikvision-china-surveillance-chinese-tech-europe/.

231. Exec. Order No. 13943, Addressing the Threat Posed by WeChat, and Taking Additional Steps to Address the National Emergency with Respect to the Information and Communications Technology and Services Supply Chain, 85 Fed. Reg. 48641 (Aug. 11, 2020); Exec. Order No. 13942, Addressing the Threat Posed by TikTok, and Taking Additional Steps to Address the National Emergency With Respect to the Information and Communications Technology

and Services Supply Chain, 85 Fed. Reg. 48637 (Aug. 11, 2020); Regarding the Acquisition of Musical.ly by ByteDance Ltd., 85 Fed. Reg. 51297 (Aug. 19, 2020).

232. Angela Huyue Zhang, CHINESE ANTITRUST EXCEPTIONALISM 240 (2021).

233. *Id.*

234. Tim Wu, A TikTok Ban Is Overdue, N.Y. TIMES (Aug. 18, 2020), https://www.nytimes.com/2020/08/18/opinion/tiktok-wechat-ban-trump.html.

235. Fact Sheet: Executive Order Addressing the Threat From Securities Investments That Finance Certain Companies of the People's Republic of China, WHITE HOUSE (June 3, 2021), https://www.whitehouse.gov/briefing-room/statements-releases/2021/06/03/fact-sheet-executive-order-addressing-the-threat-from-securities-investments-that-finance-certain-companies-of-the-peoples-republic-of-china/; Exec. Order. No. 13959, Addressing the Threat from Securities Investments That Finance Communist Chinese Military Companies, 85 Fed. Reg. 73185 (Nov. 12, 2020), as amended by Exec. Order. No. 14032, Addressing the Threat from Securities Investments That Finance Certain Companies of the People's Republic of China, 86 Fed. Reg. 30145 (June 7, 2021).

236. Justin Sherman, The U.S. Is Continuing Its Campaign Against Huawei, LAWFARE (July 20, 2021), https://www.lawfareblog.com/us-continuing-its-campaign-against-huawei.

237. Chuin-Wei Yap et al., Huawei's Yearslong Rise Is Littered with Accusations of Theft and Dubious Ethics, WALL ST. J. (May 25, 2019), https://www.wsj.com/articles/huaweis-yearslong-rise-is-littered-with-accusations-of-theft-and-dubious-ethics-11558756858.

238. Paul Mozur, U.S. Subpoenas Huawei Over Its Dealings in Iran and North Korea, N.Y. TIMES (June 2, 2016), https://www.nytimes.com/2016/06/03/technology/huawei-technologies-subpoena-iran-north-korea.html.

239. James Kynge, Huawei Suffers Biggest-Ever Decline in Revenue After US Blacklisting, FIN. TIMES (Aug. 6, 2021), https://www.ft.com/content/dc170be7-262e-4616-9ef9-2a49c611c26b.

CHAPTER 3

1. Elon Musk (@elonmusk), TWITTER (Oct. 27, 2022), https://twitter.com/elonmusk/status/1585841080431321088.

2. Thierry Breton (@ThierryBreton), TWITTER (Oct. 28, 2022), https://twitter.com/ThierryBreton/status/1585902196864045056.

3. See generally Anu Bradford, *Europe's Digital Constitution*, 64 VA. J. INT'L L. (forthcoming 2023), which initially developed the argument used in this chapter to describe the European rights-driven regulatory model.

4. *See* European Declaration on Digital Rights and Principles for the Digital Decade, of the European Parliament, Council, and Comm'n, Chapter 1 (Dec. 15, 2022).

5. The EU's commitment to the social market economy is explicitly mentioned as a common objective for Europe; *see* Consolidated Version of the Treaty on European Union art. 3, 2012 O.J. (C 326) 13 [hereafter TEU].

6. *See* Peter A. Hall & David Soskice, VARIETIES OF CAPITALISM: THE INSTITUTIONAL FOUNDATIONS OF COMPARATIVE ADVANTAGE (2001).

7. Paul Nemitz, Constitutional Democracy and Technology in the Age of Artificial Intelligence, PHIL. TRANS. R. SOC. A. 376, 1 (2018).

8. *Id*, at 1, 5.

9. *See, e.g.,* Special Eurobarometer 477: Report Democracy and Elections, at 5, EUR. COMM'N (Nov. 2018), https://europa.eu/eurobarometer/api/deliverable/downl oad/file?deliverableId=67373; Special Eurobarometer 503: Report Attitudes Towards Digitalisation on Daily Lives, at 49, EUR. COMM'N (Mar. 2020), https:// europa.eu/eurobarometer/api/deliverable/download/file?deliverableId=72615.

10. Andreas Laudner, The Polarization of the European Party System—New Data, New Approach, New Results 7 (Sep. 5, 2014) (paper presented in panel P361, "The Methodological Challenges of Designing Cross-National Voting Advice Applications" at the ECPR General Conference).

11. Regulation (EU) 2022/1925 of the European Parliament and of the Council of September 14, 2022, on contestable and fair markets in the digital sector and amending Directives (EU) 2019/1937 and (EU) 2020/1828 (Digital Markets Act), 2022 O.J. (L 265) 1.

12. European Parliament's plenary adopts the Digital Services Act and Digital Markets Act, ECOMMERCE EUROPE (July 7, 2022), https://ecommerce-europe.eu/ news-item/european-parliaments-plenary-adopts-the-digital-services-act-and-digital-markets-act/.

13. *See* Communication from the Commission to the European Parliament, the Council, the European Economic and Social Committee and the Committee of the Regions, 2030 Digital Compass: The European Way for the Digital Decade, at 1, COM (2021) 118 final (Mar. 9, 2021).

14. Mark Minevich, Can Europe Dominate in Innovation Despite US Big Tech Lead?, FORBES (Dec. 3, 2021), https://www.forbes.com/sites/markminevich/ 2021/12/03/can-europe-dominate-in-innovation-despite-us-big-tech-lead/?sh= 571e5b9b1d75.

15. *See, e.g.,* Andrew McAfee, EU Proposals to Regulate AI Are Only Going to Hinder Innovation, FIN. TIMES (July 25, 2021), https://www.ft.com/content/ a5970b6c-e731-45a7-b75b-721e90e32e1c.

16. Mark Scott, E.U. Rules Look to Unify Digital Market, But U.S. Sees Protectionism, N.Y. TIMES (Sep. 13, 2016), https://www.nytimes.com/2016/09/14/technology/ eu-us-tech-google-facebook-apple.html.

17. Editorial, Tax Affairs of American Tech Groups Come Under Fire, FIN. TIMES (Oct. 3, 2017), https://www.ft.com/content/8cdba452-a779-11e7-ab55-27219 df83c97.

18. TEU, *supra* note 5.

19. Koen Lenaerts, The ECHR and the CJEU: Creating Synergies in the Field of Fundamental Rights Protection, (Jan. 26, 2018), https://www.echr.coe.int/Documents/Speech_20180126_Lenaerts_JY_ENG.pdf.

20. Charter of Fundamental Rights of the European Union, art. 7, 8. 11, and 21, 2012 O.J. (C 326) 391, 397–400.

21. Margrethe Vestager & Josep Borrell, Why Europe's Digital Decade Matters, EEAS (Mar. 10, 2021), https://eeas.europa.eu/headquarters/headquarters-home page_en/94664/WhyEurope'sDigitalDecadeMatters

22. Koen Lenaerts, Making the EU Charter of Fundamental Rights a Reality for All, Keynote Speech, EU AGENCY FOR FUNDAMENTAL RIGHTS (Nov. 12, 2019), p. 19, https://ec.europa.eu/info/sites/default/files/charter_lenaerts12.11.19.pdf.

23. Valentina Pop, ECJ President on EU Integration, Public Opinion, Safe Harbor, Antitrust, WALL ST. J. (Oct. 14, 2015), https://www.wsj.com/articles/BL-RTBB-5170.

24. Orla Lynskey, THE FOUNDATIONS OF EU DATA PROTECTION LAW 11 (2015).

25. Charter of Fundamental Rights of the European Union, art. 1, 2012 O.J. (C 326) 391, 396 [hereinafter Charter]; *see also* Wojciech Wiewiórowski, Protecting Privacy and Data Protection in a Responsible, Sustainable Future, SPEECH AT THE PRESENTATION OF THE EDPS STRATEGY 2020–2024 (June 30, 2020), https://edps.europa.eu/sites/default/files/publication/20-06-30_strategy_speech_en.pdf.

26. Thomas Shaw, Privacy Law and History: WWII–Forward, THE PRIVACY ADVISOR (Mar. 1, 2013), https://iapp.org/news/a/2013-03-01-privacy-law-and-history-wwii-forward/.

27. Alvar C. H. Freude & Trixy Freude, Echoes of History: Understanding German Data Protection, NEWPOLITIK 2, at 85 et seq. (Oct. 1, 2016), https://www.bertelsmann-stiftung.de/de/publikationen/publikation/did/newpolitik.

28. *See* Council of Europe, European Convention for the Protection of Human Rights and Fundamental Freedoms, art. 8, opened for signature Nov. 4, 1950, ETS 5 [hereinafter ECHR]. The European Court of Human Rights, which is vested with the task of enforcing the ECHR, has extended the right to privacy to data protection; *see* Copland v. United Kingdom, 253 Eur.Ct.H.R. (2007).

29. Charter, *supra* note 25, art. 7, 8; *see* Treaty on the Functioning of the European Union art. 16, 2012 O.J. (C 326) 55.

30. Regulation 2016/679 of the European Parliament and of the Council on the Protection of Natural Persons with regard to the Processing of Personal Data and on the Free Movement of Such Data, and Repealing Directive 95/46/EC, 2016 O.J. (L 119) 1 [hereinafter GDPR].

31. *Id,*. art. 5(1)(a).

32. *Id.*, art. 5(1)(b)–1(c).

33. Id., art. 17.

34. *Id.*, art. 25.

35. *Id.*, art. 51, 68.

36. *Id.*, art. 83.

37. Case C-131/12, Google Spain SL v. Agencia Española de Protección de Datos, ECLI:EU:C:2014:317.

38. Jennifer Daskal, Borders and Bits, 71 VAND. L.R. 179, 214 (2018).

39. *See* Requests to Delist Content Under European Privacy Law, GOOGLE (May 29, 2014), https://transparencyreport.google.com/eu-privacy/overview (these numbers are accurate of Aug. 15, 2022. Google updates the figures periodically).

40. GDPR, *supra* note 30, recital 4.

41. *See, e.g.,* Joined Cases C-293/12 and C-594/12, Digital Rights Ireland Ltd v. Minister for Communications, Marine and Natural Resources, ECLI:EU:C:2014:238; Case C-623/17, Privacy International v. Secretary of State for Foreign and Commonwealth Affairs, ECLI:EU:C:2020:790; Joined Cases C-511/18, C-512/18 & C-520/18, La Quadrature du Net and Others v. Premier Ministre, ECLI:EU:C:2020:791.

42. Jeffrey Dastin, Amazon Scraps Secret AI Recruiting Tool That Showed Bias Against Women, REUTERS (Oct. 10, 2018), https://www.reuters.com/article/us-amazon-com-jobs-automation-insight/amazon-scraps-secret-ai-recruiting-tool-that-showed-bias-against-women-idUSKCN1MK08G.

43. Melissa Heikkilä, Dutch Scandal Serves as a Warning for Europe Over Risks of Using Algorithms, POLITICO (Mar. 29, 2022), https://www.politico.eu/article/dutch-scandal-serves-as-a-warning-for-europe-over-risks-of-using-algorithms/.

44. Autoriteit Persoonsgegevens, Boete Belastingdienst voor zwarte lijst FSV (Apr. 12, 2022), https://autoriteitpersoonsgegevens.nl/nl/nieuws/boete-belastingdienst-voor-zwarte-lijst-fsv.

45. Proposal for a Regulation of the European Parliament and of the Council Laying Down Harmonised Rules on Artificial Intelligence (Artificial Intelligence Act) and Amending Certain Union Legislative Acts, COM (2021) 206 final, 2021/0106 (COD) (Apr. 21, 2021).

46. *Id.*, para. 15.

47. *Id.*, para. 18.

48. High-Level Expert Group on Artificial Intelligence, Ethics Guidelines for Trustworthy AI, EUR. COMM'N (Apr. 8, 2019).

49. White Paper on Artificial Intelligence—A European Approach to Excellence and Trust, at p. 1, para 3 and p. 2, paras. 2–3, EUR. COMM'N, COM (2020) 65 final (Feb. 19, 2020).

50. Proposal for a Regulation Laying Down Harmonised Rules on Artificial Intelligence, *supra* note 45, art. 14.

51. Artificial Intelligence at Google: Our Principles, GOOGLE, https://ai.google/principles/; Microsoft Responsible AI Standard, v2, MICROSOFT (June 2022), https://query.prod.cms.rt.microsoft.com/cms/api/am/binary/RE4ZPmV; Facebook's Five Pillars of Responsible AI, FACEBOOK (June 22, 2021), https://ai.facebook.com/blog/facebooks-five-pillars-of-responsible-ai/.

52. Nemitz, *supra* note 7, at 1, 7.

53. As called for e.g. in Paul Nemitz, Democracy Through Law: The Transatlantic Reflection Group and Its Manifesto in Defence of Democracy and the Rule of Law in the Age of "Artificial Intelligence," EUR. LAW. J. 2021, 1.

54. *See* Noah Feldman, Free Speech in Europe Isn't What Americans Think, BLOOMBERG (Mar. 19, 2017), https://www.bloomberg.com/view/articles/2017-03-19/free-speech-in-europe-isn-t-what-americans-think; *see also* Jeffrey Rosen, The Delete Squad: Google, Twitter, Facebook and the New Global Battle Over the Future of Free Speech, NEW REPUBLIC (Apr. 29, 2013), https://newrepublic.com/article/113045/free-speech-internet-ssilicon-valley-%EF%BF%BCmaking-rules.

55. European Commission Against Racism and Intolerance, General Policy Recommendation No. 15 on Combating Hate Speech, ECRI (2016), 3 (Dec. 8, 2015), https://rm.coe.int/ecri-general-policy-recommendation-no-15-on-combating-hate-speech/16808b5b01.

56. Piotr Bakowski, Combating Hate Speech and Hate Crime in the EU, EUR. PARLIAMENT (June 6, 2022), https://www.europarl.europa.eu/RegData/etudes/ATAG/2022/733520/EPRS_ATA(2022)733520_EN.pdf.

57. Code of Conduct on Countering Illegal Hate Speech Online, EUR. COMM'N (June 30, 2016), https://ec.europa.eu/newsroom/just/document.cfm?doc_id=42985.

58. European Commission Daily News, Snapchat Joins the EU Code of Conduct to Fight Illegal Hate Speech Online, EUR. COMM'N (May 7, 2018), http://europa.eu/rapid/press-release_MEX-18-3723_en.htm.

59. Didier Reynders, Countering Illegal Hate Speech Online: 6th Evaluation of the Code of Conduct, EUR. COMM'N (Oct. 7, 2021), https://ec.europa.eu/info/sites/default/files/factsheet-6th-monitoring-round-of-the-code-of-conduct_october20 21_en_1.pdf. The exact time period was March 1 to April 14, 2021 (six weeks).

60. Regulation (EU) 2021/784 of the European Parliament and of the Council of April 29, 2021, on addressing the dissemination of terrorist content online, 2021 O.J. (L 172) 79.

61. *See* Joris van Hoboken, The Proposed EU Terrorism Content Regulation: Analysis and Recommendations with Respect to Freedom of Expression Implications, TRANSATLANTIC WORKING GROUP (May 3, 2019), https://www.ivir.nl/publicaties/download/TERREG_FoE-ANALYSIS.pdf.

62. Regulation on addressing the dissemination of terrorist content online, *supra* note 60.

63. *Id.*, at 90.

64. *Id.*, at 95.

65. Regulation (EU) 2022/2065 of the European Parliament and of the Council of October 19, 2022, on a Single Market for Digital Services and amending Directive 2000/31/EC (Digital Services Act), 2022 O.J. (L 277) 1.

66. *Id.*, section 4.

67. Proposal for a Regulation of the European Parliament and of the Council on a Single Market for Digital Services (Digital Services Act) and amending Directive 2000/31/EC, COM (2020) 825 final, 2020/0361 (COD) (Dec. 15, 2020), p. 4.

68. Digital Services Act, *supra* note 65, preamble, para. 62.

69. *Id.*, art. 26.

70. TEU, *supra* note 5, art. 2.

71. Conclusions of the Presidency, EUROPEAN COUNCIL IN COPENHAGEN 21–22 JUNE 1993, SN 180/1/93 REV 1, at 7A iii.

72. Sarah Repucci & Amy Slopowitz, Democracy Under Siege, FREEDOM HOUSE, https://freedomhouse.org/report/freedom-world/2021/democracy-under-siege.

73. R. S. Foa, A. Klassen, M. Slade, A. Rand, & R. Collins, THE GLOBAL SATISFACTION WITH DEMOCRACY REPORT 2020, 2, https://www.bennettinstitute.cam.ac.uk/media/uploads/files/DemocracyReport2020_nYqqWi0.pdf.

74. Hans Kundnani, The Future of Democracy in Europe: Technology and the Evolution of Representation 7 (2020), https://www.chathamhouse.org/sites/default/files/CHHJ7131-Democracy-Technology-RP-INTS-200228.pdf.

75. *See, e.g.,* Elisa Lironi, Harnessing Digital Tools to Revitalize European Democracy, CARNEGIE EUROPE (Nov. 28, 2018), https://carnegieeurope.eu/2018/11/28/harnessing-digital-tools-to-revitalize-european-democracy-pub-77806.

76. David Kaye, SPEECH POLICE: THE GLOBAL STRUGGLE TO GOVERN THE INTERNET 13 (2019).

77. Shoshana Zuboff, THE AGE OF SURVEILLANCE CAPITALISM (2019).

78. Communication from the Commission to the European Parliament, the Council, the European Economic and Social Committee and the Committee of the Regions on the European Democracy Action Plan, at 3, COM (2020) 790 final (Mar. 12, 2020).

79. *Id.*

80. Communication from the Commission to the European Parliament, the Council, the European Economic and Social Committee and the Committee of the Regions – Tackling online disinformation: a European Approach, at 1, COM(2018) 236 final (Apr. 26, 2018); *see also* Resolution on Foreign Electoral Interference and Disinformation in National and European Democratic Processes, EUR. PARL. DOC. TA (2019) 0031 para. 4 (2019) (emphasizing the importance of "free and fair elections").

81. *See* Commission Joint Communication to the European Parliament, the European Council, the Council, the European Economic and Social Committee and the Committee of the Regions, Action Plan against Disinformation, at 11, JOIN (2018) 36 final (Dec. 2, 2018).

82. Communication from the Commission, Tackling online disinformation: A European Approach, *supra* note 80, at 1.

83. Signatories of the 2022 Strengthened Code of Practice on Disinformation, EUR. COMM'N (June 16, 2022), https://digital-strategy.ec.europa.eu/en/library/signatories-2022-strengthened-code-practice-disinformation.

84. The Strengthened Code of Practice on Disinformation 2022, EUR. COMM'N (June 16, 2022), https://digital-strategy.ec.europa.eu/en/library/2022-strengthened-code-practice-disinformation.

85. European Commission Statement Statement/19/6166, Code of Practice on Disinformation one year on: online platforms submit self-assessment reports (Oct. 29, 2019).

86. European Commission Press Release IP/20/1568, Disinformation: EU assesses the Code of Practice and publishes platform reports on coronavirus related disinformation (Sep. 10, 2020).

87. Digital Services Act, *supra* note 65, preamble, para. 57.

88. *Id.*, art. 26–27.

89. *Id.*, art. 28.

90. *Id.*, art. 31.

91. *Id.*, art. 42.

92. *See* Meta Reports Fourth Quarter and Full Year 2021 Results, META PLATFORMS, INC. (Feb. 2, 2022), https://s21.q4cdn.com/399680738/files/doc_financials/2021/q4/FB-12.31.2021-Exhibit-99.1-Final.pdf.

93. *See* Duncan B. Hollis & Jens David Ohlin, DEFENDING DEMOCRACIES: COMBATING FOREIGN ELECTION INTERFERENCE IN A DIGITAL AGE, 1–16 (2021); *see also* Motion for a European Parliament resolution on foreign interference in all democratic processes in the European Union, including disinformation (2020/2268(INI) (Aug. 8, 2022).

94. *See, e.g.*, Mark Lander and Stephen Castle, "No One" Protected British Democracy from Russia, U.K. Report Concludes, N.Y. TIMES (July 21, 2020), https://www.nytimes.com/2020/07/21/world/europe/uk-russia-report-brexit-interference.html.

95. Communication from the Commission to the European Parliament, the Council, the European Economic and Social Committee and the Committee of the Regions, On the European Democracy Action Plan, at 4, COM (2020) 790 final (Dec. 3, 2020).

96. Tim Mak, Cambridge Analytica Scandal Raises New Ethical Questions About Microtargeting, NPR (MAR. 22, 2018), https://www.npr.org/2018/03/22/596180048/cambridge-analytica-scandal-raises-new-ethical-questions-about-microtargeting.

97. Proposal for a regulation of the European Parliament and of the Council on the transparency and targeting of political advertising, COM (2021) 731 final, 2021/0381 (COD) (Nov. 25, 2021).

98. On the European Democracy Action Plan, COM (2020) 790 final (Mar. 12, 2020).

99. *Id.*

100. Council of the European Union, Human Rights Guidelines on Freedom of Expression Online and Offline, at 2 (May 12, 2014), https://www.consilium.eur opa.eu/uedocs/cms_data/docs/pressdata/EN/foraff/142549.pdf.

101. Directive 2019/790, of the European Parliament and of the Council of April 17, 2019 on Copyright and Related Rights in the Digital Single Market and Amending Directives 96/9/EC and 2001/29/EC, 2019 O.J. (L 130) 92 [Copyright Directive].

102. Communication from the Commission Promoting a Fair, Efficient and Competitive European Copyright-Based Economy in the Digital Single Market, at 7, COM (2016) 592 final (Sep. 14, 2016).

103. Copyright Directive, *supra* note 101, at 92, 93, 103.

104. *Id.*, at 92.

105. *See* Academics Against Press Publishers' Right, Institute for Information Law, Universiteit van Amsterdam, https://www.ivir.nl/academics-against-press-pub lishers-right/.

106. B.O.E. 2014, 268 (Spain) (Nov. 5, 2014).

107. Ashifa Kassam, Google News Says "Adiós" to Spain in Row Over Publishing Fees, GUARDIAN (Dec. 16, 2014), https://www.theguardian.com/world/2014/ dec/16/google-news-spain-publishing-fees-internet.

108. German Publishers Cave, Grant Google Free Permission to Use Snippets in Search Results, DIGITAL READER (Oct. 22, 2014), https://the-digital-reader.com/ 2014/10/22/german-publishers-cave-grant-google-free-permission-use-snipp ets-search-results/.

109. Hanna Ziady, Google agrees to pay French publishers for news, CNN (Jan. 21, 2021), https://edition.cnn.com/2021/01/21/tech/google-pays-french-publish ers/index.html.

110. Thibault Larger & Laura Kayali, French Publishers Win Decisive Battle Against Google, POLITICO (Apr. 9, 2020), https://www.politico.eu/article/french-pub lishers-win-decisive-battle-against-google/.

111. Council conclusions on the strengthening of European content in the digital economy, 2018 O.J. (C 457) 2, 5–6.

112. Communication from the Commission to the European Parliament, the Council, the European Economic and Social Committee and the Committee of the Regions—digital education action plan 2021–2027, COM (2020) 624 final (Sep. 30, 2020).

113. Directive (EU) 2018/1808 of the European Parliament and of the Council of November 14, 2018, amending Directive 2010/13/EU on the coordination of certain provisions laid down by law, regulation or administrative action in member states concerning the provision of audiovisual media services in view of changing market realities (Audiovisual Media Services Directive), art. 1, 2018 O.J. (L 303) 69, 89.

114. Employment and Social Developments in Europe 2020, Leaving no one behind and striving for more: Fairness and solidarity in the European social market economy, at 17, EUR. COMM'N (Sep. 15, 2020).

115. Beatrice D'Hombres & Frank Neher (eds.), BEYOND AVERAGES—FAIRNESS IN AN ECONOMY THAT WORKS FOR PEOPLE 28 (2020).

116. Justice and Fairness in Europe, ESS Topline Result Series, Issue 10, at 4–10, (2020).

117. Margrethe Vestager, Foreword to the Annual Competition Report 2016, EUR. COMM'N, https://ec.europa.eu/competition/publications/annual_report/2016/fw_en.pdf. Emphasis added.

118. Jean-Claude Juncker, State of the Union 2016, EUR. COMM'N (Sep. 14, 2016), at 5–22.

119. Case AT.39740—Google Search (Shopping), C (2017) 4444 final (June 27, 2017).

120. Case T-612/17—Google and Alphabet v. Commission (Google Shopping), ECLI:EU:T:2021:763,

121. Digital Markets Act, *supra* note 11.

122. Regulation of the European Parliament and of the Council on contestable and fair markets in the digital sector (Digital Markets Act), Exploratory Memorandum, COM (2020) 842 final, 2020/0374 (COD) (Dec. 15, 2020).

123. *Id.*

124. Louis Kaplow, On the Choice of Welfare Standards in Competition Law, Harvard John M. Olin Discussion Paper Series, No. 693, 2011, at 4–12.

125. BEPS 2.0: Pillar One and Pillar Two Insights and perspectives into BEPS 2.0, KPMG, https://home.kpmg/xx/en/home/insights/2020/10/beps-2-0-pillar-one-and-pillar-two.html.

126. LOI n° 2019-759 du 24 juillet 2019 portant création d'une taxe sur les services numériques et modification de la trajectoire de baisse de l'impôt sur les sociétés (1) (FR).

127. Robert E. Lighthizer, Report on France's Digital Services Tax Prepared in the Investigation under Section 301 of the Trade Act of 1974, US TRADE REPRESENTATIVE (Dec. 2, 2019), at 25 et seq.

128. Angelique Chrisafis, France Hits Back at US Over Tax on Digital Giants, THE GUARDIAN (July 11, 2019), https://www.theguardian.com/world/2019/jul/11/france-us-tax-big-digital-companies-donald-trump-amazon-facebook.

129. KPMG, *supra* note 125.

130. Proposal for a Council Directive laying down rules relating to the corporate taxation of a significant digital presence, COM (2018) 147 final, 2018/0072 (CNS) (Mar. 21, 2018); Proposal for a Council Directive on the common system of a digital services tax on revenues resulting from the provision of certain digital services, COM (2018) 148 final, 2018/0073 (CNS) (Mar. 21, 2018).

131. Ursula von der Leyen, State of the Union Address 2020, EUR. COMM'N (Sep. 16, 2020), https://ec.europa.eu/commission/presscorner/detail/en/SPE ECH_20_1655.

132. Bjarke Smith-Meyer, Brussels Pushes on with EU Digital Levy Despite US Resistance, POLITICO (July 8, 2021), https://www.politico.eu/article/brussels-pushes-on-with-eu-digital-levy-despite-us-resistance/.

133. European Commission, Inception Impact Assessment, Ref. Ares (2021) 312667 (Jan. 14, 2021).

134. KPMG, *supra* note 125.

135. Commission Decision (EU) 2017/1283 of August 30, 2016 on State aid SA.38373 (2014/C) (ex 2014/NN) (ex 2014/CP) implemented by Ireland to Apple, 2017 O.J. (L187) 1.

136. Cases T-778/16 and T-892/16, *Ireland v. Commission*, ECLI:EU:T:2020:338.

137. Statement by Executive Vice-President Margrethe Vestager on the Commission's decision to appeal the General Court's judgment on the Apple tax State aid case in Ireland, EUR. COMM'N (Sep. 25, 2020), https://ec.europa.eu/commission/presscorner/detail/en/statement_20_1746.

138. First phase consultation of social partners under Article 154 TFEU on possible action addressing the challenges related to working conditions in platform work, C (2021) 1127 final (Feb. 24, 2021), at 5.

139. Questions and Answers: First stage social partners consultation on improving the working conditions in platform work, at 1–2 (Feb. 24, 2021), https://ec.eur opa.eu/commission/presscorner/detail/en/qanda_21_656.

140. *Id.*, at 1.

141. *Id.*

142. European Parliament, Report on a strong social Europe for Just Transitions, at 19, 2020/2084(INI) (Nov. 24, 2020).

143. Proposal for a Directive of the European Parliament and of the Council on improving working conditions in platform work, COM (2021) 762 final, 2021/0414 (COD) (Dec. 9, 2021).

144. *Id.*, art. 4; Impact Assessment Report Accompanying the document Proposal for a Directive of the European Parliament and of the Council to improve the working conditions in platform work in the European Union, annex 4, SWD (2021) 396.

145. Proposal for a Directive of the European Parliament and of the Council on improving working conditions in platform work, *supra* note 143, art. 5.

146. *Id.*

147. First phase consultation of social partners under Article 154 TFEU on possible action addressing the challenges related to working conditions in platform work, *supra* note 138, at 8.

148. *Id.*

149. *Id.*, at 25; French Constitutional Court, Ruling of March 4, 2020, Mr X v. Uber France and Uber BV, No. 374 FP-P+B+R+I; Appeal No. S 19-13.316, ECLI:FR:CCAS:2020:SO00374; Supreme Court of Spain, Glovoapp, 23 SL 805/2020, STS 2924/2020, ECLI:ES:TS:2020:2924; UK Supreme Court, Uber BV v. Aslam, UKSC [2021], paras. 1–2.

150. First phase consultation of social partners under Article 154 TFEU on possible action addressing the challenges related to working conditions in platform work, *supra* note 138 at 25; *see also* Decree of 28 May 2020, Uber Italy S.r.l, 9/2020, https://www.giurisprudenzapenale.com/wp-content/uploads/2020/06/tribunale-mi-uber-34-anonim.pdf.

151. Reuters Staff, Court Lifts Restrictions on Uber Eats Italy After Working Conditions Investigation, REUTERS (Mar. 4, 2021), https://www.reuters.com/article/us-uber-italy-verdict/court-lifts-restrictions-on-uber-eats-italy-after-working-conditions-investigation-idUSKBN2AW24Y.

152. Employment and Social Developments in Europe 2020, Leaving no one behind and striving for more: Fairness and solidarity in the European social market economy, at 17, EUR. COMM'N (Sep. 15, 2020).

153. Commission staff working document: Impact Assessment Report Accompanying the Document Proposal for a Regulation of the European Parliament and of the Council on a Single Market for Digital Services (Digital Services Act) and amending Directive 2000/31/EC, at 10–11, SWD (2020) 348 final, Part 1/2.

154. Copyright Directive, *supra* note 101, at preamble, para 1, 92.

155. Thanks to Joris van Hoboken for highlighting this argument in our conversations.

156. Fact Check on the EU Budget, EUR. COMM'N (May 2020), https://ec.europa.eu/info/strategy/eu-budget/eu-budget-added-value/fact-check_en. However, the Recovery Fund established to help the European economies rebuild after the pandemic is temporarily increasing the public funding available from the EU. *See* Recovery plan for Europe, EUR. COMM'N, https://ec.europa.eu/info/strategy/recovery-plan-europe_en.

157. In 2020, US government spending amounted to 29.6% of GDP. In preceding years, the average was closer to 20%. *See* Mandatory Spending in Fiscal Year 2020: An Infographic CBO, https://www.cbo.gov/publication/57171 and Discretionary Spending in Fiscal Year 2020: An Infographic CBO, https://www.cbo.gov/publication/57172.

158. Giandomenico Majone, From the Positive to the Regulatory State: Causes and Consequences of Changes in the Mode of Governance, 17(2) JNL PBL. POL. 139, 150–151 (1997).

159. Mark Thatcher, Supranational neo-liberalism: The EU's regulatory model of economic markets, in Vivien A Schmidt & Mark Thatcher (Eds.), RESILIENT LIBERALISM IN EUROPE'S POLITICAL ECONOMY (2013), p. 171.

160. Giovanni de Gregorio, The Rise of Digital Constitutionalism in the European Union, 19(1) INTERNATIONAL JOURNAL OF CONSTITUTIONAL LAW 41, 43–49 (2021).

161. Abraham L. Newman, Digital Policy-Making in the European Union, Helen Wallace, Mark A. Pollack, Christilla Roederer-Rynning, & Alasdair R. Young (eds.), POLICY-MAKING IN THE EUROPEAN UNION 275 (2020).

162. Speech by President-Elect von der Leyen in the European Parliament Plenary on the Occasion of the Presentation of Her College of Commissioners and Their Programme, EUR. COMM'N (Nov. 27, 2019), https://ec.europa.eu/com mission/presscorner/detail/en/SPEECH_19_6408.

163. EUR. COMM'N, SHAPING EUROPE'S DIGITAL FUTURE 3 (2020), https://ec.europa. eu/info/sites/default/files/communication-shaping-europes-digital-future-feb2020_en_4.pdf.

164. Jeremy Shapiro, Introduction: Europe's digital sovereignty, in Carla Hobbs (ed.), EUROPE'S DIGITAL SOVEREIGNTY: FROM RULEMAKER TO SUPERPOWER IN THE AGE OF US–CHINA RIVALRY, 6, 10 (2020).

165. Robbie Gramer, Trump Turning More Countries in Europe Against Huawei, FOREIGN POLICY (Oct. 27, 2020), https://foreignpolicy.com/2020/10/27/ trump-europe-huawei-china-us-competition-geopolitics-5g-slovakia/; *see for* Poland: Jill Colvin, US and Poland Sign Agreement to Cooperate on 5G Technology, AP NEWS (Sep. 2, 2019), https://apnews.com/article/europe-don ald-trump-ap-top-news-international-news-politics-9a90e16d903947709 998dd7a2dde8733; *see for* Romania: Romania, US Sign Memorandum on 5G Technologies "In Line with Rule of Law Principles," ROMANIA INSIDER (Aug. 22, 2019), https://www.romania-insider.com/romania-us-5g-memorandum.

166. Natalia Drozdiak, EU's Breton Says Time to Fix "Naïve" Approach to Chip Supply, BLOOMBERG (May 5, 2021), https://www.bloomberg.com/news/articles/ 2021-05-05/europe-looks-to-secure-chip-supply-after-naive-past-approach.

167. Inside the Future: Europe's Plan to Thrive in the Global Microchip Race, EUR. COMM'N (May 21, 2021), https://ec.europa.eu/commission/commissioners/ 2019-2024/breton/announcements/inside-future-europes-plan-thrive-global-microchip-race_en.

168. Drozdiak, *supra* note 166.

169. Mark Scott & Joshua Posaner, Europe's Big Battery Bet, POLITICO (July 26, 2020), https://www.politico.eu/article/europe-battery-electric-tesla-china/.

170. In-depth reviews of strategic areas for Europe's interests, EUR. COMM'N, https://ec.europa.eu/info/strategy/priorities-2019-2024/europe-fit-digital-age/european-industrial-strategy/depth-reviews-strategic-areas-europes-inter ests_en#lithium-li-ion-batteries.

171. Éanna Kelly, Decoding Europe's New Fascination with "Tech Sovereignty," SCIENCE BUSINESS (Sep. 3, 2020), https://sciencebusiness.net/technology-strat egy-board/news/decoding-europes-new-fascination-tech-sovereignty.

172. Regulation (EU) 2019/452 of the European Parliament and of the Council of Mar. 19, 2019, Establishing a Framework for the Screening of Foreign Direct Investments into the Union, 2019 O.J. (L 791), 1–14.

173. European Parliament, Provisional agreement resulting from interinstitutional negotiations, Subject: Proposal for a regulation of the European Parliament and of the Council on foreign subsidies distorting the internal market (COM(2021)0223—C9-0167/2021—2021/0114(COD)) (July 11, 2022), https://www.europarl.europa.eu/meetdocs/2014_2019/plmrep/COMMITTEES/INTA/DV/2022/07-13/1260231_EN.pdf.

174. Regulation (EU) 2021/821 of the European Parliament and of the Council of 20 May 2021 setting up a Union regime for the control of exports, brokering technical assistance, transit and transfer of dual-use items (recast), 2021 O.J. (L 206) 1; Strengthened EU Export Control Rules Kick In, EUR. COMM'N (Sep. 9, 2021), https://ec.europa.eu/commission/presscorner/detail/en/IP_21_4601.

175. Proposal for a Directive of the European Parliament and of the Council on measures for a high common level of cybersecurity across the Union, repealing Directive (EU) 2016/1148, COM (2020) 823 final, 2020/0359 (COD) (Dec. 16, 2020).

176. EU Imposes the First Ever Sanctions Against Cyber-Attacks, EUR. COUNCIL (July 30, 2020), https://www.consilium.europa.eu/en/press/press-releases/2020/07/30/eu-imposes-the-first-ever-sanctions-against-cyber-attacks/ .

177. Scott & Posaner, Europe's Big Battery Bet, *supra* note 169.

178. About EBA250, KIC INNOENERG, https://www.eba250.com/about-eba250/.

179. Communication from the Commission to the European Parliament, the Council, the European Economic and Social Committee and the Committee of the Regions Fostering a European Approach to Artificial Intelligence, at 2, COM (2021) 205 final (Apr. 21, 2021). [hereinafter European approach to Artificial Intelligence]

180. *See* Communication from the Commission to the European Parliament, the European Council, the Council, the European Central Bank, the European Economic and Social Committee, the Committee of the Regions and the European Investment Bank Annual Sustainable Growth Strategy 2021, COM (2020) 575 final (Sep. 17, 2020).

181. *See* Frances G. Burwell & Kenneth Propp, The European Union and the Search for Digital Sovereignty: Building "Fortress Europe" or Preparing for a New World?, ATLANTIC COUNCIL (June 2020), at 5.

182. Jonathan Ponciano, The World's Largest Technology Companies in 2021: Apple's Lead Widens as Coinbase, DoorDash Storm Into Ranks, FORBES (May 13, 2021), https://www.forbes.com/sites/jonathanponciano/2021/05/13/worlds-largest-tech-companies-2021/?sh=58e288b769bc.

183. The Complete List of Unicorn Companies, CBINSIGHTS (last accessed Aug. 17, 2022), https://www.cbinsights.com/research-unicorn-companies.

184. The EU Wants to Set the Rules for the World of Technology, THE ECONOMIST (Feb. 22, 2020), https://www.economist.com/business/2020/02/20/the-eu-wants-to-set-the-rules-for-the-world-of-technology.

185. Carmelo Cennamo & D. Daniel Sokol, Can the EU Regulate Platforms without Stifling Innovation?, HARVARD BUS. REV. (Mar. 1, 2021), https://hbr.org/2021/03/can-the-eu-regulate-platforms-without-stifling-innovation.

186. McAfee, *supra* note 15.

187. Zen Soo, Alibaba's Jack Ma Says He Is "Worried" Europe Will Stifle Innovation with Too Much Tech Regulation, S. CHINA MORNING POST (May 17, 2019), https://www.scmp.com/tech/big-tech/article/3010606/alibabas-jack-ma-says-he-worried-europe-will-stifle-innovation-too.

188. Gary Shapiro, How the EU's War on U.S. Innovation Stifles European Creativity, INVESTOR'S BUS. DAILY (Sep. 12, 2016), https://www.investors.com/politics/commentary/how-the-eus-war-on-u-s-innovation-stifles-european-creativity/.

189. The Impact of the Digital Markets Act on Innovation, OXERA (commissioned by Amazon, Nov. 2020) at 1, https://www.oxera.com/wp-content/uploads/2020/11/The-impact-of-the-Digital-Markets-Act-on-innovation_FINAL-3.pdf.

190. Directive 2000/31/EU of the European Parliament and of the Council of 8 June 2000 on certain legal aspects of information society services, in particular electronic commerce, in the Internal Market, 2000 O.J. (L 178) 1, 1–16.

191. Brad Smith, Facial Recognition Technology: The Need for Public Regulation and Corporate Responsibility, MICROSOFT (July 13, 2018), https://blogs.microsoft.com/on-the-issues/2018/07/13/facial-recognition-technology-the-need-for-public-regulation-and-corporate-responsibility/.

192. *See* Stephanie Hare, We Must Face Up to the Threat Posed by Biometrics, FIN. TIMES (Aug. 8, 2018), https://www.ft.com/content/b4d47e04-9727-11e8-95f8-8640db9060a7.

193. European Approach to Artificial Intelligence, *supra* note 179, at 5.

194. Anu Bradford, THE BRUSSELS EFFECT: HOW THE EUROPEAN UNION RULES THE WORLD 238 (2020).

195. Vincent Manancourt & Mark Scott, Whatsapp Hit With €225M Privacy Fine, POLITICO (Sep. 2, 2021), https://www.politico.eu/article/whatsapp-facebook-privacy-fine-european-commission-data-protection/.

196. Madhumita Murgia & Javier Espinoza, Ireland Fails to Enforce EU Law Against Big Tech, FIN. TIMES (Sep. 13, 2021), https://www.ft.com/content/5b986586-0f85-47d5-8edb-3b49398e2b08.

197. Commission Evaluation Report on the Implementation of the General Data Protection Regulation Two Years After Its Application, EUR. PARL. DOC. 2020/2717(RSP) (Mar. 25, 2021).

198. Report on Meeting on 27th April 2021 on the Topic of GDPR, GOV'T OF IR. JOINT COMMITTEE ON JUSTICE, (July 2021), https://data.oireachtas.ie/ie/oireachtas/

committee/dail/33/joint_committee_on_justice/reports/2021/2021-07-22_rep
ort-on-meeting-on-27th-april-2021-on-the-topic-of-gdpr_en.pdf.

199. According to a website that tracks GDPR enforcement activity, as of August 2022, 1214 fines had been issued across the EU since the entry into force of the GDPR, amounting to approximately 1.7 billion euros. GDPR Enforcement Tracker: Fines Statistics, CMS, https://www.enforcementtracker.com/?insig hts; of this combined figure, 746 million euros can be attributed to a single fine imposed by Luxembourg against Amazon in July 2021, *see also* Stephanie Bodoni, Amazon Gets Record $888 Million EU Fine Over Data Violations, BLOOMBERG (July 30, 2021), https://www.bloomberg.com/news/articles/2021-07-30/amazon-given-record-888-million-eu-fine-for-data-privacy-breach.

200. Press Release, FTC Imposes $5 Billion Penalty and Sweeping New Privacy Restrictions on Facebook, FTC (July 24, 2019), https://www.ftc.gov/news-eve nts/news/press-releases/2019/07/ftc-imposes-5-billion-penalty-sweeping-new-privacy-restrictions-facebook.

201. Michail Batikas, Stefan Bechtold, Tobias Kretschmer, & Christian Peukert, European Privacy Law and Global Markets for Data, CEPR DISCUSSION PAPERS 14475 (2020); Kevin E. Davis & Florencia Marotta-Wurgler, Contracting for Personal Data, 94 N.Y.U. L. REV. 662 (2019); René Mahieu, Hadi Asghari, Christopher Parsons, Joris van Hoboken, Masashi Crete-Nishihata, Andrew Hilts, & Siena Anstis, Measuring the Brussels Effect Through Access Requests: Has the European General Data Protection Regulation Influenced the Data Protection Rights of Canadian Citizens?, 11 JOURNAL OF INFORMATION POLICY 301 (2021).

202. Rob Price, Why Facebook's Stock Jumped Despite Facing a Record-Breaking $5 Billion FTC Penalty: "A Slap on the Wrist," BUSINESS INSIDER (July 12, 2019), https://www.businessinsider.com/facebook-stock-rose-news-5-billion-ftc-set tlement-why-critics-2019-7.

203. Conor Dougherty, Inside Yelp's Six-Year Grudge Against Google, N.Y. TIMES (July 1, 2017), https://www.nytimes.com/2017/07/01/technology/yelp-google-european-union-antitrust.html; Nitasha Tiku, Don't Expect Big Changes From Europe's Record Google Fine, WIRED (July 18, 2018), https://www.wired.com/story/dont-expect-big-changes-from-europes-record-google-fine/.

204. Special Report on the Commission's EU Merger Control and Antitrust Proceedings: A Need to Scale Up Market Oversight, ECA (2020) 24/2020.

205. Adam Satariano, Europe Is Reining in Tech Giants. But Some Say It's Going Too Far, N.Y. TIMES (May 6, 2019), https://www.nytimes.com/2019/05/06/tec hnology/europe-tech-censorship.html.

206. Jacob Mchangama & Natalie Alkiviadou, THE DIGITAL BERLIN WALL: HOW GERMANY (ACCIDENTALLY) CREATED A PROTOTYPE FOR GLOBAL ONLINE CENSORSHIP—ACT TWO 2, 21–22 (2020).

207. Oreste Pollicino, Fundamental Rights as Bycatch—Russia's Anti-Fake News Legislation, VERFASSUNGSBLOG (Mar. 28. 2019), https://verfassungsblog.de/fundamental-rights-as-bycatch-russias-anti-fake-news-legislation/.

208. Isabelle Canaan, NetzDG and the German Precedent for Authoritarian Learning, 28 COLUM. J. EUR. L. 101 (2022).

209. Jacob Mchangama & Natalie Alkiviadou, THE DIGITAL BERLIN WALL: HOW GERMANY (ACCIDENTALLY) CREATED A PROTOTYPE FOR GLOBAL ONLINE CENSORSHIP—ACT TWO (2020).

210. Tarleton Gillespie, CUSTODIANS OF THE INTERNET (2021).

211. Kaye, *supra* note 76.

212. Digital Services Act, *supra* note 65.

213. Clément Perarnaud, A Step Back to Look Ahead: Mapping Coalitions on Data Flows and Platform Regulation in the Council of the EU (2016–2019), 10(2) INTERNET POLICY REVIEW 1, 12–13 (2021).

214. *Id.*

215. Finland Invites Ministers from Digitally Advanced EU Countries to Discuss Europe's Competitiveness, MINISTRY OF JUSTICE FINLAND (Jan. 21, 2021), https://oikeusministerio.fi/en/-//1410877/finland-invites-ministers-from-digitally-advanced-eu-countries-to-discuss-europe-s-competitiveness.

216. Innovative and Trustworthy AI: Two Sides of the Same Coin, POSITION PAPER ON BEHALF OF DENMARK, BELGIUM, THE CZECH REPUBLIC, FINLAND, FRANCE, ESTONIA, IRELAND, LATVIA, LUXEMBOURG, THE NETHERLANDS, POLAND, PORTUGAL, SPAIN AND SWEDEN (Oct. 8, 2020), https://em.dk/media/13914/non-paper-innovative-and-trustworthy-ai-two-side-of-the-same-coin.pdf.

217. Thibault Larger, Mark Scott, Laura Kayali, & Nicholas Vinocur, Inside the EU's Divisions on How to Go After Big Tech, POLITICO (Dec. 14, 2020), https://www.politico.eu/article/margrethe-vestager-thierry-breton-europe-big-tech-regulation-digital-services-markets-act/.

218. Mehreen Khan & Laura Noonan, Europe's Low-Tax Nations Braced for Struggle Over US Corporate Tax Plan, FIN. TIMES (Apr. 14, 2021), https://www.ft.com/content/1a8e5bf7-49e0-4987-98c8-893f08d9c77c.

219. Arthur Messaud & Noémie Levain, CJEU Rulings v. French Intelligence Legislation, ABOUT: INTEL (May 14, 2021), https://aboutintel.eu/cjeu-french-intelligence-legislation/.

220. Theodore Christakis & Kenneth Propp, How Europe's Intelligence Services Aim to Avoid the EU's Highest Court—and What It Means for the United States, LAWFARE (Mar. 8, 2021), https://www.lawfareblog.com/how-europes-intelligence-services-aim-avoid-eus-highest-court-and-what-it-means-united-states.

221. Case C-511/18—*La Quadrature du Net and Others v. Premier Ministre*, ECLI:EU:C:2020:791.

222. Messaud & Levain, CJEU Rulings v. French Intelligence Legislation.

223. Naomi O'Leary, Graham Dwyer Case: EU States Join Ireland in Challenge to Data Law, THE IRISH TIMES (Sep. 13, 2021), https://www.irishtimes.com/news/crime-and-law/graham-dwyer-case-eu-states-join-ireland-in-challenge-to-data-law-1.4673050.

224. *See* European Parliament Press Release, Pegasus: MEPs Grilled NSO Group Representatives About Spyware Abuse Allegations (June 20, 2022), https://www.europarl.europa.eu/news/en/press-room/20220620IPR33414/pegasus-meps-grilled-nso-group-representatives-about-spyware-abuse-allegations; *see* Antoaneta Roussi, EU and Greece Veer Toward Standoff Over Wiretapping Scandal, POLITICO (Aug. 29, 2022), https://www.politico.eu/article/eu-and-greece-near-standoff-over-phone-tapping-scandal/.

225. *See* Charles Martinet & Romain Bosc, Europe Uses Spyware on Its Own Citizens, CTR. FOR EUR. POL'Y ANALYSIS (Oct. 27, 2022), https://cepa.org/article/europe-uses-spyware-on-its-own-citizens/.

226. Valerie Hopkins, Hungary Follows Poland in Taking on Big Tech "Censors," FIN. TIMES (Feb. 3, 2021), https://www.ft.com/content/6a315d26-c6fe-4906-886d-04cec27a6788.

227. Tim Hume, Poland Wants to Ban Social Media Companies From Banning Hate Speech, VICE (Jan. 15, 2021), https://www.vice.com/en/article/v7mpkj/poland-wants-to-ban-social-media-companies-from-banning-hate-speech; for a resurfacing of the discussion in 2022, *see also* Aleksandra Krzysztoszek, Polish Justice Ministry Proposes Online Free Speech Law After Facebook Debacle, EURACTIV (Jan. 18, 2022), https://www.euractiv.com/section/politics/short_news/polish-justice-ministry-proposes-online-free-speech-law-after-facebook-debacle/.

228. Tim Hume, *supra* note 227.

229. Sam Fleming, Michael Peel, & Valerie Hopkins, EU Identity Crisis: Poland, Hungary and the Fight Over Brussels' Values, FIN. TIMES (Dec. 4, 2020), https://www.ft.com/content/bfa58276-1868-4011-9891-ccd363dc68dc.

CHAPTER 4

1. *See* Apple, Privacy, https://www.apple.com/privacy/#:~:text=Privacy%20is%20a%20fundamental%20human,of%20innovation%20we%20believe%20in.

2. *See* Jack Nicas, Raymond Zhong, & Daisuke Wakabayashi, Censorship, Surveillance and Profits: A Hard Bargain for Apple in China, N.Y. TIMES (May 17, 2021), https://www.nytimes.com/2021/05/17/technology/apple-china-censorship-data.html.

3. *See id.*

4. *See id.*

5. *See* Paige Leskin, Here Are All the Major US Tech Companies Blocked Behind China's "Great Firewall," BUS. INSIDER (Oct. 10, 2019), https://www.businessinsider.com/major-us-tech-companies-blocked-from-operating-in-china-2019-5.

6. *See* Nicas, Zhong, & Wakabayashi, *supra* note 2.

7. *See* Sarah Jackson, Apple CEO Tim Cook Reportedly Signed a Secret $275 Billion Deal With China in 2016 to Skirt Challenges With Government Regulators, BUS. INSIDER (Dec. 7, 2021), https://www.businessinsider.com/apple-tim-cook-275-billion-china-deal-regulatory-crackdown-report-2021-12?r=US&IR=T.

8. *See* Vlad Savov, Apple's Balancing Act in China Gets Trickier During Xi's Crackdown, BLOOMBERG (Oct. 12, 2021), https://www.bloomberg.com/news/articles/2021-10-12/apple-s-china-balancing-act-gets-trickier-during-xi-s-crackdown?leadSource=uverify%20wall.

9. *See* Jackson, *supra* note 7.

10. *See* Paul Mozur, Daisuke Wakabayashi, & Nick Wingfield, Apple Opening Data Center in China to Comply With Cybersecurity Law, N.Y. TIMES (July 12, 2017), https://www.nytimes.com/2017/07/12/business/apple-china-data-center-cybersecurity.html.

11. *See* Jackson, *supra* note 7; Wayne Ma, Inside Tim Cook's Secret $275 Billion Deal With Chinese Authorities, THE INFORMATION (Dec. 7, 2021), https://www.theinformation.com/articles/facing-hostile-chinese-authorities-apple-ceo-signed-275-billion-deal-with-them.

12. *See* Melanie Lee & Jennifer Saba, Google Gets Nod From China to Keep Search Page, REUTERS (July 9, 2010), https://www.reuters.com/article/idINIndia-50007020100709.

13. *See* Miguel Helft, YouTube Blocked in China, Google Says, N.Y. TIMES (Mar. 24, 2009), https://www.nytimes.com/2009/03/25/technology/internet/25youtube.html.

14. *See* Matt Sheehan, How Google Took on China—and Lost, MIT TECH. REV. (Dec. 19, 2018), https://www.technologyreview.com/2018/12/19/138307/how-google-took-on-china-and-lost/.

15. *See* Sherisse Pham, Google Now Has Two Apps in China, but Search Remains Off Limits, CNN (May 31, 2018), https://money.cnn.com/2018/05/31/technology/google-in-china-files-app/.

16. Market Share of Mobile Operating Systems in China from January 2013 to December 2021, STATISTA (July 27, 2022), https://www.statista.com/statistics/262176/market-share-held-by-mobile-operating-systems-in-china/#:~:text=Android%20is%20also%20the%20most,share%20as%20of%20March%202021.

17. *See* William Yuen Yee, Google Parent Company Alphabet Is Back in China (Because It Never Left), THE CHINA PROJECT (June 18, 2020), https://thechinaproject.com/2020/06/18/google-parent-company-alphabet-is-back-in-china-because-it-never-left/.

18. *See* Sheehan, *supra* note 14.

19. *See* Fei-Fei Li, Opening the Google AI China Center, GOOGLE (Dec. 13, 2017), https://blog.google/around-the-globe/google-asia/google-ai-china-center/.

20. *See* Karen Weise & Paul Mozur, LinkedIn to Shut Down Service in China, Citing "Challenging" Environment, N.Y. TIMES (Oct. 14, 2021), https://www.nytimes.com/2021/10/14/technology/linkedin-china-microsoft.html.

21. *See* Aaron Tilley & Liza Lin, LinkedIn Social Network Is Leaving China, but Microsoft Remains, WALL ST. J. (Oct. 15, 2021), https://www.wsj.com/articles/linkedin-social-network-is-leaving-china-but-microsoft-remains-11634321277.

22. *See* Shuhei Yamada, Alibaba and Tencent Rule Another Chinese Market: Video Calls, NIKKEI ASIA (Jan. 6, 2022), https://asia.nikkei.com/Business/China-tech/Alibaba-and-Tencent-rule-another-Chinese-market-video-calls.

23. *See* Tilley & Lin, *supra* note 21.

24. *See* 21Vianet Partnership With Shanghai Municipal Government and Microsoft, 21VIANET BLUE CLOUD (Nov. 1, 2012), https://en.21vbluecloud.com/21vianet-partnership-with-shanghai-municipal-government-and-microsoft.html; Office 365 operated by 21Vianet, MICROSOFT (Apr. 19, 2022), https://docs.microsoft.com/en-us/microsoft-365/admin/services-in-china/services-in-china?view=o365-21vianet.

25. *See* Dan Swinhoe, Microsoft Announces New Azure China Data Center Region in Hebei, DATA CENTER DYNAMICS (Mar. 2, 2021), https://www.datacenterdynamics.com/en/news/microsoft-announces-new-azure-china-data-center-region-hebei/.

26. *See* Zhaoyin Feng, Microsoft Shutting Down LinkedIn in China, BBC NEWS (Oct. 14, 2021), https://www.bbc.com/news/technology-58911297.

27. *See* Weise & Mozur, *supra* note 20.

28. *See* Alyssa Abkowitz, Deepa Seetharaman, & Eva Dou, Facebook Is Trying Everything to Re-Enter China—and It's Not Working, WALL ST. J. (Jan. 30, 2017), https://www.wsj.com/articles/mark-zuckerbergs-beijing-blues-1485791106.

29. *See id.*

30. *See* Ryan Vlastelica, Instagram Reportedly Blocked in China Amid HK Protests, REUTERS (Sep. 28, 2014), https://www.reuters.com/article/uk-china-instagram/instagram-reportedly-blocked-in-china-amid-hk-protests-idUKKCN0HN0WC20140928.

31. *See* Keith Bradsher, China Blocks WhatsApp, Broadening Online Censorship, N.Y. TIMES (Sep. 25, 2017), https://www.nytimes.com/2017/09/25/business/china-whatsapp-blocked.html.

32. *See* Paresh Dave & Katie Paul, Facebook Defies China Headwinds With New Ad Sales Push, REUTERS (Jan. 7, 2020), https://www.reuters.com/article/us-facebook-china-focus/facebook-defies-china-headwinds-with-new-ad-sales-push-idUSKBN1Z616Q.

33. *See* Arjun Kharpal, Amazon Is Shutting Down Its China Marketplace Business. Here's Why It Has Struggled, CNBC (Apr. 18, 2019), https://www.cnbc.com/2019/04/18/amazon-china-marketplace-closing-down-heres-why.html.

34. *See* Iris Deng, Beijing Nudges "Made in China, Sold on Amazon" Model Along in Bid to Help Smaller Exporters, s. CHINA MORNING POST (June 29, 2021), https://www.scmp.com/tech/policy/article/3139192/beijing-nudges-made-china-sold-amazon-model-along-bid-help-smaller?module=inline&module=inline&pgtype=article&pgtype=article.

35. *See* Matt Leonard, Amazon Publishes List of More Than 1K Private Label Suppliers, SUPPLY CHAIN DIVE (Nov. 21, 2019), https://www.supplychaindive.com/news/amazon-publishes-list-of-more-than-1k-private-label-suppliers/567828/ (citing Amazon Supplier List, AMAZON (Nov. 14, 2019), https://d39w7f4ix9f5s9.cloudfront.net/cb/19/77dfc5b441c892cd6e2be166ba70/final-amazon-supplier-list-2019-11-14-updated-1005am.pdf).

36. *See* Iris Deng, "Made in China, Sold on Amazon" Merchants Scramble to Minimise Losses After US Platform Closes over 50,000 Chinese Shops, s. CHINA MORNING POST (July 26, 2021), https://www.scmp.com/tech/big-tech/article/3142599/made-china-sold-amazon-merchants-scramble-minimise-losses-after-us?module=inline&pgtype=article.

37. *See* Steve Stecklow & Jeffrey Dastin, Special Report: Amazon Partnered With China Propaganda Arm, REUTERS (Dec. 17, 2021), https://www.reuters.com/world/china/amazon-partnered-with-china-propaganda-arm-win-beijings-favor-document-shows-2021-12-17/.

38. *See* Tim Maurer & Garrett Hinck, Cloud Security: A Primer for Policymakers, CARNEGIE ENDOWMENT FOR INT'L PEACE 20 (Aug. 2020), https://carnegieendowment.org/files/Maurer_Hinck_Cloud_Security-V3.pdf.

39. *See* Haibin Peng, Amazon to Expand China Cloud Business as Demand Swells, YICAI GLOBAL (Mar. 26, 2021), https://www.yicaiglobal.com/news/amazon-to-expand-china-cloud-business-as-demand-swells.

40. *See* Rita Liao, Kindle's China Future in Doubt After Disappearing From Online Shelves, TECHCRUNCH (Jan. 4, 2022), https://techcrunch.com/2022/01/04/amazon-kindle-china/; Stecklow & Dastin, *supra* note 37.

41. Lambert Bu, Violet Chung, Nick Leung, Kevin Wei Wang, Bruce Xia, & Chenan Xia, The Future of Digital Innovation in China: Megatrends Shaping One of the World's Fastest Evolving Digital Ecosystems, MCKINSEY (Sep. 30, 2021), https://www.mckinsey.com/featured-insights/china/the-future-of-digital-innovation-in-china-megatrends-shaping-one-of-the-worlds-fastest-evolving-digital-ecosystems; Number of Internet Users in China From 2008 to 2021, STATISTA (May 12, 2022), https://www.statista.com/statistics/265140/number-of-internet-users-in-china/.

42. *See* Nicas, Zhong, & Wakabayashi, *supra* note 2.

43. *See* Isobel Asher Hamilton, China's Grip on Apple Tightens as It Boots a Hong Kong Police-Tracking App and News App Quartz, BUS. INSIDER (Oct. 10, 2019), https://www.businessinsider.com/apple-boots-hong-kong-police-tracking-app-hkmap-live-2019-10?r=US&IR=T.

44. *See* James Clayton, Apple Takes Down Quran App in China, BBC (Oct. 15, 2021), https://www.bbc.com/news/technology-58921230.

45. *See id.*

46. *See* Madeline Farber, Apple CEO Tim Cook Really Does Not Like President Trump's Travel Ban, FORTUNE (Feb. 9, 2017), https://fortune.com/2017/02/09/apple-ceo-tim-cook-donald-trump-travel-ban/.

47. *See* Jackson, *supra* note 7.

48. *See id.*

49. *See* Clive Thompson, Google's China Problem (and China's Google Problem), N.Y. TIMES (Apr. 23, 2006), https://www.nytimes.com/2006/04/23/magazine/googles-china-problem-and-chinas-google-problem.html.

50. *See* Andrew McLaughlin, Google in China, GOOGLE (Jan. 27, 2006), https://googleblog.blogspot.com/2006/01/google-in-china.html.

51. *See* Thompson, *supra* note 49.

52. *See id.*

53. *See* Miguel Helft & David Barboza, Google Shuts China Site in Dispute Over Censorship, N.Y. TIMES (Mar. 22, 2010), https://www.nytimes.com/2010/03/23/technology/23google.html.

54. *See* Sheehan, *supra* note 14.

55. *See id.*

56. *See* Michael Wines, Far-Ranging Support for Google's China Move, N.Y. TIMES (Jan. 14, 2010), https://www.nytimes.com/2010/01/15/world/asia/15china.html.

57. *See* Ryan Gallagher, Google Plans to Launch Censored Search Engine in China, Leaked Documents Reveal, THE INTERCEPT (Aug. 1, 2018), https://theintercept.com/2018/08/01/google-china-search-engine-censorship/.

58. *See* Yuan Li & Daisuke Wakabayashi, Google, Seeking a Return to China, Is Said to Be Building a Censored Search Engine, N.Y. TIMES (Aug. 1, 2018), https://www.nytimes.com/2018/08/01/technology/china-google-censored-search-engine.html?hp&action=click&pgtype=Homepage&clickSource=story-heading&module=second-column-region&region=top-news&WT.nav=top-news.

59. *See* Kate Conger & Daisuke Wakabayashi, Google Employees Protest Secret Work on Censored Search Engine for China, N.Y. TIMES (Aug. 16, 2018), https://www.nytimes.com/2018/08/16/technology/google-employees-protest-search-censored-china.html.

60. *See id.*

61. *See* Sheehan, *supra* note 14.

62. *See* David Shepardson & Paresh Dave, Google's China Plan Spurs Inquiry From U.S. Lawmakers, Staff Departures, REUTERS (Sep. 13, 2018), https://www.reuters.com/article/us-china-google-lawmakers/googles-china-plan-spurs-inquiry-from-u-s-lawmakers-staff-departures-idUSKCN1LT32O.

63. *See* Rob Price & Joe Perticone, Congress Grills Google CEO Sundar Pichai for the First Time, BUS. INSIDER (Dec. 11, 2018), https://www.businessinsider.com/google-ceo-sundar-pichai-testifies-before-congress-2018-12?r=UK#.

64. *See* Jeb Su, Confirmed: Google Terminated Project Dragonfly, Its Censored Chinese Search Engine, FORBES (July 19, 2019), https://www.forbes.com/sites/jeanbaptiste/2019/07/19/confirmed-google-terminated-project-dragonfly-its-censored-chinese-search-engine/?sh=10c7d6927e84.

65. *See* Mike Isaac, Facebook Said to Create Censorship Tool to Get Back Into China, N.Y. TIMES (Nov. 22, 2016), https://www.nytimes.com/2016/11/22/technology/facebook-censorship-tool-china.html.

66. *See* Abkowitz, Seetharaman, & Dou, *supra* note 28.

67. *See* Paul Mozur, In China, Facebook Tests the Waters With a Stealth App, N.Y. TIMES (Aug. 11, 2017), https://www.nytimes.com/2017/08/11/technology/facebook-china-moments-colorful-balloons.html.

68. *See id.*

69. *See* Kara Swisher, Zuckerberg: The Recode Interview, VOX (Oct. 8, 2018), https://www.vox.com/2018/7/18/17575156/mark-zuckerberg-interview-facebook-recode-kara-swisher.

70. *See* Dave & Paul, *supra* note 32.

71. *See* Muyi Xiao, Paul Mozur, & Gray Beltran, Buying Influence: How China Manipulates Facebook and Twitter, N.Y. TIMES (Dec. 20, 2021), https://www.nytimes.com/interactive/2021/12/20/technology/china-facebook-twitter-influence-manipulation.html?smid=tw-share.

72. Stecklow & Dastin, *supra* note 37.

73. *See id.*

74. *See id.*

75. *See id.*

76. *See id.*

77. *See* What's New: Announcing a Broader Operating Relationship Between Amazon Web Services and Sinnet, AMAZON (Aug. 1, 2016), https://www.amazonaws.cn/en/new/2016/announcing-operating-relationship-between-aws-and-sinnet/.

78. *See* Paul Mozur, Joining Apple, Amazon's China Cloud Service Bows to Censors, N.Y. TIMES (Aug. 1, 2017), https://www.nytimes.com/2017/08/01/business/amazon-china-internet-censors-apple.html.

79. *See* Stecklow & Dastin, *supra* note 37.

80. *See id.*

81. *See* David Barboza & Tom Zeller Jr., Microsoft Shuts Blog's Site After Complaints by Beijing, N.Y. TIMES (Jan. 6, 2006), https://www.nytimes.com/2006/01/06/technology/microsoft-shuts-blogs-site-after-complaints-by-beijing.html.

82. *See* Paul Mozur & Karen Weise, China Appears to Block Microsoft's Bing as Censorship Intensifies, N.Y. TIMES (Jan. 23, 2019), https://www.nytimes.com/2019/01/23/business/china-microsoft-bing.html.

83. *See* Paul Mozur & Vindu Goel, To Reach China, LinkedIn Plays by Local Rules, N.Y. TIMES (Oct. 5, 2014), https://www.nytimes.com/2014/10/06/technology/to-reach-china-linkedin-plays-by-local-rules.html; Weise & Mozur, LinkedIn to Shut Down *supra* note 20.

84. *See* Mozur & Goel, *supra* note 83.

85. *See* Paul Mozur, Raymond Zhong, & Steve Lohr, China Punishes Microsoft's LinkedIn Over Lax Censorship, N.Y. TIMES (Mar. 18, 2021), https://www.nyti mes.com/2021/03/18/technology/china-linkedin-censorship.html.

86. *See* Weise & Mozur, LinkedIn to Shut Down, *supra* note 20.

87. *See id.*

88. *See* Nicas, Zhong, & Wakabayashi, *supra* note 2.

89. *See* An Update on LinkedIn China, LINKEDIN (Mar. 9, 2021), https://news.linke din.com/2021/march/an-update-on-linkedin-china.

90. *See* Stecklow & Dastin, *supra* note 37.

91. *See* Paul Mozur & Don Clark, China's Surveillance State Sucks Up Data. U.S. Tech Is Key to Sorting It., N.Y. TIMES (Nov. 22, 2020), https://www.nytimes. com/2020/11/22/technology/china-intel-nvidia-xinjiang.html.

92. *See* Mara Hvistendahl, How Oracle Sells Repression in China, THE INTERCEPT (Feb. 18, 2021), https://theintercept.com/2021/02/18/oracle-china-police-surve illance/.

93. *See id.*

94. *See* Liza Lin, Intel Apologizes After Asking Suppliers to Avoid China's Xinjiang Region, WALL ST. J. (Dec. 23, 2021), https://www.wsj.com/articles/intel-apologi zes-after-asking-suppliers-to-avoid-chinas-xinjiang-region-11640261303.

95. *See id.*

96. *See* Facebook Has Been Bending to the Will of Arab Despots, THE ECONOMIST (July 2, 2020), https://www.economist.com/middle-east-and-africa/2020/07/ 02/facebook-has-been-bending-to-the-will-of-arab-despots.

97. *See* John Reed, Facebook and Google Accused of Complicity in Vietnam Censorship, FIN. TIMES (Nov. 30, 2020), https://www.ft.com/content/0e59e 232-adc9-443f-9aee-4920a00dd1a4.

98. *See* Anton Troianovski & Adam Satariano, Google and Apple, Under Pressure From Russia, Remove Voting App, N.Y. TIMES (Sep. 17, 2021), https://www.nyti mes.com/2021/09/17/world/europe/russia-navalny-app-election.html.

99. *See* Hannah Murphy, Javier Espinoza, Max Seddon, & Cristina Criddle, Big Tech Caught in Information War Between West and Russia, FIN. TIMES (Feb. 28, 2022), https://www.ft.com/content/e0a31741-ee65-42c0-b045-59c382a8a081.

100. *See id.; see also* Joe Flint, Netflix Won't Add Russian Broadcasters to Service, Defying New Regulation, WALL ST. J. (Feb. 28, 2022), https://www.wsj.com/ articles/netflix-wont-add-russian-channels-to-service-defying-new-regulation-11646076964.

101. *See* Dan Milmo, Russians Seek to Evade Social Media Ban With Virtual Private Networks, THE GUARDIAN (Mar. 12, 2022), https://www.theguardian.com/ world/2022/mar/12/russians-seek-to-evade-social-media-ban-with-virtual-private-networks; Pjotr Sauer, Russia Bans Facebook and Instagram Under "Extremism" Law, THE GUARDIAN (Mar. 21, 2022), https://www.theguardian.

com/world/2022/mar/21/russia-bans-facebook-and-instagram-under-extrem
ism-law.

102. *See* Sheehan, *supra* note 14.

103. John Moreno, TikTok Surpasses Google, Facebook as World's Most Popular Web Domain, FORBES (Dec. 29, 2021), https://www.forbes.com/sites/joha nmoreno/2021/12/29/tiktok-surpasses-google-facebook-as-worlds-most-popu lar-web-destination/?sh=297a3d4243ef.

104. Lucas Niewenhuis, The Difference Between TikTok and Douyin, SUPCHINA (Sep. 25, 2019), https://supchina.com/2019/09/25/the-difference-between-tik tok-and-douyin/.

105. Emily Dreibelbis, Shein Unseats Amazon as Most Downloaded US Shopping App, PC MAGAZINE (July 19, 2022), https://www.pcmag.com/news/shein-unse ats-amazon-as-most-downloaded-us-shopping-appn.

106. Shein Now Leads Fast Fashion, EARNEST RESEARCH REPORT (June 24, 2021), https://www.earnestresearch.com/data-bites/shein-leads-fast-fashion/.

107. Tracy Qu, Kuaishou Pulls Its Video App From US After Failing to Dent TikTok's Market Dominance, S. CHINA MORNING POST (Aug. 4, 2021), https:// www.scmp.com/tech/big-tech/article/3143800/kuaishou-pulls-its-video-app- us-after-failing-make-dent-tiktoks.

108. Rita Liao, With 170M Users, Bilibili Is the Nearest Thing China Has to YouTube, TECHCRUNCH (May 19, 2020), https://techcrunch.com/2020/05/18/ with-170m-users-bilibili-is-the-nearest-thing-china-has-to-youtube/.

109. Global Search Engine Market Share Held by Baidu From January 2018 to September 2021, STATISTA (July 7, 2022), https://www.statista.com/statistics/ 1219413/market-share-held-by-baidu-worldwide/.

110. Michael Schuman, Why America Is Afraid of TikTok, THE ATL. (July 30, 2020), https://www.theatlantic.com/international/archive/2020/07/tiktok-ban- china-america/614725/.

111. Rachel Kraus, TikTok Surpasses 2 Billion Global Downloads, MASHABLE (Apr. 29, 2020), https://mashable.com/article/tiktok-2-billion-downloads.

112. Alex Sherman, TikTok Reveals Detailed User Numbers for the First Time, CNBC (Aug. 24, 2020), https://www.cnbc.com/2020/08/24/tiktok-reveals- us-global-user-growth-numbers-for-first-time.html.

113. Schuman, *supra* note 110.

114. Demetri Sevastopulo and James Fontanella-Khan, TikTok to Be Banned from US App Stores from Sunday, FIN. TIMES (Sep. 18. 2020), https://www.ft.com/ content/c460ce4c-c691-4df5-af49-47a395429fe8.

115. Schuman, *supra* note 110.

116. Emily Baker-White, Leaked Audio from 80 Internal TikTok Meetings Shows That US User Data Has Been Repeatedly Accessed from China, BUZZFEED NEWS (June 17, 2022), https://www.buzzfeednews.com/article/emilybakerwh ite/tiktok-tapes-us-user-data-china-bytedance-access.

117. *Id.*

118. Schuman, *supra* note 110.

119. Fadel Allassan, Trump Says TikTok Will Be Banned If Not Sold by Sept. 15, Demands Cut of Sale Fee, AXIOS (Aug. 3, 2020), https://www.axios.com/trump-tiktok-banned-microsoft-fd45748d-1ee8-4f4a-812a-09ec76d6f8e2.html.

120. Exec. Order No. 13942, 85 Fed. Reg. 48,637 (Aug. 6, 2020).

121. Order of Aug. 14, 2020 Regarding the Acquisition of Musical.ly by ByteDance Ltd., 85 Fed. Reg. 51,297 (Aug. 19, 2020).

122. David E. Sanger, David McCabe, & Erin Griffith, Oracle Chosen as TikTok's Tech Partner, as Microsoft's Bid Is Rejected, N.Y. TIMES (Sep. 13, 2020), https://www.nytimes.com/2020/09/13/technology/tiktok-microsoft-oracle-bytedance.html.

123. Paul Mozur, Raymond Zhong, & David McCabe, TikTok Deal Is Complicated by New Rules From China Over Tech Exports, N.Y. TIMES (Aug. 29, 2020), https://www.nytimes.com/2020/08/29/technology/china-tiktok-export-controls.html; Press Release, Chinese Ministry of Commerce and Ministry of Science and Technology Publish Updated Catalogue of China's Prohibited and Restricted Export Technologies (in Chinese), MOFCOM (Aug. 28, 2020), http://www.mofcom.gov.cn/article/b/xxfb/202008/20200802996641.shtml; (中国禁止出口限制出口技术目录)调整内容 (Adjusted Table of Contents for Catalogue of China's Prohibited and Restricted Export Technologies), http://images.mofcom.gov.cn/fms/202008/20200828200911003.pdf.

124. TikTok, Inc. v. Trump, No. 20-cv-02658 (D.D.C. Sep. 23, 2020) (order granting motion for preliminary injunction).

125. TikTok, Inc. v. Trump, No. 20-cv-02658 (D.D.C. Sep. 27, 2020) (mem. opinion).

126. TikTok, Inc. v. Trump, 507 F.Supp.3d 92 (D.D.C. 2020).

127. Exec. Order 14034, 86 Fed. Reg. 31,423 (June 11, 2021).

128. Jimmy Quinn, Biden Allegedly Slow-Walking TikTok Investigation, GOP Demands Answers, NAT'L REV. (Aug. 9, 2022), https://www.nationalreview.com/corner/biden-allegedly-slow-walking-tiktok-investigation-gop-demands-answers/.

129. Letter from Members of Congress to Gina Raimondo, Sec'y, Dep't of Comm. (Aug. 4, 2022), https://www.nationalreview.com/wp-content/uploads/2022/08/8.4.22-Letter-to-DoC-on-ICTR-Rule-Enforcement12.pdf.

130. Daisuke Wakabayashi, Cecilia Kang, & Kellen Browning, "It's So Essential": WeChat Ban Makes U.S.–China Standoff Personal, N.Y. TIMES (Sep. 18, 2020), https://www.nytimes.com/2020/09/18/technology/wechat-ban-united-states-china.html.

131. *Id.*

132. Ana Swanson, Mike Isaac, & Paul Mozur, Trump Targets WeChat and TikTok, in Sharp Escalation With China, N.Y. TIMES (Aug. 6, 2020), https://www.nytimes.com/2020/08/06/technology/trump-wechat-tiktok-china.html.

133. Exec. Order 13943, 85 Fed. Reg. 48,641 (Aug. 11, 2020).

134. Press Release, Dep't of Comm., Commerce Department Prohibits WeChat and TikTok Transactions to Protect the National Security of the United States (Sep. 18, 2020), https://2017-2021.commerce.gov/news/press-releases/2020/09/commerce-department-prohibits-wechat-and-tiktok-transactions-protect.html.

135. U.S. WeChat Users Alliance v. Trump, Case No. 20-cv-05910-LB at 18 (N.D. Cal. Sep. 19, 2020) (order granting motion for preliminary injunction).

136. *Id.*

137. Exec. Order 14034, 86 Fed. Reg. 31,423 (June 11, 2021).

138. Ma Zhihan, Analysis and Implications of US WeChat Ban and Lawsuit (in Chinese), SHIWAPO GUOJIFA (SHIWAPO INTERNATIONAL LAWS) (Sep. 22, 2020), https://mp.weixin.qq.com/s/xO3wUnPU214K5X9uP-9xxQ.

139. How Can WeChat Break Out of US Review Trap? (in Chinese), CAIJING (Apr. 16, 2021), https://m.caijing.com.cn/api/show?contentid=4757198.

140. TikTok, Inc. v. Trump, 507 F.Supp.3d 92, 111 (D.D.C. 2020).

141. *Id.*

142. Elliot Lewis, Republican Senators Push TikTok for Answers on Data Privacy, NBC NEWS (June 29, 2022), https://www.nbcnews.com/tech/tech-news/republican-senators-push-tiktok-answers-data-privacy-rcna35897.

143. Letter from Senator Josh Hawley to Janet Yellen, Sec'y, Dep't of Treasury (Sep. 19, 2022), https://www.hawley.senate.gov/sites/default/files/2022-09/JDH%20Letter%20to%20Yellen%20re%20TikTok_0.pdf.

144. TikTok and the Splintering of the Global Internet, FIN. TIMES (Aug. 3, 2020), https://www.ft.com/content/6a1b9b4d-ddbc-4b62-9101-221510fb7b45.

145. Arthur Parashar, UK Parliament Shuts Down Its TikTok Account After Concern from MPs About the Social Media Firm's Links to China, DAILY MAIL (Aug. 4, 2022), https://www.dailymail.co.uk/news/article-11077205/UK-Parliament-SHUTS-TikTok-account-MPs-concern-social-media-firms-links-China.html.

146. Tom Simonite, Europe's New Law Will Force Secretive TikTok to Open Up, WIRED (May 4, 2022), https://www.wired.com/story/tiktok-transparency-dsa-europe/.

147. Taylor Lorenz & Drew Harwell, Facebook Paid GOP Firm to Malign TikTok, WASH. POST (Mar. 30, 2022), https://www.washingtonpost.com/technology/2022/03/30/facebook-tiktok-targeted-victory/.

148. Mark Zuckerberg, CEO, Meta, Speech at Georgetown University (Oct. 17, 2019), *in* Tony Romm, Zuckerberg: Standing for Voice and Free Expression, WASH. POST (Oct. 17, 2019), https://www.washingtonpost.com/technology/2019/10/17/zuckerberg-standing-voice-free-expression/.

149. Tim Wu, A TikTok Ban Is Overdue, N.Y. TIMES (Aug. 18, 2020), https://www.nytimes.com/2020/08/18/opinion/tiktok-wechat-ban-trump.html.

150. *Id.*

151. *Id.*
152. Wakabayashi, Kang, & Browning, *supra* note 130.
153. The Big Unfriending: Donald Trump Has Caused Panic Among Millions of WeChat Users, THE ECONOMIST (Aug. 13, 2020), https://www.economist.com/china/2020/08/13/donald-trump-has-caused-panic-among-millions-of-wechat-users.
154. Schuman, *supra* note 110; Samm Sacks, Banning TikTok Is a Terrible Idea, THE CHINA PROJECT (July 16, 2020), https://thechinaproject.com/2020/07/16/banning-tiktok-is-a-terrible-idea/.
155. Josephine Wolff, So What Does Trump Have Against TikTok?, N.Y. TIMES (Aug. 7, 2020), https://www.nytimes.com/2020/08/07/opinion/tiktok-wechat-china-trump-executive-order.html.
156. Schuman, *supra* note 110.
157. Wolff, *supra* note 155.
158. David. E. Sanger, TikTok Deal Exposes a Security Gap, and a Missing China Strategy, N.Y. TIMES (Sep. 20, 2020), https://www.nytimes.com/2020/09/20/us/politics/tiktok-trump-national-security.html.
159. Hvistendahl, *supra* note 92.
160. Yuan Yang, What Trump's TikTok Deal Learnt from China's Approach to Apps, FIN. TIMES (Sep. 22, 2020), https://www.ft.com/content/f60bf804-3bf4-44cd-9dbd-ba34d04a26b0.
161. Graham Webster, App Bans Won't Make US Security Risks Disappear, MIT TECH. REV. (Sep. 21, 2020), https://www.technologyreview.com/2020/09/21/1008620/wechat-tiktok-ban-china-us-security-policy-opinion/.
162. Jing Yang, Keith Zhai, & Corrie Driebusch, Didi Tried Balancing Pressure From China and Investors. It Satisfied Neither, WALL ST. J. (July 9, 2021), https://www.wsj.com/articles/didi-ipo-china-regulators-investors-trouble-11625873909?mod=article_inline.
163. *Id.*
164. Yuan Yang and Sun Yu, Beijing Asked Didi to Change Mapping Function Over Security Fears, FIN. TIMES (July 8, 2021), https://www.ft.com/content/dafbd0a2-106b-4dcc-a4c3-4ff77178bc33.
165. Didi's China Rivals Go Full Speed for Customers After App Ban, NIKKEI ASIA (July 28, 2021), https://asia.nikkei.com/Business/China-tech/Didi-s-China-rivals-go-full-speed-for-customers-after-app-ban.
166. Yoko Kubota and Liza Lin, In the New China, Didi's Data Becomes a Problem, WALL ST. J. (July 18, 2021), https://www.wsj.com/articles/in-the-new-china-didis-data-becomes-a-problem-11626606002.
167. *Id.*
168. Chinese Regulators Send Teams to Didi for Cybersecurity Review, REUTERS (July 16, 2021), https://www.reuters.com/technology/chinese-regulators-send-on-site-teams-conduct-cybersecurity-review-didi-2021-07-16/.

169. Arendse Huld, How Did Didi Run Afoul of China's Cybersecurity Regulators? Understanding the US$1.2 Billion Fine, CHINA BRIEFING (Aug. 2, 2020), https://www.china-briefing.com/news/didi-cyber-security-review-which-laws-did-didi-break/.

170. Press Release, The Cyberspace Administration of China's Decision to Impose Administrative Penalties Related to Its Cybersecurity Review of Didi Global Co., Ltd. (in Chinese) (July 21, 2022), http://www.cac.gov.cn/2022-07/21/c_1 660021534306352.htm *translated in* Graham Webster, Translation: Chinese Authorities Announce $1.2B Fine in DiDi Case, Describe "Despicable" Data Abuses, DIGICHINA (July 21, 2022), https://digichina.stanford.edu/work/tran slation-chinese-authorities-announce-2b-fine-in-didi-case-describe-despicable-data-abuses/.

171. Arjun Kharpal, Didi Drops After Tencent Clarifies It Did Not Buy New Shares in the Chinese Ride-Hailing Giant, CNBC (Feb. 11, 2022), https://www.cnbc.com/2022/02/11/didi-shares-drop-after-tencent-said-it-did-not-buy-new-sha res.html.

172. *Id.*

173. Weizhen Tan, Less Than 6 Months After Its IPO, China's Didi Says It Will Delist from the New York Stock Exchange, CNBC (Dec. 2, 2021), https://www.cnbc.com/2021/12/03/didi-on-delisting-from-us-and-list-in-hong-kong.html.

174. China's Didi Plans Hong Kong "Listing by Introduction," Picks Banks—Sources, REUTERS (Dec. 29, 2021), https://www.reuters.com/markets/us/chi nas-didi-plans-hong-kong-listing-by-introduction-picks-banks-sources-2021-12-29/.

175. Chinese Ride-Hailing Firm Didi Sued in US as Shares Slide, BBC NEWS (July 9, 2021), https://www.bbc.com/news/business-57744983; Kessler Topaz Meltzer & Check, LLP: Investor Class Action Filed Against DiDi Global Inc.—Didi for Securities Fraud Violations, https://www.ktmc.com/new-cases/didi-glo bal-inc-didi-1.

176. Ronald A. Oleynik, Antonia I. Tzinova, & Andrew K. McAllister, U.S. Government to Take Actions Against U.S.-Listed Chinese Companies, HOLLAND & KNIGHT (July 28, 2020), https://www.hklaw.com/en/insights/publications/ 2020/07/us-government-to-take-actions-against-us-listed-compan ies#:~:text=On%20April%202%2C%202020%2C%20Luckin,renminbi%20 (approximately%20%24313.5%20million).

177. Holding Foreign Companies Accountable Act, 15 U.S.C. §§ 7214(i), 7214a.

178. Andrew Olmem, Christina Thomas, & Jason Elder, Congress Passes the "Holding Foreign Companies Accountable Act," HARV. L. SCHOOL F. ON CORP. GOVERNANCE (Nov. 13, 2022), https://corpgov.law.harvard.edu/2021/01/10/ congress-passes-the-holding-foreign-companies-accountable-act/.

179. Katanga Johnson, U.S. SEC Mandates Chinese Companies Detail Ownership Structure, Audits, REUTERS (Dec. 2, 2021), https://www.reuters.com/business/

us-sec-mandates-foreign-companies-spell-out-ownership-structure-disclose-2021-12-02/.

180. Ryan McMorrow & Sun Yu, China to Tighten Rules for Tech Companies Seeking Foreign Funding, FIN. TIMES (Dec. 7, 2021), https://www.ft.com/content/7689489c-cdad-4596-a7c6-0774ed68bf5a.

181. Gary Gensler, Chairman, Sec. & Exch. Comm'n, Statement on Investor Protection Related to Recent Developments in China (July 30, 2021), https://www.sec.gov/news/public-statement/gensler-2021-07-30.

182. *Id.*

183. Joel L. Rubinstein et al., SEC Posts Sample Letter to China-Based Companies, Amid a Stalled Process for SEC Clearance of Their Offerings, WHITE & CASE (Jan. 7, 2022), https://www.whitecase.com/publications/alert/sec-posts-sample-letter-china-based-companies-amid-stalled-process-sec-clearance.

184. Matt Haldane, What China's New Data Laws Are and Their Impact on Big Tech, s. SOUTH CHINA MORNING POST (Sep. 1, 2021), https://www.scmp.com/tech/policy/article/3147040/what-chinas-new-data-laws-are-and-their-impact-big-tech.

185. Iris Deng, Beijing Tightens Grip on China Tech With Proposal for Cybersecurity Reviews on All Foreign Public Listings, s. CHINA MORNING POST (July 10, 2021), https://www.scmp.com/tech/big-tech/article/3140611/beijing-tightens-grip-china-tech-proposal-cybersecurity-reviews-all?module=inline&pgtype=article; Noriyuki Doi and Naoki Matusda, China to Require Review of Overseas IPOs by Companies with Data on 1m Users, NIKKEI ASIA (July 10, 2021), https://asia.nikkei.com/Business/China-tech/China-to-require-review-of-overseas-IPOs-by-companies-with-data-on-1m-users.

186. ZHONGHUA RENMIN GONGHEGUO GEREN XINXI BAOHUFA (中华人民共和国个人信息保护法) (Personal Information Protection Law) (2021), http://www.npc.gov.cn/npc/c30834/202108/a8c4e3672c74491a80b53a172bb753fe.shtml.

187. Data Security Law of the People's Republic of China (2021), http://www.npc.gov.cn/englishnpc/c23934/202112/1abd8829788946ecab270e469b13c39c.shtml.

188. Haldane, *supra* note 184.

189. Ryan D. Junck et al., China's New Data Security and Personal Information Protection Laws: What They Mean for Multinational Companies, SKADDEN (Nov. 3, 2021), https://www.skadden.com/insights/publications/2021/11/chinas-new-data-security-and-personal-information-protection-laws.

190. Yiming Ben Hu, China's Personal Information Protection Law and Its Global Impact, THE DIPLOMAT (Aug. 31, 2021), https://thediplomat.com/2021/08/chinas-personal-information-protection-law-and-its-global-impact/.

191. Junck et al., *supra* note 189.

192. *Id.*

193. Bob Pisani, SEC Finalizes Rule That Allows It to Delist Foreign Stocks for Failure to Meet Audit Requirements, CNBC (Dec. 2, 2021), https://www.cnbc.com/2021/12/02/sec-issues-final-regs-that-allow-it-to-delist-foreign-compan ies-that-dont-comply-with-audit-rules.html.

194. Tabby Kinder & Matt O'Dwyer, Big Four Auditors Squeezed Between US and China, FIN. TIMES (Apr. 29, 2021), https://www.ft.com/content/27a148ba-adba-425e-8d59-c22c3bb36ad8.

195. Narayanan Somasundaram, Beijing's Didi Blast Shakes $2tn of China Stocks in US, NIKKEI ASIA (July 12, 2021), https://asia.nikkei.com/Spotlight/Market-Spotlight/Beijing-s-Didi-blast-shakes-2tn-of-China-stocks-in-US.

196. Saheli Roy Choudhury, It's "Game Over" for U.S.-Listed Chinese Companies, Global Asset Manager Says, CNBC (Dec. 15, 2021), https://www.cnbc.com/2021/12/15/us-china-most-chinese-companies-could-delist-from-us-says-tcw-group.html.

197. Elaine Yu, Chinese Audio Platform to List in Hong Kong After Scrapping U.S. IPO Plans, WALL ST. J. (Sep. 14, 2021), https://www.wsj.com/articles/chin ese-audio-platform-to-list-in-hong-kong-after-scrapping-u-s-ipo-plans-11631616 407?mod=article_inline.

198. Hudson Lockett & Tabby Kiner, Wall Street Banks Redirect China IPOs to Hong Kong After Didi Shock, FIN. TIMES (July 21, 2021), https://www.ft.com/content/90620c2c-ea07-4425-9a18-f3b4587ed3ad.

199. Drew Singer, Didi's IPO Underwriters Go Silent as Volatility Dominates, BLOOMBERG (July 26, 2021), https://www.bloomberg.com/news/articles/2021-07-26/didi-s-ipo-underwriters-go-silent-as-volatility-dominates.

200. Gearoid Reidy & Min Jeong Lee, SoftBank, Biggest Investor in Didi, Sinks After China Blocks, BLOOMBERG (July 4, 2021), https://www.bloomberg.com/news/articles/2021-07-05/softbank-tumbles-as-china-blo cks-didi-app-just-days-after-ipo.

201. Didi Listing Provides a Cautionary Tale, FIN. TIMES (July 7, 2021), https://www.ft.com/content/6c52658d-4272-4e41-9570-db49f641c832.

202. Beijing Stock Exchange Launches With Focus on "Little Giants," BLOOMBERG (Nov. 13, 2021), https://www.bloomberg.com/news/articles/2021-11-13/beijing-stock-exchange-launches-with-focus-on-little-giants; Alexandra Stevenson & Paul Mozur, With Its Exit, Didi Sends a Signal: China No Longer Needs Wall Street, N.Y. TIMES (Dec. 2, 2021), https://www.nytimes.com/2021/12/02/busin ess/china-didi-delisting.html.

203. China to Tighten Foreign IPOs, May Ban Some on National Security, BLOOMBERG (Dec. 24, 2021), https://www.bloomberg.com/news/articles/2021-12-24/china-to-tighten-foreign-ipos-may-ban-some-on-national-security.

204. Shidong Zhang, Daniel Ren, & Coco Feng, Investors Likely to Cheer Clarity on VIE Companies as China Unveils Requirements on Offshore IPOs, S. CHINA

MORNING POST (Dec. 27, 2021), https://www.scmp.com/business/markets/arti cle/3161086/investors-likely-cheer-clarity-vie-companies-china-unveils.

205. Tabby Kinder, China Changes Audit Secrecy Rules in Bid to Stop US Delistings, FIN. TIMES (Apr. 2, 2022), https://www.ft.com/content/c3d52cf3-a9b7-4a59-99e4-21cdaaebebe6.

206. Tabby Kinder, Cheng Leng, Ryan McMorrow, & Sun Yu, China Plans Three-Tier Data Strategy to Avoid US Delistings, FIN. TIMES (July 24, 2022), https://www.ft.com/content/3d3d2403-7b72-4f4b-a453-c66c7d132831?shareType=nongift.

207. *Id.*

208. *Id.*

209. Patrick Temple-West & Tabby Kinder, US and China Reach Landmark Audit Inspection Deal, FIN. TIMES (Aug 26, 2022), https://www.ft.com/content/a9d18d7e-1e75-49fb-842d-d8554b420553.

210. *Id.*

211. Gary Gensler, Chairman, Sec. & Exch. Comm'n, Statement on Agreement Governing Inspections and Investigations of Audit Firms Based in China and Hong Kong (Aug. 26, 2022), https://www.sec.gov/news/statement/gensler-audit-firms-china-hong-kong-20220826.

212. Qianer Liu & Tabby Kinder, Alibaba and Yum China First in Line for Audit Checks by US Regulator, FIN. TIMES (Aug. 31, 2022), https://www.ft.com/cont ent/0b17a16a-87a1-41ff-80c0-aaf3bb1c8967?shareType=nongift.

213. Kinder, Leng, McMorrow, & Yu, *supra* note 206.

214. Tabby Kinder, Cheng Leng, & Hudson Lockett, Landmark US-China Audit Deal Spurs Hunt for Devils in the Details, FIN. TIMES (Aug. 29, 2022), https://www.ft.com/content/322e1486-7c11-4582-aa36-39799bf30c51?shareType=nongift.

215. *Privacy. That's Apple.*, APPLE, https://www.apple.com/privacy/ (last visited Nov. 13, 2022).

216. Nicas, Zhong, & Wakabayashi, *supra* note 2.

217. Sophie Mellor, Experts Say Russia's War on Ukraine Is Accelerating the "Splinternet." But What Is the Splinternet?, FORTUNE (Mar. 22, 2022), https://fortune.com/2022/03/22/Russia-war-ukraine-great-firewall-splinternet-internet/.

218. Matt Henry & Matthew Carney, China and the US Are Locked in a Superpower Tech War to "Win the 21st Century," ABC NEWS (July 7, 2021), https://www.abc.net.au/news/2021-07-08/trump-facebook-twitter-china-us-superpower-tech-war/100273812.

219. Nathaniel Fick et al., COUNCIL ON FOREIGN REL., CONFRONTING REALITY IN CYBERSPACE 3, https://www.cfr.org/report/confronting-reality-in-cyberspace/download/pdf/2022-07/CFR_TFR80_Cyberspace_Full_SinglePages_062 12022_Final.pdf.

220. Zuckerberg, *supra* note 148.

221. Henry & Carney, *supra* note 218.

222. Chris Stokel-Walker, Russia Inches Toward Its Splinternet Dream, WIRED (April 1, 2022), https://www.wired.com/story/russia-splinternet-censorship/.

223. *Id.*

224. James Ball, Russia Is Risking the Creation of a "Splinternet"—And It Could Be Irreversible, TECH. REV. (Mar. 17, 2022), https://www.technologyreview.com/2022/03/17/1047352/russia-splinternet-risk/.

225. *Id.*

CHAPTER 5

1. *See, e.g.,* OFF. U.S. TRADE REPRESENTATIVE, FINDINGS OF THE INVESTIGATION INTO CHINA'S ACTS, POLICIES, AND PRACTICES RELATED TO TECHNOLOGY TRANSFER, INTELLECTUAL PROPERTY, AND INNOVATION UNDER SECTION 301 OF THE TRADE ACT OF 1974, https://ustr.gov/sites/default/files/Section%20301%20FINAL. PDF; U.S. TRADE REPRESENTATIVE, 2017 REPORT TO CONGRESS ON CHINA'S WTO COMPLIANCE (2018), https://ustr.gov/sites/default/files/files/Press/Reports/China%202017%20WTO%20Report.pdf; WHITE HOUSE OFF. TRADE & MFG. POL'Y, HOW CHINA'S ECONOMIC AGGRESSION THREATENS THE TECHNOLOGIES AND INTELLECTUAL PROPERTY OF THE UNITED STATES AND THE WORLD (2018), https://trumpwhitehouse.archives.gov/wp-content/uploads/2018/06/FINAL-China-Technology-Report-6.18.18-PDF.pdf.

2. Notice of OFAC Sanctions Actions, 86 Fed. Reg. 15552 (Mar. 23, 2021), https://www.govinfo.gov/content/pkg/FR-2021-03-23/pdf/2021-05919.pdf; Sabrina Rodriguez, Trump Signs Hong Kong Sanctions Bill in Blow for China, POLITICO, https://www.politico.com/news/2020/07/14/trump-hong-kong-china-sancti ons-361636 (July 14, 2020); Pranshu Verma & Edward Wong, U.S. Imposes Sanctions on Chinese Officials Over Mass Detention of Muslims, N.Y. TIMES, https://www.nytimes.com/2020/07/09/world/asia/trump-china-sanctions-uighurs.html (Aug. 7, 2020); Associated Press, Biden Administration Imposes Sanctions Against China Over Abuse of Uyghurs, NBC NEWS (Dec. 16, 2021), https://www.nbcnews.com/politics/national-security/biden-administration-imposes-sanctions-against-china-over-abuse-uyghurs-n1286100.

3. EU Challenges China at the WTO to Defend Its High-Tech Sector, EUROPEAN COMM'N (Feb. 18, 2022), https://ec.europa.eu/commission/presscorner/det ail/en/ip_22_1103.

4. Reality Check: Falsehoods in US Perceptions of China, MINISTRY FOREIGN AFFS. CHINA (June 19, 2022), https://www.mfa.gov.cn/eng/wjbxw/202206/t202206 19_10706059.html.

5. Chen Dingding (陈定定), Kang Xiaomeng (康晓蒙), & Xia Yu (夏雨), "Yacangshi" dao "Daohuosuo": Zhongmei Jingmao Guanxi Fenxi ("压舱石"到"导火索": 中美经贸关系分析) [From "Ballast" to "Fuse": An Analysis of

the China-U.S. Economic and Trade Relationship], Guoji Zhengzhi Kexue (国际政治科学) [Q. J. INT'L POL.], 2019(4), at 57, http://qjip.tsinghuajournals.com/article/2019/2096-1545/101393D-2019-4-103.shtml.

6. *Id.* at 58 (unofficial translation).

7. Recovery Plan: Powering Europe's Strategic Autonomy—Speech by President Charles Michel at the Brussels Economic Forum, EUROPEAN COUNCIL EUROPEAN UNION (Sep. 8, 2020), https://www.consilium.europa.eu/en/press/press-relea ses/2020/09/08/recovery-plan-powering-europe-s-strategic-autonomy-spe ech-by-president-charles-michel-at-the-brussels-economic-forum/.

8. Jeremy Shapiro, Introduction: Europe's Digital Sovereignty, in Europe's Digital Sovereignty: From Rulemaker to Superpower in the Age of US–China Rivalry 6 (Carla Hobbs ed., 2020), https://ecfr.eu/wp-content/uploads/europe_dig-ital_sovereignty_rulemaker_superpower_age_us_china_rivalry.pdf.

9. Emma Rafaelof, U.S.-CHINA ECON. AND SEC. REV. COMM'N, UNFINISHED BUSINESS: EXPORT CONTROL AND FOREIGN INVESTMENT REFORMS 9 (2021), https://www.uscc.gov/sites/default/files/2021-06/Unfinished_Business-Export_Control_and_Foreign_Investment_Reforms.pdf.

10. Export Control Reform Act of 2018, 50 U.S.C. §§ 4801–4852; *see* discussion in Cong. Rsch. Serv., U.S. EXPORT CONTROLS AND CHINA 1 (2022), https://sgp.fas.org/crs/natsec/IF11627.pdf.

11. Revisions and Clarification of Export and Reexport Controls for the People's Republic of China (PRC); New Authorization Validated End-User; Revision of Import Certificate and PRC End-User Statement Requirements, 72 Fed. Reg. 33646, 33646 (June 19, 2007).

12. Export Control Reform Act of 2018 § 1758, 50 U.S.C. § 4817.

13. Review of Controls for Certain Emerging Technologies, 83 Fed. Reg. 58201 (ad-vanced notice of proposed rulemaking Nov. 19, 2018); Rafaelof, *supra* note 9, at 9; Akin Gump Strauss Hauer & Feld LLP, THE EXPORT CONTROL REFORM ACT OF 2018 AND POSSIBLE NEW CONTROLS ON EMERGING AND FOUNDATIONAL TECHNOLOGIES 3–4 (2018), https://www.akingump.com/en/news-insights/the-export-control-reform-act-of-2018-and-possible-new-controls.html#:~:text= ECRA%20became%20law%20on%20August,its%20country%2Dspeci fic%20licensing%20requirements.

14. Rafaelof, *supra* note 9, at 5–6.

15. *See id.* at 7.

16. CONG. RSCH. SERV., *supra* note 10, at 1.

17. Kate O'Keeffe, U.S. Approves Nearly All Tech Exports to China, Data Shows, WALL ST. J. (Aug. 16, 2022), https://www.wsj.com/articles/u-s-approves-nearly-all-tech-exports-to-china-data-shows-11660596886.

18. *Id.*

19. Entity List, BUREAU OF INDUS. AND SEC., https://www.bis.doc.gov/index.php/pol icy-guidance/lists-of-parties-of-concern/entity-list.

20. David Dodwell, Like All Wars, the US Tech War on China Is Proving Costly and Pointless, s. CHINA MORNING POST (June 6, 2022), https://www.scmp.com/comment/opinion/article/3180475/all-wars-us-tech-war-china-proving-costly-and-pointless.

21. Supplement No. 4 to Part 744—Entity List, 15 C.F.R. Part 744 (Supp. 2022).

22. Matt Henry & Matthew Carney, China and the US Are Locked in a Superpower Tech War to "Win the 21st Century," ABC NEWS, https://www.abc.net.au/news/2021-07-08/trump-facebook-twitter-china-us-superpower-tech-war/100273812 (July 8, 2021); Asa Fitch & Kate O'Keeffe, Qualcomm Lobbies U.S. to Sell Chips for Huawei 5G Phones, WALL ST. J. (Aug. 8, 2020), https://www.wsj.com/articles/qualcomm-lobbies-u-s-to-sell-chips-for-huawei-5g-phones-11596888001?mod=tech_lead_pos7.

23. Supplement No. 4 to Part 744—Entity List, 15 C.F.R. Part 744 (Supp. 2022).

24. Export Administration Regulations: Amendments to General Prohibition Three (Foreign-Produced Direct Product Rule) and the Entity List, 15 C.F.R. pts. 730, 732, 736, 744.

25. Lauly Li, Cheng Ting-Fang, & Yifan Yu, How a Handful of US Companies Can Cripple Huawei's Supply Chain, NIKKEI ASIA (Aug. 19, 2020), https://asia.nikkei.com/Spotlight/Huawei-crackdown/How-a-handful-of-US-companies-can-cripple-Huawei-s-supply-chain.

26. Kathrin Hille, Eleanor Olcott, & James Kynge, US–China Business: The Necessary Reinvention of Huawei, FIN. TIMES (Sep. 18, 2021), https://www.ft.com/content/9e98a0db-8d0a-4f78-90d3-25bfebcf3ac9.

27. Kathrin Hille, Huawei Revenues Fall 30% in 2021 but Company Is Cautiously Optimistic, FIN. TIMES (Dec. 30, 2021), https://www.ft.com/content/22d89af2-c3e2-479b-8baf-5e079ff73458; Arjun Kharpal, From No. 1 to No. 6, Huawei Smartphone Shipments Plunge 41% as U.S. Sanctions Bite, CNBC, https://www.cnbc.com/2021/01/28/huawei-q4-smartphone-shipments-plunge-41perc ent-as-us-sanctions-bite.html (Jan. 28, 2021).

28. Matthew Levy et al., Biden Administration Completes Its Second 50 Days with Continued Pressure on Targeted Countries Using Increased Sanctions and Export Controls, JD SUPRA (April 30, 2021), https://www.jdsupra.com/legalnews/biden-administration-completes-its-1089734/; Ellen Nakashima, Biden Administration Slaps Export Controls on Chinese Firms for Aiding PLA Weapons Development, WASH. POST (Apr. 8, 2021), https://www.washingtonp ost.com/national-security/biden-administration-slaps-export-controls-on-chin ese-firms-for-aiding-pla-weapons-development/2021/04/07/0c45bf0a-97f6-11eb-b28d-bfa7bb5cb2a5_story.html.

29. Letter from Michael T. McCaul, Chairman, China Task Force, and 13 China Task Force Members, to Gina Raimondo, Secretary, Dep't of Com. (Oct. 22, 2021), https://gop-foreignaffairs.house.gov/wp-content/uploads/2021/10/CTF-Letter-to-Sec.-Raimondo-on-Export-Control-Actions.pdf.

30. Timothy Brightbill et al., Senate Passes Sweeping Bill Aimed at Competition with China, JD SUPRA (June 10, 2021), https://www.jdsupra.com/legalnews/senate-passes-sweeping-bill-aimed-at-2835027/.

31. Brown, Toomey Reach Bipartisan Agreement on Amendment to China Competition Bill, SHEPPARD BROWN U.S. SENATOR FOR OHIO (May 12, 2021), https://www.brown.senate.gov/newsroom/press/release/brown-toomey-bipartisan-amendment-china-competition-bill.

32. Ana Swanson & Edward Wong, With New Crackdown, Biden Wages Global Campaign on Chinese Technology, N.Y. TIMES (Oct. 13, 2022), https://www.nytimes.com/2022/10/13/us/politics/biden-china-technology-semiconductors.html?smid=nytcore-ios-share&referringSource=articleShare.

33. Implementation of Additional Export Controls: Certain Advanced Computing and Semiconductor Manufacturing Items; Supercomputer and Semiconductor End Use; Entity List Modification, 87 Fed. Reg. 62186, 62189-62192 (Oct. 13, 2022) (to be codified at 15 C.F.R. pts. 734–774).

34. Swanson & Wong, *supra* note 32.

35. Ana Swanson, Biden Administration Clamps Down on China's Access to Chip Technology, N.Y. TIMES (Oct. 7, 2022), https://www.nytimes.com/2022/10/07/business/economy/biden-chip-technology.html.

36. Kathrin Hille, China's Chip Breakthrough Poses Strategic Dilemma, FIN. TIMES (Aug. 15, 2022), https://www.ft.com/content/f0ddae61-a8a3-456d-8768-971c71ccb6dd; Press Release, Bureau of Industry and Security, Commerce Adds China's SMIC to the Entity List, Restricting Access to Key Enabling U.S. Technology (Dec. 18. 2020), https://2017-2021.commerce.gov/news/press-releases/2020/12/commerce-adds-chinas-smic-entity-list-restricting-access-key-enabling.html.

37. Swanson & Wong, *supra* note 32.

38. Gregory C. Allen, Choking Off China's Access to the Future of AI, CENTER FOR STRATEGIC & INT'L STUDIES (Oct. 11, 2022), https://www.csis.org/analysis/choking-chinas-access-future-ai.

39. China's Chip Industry Set for Deep Pain from US Export Controls, FIN. TIMES (Oct. 8, 2022), https://www.ft.com/content/e950f58c-0d8f-4121-b4f2-ece71d2cb267?shareType=nongift.

40. *Id.*

41. Swanson & Wong, *supra* note 32.

42. *Id.*

43. Jeff Moon, China's Retaliation Playbook Can't Meet the US Export Control Challenge, HILL (Oct. 20, 2022), https://thehill.com/opinion/international/3697077-chinas-retaliation-playbook-cant-meet-the-us-export-control-challenge/.

44. *Id.*

45. Cheng Ting-Fang, China's "Sea Turtle" Tech Executives Stranded by U.S. Crackdown, NIKKEI ASIA (Oct. 11, 2022), https://asia.nikkei.com/Business/Tech/Semiconductors/China-s-sea-turtle-tech-executives-stranded-by-U.S.-crackdown.

46. Chris Miller, The US–China Chip War Is Reshaping Tech Supply Chains, FIN. TIMES (Oct. 7, 2022), https://www.ft.com/content/3bab2b03-0cd9-4e91-86ab-dcda499fb231(on file with author).

47. David Shepardson & Karen Freifeld, Trump Administration Hits China's Huawei with One-Two Punch, REUTERS (May 15, 2019), https://www.reuters.com/article/us-usa-china-trump-telecommunications/trump-administration-hits-chinas-huawei-with-one-two-punch-idUSKCN1SL2QX.

48. Michael R. Pompeo, The United States Further Restricts Huawei Access to U.S. Technology, U.S. DEP'T OF STATE (Aug. 17, 2020), https://2017-2021.state.gov/the-united-states-further-restricts-huawei-access-to-u-s-technology/index.html.

49. Shepardson & Freifeld, *supra* note 47.

50. Dan Sabbagh, US Senator: Huawei 5G Is Like Soviets Building West's Submarines, GUARDIAN (June 2, 2020), https://www.theguardian.com/technology/2020/jun/02/us-senator-huawei-5g-is-like-soviets-building-wests-submarines.

51. Secure Equipment Act of 2021, 47 U.S.C. 1601 note; Bill Signed: H.R. 3919, WHITE HOUSE (Nov. 11, 2021), https://www.whitehouse.gov/briefing-room/legislation/2021/11/11/bill-signed-h-r-3919/#:~:text=signed%20into%20law%3A-,H.R.,unacceptable%20risk%20to%20national%20security.

52. *Id.*

53. Joseph Marks & Aaron Schaffer, A Plan to Strip Huawei From Rural Telecoms Is Still Short Billions, WASH. POST (June 15, 2022), https://www.washingtonpost.com/politics/2022/06/15/plan-strip-huawei-rural-telecoms-is-still-short-billions/.

54. Helen Davidson, China's Act of "Hostage Diplomacy" Comes to End as Two Canadians Freed, GUARDIAN (Sep. 25, 2021), https://www.theguardian.com/world/2021/sep/25/canadian-pm-trudeau-says-detained-citizens-michael-kovrig-and-michael-spavor-have-left-china?CMP=Share_iOSApp_Other.

55. Paul Triolo et al., EURASIA GROUP, THE DIGITAL SILK ROAD: EXPANDING CHINA'S DIGITAL FOOTPRINT 6–8 (2020), https://www.eurasiagroup.net/files/upload/Digital-Silk-Road-Expanding-China-Digital-Footprint.pdf.

56. David Sacks, China's Huawei Is Winning the 5G Race. Here's What the United States Should Do to Respond, COUNCIL ON FOREIGN REL. (Mar. 29, 2021), https://www.cfr.org/blog/china-huawei-5g.

57. Andy Blatchford, Canada Joins Five Eyes in Ban on Huawei and ZTE, POLITICO (May 19, 2022), https://www.politico.com/news/2022/05/19/canada-five-eyes-ban-huawei-zte-00033920.

58. Harsh V. Pant & Aarshi Tirkey, India Draws a Line in the 5G Sand, FOREIGN POL'Y, https://foreignpolicy.com/2021/05/18/india-draws-a-line-in-the-5g-sand/.

59. Maria Abi-Habib, India Bans Nearly 60 Chinese Apps, Including TikTok and WeChat, N.Y. TIMES, https://www.nytimes.com/2020/06/29/world/asia/tik-tok-banned-india-china.html (June 30, 2020).

60. Huawei Bills in Networks More Than Double That of Nokia and Ericsson Combined, OBSERVATORIO NACIONAL 5G [NAT'L 5G OBSERVATORY] (Mar. 25, 2021), https://on5g.es/en/huawei-bills-in-networks-more-than-double-that-of-nokia-and-ericsson-combined/.

61. Chuin-Wei Yap, State Support Helped Fuel Huawei's Global Rise, WALL ST. J. (Dec. 25, 2019), https://www.wsj.com/articles/state-support-helped-fuel-huaweis-global-rise-11577280736.

62. Nicole Willing, Reliance Borrows $750M for Huawei Gear, LIGHT READING (May 16, 2008), https://www.lightreading.com/ethernet-ip/reliance-borrows-$750m-for-huawei-gear/d/d-id/656560.

63. Yap, *supra* note 61.

64. Lindsay Maizland & Andrew Chatzky, Huawei: China's Controversial Tech Giant, COUNCIL ON FOREIGN REL. (Aug. 6, 2020), https://www.cfr.org/backgrounder/huawei-chinas-controversial-tech-giant.

65. Huong Le Thu, Cybersecurity and Geopolitics: Why Southeast Asia Is Wary of a Huawei Ban, STRATEGIST (Oct. 5, 2019), https://www.aspistrategist.org.au/cybersecurity-and-geopolitics-why-southeast-asia-is-wary-of-a-huawei-ban/.

66. Katherine Atha et al., SOS Int'l LLC, CHINA'S SMART CITIES DEVELOPMENT 65 (2020), https://www.uscc.gov/sites/default/files/China_Smart_Cities_Development.pdf.

67. Tom Westbrook, PNG Upholds Deal with Huawei to Lay Internet Cable, Derides Counter-Offer, REUTERS (Nov. 26, 2018), https://www.reuters.com/article/us-papua-huawei-tech-idUSKCN1NV0DR.

68. Harry G. Broadman, As CFIUS Turns 45 Years Old, U.S. Regulation of Foreign Investment Is the Strictest Among Advanced Countries, FORBES (Nov. 30, 2019), https://www.forbes.com/sites/harrybroadman/2019/11/30/as-cfius-turns-45-years-old-us-regulation-of-foreign-investment-is-the-strictest-among-advanced-countries/?sh=3f2732025ecf.

69. Foreign Investment Risk Review Modernization Act of 2018, Pub. L. No. 115–232, 123 Stat. 2174 (amending 50 U.S.C. § 4565).

70. *Id.*

71. *Id.* § 1703 (amending 50 U.S.C. § 4565(a)).

72. Greg Roumeliotis, U.S. Blocks Chip Equipment Maker Xcerra's Sale to Chinese State Fund, REUTERS (Feb. 22, 2018), https://www.reuters.com/article/xcerra-ma-hubeixinyan/u-s-blocks-chip-equipment-maker-xcerras-sale-to-chinese-state-fund-idUSL2N1QD01X.

73. Ekso Bionics Holdings, Inc., Ekso Bionics Announces CFIUS Determination Regarding China Joint Venture, GLOBENEWSWIRE (May 20, 2020), https://www.globenewswire.com/news-release/2020/05/20/2036681/0/en/Ekso-Bionics-Announces-CFIUS-Determination-Regarding-China-Joint-Venture.html; discussed in Rafaelof, *supra* note 9, at 9.

74. CFIUS by the Numbers: Key Takeaways From the 2020 Annual Report, MORRISON FOERSTER (Aug. 6, 2021), https://www.mofo.com/resources/insights/210806-cfius-by-the-numbers.html.

75. Information About the Department of Justice's China Initiative and a Compilation of China-Related Prosecutions Since 2018, DEP'T JUST., https://www.justice.gov/archives/nsd/information-about-department-justice-s-china-initiative-and-compilation-china-related (Nov. 19, 2021).

76. Caroline Wagner, Intense Scrutiny of Chinese-Born Researchers in the US Threatens Innovation, CONVERSATION (Jan. 26, 2021), https://theconversation.com/intense-scrutiny-of-chinese-born-researchers-in-the-us-threatens-innovation-153688.

77. *Id.*

78. Ellen Barry, "In the End, You're Treated Like a Spy," Says M.I.T. Scientist, N.Y. TIMES (Jan. 24, 2022), https://www.nytimes.com/2022/01/24/science/gang-chen-mit-china.html.

79. Ken Dilanian, How a Federal Push to Stop Chinese Scientists from Stealing U.S. Secrets Has Sputtered in Court, NBC NEWS (Oct. 19, 2021), https://www.nbcnews.com/politics/justice-department/how-federal-push-stop-chinese-scientists-stealing-u-s-secrets-n1281831.

80. Margaret K. Lewis, Criminalizing China, 111 J. CRIM. L. & CRIMINOLOGY 145, 146 (2021).

81. Assistant Attorney General Matthew Olsen Delivers Remarks on Countering Nation-State Threats, U.S. DEP'T JUST. (Feb. 23, 2022), https://www.justice.gov/opa/speech/assistant-attorney-general-matthew-olsen-delivers-remarks-countering-nation-state-threats.

82. Michael German, End of Justice Department's "China Initiative" Brings Little Relief to U.S. Academics, BRENNAN CTR. FOR JUST. (Mar. 25, 2022), https://www.brennancenter.org/our-work/analysis-opinion/end-justice-departments-china-initiative-brings-little-relief-us.

83. Humeyra Pamuk, David Brunnstrom, & Ryan Woo, U.S. Cancels Visas of More Than 1,000 Chinese Nationals Deemed Security Risks, REUTERS (Sep. 15, 2020), https://www.reuters.com/article/usa-china-visas/u-s-cancels-visas-of-more-than-1000-chinese-nationals-deemed-security-risks-idUSKBN2602SH.

84. *Id.*; Emily Feng, As U.S. Revokes Chinese Students' Visas, Concerns Rise About Loss of Research Talent, NPR, https://www.npr.org/2020/09/23/915939365/critics-question-u-s-decision-to-revoke-chinese-students-visas (Sep. 24, 2020).

85. Rubio, Scott, Colleagues Introduce Bill to Reestablish DOJ's China Initiative, MARCO RUBIO US SENATOR FOR FLA. (Mar. 31, 2022), https://www.rubio.senate. gov/public/index.cfm/2022/3/rubio-scott-colleagues-introduce-bill-to-reestabl ish-doj-s-china-initiative.

86. Rory Truex, What the Fear of China Is Doing to American Science, ATLANTIC (Feb. 16, 2021), https://www.theatlantic.com/ideas/archive/2021/02/fears-about-china-are-disrupting-american-science/618031/; *see also* Cotton, Blackburn, Kustoff Unveil Bill to Restrict Chinese STEM Graduate Student Visas & Thousand Talents Participants, TOM COTTON SENATOR FOR ARKANSAS (May 27, 2020), https://www.cotton.senate.gov/news/press-releases/cotton-blackburn-kustoff-unveil-bill-to-restrict-chinese-stem-graduate-student-visas-and-thous and-talents-participants.

87. Hartzler Introduces Legislation to Ban Communist China Officials and Families From Attending American Universities, VICKY HARTZLER (Feb. 16, 2022), https:// hartzler.house.gov/media-center/press-releases/hartzler-introduces-legislation-ban-communist-china-officials-and.

88. Truex, *supra* note 86.

89. Sha Hua, Visa Restrictions on Chinese Students Endanger U.S. Innovation Edge, Universities Say, WALL ST. J. (Nov. 2, 2021), https://www.wsj.com/articles/ visa-restrictions-on-chinese-students-endanger-u-s-innovation-edge-universit ies-say-11635856001.

90. Amy Qin, As U.S. Hunts for Chinese Spies, University Scientists Warn of Backlash, N.Y. TIMES (Nov. 28, 2021), https://www.nytimes.com/2021/11/28/ world/asia/china-university-spies.html.

91. Jeffrey Mervis, More Restrictive U.S. Policy on Chinese Graduate Student Visas Raises Alarm, SCIENCE (June 11, 2018), https://www.science.org/content/article/ more-restrictive-us-policy-chinese-graduate-student-visas-raises-alarm.

92. Truex, *supra* note 86.

93. Eric Lipton, David E. Sanger, & Scott Shane, The Perfect Weapon: How Russian Cyberpower Invaded the U.S., N.Y. TIMES (Dec. 13, 2016), https://www.nytimes. com/2016/12/13/us/politics/russia-hack-election-dnc.html.

94. Erica Moret & Patryk Pawlak, EUROPEAN UNION INST. FOR SEC. STUD., THE EU CYBER DIPLOMACY TOOLBOX: TOWARDS A CYBER SANCTIONS REGIME? (2017), https://www. iss.europa.eu/sites/default/files/EUISSFiles/Brief%2024%20Cyber%20sancti ons.pdf.

95. Russell Brandom, US Institutes New Russia Sanctions in Response to SolarWinds Hack, VERGE (April 15, 2021), https://www.theverge.com/2021/4/15/ 22385371/russia-sanctions-solarwinds-biden-white-house-putin-hack.

96. Hannah Murphy, Kiran Stacey, & Helen Warrell, US Accuses China of Masterminding Cyber Attacks Worldwide, FIN. TIMES (July 19, 2021), https:// www.ft.com/content/54803790-ac33-4616-a0b5-7c39e3ea0b29?shareType= nongift.

97. Indictment, U.S. v. Ding, No. 21-cr-1622-GPC (S. D. Cal. May 28, 2021), https://www.justice.gov/opa/press-release/file/1412916/download, discussed in Katie Benner, The Justice Dept. Accuses Chinese Security Officials of a Hacking Attack Seeking Data on Viruses Like Ebola, N.Y. TIMES (July 19, 2021), https://www.nytimes.com/2021/07/19/us/politics/chinese-hackers-justice-dept.html.

98. Zolan Kanno-Youngs & David E. Sanger, U.S. Accuses China of Hacking Microsoft, N.Y. TIMES, https://www.nytimes.com/2021/07/19/us/politics/microsoft-hacking-china-biden.html (Aug. 26, 2021).

99. Nicole Perlroth, How China Transformed Into a Prime Cyber Threat to the U.S., N.Y. TIMES, https://www.nytimes.com/2021/07/19/technology/china-hacking-us.html (July 20, 2021).

100. Murphy et al., *supra* note 96.

101. *Id.*

102. Edward White & Christian Shepherd, China Hits Back at US-Led Accusations over Cyber Attacks, FIN. TIMES (July 20, 2021), https://www.ft.com/content/fe589e37-2f85-428e-a0ef-cbb5a5211157.

103. Kanno-Youngs & Sanger, *supra* note 98.

104. *Id.*

105. Dan Wang, China's Sputnik Moment? How Washington Boosted Beijing's Quest for Tech Dominance, FOREIGN AFFS. (July 29, 2021), https://www.foreignaffairs.com/articles/united-states/2021-07-29/chinas-sputnik-moment.

106. Chukou Guanzhi Fa (出口管制法) [Export Control Law] (promulgated by the Standing Comm. Nat'l People's Cong., Oct. 17, 2020, effective Dec. 1, 2020), 2020 STANDING COMM. NAT'L PEOPLE'S CONG. GAZ. 778, translated in Export Control Law of the People's Republic of China, NAT'L PEOPLE'S CONG. CHINA (Oct. 17, 2020), http://www.npc.gov.cn/englishnpc/c23934/202112/63aff482fece44a591b45810fa2c25c4.shtml (China).

107. China Enacts Export Control Law Following Its Announcement of the Unreliable Entities List, WHITE & CASE (Jan. 15, 2021), https://www.whitecase.com/publications/alert/china-enacts-export-control-law-following-its-announcement-unreliable-entities.

108. China's "Unreliable Entity List" Creates New Countervailing Risks for Companies Navigating U.S. Sanctions and Long-Arm Enforcement, MORRISON FOERSTER (Oct. 7, 2020), https://www.mofo.com/resources/insights/201007-china-mofcom-unreliable-entity-list.html.

109. Evelyn Cheng, China Releases Details on Its Own Blacklist, Raising Uncertainty for Foreign Businesses, CNBC, https://www.cnbc.com/2020/09/21/china-releases-details-on-unreliable-entity-list-raising-uncertainty-for-foreign-businesses.html (Sep. 23, 2020).

110. Bukekao Shiti Qingdan Guiding (不可靠实体清单规定) [Provisions on the Unreliable Entity List] (promulgated by Ministry of Com., Sep. 19, 2020, effective Sep. 19, 2020), art. 2, St. Council Gaz., Nov. 30, 2020, at 68 (China),

translated in MOFCOM Order No. 4 of 2020 on Provisions on the Unreliable Entity List, MINISTRY COM. CHINA (Sep. 19, 2020), http://english.mofcom.gov.cn/article/policyrelease/questions/202009/20200903002580.shtml.

111. MORRISON FOERSTER, *supra* note 108.

112. Jon Bateman, U.S. Sanctions on Hikvision Would Dangerously Escalate China Tech Tensions, CARNEGIE ENDOWMENT FOR INT'L PEACE (May 6, 2022), https://carnegieendowment.org/2022/05/06/u.s.-sanctions-on-hikvision-would-dangerously-escalate-china-tech-tensions-pub-87089.

113. Margot Patrick & Frances Yoon, HSBC Stock Hits 25-Year Low, WALL ST. J. (Sep. 21, 2020), https://www.wsj.com/articles/hsbc-stock-hits-25-year-low-11600672778?mod=article_inline.

114. *Id.*; China's First Entity List May Target Foreign Entities Blocking Chinese Firms' Supplies: Experts, GLOBAL TIMES (Sep. 19, 2020), https://www.globaltimes.cn/content/1201374.shtml.

115. Mike Bird, China's Attack on "Unreliable Entities" Is a Double-Edged Sword for Beijing, WALL ST. J. (Sep. 22, 2020), https://www.wsj.com/articles/chinas-attack-on-unreliable-entities-is-a-double-edged-sword-for-beijing-11600767713.

116. *Id.*

117. Shuju Anquan Fa (数据安全法) [Data Security Law] (promulgated by the Standing Comm. Nat'l People's Cong., June 10, 2021, effective Sep. 1, 2021), 2021 STANDING COMM. NAT'L PEOPLE'S CONG. GAZ. 951 (China), translated in Data Security Law of the People's Republic of China, NAT'L PEOPLE'S CONG. CHINA (June 10, 2021), http://www.npc.gov.cn/englishnpc/c23934/202112/1abd8829788946ecab270e469b13c39c.shtml (China).

118. Liu JunChen (刘俊臣), Guanyu "Zhonghua Renmin Gongheguo Shuju Anquan Fa (Cao'an)" de Shuoming (关于《中华人民共和国数据安全法（草案）》的说明) [Explanation of the Draft Data Security Law], 2021 STANDING COMM. NAT'L PEOPLE'S CONG. GAZ. 956 (China); the same sentence appears in Xinhua She (新华社) [Xinhua News Agency], Shuju Anquan Fa: Huhang Shuju Anquan, Zhuli Shuzi Fazhan (数据安全法：护航数据安全，助力数字经济发展) [Data Security Law: Safeguarding Data Security, and Supporting the Development of Digital Economy], Renmin Wang (人民网) [PEOPLE.CN], http://finance.people.com.cn/n1/2021/0611/c1004-32128289.html, and translated in Wei Sheng, China Passes Data Security Law as It Continues to Crack Down on Tech Giants, TECHNODE (June 11, 2021), https://technode.com/2021/06/11/china-passes-data-security-law-as-it-continues-to-crack-down-on-tech-giants/.

119. Wangluo Anquan Fa (网络安全法) [Cybersecurity Law] (promulgated by the Standing Comm. Nat'l People's Cong., Nov. 07, 2016, effective June 1, 2017), 2016 STANDING COMM. NAT'L PEOPLE'S CONG. GAZ. 899 (China), translated in PKULaw, CLI.1.283838(EN).

120. Zuduan Waiguo Falü yu Cuoshi Budang Yuwai Shiyong Banfa (阻断外国法律与措施不当域外适用办法) [Rules on Counteracting Unjustified

Extra-territorial Application of Foreign Legislation and Other Measures] (promulgated by Ministry of Com., Jan. 9, 2021, effective Jan. 9, 2021), ST. COUNCIL GAZ., Mar. 20, 2021, at 45, translated in MOFCOM Order No. 1 of 2021 on Rules on Counteracting Unjustified Extra-territorial Application of Foreign Legislation and Other Measures, MINISTRY COM. CHINA (Jan. 9, 2021), http:// english.mofcom.gov.cn/article/policyrelease/announcement/202101/2021010 3029708.shtml (China).

121. *Id.*

122. Lester Ross, Kenneth Zhou, & Tingting Liu, China Issues Blocking Rules to Counter Foreign Sanctions and Other Measures, WILMERHALE (Jan. 12, 2021), https://www.wilmerhale.com/en/insights/client-alerts/20210121-china-issues-blocking-rules-to-counter-secondary-sanctions.

123. Council Regulation No 2271/96, 1996 O.J. (L309) 1 (EC), https://eur-lex.eur opa.eu/legal-content/EN/TXT/?uri=CELEX%3A01996R2271-20180807.

124. Ross et al., *supra* note 122.

125. Gibson Dunn, 2021 YEAR-END SANCTIONS AND EXPORT CONTROLS UPDATE 47 (2022), https://www.gibsondunn.com/wp-content/uploads/2022/02/2021-year-end-sanctions-and-export-controls-update.pdf.

126. Tom Mitchell, China Launches Measures to Protect Companies from US Sanctions, FIN. TIMES (Jan. 9, 2021), https://www.ft.com/content/33c307b7-7157-442d-90b4-f48308429d02.

127. Fan Waiguo Zhicai Fa (反外国制裁法) [Anti-foreign Sanctions Law] (promulgated by the Standing Comm. Nat'l People's Cong., June 10, 2021, effective June 10, 2021), 2021 STANDING COMM. NAT'L PEOPLE'S CONG. GAZ. 1041 (China), translated in PKULaw, CLI.1.5015159(EN).

128. China's New Anti-Foreign Sanctions Law: Understanding Its Scope and Potential Liabilities, MORRISON FOERSTER (June 30, 2021), https://www.mofo. com/resources/insights/210630-chinas-new-anti-foreign-sanctions-law.html.

129. Emily Feng, China's New Anti-Foreign Sanctions Law Sends a Chill Through the Business Community, NPR (June 11, 2021), https://www.npr.org/2021/06/ 11/1005467033/chinas-new-anti-foreign-sanctions-law-sends-a-chill-through-the-business-communi.

130. Foreign Ministry Spokesperson Announces China's Sanctions on U.S. House Speaker Nancy Pelosi, MINISTRY FOREIGN AFFS. CHINA (Aug. 5, 2022), https:// www.fmprc.gov.cn/mfa_eng/xwfw_665399/s2510_665401/202208/t202208 05_10735509.html.

131. MORRISON FOERSTER, *supra* note 128.

132. Waishang Touzi Anquan Shencha Banfa (外商投资安全审查办法) [Measures for Security Review of Foreign Investment] (promulgated by Nat'l Dev. and Reform Comm'n & Ministry of Com., Dec. 19, 2020, effective Jan. 18, 2021), ST. COUNCIL GAZ., Jan. 30, 2021, at 11 (China), translated in PKULaw, CLI.4.349133(EN).

133. *See* Ropes & Gray, COMPARING CHINA'S NEW MEASURES ON NATIONAL SECURITY REVIEW OF FOREIGN INVESTMENTS WITH THE U.S. CFIUS REVIEW PROCESS (2021), https://www.ropesgray.com/en/newsroom/alerts/2021/January/Compar ing-Chinas-New-Measures-on-National-Security-Review-of-Foreign-Investme nts-with-the.

134. The New FISR Measures—A Step Further in China's National Security Review of Foreign Investments, WHITE & CASE (Jan. 21, 2021), https://www.whitecase. com/publications/alert/new-fisr-measures-step-further-chinas-national-secur ity-review-foreign.

135. *Id.*

136. Measures for Security Review of Foreign Investment art. 12.

137. *E.g.*, Waishang Touzi Zhunru Tebie Guanli Cuoshi (Fumian Qingdan) (2021 Nian Ban) (外商投资准入特别管理措施（负面清单）（2021年版）) [Special Administrative Measures (Negative List) for the Access of Foreign Investment (2021)] (promulgated by Nat'l Dev. & Reform Comm'n & Ministry of Com., Dec. 27, 2021, effective Jan. 1, 2022), ST. COUNCIL GAZ., Mar. 20, 2022, at 48, translated in PKULaw, CLI.4.5112872(EN).

138. Wendy Wu & Catherine Wong, No Breakthrough but Some Consensus in China-US Trade Talks, Beijing Says, S. CHINA MORNING POST (May 4, 2018), https://www.scmp.com/news/china/diplomacy-defence/article/2144705/ no-breakthrough-some-consensus-china-us-trade-talks; OFF. U.S. TRADE REPRESENTATIVE, UPDATE CONCERNING CHINA'S ACTS, POLICIES AND PRACTICES RELATED TO TECHNOLOGY TRANSFER, INTELLECTUAL PROPERTY, AND INNOVATION 4, 25–26 (2018), https://ustr.gov/sites/default/files/enforcement/301Investi gations/301%20Report%20Update.pdf.

139. Tanner Brown, As China Opens Services Sector, Overseas Businesses Are Invited to Sell Anti-Censorship Tools — But Only to Other Foreign Companies, MARKET WATCH, https://www.marketwatch.com/story/as-china-opens-services- sector-overseas-businesses-are-invited-to-sell-anti-censorship-tools-but-only- to-other-foreign-companies-11600839121 (Sep. 23, 2020).

140. Foreign Investment Banned in Rare-Earth Sector, New Negative Lists Show, GLOBAL TIMES (Dec. 27, 2021), https://www.globaltimes.cn/page/202112/1243 515.shtml.

141. Casey: Stop China From Dominating Rare Earth Elements Market, BOB CASEY: U.S. SENATOR FOR PENNSYLVANIA (Mar. 15, 2011), https://www.casey.sen ate.gov/news/releases/casey-stop-china-from-dominating-rare-earth-eleme nts-market.

142. Lester Ross, Kenneth Zhou, & Tingting Liu, China's New Negative List for Foreign Direct Investment, WILMERHALE (Jan. 11, 2022), https://www.wilmerh ale.com/en/insights/client-alerts/20220111-chinas-new-negative-list-for-fore ign-direct-investment.

143. Michael Martina, Insight: Flexing Antitrust Muscle, China Is a New Merger Hurdle, REUTERS (May 2, 2013), https://www.reuters.com/article/us-mergers-regulation-china-insight/insight-flexing-antitrust-muscle-china-is-a-new-merger-hurdle-idUSBRE94116920130502.

144. *Id.*

145. Yvonne Lau, After Second Failed Blackstone Deal, Can Soho China Find a New Suitor?, FORTUNE (Sep. 13, 2021), https://fortune.com/2021/09/13/soho-china-blackstone-deal-new-buyer/.

146. *Id.*

147. Don Clark, Qualcomm Scraps $44 Billion NXP Deal After China Inaction, N.Y. TIMES (July 25, 2018), https://www.nytimes.com/2018/07/25/technology/qualcomm-nxp-china-deadline.html.

148. Applied Materials Walks Away From $3.5bn Kokusai Electric Deal, NIKKEI ASIA, https://asia.nikkei.com/Business/Business-deals/Applied-Materials-walks-away-from-3.5bn-Kokusai-Electric-deal (Mar. 30, 2021).

149. Stephenie Yang, China Clears Cisco-Acacia Deal With Conditions, WALL ST. J. (Jan. 19, 2021), https://www.wsj.com/articles/china-clears-cisco-acacia-deal-with-conditions-11611064728.

150. *Id.*

151. Coco Feng, LinkedIn Launches New App in China Without Social Feed After Shutting Main Service, S. CHINA MORNING POST (Dec. 16, 2021), https://www.scmp.com/tech/big-tech/article/3159968/linkedin-launches-new-app-china-without-social-feed-after-shutting.

152. Wang, *supra* note 105.

153. Jude Blanchette & Andrew Polk, Dual Circulation and China's New Hedged Integration Strategy, CNTR. FOR STRATEGIC INT'L STUD. (Aug. 24, 2020), https://www.csis.org/analysis/dual-circulation-and-chinas-new-hedged-integration-strategy.

154. Zhonggong Zhongyang Zhengzhiju Changwu Weiyuanhui Zhaokai Huiyi Zhonggong Zhongyang Zongshuji Xi Jinping Zhuchi Huiyi (中共中央政治局常务委员会召开会议 中共中央总书记习近平主持会议) [Standing Committee of the Political Bureau of the CPC Central Committee; General Secretary Xi Jinping Presided], Renmin Wang (人民网) [PEOPLE.CN] (May 15, 2020), http://cpc.people.com.cn/n1/2020/0515/c64094-31709627.html?mc_cid=28966ada58&mc_eid=902fe70bde (China).

155. *See, e.g.,* Zhonghua Renmin Gongheguo Guomin Jingji He Shehui Fazhan Dishisige Wunian Guihua he 2035 Nian Yuanjing Mubiao Gangyao (中华人民共和国国民经济和社会发展第十四个五年规划和 2035 年远景目标纲要) [Outline of the People's Republic of China 14th Five-Year Plan for National Economic and Social Development and Long-Range Objectives for 2035] (promulgated by Nat'l. People's Cong., Mar. 12, 2021), 2021 STANDING COMM. NAT'L PEOPLE'S CONG. GAZ. 429, 447–448 (China), translated in Ctr. for Sec.

& Emerging Tech., OUTLINE OF THE PEOPLE'S REPUBLIC OF CHINA 14TH FIVE-YEAR PLAN FOR NATIONAL ECONOMIC AND SOCIAL DEVELOPMENT AND LONG-RANGE OBJECTIVES FOR 2035 32–36 (2021), https://cset.georgetown.edu/wp-content/uploads/t0284_14th_Five_Year_Plan_EN.pdf; Gongyehua He Xinxihua Bu Guanyu Yinfa "Shisiwu" Xinxihua He Gongyehua Shendu Ronghe Fazhan Guihua de Tongzhi (工业和信息化部关于印发"十四五"信息化和工业化深度融合发展规划的通知) [Notice of the Ministry of Industry and Information Technology Issuing the "14th Five-Year" Informationization and Industrialization In-Depth Integration and Development Plan] (promulgated by the Ministry of Indus. & Info. Tech., Nov. 17, 2021), 3, https://www.miit.gov.cn/cms_files/filemanager/1226211233/attach/20226/352cb6af2a194ce0a8de07c8561d030b.pdf (China).

156. Will the Dual Circulation Strategy Enable China to Compete in a Post-Pandemic World?, CHINA POWER, https://chinapower.csis.org/china-covid-dual-circulation-economic-strategy/.

157. Wang, *supra* note 105.

158. Li Xiang, Bolder Reforms to Strengthen Nation's Market, CHINA DAILY (Mar. 1, 2022), http://global.chinadaily.com.cn/a/202203/01/WS621d5c34a310cdd39bc8963f.html.

159. Alicia García-Herrero, What Is Behind China's Dual Circulation Strategy, CHINA LEADERSHIP MONITOR, Fall 2021, at 1, 6, 12.

160. *Id.*

161. Greg Ip, China Wants Manufacturing—Not the Internet—to Lead the Economy, WALL ST. J. (Aug. 4, 2021), https://www.wsj.com/articles/china-wants-manufacturingnot-the-internetto-lead-the-economy-11628078155.

162. Wang, *supra* note 105.

163. *Id.*

164. Indermit Gill, Whoever Leads in Artificial Intelligence in 2030 Will Rule the World Until 2100, BROOKINGS (Jan. 17, 2020), https://www.brookings.edu/blog/future-development/2020/01/17/whoever-leads-in-artificial-intelligence-in-2030-will-rule-the-world-until-2100/.

165. Jacques Bughin, Jeongmin Seong, James Manyika, Michael Chui, & Raoul Joshi, Notes from the AI Frontier: Modeling the Impact of AI on the World Economy, MCKINSEY & COMPANY (Sep. 4, 2018), https://www.mckinsey.com/featured-insights/artificial-intelligence/notes-from-the-ai-frontier-modeling-the-impact-of-ai-on-the-world-economy.

166. World Bank Group, HARNESSING ARTIFICIAL INTELLIGENCE FOR DEVELOPMENT IN THE POST-COVID-19 ERA (2021), https://openknowledge.worldbank.org/handle/10986/35619.

167. PwC, SIZING THE PRIZE: WHAT'S THE REAL VALUE OF AI FOR YOUR BUSINESS AND HOW CAN YOU CAPITALISE? 3 (2017), https://www.pwc.com/gx/en/issues/data-and-analytics/publications/artificial-intelligence-study.html.

168. Xinyidai Rengong Zhineng Fazhan Guihua (新一代人工智能发展规划) [Plan for Development of the New Generation of Artificial Intelligence] (promulgated by St. Council, July 8, 2017), ST. COUNCIL GAZ., Aug. 10, 2017, at 7 (China), translated in Graham Webster et al., Full Translation: China's "New Generation Artificial Intelligence Development Plan" (2017), DIGICHINA (Aug. 1, 2017), https://www.newamerica.org/cybersecurity-initiative/digichina/blog/full-translation-chinas-new-generation-artificial-intelligence-development-plan-2017/.

169. Premier Li Promotes Future of AI as Economic Driver, ST. COUNCIL (Jul. 24, 2017), http://english.www.gov.cn/premier/news/2017/07/24/content_2814 75750043336.htm.

170. *Id.*

171. Exec. Order No. 13859, Maintaining American Leadership in Artificial Intelligence, 84 Fed. Reg. 3967 (Feb. 11, 2019).

172. Nat'l Sec. Comm'n on A.I., FINAL REPORT (2021), https://www.nscai.gov/wp-content/uploads/2021/03/Full-Report-Digital-1.pdf.

173. European Council on Foreign Rel., GEO-TECH POLITICS: WHY TECHNOLOGY SHAPES EUROPEAN POWER 2 (2021), https://ecfr.eu/wp-content/uploads/Geo-tech-politics-Why-technology-shapes-European-power.pdf.

174. Nat'l Sec. Comm'n on A.I., *supra* note 172, at 12.

175. Daitian Li, Tony W. Tong, & Yangao Xiao, Is China Emerging as the Global Leader in AI?, HARV. BUS. REV. (Feb. 18, 2021), https://hbr.org/2021/02/is-china-emerging-as-the-global-leader-in-ai.

176. Kai Fu-Lee, AI SUPERPOWERS: CHINA, SILICON VALLEY, AND THE NEW WORLD ORDER 34–68 (2018).

177. *See generally id.*

178. Plan for Development of the New Generation of Artificial Intelligence, *supra* note 168, 14–15 (China), translated in Webster et al., *supra* note 168.

179. Jake Sullivan (@JakeSullivan46), TWITTER (Mar. 9, 2021, 10:49 a.m.), https://twitter.com/jakesullivan46/status/1369314351820242947?lang=en.

180. Plan for Development of the New Generation of Artificial Intelligence, *supra* note 168, at 18 (China), translated in Webster et al., *supra* note 168.

181. *Id.* at 7.

182. Julian E. Barnes & Josh Chin, The New Arms Race in AI, WALL ST. J. (Mar. 2, 2018), https://www.wsj.com/articles/the-new-arms-race-in-ai-1520009261.

183. Nat'l Sec. Comm'n on A.I., *supra* note 172, at 9.

184. Drew Harwell, Defense Department Pledges Billions Toward Artificial Intelligence Research, WASH. POST (Sep. 7, 2018), https://www.washingtonpost.com/technology/2018/09/07/defense-department-pledges-billions-toward-artificial-intelligence-research/.

185. Jackson Barnett, Austin Commits to $1.5B for DOD's Joint AI Center Over Next 5 Years, FEDSCOOP (July 13, 2021), https://www.fedscoop.com/lloyd-austin-dod-jaic-funding/.

186. Roland Tricot, OECD, VENTURE CAPITAL INVESTMENTS IN ARTIFICIAL INTELLIGENCE: ANALYSING TRENDS IN VC IN AI COMPANIES FROM 2012 THROUGH 2020, at 5 (OECD Digit. Econ. Papers, No. 319, 2021), https://www.oecd-ilibrary.org/docserver/f97beae7-en.pdf?expires=1661891287&id=id&accname=guest&checksum=3EAE92AFA4A1228B546641C79DBCDF00.

187. Axelle Lemaire et al., Roland Berger & Asgard, HUMAN VENTURE CAPITAL, ARTIFICIAL INTELLIGENCE—A STRATEGY FOR EUROPEAN STARTUPS: RECOMMENDATIONS FOR POLICYMAKERS 7 (2018), https://www.rolandberger.com/publications/publication_pdf/roland_berger_ai_strategy_for_european_startups.pdf.

188. Zhongguo Xinxi Tongxin Yanjiuyuan Shuju Yanjiu Zhongxin (中国信息通信研究院数据研究中心) [China Acad. Info. & Commc'ns Tech. Data Rsch. Ctr.], Quanqiu Rengong Zhineng Chanye Shuju Baogao (全球人工智能产业数据报告) [GLOBAL ARTIFICIAL INTELLIGENCE INDUSTRY DATA REPORT] (2019), http://m.caict.ac.cn/sytj/201905/P020190523542892859794.pdf (China), discussed in Daitian Li, Tony W. Tong, & Yangao Xiao, Is China Emerging as the Global Leader in AI?, HARV. BUS. REV. (Feb. 18, 2021), https://hbr.org/2021/02/is-china-emerging-as-the-global-leader-in-ai.

189. Li et al., *supra* note 188 (discussing Qinghua Daxue Zhongguo Keji Zhengce Yanjiu Zhongxin (清华大学中国科技政策研究中心) [China Inst. for Sci. & Tech. Pol'y Tsinghua Univ.], Zhongguo Rengong Zhineng Fazhan Baogao (中国人工智能发展报告) [CHINA AI DEVELOPMENT REPORT] 2 (2018), Chinese version available at http://www.clii.com.cn/lhrh/hyxx/201807/P020180724021759.pdf (China).

190. Stanford Inst. for Human-Centered A.I., ARTIFICIAL INTELLIGENCE INDEX REPORT 2022 39–40 (2022), https://aiindex.stanford.edu/wp-content/uploads/2022/03/2022-AI-Index-Report_Master.pdf.

191. China Inst. for Sci. & Tech. Pol'y Tsinghua Univ., *supra* note 189, at 11, discussed in Li et al., *supra* note 188.

192. The Global AI Talent Tracker, MACRO POLO, https://macropolo.org/digital-projects/the-global-ai-talent-tracker/.

193. Cheng Ting-Fang & Lauly Li, US–China Tech War: Beijing's Secret Chipmaking Champions, Nikkei Asia (May 5, 2021), https://asia.nikkei.com/Spotlight/Most-read-in-2021/US-China-tech-war-Beijing-s-secret-chipmaking-champions.

194. Yoko Kubota, China Sets Up New $29 Billion Semiconductor Fund, WALL ST. J. (Oct. 25, 2019), www.wsj.com/articles/china-sets-up-new-29-billion-semiconductor-fund-11572034480; Yusho Cho, Eyeing US, China Wields $33bn Subsidies to Bolster Chips, Defense, NIKKEI ASIA (May 17, 2021),

asia.nikkei.com/Politics/International-relations/US-China-tensions/
Eyeing-US-China-wields-33bn-subsidies-to-bolster-chips-defense.

195. FACT SHEET: CHIPS and Science Act Will Lower Costs, Create Jobs, Strengthen Supply Chains, and Counter China, WHITE HOUSE BRIEFING ROOM (Aug. 9, 2022), https://www.whitehouse.gov/briefing-room/statements-relea ses/2022/08/09/fact-sheet-chips-and-science-act-will-lower-costs-create-jobs-strengthen-supply-chains-and-counter-china/.

196. Natalie Andrews, House Passes Chips Act to Boost U.S. Semiconductor Production, WALL ST. J. (July 28, 2022), https://www.wsj.com/articles/house-passes-chips-act-to-boost-u-s-semiconductor-production-11659035676.

197. Jiyoung Sohn, The U.S. Is Investing Big in Chips. So Is the Rest of the World, WALL ST. J. (July 31, 2022), https://www.wsj.com/articles/the-u-s-is-investing-big-in-chips-so-is-the-rest-of-the-world-11659259807.

198. *See* Laura Silver, Kat Devlin, & Christine Huang, PEW RSCH. CTR., UNFAVORABLE VIEWS OF CHINA REACH HISTORIC HIGHS IN MANY COUNTRIES (2020), https:// www.pewresearch.org/global/wp-content/uploads/sites/2/2020/10/PG_2 020.10.06_Global-Views-China_FINAL.pdf; *see also* Kaiser Kuo, How Do Chinese People View the United States?, SUPCHINA (Nov. 26, 2021), https:// supchina.com/2021/11/26/how-do-chinese-people-view-the-united-states/.

199. *See generally* Karl Aiginger & Dani Rodrik, Rebirth of Industrial Policy and an Agenda for the Twenty-First Century, 20 J. INDUS., COMPETITION & TRADE 189 (2020), https://link.springer.com/content/pdf/10.1007/s10 842-019-00322-3.pdf.

200. *See* Trump's Foreign Policy Moments, COUNCIL FOREIGN REL., https://www. cfr.org/timeline/trumps-foreign-policy-moments; Doug Palmer, Turn It up to 11: Trump's Trade Carnage Went Beyond Tariff Wars, POLITICO (Jan. 4, 2021), https://www.politico.com/news/2021/01/04/trump-trade-carnage-tariff-wars-454512; David J. Lynch, Josh Dawsey, & Damian Paletta, Trump Imposes Steel and Aluminum Tariffs on the E.U., Canada and Mexico, WASH. POST (May 31, 2018), https://www.washingtonpost.com/business/economy/ trump-imposes-steel-and-aluminum-tariffs-on-the-european-union-canada-and-mexico/2018/05/31/891bb452-64d3-11e8-a69c-b944de66d9e7_story. html; Humeyra Pamuk & Andrea Shalal, Trump Administration Pushing to Rip Global Supply Chains from China: Officials, REUTERS (May 4, 2020), https://www.reuters.com/article/us-health-coronavirus-usa-china/trump-administration-pushing-to-rip-global-supply-chains-from-china-officials-idUSKBN22G0BZ.

201. Remarks by President Biden on the American Jobs Plan, WHITE HOUSE (Mar. 31, 2021), https://www.whitehouse.gov/briefing-room/speeches-remarks/2021/ 03/31/remarks-by-president-biden-on-the-american-jobs-plan/.

202. Kori Schake, Biden Brings More Class Warfare to Foreign Policy, ATLANTIC (May 27, 2021), https://www.theatlantic.com/ideas/archive/2021/05/biden-foreign-policy-america-first-middle-class/618999/.

203. Nikki Haley, Free Enterprise, Not Central Planning, Will Beat China, WALL ST. J. OP. (Aug. 15, 2022), https://www.wsj.com/articles/central-planning-wont-beat-china-ccp-threat-america-free-markets-chips-and-science-act-beijing-legi slation-policy-11660595174.

204. Agatha Kratz & Janka Oertel, EUROPEAN COUNCIL ON FOREIGN REL, HOME ADVANTAGE: HOW CHINA'S PROTECTED MARKET THREATENS EUROPE'S ECONOMIC POWER (2021), https://ecfr.eu/wp-content/uploads/Home-advantage-How-Chi nas-protected-market-threatens-Europes-economic-power.pdf.

205. President Macron Interviewed by Le Grand Continent (12 November 2020), FR. DIPL. (Nov. 12, 2020), https://www.diplomatie.gouv.fr/en/french-foreign-policy/news/2020/article/president-macron-interviewed-by-le-grand-contin ent-12-nov-2020; EUROPEAN COUNCIL, *supra* note 7.

206. Scott Malcomson, The New Age of Autarky: Why Globalization's Biggest Winners Are Now on a Mission for Self-Sufficiency, FOREIGN AFFS. (Apr. 26, 2021), https://www.foreignaffairs.com/articles/united-states/2021-04-26/new-age-autarky.

207. Jeanne Whalen & Chris Alcantara, Nine Charts to Show Who's Winning the US–China Tech Race, WASH. POST (Sep. 21, 2021), https://www.washingtonpost.com/technology/2021/09/21/us-china-tech-competition/.

208. *Id.*

209. Graham Allison, The Thucydides Trap: Are the U.S. and China Headed for War?, ATLANTIC (Sep. 24, 2015), https://www.theatlantic.com/international/archive/2015/09/united-states-china-war-thucydides-trap/406756/.

210. *Id.*

211. *See, e.g.,* Thomas J. Shattuck, Believe Biden When He Says America Will Defend Taiwan, FOREIGN POL'Y RSCH. INST. (May 25, 2022), https://www.fpri.org/article/2022/05/believe-biden-when-he-says-america-will-defend-tai wan/; *see generally* Jessica Chen Weiss, The China Trap: U.S. Foreign Policy and the Perilous Logic of Zero-Sum Competition, FOREIGN AFFS., Sep./Oct. 2022, at 10.

212. John Lee & Jan-Peter Kleinhans, Would China Invade Taiwan for TSMC?, DIPLOMAT (Dec. 15, 2020), https://thediplomat.com/2020/12/would-china-inv ade-taiwan-for-tsmc/.

213. Henry & Carney, *supra* note 22.

214. Chen Bo (陈波), Maoyizhan Kaida Sannianduo, Meiguo Dalege Jimo (贸易战开打三年多，美国打了个"寂寞") [The Trade War Has Been Going for Three Years, but U.S. Has Gained Nothing], Zhongguo Ribao Zhongwen Wang (中国日报中文网) [CHINA DAILY CHINESE] (Oct. 19, 2021), https://cn.chinadaily.com.cn/a/202110/09/WS61619205a3107be4979f1989.html (China).

215. Thomas J. Christensen, There Will Not Be a New Cold War, FOREIGN AFFS. (Mar. 24, 2021), https://www.foreignaffairs.com/articles/united-states/2021-03-24/there-will-not-be-new-cold-war.

216. Lawrence J. Lau, ON TWIN CIRCULATIONS (试论双循环) 8 (2020), https://www.igef.cuhk.edu.hk/igef_media/people/lawrencelau/presentations/english/200912.pdf.

217. García-Herrero, *supra* note 159, at 6–7.

218. Stephen Ezel, INFO. TECH. & INNOVATION FOUND., MOORE'S LAW UNDER ATTACK: THE IMPACT OF CHINA'S POLICIES ON GLOBAL SEMICONDUCTOR INNOVATION 12 (2021), https://itif.org/publications/2021/02/18/moores-law-under-attack-impact-chinas-policies-global-semiconductor.

219. IC Insights, SALES OF LOGIC ICS ACCOUNT FOR LARGEST SHARE OF CHINA'S IC MARKET IN 2020 (2021), https://www.icinsights.com/data/articles/documents/1347.pdf, discussed in García-Herrero, *supra* note 159, 6–7.

220. H.R. 4346, 117th Cong. (2022). *See also* Tobias Mann, The CHIPS Act Won't End US Reliance on Foreign Foundries, REGISTER (Aug. 18, 2022), https://www.theregister.com/2022/08/18/chips_act_made_usa/.

221. Ana Swanson & Cecilia Kang, Trump's China Deal Creates Collateral Damage for Tech Firms, N.Y. TIMES (Jan. 20, 2020), https://www.nytimes.com/2020/01/20/business/economy/trump-us-china-deal-micron-trade-war.html.

222. The Debate Over Export Controls on Semiconductor Manufacturing Equipment to China, SEMI-LITERATE (Dec. 7, 2020), https://semiliterate.substack.com/p/the-debate-over-export-controls-on?s=r.

223. Cadence Designs System, Inc., COMMENTS OF CADENCE DESIGN SYSTEMS, INC. ADVANCE NOTICE OF PROPOSED RULEMAKING REGARDING REVIEW OF CONTROLS FOR CERTAIN FOUNDATIONAL TECHNOLOGIES 8–22 (2020), https://www.regulations.gov/document/BIS-2020-0029-0032.

224. Intel Corporation, INTEL CORPORATION RESPONSE TO THE NOTICE OF PROPOSED RULEMAKING SEEKING PUBLIC COMMENT ON THE DEFINITION OF AND CRITERIA FOR IDENTIFYING FOUNDATIONAL TECHNOLOGIES 8 (2020), https://www.regulations.gov/comment/BIS-2020-0029-0061.

225. SIA Statement on Export Control Rule Changes, SEMICONDUCTOR INDUSTRY ASSOCIATION (Aug. 17, 2020), https://www.semiconductors.org/sia-statement-on-export-control-rule-changes-2/.

226. Kathrin Hille, Huawei Woes Hide "Toothless" US Export Controls Against Chinese Tech, FIN. TIMES (Aug. 18, 2021), https://www.ft.com/content/2f5fc6c9-ca2b-496c-9783-b47bf060769d.

227. *Id.*

228. *Id.*

229. Weiss, *supra* note 211.

230. *Id.*

231. *Id.*

CHAPTER 6

1. In re A Warrant to Search a Certain E-Mail Account Controlled & Maintained by Microsoft Corp., 15 F. Supp. 3d 466, 467–468. (S.D.N.Y. 2014); *see also* Robert Barnes, Supreme Court to Consider Major Digital Privacy Case on Microsoft Email Storage, WASH. POST (Oct. 16, 2017), https://www.washingtonpost.com/polit ics/courts_law/supreme-court-to-consider-major-digital-privacy-case-on-micros oft-email-storage/2017/10/16/b1e74936-b278-11e7-be94-fabb0fie9ffb_story.html.

2. In re Warrant to Search a Certain Email Account Controlled & Maintained by Microsoft Corp., 128 HARV. L. REV. 1019, 1019 (2015).

3. Cyrus Farivar, Microsoft Wins: Court Rules Feds Can't Use SCA to Nab Overseas Data, ARS TECHNICA (July 14, 2016), https://arstechnica.com/tech-policy/2016/ 07/microsoft-wins-court-rules-feds-cant-use-sca-to-nab-overseas-data/.

4. Petition for Writ of Certiorari at 12–13, *US v. Microsoft*, 138 S.Ct. 1186 (2017) (No. 12-7).

5. US v. Microsoft, 138 S. Ct. 1186, 1188 (2018).

6. H.R. 4943, 115th Cong. (2018).

7. William Schwartz, Andrew Goldstein, & Daniel Grooms, The New Data Wars: How the CLOUD Act Is Likely To Trigger Legal Challenges, N.Y. L. J. (Mar. 31, 2020), https://cdp.cooley.com/wp-content/uploads/2020/04/NYLJo 3302020444632Cooley.pdf.

8. Hearing on Law Enforcement Access to Data Stored Across Borders: Facilitating Cooperation and Protecting Rights Before the S. Judiciary Comm. Subcomm. on Crime and Terrorism, 115th Cong. 2, 8 (2017 (statement of Brad Smith, CEO, Microsoft Corp.).

9. Eugenia Lostri, The CLOUD Act, CSIS (Oct. 2, 2020), https://www.csis.org/ blogs/technology-policy-blog/cloud-act.

10. Proposal for a Regulation of the European Parliament and of the Council on European Production and Preservation Orders for Electronic Evidence in Criminal Matters, COM (2018) 225 (final) (Apr. 4, 2018); Kenneth Propp, Has the Time for an EU-U.S. Agreement on E-Evidence Come and Gone?, LAWFARE (June 2, 2022), https://www.lawfareblog.com/has-time-eu-us-agreement-e-evidence-come-and-gone.

11. European Data Protection Board and European Data Protection Supervisor, Initial Legal Assessment of the Impact of the US CLOUD Act on the EU Legal Framework for the Protection of Personal Data and the Negotiations of an EU-US Agreement on Cross-Border Access to Electronic Evidence at 3 (July 10, 2019), https://edps.europa.eu/sites/default/files/publication/19-07-10_edpb_ edps_cloudact_annex_en.pdf, at 3–4.

12. Charlene Barshefsky, EU Digital Protectionism Risks Damaging Ties With the US, FIN. TIMES (Aug. 2, 2020), https://www.ft.com/content/9edea4f5-5f34-4e17-89cd-f9b9ba698103.

13. *Id.*

14. Henry Farrell & Abraham Newman, The Transatlantic Data War, FOREIGN AFF. MAG. (Jan./Feb. 2016), https://www.foreignaffairs.com/articles/united-states/ 2015-12-14/transatlantic-data-war.

15. Wilbur Ross, EU Data Privacy Laws Are Likely to Create Barriers to Trade, FIN. TIMES (May 30, 2018), https://www.ft.com/content/9d261f44-6255-11e8-bdd1- cc0534df682c.

16. Daniel Lyons, GDPR: Privacy as Europe's Tariff by Other Means?, AM. ENTER. INST.: AEIDEAS (July 3, 2018), https://www.aei.org/technology-and-innovation/ gdpr-privacy-as-europes-tariff-by-other-means/.

17. Ashley Rodriguez, Google Says it Spent "Hundreds of Years of Human Time" Complying with Europe's Privacy Rules, QUARTZ (Sep. 26, 2018), https:// qz.com/1403080/google-spent-hundreds-of-years-of-human-time-complying- with-gdpr/.

18. *See* Uniting and Strengthening America by Providing Appropriate Tools Required to Intercept and Obstruct Terrorism (USA PATRIOT) Act of 2001, Pub. L. No. 107-56, § 223, 115 Stat. 272, 293 (2001); *see also* 18 U.S.C. §§ 2520(f), 2707(d), 2712(c) (2006).

19. *See generally* Uniting and Strengthening American by Fulfilling Rights and Ensuring Effective Discipline Over Monitor (USA FREEDOM) Act of 2015, Pub. L. No. 114-23, 129 Stat. 268; Presidential Policy Directive—Signals Intelligence Activities, Policy Directive/PPD-28, The White House Archives (Jan. 17, 2014), https://obamawhitehouse.archives.gov/the-press-office/2014/01/17/president ial-policy-directive-signals-intelligence-activities.

20. *See, e.g.,* Fed. Bureau of Investigation v. Fazaga, 142 S. Ct. 1051 (2022).

21. *See* Joined Cases C-293/12 & C-594/12, Digital Rights Ireland Ltd v. Minister for Communications, 2014 E.C.R. I-238.

22. *Id.* at §56.

23. Case C-623/17, Privacy International v. Secretary of State for Foreign and Commonwealth Affairs, (2020) E.C.R. 970; Joined Cases C-511/18, C-512/18 & C-520/18, La Quadrature du Net and Others v. Premier Ministre, (2020) E.C.R. 791.

24. Joined Cases C-511/18, C-512/18 & C-520/18, La Quadrature du Net and Others v. Premier Ministre, (2020) E.C.R. 791 at ¶ 137.

25. *Id.* at ¶¶ 138, 168.

26. *See* Peter Swire, "Schrems II" Backs the European Legal Regime Into a Corner— How Can It Get Out?, INT'L ASS. OF PRIVACY PROFESSIONALS (July 16, 2020), https://iapp.org/news/a/schrems-ii-backs-the-european-legal-regime-into-a-cor ner-how-can-it-get-out/.

27. *See* Loi 2015-912 du 24 juillet 2015 relative au renseignement [French Intelligence Act of 24 July 2015], JOURNAL OFFICIEL DE LA RÉPUBLIQUE FRANCAISE [J.O.] [OFFICIAL GAZETTE OF FRANCE], July 26, 2015, No. 0171; Theodore Christakis & Kenneth Propp, How Europe's Intelligence Services Aim to Avoid the EU's

Highest Court—and What It Means for the United States, LAWFARE (Mar. 8, 2021), https://www.lawfareblog.com/how-europes-intelligence-services-aim-avoid-eus-highest-court-and-what-it-means-united-states.

28. Michael Holden, Attorney General Lynch Chides European Decisions to Restrict Data Sharing, REUTERS (Dec. 9, 2015), https://www.reuters.com/article/us-usa-security-europe-idUSKBN0TS0UV20151209#jhyFZ4HCXWVwi27q.97.

29. Nicholas Vinocur, Why Trump's Administration Is Going After the GDPR, POLITICO (June 29, 2020), https://www.politico.com/news/2020/06/29/trump-administration-gdpr-345254.

30. EUROPEAN COMM'N, FEEDBACK FROM: CROWDSTRIKE (2020), https://ec.europa.eu/info/law/better-regulation/have-your-say/initiatives/12322-Data-protection-report-on-the-General-Data-Protection-Regulation/details/F514249_en.

31. See Jennifer Daskal, What Comes Next: The Aftermath of European Court's Blow to Transatlantic Data Transfers, JUST SEC. (July 17, 2020), https://www.justsecurity.org/71485/what-comes-next-the-aftermath-of-european-courts-blow-to-transatlantic-data-transfers/.

32. Regulation 2016/ 679 of the European Parliament and of the Council on the Protection of Natural Persons with regard to the Processing of Personal Data and on the Free Movement of Such Data, and Repealing Directive 95/ 46/ EC, 2016 O.J., (L 119) 1 [hereinafter GDPR].

33. James Sullivan, The EU-U.S. and Swiss–U.S. Privacy Shield Frameworks: Why They Matter, INT'L TRADE ADMIN.: TRADEOLOGY (Sep. 13, 2019), https://blog.trade.gov/2019/09/13/the-eu-u-s-and-swiss-u-s-privacy-shield-frameworks-why-they-matter/.

34. See Marcin Szczepański, EUR. PARLIAMENTARY RESEARCH SERV., EU-US TRADE AND TECHNOLOGY COUNCIL NEW FORUM FOR TRANSATLANTIC COOPERATION (Sep. 2021), at 3, https://www.europarl.europa.eu/RegData/etudes/BRIE/2021/698037/EPRS_BRI(2021)698037_EN.pdf; see Adam Conner-Simmons, U.S., EU Leaders Talk Web Policy and World Economy at MIT, MIT NEWS (Mar. 11, 2016), https://news.mit.edu/2016/us-eu-leaders-web-policy-world-economy-0311.

35. See Comm'n Decision (2000/520/EC) of 26 July 2000 Pursuant to Directive 95/46/EC of the European Parliament and of the Council on the Adequacy of the Protection Provided by the Safe Harbour Privacy Principles and Related Frequently Asked Questions Issued by the U.S. Dep't of Commerce, 2000 O.J. (L 215), 7.

36. See U.S.-EU Safe Harbor List, U.S. DEP'T. OF COM., https://www.export.gov/safeharbor_eu; Steve Schmidt, Customer Update—AWS and EU Safe Harbor, AWS SECURITY BLOG (Oct. 9, 2015), https://aws.amazon.com/blogs/security/customer-update-aws-and-eu-safe-harbor/; Lucinda Southern, What the EU's Safe Harbor Verdict Means for Platforms, Brands—and You, DIGIDAY (Oct. 7, 2015), https://digiday.com/media/eus-safe-harbor-verdict-means-platforms-brands/.

37. *See* Case C- 362/ 14, Maximillian Schrems v. Data Prot. Comm'r, 2015 E.C.R. 650 [hereinafter Schrems I].

38. *Id*. at ¶73 (emphasis added).

39. *See* Hannah Kuchler, Max Schrems: The Man Who Took on Facebook—and Won, FIN. TIMES (Apr. 5, 2018), https://www.ft.com/content/86d1ce50-3799-11e8-8eee-e06bde01c544.

40. *See* Schrems v. Data Protection Comm'r [2014] IEHC 310 (H.Ct.) (Ir.).

41. Schrems I, *supra* note 37.

42. Comm'n Implementing Decision (EU) 2016/1250 of 12 July 2016 Pursuant to Directive 95/46/EC of the European Parliament and of the Council on the Adequacy of the Protection Provided by the EU-U.S. Privacy Shield (notified under document C(2016) 4176), 2016 O.J. (L 207), 1.

43. *See* Privacy Shield Framework List of Companies, U.S. DEPT. OF COM., https://www.privacyshield.gov/list.

44. *See* European Commission Press Release IP/16/2461, European Commission Launches EU-U.S. Privacy Shield: Stronger Protection for Transatlantic Data Flows (July 12, 2016), https://ec.europa.eu/commission/presscorner/detail/en/IP_16_2461.

45. *See* Judicial Redress Act of 2015 § 2, Pub. L. No. 114-126, 130 Stat. 282, 3493–3494 (2016).

46. *See* EUR. DATA PROT. BOARD: EU–U.S. PRIVACY SHIELD—SECOND ANNUAL JOINT REVIEW (Jan. 22, 2019), https://edpb.europa.eu/sites/edpb/files/files/file1/20190122edpb_2ndprivacyshieldreviewreport_final_en.pdf; *see also* Resolution on the Adequacy of the Protection Afforded by the EU-US Privacy Shield, EUR. PARL. DOC. RSP 2645 (2018), http://www.europarl.europa.eu/sides/getDoc.do?type=MOTION&reference=B8-2018-0305&language=EN; Barney Thompson & Mehreen Khan, Brussels Losing Patience with US Over Data-Sharing Agreement, FIN. TIMES (Sep. 18, 2017), https://www.ft.com/content/ed13ad0a-9bb8-11e7-8cd4-932067fbf946.

47. *See generally* Case C-311/18, Data Prot. Comm'r v. Facebook Ireland Ltd. and Schrems, 2020 E.C.R. 559.

48. *Id*. at, ¶180–182.

49. *Id*. at ¶183.

50. *Id*. at ¶¶ 64–65, 178–180.

51. *See id*. at ¶109.

52. *See* Meta Platforms, Annual Report (Form 10-K) (Feb. 2, 2022), https://d18rnop25nwr6d.cloudfront.net/CIK-0001326801/14039b47-2e2f-4054-9dc5-71bcc7cf01ce.pdf.

53. Markus Reinisch, Meta Is Absolutely Not Threatening to Leave Europe, META NEWSROOM (Feb. 8, 2022), https://about.fb.com/news/2022/02/meta-is-absolutely-not-threatening-to-leave-europe/.

54. Vincent Manancourt, EU's Rejection of US Surveillance Also Tests Its Commitment to Privacy, POLITICO (July 17, 2020), https://www.politico.eu/article/rejection-of-us-surveillance-tests-eu-mettle-on-privacy-shield/.

55. *See* Greg Nojeim, Schrems II and the Need for Intelligence Surveillance Reform, CTR. FOR DEMOCRACY & TECH. (Jan. 13, 2021), https://cdt.org/insights/schrems-ii-and-the-need-for-intelligence-surveillance-reform/.

56. *See* Chris D. Linebaugh & Edward C. Liu, CONG. RESEARCH SERV., EU DATA TRANSFER REQUIREMENTS AND U.S. INTELLIGENCE LAWS: UNDERSTANDING SCHREMS II AND ITS IMPACT ON THE EU-U.S. PRIVACY SHIELD 12–13 (2021), https://crsreports.congress.gov/product/pdf/R/R46724.

57. *See* Henry Farrell & Abraham L. Newman, Schrems II Offers an Opportunity— If the U.S. Wants to Take It, LAWFARE (July 28, 2020), https://www.lawfareblog.com/schrems-ii-offers-opportunity-if-us-wants-take-it.

58. *See* Joshua P. Meltzer, Why Schrems II Requires US–EU Agreement on Surveillance and Privacy, BROOKINGS INST.: TECH STREAM (Dec. 8, 2020), https://www.brookings.edu/techstream/why-schrems-ii-requires-us-eu-agreement-on-surveillance-and-privacy/.

59. Press Release, Republican Energy & Commerce Comm., Walden, Rodgers Statement on EU-U.S. Privacy Shield Ruling (July 16, 2020), https://republicans-energycommerce.house.gov/news/press-release/walden-rodgers-statement-on-eu-u-s-privacy-shield-ruling/.

60. *See* U.S. PRIVACY & CIVIL LIBERTIES OVERSIGHT BD., STATEMENT BY CHAIRMAN ADAM KLEIN ON THE TERRORIST FINANCE TRAFFICKING PROGRAM (2020), https://documents.pclob.gov/prod/Documents/EventsAndPress/b8ce341a-71d5-4cdd-a101-219454bfa459/TFTP%20Chairman%20Statement%2011_19_20.pdf.

61. Stewart Baker, How Can the U.S. Respond to Schrems II, LAWFARE (July 21, 2020), https://www.lawfareblog.com/how-can-us-respond-schrems-ii.

62. *See* Swire, *supra* note 26.

63. *See* Daskal, *supra* note 31.

64. *See* Berlin Commissioner Issues Statement on Schrems II Case, Asks Controllers to Stop Data Transfers to the US, ONETRUST DATA GUIDANCE (July 17, 2020), https://www.dataguidance.com/news/berlin-berlin-commissioner-issues-statement-schrems-ii-case-asks-controllers-stop-data.

65. Mark Scott, What's Driving Europe's New Aggressive Stance on Tech, POLITICO (Oct. 27, 2019), https://www.politico.eu/article/europe-digital-technological-sovereignty-facebook-google-amazon-ursula-von-der-leyen/.

66. Anupam Chander, Is Data Localization a Solution for Schrems II?, 23 J. OF INT'L ECON. L. 771, 772 (2020), https://academic.oup.com/jiel/article-abstract/23/3/771/5909035?redirectedFrom=fulltext.

67. *See generally id.*

68. Eur. External Action Serv., SUBMISSION ON DRAFT PERSONAL DATA PROTECTION BILL OF INDIA 2018 BY THE DIRECTORATE-GENERAL FOR JUSTICE & CONSUMERS TO THE

MINISTRY OF ELECTRONICS AND INFORMATION TECHNOLOGY (2018), https://eeas. europa.eu/delegations/india/53963/.

69. *See* U.S. Mission to the Eur. Union, U.S. SECRETARY OF COMMERCE WILBUR ROSS STATEMENT ON SCHREMS II RULING AND THE IMPORTANCE OF EU-U.S. DATA FLOWS (2020), https://useu.usmission.gov/u-s-secretary-of-commerce-wilbur-ross-statement-on-schrems-ii-ruling-and-the-importance-of-eu-u-s-data-flows/ ; *see* European Commission Statement/20/1366, Opening Remarks by Vice-President Jourová and Commissioner Reynders at the Press Point Following the Judgment in Case C-311/18 Facebook Ireland and Schrems (July 16, 2020), https://ec.europa.eu/commission/presscorner/detail/en/statement_20_1366.

70. *See* Daniel Michaels & Sam Schechner, U.S., EU Reach Preliminary Deal on Data Privacy, WALL ST. J. (Mar. 25, 2022), https://www.wsj.com/articles/u-s-eu-reach-preliminary-deal-on-data-privacy-11648200085.

71. Exec. Order No. 14,086, 87 Fed. Reg. 62,283 (Oct. 14, 2022).

72. FACT SHEET: President Biden Signs Executive Order to Implement the European Union–U.S. Data Privacy Framework, WHITE HOUSE BRIEFING ROOM (Oct. 7, 2022), https://www.whitehouse.gov/briefing-room/statements-relea ses/2022/10/07/fact-sheet-president-biden-signs-executive-order-to-implem ent-the-european-union-u-s-data-privacy-framework/. [hereinafter *EU-US Data Privacy Framework Executive Order*]

73. F. Paul Pittman and Shira Shamir, Biden Executive Order Seeks to Solidify European Union–U.S. Data Privacy Framework, WHITE & CASE (Oct. 19, 2022), https://www.whitecase.com/insight-alert/biden-executive-order-seeks-solidify-european-union-us-data-privacy-framework.

74. *EU-US Data Privacy Framework Executive Order, supra* note 72.

75. *Id.*

76. Pittman & Shamir, *supra* note 73.

77. Questions & Answers: EU-U.S. Data Privacy Framework, EUROPEAN COMM'N PRESS CORNER (Oct. 7, 2022), https://ec.europa.eu/commission/presscorner/det ail/en/QANDA_22_6045.

78. New US Executive Order Unlikely to Satisfy EU Law, NOYB (Oct. 7, 2022), https://noyb.eu/en/new-us-executive-order-unlikely-satisfy-eu-law.

79. *Id.*

80. *Id.*

81. *See* Fed. Bureau of Investigation v. Fazaga, 142 S. Ct. 1051 (2022).

82. Patrick Toomey & Ashley Gorski, The Supreme Court Just Made a US–EU Privacy Shield Agreement Even Harder, THE HILL (Mar. 21, 2022), https://theh ill.com/opinion/judiciary/598899-the-supreme-court-just-made-a-us-eu-priv acy-shield-agreement-even-harder?rl=1

83. To Make Real Progress, ACLU Calls on Congress to Enact Meaningful Surveillance Reform, ACLU (Oct. 7, 2022), https://www.aclu.org/press-releases/ new-biden-executive-order-eu-us-data-transfers-fails-adequately-protect-privacy.

84. *Id.*

85. Federica Laricchia, Apple: Net Sales in Europe 2011–2021, STATISTA (Feb. 1, 2022), https://www.statista.com/statistics/349086/apple-net-sales-in-europe/.

86. European Commission Press Release, State Aid: Ireland Gave Illegal Tax Benefits to Apple Worth Up to €13 Billion (Aug. 30, 2016), https://ec.europa.eu/commission/presscorner/detail/en/IP_16_2923.

87. Reuven Avi-Yonah, Young Ran (Christine) Kim, & Karen Sam, A New Framework for Digital Taxation, 63 HARV. INT'L L. J. 279 (2022), at 297 .

88. Ruth Mason, The Transformation of International Tax Law, 114 AM. J. OF INT'L TAX 353, 358 (2020).

89. Edward D. Kleinbard, Stateless Income, 9 FLA. TAX REV. 699 (2011).

90. *See* Lillian Faulhaber, Taxing Tech: The Future of Digital Taxation, 39.2 VA. TAX REV. 145, 164–165 (2019).

91. Mason, *supra* note 88.

92. Avi-Yonah et al., *supra* note 87 at 287.

93. *Commission Proposal for a Directive Laying Down Rules Relating to the Corporate Taxation of Significant Digital Presence*, COM (2018) 147 final (Mar. 21, 2018), https://ec.europa.eu/taxation_customs/system/files/2018-03/proposal_significant_digital_presence_21032018_en.pdf; https://ec.europa.eu/taxation_customs/system/files/2018-03/proposal_common_system_digital_services_tax_21032018_en.pdf.

94. Foo Yun Chee, EU's Planned Digital Levy to Cover Hundreds of Firms, Vestager Says, REUTERS (July 2, 2021), https://www.reuters.com/business/exclusive-eus-planned-digital-levy-cover-hundreds-firms-vestager-says-2021-07-02/.

95. *See* Alan Rappeport, E.U. Delays Digital Levy as Tax Talks Proceed, N.Y. TIMES (July 12, 2021), https://www.nytimes.com/2021/07/12/us/politics/eu-digital-tax.html.

96. *See id.*

97. Gary Clyde Hufbauer & Zhiyao (Lucy) Lu, The European Union's Proposed Digital Services Tax: A De Facto Tariff 3 (Peterson Inst. for Int'l Econ., Policy Brief No. 18-15, 2018).

98. *See, e.g.*, Amanda Parsons, Tax's Digital Labor Dilemma, 71 DUKE L. J. 1781 (2022); Wei Cui, The Digital Services Tax: A Conceptual Defense, 73 TAX L. REV. 69 (2019); Avi-Yonah et al., *supra* note 87 at 301, 332.

99. Hufbauer & Lu, *supra* note 97.

100. Alan Rappeport, Milan Schreuer, Jim Tankersley, & Natasha Singer., Europe's Planned Digital Tax Heightens Tensions With U.S., N.Y. TIMES (Mar. 19, 2018), https://www.nytimes.com/2018/03/19/us/politics/europe-digital-tax-trade.html.

101. Nigel Cory, The Ten Worst Digital Protectionism and Innovation Mercantilist Policies of 2018 (Info. Tech. & Innovation Found., January 2019), at 11, https://www2.itif.org/2019-worst-mercantilist-policies.pdf.

102. *See id.*

103. Donald J. Trump (@realDonaldTrump), TWITTER (July 26, 2019), https://twit ter.com/realDonaldTrump/status/1154791664625606657.

104. Notices, 84 Fed. Reg. 34042 (July 16, 2019), https://ustr.gov/sites/default/files/ enforcement/301Investigations/Initiation_of_Section_301_Investigation.pdf.

105. AMBASSADOR ROBERT E. LIGHTHIZER, OFFICE OF THE U.S. TRADE REPRESENTATIVE, REPORT ON FRANCE'S DIGITAL SERVICES TAX 1 (2019), https://ustr.gov/sites/defa ult/files/Report_On_France%27s_Digital_Services_Tax.pdf.

106. *See* Andrea Shalal, U.S. Suspends French Tariffs Over Digital Services Tax, REUTERS (Jan. 7, 2021), https://www.reuters.com/article/us-usa-trade-france/ u-s-suspends-french-tariffs-over-digital-services-tax-idUSKBN29C2KQ.

107. Press Release, Office of the U.S. Trade Representative, USTR Initiates Section 301 Investigations of Digital Services Taxes (June 2, 2020), https://ustr.gov/ about-us/policy-offices/press-office/press-releases/2020/june/ustr-initiates-section-301-investigations-digital-services-taxes.

108. *See* David Lawder, USTR Says Austria, Spain, UK Digital Taxes Discriminate Against U.S. Firms, REUTERS (Jan. 14, 2021), https://www.reuters.com/article/ us-usa-trade-digital-tax/ustr-says-austria-spain-uk-digital-taxes-discriminate-against-u-s-firms-idUSKBN29J2AZ.

109. *See* OFFICE OF THE U.S. TRADE REPRESENTATIVE, REPORT ON ITALY'S DIGITAL SERVICES TAX i–ii (2021), https://ustr.gov/sites/default/files/enforcement/ 301Investigations/Report%20on%20Italy%E2%80%99s%20Digital%20S ervices%20Tax.pdf.

110. *Id.*

111. *See* Press Release, Office of the U.S. Trade Representative, USTR Announces, and Immediately Suspends, Tariffs in Section 301 Digital Services Taxes Investigations (June 2, 2020), https://ustr.gov/about-us/policy-offices/press-office/press-releases/2021/june/ustr-announces-and-immediately-suspends-tariffs-section-301-digital-services-taxes-investigations.

112. Ruth Mason & Leopoldo Parada, Digital Battlefront in the Tax Wars 1184–1186 (Virginia L. & Econ., Research Paper No. 2018-16, 2018).

113. Avi-Yonah et al., *supra* note 87 at 240.

114. *Id.* at 37.

115. *See* Shalal, *supra* note 106.

116. *See* Zach Meyers, The US Proposals on Digital Services Taxes and Minimum Tax Rates: How the EU Should Respond, CTR. FOR EUR. REFORM (Apr. 15, 2021), https://www.cer.eu/insights/us-proposals-digital-services-taxes-and-mini mum-tax-rates-how-eu-should-respond.

117. *See* U.S. Treasury Secretary Sends Letter to OECD Secretary-General on Work to Address the Tax Challenges of the Digitalization of the Economy, ORBITAX (Dec. 5, 2019), https://www.orbitax.com/news/archive.php/U.S.-Treasury-Secretary-Sends--40283.

118. Laura Davidson, Digital Tax Talks May Result in Trade War Even If Democrats Win, BLOOMBERG LAW (Feb. 27, 2020), https://www.bloomberglaw.com/bloom berglawnews/daily-tax-report/X358INE0000000?bna_news_filter=daily-tax-report#jcite.

119. Mason, *supra* note 88.

120. James Politi & Aime Williams, US Political Battlelines Form on Biden Global Tax Plan, FIN. TIMES (April 10, 2021), https://www.ft.com/content/84f0a9f2-2c1e-42e3-a8ee-82e64ba9c6c3.

121. Richard Partington, Biden's Plans Are "Once in a Lifetime" Chance to End Global Tax Abuse, Says OECD Boss, THE GUARDIAN (Apr. 29, 2021), https://www.theguardian.com/business/2021/apr/29/bidens-plans-are-once-in-a-lifet ime-chance-to-end-global-tax-abuse-says-oecd-boss.

122. Andrea Shalal, Michael Nienaber, & Leigh Thomas, U.S. Drops "Safe Harbor" Demand, Raising Hopes for Global Tax Deal, REUTERS (Feb. 26, 2021), https://www.reuters.com/article/us-g20-usa-oecd/u-s-drops-safe-harbor-demand-rais ing-hopes-for-global-tax-deal-idUSKBN2AQ2E6.

123. Org. of Econ. Dev., INTERNATIONAL COMMUNITY STRIKES A GROUND-BREAKING TAX DEAL FOR THE DIGITAL AGE (2021), https://www.oecd.org/tax/international-community-strikes-a-ground-breaking-tax-deal-for-the-digital-age.htm.

124. The agreement specifies that 25% of residual profit (defined as profit in excess of 10% of revenue) will be allocated to market jurisdiction. *See Two-Pillar Solution to Address the Tax Challenges Arising From the Digitalisation of the Economy* (Org. of Econ. Dev., OECD/G20 Base Erosion and Profit Shifting Project, Oct. 2021), at 6, https://www.oecd.org/tax/beps/brochure-two-pillar-solution-to-address-the-tax-challenges-arising-from-the-digitalisation-of-the-economy-october-2021.pdf.

125. The rules apply to multinational enterprises with global sales exceeding EUR 20 billion and a profit margin above 10 percent. The financial services firms and firms in extractive industries are excluded.

126. The global minimum tax applies to all MNEs with annual revenue over 750 million euros. *See Two-Pillar Solution to Address the Tax Challenges Arising from the Digitalisation of the Economy, supra* note 124 at 4.

127. *See* U.S. Reaches Agreement to end European Digital Services Taxes, DEUTSCHE WELLE (Oct. 22, 2021), https://www.dw.com/en/us-reaches-agreement-to-end-european-digital-services-taxes/a-59584827.

128. Alan Rappeport, U.S. Agrees to Drop Tariffs on Countries That Imposed Digital Services Taxes as a Global Tax Overhaul Moves Ahead, N.Y. TIMES (Nov. 1, 2021), https://www.nytimes.com/2021/10/21/business/global-tax-agreem ent-digital-services.html.

129. *See* Davidson, *supra* note 118; Teaganne Finn, Manchin Says Build Back Better in Its Current Form Is "Dead," Leaves Door Open to New Talks, NBC NEWS

(Feb. 1, 2022), https://www.nbcnews.com/politics/congress/manchin-says-build-back-better-its-current-form-dead-leaves-n1288359.

130. *See* Sam Fleming & Mary McDougall, EU to Revive Digital Levy Plan if Global Tax Deal Fails, Warns Minister, FIN. TIMES (Nov. 8, 2022), https://www.ft.com/content/7eabcd39-ef14-43f3-addb-4fd07bde8af7.

131. *See* European Commission Press Release IP/22/1703, Antitrust: Commission Opens Investigation Into Possible Anticompetitive Conduct by Google and Meta, in Online Display Advertising (Mar. 11, 2022), https://ec.europa.eu/commission/presscorner/detail/en/ip_22_1703.

132. *See* European Commission Press Release IP/21/2061, Antitrust: Commission Sends Statement of Objections to Apple on App Store Rules for Music Streaming Providers (Apr. 30, 2021), https://ec.europa.eu/commission/presscorner/detail/en/speech_21_2093.

133. *See* European Commission Press Release IP/21/2848, Commission Opens Investigation Into Possible Anticompetitive Conduct of Facebook (June 4, 2021), https://ec.europa.eu/commission/presscorner/detail/en/IP_21_2848.

134. *See* Press Release, Antitrust: Commission accepts commitments by Amazon barring it from using marketplace seller data, and ensuring equal access to Buy Box and Prime, Eur. Comm'n (Dec. 20, 2022), https://ec.europa.eu/commission/presscorner/detail/en/ip_22_7777.

135. *Big Tech Competition Probes*, THE INFORMATION, https://www.theinformation.com/big-tech-probe.

136. *See* European Commission Press Release IP/19/1770, Antitrust: Commission Fines Google €1.49 Billion for Abusive Practices in Online Advertising (Mar. 20, 2019), http://europa.eu/rapid/press-release_IP-19-1770_en.htm; Google lost its appeal against the Commission decision; however, the fine did get reduced to $4.13 billion. *See* Case T-604/18, Google & Alphabet v. Comm'n, 2018 O.J., (C 445) 21.

137. *See* European Commission Press Release IP/18/4581, Antitrust: Commission Fines Google €4.34 Billion for Illegal Practices Regarding Android Mobile Devices to Strengthen Dominance of Google's Search Engine (July 18, 2018), http://europa.eu/rapid/press-release_IP-18-4581_en.htm]. Google appealed the case before the European Courts, but lost the appeal before the General Court. *See* Case T-612/17, Google & Alphabet v. Comm'n, 2017 O.J. (C 369) 37.

138. Comm'n Decision in Case No. AT.39740 (Google Search—Shopping), C(2017) 4444 final (June 27, 2017) *cited in* 2018 O.J. (C 9) 11, http://ec.europa.eu/competition/antitrust/cases/dec_docs/39740/39740_14996_3.pdf. Google has appealed the case before the European Courts. *See* Case T-612/17, Google & Alphabet v. Comm'n, 2017 O.J. (C 369) 37.

139. In 2018, the Commission fined Qualcomm $1.2 billion for its exclusive dealing contracts with Apple on the computer chips market. *See* Summary of Comm'n

Decision in Case No. AT.40220 (Qualcomm—Exclusivity Payments), 2018 O.J. (C 295) 25 (No public version of the full Decision available as of April 13, 2019).

140. *See* Commission Decision in Case No. COMP/C-3/37.990 (Intel), D(2009) 3726 final (May 13, 2009) *cited in* 2009 O.J. (C 227) 13. In September 2017, the European Court of Justice overturned the fine levied by the Commission in its decision. *See* Case C-413/14 P, Intel v. Comm'n, Judgment of September 6, 2017 (Grand Chamber), https://eur-lex.europa.eu/legal-content/EN/TXT/PDF/?uri=CELEX:62014CJ0413.

141. *See* Commission Decision in Case No. COMP/C-3/37.792 (Microsoft), C(2004) 900 final (Mar. 24, 2004), *cited in* 2007 O.J. (L 32) 23.

142. *See* Commission Decision in Case No. COMP/M.2220 (General Electric/Honeywell), 2004 O.J. (L 48) 1.

143. *See* Press Release, Italian Competition Authority, Amazon Fined Over 1,128 Billion for Abusing Its Dominant Position (Dec. 9, 2021), https://en.agcm.it/en/media/press-releases/2021/12/A528.

144. *See* Commission Decision in Case No. SA.38373 (Ireland/Apple State Aid), 2017 O.J. (L 187) 1.

145. *Id.*

146. Cases T-778/16 & T-892/16, Ireland and Apple v. Commission (2020), E.C.R. 338.

147. European Commission Statement/20/1746, Statement by Executive Vice-President Margrethe Vestager on the Commission's Decision to Appeal the General Court's Judgment on the Apple Tax State Aid Case in Ireland (Sep. 25, 2020), https://ec.europa.eu/commission/presscorner/detail/en/statement_20_1746.

148. Regulation (EU) 2022/1925 of the European Parliament and of the Council of 14 September 2022 on contestable and fair markets in the digital sector and amending Directives (EU) 2019/1937 and (EU) 2020/1828 (Digital Markets Act) 2022 O.J. (L265) 1.

149. *Id.* at arts. 5–6.

150. Mark Scott, E.U. Commission Opens Inquiry Into E-Commerce Sector, N.Y. TIMES (May 6, 2015), https://www.nytimes.com/2015/05/07/business/international/european-commission-e-commerce-inquiry-american-tech-companies.html.

151. Julia Fioretti, Apple Appeals Against EU Tax Ruling, Brussels Says No Cause for Lower Tax Bill, REUTERS (Dec. 18, 2016), https://www.reuters.com/article/us-eu-apple-taxavoidance-idUSKBN14800O7.

152. Interview by Kara Swisher with Barack Obama, President of the United States of America, in Stanford, Cal. (Feb. 15, 2015), https://www.vox.com/2015/2/15/11559056/white-house-red-chair-obama-meets-swisher.

153. U.S. Dep't of the Treasury, THE EUROPEAN COMMISSION'S RECENT STATE AID INVESTIGATIONS OF TRANSFER PRICING RULINGS (Aug. 24, 2016), https://home. treasury.gov/system/files/131/WhitePaper-EU-State-Aid-8-24-2016.pdf.

154. Adam Satariano & Jack Nicas, E.U. Fines Google $5.1 Billion in Android Antitrust Case, N.Y. TIMES (July 18, 2018) https://www.nytimes.com/2018/07/18/technology/google-eu-android-fine.html.

155. John Cassidy, Why Did the European Commission Fine Google Five Billion Dollars?, NEW YORKER (July 20, 2018), https://www.newyorker.com/news/our-columnists/why-did-the-european-commission-fine-google-five-billion-dollars.

156. Javier Espinoza & James Politi, US Warns EU Against "Anti-American" Tech Policies, THE IRISH TIMES (June 15, 2021), https://www.irishtimes.com/business/technology/us-warns-eu-against-anti-american-tech-policies-1.4594181.

157. Stuart Lauchlan, US, EU Tech Policy Is Divided by More Than the Atlantic. Can the New Trade and Technology Council Realistically Bridge the Gap?, DIGINOMICA (Sep. 29, 2021), https://diginomica.com/us-eu-tech-policy-divided-more-atlantic-can-new-trade-and-technology-council-realistically-bridge.

158. Rep. Suzan DelBene (@RepDelBene), TWITTER (June 10, 2021), https://twitter.com/RepDelBene/status/1403124892871139328.

159. *See* Javier Espinoza, How Big Tech Lost the Antitrust Battle With Europe, FIN. TIMES (Mar. 21, 2022), https://www.ft.com/content/cbb1fe40-860d-4013-bfcf-b75ee6e30206?shareType=nongift.

160. *See* Javier Espinoza, Big Tech Attacks Tough EU Measures Aimed at Tackling Its Market Power, FIN. TIMES (Mar. 25, 2022), https://www.ft.com/content/0bc9378b-3e27-45e2-92d8-7c462427f876?shareType=nongift.

161. Senate Finance Committee (@SenFinance), TWITTER (July 18, 2018), https://twitter.com/SenFinance/status/1019605981968371712.

162. Myron Brilliant, Data Drives the Trans-Atlantic Economy. Can the U.S. and Europe See Eye to Eye?, BARRON'S (Sep. 28, 2021), https://www.barrons.com/articles/data-drives-the-trans-atlantic-economy-can-the-u-s-and-europe-see-eye-to-eye-51632784047.

163. Nick Clegg, Europe Should Tear Down Digital Walls Not Build New Ones, FIN. TIMES (Oct. 19, 2020), https://www.ft.com/content/98cf847c-96f9-4558-9a30-7d72ea4e79c2.

164. *Id.*

165. *See* Anu Bradford, THE BRUSSELS EFFECT 241–247 (2020).

166. *See* Ian Wishart, Microsoft Files Anti-Corruption Complaint Against Google, POLITICO (Mar. 31, 2011), https://www.politico.eu/article/microsoft-files-anti-competition-complaint-against-google/.

167. Epic Games Files EU Antitrust Complaint Against Apple, EPIC GAMES (Feb. 17, 2021), https://www.epicgames.com/site/en-US/news/epic-games-files-eu-antitrust-complaint-against-apple.

Notes

168. James Kanter, Yelp Joins Critics of European Union Antitrust Settlement With Google, N.Y. TIMES (July 8, 2014), https://www.nytimes.com/2014/07/09/tec hnology/yelp-joins-critics-of-european-union-settlement-with-google.html.

169. David Lawsky, Intel to Pay AMD $1.25 Billion, Settle Disputes, REUTERS (Nov. 12, 2009), https://www.reuters.com/article/us-intel-amd-idUSTRE5AB2LL2 0091112.

170. *See* Bradford, *supra* note 165.

171. *See* Anu Bradford, Robert J. Jackson Jr., & Jonathon Zytnick, Is EU Merger Control a Tool for Protectionism? An Empirical Analysis, 15 J. OF EMPIRICAL LEGAL STUD. 165 (2018).

172. *See* Anu Bradford, CAN EU MERGER CONTROL RESIST THE TURN TOWARDS PROTECTIONISM? (Levy & Kokkoris eds.) (forthcoming in 2023).

173. Case M.8677, Siemens/Alstom, 2019, ¶1783; EUROPEAN POLITICAL STRATEGY CTR. (EUROPEAN COMM'N), EU INDUSTRIAL POLICY AFTER SIEMENS-ALSTOM (2019), https://op.europa.eu/en/publication-detail/-/publication/03fb102b-10e2-11ea-8c1f-01aa75ed71a1.

174. Jorge Valero, Six Takeaways From Siemens-Alstom Rejection, EURACTIV (Feb. 6, 2019), https://www.euractiv.com/section/competition/news/six-takeaways-from-siemens-alstom-rejection/.

175. *Id.*

176. Bundesministerium für der Wirtschaft und Energie, A Franco-German Manifesto for a European Industrial Policy Fit for the 21st Century, https://www.bmwi.de/Redaktion/DE/Downloads/F/franco-german-manifesto-for-a-european-industrial-policy.pdf%3F__blob%3DpublicationFile%26v%3D2.

177. Bundesministeriums für Wirtschaft und Energie, Ministère de l'Économie et des Finances, Ministerstwo Przedsiębiorczości i Technologii, Modernising EU Competition Policy, https://www.bmwi.de/Redaktion/DE/Downloads/M-O/modernising-eu-competition-policy.pdf?__blob=publicationFile.

178. Barshefsky, *supra* note 12.

179. EU Industrial Policy After Siemens-Alstom (European Political Strategy Ctr., Mar. 18, 2019), at 4, https://op.europa.eu/en/publication-detail/-/publication/03fb102b-10e2-11ea-8c1f-01aa75ed71a1.

180. Javier Espinoza, EU Tech Policy Is Not Anti-American, Says Margrethe Vestager, THE IRISH TIMES (June 20, 2021), https://www.irishtimes.com/business/technology/eu-tech-policy-is-not-anti-american-says-margrethe-vestager-1.4598477.

181. Javier Espinoza, EU Should Focus on Top 5 Tech Companies, Says Leading MEP, FIN. TIMES (May 31, 2021), https://www.ft.com/content/49f3d7f2-30d5-4336-87ad-eeaoeeoecc7b?shareType=nongift.

182. Dita Charanzová, Turning Europe's Internet Into a "Walled Garden" Is the Wrong Path to Take, FIN. TIMES (Feb. 17, 2021), https://www.ft.com/content/d861af6a-eb92-4415-881a-be798f018401.

183. *Id.*

184. Le Grand Continent, "Interview du Président Emmanuel Macron à la Revue le Grand Continent," https://legrandcontinent.eu/fr/2020/11/16/macron/; President Charles Michel, Speech at the Brussels Economic Forum: Recovery Plan: Powering Europe's Strategic Autonomy, https://www.consilium.europa. eu/en/press/press-releases/2020/09/08/recovery-plan-powering-europe-s-strategic-autonomy-speech-by-president-charles-michel-at-the-brussels-econo mic-forum/.

185. Emily A. Vogels, 56% of Americans Support More Regulation of Major Technology Companies, PEW RESEARCH CTR. (July 20, 2021), https://www.pewr esearch.org/fact-tank/2021/07/20/56-of-americans-support-more-regulation-of-major-technology-companies/.

186. Tanya Snyder & Janosch Delcker, US Pushes Light Regulations for AI, in Contrast to Europe, POLITICO (Jan. 9, 2020), https://www.politico.eu/article/us-pushes-light-regulations-for-ai-in-contrast-to-europe/.

187. Jake Sullivan (@JakeSullivan46), TWITTER (Apr. 21, 2021), https://twitter.com/ JakeSullivan46/status/1384970668341669891.

188. *See* Cristiano Lima, Biden's Commerce Chief Is Under Fire From Warren, Progressives for Defending U.S. Tech Giants, WASH. POST (Dec. 15, 2021), https://www.washingtonpost.com/politics/2021/12/15/bidens-commerce-chief-is-under-fire-warren-progressives-defending-us-tech-giants/.

189. *See* European Commission Press Release IP/21/2990, EU-US Launch Trade and Technology Council to Lead Values-Based Global Digital Transformation (June 15, 2021), https://ec.europa.eu/commission/presscorner/detail/en/ IP_21_2990; *see* White House Briefing Room, U.S.-EU Trade and Technology Council Inaugural Statement (Sep. 29, 2021), https://www.whitehouse.gov/ briefing-room/statements-releases/2021/09/29/u-s-eu-trade-and-technology-council-inaugural-joint-statement/?utm_source=link.

190. White House Briefing Room, Remarks by National Security Advisor Jake Sullivan at the National Security Commission on Artificial Intelligence Global Emerging Technology Summit (July 13, 2021), https://www.whitehouse.gov/ nsc/briefing-room/2021/07/13/remarks-by-national-security-advisor-jake-sullivan-at-the-national-security-commission-on-artificial-intelligence-glo bal-emerging-technology-summit/. [hereinafter *Sullivan artificial intelligence remarks*]

191. *See* European Commission Press Release IP/21/2990, EU-US Launch Trade and Technology Council to Lead Values-Based Global Digital Transformation (June 15, 2021), https://ec.europa.eu/commission/presscorner/detail/en/ IP_21_2990.

192. *See* Konstantinos Komaitis & Justin Sherman, The EU-US Tech Council Shouldn't Just Focus on China, BROOKINGS INST. (July 20, 2021), https://www.brookings. edu/techstream/the-eu-us-tech-council-shouldnt-just-focus-on-china/.

193. European Commission Statement 21/451, EU-US Trade and Technology Council Inaugural Statement (Sep. 29, 2021), https://ec.europa.eu/commiss ion/presscorner/detail/en/STATEMENT_21_4951.

194. *See* Chad P. Brown & Cecilia Malmström, What Is the US–EU Trade and Technology Council? Five Things You Need to Know, PETERSON INST. FOR INT'L ECON. (Sep. 24, 2021), https://www.piie.com/blogs/trade-and-investment-pol icy-watch/what-us-eu-trade-and-technology-council-five-things-you-need.

195. Mark Scott & Jacopo Barigazzi, US and Europe to Forge Tech Alliance Amid China's Rise, POLITICO (June 9, 2021), https://www.politico.eu/article/eu-us-trade-tech-council-joe-biden-china/.

196. David J. Lynch, EU and US Try to Forge Closer Alliance on Trade and Tech After Recent Discord, WASH. POST (Sep. 28, 2021), https://www.washingtonp ost.com/us-policy/2021/09/28/eu-us-council-trade-technology/.

197. Robert D. Atkinson, Advancing US Goals in the US–EU Trade and Technology Council 2 (Info. Tech. & Innovation Found., Sep. 13, 2021), https://itif.org/publi cations/2021/09/13/advancing-us-goals-us-eu-trade-and-technology-council/.

198. *See* China Overtakes US as EU's Biggest Trading Partner, BBC (Feb. 17, 2021), https://www.bbc.com/news/business-56093378.

199. *See* Lynch, *supra* note 196.

200. Henry Foy, EU Ministers Advised to Take Tougher Line on China, FIN. TIMES (Oct 17, 2022), https://www.ft.com/content/b83615cb-6db0-4e67-85a3-7aab1 31abeb5?shareType=nongift.

201. *See* Frances Burwell, The US–EU Trade and Technology Council: Seven Steps Toward Success, ATLANTIC COUNCIL: NEW ATLANTICIST (Sep. 24, 2021), https:// www.atlanticcouncil.org/blogs/new-atlanticist/the-us-eu-trade-and-technol ogy-council-seven-steps-toward-success/.

202. *Sullivan artificial intelligence remarks, supra* note 190.

203. Angela Dewan & Luke McGee, Biden Says "America Is Back," but "America First" Has Haunted His First 100 Days, CNN (Apr. 28, 2021), https://www.cnn. com/2021/04/28/world/biden-100-days-foreign-policy-intl/index.html.

204. *See* Scott & Barigazzi, *supra* note 195.

CHAPTER 7

1. Jack Goldsmith, The Failure of Internet Freedom, KNIGHT FIRST AMENDMENT AT COLUMBIA UNIVERSITY (June 13, 2018), https://knightcolumbia.org/content/ failure-internet-freedom.

2. *Id.*

3. *See generally* Steven Schwarcz, Private Ordering, 97 NORTHWESTERN L. REV. 319 (2002), https://scholarship.law.duke.edu/cgi/viewcontent.cgi?article= 1838&context=faculty_scholarship.

4. Kate Klonick, The New Governors: The People, Rules, and Processes Governing Online Speech, 131 HARV. L. REV. 1598 (2018)

5. Ian Bremmer, The Technopolar Moment: How Digital Powers Will Reshape the Global Order, FOREIGN AFFS. (Dec. 2021), https://www.foreignaffairs.com/artic les/world/2021-10-19/ian-bremmer-big-tech-global-order.

6. Leading Brands Worldwide in 2021, by Brand Value, STATISTA (July 27, 2022), https://www.statista.com/statistics/264826/most-valuable-brands-worldwide-in-2009/.

7. Most Popular Social Networks Worldwide as of January 2022, Ranked by Number of Monthly Active Users, STATISTA (July 26, 2022), https://www.statista.com/statistics/272014/global-social-networks-ranked-by-number-of-users/.

8. Jennifer Elias, TikTok Looms Large in Tech Earnings Reports as Digital Ad Giants Struggle to Keep Up, CNBC TECH (Apr. 29, 2022), https://www.cnbc.com/2022/04/29/tiktok-looms-large-in-tech-earnings-from-google-facebook-amazon.html.

9. Number of Daily Active Facebook Users Worldwide as of 2nd Quarter 2022, STATISTA (July 28, 2022), https://www.statista.com/statistics/346167/facebook-glo bal-dau/; Most Popular Social Networks Worldwide as of January 2022, Ranked by Number of Monthly Active Users, STATISTA (July 26, 2022), https://www.stati sta.com/statistics/272014/global-social-networks-ranked-by-number-of-users/.

10. Percentage of Global Population Using Facebook as of May 2022, by Region, STATISTA (Aug. 1, 2022), https://www.statista.com/statistics/241552/share-of-glo bal-population-using-facebook-by-region/.

11. Social Media Stats Worldwide, STATCOUNTER, https://gs.statcounter.com/social-media-stats#monthly-202101-202112 (last visited, Sep. 30, 2022).

12. Statista, *supra* note 9.

13. Facebook Users by Country 2022, WORLD POP. REV., https://worldpopulatio nreview.com/country-rankings/facebook-users-by-country (last visited Sep. 30, 2022) (excludes Afghanistan),

14. Facebook's Average Revenue per User as of 2nd Quarter 2022, by Region, STATISTA (July 28, 2022), https://www.statista.com/statistics/251328/facebooks-average-revenue-per-user-by-region/.

15. Facebook Revenue by Geography, STATSTIC, https://statstic.com/facebook-reve nue-by-geography/ (last visited Sep. 30, 2022).

16. About WhatsApp, WHATSAPP, https://www.whatsapp.com/about/ (last visited Oct. 14, 2022).

17. Number of WhatsApp Users in Selected Countries Worldwide as of June 2021, STATISTA (May 25, 2022), https://www.statista.com/statistics/289778/countries-with-the-most-facebook-users/.

18. Panoramas, WhatsApp's Popularity Abroad vs. in the US, Univ. of Pittsburgh, https://www.panoramas.pitt.edu/news-and-politics/whatsapp%E2%80%99s-popularity-abroad-vs-us (last visited Oct. 14, 2022).

19. Sources differ, but 86 percent is the lowest reported. Worldwide Desktop Market Share of Leading Search Engines From January 2010 to July 2022, STATISTA (July 27, 2022), https://www.statista.com/statistics/216573/worldwide-market-share-of-search-engines/.

20. Search Engine Market Share Worldwide, STATCOUNTER, https://gs.statcounter.com/search-engine-market-share/ (last visited Oct. 14, 2022); Current State of Google and Search Engine Marketing in Asia, PRINCIPLE, https://us.principle-c.com/blog/apac/current-state-of-google-and-search-engine-marketing-in-asia/ (last visited Oct. 14, 2022); Josh Ternyak, Search Engine Market Share by Country & Worldwide, JT (Aug. 19, 2022), https://www.joshternyak.com/data/search-engine-market-share.

21. Internet Penetration Rate in Asia Compared to the Global Penetration Rate from 2010 to 2022, STATISTA (Sep. 28, 2022), https://www.statista.com/statistics/265156/internet-penetration-rate-in-asia/.

22. Share of Desktop Search Traffic Originating from Google in Selected Countries as of July 2022, STATISTA (July 19, 2022), https://www.statista.com/statistics/220534/googles-share-of-search-market-in-selected-countries/.

23. *Id.*

24. *Apple Revenue 2010–2022*, Macrotrends, https://www.macrotrends.net/stocks/charts/AAPL/apple/revenue#:~:text=Apple%20annual%20revenue%20for%202022,a%205.51%25%20increase%20from%202019 (last visited Nov. 14, 2022).

25. David Curry, Apple Statistics (2022), BUSINESSOFAPPS (Oct. 7, 2022), https://www.businessofapps.com/data/apple-statistics.

26. *Id.*

27. Apple's iPhone Revenue from 3rd Quarter 2007 to 3rd Quarter 2022, STATISTA (Aug. 30, 2022), https://www.statista.com/statistics/263402/apples-iphone-revenue-since-3rd-quarter-2007/.

28. Mobile Vendor Market Share Africa, STATCOUNTER, https://gs.statcounter.com/vendor-market-share/mobile/africa (last visited Oct. 14, 2022).

29. Revenue From Services as a Share of Apple's Total Global Revenue from 3rd Quarter 2015 to 3rd Quarter 2022, STATISTA (Aug. 30, 2022), https://www.statista.com/statistics/1101212/services-revenue-as-share-of-apples-total-revenue/.

30. Microsoft Annual Revenue by Geography: Fiscal 2002–2021, DAZEINFO (Aug. 20, 2021), https://dazeinfo.com/2019/11/11/microsoft-revenue-by-geography-by-year-graphfarm/

31. Microsoft's Revenue Breakdown by Segment (2016–2022), BUS. QUANT, https://businessquant.com/microsoft-revenue-by-segment (last visited Oct. 14, 2022).

32. Dave Tracey, Who's Using Microsoft Azure? [2020], CONTINO (Feb. 20, 2020), https://www.contino.io/insights/whos-using-microsoft-azure-2020.

33. Jared Spataro, Remote Work Trend Report: Meetings, MICROSOFT (Apr. 9, 2020), https://www.microsoft.com/en-us/microsoft-365/blog/2020/04/09/

remote-work-trend-report-meetings/?wt.mc_id=AID2409697_QSG_SCL_424 041&ocid=AID2409697_QSG_SCL_424041.

34. David Curry, Microsoft Teams Revenue and Usage Statistics (2022), BUSINESSOFAPPS (Sep. 6, 2022), https://www.businessofapps.com/data/micros oft-teams-statistics/; Number of Daily Active Users (DAU) of Microsoft Teams Worldwide as of April 2021, STATISTA (Feb. 14, 2022), https://www.statista.com/ statistics/1033742/worldwide-microsoft-teams-daily-and-monthly-users/.

35. Number of Office 365 Company Users Worldwide as of June 2022, by Leading Country, STATISTA (Feb. 23, 2022), https://www.statista.com/statistics/983321/ worldwide-office-365-user-numbers-by-country/.

36. David Curry, Amazon Statistics (2022), BUSINESSOFAPPS (Aug. 11, 2022), https:// www.businessofapps.com/data/amazon-statistics/.

37. Jasmine Enberg, Amazon Around the World: "Primed" for International Expansion, but Faces Challenges from Alibaba, MercadoLibre, Flipkart and Others, INSIDER INTEL. (Nov. 13, 2018), https://www.emarketer.com/content/ amazon-around-the-world.

38. Amazon's Revenue by Region, BUS. QUANT, https://businessquant.com/ama zon-revenue-by-region (last visited Oct. 14, 2022); Annual Net Sales Revenue of Amazon from 2006 to 2021, by Segment, STATISTA (July 27, 2022), https://www. statista.com/statistics/266289/net-revenue-of-amazon-by-region.

39. Amazon's Revenue by Region, *supra* note 36.

40. 74 Amazon Statistics You Must Know: 2021/2022 Market Share Analysis & Data, FINANCESONLINE, https://financesonline.com/amazon-statistics/ (last visited Oct. 14, 2022).

41. Benjamin Parkin, Farhan Bokhari, & Ryan McMorrow, From Nappies to Cricket: China's Alibaba Targets South Asia, FIN. TIMES (June 21, 2022), https:// www.ft.com/content/2284ab4e-72b6-4858-a20c-a3567f324318.

42. Jacky Wong, Tencent Looks Abroad as Beijing Tightens the Screws at Home, WALL ST. J. (Aug. 18, 2021), https://www.wsj.com/articles/tencent-looks-abroad- as-beijing-tightens-the-screws-at-home-11629286711.

43. Zeyi Yang, How Chinese Tech Companies Took Over the World in 2021, PROTOCOL (Dec. 29, 2021), https://www.protocol.com/china/china-world-2021- review.

44. Huawei's Revenue from 2012 to 2021, by Geographical Region, STATISTA (July 27, 2022), https://www.statista.com/statistics/368509/revenue-of-huawei-by- region/.

45. Huawei Investment & Holding Co., Ltd., 2021 ANNUAL REPORT 21 (2021), https:// www-file.huawei.com/minisite/media/annual_report/annual_report_2021_ en.pdf?version=0401.

46. Yang, *supra* note 43.

47. Geoffrey T. Dancik, The Creation of an Information, Communication, and Technology (ICT) Industry Cluster: Dubai's Internet City, UNIV. OF MICH. (Dec. 16, 2005), http://websites.umich.edu/~econdev/gd_dubai/index.html.

48. Sam Bridge, Dubai Is Middle East's Silicon Valley, Says Ruler, ARABIAN BUS., (Sep. 11, 2019), https://www.arabianbusiness.com/industries/technology/427 823-dubai-is-middle-easts-silicon-valley-says-ruler.

49. Conor Gaffey, Silicon Lagoon: Africa's Tech Revolution Heads West, NEWSWEEK MAG. (Nov. 29, 2016), https://www.newsweek.com/2016/12/09/nigeria-start ups-yaba-lagos-mark-zuckerberg-525824.html.

50. Eniola Daniel, Ogun Will Soon Become Nigeria's Silicon Valley, Says Pantami, THE GUARDIAN (Aug. 3, 2022), https://guardian.ng/news/nigeria/ogun-will-soon-become-nigerias-silicon-valley-says-pantami/

51. Goldsmith, *supra* note 1.

52. Press Release, Hillary Clinton, Sec. of State, Remarks on Internet Freedom (Jan. 21, 2010), https://2009-2017.state.gov/secretary/20092013clinton/rm/2010/01/135519.htm.

53. 47 U.S.C. § 230.

54. Goldsmith, *supra* note 1.

55. World Telecommunication Development Conference, TELECOMM. DEV. CONFS., https://www.itu.int/en/history/Pages/TelecommunicationDevelopmentConf erences.aspx?conf=4.144 .

56. Read the Framework, THE WHITE HOUSE, https://clintonwhitehouse4.archives. gov/WH/New/Commerce/read.html.

57. Ira C. Magaziner, Creating a Framework for Global Electronic Commerce, FUTURE INSIGHT (July 1999), http://www.pff.org/issues-pubs/futureinsights/fi6.1globaleconomiccommerce.html.

58. *Id.*

59. Stuart S. Malawer, Global Governance of E-Commerce and Internet Trade: Recent Developments, VA. LAW. (June 2001), https://www.worldtradelaw.net/document. php?id=articles/malawerecommerce.pdf&mode=download.

60. Press Release, William J. Clinton, President of the United States (1998), https:// www.wto.org/english/thewto_e/minist_e/min98_e/anniv_e/clinton_e.htm.

61. Joint Statement, U.S.–Japan, ELEC. COM. (May 15, 1998), https://www.mofa. go.jp/policy/economy/e_commerce/statemt9805.html.

62. Jeri Clausing, Japan Backs Administration's Market-Driven Approach to E-Commerce, N.Y. TIMES (May 15, 1998), https://archive.nytimes.com/www.nyti mes.com/library/tech/98/05/cyber/articles/15commerce.html.

63. Data Protection Directive, EC No. 1882, 2003 (Dec. 13, 1995).

64. Press Release, William J. Clinton, President of the United States, Statement of the United States and the European Union on Building Consumer Confidence in E-Commerce and the Role of Alternative Dispute Resolution (Dec. 18, 2000),

https://www.presidency.ucsb.edu/documents/statement-the-united-states-and-the-european-union-building-consumer-confidence-e-commerce.

65. Malawer, *supra* note 59.

66. Press Release, William J. Clinton, President of the United States, Joint Statement From Australia and the United States on Electronic Commerce (Nov. 30, 1998), https://www.presidency.ucsb.edu/documents/joint-statement-from-australia-and-the-united-states-electronic-commerce.

67. Press Release, George W. Bush, President of the United States, U.S.-Jordan Free Trade Agreement (Sep. 28, 2001), https://georgewbush-whitehouse.archives.gov/news/releases/2001/09/20010928-12.html.

68. *Id.*

69. *Development Initiative*, FED. COMM. COMM'N, https://www.fcc.gov/general/development-initiative (last visited Oct. 14, 2022).

70. *Id.*

71. From Global Digital Divide to Digital Opportunity, The White House (July 22, 2000), https://clintonwhitehouse4.archives.gov/textonly/WH/EOP/nec/html/G8DigDivTaskForce000722.html.

72. *Id.*

73. Statement, William J. Clinton, President of the United States (1998) https://www.wto.org/english/thewto_e/minist_e/min98_e/anniv_e/clinton_e.htm.

74. WTO document G/L/160 of April 2, 1997, "Implementation of the Ministerial Declaration on Trade in Information Technology Products."

75. Michael Anderson & Jacob Mohs, The Information Technology Agreement: An Assessment of World Trade in Information Technology Products, 1 J. OF INT'L COMM. & ECON. 110 (Jan. 2010), https://www.usitc.gov/publications/332/journals/05_andersonmohs_itagreement.pdf.

76. WTO Document WT/MIN(98)/DEC/2 of 25 May 1998, "The Geneva Ministerial Declaration on Global Electronic Commerce."

77. Kal Raustiala, An Internet Whole and Free: Why Washington Was Right to Give Up Control, FOREIGN AFFS. (March 2017), https://www.foreignaffairs.com/articles/world/2017-02-13/internet-whole-and-free.

78. RFE/RL Language Services, RADIOFREEEUROPE, https://pressroom.rferl.org/rferl-language-services.

79. RAND Corporation, INTERNET FREEDOM AND POLITICAL SPACE 155, 173 (2013), https://www.rand.org/pubs/research_reports/RR295.html#download.

80. S. 3093, 107th Cong. § 2 (2002), https://www.govinfo.gov/content/pkg/BILLS-107s3093is/html/BILLS-107s3093is.htm.

81. *Id.*

82. *Id.*

83. Thomas Lum, Patricia Moloney Figiola, & Matthew C. Weed, China Internet Freedom and U.S. Policy, CONG. RSCH. SERV. (July 13, 2012), https://sgp.fas.org/crs/row/R42601.pdf.

84. Global Internet Freedom Task Force (GIFT) Strategy: A Blueprint for Action, U.S. DEP'T OF STATE (Dec. 28, 2006), https://2001-2009.state.gov/g/drl/rls/78340.htm.

85. Goldsmith, *supra* note 1.

86. Thomas Lum, Patricia Moloney Figiola, & Matthew C. Weed, China Internet Freedom, and U.S. Policy, CONG. RSCH. SERV. (July 13, 2012), https://sgp.fas.org/crs/row/R42601.pdf.

87. Press Release, Hillary Clinton, Sec. of State, Remarks on Internet Freedom (Jan. 21, 2010), https://2009-2017.state.gov/secretary/20092013clinton/rm/2010/01/135519.htm.

88. *Id.*

89. Goldsmith, *supra* note 1.

90. Jessi Hempel, Social Media Made the Arab Spring But Couldn't Save It, WIRED (Jan. 26, 2016), https://www.wired.com/2016/01/social-media-made-the-arab-spring-but-couldnt-save-it/.

91. Carol Huang, Facebook and Twitter Key to Arab Spring Uprisings: Report, UAE (June 5, 2011), https://www.thenationalnews.com/uae/facebook-and-twitter-key-to-arab-spring-uprisings-report-1.428773/.

92. Ron Nixon, U.S. Groups Helped Nurture Arab Uprisings, N.Y. TIMES (Apr. 14, 2011), https://www.nytimes.com/2011/04/15/world/15aid.html.

93. Benjamin Wagner, Kirsten Gollatz, & Andrea Calderaro, Internet & Human Rights in Foreign Policy: Comparing Narratives in the US and EU Internet Governance Agenda, CADMUS (2014), https://cadmus.eui.eu/handle/1814/32433.

94. Current U.S. Policy: Continuity and Growth, COUNCIL ON FOREIGN RELS. (2013), https://www.cfr.org/annual-report-2013.

95. Lum, Moloney Figiola, & Weed, *supra* note 86.

96. U.N. Human Rights Council: First Resolution on Internet Free Speech, LIBR. OF CONG. (July 12, 2012), https://www.loc.gov/item/global-legal-monitor/2012-07-12/u-n-human-rights-council-first-resolution-on-internet-free-speech/.

97. Clinton, Remarks on Internet Freedom, *supra* note 52.

98. Benjamin Wagner, Kirsten Gollatz, & Andrea Calderaro, Internet & Human Rights in Foreign Policy: Comparing Narratives in the US and EU Internet Governance Agenda, CADMUS (2014), https://cadmus.eui.eu/handle/1814/32433.

99. Terms of Reference, FREEDOM ONLINE COAL. (Sep. 6, 2012), https://freedomonlinecoalition.com/wp-content/uploads/2021/05/Nairobi-Terms-of-Reference.pdf.

100. Lum, Moloney Figiola, & Weed, *supra* note 86.

101. *Id.*

102. Jay Newton-Small, Hillary's Little Startup: How the U.S. Is Using Technology to Aid Syria's Rebels, TIME (June 13, 2012), https://world.time.com/2012/

06/13/hillarys-little-startup-how-the-u-s-is-using-technology-to-aid-syrias-rebels/.

103. Fergus Hanson, Revolution @State: The Spread of Democracy, LOWRY INST. FOR INT'L POL'Y (March 2012), https://www.brookings.edu/wp-content/uplo ads/2016/06/03_ediplomacy_hanson.pdf.

104. Clinton, Remarks on Internet Freedom, *supra* note 52.

105. James Glanz & John Markoff, U.S. Underwrites Internet Detour Around Censors, N.Y. TIMES (June 12, 2011), https://www.nytimes.com/2011/06/12/world/12internet.html.

106. Fergus Hanson, Revolution @State: The Spread of Democracy, LOWRY INST. FOR INT'L POL'Y (March 2012), https://www.brookings.edu/wp-content/uplo ads/2016/06/03_ediplomacy_hanson.pdf.

107. Newton-Small, *Hillary's Little Startup, supra* note 102.

108. Lum, Moloney Figiola, & Weed, *supra* note 86.

109. *Id.*

110. Benjamin Wagner, Kirsten Gollatz, & Andrea Calderaro, Internet & Human Rights in Foreign Policy: Comparing Narratives in the US and EU Internet Governance Agenda, CADMUS (2014), https://cadmus.eui.eu/handle/1814/32433.

111. Google Chief Urges Burma to Open Telecoms, RADIO FREE ASIA (Mar. 22, 2013), https://www.rfa.org/english/news/myanmar/google-03222013191201.html.

112. *Id.*

113. Mark Landler & Brian Stelter, Washington Taps Into a Potent New Force in Diplomacy, N.Y. TIMES (June 16, 2009), https://www.nytimes.com/2009/06/17/world/middleeast/17media.html.

114. Rebecca MacKinnon, A Clunky Cyberstrategy: Washington Preaches Internet Freedom but Practices Surveillance, FOREIGN AFFRS. (Apr. 26, 2012), https://www.foreignaffairs.com/articles/americas/2012-04-26/clunky-cyberstrategy.

115. Bobbie Johnson, Obama Urged to Punish US Firms for Aiding Internet Censorship, THE GUARDIAN (June 30, 2009), https://www.theguardian.com/world/2009/jun/30/us-firms-aiding-censorship.

116. The Internet in China: A Tool for Freedom or Suppression?: Joint Hearing Before the Subcomm. on Africa, Global Human Rights and Int'l Operations & on Asia and the Pacific, 109th Cong. 102 (2006) (statement of Representative Christopher Smith).

117. Lum, Moloney Figiola, & Weed, *supra* note 86.

118. National Cyber Strategy of the United States of America, THE WHITE HOUSE (Sep. 2018), https://trumpwhitehouse.archives.gov/wp-content/uploads/2018/09/National-Cyber-Strategy.pdf.

119. Spencer S. Hsu, Trump Administration Is Crippling International Internet Freedom Effort by Withholding Funds, Officials Say, WASH. POST (July 31, 2020), https://www.washingtonpost.com/local/legal-issues/trump-adminis

tration-withholds-20-million-crippling-international-internet-freedom-effort-officials-say/2020/07/31/eea0a9c0-d2a1-11ea-8d32-1ebf4e9d8e0d_story.html.

120. Jon Allsop, The Fight for Voice of America, COLUM. JOURNALISM REV. (Dec. 9, 2020), https://www.cjr.org/the_media_today/michael_pack_voice_of_america_transition.php; Alex Ward, Voice of America Reporters: Trump-Backed CEO 'Is Failing' the US, VOX (Aug. 31, 2020), https://www.vox.com/2020/8/31/21408467/voice-of-america-letter-michael-pack-trump.

121. Justin Sherman, Trump's Un-American Failure to Protect Internet Freedom, WIRED (Oct. 22, 2020), https://www.wired.com/story/trumps-un-american-failure-to-protect-internet-freedom/

122. Shannon Bond & Avie Schneider, Trump Threatens to Shut Down Social Media After Twitter Adds Warning to His Tweets, NPR (May 27, 2020), https://www.npr.org/2020/05/27/863011399/trump-threatens-to-shut-down-social-media-after-twitter-adds-warning-on-his-twee.

123. Tom Wheeler, Could Donald Trump Claim a National Security Threat to Shut Down the Internet?, BROOKINGS (June 25, 2020), https://www.brookings.edu/blog/techtank/2020/06/25/could-donald-trump-claim-a-national-security-threat-to-shut-down-the-internet/.

124. Reining in Big Tech's Censorship of Conservatives, COMM. ON THE J. (Oct. 6, 2020), https://republicans-judiciary.house.gov/wp-content/uploads/2020/10/2020-10-06-Reining-in-Big-Techs-Censorship-of-Conservatives.pdf.

125. S. 4534, 116th Cong. 2 (2020) (amending § 230 of the Communications Act of 1934), https://www.commerce.senate.gov/services/files/94D0F3C6-B927-46D2-A75C-17C78D0D92AA.

126. Paul M. Barrett & J. Grant Sims, FALSE ACCUSATION: THE UNFOUNDED CLAIM THAT SOCIAL MEDIA COMPANIES CENSOR CONSERVATIVES (2021), https://bhr.stern.nyu.edu/bias-report-release-page.

127. Yochai Benkler, Robert Fairs, & Hal Roberts, NETWORK PROPAGANDA: MANIPULATION, DISINFORMATION, AND RADICALIZATION IN AMERICAN POLITICS 354 (2018).

128. Freedom House, FREEDOM ON THE NET (2021), https://freedomhouse.org/country/united-states/freedom-net/2021.

129. Press Release, Anthony J. Blinken, Sec. of State, The Modernization of American Democracy (Oct. 27, 2021), https://www.state.gov/secretary-antony-j-blinken-on-the-modernization-of-american-diplomacy/

130. Press Release, Office of the Spokesperson, U.S. Dep't of State, Establishment of the Bureau of Cyberspace and Digital Policy (Apr. 4, 2022), https://www.state.gov/establishment-of-the-bureau-of-cyberspace-and-digital-policy/.

131. Steven Feldstein, Can the State Department's Cyber Bureau Tackle Digital Repression?, THE NAT'L INT. (June 2, 2022), https://nationalinterest.org/blog/techland-when-great-power-competition-meets-digital-world/can-state-department%E2%80%99s-cyber-bureau.

132. Sean Lyngaas, State Department Launches Cyberbureau Amid Concerns Over Russia and China's Digital Authoritarianism, CNN POL. (Apr. 4, 2022), https://www.cnn.com/2022/04/04/politics/state-department-cyber-bureau/index.html.

133. Lauren Feiner, Bipartisan Lawmakers Want Biden to Tell Europe to Stop "Unfairly" Targeting U.S. Tech Companies, CNBC (Feb. 23, 2022).

134. Fact Sheet: Executive Order on Promoting Competition in the American Economy, THE WHITE HOUSE (July 9, 2021), https://www.whitehouse.gov/briefing-room/statements-releases/2021/07/09/fact-sheet-executive-order-on-promoting-competition-in-the-american-economy/.

135. Alexandra Stevenson, Facebook Admits It Was Used to Incite Violence in Myanmar, N.Y. TIMES (Nov. 6, 2018), https://www.nytimes.com/2018/11/06/technology/myanmar-facebook.html.

136. Dan Milmo, Rohingya Sue Facebook for £150bn Over Myanmar Genocide, THE GUARDIAN (Dec. 6, 2021), https://www.theguardian.com/technology/2021/dec/06/rohingya-sue-facebook-myanmar-genocide-us-uk-legal-action-social-media-violence.

137. Vyacheslav Polonski, IMPACT OF SOCIAL MEDIA ON THE OUTCOME OF THE EU REFERENDUM (2016), http://www.referendumanalysis.uk/eu-referendum-analysis-2016/section-7-social-media/impact-of-social-media-on-the-outcome-of-the-eu-referendum/.

138. Digital, Culture, Media & Sport Committee, DISINFORMATION AND "FAKE NEWS": FINAL REPORT, 2017–2019, HC 1791, § 6 (UK), https://publications.parliament.uk/pa/cm201719/cmselect/cmcumeds/1791/1791.pdf.

139. Aurelien Breeden, Child Abduction Rumors Lead to Violence Against Roma in France, N.Y. TIMES (Mar. 28, 2019), https://www.nytimes.com/2019/03/28/world/europe/roma-kidnap-rumors-france.html.

140. Agence France-Presse, Roma Attacked in Paris After Fake News Reports, GUARDIAN (Mar. 27, 2019), https://www.theguardian.com/world/2019/mar/27/roma-call-for-protection-after-vigilante-attacks-inspired-by-fake-news.

141. Judit Szakács & Éva Bognár, EUROPEAN PARLIAMENT SPECIAL COMMITTEE ON FOREIGN INTERFERENCE IN ALL DEMOCRATIC PROCESSES IN THE EUROPEAN UNION, THE IMPACT OF DISINFORMATION CAMPAIGNS ABOUT MIGRANTS AND MINORITY GROUPS IN THE EU 14 (2021).

142. Jakub Janda & Ilyas Sharibzhanov, Six Outrageous Lies Russian Disinformation Peddled about Europe in 2016, ATLANTIC COUNCIL (Feb. 8, 2017), https://www.atlanticcouncil.org/blogs/ukrainealert/six-outrageous-lies-russian-disinformation-peddled-about-europe-in-2016/.

143. Andreas Rinke & Paul Carrel, German-Russian Ties Feel Cold War–Style Chill Over Rape Case, REUTERS (Feb. 1, 2016), https://www.reuters.com/article/us-germany-russia/german-russian-ties-feel-cold-war-style-chill-over-rape-case-idUSKCN0VA31O.

144. The Facebook Papers and Their Fallout, N.Y. TIMES (Oct. 25, 2021), https://www.nytimes.com/2021/10/25/business/facebook-papers-takeaways.html.

145. Sheera Frenkel & Davey Alba, In India, Facebook Grapples With an Amplified Version of Its Problems, N.Y. TIMES (Oct. 23, 2021), https://www.nytimes.com/2021/10/23/technology/facebook-india-misinformation.html.

146. Sameer Yasir & Maria Abi-Habib, Kashmir Suffers From the Worst Attack There in 30 Years, N.Y. TIMES (Feb. 14, 2019), https://www.nytimes.com/2019/02/14/world/asia/pulwama-attack-kashmir.html.

147. Frenkel & Alba, *supra* note 145.

148. *Id.*

149. Christchurch Shootings: 49 Dead in New Zealand Mosque Attacks, BBC (Mar. 15, 2019), https://www.bbc.com/news/world-asia-47578798.

150. *See* Victor Mallet & Hannah Murphy, Social Media Groups Under Fire in France Over Islamist Killing, FIN. TIMES (Oct. 20, 2020), https://www.ft.com/content/b2af266c-5a84-4ddd-8d49-ab41f29a7b06.

151. Dipesh Gadher, London Bridge Terror Attack Planned on WhatsApp, THE TIMES (May 12, 2019), https://www.thetimes.co.uk/article/london-bridge-terror-attack-planned-on-whatsapp-32r38jz8v.

152. WhatsApp Must Not Be "Place for Terrorists to Hide," BBC (Mar. 26, 2017), https://www.bbc.com/news/uk-39396578.

153. *Id.*

154. Sheera Frenkel & Ben Decker, Taliban Ramp Up on Social Media, Defying Bans by the Platforms, N.Y. TIMES (Aug. 18, 2021), https://www.nytimes.com/2021/08/18/technology/taliban-social-media-bans.html.

155. *Id.*

156. Jessica Brandt, Bret Schafer, Elen Aghekyan, Valerie Wirtschafter, & Adya Danaditya, WINNING THE WEB: HOW BEIJING EXPLOITS SEARCH RESULTS TO SHAPE VIEWS OF XINJIANG AND COVID-19 (2022), https://www.brookings.edu/wp-content/uploads/2022/05/FP_20220525_china_seo_v2.pdf.

157. *Id.*

158. Nina Otte-Witte, Disinformation Campaigns: "Lies Can Turn Deadly or Threaten the Stability of Societies," AKADEMIE (Sep. 24, 2021), https://www.dw.com/en/disinformation-campaignslies-can-turn-deadly-or-threaten-the-stability-of-societies/a-59299651.

159. Silja Frölich, Dictators in Africa Using Social Media to Cling to Power, DW (Jan. 9, 2022), https://www.dw.com/en/dictators-in-africa-using-social-media-to-cling-to-power/a-60360543.

160. *Id.*

161. *Id.*

162. Zecharias Zelalem & Peter Guest, Why Facebook Keeps Failing in Ethiopia, REST OF WORLD (Nov. 13, 2021), https://restofworld.org/2021/why-facebook-keeps-failing-in-ethiopia/.

163. *Id.*

164. Frenkel & Alba, *supra* note 145.

165. *Id.*

166. Jillian Deutsch, Facebook Whistle-Blower Haugen Applauded in European Parliament, BLOOMBERG (Nov. 8, 2021), https://www.bloomberg.com/news/articles/2021-11-08/facebook-defends-meta-rebrand-ahead-of-whistle-blower-hearing.

167. Danielle Citron, THE FIGHT FOR PRIVACY: PROTECTING DIGNITY, IDENTITY, AND LOVE IN THE DIGITAL AGE 157 (2022),

168. Goldsmith, *supra* note 1; Fergus Hanson, Internet Freedom: The Role of the U.S. State Department, BROOKINGS (Oct. 25, 2012), https://www.brookings.edu/research/internet-freedom-the-role-of-the-u-s-state-department/.

169. Goldsmith, *supra* note 1.

170. Zhang Jiawei, China Doesn't Need a Politicized Google, CHINA DAILY (Mar. 20, 2010), https://www.chinadaily.com.cn/china/2010-03/20/content_9618252.htm.

171. Lum, Moloney Figiola, & Weed, *supra* note 86.

172. Sami Ben Gharbia, The Internet Freedom Fallacy and Arab Digital Activism, FUTURECHALLENGES (Sep. 17, 2010), https://nawaat.org/2010/09/17/the-internet-freedom-fallacy-and-the-arab-digital-activism/.

173. Will Englund, Russia Hears an Argument for Web Freedom, WASH. POST (Oct. 28, 2011), https://www.washingtonpost.com/world/europe/russia-hears-an-argument-for-web-freedom/2011/10/28/gIQAFybZPM_story.html.

174. Brazil as the Global Guardian of Internet Freedom?, HUMAN RIGHTS WATCH (Feb. 13, 2015), https://www.hrw.org/news/2015/02/13/brazil-global-guardian-internet-freedom#.

175. Goldsmith, *supra* note 1.

176. Press Release, Office of the Press Secretary, Remarks by the President to the UN General Assembly (Sep. 25, 2012), https://obamawhitehouse.archives.gov/the-press-office/2012/09/25/remarks-president-un-general-assembly

177. Jessi Hempel, Social Media Made the Arab Spring But Couldn't Save It, WIRED (Jan. 26, 2016), https://www.wired.com/2016/01/social-media-made-the-arab-spring-but-couldnt-save-it/.

178. *Id.*

179. Daria Litvinova, This Social Media App Is Driving the Belarus Protests, THE CHRISTIAN SCIENCE MONITOR (Aug. 21, 2020), https://www.csmonitor.com/World/Europe/2020/0821/This-social-media-app-is-driving-the-Belarus-protests.

180. Adrian Shahbaz & Allie Funk, Freedom on the Net 2021: The Global Drive to Control Big Tech, FREEDOM HOUSE, 2–4, https://freedomhouse.org/report/freedom-net/2021/global-drive-control-big-tech#Key.

181. Ira C. Magaziner, Creating a Framework for Global Electronic Commerce, FUTURE INSIGHT (July 1999), http://www.pff.org/issues-pubs/futureinsights/fi6.1globaleconomiccommerce.html.

182. Directive 2000/31/EC of the European Parliament and of the Council (June 8, 2000), https://eur-lex.europa.eu/legal-content/EN/TXT/PDF/?uri=CELEX:32000L0031&from=EN.

183. *See supra* Chapter 3.

184. Goldsmith, *supra* note 1.

CHAPTER 8

1. Matthew S. Erie & Thomas Streinz, The Beijing Effect: China's "Digital Silk Road" as Transnational Data Governance, 54 N.Y.U. J. INT'L L. & POL. 1 (2021).

2. *See id.* at 53.

3. James Kynge et al., Exporting Chinese Surveillance: The Security Risks of "Smart Cities," FIN. TIMES (June 9, 2021), https://www.ft.com/content/76fda c7c-7076-47a4-bcb0-7e75af0aadab.

4. *See id.*

5. *See generally* Erie & Streinz, *supra* note 1.

6. *See* Elizabeth C. Economy, THE THIRD REVOLUTION: XI JINPING AND THE NEW CHINESE STATE 58 (2018).

7. Kynge et al., *supra* note 3.

8. *See, e.g.,* Christopher Ashley Ford, Huawei and Its Siblings, the Chinese Tech Giants: National Security and Foreign Policy Implications, U.S. DEP'T OF STATE (Sep. 11, 2019), https://2017-2021.state.gov/huawei-and-its-siblings-the-chin ese-tech-giants-national-security-and-foreign-policy-implications/index.html.

9. Lindsay Maizland & Andrew Chatzky, Huawei: China's Controversial Tech Giant, COUNCIL ON FOREIGN REL. (Aug. 6, 2020), https://www.cfr.org/backg rounder/huawei-chinas-controversial-tech-giant; Michael Schuman, Why America Is Afraid of TikTok, ATLANTIC (July 30, 2020), https://www.theatlan tic.com/international/archive/2020/07/tiktok-ban-china-america/614725/.

10. David Sacks, Countries in China's Belt and Road Initiative: Who's In & Who's Out, COUNCIL ON FOREIGN RELATIONS (Mar. 24, 2021), https://www.cfr.org/blog/countries-chinas-belt-and-road-initiative-whos-and-whos-out.

11. Nat'l Dev. & Reform Comm'n, Ministry of Foreign Affs. & Ministry of Com., Vision and Actions on Jointly Building Silk Road Economic Belt and 21st-Century Maritime Silk Road, NAT'L DEV. & REFORM COMM'N (Mar. 28, 2015), https://www.fmprc.gov.cn/eng/topics_665678/2015zt/xjpcxbayzlt2015nnh/201503/t2015 0328_705553.html#:~:text=The%20Chinese%20government%20has%20draf ted,African%20countries%20more%20closely%20and (China).

12. *See* Joshua Kurlantzick, China's Digital Silk Road Initiative: A Boon for Developing Countries or a Danger to Freedom?, DIPLOMAT (Dec. 17, 2020),

https://thediplomat.com/2020/12/chinas-digital-silk-road-initiative-a-boon-for-developing-countries-or-a-danger-to-freedom/.

13. *See* Robert Greene & Paul Triolo, Will China Control the Global Internet via Its Digital Silk Road?, CARNEGIE ENDOWMENT FOR INT'L PEACE (May 8, 2020), https://carnegieendowment.org/2020/05/08/will-china-control-global-internet-via-its-digital-silk-road-pub-81857.

14. *Id.*

15. *See* Andrew Kitson & Kenny Liew, China Doubles Down on Its Digital Silk Road, CTR. FOR STRATEGIC & INT'L STUDIES (Nov. 14, 2019), https://reconasia.csis.org/china-doubles-down-its-digital-silk-road/.

16. Richard Ghiasy & Rajeshwari Krishnamurthy, China's Digital Silk Road & the Global Digital Order, DIPLOMAT (Apr. 13, 2021), https://thediplomat.com/2021/04/chinas-digital-silk-road-and-the-global-digital-order/.

17. Arjun Kharpal, Huawei Says It Would Never Hand Data to China's Government. Experts Say It Wouldn't Have a Choice, CNBC (Mar. 5, 2019), https://www.cnbc.com/2019/03/05/huawei-would-have-to-give-data-to-china-government-if-asked-experts.html .

18. Kynge et al., *supra* note 3.

19. *See* Katherine Atha et al., SOS INT'L LLC, CHINA'S SMART CITIES DEVELOPMENT: RESEARCH REPORT PREPARED ON BEHALF OF THE U.S.-CHINA ECONOMIC AND SECURITY REVIEW COMMISSION 27–29, 55–80 (2020), https://www.uscc.gov/sites/default/files/China_Smart_Cities_Development.pdf; *see also* Kynge et al., *supra* note 3.

20. Kharpal, *supra* note 17.

21. Atha et al., *supra* note 19, at 55.

22. Kynge et al., *supra* note 3.

23. Steven Feldstein, The Global Expansion of AI Surveillance 8 (Carnegie Endowment for Int'l Peace Working Paper, Sep. 2019), https://carnegieendowment.org/files/WP-Feldstein-AISurveillance_final1.pdf.

24. Álvaro Artigas, INSTITUT BARCELONA D'ESTUDIS INTERNACIONALS [BARCELONA INSTITUTE OF INTERNATIONAL STUDIES], SURVEILLANCE, SMART TECHNOLOGIES AND THE DEVELOPMENT OF SAFE CITY SOLUTIONS: THE CASE OF CHINESE ICT FIRMS AND THEIR INTERNATIONAL EXPANSION TO EMERGING MARKETS 33–35 (IBEI Working Papers, 2017/52, 2017), https://www.ibei.org/surveillance-smart-technologies-and-the-development-of-safe-city-solutions-the-case-of-chinese-ict-firms-and-their-international-expansion-to-emerging-markets_112561.pdf.

25. Atha et al., *supra* note 19, at 71–78.

26. Adam Segal, When China Rules the Web: Technology in Service of the State, FOREIGN AFFS., Sep./Oct. 2018, at 17 [hereinafter: Segal, *When China Rules the Web*]

27. Joe Parkinson, Nicholas Bariyo, & Josh Chin, Huawei Technicians Helped African Governments Spy on Political Opponents, WALL ST. J. (Aug. 15, 2019),

https://www.wsj.com/articles/huawei-technicians-helped-african-governme
nts-spy-on-political-opponents-11565793017.

28. Al-Masry Al-Youm, Egypt, Huawei Sign MoU for Cloud Computing AI
Networks, EGYPT INDEP. (Feb. 26, 2019), https://egyptindependent.com/egypt-
huawei-sign-mou-for-cloud-computing-ai-networks/.

29. James Barton, Telecom Egypt Secures $200M of Chinese Financing, DEVELOPING
TELECOMS (May 30, 2018), https://developingtelecoms.com/business/operator-
news/7841-telecom-egypt-secures-200m-of-chinese-financing.html.

30. Hikvision Enhances Suez Governorate's Bus Fleet Operation, HIKVISION,
https://www.hikvision.com/en/newsroom/success-stories/traffic/hikvision-
enhances-suez-governorate-s-bus-fleet-operation/.

31. Atha et al., *supra* note 19, at 68–70.

32. *Id.* at 70.

33. *Id.*

34. *Id.* at 75 (quoting a Nairobi police force official speaking in a video posted on
(yet subsequently removed from) Huawei's website).

35. Chris Burt, Zimbabwe to Use Hikvision Facial Recognition Technology for
Border Control, BIOMETRIC UPDATE (Jun 14, 2018), https://www.biometricupd
ate.com/201806/zimbabwe-to-use-hikvision-facial-recognition-technology-for-
border-control.

36. Problem Masau, Chinese Tech Revolution Comes to Zimbabwe, HERALD
(Oct. 9, 2019, 00:10), https://www.herald.co.zw/chinese-tech-revolution-
comes-to-zim/.

37. *See* Amy Hawkins, Beijing's Big Brother Tech Needs African Faces, FOREIGN
POL'Y (July 28, 2018), https://foreignpolicy.com/2018/07/24/beijings-big-brot
her-tech-needs-african-faces/.

38. Lynsey Chutel, China Is Exporting Facial Recognition Software to Africa,
Expanding Its Vast Database, QUARTZ AFRICA (July 20, 2022), https://qz.com/
africa/1287675/china-is-exporting-facial-recognition-to-africa-ensuring-ai-
dominance-through-diversity/ .

39. Joy Buolamwini & Timnit Gebru, Gender Shades: Intersectional Accuracy
Disparities in Commercial Gender Classification, 81 PROC. MACH. LEARNING
RSCH. 77 (2018), http://proceedings.mlr.press/v81/buolamwini18a/buolam
wini18a.pdf].

40. Hawkins, *supra* note 37.

41. *Id.*

42. Ashnah Kalemera, Tanzania Issues Regressive Online Content Regulations,
CIPESA (Apr. 12, 2018), https://cipesa.org/2018/04/tanzania-enacts-regress
ive-online-content-regulations/.

43. Jisuanji Xinxi Wangluo Guoji Lianwang Anquan Baohu Guanli Banfa (计算
机信息网络国际联网安全保护管理办法) [Measures for Security Protection
Administration of International Interconnection of Computer-Based Information

Networks] (promulgated by St. Council Dec. 16, 1997, effective Dec. 30, 1997, revised Jan. 8, 2011, effective Jan. 8, 2011), art. 5 § 5, ST. COUNCIL GAZ. SUPP., Apr. 28, 2011, at 332, 333 (China), translated in PKULaw, CLI.2.174847(EN).

44. Wangluo Duanshiping Neirong Shenhe Biaozhun Xize (网络短视频内容审核标准细则) [Standards and Detailed Rules for the Review of Online Short Video Content] (promulgated by China Netcasting Service Association Jan. 2019, effective Jan. 2019, revised Dec. 2021, effective Dec. 2021) art. 2 § 14, http://www.cnsa.cn/art/2021/12/16/art_1488_27573.html (China), translated in Standards and Detailed Rules for the Review of Online Short Video Content (2021), CHINA L. TRANSLATE (Dec. 16, 2021), https://www.chinalawtranslate.com/en/short-video-content/.

45. Kurlantzick, *supra* note 12.

46. Adam Segal, China's Vision for Cyber Sovereignty and the Global Governance of Cyberspace, in AN EMERGING CHINA-CENTRIC ORDER: CHINA'S VISION FOR A NEW WORLD ORDER IN PRACTICE 85, 94 (Nat'l Bureau of Asian Research, Special Report #87, Aug. 2020), https://www.nbr.org/wp-content/uploads/pdfs/publications/sr87_aug2020.pdf [hereinafter: Segal, *China's Vision*]

47. Adrian Shahbaz, The Rise of Digital Authoritarianism, in FREEDOM HOUSE, FREEDOM ON THE NET 2018, at 8 (2018), https://freedomhouse.org/sites/default/files/FOTN_2018_Final.pdf.

48. *See* Chan Jia Hao, China's Digital Silk Road: A Game Changer for Asian Economies, DIPLOMAT (Apr. 30, 2019), https://thediplomat.com/2019/04/chinas-digital-silk-road-a-game-changer-for-asian-economies/.

49. Erie & Streinz, *supra* note 1, at 69–70, 72–73.

50. Hugh Harsono, China's Surveillance Technology Is Keeping Tabs on Populations Around the World, DIPLOMAT (June 19, 2020), https://thediplomat.com/2020/06/chinas-surveillance-technology-is-keeping-tabs-on-populations-around-the-world.

51. *See* Brian Harding, China's Digital Silk Road & Southeast Asia, CTR. FOR STRATEGIC & INT'L STUD. (Feb. 15, 2019), https://www.csis.org/analysis/chinas-digital-silk-road-and-southeast-asia.

52. Paul Mozur, Jonah M. Kessel, & Melissa Chan, Made in China: Exported to the World, N.Y. TIMES (Apr. 24, 2019), https://www.nytimes.com/2019/04/24/technology/ecuador-surveillance-cameras-police-government.html.

53. Atha et al., *supra* note 19, at 67.

54. Mozur et al., *supra* note 52.

55. Zack Wittaker, US Towns Are Buying Chinese Surveillance Tech Tied to Uighur Abuses, TECHCRUNCH (May 24, 2021), https://techcrunch.com/2021/05/24/united-states-towns-hikvision-dahua-surveillance/.

56. Prague Sec. Stud. Inst., THE SUM OF ALL FEARS—CHINESE AI SURVEILLANCE IN SERBIA 3 (2020), https://www.pssi.cz/download//docs/8447_the-sum-of-all-fears-chinese-ai-surveillance-in-serbia.pdf.

57. *Id.*

58. Economist Intel. Unit, DEMOCRACY INDEX 2020: IN SICKNESS AND IN HEALTH? 33 (2020).

59. Feldstein, *supra* note 23, at 26–28.

60. *See generally* Ryan Fedasiuk, Emily Weinstein, & Anna Puglisi, CTR. FOR SEC. AND EMERGING TECH, CHINA'S FOREIGN TECHNOLOGY WISH LIST (2021), https://cset. georgetown.edu/wp-content/uploads/CSET-Chinas-Foreign-Technology-Wish-List.pdf.

61. *Id.* at 20.

62. *See* Secretary Michael R. Pompeo at a Press Availability with Danish Foreign Minister Jeppe Kofod, U.S. EMBASSY & CONSULATE DEN., https://dk.usembassy. gov/secretary-michael-r-pompeo-at-a-press-availability-with-danish-foreign-minister-jeppe-kofod/; Jennifer Hansler, Pompeo Blasts Beijing as Deadline Nears for China to Shutter Houston Consulate, CNN (July 23, 2020), https:// www.cnn.com/2020/07/23/politics/pompeo-china-nixon-library-speech/ index.html.

63. Erie & Streinz, *supra* note 1, 35–47, 61–67.

64. *See* Segal, *When China Rules the Web, supra* note 26, at 16.

65. Letter from the Permanent Representatives of China, the Russian Federation, Tajikistan & Uzbekistan to the U.N. Addressed to the Secretary-General (Sep. 14, 2011), https://undocs.org/A/66/359 (select "English").

66. *See* Adam Segal, COUNCIL OF FOREIGN RELATIONS, CHINA'S ALTERNATIVE CYBER GOVERNANCE REGIME 4 (2020), https://www.uscc.gov/sites/default/files/test imonies/March%2013%20Hearing_Panel%203_Adam%20Segal%20CFR.pdf.

67. BRICS LEADERS XIAMEN DECLARATION 25 (2017), http://www.brics.utoronto.ca/ docs/170904-xiamen.pdf.

68. Colum Lynch & Elias Groll, As U.S. Retreats Farther From World Organizations, China Steps in to Fill the Void, FOREIGN POL'Y (Oct. 6, 2017), https://foreignpol icy.com/2017/10/06/as-u-s-retreats-from-world-organizations-china-steps-in-the-fill-the-void/.

69. Segal, *China's Vision, supra* note 46, at 91–92.

70. Franz-Stefan Gady, The Wuzhen Summit & Chinese Internet Sovereignty, CHINA U.S. FOCUS (Dec. 8, 2014), https://www.chinausfocus.com/peace-secur ity/the-wuzhen-summit-and-chinese-internet-sovereignty.

71. International Strategy of Cooperation on Cyberspace, MINISTRY FOREIGN AFFS. CHINA (Mar. 1, 2017), https://www.fmprc.gov.cn/mfa_eng/wjb_663304/zzjg_ 663340/jks_665232/kjlc_665236/qtwt_665250/201703/t20170301_599869. html#:~:text=International%20Strategy%20of%20Cooperation%20on%20 Cyberspace%20provides%20a%20comprehensive%20explanation,exter nal%20relations%20on%20that%20front.

72. Arjun Kharpal, Power Is "Up for Grabs": Behind China's Plan to Shape the Future of Next-Generation Tech, CNBC (Apr. 26, 2020), https://www.cnbc.com/2020/04/27/china-standards-2035-explained.html.

73. Valentina Pop, Sha Hua, & Daniel Michaels, From Lightbulbs to 5G, China Battles West for Control Over Vital Technology Standards, WALL ST. J. (Feb. 8, 2021), https://www.wsj.com/articles/from-lightbulbs-to-5g-china-battles-west-for-control-of-vital-technology-standards-11612722698.

74. *Id.*

75. Jorge L. Contreras, Global Rate Setting: A Solution for Standards-Essential Patents?, 94 WASH. L. REV. 701, 704 (2019).

76. Biography—Houlin Zhao, ITU, https://www.itu.int/en/osg/Pages/biography-zhao.aspx.

77. Daniel Fuchs & Sarah Eaton, How China & Germany Became Partners on Technical Standardization, WASH. POST (Nov. 16, 2020), https://www.washingtonpost.com/politics/2020/11/16/how-china-germany-became-partners-technical-standardization/.

78. Int'l Elec. Comm'n, IEC LEADERSHIP (2021), https://www.iec.ch/leadership.

79. Newley Purnell & Stu Woo, China's Huawei Is Determined to Lead the Way on 5G Despite U.S. Concerns, WALL ST. J. (Mar. 30, 2018), https://www.wsj.com/articles/washington-woes-aside-huawei-is-determined-to-lead-the-way-on-5g-1522402201.

80. *See* WG 11 Smart Cities, JTC1 (Oct. 2021), https://jtc1info.org/sd-2-history/jtc1-working-groups/wg-11/]; *see also* Atha et al., *supra* note 19, at 58.

81. *See* James Kynge & Nian Liu, From AI to Facial Recognition: How China Is Setting the Rules in New Tech, FIN. TIMES (Oct. 7, 2020), https://www.ft.com/content/188d86df-6e82-47eb-a134-2e1e45c777b6.

82. *Id.*

83. Segal, *China's Vision, supra* note 46, at 98.

84. Eurasia Group, THE DIGITAL SILKROAD: EXPANDING CHINA'S DIGITAL FOOTPRINT 12 (Apr. 8, 2020), https://www.eurasiagroup.net/files/upload/Digital-Silk-Road-Expanding-China-Digital-Footprint.pdf.

85. Pop et al., *supra* note 73.

86. Anna Gross & Madhumita Murgia, China & Huawei Propose Reinvention of the Internet, FIN. TIMES (Mar. 27, 2020), https://www.ft.com/content/c78be2cf-a1a1-40b1-8ab7-904d7095e0f2.

87. *See* Nicholas Rühlig & Tobias ten Brink, The Externalization of China's Technical Standardization Approach, 52 DEVELOPMENT & CHANGE 1196, 1216 (2021).

88. Gross & Murgia, China & Huawei Propose Reinvention of the Internet, *supra* note 86.

89. *Id.*

90. *See* Madhumita Murgia & Anna Gross, Inside China's Controversial Mission to Reinvent the Internet, FIN. TIMES (Mar. 27, 2020), https://www.ft.com/cont

ent/ba94c2bc-6e27-11ea-9bca-bf503995cd6f; *see also* Gross & Murgia, China & Huawei Propose Reinvention of the Internet, *supra* note 86.

91. Milton Mueller, About that Chinese "Reinvention" of the Internet, INTERNET GOVERNANCE PROJECT (March 30, 2022), https://www.internetgovernance.org/2020/03/30/about-that-chinese-reinvention-of-the-internet/.

92. *Id.*

93. Alissa Cooper, Liaison Statement, Response to "LS on New IP, Shaping Future Network," IETF DATATRACKER (March 30, 2020), https://datatracker.ietf.org/liaison/1677/.

94. Javier Espinoza & Valentina Pop, EU to Outline Tech Standards Plan to Counter China Influence, FIN. TIMES (Feb. 2, 2022), https://www.ft.com/content/531194f3-feb3-4222-a949-f9f17618b618.

95. Luca Bertuzzi, China Rebrands Proposal on Internet Governance, Targeting Developing Countries, EURACTIV (June 6, 2022), https://www.euractiv.com/section/digital/news/china-rebrands-proposal-on-internet-governance-targeting-developing-countries/.

96. *Id.*

97. *Id.*

98. *See* Rühlig & ten Brink, *supra* note 87, at 1205–1206.

99. *See id.* at 1210.

100. Federal'nyĭ Zakon RF o vnesenii izmenenij v Federal'nyj zakon o svjazi I Federal'nyj zakon Ob informacii, informacionnyh tehnologijah I o zašite informacii [Federal Law of the Russian Federation on Amendments to the Federal Law on Communications and the Federal Law on Information, Information Technologies and Information Protection], SOBRANIE ZAKONODATEL'STVA ROSSIĬSKOĬ FEDERATSII [SZ RF] [Russian Federal Collection of Legislation] 2019, No. 90.

101. Alex Hern & Marc Bennetts, Great Firewall Fears as Russia Plans to Cut Itself Off From Internet, GUARDIAN (Feb. 12, 2019), https://www.theguardian.com/world/2019/feb/12/great-firewall-fears-as-russia-plans-to-cut-itself-off-from-internet.

102. Russia: Growing Internet Isolation, Control, Censorship, HUMAN RIGHTS WATCH (June 18, 2020), https://www.hrw.org/news/2020/06/18/russia-growing-internet-isolation-control-censorship.

103. Anton Troianovski, China Censors the Internet. So Why Doesn't Russia?, N.Y. TIMES (February 21, 2021), https://www.nytimes.com/2021/02/21/world/europe/russia-internet-censorship.html.

104. *Id.*

105. Federal'nyĭ Zakon RF o dejatel'nosti inostrannyh lic v informacionno-telekommunikacionnoj seti "Interne" na territorii Rossijskoj Federacii [Federal Law of the Russian Federation on the Activities of Foreign Persons on the Internet Telecommunications Network "Internet" in the Territory of the

Russian Federation], SOBRANIE ZAKONODATEL'STVA ROSSIĬSKOĬ FEDERATSII [SZ
RF] [Russian Federal Collection of Legislation] 2021, No. 236; *See* Putin Signs
Law Forcing Foreign Social Media Giants to Open Russian Offices, REUTERS
(July 1, 2021), https://www.reuters.com/technology/putin-signs-law-forcing-
foreign-it-firms-open-offices-russia-2021-07-01/.

106. Federal'nyĭ Zakon RF o vnesenii izmenenij v otdel'nye zakonodatel'nye
akty Rossijskoj Federacii v časti utočnenija porjadka obrabotki personal'nyh
dannyh v informacionno-telekommunikacionnyh setjah [Federal Law of the
Russian Federation on Amendments to Certain Legislative Acts of the Russian
Federation to Clarify the Procedure of Personal Data Processing in Information
and Telecommunication Networks], SOBRANIE ZAKONODATEL'STVA ROSSIĬSKOĬ
FEDERATSII [SZ RF] [Russian Federal Collection of Legislation] 2014, No. 242.

107. LinkedIn Blocked by Russian Authorities, BBC (Nov. 17, 2016), https://www.
bbc.com/news/technology-38014501.

108. Facebook, Twitter Told to Open Databases in Russia by July—Ifax, REUTERS
(May 26, 2021), https://www.reuters.com/technology/russia-force-facebook-
twitter-open-databases-russian-territory-by-july-ifax-2021-05-26/.

109. Russia Opens Case Against Google for Breaching Personal Data Law, REUTERS
(June 30, 2021), https://www.reuters.com/technology/google-risks-russia-fine-
over-personal-data-law-regulator-2021-06-30/.

110. Ananaya Agrawal, Russia Fines Google, Sues WhatsApp for Violating Data
Localisation Law, JURIST (August 1, 2021), https://www.jurist.org/news/2021/
08/russia-fines-google-sues-whatsapp-for-violating-data-localisation-law/.

111. Federal'nyĭ Zakon RF o vnesenii izmenenij v Federal'nyj zakon o protivodejstvii
terrorizm i otdel'nye zakonodatel'nye akty Rossijskoj Federacii v časti
ustanovlenija dopolnitel'nyh mer protivodejstvija terrorizmu i obespečenija
obŝestvennoj bezopasnosti [Federal Law of the Russian Federation on
Amendments to the Federal Law on Counteraction of Terrorism, and Other
Legal Acts of the Russian Federation in the Part Establishing Additional
Measures to Counteract Terrorism and Ensure Public Safety], SOBRANIE
ZAKONODATEL'STVA ROSSIĬSKOĬ FEDERATSII [SZ RF] [Russian Federal Collection of
Legislation] 2016–2018, No. 374.

112. Russia: Growing Internet Isolation, Control, Censorship, HUMAN RIGHTS
WATCH, *supra* note 102.

113. Federal'nyj Zakon RF o vnesenii izmenenij v Kodeks Rossijskoj Federacii Ob
Administrativnyh Pravonaruŝenijah [Federal Law of the Russian Federation on
Amendments to the Code of Administrative Offenses of the Russian Federation],
SOBRANIE ZAKONODATEL'STVA ROSSIĬSKOĬ FEDERATSII [SZ RF] [Russian Federal
Collection of Legislation] 2020, No. 511. *See* The Putin Regime Will Never Tire
of Imposing Internet Control: Developments in Digital Legislation in Russia,
COUNCIL ON FOREIGN RELATIONS (February 22, 2021), https://www.cfr.org/blog/
putin-regime-will-never-tire-imposing-internet-control-developments-digi

tal-legislation-russia; *see also* Russia: Social Media Pressured to Censor Posts, HUMAN RIGHTS WATCH (Feb. 25, 2021), https://www.hrw.org/news/2021/02/05/russia-social-media-pressured-censor-posts.

114. Russia Fines Google, Facebook for Failing to Delete Banned Content, REUTERS (May 25, 2021), https://www.reuters.com/technology/russia-fines-google-4-mln-roubles-failing-delete-content-tass-2021-05-25/.

115. Federal'nyĭ Zakon RF o vnesenii izmenenij v Federal'nyj zakon o merah vozdejstvija na lic, pričastnyh k narušenijam osnovopolagajuših prav I svobod čeloveka, prav i svobod graždan [Federal Law of the Russian Federation on Amendments to the Federal Law on Measures of Influence on Persons Involved in Violations of Fundamental Human Rights and Freedoms, Rights and Freedoms of Citizens of the Russian Federation], SOBRANIE ZAKONODATEL'STVA ROSSIĬSKOĬ FEDERATSII [SZ RF] [Russian Federal Collection of Legislation] 2020, No. 482.

116. Google Appeals Court Order to Unblock YouTube Account of Sanctioned Businessman, REUTERS (May 20, 2021), https://www.reuters.com/technology/google-appeals-court-order-unblock-youtube-account-sanctioned-businessman-2021-05-20/.

117. Max Seddon, YouTube Feels the Heat as Russia Ramps Up "Digital Sovereignty" Drive, FIN. TIMES (May 22, 2021), https://www.ft.com/content/918d2e15-b4d7-4d02-8961-6dfc4e76d68f.

118. *Id.*

119. *See* Leonid Kovachich & Andrei Kolesnikov, Digital Authoritarianism with Russian Characteristics?, CARNEGIE MOSCOW CTR. (April 21, 2021), https://carnegiemoscow.org/2021/04/21/digital-authoritarianism-with-russian-characteristics-pub-84346.

120. Max Seddon & Madhumita Murgia, Apple and Google Drop Navalny App After Kremlin Piles on Pressure, FIN. TIMES (Sep. 17, 2021), https://www.ft.com/content/faaada81-73d6-428c-8d74-88d273adbad3; Putin Calls for Internet Bound by Moral Rules, Criticises Opposition Rallies, REUTERS (Mar. 4, 2021), https://www.reuters.com/article/us-russia-internet/putin-calls-for-internet-bound-by-moral-rules-criticises-opposition-rallies-idUSKCN2AW2D4.

121. Federal'nyĭ Zakon RF o vnesenii izmenenija v stat'ju 128I Ugolovnogo kodeksa Rossijskoj Federacii [Federal Law of the Russian Federation on Amendments to Article 128-1 of the Criminal Code of the Russian Federation], SOBRANIE ZAKONODATEL'STVA ROSSIĬSKOĬ FEDERATSII [SZ RF] [Russian Federal Collection of Legislation], Dec. 30, 2020, No. 538. *See* Putin Signs Bill Criminalizing Online Slander Into Law, TASS (Dec. 30, 2020), https://tass.com/politics/1241379.

122. Olga Melnikova (Ольга Мельникова), Международный Союз Электросвязи—Технический Регулятор Или Арена Нового Противостояния [International Telecommunication Union—Technical Regulator or Arena of New

Confrontation], Международная Жизнь [INT'L AFFS.] (Dec. 7, 2021), https://interaffairs.ru/news/show/30759 (translation by Google Translate).

123. Zhonghua Renmin Gongheguo Zhengfu he Eluosi Lianbang Zhengfu Guanyu zai Baozhang Guoji Xinxi Anquan Lingyu Hezuo Xieding (中华人民共和国政府和俄罗斯联邦政府关于在保障国际信息安全领域合作协定) [Agreement Between the Government of the Russian Federation and the Government of the People's Republic of China on Cooperation in Ensuring International Information Security], Russ.-China, May 8, 2015. *See* Valentin Weber, The Sinicization of Russia's Cyber Sovereignty Model, COUNCIL ON FOREIGN REL. (April 1, 2020), https://www.cfr.org/blog/sinicization-russias-cyber-sovereig nty-model.

124. Miranda Lupion, Sino-Russian Advocacy for "Internet Sovereignty" and State-Led Internet Governance, in DIGITAL SILK ROAD IN CENTRAL ASIA: PRESENT AND FUTURE 9, 11 (Nargis Kassenova & Brendan Duprey eds., 2021), https://davi scenter.fas.harvard.edu/sites/default/files/files/2021-06/Digital_Silk_Road_ Report.pdf.

125. Weber, *supra* note 123.

126. *See generally* Dennis Broeders, Liisi Adamson, & Rogier Creemers, THE HAGUE PROGRAM FOR CYBER NORMS, A COALITION OF THE UNWILLING? CHINESE & RUSSIAN PERSPECTIVES ON CYBERSPACE 3–4 (2021).

127. Troianovski, *supra* note 103.

128. Kovachich & Kolesnikov, *supra* note 119; *see* Max Seddon & Henry Foy, Russian Technology: Can the Kremlin Control the Internet?, FIN. TIMES (June 5, 2019), https://www.ft.com/content/93be9242-85e0-11e9-a028-86cea8523dc2.

129. Cat and Mouse: How China Makes Sure Its Internet Abides by the Rules, ECONOMIST (Apr. 6, 2013), https://www.economist.com/special-report/2013/04/06/cat-and-mouse.

130. Russia Lifts Ban on Telegram Messaging App After Failing to Block It, REUTERS (June 18, 2020), https://www.reuters.com/article/us-russia-telegram-ban/russia-lifts-ban-on-telegram-messaging-app-after-failing-to-block-it-idUSKB N23P2FT.

131. Max Seddon & Siddharth Venkataramakrishnan, Russia Attempts to Slow Down Access to Twitter, FIN. TIMES (Mar. 10, 2021), https://www.ft.com/cont ent/7b46cb83-1e42-45c1-9a25-86da0fca24cc.

132. *Id.*

133. *See* Laura Dudley, Part Three: Huawei's Role in the China-Russia Technological Partnership, COUNCIL ON FOREIGN RELATIONS (Dec. 16, 2020), https://www.cfr. org/blog/part-three-huaweis-role-china-russia-technological-partnership.

134. Alexander Gabuev, Huawei's Courtship of Moscow Leaves West in the Cold, FIN. TIMES (June 21, 2020), https://www.ft.com/content/f36a558f-4e4d-4c00-8252-d8c4be45bde4.

135. Kovachich & Kolesnikov, *supra* note 119.

136. *Id.*

137. Russian Law Requires Smart Devices to Come Pre-Installed With Domestic Software, REUTERS (April 1, 2021), https://www.reuters.com/article/us-russia-technology-software/russian-law-requires-smart-devices-to-come-pre-installed-with-domestic-software-idUSKBN2BO4P2.

138. Mark Gurman, Apple Agrees to Let Russians Pre-Install Local Apps on iPhones, BLOOMBERG (March 16, 2021), https://www.bloomberg.com/news/articles/2021-03-16/apple-agrees-to-let-russians-pre-install-local-apps-on-iphones.

139. Pjotr Sauer, Russia Bans Facebook and Instagram Under "Extremism" Law, GUARDIAN (Mar. 21, 2022), https://www.theguardian.com/world/2022/mar/21/russia-bans-facebook-and-instagram-under-extremism-law.

140. Jillian Deutsch, RT, Sputnik Content Officially Banned Across European Union, BLOOMBERG (Mar. 2, 2022), https://www.bloomberg.com/news/articles/2022-03-02/rt-sputnik-content-officially-banned-across-european-union.

141. *See* William Yang, Ukraine War: How Russian Propaganda Dominates Chinese Social Media, DW (June 4, 2022), https://www.dw.com/en/ukraine-war-how-russian-propaganda-dominates-chinese-social-media/a-61375386.

142. *See* Greene & Triolo, *supra* note 13.

143. Robyn Dixon, China's New Surveillance Program Aims to Cut Crime. Some Fear It'll Do Much More, L.A. TIMES (Oct. 27, 2018), https://www.latimes.com/world/asia/la-fg-china-sharp-eyes-20181027-story.html.

144. Charlie Campbell, "The Entire System Is Designed to Suppress Us." What the Chinese Surveillance State Means for the Rest of the World, TIME (Nov. 21, 2019), https://time.com/5735411/china-surveillance-privacy-issues/.

145. *See generally* Feldstein, *supra* note 23.

146. Paul Mozur, Jonah M. Kessel, & Melissa Chan, Made in China, Exported to the World: The Surveillance State, N.Y. TIMES (Apr. 24, 2019), https://www.nytimes.com/2019/04/24/technology/ecuador-surveillance-cameras-police-government.html.

147. Hawkins, *supra* note 37.

148. Freedom House, FREEDOM ON THE NET 2021, at 4 (2021), https://freedomhouse.org/sites/default/files/2021-09/FOTN_2021_Complete_Booklet_09162021_FINAL_UPDATED.pdf.

149. *Id.* at 9 (2021).

150. Kaan Sahin, The West, China, and AI Surveillance, ATL. COUNCIL (Dec. 18, 2020), https://www.atlanticcouncil.org/blogs/geotech-cues/the-west-china-and-ai-surveillance/; for the effectiveness of the Chinese measures, *see, e.g.,* Kai Kupferschmidt & Jon Cohen, China's Aggressive Measures Have Slowed the Coronavirus. They May Not Work in Other Countries, SCIENCE (Mar. 2, 2020), https://www.science.org/content/article/china-s-aggressive-measures-have-slowed-coronavirus-they-may-not-work-other-countries.

151. *See* Aidan Powers-Riggs, Covid-19 Is Proving a Boon for Digital Authoritarianism, CTR. FOR STRATEGIC AND INT'L STUD. (Aug. 17, 2020), https://www.csis.org/blogs/new-perspectives-asia/covid-19-proving-boon-digital-authoritarianism.

152. Feldstein, *supra* note 23, at 1–2.

153. Ronen Bergman & Mark Mazzetti, The Battle for the World's Most Powerful Cyberweapon, N.Y. TIMES MAG., https://www.nytimes.com/2022/01/28/magazine/nso-group-israel-spyware.html.

154. *Id.*

155. David E. Sanger et al., U.S. Blacklists Israeli Firm NSO Group Over Spyware, N.Y. TIMES (Nov. 3, 2021), https://www.nytimes.com/2021/11/03/business/nso-group-spyware-blacklist.html.

156. Feldstein, *supra* note 23, at 13–14.

157. Liza Lin & Josh Chin, U.S. Tech Companies Prop Up China's Vast Surveillance Network, WALL ST. J. (Nov. 26, 2019), https://www.wsj.com/articles/u-s-tech-companies-prop-up-chinas-vast-surveillance-network-11574786846.

158. Pop et al., *supra* note 73.

159. Kynge et al., *supra* note 3.

160. Assessing China's Digital Silk Road Initiative, COUNCIL ON FOREIGN REL., https://www.cfr.org/china-digital-silk-road/.

161. Greene & Triolo, *supra* note 13.

162. Erie & Streinz, *supra* note 1, at 5.

163. *See* Parkinson et al., *supra* note 27.

164. *Id.*

165. Daniel Cave, The African Union Headquarters Hack & Australia's 5G Network, AUSTRALIAN STRATEGIC POLICY INST.: THE STRATEGIST (July 13, 2018), https://www.aspistrategist.org.au/the-african-union-headquarters-hack-and-australias-5g-network/.

166. Abhishek G. Bhaya, China, African Leaders Slam French Report on AU Headquarters Hacking as "Ridiculous," "Nonsense," CGTN, https://news.cgtn.com/news/346b6a4e30677a6333566d54/share_p.html (last updated Jan. 31, 2018).

167. Ghalia Kadiri & Joan Tilouine, A Addis-Abeba, le Siège de l'Union Africaine Espionné par Pékin [In Addis Ababa, the Headquarters of the African Union Spied on by Beijing], LE MONDE [THE WORLD] (Jan. 26, 2018), https://www.lemonde.fr/afrique/article/2018/01/26/a-addis-abeba-le-siege-de-l-union-africaine-espionne-par-les-chinois_5247521_3212.html (Fr.).

168. Raphael Satter, Exclusive—Suspected Chinese Hackers Stole Camera Footage from African Union—Memo, REUTERS (Dec. 16, 2020), https://www.reuters.com/article/us-ethiopia-african-union-cyber-exclusiv-idINKBN28Q1DB.

169. *Id.*

170. *See* Asebe Regassa Debelo, SOC. SCIENCE RESEARCH COUNCIL, THE AFRICAN UNION'S PEACE & SECURITY PARTNERSHIPS WITH CHINA 2 (African Peacebuilding

Network, Briefing Note No. 12, July 2017), https://s3.amazonaws.com/ssrc-cdn1/crmuploads/new_publication_3/the-african-union-s-peace-and-security-partnership-with-china.pdf.

171. Feldstein, *supra* note 23, at 1–2.

172. David E. Sanger & Nicole Perlroth, N.S.A. Breached Chinese Servers Seen as Security Threat, N.Y. TIMES (Mar. 22, 2014), https://www.nytimes.com/2014/03/23/world/asia/nsa-breached-chinese-servers-seen-as-spy-peril.html.

173. *See* Bailey Cahall et al., Do NSA's Bulk Surveillance Programs Stop Terrorists?, NEW AMERICA (Jan. 13, 2014), https://www.newamerica.org/international-security/policy-papers/do-nsas-bulk-surveillance-programs-stop-terrorists/.

174. Judicial Oversight of Section 702 of the Foreign Intelligence Surveillance Act, NAT'L SEC. AGENCY/CENT. SEC. SERV. (Sep. 14, 2017), https://www.nsa.gov/Press-Room/Speeches-Testimony/Article-View/Article/1619167/judicial-oversight-of-section-702-of-the-foreign-intelligence-surveillance-act/.

175. Feldstein, *supra* note 23, at 1–2.

176. Foreign Ministry Spokesperson Zhao Lijian's Regular Press Conference on July 25, 2022, MINISTRY FOREIGN AFFS. CHINA, https://www.fmprc.gov.cn/mfa_eng/xwfw_665399/s2510_665401/2511_665403/202207/t20220725_10727739.html.

177. Stu Woo, China Threatens Retaliation Against Ericsson If Sweden Doesn't Drop Huawei 5G Ban, WALL ST. J. (May 11, 2021), https://www.wsj.com/articles/china-threatens-retaliation-against-ericsson-if-sweden-doesnt-drop-huawei-5g-ban-11620740192?st=zz8ozjuxm9odwax&reflink=desktopwebshare_permalink.

178. *Id.*

179. Mike Cherney, China Sours on Australian Wine as Trade Spat Spirals, WALL ST. J. (Aug. 18, 2020), https://www.wsj.com/articles/china-sours-on-australian-wine-as-trade-spat-spirals-11597750564?mod=article_inline.

180. *Id.*; Stuart Condie, China Escalates Australia Trade Dispute With Wine Tariffs, WALL ST. J. (Nov. 27, 2020), https://www.wsj.com/articles/china-escalates-australia-trade-dispute-with-wine-tariffs-11606472504?st=xuw8ebrx2n7upit&reflink=desktopwebshare_permalink.

181. Condie, *supra* note 180.

182. Lily Kuo, Taiwan Loses Another Diplomatic Partner as Nicaragua Recognizes China, WASH. POST (Dec. 10, 2021), https://www.washingtonpost.com/world/asia_pacific/nicaragua-taiwan-china/2021/12/09/741098d8-5954-11ec-8396-5552bef55c3c_story.html.

183. Shannon Tiezzi, China, Nicaragua Seal Diplomatic Ties as Taiwan Loses Another Official Partner, DIPLOMAT (Dec. 10, 2021), https://thediplomat.com/2021/12/china-nicaragua-seal-diplomatic-ties-as-taiwan-loses-another-official-partner/.

184. *See, e.g.,* Jared Cohen & Richard Fontaine, Uniting the Techno-Democracies: How to Build Digital Cooperation, FOREIGN AFFS., Nov./Dec. 2020, at 112.

185. The Clean Network, U.S. DEP'T STATE (2020), https://2017-2021.state.gov/the-clean-network/index.html.

186. *Id.*

187. *Id.*

188. *Id.*

189. *See* Prague 5G Security Conference Announced Series of Recommendations: The Prague Proposals, GOV'T CZECH (May 3, 2019), https://www.vlada.cz/en/media-centrum/aktualne/prague-5g-security-conference-announced-series-of-reco mmendations-the-prague-proposals-173422/.

190. *See* Michael Kahn & Jan Lopatka, Western Allies Agree 5G Security Guidelines, Warn of Outside Influence, REUTERS (May 3, 2019), https://www.reuters.com/ article/us-telecoms-5g-security/western-allies-agree-5g-security-guidelines-warn-of-outside-influence-idUSKCN1S91D2; Lenka Ponikelska, Countries Seek United 5G Security Approach Amid Huawei Concerns, BLOOMBERG, https://www.bloomberg.com/news/articles/2019-05-03/countries-seek-uni ted-5g-security-approach-amid-huawei-concerns (May 3, 2019).

191. Michael Mink, How the Clean Network Alliance of Democracies Turned the Tide on Huawei in 5G, LIFE & NEWS (Dec. 2, 2020), https://www.lifeandnews. com/articles/how-the-clean-network-alliance-of-democracies-turned-the-tide-on-huawei-in-5g/.

192. *See id.*

193. *See* Cotton Demands Answers to Biden Strategy to Counter Huawei, TOM COTTON: SENATOR FOR ARK. (Sep. 22, 2021), https://www.cotton.senate.gov/ news/press-releases/cotton-demands-answers-about-biden-strategy-to-coun ter-huawei.

194. David E. Sanger & Michael Crowley, As Biden and Xi Begin a Careful Dance, a New American Policy Takes Shape, N.Y. TIMES (Mar. 17, 2021), https://www.nyti mes.com/2021/03/17/us/politics/us-china-relations.html.

195. *See id.*

196. *See* Statements and Releases, Fact Sheet: President Biden and G7 Leaders Launch Build Back Better World (B3W) Partnerships, WHITE HOUSE (June 12, 2021), https://www.whitehouse.gov/briefing-room/statements-releases/2021/ 06/12/fact-sheet-president-biden-and-g7-leaders-launch-build-back-better-world-b3w-partnership/.

197. *See id.*

198. *See* Mordechai Chaziza, The "Build Back Better World": An Alternative to China's BRI for the Middle East?, MIDDLE EAST INST. (July 20, 2021), https:// www.mei.edu/publications/build-back-better-world-alternative-chinas-bri-mid dle-east.

199. Steve Holland & Guy Faulconridge, G7 Rivals China With Grand Infrastructure Plan, REUTERS (June 13,2021), https://www.reuters.com/world/g7-counter-chi nas-belt-road-with-infrastructure-project-senior-us-official-2021-06-12/.

200. Global Gateway, EUROPEAN COMM'N, https://ec.europa.eu/info/strategy/pri orities-2019-2024/stronger-europe-world/global-gateway_en; Anna Cooban, Europe Unveils Its $340 Billion Answer to China's Belt and Road Infrastructure Initiative, CNN (Dec. 1, 2021), https://www.cnn.com/2021/12/01/business/glo bal-gateway-eu-china-belt-road/index.html.

201. *See* Patsy Widakuswara, US to Offer Alternative to China's Belt and Road Initiative, VOA NEWS (June 12, 2021), https://www.voanews.com/a/usa_us-offer-alternative-chinas-belt-and-road-initiative/6206928.html.

202. *See* Chaziza, *supra* note 198.

203. *See* Peter Martin, Eric Martin, & Saleha Mohsin, Biden Team Weighs Digital Trade Deal to Counter China in Asia, BLOOMBERG (July 13, 2021), https://www. bloomberg.com/news/articles/2021-07-12/biden-team-weighs-digital-trade-deal-to-counter-china-in-asia.

204. *See id.*

205. Fact Sheet: Quad Leaders' Summit, WHITE HOUSE (Sep. 24, 2021), https://www. whitehouse.gov/briefing-room/statements-releases/2021/09/24/fact-sheet-quad-leaders-summit/; FACT SHEET: Quad Leaders' Tokyo Summit 2022, WHITE HOUSE (May 23, 2022), https://www.whitehouse.gov/briefing-room/sta tements-releases/2022/05/23/fact-sheet-quad-leaders-tokyo-summit-2022/.

206. Quad Principles on Technology Design, Development, Governance, and Use, WHITE HOUSE (Sep. 24, 2021), https://www.whitehouse.gov/briefing-room/ statements-releases/2021/09/24/quad-principles-on-technology-design-deve lopment-governance-and-use/.

207. *Id.*

208. Biden's New China Doctrine, ECONOMIST (July 17, 2021), https://www.econom ist.com/leaders/2021/07/17/bidens-new-china-doctrine.

209. James Crabtree, Biden's Digital Trade Idea Reveals Emerging US Strategy for Asia, NIKKEI ASIA (Aug. 11, 2021), https://asia.nikkei.com/Opinion/Biden-s-digital-trade-idea-reveals-emerging-US-strategy-for-Asia.

210. Xi Jinping, President of China, Full Text: Remarks by Xi Jinping at the APEC Informal Economic Leaders' Retreat, XINHUA NET (July 16, 2021), http://www. news.cn/english/2021-07/16/c_1310065704.htm.

CHAPTER 9

1. Regulation 2016/679 of the European Parliament and of the Council on the Protection of Natural Persons With Regard to the Processing of Personal Data and on the Free Movement of Such Data, and Repealing Directive 95/46/EC, 2016 O.J., (L 119) 1 [hereinafter GDPR].

2. Hard Questions Q&A with Mark Zuckerberg, FACEBOOK NEWSROOM (Apr. 4, 2018), https://newsroom.fb.com/news/2018/04/hard-questions-protecting-peoples-information/.

3. E-mail from Google to Google User (May 14, 2018), available at https://groups.google.com/g/mtechcs09_nitkkr/c/B5lWXsJv8aQ?pli=1.

4. Alex Hern, Apple Launches iOS 11.3 with Raft of Privacy Features, GUARDIAN (Mar. 29, 2018), https://www.theguardian.com/technology/2018/mar/29/apple-launches-ios- 113-privacy-features-gdpr-data-protection.

5. *See* Preparing for a New Era in Privacy Regulation, MICROSOFT (Apr. 16, 2018), https://www.microsoft.com/en-us/microsoft-365/blog/2018/04/16/preparing-for-a-new-era-in-privacy-regulation-with-the-microsoft-cloud/.

6. Anu Bradford, THE BRUSSELS EFFECT: HOW THE EUROPEAN UNION RULES THE WORLD (2020).

7. Graham Greenleaf, Global Data Privacy Laws 2021: Despite COVID Delays, 145 Laws Show GDPR Dominance, 169 PRIVACY L. & BUS. INT'L REP. 1 (2021) (manuscript at 1), http://classic.austlii.edu.au/au/journals/UNSWLRS/2021/60.html.

8. Paul M Schwartz & Karl-Nikolaus Peifer, Transatlantic Data Privacy Law, 106 GEO. L. J. 115, 122 (2017).

9. Graham Greenleaf, ASIAN DATA PRIVACY LAWS: TRADE & HUMAN RIGHTS PERSPECTIVES 57 (2014).

10. Graham Greenleaf, The Influence of European Data Privacy Standards Outside Europe: Implications for Globalization of Convention 108, 2 INT'L DATA PRIVACY L. 68, 75 (2012); *see, e.g.*, María Paz Canales, Protección de datos en América Latina, urgente y necesaria [Data Protection in Latin America, Urgent and Necessary], DERECHODIGITALES (July 7, 2017), https://www.derechosdigitales.org/11282/proteccion-de-datos-en-america-latina-urgente-y-necesaria/ (translation supplied).

11. GDP (Current US$)—European Union, WORLD BANK, https://data.worldbank.org/indicator/NY.GDP.MKTP.CD?locations=EU (last visited Oct. 9, 2022). The GDP figure is the nominal GDP.

12. European Union GDP Per Capita PPP, TRADING ECONOMICS, https://tradingeconomics.com/european-union/gdp-per-capita-ppp (last visited Oct. 9, 2022).

13. Facebook Monthly Active Users (MAU) in Europe as of 2nd Quarter 2022, STATISTA (July 2022), https://www.statista.com/statistics/745400/facebook-europe-mau-by-quarter/.

14. Search Engine Market Share Europe—February 2022, STATCOUNTER, https://gs.statcounter.com/search-engine-market-share/all/europe (last visited Oct. 9, 2022); Prachi Bhardwaj & Jenny Cheng, This Chart Shows How Dominant Google Is in Europe and the UK: About 9 Out of Every 10 Consumers There Use Google's Search Engine, BUS. INSIDER (July 18, 2018), https://www.businessinsider.com/google-share-search-platform-browser-use-uk-charts-2018-7?r=US&IR=T].

15. There was a total of 209.1 million users in Germany, France, Italy, and Spain as of April 2022; *see* Leading Countries Based on YouTube Audience Size as of April 2022, STATISTA (Apr. 2022), https://www.statista.com/statistics/280685/number-of-monthly-unique-youtube-users/. There are approximately 2.1 billion YouTube users worldwide; *see* L. Ceci, YouTube Statistics & Facts (2022), STATISTA (Apr. 4, 2022), https://www.statista.com/topics/2019/youtube/#dossierKeyfigures.

16. Prateek Kulkarni, Apple's Revenue by Region (2015–2022), BUS. QUANT, https://businessquant.com/apple-revenue-by-region#:~:text=Europe%20was%20the%20second%20biggest,of%20the%20company's%20total%20revenue (last visited Oct. 9, 2022).

17. Amazon's Share of Online Retail Sales in Selected Regions as of September 2020, STATISTA, https://www.statista.com/statistics/1183515/amazon-market-share-region-worldwide/ (last visited Oct. 9, 2022); *E-Commerce in Europe 2020*, POSTNORD 19 (2020), https://www.postnord.se/siteassets/pdf/rapporter/e-commerce-in-europe-2020.pdf.

18. *See* David Bach & Abraham L. Newman, The European Regulatory State and Global Public Policy: Micro-Institutions, Macro-Influence, 14 J. EUR. PUB. POL'Y 827, 831 (2007).

19. Hussein Kassim, John Peterson, & Michael W. Bauer, THE EUROPEAN COMMISSION OF THE TWENTY-FIRST CENTURY 39 (2013); *see* Liesbet Hooghe, *Images of Europe: How Commission Officials Conceive Their Institution's Role*, 50 J. COMMON MKT. STUD. 87, 101 (2012).

20. GDPR, *supra* note 1, art 83.

21. Jennifer Daskal, Borders and Bits, 71 VAND. L.R. 179, 232–234 (2018).

22. Dorothee Heisenberg, NEGOTIATING PRIVACY: THE EUROPEAN UNION, THE UNITED STATES, AND PERSONAL DATA PROTECTION 119 (2005).

23. *See, e.g.*, Privacy Policy & Terms, GOOGLE (Jan. 22, 2019), https://policies.google.com/privacy?hl=en&gl=ZZ; Privacy Statement, NETFLIX (Nov. 2, 2021), https://help.netflix.com/legal/privacy.

24. *See* Ryan Singel, EU Tells Search Engines to Stop Creating Tracking Databases, WIRED (Apr. 8, 2008), http://www.wired.com/threatlevel/2008/04/eu-tells-search/.

25. *See* Brandon Mitchener, Standard Bearers: Increasingly, Rules of Global Economy Are Set in Brussels, WALL ST. J., Apr. 23, 2002, at A1; Editorial, *Regulatory Imperialism*, WALL ST. J. (Oct. 26, 2007), https://www.wsj.com/articles/SB119334720539572002.

26. *See, e.g.*, Legal Confusion on Internet Privacy: The Clash of Data Civilizations, ECONOMIST, June 19, 2010; Kevin J. O'Brien, Anger in Europe Over Google and Privacy, N.Y. TIMES, May 17, 2010, at B5; *see also* Mark Berniker, EU: Microsoft Agrees to NET Passport Changes, DATAMATION (Jan. 30, 2003), https://www.dat

amation.com/entdev/article.php/1576901/EU-Microsoft-Agrees-to-NET-Passp
ort-Changes.htm.

27. Daniel Michaels, Hot U.S. Import: European Regulations, WALL ST. J. (May 7, 2018), https://www.wsj.com/articles/techs-pickup-of-new-data-privacy-rules-reflects-eus-growing-influence-1525685400.

28. GDPR, *supra* note 1, art. 25.

29. *Privacy Governance*, APPLE, https://www.apple.com/legal/privacy/en-ww/gov ernance/; *see* Preparing for a New Era in Privacy Regulation, MICROSOFT (Apr. 16, 2018), https://www.microsoft.com/en-us/microsoft-365/blog/2018/04/16/ preparing-for-a-new-era-in-privacy-regulation-with-the-microsoft-cloud/.

30. Mark Scott, E.U. Fines Facebook $122 Million Over Disclosures in WhatsApp Deal, N.Y. TIMES (Jan. 20, 2018), https://www.nytimes.com/2017/05/18/technol ogy/facebook-european-union-fine-whatsapp.html.

31. David Ingram, Exclusive: Facebook to Put 1.5 Billion Users Out of Reach of New EU Privacy Law, REUTERS (Apr. 18, 2018), https://www.reuters.com/article/us-facebook-privacy-eu-exclusive/exclusive-facebook-to-change-user-terms-limit ing-effect-of-eu-privacy-law-idUSKBN1HQ00P.

32. Matthew Newton & Julia Summers, Russian Data Localization Laws: Enriching "Security" & the Economy, HENRY M. JACKSON SCH. INT'L STUDIES (2018), https://jsis.washington.edu/news/russian-data-localization-enriching-secur ity-economy/; Yuxi Wei, Chinese Data Localization Law: Comprehensive but Ambiguous, HENRY M. JACKSON SCH. INT'L STUDIES (2018), https://jsis.washing ton.edu/news/chinese-data-localization-law-comprehensive-ambiguous/.

33. Olga Razumovskaya & Laura Mills, Russia to Block LinkedIn Over Data-Privacy Dispute, WALL ST. J. (Nov. 11, 2016), https://www.wsj.com/articles/russia-may-block-linkedin-if-company-loses-court-case-on-personal-data-law-1478775414.

34. Paul Mozur & Vindu Goel, To Reach China, LinkedIn Plays by Local Rules, N.Y. TIMES (Oct. 5, 2014), https://www.nytimes.com/2014/10/06/technology/to-reach-china-linkedin-plays-by-local-rules.html.

35. Karen Weise & Paul Mozur, LinkedIn to Shut Down Service in China, Citing "Challenging" Environment, N.Y. TIMES (Oct. 14, 2021), https://www.nytimes. com/2021/10/14/technology/linkedin-china-microsoft.html.

36. India's Misguided Move Towards Data Localisation, FIN. TIMES (Sep. 29, 2018), https:// www.ft.com/content/92bb34a8-b4e5-11e8-bbc3-ccd7deo85ffe.

37. René Mahieu et al., Measuring the Brussels Effect Through Access Requests: Has the European General Data Protection Regulation Influenced the Data Protection Rights of Canadian Citizens?, 11 J. JNFO. POL'Y. 301 (2021).

38. Kevin Davis & Florencia Marotta-Wurgler, Contracting for Personal Data, 94 N.Y. UNIV. L.R. 662–705 (2019).

39. Michail Batikas et al., European Privacy Law and Global Markets for Data, CENTRE ECON. POL'Y. RES. (Mar. 25, 2020).

40. David Vogel, TRADING UP: CONSUMER AND ENVIRONMENTAL REGULATION IN A GLOBAL ECONOMY (1995).

41. Tim Cook Calls for US Federal Privacy Law to Tackle "Weaponized" Personal Data, GUARDIAN (Oct. 24, 2018), https://www.theguardian.com/technology/2018/oct/24/tim-cook-us-federal-privacy-law-weaponized-personal-data.

42. Mark Zuckerberg, The Internet Needs New Rules. Let's Start in These Four Areas, WASH. POST (Mar. 30, 2019), https://www.washingtonpost.com/opinions/mark-zuckerberg-the-internet-needs-new-rules-lets-start-in-these-four-areas/2019/03/29/9e6f0504-521a-11e9-a3f7-78b7525a8d5f_story.html.

43. *See generally* California Consumer Privacy Act of 2018, CAL. CIV. CODE § 1798.100 (2018) *amended by* initiative Proposition 24, Sec. 4 (California Privacy Rights Act of 2020).

44. Meghashyam Mali, Tech Mobilizes Against California Privacy Law, THE HILL (July 1, 2018), https://thehill.com/policy/technology/394928-tech-mobilizes-against-california-privacy-law.

45. *See* GDPR *supra* note 1, art. 45; *see also* Communication from the Commission to the European Parliament and the Council Exchanging and Protecting Personal Data in a Globalised World (COM) (2017) 7 final (Jan. 10, 2017).

46. Eur. Comm'n, Adequacy Decisions, EUROPA, https://ec.europa.eu/info/law/law-topic/data-protection/international-dimension-data-protection/adequacy-decisions_en.

47. Protección de los atos Personales [Personal Data Protection Act], Ley 25.326, (Nov. 2, 2000), BOLETÍN OFICIAL [B.O.] 1 (Arg.), http://www.uba.ar/archivos_secyt/image/Ley%2025326.pdf.

48. Civil Rights Association, The Future of Personal Data Protection in Argentina: Reflections of a Working Group at 3, 6–8 (June 2016), https://adcdigital.org.ar/wp-content/uploads/2016/07/Reflexiones-futuro-datos-personales-ADC.pdf (translation supplied).

49. Press Release, Eur. Comm'n, The European Union and Japan Agreed to Create the World's Largest Area of Safe Data Flows (July 17, 2018); *see also* Stephen Gardner, EU, South Korea Look to Data Transfer Privacy Deal in 2018, BLOOMBERG (Nov. 20, 2017), https://www.bna.com/eu-south-korea-n73014472278/.

50. Brian Yap, Multinationals Struggle to Adapt to Japan's New Privacy Law, BLOOMBERG (Aug. 31, 2017), https://www.bna.com/multinationals-struggle-adapt-n73014464003/.

51. Privacy Act Review Issues Paper, GOVT. AUSTL. (2020), https://www.ag.gov.au/system/files/2020-10/privacy-act-review--issues-paper-october-2020.pdf; Digital Platforms Inquiry, AUSTL. COMPETITION & CONSUMER COMM'N, https://www.accc.gov.au/system/files/Digital%20platforms%20inquiry%20-%20final%20report.pdf.

52. Digital Platforms Inquiry, AUSTL. COMPETITION & CONSUMER COMM'N, https://www.accc.gov.au/system/files/Digital%20platforms%20inquiry%20-%20fi nal%20report.pdf.

53. *Id.* at 480.

54. *Id.* at 466.

55. *Id.* at 471.

56. *Id.* at 461.

57. *Id.* at 439.

58. Austl. Treasury, Government Response and Implementation Roadmap for the Digital Platforms Inquiry, GOVT. AUSTL. 17–18 (2019), https://treasury.gov.au/sites/default/files/2019-12/Government-Response-p2019-41708.pdf.

59. Zhonghua Renmin Gongheguo Geren Xinxi Baohu Fa [PRC Personal Information Protection Law] (promulgated by the Standing Comm. Nat'l People's Cong., Aug. 20, 2021, effective Nov. 1, 2021), http://www.npc.gov.cn/npc/c30834/202108/a8c4e3672c74491a80b53a172bb753fe.shtml.

60. Gil Zhang & Kate Yin, A Look at China's Draft of Personal Information Protection Law, IAPP (oct. 26, 2020), https://iapp.org/news/a/a-look-at-chinas-draft-of-personal-data-protection-law/.

61. Rogier Creemers et al., China's Draft "Personal Information Protection Law" (Full Translation), NEW AMERICA (oct. 21, 2020), https://www.newamerica.org/cybersecurity-initiative/digichina/blog/chinas-draft-personal-information-pro tection-law-full-translation/.

62. *Id.* (Article 29). *See also* George Qi et al., China Releases Draft Personal Data Protection Law, NAT'L L. REV. (Jan. 21, 2021), https://www.natlawreview.com/arti cle/china-releases-draft-personal-information-protection-law.

63. Alexa Lee, Personal Data, Global Effects: China's Draft Privacy Law in the International Context, NEW AMERICA (Jan. 4, 2021), https://www.newamerica.org/cybersecurity-initiative/digichina/blog/personal-data-global-effects-chi nas-draft-privacy-law-in-the-international-context/; Stephanie Hare, These New Rules Were Meant to Protect Our Privacy. They Don't Work, GUARDIAN (Nov. 10, 2019), https://www.theguardian.com/commentisfree/2019/nov/10/these-new-rules-were-meant-to-protect-our-privacy-they-dont-work.

64. Creemers et al., *supra* note 61.

65. Lee, *supra* note 63; Hare, *supra* note 63.

66. India Introduces Updated Draft of Personal Data Protection Bill, COVINGTON & BURLING LLP (Feb. 5, 2020), https://www.cov.com/-/media/files/corporate/publi cations/2020/02/india-introduces-updated-draft-of-personal-data-protection-bill.pdf.

67. Kurt Wimmer et al., Comparison: Indian Personal Data Protection Bill 2019 vs. GDPR, IAPP (Mar. 2022), https://iapp.org/media/pdf/resource_center/india_pdpb2019_vs_gdpr_iapp_chart.pdf.

68. *Id.*

69. Arindrajit Basu & Justin Sherman, Key Global Takeaways From India's Revised Personal Data Protection Bill, LAWFARE (Jan. 23, 2020), https://www.lawfareblog.com/key-global-takeaways-indias-revised-personal-data-protection-bill.

70. Vijay Govindarajan, Anup Srivastava, & Luminita Enache, How India Plans to Protect Consumer Data, HARV. BUS. REV. (Dec. 18, 2019), https://hbr.org/2019/12/how-india-plans-to-protect-consumer-data.

71. Sameer Yasir & Karan Deep Singh, India Withdraws a Proposed Law on Data Protection, N.Y. TIMES (Aug. 4, 2022), https://www.nytimes.com/2022/08/04/business/india-data-privacy.html

72. Graham Greenleaf, Nigeria Regulates Data Privacy: African and Global Significance, 158 PRIVACY L. & BUS. INT'L REP. 23 (2019) (manuscript at 1), http://www.austlii.edu.au/au/journals/UNSWLRS/.

73. OneTrust DataGuidance, COMPARING PRIVACY LAWS: GDPR V. NIGERIAN DATA PROTECTION REGULATION (2020), https://www.dataguidance.com/sites/default/files/gdpr_v._nigeria.pdf.

74. PwC, THE NDPR AND THE DATA PROTECTION BILL 2020 2 (2020), https://www.pwc.com/ng/en/assets/pdf/the-ndpr-data-protection-bill-2020.pdf.

75. Data Protection Bill (2020) (Nigeria), https://www.ncc.gov.ng/documents/911-data-protection-bill-draft-2020/file, at § 35.

76. Lei Geral de Protecao de Dados Pessoais (General Data Protection Law), Law No. 13,709/2018, https://iapp.org/media/pdf/resource_center/Brazilian_General_Data_Protection_Law.pdf.

77. *See* Abigayle Erickson, Comparative Analysis of the EU's GDPR and Brazil's LGPD: Enforcement Challenges with the LGPD, 44 BROOKLYN J. INT'L L. 859, 833 (2019).

78. Stacey Gray et al., Emerging Patchwork or Laboratories of Democracy? Privacy Legislation in Virginia and Other States, FUTURE OF PRIVACY F. (Feb. 12, 2021), https://fpf.org/blog/emerging-patchwork-or-laboratories-of-democracy-privacy-legislation-in-virginia-and-other-states/.

79. *Compare* CAL. CIV. CODE § 1798.110(a) (West) *with* GDPR, *supra* note 1, at art. 5(1)(b), 12.

80. *Compare* CAL. CIV. CODE § 1798.100(a) (West) *with* GDPR, *supra* note 1, at art. 15.

81. *Compare* CAL. CIV. CODE § 1798.105(a) (West) *with* GDPR, *supra* note 1, at art. 17.

82. *Compare* CAL. CIV. CODE § 1798.199.40(c) (West) (effective Jan. 1, 2023) *with* GDPR, *supra* note 1, at art. 5.

83. IAPP Westin Rsch. Ctr., State Comprehensive-Privacy Law Comparison, IAPP, https://iapp.org/resources/article/state-comparison-table/ (last updated Oct. 7, 2022).

84. *See* VA. CODE ANN. § 59.1–571 (2021); A. 3283, 219th Leg., Reg. Sess. § 2 (N.J., 2020); HF 1492, 92nd Leg., Reg. Sess. § 2 (Minn., 2021).

85. A. 3283, 219th Leg., Reg. Sess. § 3(a) (N.J., 2020). *See also* GDPR, *supra* note 1, art 5(1)(a).

86. A. 680, 2021–2022, Reg. Sess. § 1103(6) (N.Y., 2021). *See also* GDPR, *supra* note 1, art 22(1).

87. *Brandenburg v. Ohio*, 395 U.S. 444, 447 (1969); *see also Chaplinsky v. New Hampshire*, 315 U.S. 568, 572 (1942).

88. Council Framework Decision 2008/913/JHA, Combating Certain Forms and Expressions of Racism and Xenophobia by Means of Criminal Law, art. 1 2008 O.J. (L 328) 55, 56.

89. *See* YouTube Help, HATE SPEECH, https://support.google.com/youtube/answer/2801939?hl=en (last visited Oct. 21, 2022).

90. Martin Ammori, The "New" New York Times, 127 HARV. L. REV. 2259, 2279 (2014).

91. Eur. Comm'n, Code of Conduct—Illegal Online Hate Speech, Questions and Answers, EUROPA (June 2016), https://ec.europa.eu/info/sites/info/files/code_of_conduct_hate_speech_en.pdf.

92. Julia Angwin & Hannes Grassegger, Facebook's Secret Censorship Rules Protect White Men from Hate Speech But Not Black Children, PROPUBLICA (June 28, 2017), https://www.propublica.org/article/facebook-hate-speech-censorship-internal-documents-algorithms.

93. Ira Steven Nathenson, Super-Intermediaries, Code, HumanRights, St. Thomas University School of Law Legal Studies Research Paper No. 2014-09, at 127.

94. Apple Changes Crimea Map to Meet Russian Demands, BBC (Nov. 27, 2019), https://www.bbc.com/news/technology-50573069. Apple Maps has since been updated to show Crimea as part of Ukraine when viewed outside of Russia, *see* Aisha Malik, Apple Maps Now Displays Crimea as Part of Ukraine to Viewers Outside of Russia, TECHCRUNCH (Mar. 4, 2022), https://techcrunch.com/2022/03/04/apple-maps-now-displays-crimea-as-part-of-ukraine-to-viewers-outside-of-russia/.

95. Sebnem Arsu & Mark Scott, Facebook Is Said to Block Pages Critical of Muhammad to Avoid Shutdown in Turkey, N.Y. TIMES (Jan. 26, 2015), https://www.nytimes.com/2015/01/27/world/europe/facebook-said-to-block-pages-on-muhammad-to-avoid-ban-in-turkey.html.

96. Jeffrey Rosen, Google's Gatekeepers, N.Y. TIMES (Nov. 28, 2008), http://www.nytimes.com/2008/11/30/magazine/30google-t.html.

97. Rachel Whetstone, Free Expression and Controversial Content on the Web, GOOGLE BLOG (Nov. 14, 2007), https://googleblog.blogspot.com/2007/11/free-expression-and-controversial.html.

98. Eva Galperin, Twitter Steps Down from the Free Speech Party, ELEC. FRONTIER FOUND. (May 21, 2014), https://www.eff.org/deeplinks/2014/05/twitter-steps-down-free-speech-party.

99. Ammori, *supra* note 90.

100. Julia Angwin & Hannes Grassegger, Facebook's Secret Censorship Rules Protect White Men from Hate Speech But Not Black Children, PROPUBLICA

(June 28, 2017), https://www.propublica.org/article/facebook-hate-speech-censorship-internal-documents-algorithms.

101. *Id.*

102. Ammori, *supra* note 90 (citing interviews with Dave Willner & Monika Bickert).

103. *See generally* Facebook Must Delete Hate Postings, Austria Court Rules, BBC NEWS (May 9, 2017), http://www.bbc.com/ news/world-europe-39852623; *see also* Alphabet Inc., Annual Report (Form 10-K, Feb. 5, 2018).

104. Case C-18/18, Eva Glawischnig-Piesczek v. Facebook Ireland Limited, ECLI:EU:C:2019:821, (June 4, 2019).

105. Case C-18/18, Eva Glawischnig-Piesczek v. Facebook Ireland Limited, ECLI:EU:C:2019:821, ¶50 (June 4, 2019).

106. *See* Case C-507/17, Google LLC, successor in law to Google Inc. v. Commission nationale del'informatique et des libertés (CNIL), ECLI:EU:C:2019:772, ¶64 (Sep. 24, 2019).

107. Regulation (EU) 2022/2065 of the European Parliament and of the Council of 19 October 2022 on a Single Market for Digital Services and Amending Directive 2000/31/EC (Digital Services Act), 2022 O.J. (L 277) 1.

108. *Id.* at art, 26 and 28.

109. *Id.* at art. 24, 34, 37, 40, 42, and 85.

110. Australian Code of Practice on Disinformation and Misinformation, DIG. INDUS. GRP. (2021), https://www.digi.org.au/wp-content/uploads/2021/02/Australian-Code-of-Practice-on-Disinformation-and-Misinformation-FINAL-PDF-Feb-22-2021.pdf [hereinafter Australian Code].

111. About the Code, DIG. INDUS. GRP. (2021), https://digi.org.au/disinformation-code/ [hereinafter About the Code].

112. Digital Platforms Inquiry, AUSTL. COMPETITION & CONSUMER COMM'N, https://www.accc.gov.au/focus-areas/inquiries-finalised/digital-platforms-inquiry-0 .

113. Digital Platforms Inquiry—Final Report, DIG. INDUS. GRP. 370 (2021), https://www.accc.gov.au/system/files/Digital%20platforms%20inquiry%20-%20final%20report.pdf [hereinafter Digital Platforms Inquiry—Final Report].

114. Austl. Treasury, Regulating in the Digital Age, GOVT. AUSTL. 7, (2019), https://treasury.gov.au/sites/default/files/2019-12/Government-Response-p2019-41708.pdf.

115. *About the Code, supra* note 111.

116. Misinformation and News Quality on Digital Platforms in Australia: A Position Paper to Guide Code Development, AUSTL. COMM'N & MEDIA AUTHORITY 15 (2020), https://www.acma.gov.au/sites/default/files/2020-06/Misinformation%20and%20news%20quality%20position%20paper.pdf [hereinafter Misinformation and News Quality on Digital Platforms in Australia].

117. Australian Code, *supra* note 110.

118. Eur. Comm'n, Code of Practice on Disinformation, EUROPA, https://digital-strategy.ec.europa.eu/en/policies/code-practice-disinformation.

119. Digital Platforms Inquiry—Final Report, *supra* note 113, at 371.

120. Misinformation and News Quality on Digital Platforms in Australia, *supra* note 116, at 23.

121. Online Safety Bill (2023), (HL Bill 87(*Rev*), 2021-22, 2022-23), Parliament: House of Commons, https://bills.parliament.uk/bills/3137.

122. Press Release, UK Dep't. Dig. Culture Media & Sport, Landmark Laws to Keep Children Safe, Stop Racial Hate and Protect Democracy Online Published (May 12, 2021), https://www.gov.uk/government/news/landmark-laws-to-keep-child ren-safe-stop-racial-hate-and-protect-democracy-online-published.

123. Joint Committee on the Draft Online Safety Bill, Draft Online Safety Bill Report of Session 2021–22, UK PARL. ¶¶ 103, 219, 417 (2022), https://committ ees.parliament.uk/publications/8206/documents/84092/default/; Annabelle Dickson & Clothilde Goujard, On Online Content, London Tries to Out-Regulate Brussels, POLITICO (Nov. 8, 2021), https://www.politico.eu/article/eu-digital-services-act-uk-online-safety-bill-content-moderation-safety/.

124. Press Release, UK Dep't. Dig. Culture Media & Sport, Landmark Laws to Keep Children Safe, Stop Racial Hate and Protect Democracy Online Published (May 12, 2021), https://www.gov.uk/government/news/landmark-laws-to-keep-child ren-safe-stop-racial-hate-and-protect-democracy-online-published.

125. *Id.*

126. Tech Leaders Could Face Jail Time and Big Fines Under UK's Online Safety Bill, EURONEWS (Mar. 3, 2018), https://www.euronews.com/next/2022/03/18/ tech-leaders-could-face-jail-time-and-big-fines-under-uk-s-online-safety-bill; Online Safety Bill: Factsheet, GOVT. UK (Mar. 17, 2022), https://www.gov.uk/ government/publications/online-safety-bill-supporting-documents/online-saf ety-bill-factsheet.

127. Commission Decision in Case No. COMP/C-3/37.792 (Microsoft), C(2004) 900 final, ¶ 2.1 (Mar. 24, 2004) *cited in* 2007 O.J. (L 32) 23.

128. Case AT.39740—Google Search (Shopping), C (2017) 4444 final (June 27, 2017).

129. Case T-612/17, Google and Alphabet v. Commission (Google Shopping), ECLI:EU:T:2021:763 (Nov. 10, 2021).

130. Oliver Heckmann, Changes to Google Shopping in Europe, GOOGLE BLOG (Sep. 27, 2017), https://adwords.googleblog.com/2017/09/changes-to-google-shopping-in-europe.html.

131. Rochelle Toplensky & Richard Waters, Google Changes Shopping Search to Sooth EU Antitrust Concerns, FIN. TIMES (Sep. 28, 2017), https://www.ft.com/ content/9c9d196a-a432-11e7-b797-b61809486fe2.

132. Digital Platforms Inquiry—Final Report, *supra* note 113, at 30.

133. Austl. Treasury, Government Response and Implementation Roadmap for the Digital Platforms Inquiry, GOVT. AUSTL. 15 (2019), https://treasury.gov.au/sites/ default/files/2019-12/Government-Response-p2019-41708.pdf.

134. Maria Kiselyova, Russian Competition Watchdog Opens Case Against Google, REUTERS (Feb. 20, 2015), https://www.reuters.com/article/us-russia-crisis-goo gle-investigation/russian-competition-watchdog-opens-case-against-google-idUSKBNoLOoRJ20150220.

135. *Rekabet Kurulu* [Competition Authority], *Karar Sayısı* 18-33/555-273 [Decision Number 18-33/555-273] (Sep. 19, 2018), https://www.rekabet.gov.tr/Karar?kara rId=7d9ba7e3-2b8f-4438-87a5-26609eab5443.

136. Bahadir Balki, Google Fined—This Time by the Turkish Competition Watchdog, KLUWER COMPETITION LAW BLOG (Nov. 5, 2018), http://competition lawblog.kluwercompetitionlaw.com/2018/11/05/google-fined-this-time-by-the-turkish-competition-watchdog/.

137. Jonas Valente, Brazil Probes Into Anti-Competitive Practices by Google, AGENCIABRASIL (June 13, 2019), https://agenciabrasil.ebc.com.br/en/geral/noti cia/2019-06/brazil-probes-anti-competitive-practices-google.

138. Reuters Staff, Brazil May Probe Google Over Its Cell Phone System: Report, REUTERS (Aug. 15, 2018), https://www.reuters.com/article/us-brazil-google/bra zil-may-probe-google-over-its-cell-phone-system-report-idUSKBN1L018K.

139. Satsuki Kaneko & Ryohei Yasoshima, Apple and Google Under Antitrust Scrutiny in Japan for Mobile OS, NIKKEIASIA (Oct. 7, 2021), https://asia.nik kei.com/Business/Technology/Apple-and-Google-under-antitrust-scrutiny-in-Japan-for-mobile-OS.

140. Aaron Gregg, South Korea Hits Google With $177 Million Fine for Blocking Android Alternatives, WASH. POST (Sep. 14, 2021), https://www.washingtonpost. com/business/2021/09/14/google-south-korea-aandroid-antitrust/.

141. Josh Sisco, Apple, Amazon, Google and Facebook Face at Least 70 Antitrust Probes, Cases, INFO. (July 15, 2021), https://www.theinformation.com/ big-tech-probe.

142. Press Release, UK Competition & Markets Authority, CMA Advises Government on New Regulatory Regime for Tech Giants (Dec. 8, 2020), https://www.gov. uk/government/news/cma-advises-government-on-new-regulatory-regime-for-tech-giants.

143. Key Points of the Act on Improving Transparency and Fairness of Digital Platforms (TFDPA), JAPAN MINISTRY ECON. TRADE & INDUS., https://www.meti. go.jp/english/policy/mono_info_service/information_economy/digital_platfo rms/tfdpa.html (last updated Apr. 16, 2021).

144. Designation of Digital Platform Providers Subject to Specific Regulations Under the Act on Improving Transparency and Fairness of Digital Platforms, JAPAN MINISTRY ECON. TRADE & INDUS. (Apr. 1, 2021), https://www.meti.go.jp/ english/press/2021/0401_001.html.

145. Key Points of the Act on Improving Transparency and Fairness of Digital Platforms, JAPAN MINISTRY ECON. TRADE & INDUS. 2 (2021), https://www.meti.

go.jp/english/policy/mono_info_service/information_economy/digital_platfo
rms/pdf/0401_001b.pdf.

146. Digital Platforms, JAPAN MINISTRY ECON. TRADE & INDUS., https://www.meti.
go.jp/english/policy/mono_info_service/information_economy/digital_platfo
rms/index.html (last updated Oct. 24, 2022).

147. Jeffrey J. Amato & Tomonori Maezawa, Japan: Japanese Legislature Passes Act
to Regulate Big Tech Platforms, WINSTON & STRAWN LLP (Jan. 12, 2021), https://
www.mondaq.com/antitrust-eu-competition-/1024456/japanese-legislature-
passes-act-to-regulate-big-tech-platforms.

148. Natsuko Sugihara, Japan's Digital Platform Regulations, CLIFFORD CHANCE
(Aug. 31, 2021), https://www.cliffordchance.com/insights/resources/hubs-
and-toolkits/talking-tech/en/articles/2021/08/japan-s-digital-platform-regu
lations.html.

149. Toshio Dokei et al., Recent Developments in Competition Law and Policy in
the Digital Economy in Japan, COMP. POL'Y INT'L 5 (2021), https://www.com
petitionpolicyinternational.com/wp-content/uploads/2021/03/3-recent-devel
opments-in-competition-law-and-policy-in-the-digital-economy-in-japan.pdf.

150. Song Jung-a, Google and Apple's App Stores Hit by New South Korean Law,
FIN. TIMES (Aug. 31, 2021), https://www.ft.com/content/897ab9a9-df38-4c32-
9e70-ef752c38c514; see Telecommunications Business Act, Law 6360 (S.
Korea).

151. Song Jung-a, *supra* note 150.

152. State Administration for Market Regulation, Anti-Monopoly Guidelines for the
Platform Economy Sector (Feb. 7, 2021), https://gkml.samr.gov.cn/nsjg/fldj/
202102/t20210207_325967.html.

153. Mark Thompson & Pauline Lockwood, China Hits Alibaba with Record $2.8
Billion Fine for Behaving Like a Monopoly, CNN (Apr. 12, 2021), https://edition.
cnn.com/2021/04/10/tech/alibaba-china-record-fine/index.html.

154. Chinese Streaming Firm DouYu Terminates $5.3 Bln Merger with Huya,
REUTERS (July 12, 2021), https://www.reuters.com/world/china/chinese-live-
streaming-firm-douyu-terminates-merger-deal-with-huya-2021-07-12/.

155. Raymond Zhong, China's Tech Antitrust Campaign Snares Meituan, a Food-
Delivery Giant, N.Y. TIMES (Oct. 8, 2021), https://www.nytimes.com/2021/10/
08/technology/china-meituan-antitrust-fine.html.

156. Staff of S. Comm. of the Judiciary, 116TH CONG., ON ANTITRUST, COM. & ADMIN.
L., *Investigation of Competition in Digital Markets* (2020); *see, e.g.,* American
Innovation and Choice Online Act, S. 2992, 117th Cong. (2022); Ending
Platform Monopolies Act, H.R. 3825, 117th Cong. (2021); Platform Competition
and Opportunity Act, H.R. 3826, 117th Cong. (2021); Augmenting Compatibility
and Competition by Enabling Service Switching (ACCESS) Act, 117th Cong.
(2021).

157. Dep't of Justice Press Release, Justice Department Sues Monopolist Google for Violating Antitrust Laws (Oct. 20, 2020), https://www.justice.gov/opa/pr/just ice-department-sues-monopolist-google-violating-antitrust-laws; Fed. Trade Commission Press Release, FTC Sues Facebook for Illegal Monopolization (Dec. 9, 2020), https://www.ftc.gov/news-events/press-releases/2020/12/ftc-sues-facebook-illegal-monopolization.

158. *FTC v. Facebook, Inc.*, No. 20-3590 (JEB), slip op. at 1 (D.D.C. June 28, 2021); *but see FTC v. Facebook, Inc. ("Facebook II")*, ___ F. Supp. 3d ___, Case No. 1:20-cv-03590, ECF No. 90 (D.D.C., Jan. 11, 2022) (ruling that the FTC's amended complaint filed in August 2021 can survive Facebook's Motion to Dismiss).

159. Proposal for a Regulation Laying Down Harmonised Rules on Artificial Intelligence, COM (2021) 206 final (Apr. 21, 2021).

160. Diego Zambrano, How Litigation Imports Foreign Regulation, 107 VA. L. R. (2021).

161. Arthur Mitchell et al., Regulation of Artificial Intelligence in Europe and Japan, WHITE & CASE (Aug. 24, 2020), https://www.whitecase.com/publications/insi ght/regulation-artificial-intelligence-europe-and-japan; Council for Social Principles of Human-Centric AI, Social Principles of Human-Centric AI, JAPAN CABINET OFF. (2019), https://ai.bsa.org/wp-content/uploads/2019/09/hum ancentricai.pdf.

162. Expert Group on Architecture for AI Principles to Be Practiced, AI Governance in Japan Ver. 1.0—Interim Report, JAPAN MINISTRY ECON. TRADE & INDUS. 19, 28 (2021), https://www.meti.go.jp/press/2020/01/20210115003/20210115 003-3.pdf.

163. *Id.* at 28.

164. The framework is published as a series of webpages at Dep't. Indus. Energy Sci. & Resources, Australia's Artificial Intelligence Ethics Framework, GOVT. AUSTL., https://www.industry.gov.au/data-and-publications/australias-artific ial-intelligence-ethics-framework.

165. *Id.*

166. Australia's AI Action Plan, GOVT. AUSTL. 5 (2021), https://wp.oecd.ai/app/uplo ads/2021/12/Australia_AI_Action_Plan_2021.pdf.

167. Human Rights and Technology Final Report, AUSTL. HUMAN RTS. COMM'N 58 (2021), https://tech.humanrights.gov.au/downloads.

168. *Id.*

169. Press release, Eur. Union and Austr., EU–Australia Leaders' Virtual Meeting (Nov. 26, 2020), https://ec.europa.eu/commission/presscorner/detail/en/ ip_20_2215.

170. David Shepardson, White House Proposes Regulatory Principles to Govern AI Use, REUTERS (Jan. 7, 2020), https://www.reuters.com/article/us-tech-ces-ai-white-house/white-house-proposes-regulatory-principles-to-govern-ai-use-idUSKBN1Z60GL.

171. Jake Sullivan (@JakeSullivan46), TWITTER (Apr. 21, 2021), https://twitter.com/jakesullivan46/status/1384970668341669891?lang=en.

172. Directive 2019/790, of the European Parliament and of the Council of 17 April 2019 on Copyright and Related Rights in the Digital Single Market and Amending Directives 96/9/EC and 2001/29/EC, 2019 O.J. (L 130) 92.

173. Treasury Laws Amendment (News Media and Digital Platforms Mandatory Bargaining Code) Act 2021, No. 21, 2021, https://www.legislation.gov.au/Details/C2021A00021.

174. Richard Glover, Australia Is Standing Up to Facebook and Big Tech. It Shouldn't Fight Alone, WASH. POST (Feb. 19, 2021), https://www.washingtonpost.com/opinions/2021/02/19/australia-facebook-google-news/.

175. Jamie Smyth, Hannah Murphy, & Alex Barker, Facebook Ban on News in Australia Provokes Fierce Backlash, FIN. TIMES (Feb. 18, 2021), https://www.ft.com/content/cac1ff54-b976-4ae4-b810-46c29ab26096.

176. *Id*; Gerrit De Vynck, Google Is Threatening to Pull Its Search Engine out of Australia, WASH. POST (Jan 22, 2021), https://www.washingtonpost.com/technology/2021/01/22/google-australia-publishers/.

177. James Clayton, Facebook Reverses Ban on News Pages in Australia, BBC (Feb. 23, 2021), https://www.bbc.com/news/world-australia-56165015.

178. Javier Espinoza & Alex Barker, EU Ready to Follow Australia's Lead on Making Google and Facebook Pay for News, L.A. TIMES (Feb. 8, 2021), https://www.latimes.com/world-nation/story/2021-02-08/eu-australia-google-facebook-tech-news.

179. Kanishka Singh, U.S. Opposes Canada's Digital Services Tax Proposal, REUTERS (Feb. 22, 2022), https://www.reuters.com/world/us-opposes-canadas-digital-services-tax-proposal-2022-02-22/.

180. Tim Bradshaw, Countries Vow to Press Ahead with Digital Taxes Despite US Threat, FIN. TIMES (Dec. 4, 2019), https://www.ft.com/content/6529014c-169a-11ea-9ee4-11f260415385.

181. Digital Services Tax Act, GOV'T. CANADA, https://www.canada.ca/en/department-finance/news/2021/12/digital-services-tax-act.html (last updated Feb. 14, 2022).

182. Robert Sledz, Israel Preparing Digital Services Tax Modelled Off Pending French Proposal, THOMSON REUTERS (May 7, 2019), https://tax.thomsonreuters.com/blog/israel-preparing-digital-services-tax-modelled-off-pending-french-proposal/.

183. Turkey—Digital Services Tax, BINDER DIJKER OTTE GLOBAL, https://www.bdo.global/en-gb/microsites/digital-services-taxation/countries-cit-map/turkey-digital-services-tax.

184. Status Update on Digital Services Tax Investigations of Brazil, the Czech Republic, the European Union, and Indonesia, OFF. U.S. TRADE REP. 9 (2021),

https://ustr.gov/sites/default/files/files/Press/Releases/StatusUpdate301Inv
estigationsBEUIndCR.pdf.

185. Andrew McAfee, EU Proposals to Regulate AI Are Only Going to Hinder Innovation, Financial times (July 25, 2021), https://www.ft.com/content/a5970b6c-e731-45a7-b75b-721e90e32e1c.

186. Charlene Barshefsky, EU Digital Protectionism Risks Damaging Ties With the US, fin. times (Aug. 2, 2020), https://www.ft.com/content/9edea4f5-5f34-4e17-89cd-f9b9ba698103.

187. *See, e.g.*, Editorial, Regulatory Imperialism, wall st. j. (Oct. 26, 2007), https://www.wsj.com/articles/SB119334720539572002.

188. Mark Scott & Laurens Cerulus, Europe's New Data Protection Rules Export Privacy Standards Worldwide, politico (Jan. 31, 2018), https://www.politico.eu/article/europe-data-protection-privacy-standards-gdpr-general-protection-data-regulation/.

189. *See, e.g.*, Margrethe Vestager, Competition Commissioner, Opening Remarks at the ICN Merger Workshop: Merger Review: Building a Global Community of Practice (June 3, 2016); The Rt Hon Sir Leon Brittan QU, Vice-President of the European Commission, Address at the WTO High-Level Symposium on Trade and the Environment (Mar. 15, 1999).

190. Citizens United v. FEC, 130 S. Ct. 876 (2010).

191. Joseph H. H. Weiler et al., 1995. *European Democracy and Its Critique: Five Uneasy Pieces* (European Univ. Inst. Working Paper RSC No. 95/11, 1995), http://cadmus.eui.eu/handle/1814/1386.

192. Andreas Dür et al., political influence of business in the european union (2019).

193. Brooke Auxier, Americans' Attitudes and Experiences With Privacy Policies and Laws, pew res. (Nov. 15, 2019), https://www.pewresearch.org/internet/2019/11/15/americans-attitudes-and-experiences-with-privacy-policies-and-laws/.

194. Transcend, the data privacy feedback loop 2020, https://www.datocms-assets.com/16414/1597336087-transcenddataprivacyfeedbackloop20201.pdf.

195. Joanne Scott, From Brussels with Love: The Transatlantic Travels of European Law and the Chemistry of Regulatory Attraction, 57 am. j. comp. l. 897, 920–928 (2009); *see also, generally* Katerina Linos, the democratic foundations of policy diffusion: how health, family and employment laws spread across countries (2013).

196. Neema Singh Guliani & Jay Stanley, The Landmark European Law That Could Change Facebook and Improve Privacy in America, ACLU (Apr. 12, 2018), https://www.aclu.org/blog/privacy-technology/internet-privacy/landmark-european-law-could-change-facebook-and-improve.

197. Nuala O'Connor, Reforming the U.S. Approach to Data Protection and Privacy, council foreign relations (Jan. 30, 2018), https://www.cfr.org/report/reforming-us-approach-data-protection.

198. Warwick Ashford, GDPR Will Have Positive Ripple Effect, Says US Consumer Group, COMPUT. WKLY. (Feb. 27, 2018), https://www.computerweekly.com/news/252435774/GDPR-will-have-positive-ripple-effect-say-US-consumer-group.

199. The Lobby Network: Big Tech's Web of Influence in the EU, CORP. EUR. OBSERVATORY (Aug. 31, 2021), https://corporateeurope.org/en/2021/08/lobby-network-big-techs-web-influence-eu.

200. Adam Satariano, G.D.P.R., a New Privacy Law, Makes Europe World's Leading Tech Watchdog, N.Y. TIMES (May 24, 2018), https://www.nytimes.com/2018/05/24/technology/europe-gdpr-privacy.html.

201. Susan Ariel Aaronson et al., EU Data Protection Reform: Opportunities and Concerns, INTERECONOMICS, Volume 48, 2013, Number 5, pp. 268–286 https://www.intereconomics.eu/contents/year/2013/number/5/article/eu-data-protection-reform-opportunities-and-concerns.html.

202. *See* EUROPEAN COMM'N, Consultation on the Legal Framework for the Fundamental Right to Protection of Personal Data, https://ec.europa.eu/home-affairs/what-is-new/public-consultation/2009/consulting_0003_en.

203. *Id.*

204. Andreas Dür et al., *supra* note 192, at 4.

205. Javier Espinoza, How Big Tech Lost the Antitrust Battle with Europe, FIN. TIMES (Mar. 21, 2022), https://www.ft.com/content/cbb1fe40-860d-4013-bfcf-b75ee6e30206?shareType=nongift.

206. *Id.*

207. *See* Steve Lohr, Antitrust Cry from Microsoft, N.Y. TIMES (Mar. 31, 2011), at B1, https://www.nytimes.com/2011/03/31/technology/companies/31google.html; Brad Smith, Adding Our Voice to Concerns About Search in Europe, MICROSOFT ON THE ISSUES (Mar. 30, 2011), https://blogs.microsoft.com/on-the-issues/2011/03/30/adding-our-voice-to-concerns-about-search-in-europe/.

208. Vlad Savov, What Is Fair Search and Why Does It Hate Google So Much?, THE VERGE (Apr. 12, 2013), https://www.theverge.com/2013/4/12/4216026/who-is-fairsearch.

209. Foo Yun Chee, Facebook, Microsoft Gripes with Apple's App Store on EU's Antitrust Radar, REUTERS (Aug. 10, 2020), https://www.reuters.com/article/uk-eu-apple-facebook-microsoft-idUSKCN2566235.

210. Javier Espinoza, Epic Games Files EU Antitrust Complaint Against Apple, FIN. TIMES (Feb. 17, 2021), https://www.ft.com/content/e1259614-d954-400f-9265-f39a36c8c0c6.

211. Conor Dougherty, Inside Yelp's Six-Year Grudge Against Google, N.Y. TIMES (July 1, 2017), https://www.nytimes.com/2017/07/01/technology/yelp-google-european-union-antitrust.html.

212. Saim Saeed, News Corp, Getty Images Back EU in Google Case, POLITICO (June 27, 2017), https://www.politico.eu/article/news-corp-getty-images-back-eu-in-google-case/.

213. Diane Bartz, Big Tech Critics Ask Raimondo for Meeting After Critique of European Proposals, REUTERS (Dec. 22, 2021), https://www.reuters.com/technology/big-tech-critics-ask-raimondo-meeting-after-critique-european-proposals-2021-12-22/.

214. *See* Gregory Shaffer, Globalization and Social Protection: The Impact of EU and International Rules in the Ratcheting Up of U.S. Privacy Standards, 25 YALE J. INT'L L. 1, 54–55 (2000).

215. Philip Blenkinsop, EU Deeply Disagrees With U.S. on Trade Despite Détente, REUTERS (Aug. 30, 2018), https://www.reuters.com/article/us-usa-trade-eu/eu-deeply-disagrees-with-u-s-on-trade-despite-detente-idUSKCN1LF1E0.

216. *See* European Commission Press Release IP/21/2990, EU-US Launch Trade and Technology Council to Lead Values-Based Global Digital Transformation (June 15, 2021), https://ec.europa.eu/commission/presscorner/detail/en/IP_21_2990; *see* European Commission Statement 21/451, EU–US Trade and Technology Council Inaugural Statement (Sep. 29, 2021); https://ec.europa.eu/commission/presscorner/detail/en/STATEMENT_21_4951; *see* White House Briefing Room, U.S.–EU Trade and Technology Council Inaugural Statement (Sep. 29, 2021), https://www.whitehouse.gov/briefing-room/statements-releases/2021/09/29/u-s-eu-trade-and-technology-council-inaugural-joint-statement/?utm_source=link.

CONCLUSION

1. *See* Steven Erlanger & Adam Satariano, Europe Feels Squeeze as Tech Competition Heats Up Between U.S. and China, N.Y. TIMES (Sep. 13, 2020), https://www.nytimes.com/2020/09/11/world/europe/eu-us-china-technology.html; Yuan Yang, European Tech Accuses US of Using Sanctions to Shut It Out of China, FIN. TIMES (Dec. 22, 2020), https://www.ft.com/content/7baa8caf-ca3f-4d95-967c-e315a3ee348f.

2. *See* Tyson Barker, Europe Can't Win the Tech War It Just Started, FOREIGN POL'Y (Jan. 16, 2020), https://foreignpolicy.com/2020/01/16/europe-technology-sovereignty-von-der-leyen/; Erlanger & Satariano, *supra* note 1; David Kirton, U.S.–China Tech War Bigger Risk Than Coronavirus, EU Chamber Chief Says, REUTERS (June 18, 2020), https://www.reuters.com/article/us-china-business-europe/u-s-china-tech-war-bigger-risk-than-coronavirus-eu-chamber-chief-says-idUSKBN23P1PQ.

3. *See* Jack Goldsmith, The Failure of Internet Freedom, KNIGHT FIRST AMEND. INST. AT COLUM. UNIV. (June 13, 2018), https://knightcolumbia.org/content/failure-internet-freedom.

4. *See* Josh Sisco, Apple, Amazon, Google and Facebook Face at Least 70 Antitrust Probes, Cases, THE INFORMATION (July 15, 2021), https://www.theinformation.

com/articles/apple-amazon-google-and-facebook-face-at-least-70-antitrust-pro
bes-cases.

5. *See* Monica Anderson, Most Americans Say Social Media Companies Have Too
   Much Power, Influence in Politics, PEW RESEARCH CTR. (July 22, 2020), https://
   www.pewresearch.org/fact-tank/2020/07/22/most-americans-say-social-
   media-companies-have-too-much-power-influence-in-politics/.

6. *See* Kelly Tyko, Facebook Advertising Boycott List: Companies Halting Ads
   Include Unilever, Coca-Cola, Verizon, Ben & Jerry's, USA TODAY (June 27, 2020),
   https://www.usatoday.com/story/tech/2020/06/27/facebook-ad-boycott-hate-
   speech-biggest-brands-verizon-coca-cola/3270335001/.

7. *See, e.g.,* Competition and Antitrust Law Enforcement Reform Act, S. 225, 117th
   Cong. (2021); A Bill to Repeal Section 230 of the Communications Act of 1934,
   S. 2972, 117th Cong. (2021); SAFE DATA Act, S. 2499, 117th Cong. (2021).

8. *See* Press Release, Dep't of Justice, Justice Department Sues Monopolist Google
   for Violating Antitrust Laws (Oct. 20, 2020), https://www.justice.gov/opa/
   pr/justice-department-sues-monopolist-google-violating-antitrust-laws; Press
   Release, Fed. Trade Comm'n, FTC Sues Facebook for Illegal Monopolization
   (Dec. 9, 2020), https://www.ftc.gov/news-events/press-releases/2020/12/ftc-
   sues-facebook-illegal-monopolization.

9. *See, e.g.,* Jeff Horwitz, The Facebook Whistleblower, Frances Haugen, Says She
   Wants to Fix the Company, Not Harm It, WALL ST. J. (Oct. 3, 2021), https://www.
   wsj.com/articles/the-facebook-files-11631713039.

10. *See* Tony Romm, Facebook, Twitter Could Face Punishing Regulation for Their
    Role in U.S. Capitol Riot, Democrats Say, WASH. POST (Jan. 8, 2021), https://www.
    washingtonpost.com/technology/2021/01/08/facebook-twitter-congress-trump-
    riot/.

11. *See* Emily Bazelon, Why Is Big Tech Policing Speech? Because the Government
    Isn't, N.Y. TIMES MAG. (Jan. 26, 2021), https://www.nytimes.com/2021/01/26/
    magazine/free-speech-tech.html.

12. *See* Danielle Keats Citron & Mary Anne Franks, The Internet as a Speech
    Machine and Other Myths Confounding Section 230 Reform, 2020 U. CHI.
    LEGAL F. 45, 46–48 (2020); Mark A. Lemley, The Contradictions of Platform
    Regulation, 1 J. FREE SPEECH L. 303, 307–310 (2021).

13. *See* FTC v. Facebook, Inc., No. 20-3590 (JEB), slip op. at 1 (D.D.C. June 28, 2021);
    but see FTC v. Facebook, Inc. ("Facebook II"), 581 F. Supp. 3d 34, Case No. 1:20-
    cv-03590, ECF No. 90 (D.D.C., Jan. 11, 2022) (ruling that the FTC's amended
    complaint filed in August 2021 can survive Facebook's motion to dismiss).

14. *See* Lauren Feiner, New Poll Shows Voters Favor Tech Regulation, But Rank It
    a Low Priority, CNBC (June 23, 2021), https://www.cnbc.com/2021/06/23/new-
    poll-shows-voters-favor-tech-regulation-but-rank-it-low-priority.html.

15. *See* Bazelon, *supra* note 11.

16. *See* Adrian Shahbaz & Allie Funk, Freedom on the Net 2021: The Global Drive to Control Big Tech, FREEDOM HOUSE 2–5, https://freedomhouse.org/sites/defa ult/files/2021-09/FOTN_2021_Complete_Booklet_09162021_FINAL_UPDA TED.pdf.

17. *See* Aidan Powers-Riggs, Covid-19 Is Proving a Boon for Digital Authoritarianism, CTR. FOR STRATEGIC INT'L STUDIES (Aug. 17, 2020), https://www.csis.org/blogs/ new-perspectives-asia/covid-19-proving-boon-digital-authoritarianism.

18. *See* Jeanne Whalen & Chris Alcantara, Nine Charts That Show Who's Winning the U.S.–China Tech Race, WASH. POST (Sep. 21, 2021), https://www.washingtonp ost.com/technology/2021/09/21/us-china-tech-competition/.

19. *See* Final Report, NAT'L SEC. COMM'N ON ARTIFICIAL INTELLIGENCE (Mar. 19, 2021), https://www.nscai.gov/wp-content/uploads/2021/03/Full-Report-Digital-1.pdf.

20. *See* Cass Sunstein, Is Social Media Good or Bad for Democracy?, 15 SUR: INT'L J. ON HUM. RTS. 83, 84–87 (2018).

21. *See* Shoshana Zuboff, THE AGE OF SURVEILLANCE CAPITALISM: THE FIGHT FOR A HUMAN FUTURE AT THE NEW FRONTIER OF POWER 8–12 (2019).

22. *See* Sheera Frenkel, Whistleblower Discusses How Instagram May Lead Teenagers to Eating Disorders, N.Y. TIMES (Oct. 5, 2021), https://www.nytimes. com/live/2021/10/05/technology/facebook-whistleblower-frances-haugen?act ion=click&pgtype=Article&module=&state=default&region=footer&context= breakout_link_back_to_briefing#in-hearing-haugen-discusses-how-instagram- may-lead-teenagers-to-eating-disorders.

23. *See* Karl Manheim & Lyric Kaplan, Artificial Intelligence: Risks to Privacy and Democracy, 21 YALE J.L. & TECH. 106, 129–130 (2019).

24. *See* Josh Constine, Zuckerberg's Response to Cambridge Scandal Omits Why It Delayed Investigating, TECHCRUNCH (Mar. 21, 2018), https://techcrunch.com/ 2018/03/21/zuckerberg-cambridge-analytica/.

25. iMinds, Fragmentation of the Single Market for Online Video On Demand Services: Point of View of Content Providers (European Commission 2014), at 33.

26. *See e,g.* Digital Europe, *Single Market Barriers,* DIGITAL EUROPE (March 3 2022), https://www.digitaleurope.org/resources/single-market-barriers-continue-limit ing-the-eus-potential-for-the-twin-transition/.

27. *See* Kim Baroudy, Jonatan Janmark, Abhi Satyavarapu, Tobias Strålin, & Zeno Ziemke, Europe's Start-Up Ecosystem: Heating Up, but Still Facing Challenges, MCKINSEY & CO. (Oct. 11, 2020), https://www.mckinsey.com/industries/technol ogy-media-and-telecommunications/our-insights/europes-start-up-ecosystem- heating-up-but-still-facing-challenges.

28. European Commission Press Release MEMO/10/473, Turning Europe Into a True Innovation Union (Oct. 6, 2010).

29. *See* Why We Need a Digital Single Market, at 1 (May 6, 2015), https://ec.europa. eu/info/sites/default/files/dsm-factsheet_en.pdf; *see also* Paul-Jasper Dittrich, Balancing Ambition and Pragmatism for the Digital Single Market 4 (Jacques

Delors Inst. Pol'y Paper No. 204, 2017), https://institutdelors.eu/wp-content/uploads/2020/08/balancingambitionandpragmatismforthedigitalsinglemarket-dittrich-jdib-sept2017-2.pdf.

30. *See* Jacques Bughin, Eckart Windhagen, Sven Smit, Jan Mischke, Pal Erik Sjatil, & Bernhard Gürich, Innovation in Europe, MCKINSEY GLOBAL INSTITUTE 14 (Oct. 2019), https://www.mckinsey.com/~/media/mckinsey/featured%20insights/innovation/reviving%20innovation%20in%20europe/mgi-innovation-in-europe-discussion-paper-oct2019-vf.ashx.

31. Commission Staff Working Document, Impact Assessment Accompanying the Document Proposal for a Regulation of the European Parliament and of the Council on a Single Market for Digital Services (Digital Services Act) and amending Directive 2000/31/EC, Part 1/2 at 24, SWD (2020) 348 final (Dec. 15, 2020).

32. *See* Bughin et al., *supra* note 30, at 8.

33. Kim Baroudy, Jonatan Janmark, Abhi Satyavarapu, Tobias Strålin, & Zeno Ziemke, Europe's Start-Up Ecosystem: Heating Up, But Still Facing Challenges, MCKINSEY & CO. (Oct. 11, 2020), https://www.mckinsey.com/industries/technology-media-and-telecommunications/our-insights/europes-start-up-ecosystem-heating-up-but-still-facing-challenges.

34. *See id.*

35. *See* How Sturdy Are Europe's Tech Unicorns?, THE ECONOMIST (July 4, 2022), https://www.economist.com/business/2022/07/04/how-sturdy-are-europes-tech-unicorns.

36. *See* Natalie Sachmechi, Sequoia Capital Opening Its First New York Office, CRAINS N.Y. BUS. (July 28, 2022), https://www.crainsnewyork.com/real-estate/sequoia-capital-opening-its-first-new-york-office.

37. *See* Sam Shead, U.S. VC Heavyweight Sequoia Is Shunning London's Mayfair to Open a New Office in Marylebone, CNBC (Feb. 16, 2021), https://www.cnbc.com/2021/02/16/sequoia-shuns-londons-mayfair-for-marylebone.html.

38. *See* Sebastian Mallaby, Venture Capital's New Race for Europe, FIN. TIMES (Feb. 4, 2022), https://www.ft.com/content/6fc9455a-75fc-4952-a4ff-203e5579aefa.

39. *See* What Is the Capital Markets Union?, EUR. COMM'N, https://ec.europa.eu/info/business-economy-euro/growth-and-investment/capital-markets-union/what-capital-markets-union_en#overview.

40. *See* Luis de Guindos, Fabio Panetta, & Isabel Schnabel, Europe Needs a Fully Fledged Capital Markets Union—Now More Than Ever, ECB BLOG (Sep. 2, 2020), https://www.ecb.europa.eu/press/blog/date/2020/html/ecb.blog200902~c168038cbc.en.html.

41. *See* Müge Adalet McGowen & Dan Andrews, Design of Insolvency Regimes Across Countries, ECO/WKP(2018)52, at 6 (OECD Econ. Dep't Working Papers No. 1504), https://www.oecd.org/officialdocuments/publicdisplaydocumentpdf/?cote=ECO/WKP(2018)52&docLanguage=En.

42. *See* European Parliamentary Research Service Briefing, New EU Insolvency Rules Give Troubled Businesses a Chance to Start Anew, EPRS_BRI (2018) 623548 (June 19, 2018), https://www.europarl.europa.eu/RegData/etudes/BRIE/2018/623548/EPRS_BRI(2018)623548_EN.pdf (hereinafter New EU Insolvency Rules).

43. *See* Press Release, Council of the EU, Giving Entrepreneurs a Second Chance: New Rules on Business Insolvency Adopted (June 6, 2019), https://www.consilium.europa.eu/en/press/press-releases/2019/06/06/giving-entrepreneurs-a-second-chance-new-rules-on-business-insolvency-adopted/.

44. *See id.*; New EU Insolvency Rules, *supra* note 42.

45. *See* Emilie Ghio, Gert-Jan Boon, David Ehmke, Jennifer Gant, Line Langkjaer, & Eugenio Vaccari, Harmonizing Insolvency Law in the EU: New Thoughts on Old Ideas in the Wake of the COVID-19 Pandemic, 30 INT'L INSOLVENCY REV. 427, 431–433 (2021).

46. *See* Baroudy et al., *supra* note 33; James B. Stewart, A Fearless Culture Fuels U.S. Tech Giants, N.Y. TIMES (June 18, 2015), https://www.nytimes.com/2015/06/19/business/the-american-way-of-tech-and-europes.html (internal quotation marks omitted).

47. *See* Peter Ester, ACCELERATORS IN SILICON VALLEY 137, 142 (2017); Stewart, *supra* note 46.

48. *See* Stuart Anderson, Nat'l Found. for Am. Pol'y, Immigrants and Billion Dollar Companies, NFAP POL'Y BRIEF 1 (Oct. 2018), https://nfap.com/wp-content/uploads/2019/01/2018-BILLION-DOLLAR-STARTUPS.NFAP-Policy-Brief.2018-1.pdf.

49. *See* Bughin et al., *supra* note 30.

50. *See* The Global AI Talent Tracker, MACRO POLO, https://macropolo.org/digital-projects/the-global-ai-talent-tracker/ (last visited Mar. 29, 2022).

51. *See* A Quick Look at Global Mobility Trends, INST. INT'L EDUC. (2020), https://iie.widen.net/s/g2bqxwkwqv/project-atlas-infographics-2020.

52. *See* World University Rankings 2022, TIMES HIGHER EDUC., https://www.timeshighereducation.com/world-university-rankings/2022/world-ranking#!/page/0/length/25/sort_by/rank/sort_order/asc/cols/stats (last visited Mar. 29, 2022).

53. *See* Michael G. Finn & Leigh Ann Pennington, Stay Rates of Foreign Doctorate Recipients From U.S. Universities, 2013, NAT'L CTR. FOR SCI. & ENG'G STAT. OF THE NAT'L SCI. FOUND. BY OAK RIDGE INST. FOR SCI. & EDUC. 3–4 (Jan. 2018), https://orise.orau.gov/stem/reports/stay-rates-foreign-doctorate-recipients-2013.pdf.

54. *See* Dominic Jacquesson, INDEX VENTURES, REWARDING TALENT: A GUIDE TO STOCK OPTIONS FOR EUROPEAN ENTREPRENEURS (2017), https://www.indexventures.com/rewardingtalent/handbook.

55. *See* Not Optional—Europe Must Attract More Talent to Startups, https://www.notoptional.eu/ (last visited Mar. 29, 2022).

56. *See* Adam Satariano, New Privacy Rules Could Make This Woman One of Tech's Most Important Regulators, N.Y. TIMES (May 16, 2018), https://www.nytimes.com/2018/05/16/technology/gdpr-helen-dixon.html.

57. *See* Press Release, FACEBOOK, Facebook Reports Quarter and Full Year 2021 Results (Feb. 2, 2022), https://investor.fb.com/investor-news/press-release-details/2022/Meta-Reports-Fourth-Quarter-and-Full-Year-2021-Results/defa ult.aspx#:~:text=Facebook%20daily%20active%20users%20(DAUs,%25%20y ear%2Dover%2Dyear.

58. *See* Data Never Sleeps 8.0, DOMO, https://www.domo.com/learn/data-never-sle eps-8 (last visited Mar. 21, 2021).

59. *See* App Store, APPLE, https://www.apple.com/app-store/ (last visited Oct. 14, 2021) (noting that "Every week, over 500 dedicated experts around the world review over 100K apps.").

60. *See* Kate Klonick, The New Governors: The People, Rules, and Processes Governing Online Speech, 131 HARV. L. REV. 1598, 1654 (2018).

61. *See* Ian Bremmer, The Technopolar Moment: How Digital Powers Will Reshape the Global Order, 100 FOREIGN AFF. 112–128 (2021).

62. *See* Stephen M. Walt, Big Tech Won't Remake the Global Order, FOREIGN POL'Y (Nov. 8, 2021), https://foreignpolicy.com/2021/11/08/big-tech-wont-remake-the-global-order/.

63. *See* Jack Goldsmith & Tim Wu, WHO CONTROLS THE INTERNET? ILLUSIONS OF A BORDERLESS WORLD 65–85 (2006).

64. *See, e.g.,* David R. Johnson & David Post, Law and Borders: The Rise of Law in Cyberspace, 48 STAN. L. REV. 1367 (1996).

65. *See, e.g.,* Goldsmith & Wu, *supra* note 63.

66. *See* Commission Regulation 2022/1925, of the European Parliament and of the Council of 14 September 2022 on Contestable and Fair Markets in the Digital Sector and Amending Directives 2019/1937 and 2020/1828 (Digital Markets Act), 2022 O.J. (L 265) 1, 2–3.

67. *See* Commission Regulation 2022/2065, of the European Parliament and of the Council of 19 October 2022 on a Single Market for Digital Services and Amending Directive 2000/31/EC (Digital Services Act), 2022 O.J. (L 277) 1, 5–7.

68. *See id.* at 19, 60.

69. *See* Parmy Olson, Facebook and Google's Ad Addiction Can't Last Forever, SF GATE (Feb. 3, 2022), https://www.sfgate.com/business/article/Facebook-and-Google-s-ad-addiction-can-t-last-16829321.php.

70. *See* Data Privacy Day at Apple: Improving Transparency and Empowering Users, APPLE (Jan. 27, 2021), https://www.apple.com/newsroom/2021/01/data-privacy-day-at-apple-improving-transparency-and-empowering-users/.

71. *See* Patrick McGee, Snap, Facebook, Twitter and YouTube Lose Nearly $10bn After iPhone Privacy Changes, FIN. TIMES (Oct. 31, 2021), https://www.ft.com/content/4c19e387-ee1a-41d8-8dd2-bc6c302ee58e.

72. *See* Bart de Langhe & Stefano Puntoni, Facebook's Misleading Campaign Against Apple's Privacy Policy, HARV. BUS. REV. (Feb. 2, 2021), https://hbr.org/2021/02/facebooks-misleading-campaign-against-apples-privacy-policy; Tom Warren, Facebook Criticizes Apple's iOS Privacy Changes With Full-Page Newspaper Ads, VERGE (DEC. 16, 2020), https://www.theverge.com/2020/12/16/22178068/facebook-apple-newspaper-ads-ios-privacy-changes.

73. *See* Kurt Wagner, Facebook Users Said No to Tracking. Now Advertisers Are Panicking, BLOOMBERG (July 14, 2021), https://www.bloomberg.com/news/artic les/2021-07-14/facebook-fb-advertisers-impacted-by-apple-aapl-privacy-ios-14-changes.

74. *See* Jared Newman, Most People Are Embracing iOS 14.5's New Anti-tracking Features, FAST COMPANY (May 7, 2021), https://www.fastcompany.com/90633 965/ios-14-5-tracking-opt-out-rate.

75. *See* Kate Conger & Brian X. Chen, A Change by Apple Is Tormenting Internet Companies, Especially Meta, N.Y. TIMES (Feb. 3, 2022), https://www.nytimes.com/2022/02/03/technology/apple-privacy-changes-meta.html.

76. *See* McGee, *supra* note 71.

77. *See* Brad Smith, Microsoft's Endorsement of Australia's Proposal on Technology and the News, MICROSOFT ON THE ISSUES (Feb. 11, 2021), https://blogs.microsoft.com/on-the-issues/2021/02/11/endorsement-australias-proposal-technology-news/.

78. *See* Brad Smith, Adding Our Voice to Concerns About Search in Europe, MICROSOFT ON THE ISSUES (Mar. 30, 2011), https://docs.microsoft.com/en-us/archive/blogs/microsoft_on_the_issues/adding-our-voice-to-concerns-about-search-in-europe.

79. *See* Danny Hakim, Microsoft, Once an Antitrust Target, Is Now Google's Regulatory Scold, N.Y. TIMES (Apr. 15, 2015), https://www.nytimes.com/2015/04/16/technology/microsoft-once-an-antitrust-target-is-now-googles-regulatory-scold.html.

80. *See* Conor Dougherty, Inside Yelp's Six-Year Grudge Against Google, N.Y. TIMES (July 1, 2017), https://www.nytimes.com/2017/07/01/technology/yelp-google-european-union-antitrust.html.

81. *See* Dina Bass & Nico Grant, Google and Microsoft End Their Five-Year Cease-Fire, FORTUNE (June 30, 2021), https://fortune.com/2021/06/30/google-micros oft-lobbying-antitrust/ (internal quotation marks omitted).

82. *See* David McLaughlin, Google Slams Microsoft Over Support for Media Antitrust Bill, BLOOMBERG (Mar. 12, 2021), https://www.bloomberg.com/news/articles/2021-03-12/google-slams-microsoft-over-support-for-media-antitrust-bill (internal quotation marks omitted).

83. *See, e.g.,* Hannah Murphy & Kiran Stacey, Mark Zuckerberg Backs Reform of Legal Protections for Social Media, FIN. TIMES (Oct. 27, 2020), https://www.

ft.com/content/9e9b8a33-74af-4a42-9c6f-1e24958de46c (on file with the author).

84. *See* Tom McCarthy, Zuckerberg Says Facebook Won't Be "Arbiters of Truth" After Trump Threat, GUARDIAN (May 28, 2020), https://www.theguardian.com/technology/2020/may/28/zuckerberg-facebook-police-online-speech-trump (internal quotation marks omitted).

85. *See* Hannah Murphy, Facebook Wrestles With Advertisers' Demands as Boycott Escalates, FIN. TIMES (July 1, 2020), https://www.ft.com/content/2970cf91-dcf7-4424-bdc9-b6d92ad72d67.

86. *See* Lauren Feiner, Russia Blocks Access to Facebook, CNBC (Mar. 4, 2022), https://www.cnbc.com/2022/03/04/russia-blocks-access-to-facebook.html.

87. *See* Salvador Rodriguez, Hundreds of Facebook Employees Walk Out as Zuckerberg Plans Town Hall, CNBC (June 2, 2020), https://www.cnbc.com/2020/06/01/facebook-employees-stage-virtual-walkout-over-trump-post-moderation.html.

88. *See id.*

89. *See* Tim Bradshaw & Hannah Murphy, Facebook Employees Revolt over Zuckerberg's Stance on Trump, FIN. TIMES (June 2, 2020), https://www.ft.com/content/0ad3c5e7-a93a-414f-911b-16cb3f118688.

90. *See, e.g.,* Rima Alaily, Microsoft Supports New Rules for Gatekeepers, MICROSOFT (May 3, 2021), https://blogs.microsoft.com/eupolicy/2021/05/03/microsoft-supports-new-rules-for-gatekeepers/; Julie Brill, Microsoft's Commitment to GDPR, Privacy and Putting Customers in Control of Their Own Data, MICROSOFT (May 21, 2018), https://blogs.microsoft.com/on-the-issues/2018/05/21/microsofts-commitment-to-gdpr-privacy-and-putting-customers-in-control-of-their-own-data/; Kashmir Hill, Microsoft Plans to Eliminate Face Analysis Tools in Push for "Responsible A.I.," https://www.nytimes.com/2022/06/21/technology/microsoft-facial-recognition.html?referringSource=articleShare; Brad Smith, Technology and the Free Press: The Need for Healthy Journalism in a Healthy Democracy, MICROSOFT (Mar. 12, 2021), https://blogs.microsoft.com/on-the-issues/2021/03/12/technology-and-the-free-press-the-need-for-healthy-journalism-in-a-healthy-democracy/.

91. *See* Cecilia Kang, Lawmakers, Taking Aim at Big Tech, Push Sweeping Overhaul of Antitrust, N.Y. TIMES (June 11, 2021), https://www.nytimes.com/2021/06/11/technology/big-tech-antitrust-bills.html; Paul Mozur, Cecilia Kang, Adam Satariano, & David McCabe, A Global Tipping Point for Reining In Tech Has Arrived, N.Y. TIMES (Apr. 20, 2021), https://www.nytimes.com/2021/04/20/technology/global-tipping-point-tech.html.

92. *See* Gabriella Blum, Islands of Agreement: Managing Enduring Armed Rivalries 5, 21 (2007).

93. *See generally* Mark A. Lemley, *The Splinternet*, 70 DUKE L. J. 1397 (2021).

94. *See* Jared Cohen & Richard Fontaine, Uniting the Techno-Democracies: How to Build Digital Cooperation, 99 FOREIGN AFFAIRS 112, https://www.foreignaffairs.com/articles/united-states/2020-10-13/uniting-techno-democracies.

95. *See id.*

96. *See* Our Mission, HALIFAX INT'L SEC. FORUM, https://halifaxtheforum.org/mission (last visited Nov. 21, 2022).

97. *See* Robin Shepherd, CHINA VS. DEMOCRACY: THE GREATEST GAME 4–5 (2020), https://hfxchinahandbook.s3.amazonaws.com/EN_HFX+China+Handbook_FINAL_WEB.pdf.

98. *See* Cohen & Fontaine, *supra* note 94.

99. *See id.*

100. *See* China Strategy Group, Asymmetric Competition: A Strategy for China & Technology: Actionable Insights for China & Technology 3–4, 17, 26–27 (2020), https://s3.documentcloud.org/documents/20463382/final-memo-china-strategy-group-axios-1.pdf. *See generally* Erik Brattberg & Ben Judah, Forget the G-7, Build the D-10, FOREIGN POL'Y (June 10, 2020), https://foreignpolicy.com/2020/06/10/g7-d10-democracy-trump-europe/; Ash Jain, Like-Minded and Capable Democracies: A New Framework for Advancing a Liberal World Order (Council on Foreign Rels. Working Paper, Jan. 2013), https://cdn.cfr.org/sites/default/files/pdf/2012/11/IIGG_WorkingPaper12_Jain.pdf; Anja Manuel, THE TECH 10: A FLEXIBLE APPROACH FOR INTERNATIONAL TECHNOLOGY AND GOVERNANCE, IN DOMESTIC AND INTERNATIONAL (DIS)ORDER: A STRATEGIC RESPONSE 71 (Leah Bitounis & Niamh King eds., 2020), https://www.aspeninstitute.org/wp-content/uploads/2020/10/Foreign-Policy-2021-ePub_FINAL.pdf.

101. *See* Adrian Shabaz, The Rise of Digital Authoritarianism, FREEDOM HOUSE (2018), https://freedomhouse.org/report/freedom-net/2018/rise-digital-authoritarianism.

102. *See* Jon Bateman, Biden Is Now All-In on Taking Out China, FOREIGN POL'Y (Oct. 12, 2022), https://foreignpolicy.com/2022/10/12/biden-china-semiconductor-chips-exports-decouple/.

103. *See* The Summit for Democracy, U.S. DEP'T STATE (Feb. 2021), https://www.state.gov/summit-for-democracy/.

104. *See* A Declaration for the Future of the Internet, WHITE HOUSE (Apr. 28, 2021), https://www.whitehouse.gov/wp-content/uploads/2022/04/Declaration-for-the-Future-for-the-Internet_Launch-Event-Signing-Version_FINAL.pdf.

105. *See id.*

106. *See* Janan Ganesh, The US Cannot Be Choosy About Its Allies, FIN. TIMES (Mar. 30, 2021), https://www.ft.com/content/ff8abf95-abb4-48d9-83b6-728a0deec9ae.

107. *See* Biden's New China Doctrine, THE ECONOMIST (July 17, 2021), https://www.economist.com/leaders/2021/07/17/bidens-new-china-doctrine.

108. *See* A Letter to Our Customers and to the Community, ALIZILA (Apr. 10, 2021). https://www.alizila.com/a-letter-to-our-customers-and-to-the-community/.

109. *See* Frances Yoon, Alibaba Pledges $15.5 Billion as Chinese Companies Extol Beijing's "Common Prosperity" Push, WALL ST. J. (Sep. 3, 2021), https://www.wsj.com/articles/alibaba-pledges-15-5-billion-as-chinese-companies-extol-beijings-common-prosperity-push-11630587923.

110. *See supra* discussion in Chapter 2.

Index

For the benefit of digital users, indexed terms that span two pages (e.g., 52–53) may, on occasion, appear on only one of those pages.

artificial intelligence (AI) (*cont.*)
    Plan for Development of
        the New Generation of
        Artificial Intelligence (2017
        AI Development Plan)
        (China), 208–9
    protections against harmful
        applications of, 113–15
    regulation of, 15–16, 142, 251–52,
        337, 348–53
    research and development,
        197, 374–75
    surveillance operations, 85,
        293, 315–16
    tech standards, 305–6
    US–China tech war, 186–
        87, 207–11
    VC funding, 209–10
Asia, 260–61, 300. *see also specific*
    countries by name
Asia-Pacific Economic
    Group, 266–67
AU (African Union), 18–19, 318
Audiovisual Media Services Directive
    (EU), 123
Austin, Lloyd, 209
Australia, 337
    AI Action Plan, 350–51
    AI Ethics Framework, 350–51
    anti-censorship
        principles, 267–68
    antitrust regulation, 343–44, 345
    Clean Network, 321
    Code of Practice on
        Disinformation and
        Misinformation, 341–42
    content moderation, 341–42
    digital trade agreements, 322
    news industry regulation, 351–
        52, 383
    nonregulation principle, 266–68
    Privacy Act, 334

relations with China, 197–
    98, 319–20
restrictions on Chinese tech
    companies, 193–94, 319–20
search engine market, 260–61
techno-democracy, 389–90
Australian Communications
    and Media Authority
    (ACMA), 341–42
Australian Competition and
    Consumer Commission
    (ACCC), 334, 341, 343–44
Australian Human Rights
    Commission (AHRC), 350–51
Austria, 126–27, 239, 242
authoritarian
    governments, 364–66
authoritarianism, 135, 388–89
    beyond China, 308–13
    digital, 77–78, 99, 290–323
automated driving, 208–9
autonomy, strategic, 132–34, 186
AWS (Amazon Web Services),
    155, 160
Azure cloud-computing service
    (Microsoft), 154–55

B3W (Build Back Better World)
    initiative (G7), 321–22
Backpage, 367–68
Backpage.com, 51–52, 64
Bahrain, 284
Baidu, 73, 108, 153–54, 165, 208–9
    American funding, 93–94
    VIE structure, 174–75
Baker, Stewart, 233
Balkin, Jack, 53–54, 56–57
Bankruptcy Code (US), 374
Barbrook, Richard, 34
Barlow, John Perry, 36–37
Barreto, Alexandre, 344–45
Barshefsky, Charlene, 224

Germany *(cont.)*
  NetzDG law, 140–41
  privacy culture, 143
  protections for platform
    workers, 128–29
  relations with China, 253, 321
  smart city technologies, 296–97
  techno-democracy, 389
Ghana, 273
GIFT (Global Internet Freedom Task
    Force) (US), 271
gig workers, 128–29
Glawischnig, Eva, 339–40
Global Artificial Intelligence
    Industry Data Report, 210
global digital economy, 385–93. *see
    also* e-commerce
  bipolar, 386–88
  "A Framework for Global
    Electronic Commerce"
    (Framework) (Clinton
    administration), 48, 266–67
  multipolar, 386
  unipolar, 386
  technopolar
Global Gateway initiative
    (EU), 321–22
Global Information Infrastructure
    (proposed), 266
global internet, 16. *see also* internet
Global Internet Freedom Task Force
    (GIFT) (US), 271
global smartphone sales, 215–16
global tax reform, 240–42
  Pillar One, 241–42
  Pillar Two, 241–42
global techno-nationalism, 212–15
global telecom equipment
    market, 194
The Global Times, 83, 100
globalization
  Brussels effect, 324–26

  of Chinese infrastructure power,
    293–302
  of Chinese surveillance, 314–20
  deglobalization, 151, 165–66
  of European digital
    rights, 324–59
  of regulation, 1–29, 324–93
Gmail, 153–54
Goldman Sachs, 93, 176
Goldsmith, Jack, 37, 66–67, 265,
    287–88, 379
González, Mario Costeja, 112–13
Google, 33–34, 108, 138–39
  acquisitions, 2, 50–51
  AdSense program, 243
  advertising revenue, 260–61
  AI research, 153–54, 210–11
  Android OS, 153–54, 189–90
  annual revenue, 2
  anticompetitive practices, 56
  antitrust investigations, 50–51,
    53–54, 137–38, 140, 224, 242–47,
    249, 343, 344–45, 347, 348, 358,
    363, 383
  battles with governments, 13–15
  Chinese constraints on, 76–77,
    178, 189–90
  comparison-shopping service, 125
  compliance with Chinese laws
    and regulations, 150–51, 153–
    54, 157–58
  compliance with EU laws and
    regulations, 324–25, 338
  compliance with Russian laws and
    regulations, 163
  content moderation, 3–4, 9–10,
    120, 338–39, 341
  data collection, 38, 61
  data privacy policy, 324
  data protection, 226
  diplomatic missions, 274–75
  Disinformation Code, 120